The
Fine Furniture
& Furnishings
DISCOUNT SHOPPING GUIDE

Fourth Edition!

Why Pay Retail?

By

M. Katherine Gladchun

The Fine Furniture and Furnishings Discount Shopping Guide

M. Katherine Gladchun
Text edited by Joe Evancho

Resources, Inc
PO Box 973
Bloomfield Hills, MI 48303-0973
248-644-3440 (Phone/fax)
email: ResKate@aol.com

645
G451
1998

Cover Design: Michael Huffman, Huffman, Fisher Design

Ordering Information
For ordering information for more copies of this book, see the coupon in the back pages.
Quantity discounts are available by the case.

Library of Congress Catalog Card Number:
98-60554

ISBN:
0-9638701-2-2

Dear Reader:

This fourth edition of *THE FINE FURNITURE AND FURNISHINGS DISCOUNT SHOPPING GUIDE* is the most concise, detailed and informative book available on buying furniture and home furnishings at every day deep discount prices.

Buying for the home is not something to be done on a whim. It requires a lot of time and attention. This book shows you how to save time and money through the three phases of discount shopping: *information gathering, pre-shopping and shopping.* It shows you how to do your pre-shopping research: who to talk to, questions to ask, options to consider and things to expect. It guides you through the steps that take you to those ultimate shopping decisions: what to buy and where to buy.

It's a book for the novice and experienced home-furnishings shopper alike. There are no memberships required for the resources it introduces you to. Although many designers already own this book, you don't have to be a designer to take advantage of all it offers. Whether you live in New York City or Boise, Idaho, this book can help you save money while beautifying your home.

The success of the first three editions is a good indicator that American consumers want to know all they can about discount shopping for the home. Everything you need to know to make smart choices and save money in the process is contained within these pages.

To those who argue that discount resources undermine retail store profits, I would remind them that it's an individual's choice where he or she spends their money. Why pass up the opportunity to save if everything else is equal: service, product satisfaction, product warranty, return policies and delivery.

There's a lot of **new** information in this book. We've added many new tips and ideas for shopping by phone and in-person, along with some charts and a map. There are now over 350 discount resources. (Even sources for the kitchen sink!) Every effort has been made to keep the information in this book as up-to-date as possible. However, changes do occur. If you discover any new resources or changes in existing ones, please feel free to contact me and I will do my best to pass the information on. You can reach me by phone, fax or email.

Phone/Fax:	248-644-3440
Mail:	Resources, Inc. PO Box 973 Bloomfield Hills, MI 48303-0973
email:	ResKate@aol.com

Tell your friends they can order their own copy with the coupon on the last page.

ABOUT THIS BOOK

This book was written to help you save money. It's filled with hundreds of usable suggestions, step-by-step planning and shopping instructions, a map and a directory of every day deep-discount resources for furniture and furnishings for home and office, listed both alphabetically and geographically. It also contains an alphabetical index of manufacturers in the back of the book. If you're shopping for furniture, lighting, accessories, beds, bedding, patio furniture, carpet, bath and kitchen fixtures, wall covering, window treatments or fabric (including British and European fabrics and wallpapers), this book will be a very valuable tool for you.

For simplification, the term "**resource**" is used to describe any place where the above items can be purchased at discount prices. Someone else might call them showrooms, warehouses, shops, stores, outlets, etc. Each resource carries or represents the products of various manufacturers. The term "**manufacturer**" is used to describe or identify the makers of furniture or furnishings or the brand names for their products, e.g., Henredon, Baker, La-Z-Boy.

The book is organized into three sections:

1. **The Art of Discount Shopping**
2. **Product and Manufacturer Information**
3. **The Resource Directory**

Section 1 contains basic furniture and furnishings shopping information with tips and suggestions for shopping in person or by phone. It's full of useful information for the newcomer and veteran shopper alike, with lots of short cuts and time-saving ideas. Also included are some important phone numbers for consumer services and agencies. I recommend reading this section completely before you begin shopping.

Section 2 lists manufacturers by general product types and styles. There is also a list of over 400 manufacturers with addresses, phone numbers and in some cases a short description of their products.

Section 3—probably best described as the heart of the book—lists discount resources in alphabetical and geographic order and provides detailed information regarding each.

My experience over the past three editions has shown that this book gets borrowed a lot. Be sure to write your name and phone number in the front of your book. Oh yes, and your friends can order their own with the order form in the back pages of this book.

THE FINE FURNITURE AND FURNISHINGS DISCOUNT SHOPPING GUIDE
Fourth Edition—1998

TABLE OF CONTENTS

THE ART OF DISCOUNT SHOPPING 1
   GETTING STARTED 1
   NUMBER ONE: HOMEWORK AND LEGWORK 1
   NUMBER TWO: FINDING RELIABLE SALESPEOPLE 4
   SHOPPING THE RESOURCES 5
   TEN TIPS FOR SHOPPING BY PHONE 6
   SHOPPING IN PERSON 6
   SHOPPING NORTH CAROLINA 7
   TEN TIPS FOR SHOPPING IN PERSON 8
   HOW TO GET TO NORTH CAROLINA 8
   BEFORE YOU ORDER 12
   SHIPPING 12
   SHOPPING FOR UPHOLSTERED FURNITURE 15
   "COM" SHOPPING—CHOOSING YOUR OWN UPHOLSTERY FABRIC 19
   SHOPPING FOR CASEGOODS 20
   PROTECTING YOUR DEPOSIT 22
   IMPORTANT PHONE NUMBERS AND/OR ADDRESSES 23
   ONE FINAL NOTE: 24

PRODUCT AND MANUFACTURER LISTINGS 25
   PRODUCTS LISTING WITH SUGGESTED MANUFACTURERS 25
   MANUFACTURER LISTING 41

RESOURCE DIRECTORY 69
   GEOGRAPHIC LISTING 334

INDEX 345

THE ART OF DISCOUNT SHOPPING

PLEASE READ THIS SECTION CAREFULLY AND COMPLETELY

GETTING STARTED

There are two basic steps to successful discount shopping for fine furniture and furnishings. **1)** Be willing to do your homework, some legwork and some preliminary investigation before you buy. This means familiarizing yourself with the products you're interested in and the manufacturers who make them. **2)** Find a reliable, knowledgeable salesperson or persons who can help you with your purchases. The right salesperson for you is someone you will be comfortable with and who will be familiar with the products you're looking for. He or she will be able to offer you meaningful information and advice about various manufacturers and their products.

Once you've decided on the item you're looking for, begin the narrowing down process with manufacturers' names as your broad choices: *Henredon, Baker, Lexington, La-Z-Boy, Broyhill, etc.* Section 2 contains over 50 different products and some of the manufacturers who produce these products. If you can get it down to a specific manufacturer *and* style, that's even better: *Henredon camelback, 3-seat, loose pillow, tailored skirt sofa.* Best of all are the model or style numbers of the item or items you want: *Pearson swivel chair, model number 1136, with tufted back.* With many products there's often an assortment of options available; things like seat and back cushions, skirts, arms and finishes, so make certain you know when such options are available and what the choices are.

NUMBER ONE: HOMEWORK AND LEGWORK

Gathering Information

A critical element in the discount shopping process is information gathering. Begin by organizing information about your present home or office furniture and furnishings. Here are some suggestions on how to go about doing this:

- **Keep a record** of the furniture and furnishings in your home or office: the brand and pattern numbers of your wallpapers; paint colors with manufacturers' names and chips, if possible; furniture and drapery fabric samples with names or pattern numbers; carpet samples; window covering samples; anything that will help you in making buying decisions.

Next, start looking and thinking ahead about what you would like to do in terms of decorating and furnishing. Here's one way to begin:

- **Create a file** of items you are currently interested in, will be looking at soon, or would like someday: photos, ads, magazine or catalog pages, anything that will give you a visual reference. I recommend a binder, with clear, plastic sheet protectors to hold fabric swatches, photos, magazine pages, etc. Be sure to include floor plans of the rooms you're working on, or your entire home.

- **Jot down** on each reference piece pertinent information like a brand name, where the catalog or magazine came from, model numbers, etc. Post-its are perfect for this task, so keep a pad handy with your collection.

Whether you're accumulating information for future or immediate needs, you can use these materials to stimulate ideas, identify or explain products to a salesperson or simply have on hand for your personal reference.

Pre-Shopping

Once you've organized your information, begin putting it to use in what I call the *pre-shopping process*. This is the gathering of the hard information needed to make your final buying decisions. There are three basic ways to pre-shop:

- **By visiting local retail shops**
- **By studying manufacturers' advertisements or catalogs**
- **By contacting discount resources**

The information gathered can then be used to compare brands, quality, prices, availability, service, delivery and warranty—all important components in the decision-making process.

Local retail shops, though they don't always advertise the fact, are sometimes quite competitive. They'll meet or beat sale and discount prices when necessary. For this reason, they are a good place to begin. When searching out products, regardless of where you are looking, there are certain questions you will want answered:

- Who manufactures the products?
- What are the different brand names?
- If upholstered items, are they available in leather or fabric?
- What sizes are available?
- What kind of warranty do they carry?
- Do they represent good value?
- What is the cost?

You probably won't find all the answers in one place and will likely make several stops before you're ready to decide. The question of value, you'll probably have to answer for yourself. But, to get answers, you have to ask questions. Don't be reluctant to inquire about manufacturers, warranties or product reputation. Note the style numbers or model numbers. On tables and other case goods, the model number is usually printed on an underside or unfinished surface. Upholstered items are a little harder to identify but, if you have the opportunity, try to locate the content tag—the one that says *Do Not Remove Under Penalty Of Law*. It's usually found on a cushion or on the deck of a sofa or chair. At the very bottom of this tag, it should indicate where the item was made, either by manufacturer or city of origin. Also note color and fabric.

> **NOTE:** *Some retail stores use their own model and style numbers, so be sure you have the* **manufacturer's** *model and style numbers. One way to do this is to compare tag information between stores. Another is to get as much descriptive information as possible, e.g. Pearson swivel chair, showing model number 1136, with tufted back, gathered skirt and cherry finish. You can inquire if the piece you're interested in comes in other styles or finishes. You may be offered a brochure or photo. This descriptive information and model number can then be used for comparison purposes, either at another retail outlet or discount resource.* **Most importantly, you want to be able to identify what you like!**

Magazine ads, catalogs or other collateral material can also be used for pre-shopping. These materials usually provide good descriptive information that proves useful for making purchase decisions. They often include the manufacturer's address or an 800 number where a representative can be reached. Information acquired through these sources is usually accurate and reliable in terms of product information. Keep track of prices. Knowing the cost of the item from one source may prove to be helpful when negotiating with another resource.

Discount resources can now be brought into the pre-shopping process. With a good idea of what you're looking for in terms of products, models, styles and price, you're ready to put your **Fine Furniture and Furnishings Discount Shopping Guide** to work. Here's how:

Let's say that after doing your research, you decide you like Sherrill sofas. Look up Sherrill in the index. There you will find numbers listed. Those numbers will lead you to the resources carrying Sherrill products. Each resource is identified by name, address, phone number, fax number and hours of operation. If appropriate, special notations are also included. This information is then followed by a list of manufacturers the resource carries or represents.

Select your resource or resources, call and ask to speak to a salesperson about buying furniture. Explain which items you're interested in, along with any fabrics or options you might like. Ask for a price which includes shipping.

Now compare these prices to those you've been quoted from your local shops. If a local shop can sell you the item at a comparable price, make the deal. By measuring its prices against discount resources and finding them comparable you've assured yourself that you've gotten a good value. If there's a big difference, you have several choices.

1.   Ask the local store if they will match a competitive price. If they will, use your discount price to negotiate the best deal you can.

2.	If you prefer not to negotiate or the local store refuses to, buy from the discount resource. It's the same product, from the same manufacturer, with the same options, but at a better price.

Once you've done your legwork and research, you can also go directly to any of the resources and discuss your needs with a salesperson there. A good salesperson will not only be able to help you with the specific product you're after but should also be able to suggest some comparable products or brands. A good salesperson is invaluable at this point, which brings us to step two:

NUMBER TWO: FINDING RELIABLE SALESPEOPLE

This step is a little more instinctive and subjective. A good salesperson at a reliable resource is your best asset in the discount furniture-buying process. He or she should be familiar with comparable products and different manufacturers and be willing to introduce you to these new possibilities. A good salesperson will be listening carefully to what you want and you should be open- minded to their suggestions.

So, how do you go about finding a knowledgeable, reliable salesperson? Sometimes you just get lucky and hit pay dirt early on. Most of the time, however, it takes several phone calls and some extended conversation to locate the one that's right for you. The resources listed in this book have very capable salespeople who are familiar with the products of numerous manufacturers and many are experts on the products of specific manufacturers. Most are dedicated professional who will provide you with prompt, courteous assistance.

Here are some suggestions on how to go about locating a reliable salesperson who will help you make the most of your discount shopping experience:

1.	**Begin by selecting your resources** from the Discount Shopping Guide.
2.	**Contact each resource** and ask for a salesperson familiar with the products in which you are interested.
3.	**Explain your needs and evaluate the response**. For example, if the salesperson tells you to get a model number from your local furniture store and he or she will quote you a price, scratch that one. That might be all you need at some other time, and there are resources that operate exclusively at that level, but right now you're looking for someone who can offer advice and useful information. If, on the other hand, the salesperson asks questions about the item you're looking for or suggests that a different manufacturer may have the same product at a better price, you're getting close. More conversation will usually help you decide whether or not this person is truly interested in helping. This is where instinct and intuition come into play. Working in your favor is the fact that most resources and their salespeople understand that satisfied customers are their very best advertising. They also know that there is a growing nationwide network of discount shoppers tuned in on which resources are doing the best job for them.

4.   **Go through the same procedure with each resource** or ask one of the salespeople you've decided on to recommend a salesperson at other resources. Create a file card for each of your contacts and keep them with your discount shopping file. As you make ongoing furniture purchases you'll find that knowing salespeople who are familiar with your tastes and preferences can be very beneficial. Ask them to let you know about any special sales or promotions. Also, if you plan to visit the resource, be sure to let them know, make an appointment and bring your file so that you can discuss present and future needs.

SHOPPING THE RESOURCES

Shopping by phone

Begin by looking for a toll-free 800 number. All resources in this guide with 800 numbers at the time of publication are listed as such. However, these numbers are constantly changing, being deleted or added. If no number is listed or a number has been changed, call 800 information at 1-800-555-1212. If a resource does not have an 800 number, call the published number, explain what you're looking for and ask them to call you back. Most are happy to do so. If not, move on to a resource that will.

> **NOTE:** *With the ever-changing telephone systems throughout the US, we have been experiencing the addition of new area codes everywhere. If you find that a number you've dialed is not working properly, check to see if there has been a recent area code split within that region, or call Information to verify. Information in this book has been updated to June of 1998.*

When shopping by phone, accuracy is critical, particularly if you do not have model numbers. Even with model numbers, you must carefully explain exactly what you're after, making sure the salesperson understands completely. This helps to avoid the unnecessary grief of receiving the wrong item and the salesperson can often offer information about which you are unaware. For example, you have the model number and complete description of a side table. You also know the color you want. What you may not know is that the table comes in four different finishes from high gloss to oil. By providing the salesperson with all of the particulars, he or she will be able to precisely identify the table and advise you of the finish options and any differences in pricing.

Now, let's assume you don't know the model number or the manufacturer, but you can generally describe the piece you want—say a leather lounge chair or sofa—and you know how much you want to spend. Again, provide your salesperson with as much descriptive detail as possible: style, color, leather or fabric, where and how you'll be using this item. Perhaps you saw it advertised somewhere. If you can recall where, that will help. With enough information, your resource should be able to identify what you're after by manufacturer, model and style and confirm it by sending or faxing photo copies, literature or photographs. Because they know these products inside and out, your resource also might be able to suggest a better value, (**i.e.**, items similar to those you're interested in but better quality) at the same price or equal quality at a lower price. Do not hesitate to ask if and when an item you're considering might go on sale. There are often scheduled promotions on various manufacturers throughout the year.

Once the details are worked out, a photocopy of the manufacturer's description of the piece with a complete description of the finish should be offered to you. You may even be offered wood samples or more elaborate brochures showing color and finish, which you may be obligated to return. All of these steps should be followed in order to receive exactly what you want.

TEN TIPS FOR SHOPPING BY PHONE

1. Have your credit card ready if you will be using it for your deposit.
2. Have delivery name, address, zip code ready.
3. Have product/model numbers and all pertinent information in front of you.
4. Get the name of the resource salesperson.
5. Find out if the product is in stock.
6. Find out when it would be shipped and by whom.
7. Ask if items can be shipped separately, if necessary. This means that if two items are in stock and one is not, will they ship you the items that are ready and ship the other later? If such arrangements can be made, you may be asked to pay extra shipping costs.
8. Get the total amount involved: cost of each item, delivery/shipping, and any additional charges.
9. Tell the salesperson that you are noting all of the information and request a written confirmation.
10. File this information in a place where it can be easily retrieved..

SHOPPING IN PERSON

There are high quality discount resources located throughout the country, some probably in your area. Depending on your needs, it's a good idea to identify these locations and make it a point to check them out.

If you're considering a discount shopping trip, whether it's local or long distance, here are some things to keep in mind:

- Gather your information. Be prepared with photos, catalogs and all of your notes.
- It's also helpful to have accurate floor plans of the rooms you're working on and photos of furniture you already have and plan to keep.
- Bring swatches of fabrics you already are using and plan to keep. An arm cap from a chair or the covering from a pillow or cushion is sufficient.

- If you know your exact shopping dates, contact your salesperson and set up an appointment. If he or she is made familiar with what you're looking for, they can have catalogs, samples and ideas ready for you when you arrive, wasting less time on preliminaries.

While at the resource, make the most of your situation:

- Ask questions.
- Draw as much as you can on your salespersons' knowledge and experience
- Review catalogs; get photocopies, measurements and model numbers to help in making your final decisions.

SHOPPING NORTH CAROLINA

As you will see or may have already noticed, many of the resources listed in this book are located in Hickory or High Point, North Carolina, and for good reason. These cities, located in northwest North Carolina within a 90-minute drive of one another, are considered by many to be the mecca of discount shopping. High Point, which forms a tri-city area with Winston-Salem and Greensboro is a major textile and furniture producing area. Furniture shows held here twice yearly attract exhibitors from all over the world. Hickory, which lies to the southwest, is the home of the internationally famous Hickory Furniture Mart. Although there are literally hundreds of resources in the area, High Point and Hickory, because of the quantity and quality of their resources, are ideal shopping tour starting points. You'll also find that their salespeople are very well informed. My personal favorite is the Hickory Furniture Mart, currently a 17-acre complex with over 80 shops under one roof and plans for more expansion. Not only can you cover a lot of territory in a short period of time, the mart also features two clearance centers offering one-of-a-kind items and many manufacturer owned and authorized factory outlets. These include stock overruns, showroom samples and other excellent bargain items definitely worth checking out.

To get to North Carolina you can fly or drive. Combining a trip to the furniture resources with a business trip or vacation is often practical. You can also fly into Raleigh-Durham, Greensboro or Charlotte. Shop the airfares; they can vary dramatically. Raleigh-Durham airport is about one to 1½ hours from High Point and the Greensboro airport is about 20 minutes from High Point, but sometimes there are better air fares through Raleigh. Charlotte airport is about one hour from Hickory. There is also an airport in Hickory, but you have to take a short commuter flight to get there. With some flexibility, you should be able to get a fairly decent air fare into either city. Once you have your flights, you can reserve a car and accommodations. The listings on the following pages will give you some choices of airlines, car rentals, hotels and places to eat.

If you have only one or two days, I would recommend Hickory. The Hickory Furniture Mart, as I mentioned before, is basically under one roof and you'll be able to cover a lot of ground. Also there are hotel accommodations close by.

If you have three to five days, I would recommend starting out in either Hickory or High Point and definitely make time to visit the sister city. Hickory has the Mart, of course, and High

Point has Boyles, The Atrium, Wood Armfield, Young's, Priba, Rose Furniture and Zaki Oriental Rugs, to mention a few of my favorites. Don't miss these.

A listing of places to stay and/or eat follows. Also included are airline phone numbers and car rental agencies. These are not personal recommendations, but have been suggested by the resources. There's also a map of North Carolina on the inside back cover showing where many of the cities are located.

TEN TIPS FOR SHOPPING IN PERSON

1. Do your preliminary research: manufacturers, models, prices.
2. Take camera and tape measure.
3. Bring room measurements and floor plans, if possible.
4. Bring fabric samples of furniture you plan to keep.
5. Wear comfortable shoes, casual clothing.
6. Bring a notebook for sketches and/or measurements to remind yourself where you were and what you saw. When you take pictures of an item, jot "photo" next to your notes for review later.
7. Ask for photocopies, brochures and catalogs.
8. Be sure to visit manufacturers' outlets and clearance centers.
9. Sit in upholstered pieces or their facsimiles before you buy.
10. Check out your various options.

HOW TO GET TO NORTH CAROLINA

AIRLINES

Airline	Phone Number
Air Canada	1-800-776-3000
American Airlines	1-800-433-7300
British Airways	1-800-247-9297
Continental Airlines	1-800-525-0280

Delta	1-800-221-1212
Northwest Airlines	1-800-225-2525
TWA	1-800-221-2000
United Airlines	1-800-241-6522
US Airways	1-800-428-4322

CAR RENTAL

Company	Phone Number
Alamo	1-800-327-9633
Avis	1-800-331-1212
Budget	1-800-527-0700
Dollar	1-800-800-4000
Enterprise	1-800-325-8007
Hertz	1-800-654-3131
National	1-800-227-7368
Thrifty	1-800-FOR-CARS
Value	1-800-468-2583

WHERE TO STAY
Hickory
Comfort Inn
1125 13th Avenue Dr SE
Hickory, NC 28602-5176
Phone: (828)323-1211

Econo Lodge
325 US Highway 70 SW
Hickory, NC 28602-5018
Phone: (828)328-2111

Fairfield Inn
1950 13th Avenue Dr SE
Hickory, NC 28602-5186
Phone: (828)431-3000

Fran Mar Motel
2710 US Highway 70 SW
Hickory, NC 28602-4746
Phone: (828)327-4137

Gateway Center Hotel
909 US Highway 70 SW
Hickory, NC 28602-5022
Phone: (828)328-5101

Hampton Inn
1520 13th Avenue Dr SE
Hickory, NC 28602-5183
Phone: (828)323-1150

Hickory Bed & Breakfast
464 7th St SW
Hickory, NC 28602-2743
Phone: (828)324-0548

Holiday Inn Select
1385 Lenoir Rhyne Blvd SE
Hickory, NC 28602-5117
Phone: (828)323-1000

Holiday Inn Express
2250 US Highway 70 SE
Hickory, NC 28602-5164
Phone: (828)328-2081

Howard Johnson
483 US Highway 70 SW
Hickory, NC 28602-5019
Phone: (828)322-1600

Red Roof Inn
1184 Lenoir Rhyne Blvd SE
Hickory, NC 28602-5169
Phone: (828)323-1500

Royal Inn
30 US Highway 70 SW
Hickory, NC 28602-5013
Phone: (828)322-4311

Sleep Inn
1179 13th Avenue Dr SE
Hickory, NC 28602-5176
Phone: (828)323-1140

Shopping Tips

Hickory hotels that offer furniture shoppers rates: (Make reservations through Hickory Furniture Mart toll free number 1-800-462-MART):

Holiday Inn Express (828)328-2081
Holiday In Select (828)323-1000
Hampton Inn (828)323-1150
Fairfield Inn (828)431-3000

High Point
Days Inn
120 SW Cloverleaf/Bus I-85
High Point, NC 27263
Phone: (336)885-6000

Harbor Inn Motel
2429 W Green Dr
High Point, NC 27263
Phone: (336)883-6101

Holiday Inn-Market Square
236 S Main St
High Point, NC 27263
Phone: (336)886-7011

Howard Johnson
2000 Brentwood St
High Point, NC 27283
Phone: (336)886-4141

Innkeeper
4300 S Main St
High Point, NC 27262
Phone: (336)434-5151

Premier Bed & Breakfast
1001 Johnson St
High Point, NC 27263
Phone: (336)889-8349

Radisson Hotel
135 S Main St
High Point, NC 27262
Phone: (336)889-8888

Super 8 Motel
400 S Main St
High Point, NC 27263
Phone: (336)882-4103

The Atrium Inn
425 S Main St
High Point, NC 27260
Phone: 1-888-9-ATRIUM

Trinity Inn
120 SW Cloverleaf Place
High Point, NC 27263
Phone: (336)885-4011

Black Mountain
Red Rocker Inn (704)669-5991
* restaurant too
Monte Vista Hotel (704)669-2119
* restaurant too
Comfort Inn (704)669-0666
Travel-Eze Motel (704)669-8076

Rocky Mount
Hampton Inn (919)937-6333
Holiday Inn (919)937-6888
Comfort Inn(919)937-7765

WHERE TO EAT
Hickory
1859 Cafe
443 2nd Ave SW
Hickory, NC 28602
(828)322-1859

Angus Steak House
3795 US Hwy 70 SW
Hickory, NC 28602
(828)327-9883

Annabelles
1960 US Hwy 70 SE
Hickory, NC 28602
(828)328-5607

Old Hickory Brewery
2828 US Hwy 70 W
Hickory, NC 28602
(828)323-8753

Vintage House
271 Third (Corner 3rd Ave & 3rd St.)
Hickory, NC 28601
(828)324-1210

High Point
J Basul Nobles
114 S Main St
High Point, NC (336)889-3354

Bamboo Garden
10106 S Main St #C
Archdale, NC 27263
(336)434-1888

Act I
130 E Parris
High Point, NC 27262
(336)869-5614

Outback
260 E Parris Ave
High Point, NC 27262
(336)885-6283

Fuji's
133 E Parris Ave
High Point, NC 27262
(336)869-9000

Rocky Mount
Chaos Cappuccino Bar & Bistro
(919)443-9090

Atlantis Seafood & Oyster Bar
(919)977-2239

Carleton House
(919)977-0410

Black Mountain
Berliner Kindl (German)
(704)669-5255

Coach House Seafood
(704)669-4223

Claudia's Cafe (fine dining)
(704)669-4447

Mountain Bar-B-Cue
(704)669-7078

My Father's Pizza
(704)669-4944

Olympic Flame (Italian)
(704)669-9799

Tong Sing Restaurant (Chinese)
(704)669-5049

BEFORE YOU ORDER

Whether you're ordering by phone or in person, there are some questions that need to be answered before you make a deal:

- How long has the resource been in business?
- How do they ship and deliver to your area?
- How reliable are the freight carriers they use?
- Will the resource handle any problems that might occur with the manufacturer or the freight carrier?

These are things you need to know before you commit to a purchase. If there is a problem with the carrier or the manufacturer, you want assurances, in writing if possible, that the resource will handle the entire matter. If satisfactory assurances are not forthcoming, you would be well advised to look for another resource.

You'll also want to know about service after the sale:

- What happens if the fabric wears prematurely or the stitching fails? What will they do for you?
- What is their policy on returns and exchanges, particularly with wallpaper or fabric? Is there a re-stocking fee and how much is it?

On these matters, you should be fully satisfied with the answers, or use another resource.

Payment

Many resources will accept a down payment—usually 30% to 50% of the full amount—via Mastercard or Visa, certified check or cashier's check. See **Protecting Your Deposit** on Page 22 for advice on this subject. They then require that the balance be paid once the merchandise has arrived at their warehouse, and before delivery. Usually the balance must be paid with a certified or cashier's check. Some resources will offer further discounts if the item is paid for in full at the time of ordering. To avoid any misunderstanding, be sure to check with each resource on its payment policy. Also be aware that the shipping cost is separate and must be paid (usually) in certified funds to the shipper at the time of delivery.

SHIPPING

Shipping costs will vary depending on the number of items you order, the weight, the distance, or a combination of all three. Shipping a sofa might cost $100. Shipping a sofa, two chairs and a small table might cost $150. So, one way to economize is to save on shipping by making all your purchases from one resource if possible. Don't forget, too, that many people travel to North Carolina with a rental truck or their personal vehicle to take immediate possession of their purchases.

The Hickory Furniture Mart in Hickory in Hickory, NC not only offers excellent resources (over 80 stores as of early 1998), but highly convenient shipping practices as well. Their shipping office will consolidate all purchases made within their stores, all 80 of them. As purchases are made, tell your salesperson that you have made other purchases within the complex. That fact is noted and Hickory Furniture Mart then handles all of the logistics of gathering and shipping your purchases.

> **NOTE:** *Even though this service is made available to you, it's always a good idea to keep in touch with the shipping department and verify the status of your shipment.*

The chart beginning on Page 14 provides shipping information based on approximate weights of shipments originating from Hickory, NC.This reference chart should be used simply to get an idea of the cost of shipping from a North Carolina resource to you. It contains approximate freight charges, effective 1/1/98 and was supplied by the Hickory Furniture Mart. **Please note these charges are subject to change without notice and that shipping needs will often vary.** Additional charges can be incurred for split shipments and for other variations of typical shipping situations.

Shipping Problems

If a problem occurs during the shipment of your furniture, there are several steps to take. The most important factor, if you've done your preliminary research, is that you are dealing with a resource that says they will handle the problems on your behalf.

Minor damages, small scratches and minor blemishes that occur during shipping should be noted immediately with the shipper and you should call your resource immediately. Inform your salesperson or customer service rep of the problem. They should handle the problem from that point. They may request that you get estimates for the repair of the piece or may even recommend a local repair shop to you. They should pay for the repair or replacement of the item. Know this beforehand. Determine with the resource which course of action will be taken.

If the damage is more severe, you can return the item with the resource's approval. Do not send it back until you have spoken with the resource. If the item is totally unacceptable because of damage, do not accept it and call the resource immediately.

In my experience of furniture buying and shipping, I have encountered only minor problems with furniture deliveries. Sometimes a piece of hardware is missing. The resource can re-ship or UPS the missing piece immediately. **NOTE:** Don't forget to measure the furniture that you're buying, not only for where it will eventually be placed, but to be sure that it will fit through entrances and hallways as well. When your furniture is delivered, you have to be sure it can be carried up or down stairs, around corners and doorways and through halls and archways. This can be a bit tricky, especially with a lot of today's oversized furniture pieces.

The resources know that their best advertising is a happy customer. Many of them have worked hard to perfect their shipping and customer service policies. They want happy customers to go out and tell their friends, relatives and co-workers what a good experience they had. I have also found that most of the resources are very easy to work with if you're fair with them, too. If you do have a problem or a complaint, be polite, courteous and to-the-point. It goes a lot further than an aggressive or defensive attitude.

APPROXIMATE SHIPPING COSTS

STATE	MINIMUM	151-1000 POUNDS	1001-2000 POUNDS	2001-4000 POUNDS
Alabama	$87.00	$51.00	$43.00	$37.00
Arizona	136.00	84.00	80.00	65.00
Arkansas	106.00	67.00	64.00	61.00
California	142.00	93.00	91.00	89.00
Connecticut	104.00	57.00	51.00	46.00
Colorado	137.00	91.00	90.00	88.00
Delaware	94.00	52.00	46.00	40.00
Dist of Columbia	94.00	52.00	46.00	40.00
Florida	99.00	57.00	48.00	42.00
Georgia	89.00	47.00	41.00	35.00
Idaho	153.00	103.00	100.50	98.00
Illinois	109.00	60.00	54.00	46.00
Indiana	99.00	57.00	51.00	45.00
Iowa	132.00	84.00	82.00	80.00
Kansas	137.00	91.00	89.50	88.00
Kentucky	94.00	55.00	49.00	43.00
Louisiana	104.00	64.00	53.00	48.00
Maine	112.00	66.00	60.00	54.00
Maryland	94.00	48.00	42.00	36.00
Massachusetts	109.00	60.00	54.00	48.00
Michigan (lower)	104.00	58.00	52.00	46.00
Michigan (upper)	400.00	77.00	68.00	65.00
Minnesota	129.00	81.00	80.50	80.00
Mississippi	96.00	58.00	50.00	46.00
Missouri	110.00	64.50	58.50	55.00
Montana	470.00 *	94.00	88.00	88.00
Nebraska	122.00	73.00	68.00	66.00
Nevada	143.00	98.00	96.00	94.00
New Hampshire	110.00	65.50	59.50	53.50
New Jersey	99.00	56.00	50.00	44.00
New Mexico	121.00	81.00	79.50	78.00
New York	109.00	58.00	52.00	46.00
North Carolina (704 area)	77.00 **	30.00	26.00	23.00
North Carolina (Other)	94.00 **	35.00	31.00	28.00
North Carolina (local)	47.00 **	22.00	20.00	18.00
North Dakota	420.00 *	84.00	78.00	78.00
Ohio	99.00	56.00	50.00	44.00
Oklahoma	120.00	77.00	75.00	73.00
Oregon	168.00	110.00	107.50	105.00
Pennsylvania	99.00	56.00	50.00	44.00

STATE	MINIMUM	151-1000 POUNDS	1001-2000 POUNDS	2001-4000 POUNDS
Rhode Island	109.00	58.00	52.00	46.00
South Carolina	89.00	44.00	38.00	32.00
South Dakota	410.00*	82.00	79.00	76.00
Tennessee	94.00	52.50	42.00	34.50
Texas	117.00	76.00	70.00	68.00
Utah	150.00	97.00	95.00	93.00
Vermont	112.00	66.00	60.00	54.00
Virginia	89.00	45.00	39.00	33.00
Washington	168.00	111.00	108.50	106.00
West Virginia	94.00	52.00	46.00	40.00
Wisconsin	125.00	77.50	73.25	70.00
Wyoming	440.00*	88.00	80.00	80.00

* 500 pound minimum   ** 250 pound minimum

SHOPPING FOR UPHOLSTERED FURNITURE

Upholstered furniture presents its own unique but definitely surmountable challenges. With upholstered furniture, price is not necessarily a measure of quality. The quality of upholstered furniture lies in its construction. And its fabric must not only suit its intended appearance, but its intended use as well. When shopping for upholstered furniture, begin with an overall evaluation of the piece for the quality of its construction, then do the same for its fabrics and options. Be sure that the height of the back and the angle are comfortable and suitable to those who will be sitting in it. The seat and cushion should not feel flat, springs shouldn't squeak, the frame shouldn't wobble. There should be no noise or movement when you jab at the arms. Here are the things to look for in determining the quality of an upholstered piece:

Construction

The basic ingredients of any upholstered piece are its frame, springs, padding and fabric with the frame and springs being most important. Fabric and padding can be easily replaced; frames and springs are a different matter.

The best frames are made of hardwoods (maple, elm, hickory), kiln-dried to prevent shrinkage. Lift one end to check for wobbling or creaking. If possible, check the underside for strong joints secured in the corners with triangular corner blocks. Joints should be doweled, glued and screwed. Dripping glue, nailed joints or legs screwed, glued or nailed to the frame indicate lesser quality. Exposed woods should be sanded and finished and should feel smooth to the touch.

Springs provide the support for the cushions and padding. The more springs and the more intricate the connections, the better the quality. The best construction consists of coil springs individually mounted on a polypropylene webbing base. Each spring should be hand-tied with strong twine in eight different locations. Lesser quality pieces use fewer springs secured in fewer places.

Cushions. Check the fit of the cushions to see that they fit flush with the front edge of the seat and that they fit snugly. Cushioning material varies. The tag on the cushion should describe the type of filling. Types of fillings include:

- Down, a comfortable but non-resilient filling.
- Polyurethane foam and polyester fiberfil are the most common fillings and both are quite durable.
- HR foam (High Resiliency) is of particularly high quality.
- HC foam (High Comfort) is better than conventional, but not as good as HR.

Polyurethane foam cushions, filled with kapok or bonded shredded foam have a tendency to flatten after a period of time and cause seams and welting to shift. Compress a cushion to see how well it returns to its original shape. Zippered cushions indicate quality. When the zipper is opened, you should see that the filling has been sewn into ticking.

Fabrics. The fabric design should match on the seat and cushions and be centered on the front and back of the piece. Seams should be straight. Look for secured buttons and welting. Run your hand over the fabric to make sure there are no wrinkles. On a sofa, the pleats in the skirt should align with the separation between the cushions. The deck (the fabric under the cushions) should match or complement the fabric. If you press down on the deck, there should be sufficient padding to prevent feeling the springs or the openings between them.

Fabrics will vary from manufacturer to manufacturer because fabric grading is not standardized. Fabric quality depends on content, so always check the tags and swatches. Here are descriptions of blends of fabrics in current use:

- Knitted, woven or felted fabrics from natural fibers like cotton flax, wool and silk are soft to the touch.
- Blends with synthetics like acetate, acrylic, nylon, polyester, polypropylene and rayon are more durable and stain resistant.
- New synthetics called "microdenier fibers" are made up of very thin filaments. These filaments mimic natural fibers, but are more durable and stain-resistant.

A tighter weave indicates more durability. If you hold a fabric up to light and see more than tiny specks of light coming through, this indicates low quality. To check further for durability:

- Stretch the fabric and push with your thumbs. You should not be able to separate the threads.
- Scratch the fabric with a fingernail to see if yarns are easily pulled.
- Rub the fabric with a pencil eraser to see if it balls, pills or comes apart.
- Rub patterned fabric with a white handkerchief to see if color rubs off.
- If a fabric has a design or pattern woven into it, you should be able to see the design from the back of the material. This generally indicates better quality.

Cleaning

It's always important to know how fabrics should be cleaned and their labels should indicate the cleaning method:

W	means use water-based cleaners.
S	means use solvent-based cleaners.
W-S	indicates either type cleaner can be used.
X	means vacuum only.

Upholstery Options

Upholstered pieces are available with a wide assortment of options. When shopping for chairs, sofas, love seats, cushions or other upholstered pieces, don't forget the options. The following partial list will give you some idea of what's available:

OPTIONS:	WHAT'S AVAILABLE
Arm Sleeve	A protective cover made from your upholstery fabric. It covers front to back of the arm and down inside the seat
Arm Covers	Covers about one-third of the arm of sofa or chair.
Arm Styles	Examples: Envelope, English, Large Lawson, Conventional Lawson, Tuxedo, Rolled Tuxedo, Pleated Tuxedo, Scroll, Curved Pleated
Brass Nail Trim	Pieces can sometimes be upholstered with or without nails. Where the nails are placed can also vary.
Casters	Ask about the different types of casters or wheels on the furniture.
Combination Covers	Two or more fabrics/leather/or both are used in one piece.
Contrasting Welts and Buttons	Adds a very nice professional touch. Matching, contrasting or complementary welting is sewn into the piece. Buttons can be added on cushions or backs of chairs and sofas.
Cushions	Examples: Firmness, Number of Cushions, Shape, Decorative Edging and Trim
Decorative Edging and Trim	Fringes, cording and tassels

Decorative Skirts	Examples: Kick Pleat, Ruffle, Double Pleat, Corner Pleat, Corner Shirred, Box Pleat
Fabrics	Self-explanatory
Finishes	Exposed wood may be finished in a choice of colors or stains.
Pillows/Bolsters	Examples: Knife-edge Welted, Knife-edge Weltless, Corner-pleat Welted, Corner-pleat, Number of Pillows/Bolsters, Shape, Weltless
Quilting	Different patterns, stitches, threads.
Self-decking	This refers to upholstering the piece under the cushions with the same fabric as the rest of the item. The standard is usually done in cotton or muslin.
Sleeper Sofa	Some sofas have this option.
Soil Resistant Treatment	Treatments can vary. Different products can be used for this.
Swivels and Rockers	Some chairs can be built with swivel and/or rocker and/or both capabilities.

Leather

You'll find that leather-covered furniture is slightly more expensive than fabric-covered pieces. However, leather is definitely in demand for certain furniture applications and can last years longer than fabric. There are three grades of leather, based on the way the hide has been cut and treated:

- **Premium leather** is "full grain" which indicates that it needs no corrections. The hide is very soft and shows natural variations in the grain.
- **"Top grain"** leather is the next best grade. It has been partially or fully corrected to improve its appearance. This process involves sanding and buffing the old grain off and embossing a new grain into it. The process makes the leather feel stiffer, and top grain is considered as strong as full grained leather.
- **"Split"** is the lowest grade leather and is not recommended for upholstering because it is the weakest portion of the hide and cannot endure daily usage.

The dying process used is also an important consideration in the selection of leather. Aniline dye is better than sprayed-on color because it completely penetrates the hide, yet lets the natural grain show through. Scratch the surface of aniline dyed leather and you will see the same color beneath the surface as on it. Most leather is treated with a clear coating for protection and easy care. Unprotected leather is much softer to the touch, but having the clear-coat protection is very important if you're concerned about spills and stains.

"COM" SHOPPING—CHOOSING YOUR OWN UPHOLSTERY FABRIC

When it comes to shopping for upholstered furniture, you have even more latitude with a service called COM, an acronym for "Customer's Own Material." With COM, you are not limited to the fabrics offered by the manufacturers. Instead, you provide the manufacturer with material you have selected for your chosen upholstered piece.

For instance, you want a Henredon sofa but you don't like the Henredon fabric choices. Instead, you've found a beautiful fabric you want to use. This will now become a COM transaction. COM is normally listed as a fabric option by the manufacturer. That is, the manufacturer may offer three grades of fabric (A, B and C) with A priced at $800; Grade B at $1,000 and Grade C at $1,200. The "COM" option will normally be priced near the cost of the piece upholstered in the lowest grade fabric. To that price you must now add the cost of your preferred fabric.

You may find that you have to go to an entirely different resource to get the fabric. If so, arrangements must be made to have the fabric shipped directly to the upholstery resource. Here is the step-by-step procedure:

Ordering COM Furniture

1. Know the furniture piece you want - manufacturer, model number, etc.
2. Know the fabric you want - manufacturer, pattern number, repeat, width. *Repeat tells you how often, in inches, the design or the pattern in a fabric repeats itself. You need to know the repeat width to determine the amount of material needed and to ultimately determine fabric costs.*
3. Call the furniture resource for the COM price, shipping costs, yardage required, and any special instructions, including where to ship the fabric.
4. Contact fabric resource. Order the amount of fabric you need and be prepared to provide them with the furniture resource's shipping address, and any special manufacturer's instructions.
5. Request a "cutting for approval" so that you can confirm that you have selected the right fabric and color.
6. Also request that the yardage you need is "reserved" for you upon your approval. **IMPORTANT NOTE**: *If you plan to have accessories or complementary pieces made, order enough fabric for all the pieces at one time and have it "split-shipped." By ordering all the fabric at one time and split-shipping, you get all the fabric from the same bolt or dye lot and "split" the fabric between that shipped to the furniture resource and the remainder which is shipped to you, another resource or both. Split-shipping is very important because the same fabrics may vary dramatically from one bolt or dye lot to another.*

7. When you receive and approve the cutting, call the fabric resource and have it released for shipment to the upholstery resource. If the fabric is wrong, immediately notify the fabric resource and tell them not to ship but to send you the correct cuttings, if available. If not, you must start the fabric selection process over.

8. Request the upholstery resource to notify you when they have received the fabric. The six to 12 weeks normally required for production and delivery doesn't begin until the fabric is received. Most resources will notify you by phone or mail that they've received your fabric and when they are scheduling your item for production.

While ordering an item "COM" is a little more involved, you'll get exactly what you want. It's worth the extra effort.

SHOPPING FOR CASEGOODS

Case goods, which is a general term for all non-upholstered furniture, are simpler to order because they generally have fewer options. Stain-color and finish are the usual options. If you see a piece you like, be sure to note the color **and** finish. Like fabric, stain-color and finish can dramatically change the appearance of any piece of furniture and will sometimes alter pricing. Be sure to measure carefully the width, length and height of the space where you plan to put this piece of furniture.

Following is a list of typical case goods options:

Case goods Options
- Arm Styles
- Brass Nail Heads
- Exposed Wood Finishes: Standard, Premium
- Stains
- Swivel-tilt Base with Casters

NOTE: *Sometimes when ordering a sofa or chair with exposed wood and upholstery, you will have both upholstery and case goods options to choose from.*

Things You Should Know About Wood
- Wood names are often used to describe the color of a finish, not the wood itself. A label indicating that a piece has an "oak finish" does not necessarily mean it's made of oak.
- "Softwood" furniture is produced from conifer or cone-bearing trees with needles, such as pine, cedar and redwood. Most softwoods can be easily scratched and dented.
- "Hardwood" furniture is made from deciduous or leaf-bearing trees that shed their leaves each fall, such as ash, cherry, maple, oak and walnut.

Mahogany is an imported hardwood. Hardwoods are most often used in the construction of quality furniture.

- "Solid wood" means 100% wood construction with no veneers or substitute matter like particle board.
- "Veneers" are thin layers of hardwood bonded to a core material such as particle board or plywood. When bonded to plywood or other solid wood, veneer construction can be referred to as "all wood". Walnut and mahogany are frequently used for veneering.
- "Laminates" are photographic reproductions of wood grains on a thin layer of plastic that is bonded to particle board or some other reconstituted wood product.

Things To Look For When Shopping For Casegoods

- Does the piece have a well-balanced feeling?
- How is the piece constructed? Ask a salesperson. If it's tongue-and-groove, double-doweled joints or mortise-and-tenon, these are good features. Test it by gently pushing on a corner or putting your weight against a side. It should not wobble or creak.
- The back panels should be inset and attached with screws.
- Check the underside: Joints should be reinforced with screws, slats and rungs should be snug, joints should be free of excess glue and filler. Look for triangular corner blocks. Are they screwed and glued in place for added stability and support?
- Check for drawer dust panels between drawer spaces.
- Check to see if dining table leaves have an apron to match that of the table.
- Furniture used for storage or display should have a leveling device in the bottom corners.
- Check drawer glides and stops for smooth operation.
- Is drawer hardware sturdy and screwed from the inside?
- Do doors swing open evenly without squeaking or rubbing?
- Check door inset panels for rattling or jiggling.
- Furniture for electronic equipment should have an opening for electrical cords and cables.
- Do all movable parts operate smoothly and properly?
- Are interior lights easy to use?
- Check for smoothness by running your hand over the full surface of the piece, including legs and underside. The finish should be smooth and even with no stains, streaks, bubbles or cracks.

PROTECTING YOUR DEPOSIT

One of the major hesitations consumer have when buying furniture is the perceived risk involved when paying a 30-50% deposit on furniture they may not see for six to twelve weeks. Here are several steps you can take to protect your peace of mind and your investment:

- **Pay with a credit card**. You can dispute charges for items you paid for but never received.
- **Call the Better Business Bureau.** Check the status of a company you're planning to do business with. However, not belonging to the BBB does not mean a company is disreputable. See Page 23 for some phone numbers.
- **Call the Attorney General's Office** of the state the company is located in. Inquire if there is pending litigation against this company. See Page 23 for some phone numbers
- **Call the Consumer Department** of the manufacturer of the item you're planning on purchasing. Ask if the resource is an authorized dealer in good standing with the manufacturer. There is a listing of manufacturers and their addresses and phone numbers on Page 41 to help you.
- **Ask the resource themselves** what, if anything, they doto protect their customers from any problems they may have with the company. Some resources have surety bonds, others have backing from a higher entity or insurance policies for such situations.

IMPORTANT PHONE NUMBERS
AND/OR ADDRESSES

Below I have provided the names of several business bureaus and agencies in North Carolina. This information may be helpful to you in deciding if you want to do business with any particular resource. For other companies besides those located in North Carolina, you can call general information and request the numbers of the appropriate agencies.

AGENCIES AND BUREAUS

BETTER BUSINESS BUREAUS

BBB of Central North Carolina
3608 W Friendly Ave
Greensboro, NC 27410
336-852-4240

BBB of Western North Carolina
1200 BB&T Bldg
Asheville, NC 28801-3418
704-253-2392

BBB of Southern Piedmont
5200 Park Rd
Suite 202
Charlotte, NC 28209-3650
704-527-0012

BBB of Eastern North Carolina
3125 Poplarwood Ct
Suite 308
Raleigh, NC 27604-1088
919-872-9240

BBB of Northwest North Carolina
500 W 5th St
Suite 202
Winston-Salem, NC 27101-2728
910-752-8348

NORTH CAROLINA ATTORNEY GENERAL'S OFFICE
Michael F. Easley
P.O. Box 629
Raleigh, N.C. 27602
919-716-6000

HIGH POINT CONVENTION AND VISITORS' BUREAU
300 S Main St
High Point, N.C. 27260
336-884-5255

HICKORY CHAMBER OF COMMERCE
PO BOX 1828
Hickory, NC 28603
828-328-6111

ONE FINAL NOTE:

Don't be afraid to shop aggressively for value. Be willing to pay for good advice, but don't overpay. Keep yourself well-informed. Doing your homework helps make things go much easier.

Recognize when and if you need technical advice or help in developing a design concept. Don't be afraid to hire a designer. When you need help, the smartest thing you can do is hire someone who is professionally trained and experienced to assist you. You may want someone to handle an entire project, or you may want someone to spend a day or two with you developing ideas. Designers usually charge by the hour. Rates are usually negotiable but be prepared to pay from $35 to $150 per hour, depending on the designer. Some designers work on a "cost-plus" basis. That is, they charge a certain percentage of the cost of products and materials purchased through them. Other designers work on a combination of these systems.

Always be straightforward with the designer you've chosen to work with. If you're looking for ideas and some limited assistance and plan to purchase items on your own, make those facts known and develop a payment plan accordingly. There are a number of ways to find reputable designers:

- Through a local design center, if there's one near you.
- Through referrals.
- Through furniture stores with designers on staff.
- Through the American Society of Interior Designers (ASID) Referral service. 800-775-ASID for residential projects and 800-610-ASID for commercial jobs.

A good designer who understands your needs and your budget can be a real asset for selecting materials and products. They usually have access to labor and materials sources. If there is a need for a designer in your decorating or refurnishing plans, there's a designer out there to fill that need.

GOOD LUCK, GOOD DEALS AND GOOD SHOPPING!!

PRODUCT AND MANUFACTURER LISTINGS

PRODUCTS LISTING WITH SUGGESTED MANUFACTURERS

Following is a list of manufacturers by products. It is not to be construed as a recommendation of quality, price or preference. You may find a particular manufacturer in this list that does not appear in the cross-reference index, but this does not mean that this manufacturer's products are not available through the resources of this book. Many manufacturer produce the same product under different names or other manufacturers make comparable or superior products at very attractive prices. Many resources do not list all of the manufacturers that they carry. When searching out a specific item, you can ask about a particular manufacturer by name or ask for a comparable product. Products and manufacturers change on a daily basis, which makes it impossible for the information in this book to be completely up-to-date. Every effort has been made to assure that this book contains only the most current and accurate information. Therefore, there may be omissions of manufacturers under the individual categories. Feel free to add in your own recommendations. **The bolded entries designate the name of a resource that specializes in that particular area or product.**

ACCESSORIES
A.R.T.
Accessory Art
Artisan House
Artmaster Studios
As You Like It
Austin
Baldwin
Bassett Mirror
Bob Timberlake
Brasscrafters
Carolina Mirror
Classic Picture
Consignment Galleries
Creative Accents
Decorative Arts
Decorative Crafts
Department 56
Elliott's
Fe/26
Fine Art Ltd. - mirror
FloralArt
Flute
General Store
Guildmaster
Harris G. Strong
Hen Feathers
Interlude
J.K. Reed
John Richard Collection
Kinder-Harris

Lawrence Unlimited
Linden
Liteline
Maitland Smith
Maxton
NDI (swags, trees, wreaths tabletops)
Palecek
Plant Plant (bonsai, fruit, veggies, Xmas)
Pouliot
Pulaski
Reprocrafters
Ridgeway
Royal Doulton
Royal Worchester/Spode
Sarreid
Somerset Studios - lodge
Studio Internationale
Tempo
Uttermost
Vanguard Studios
Waterford Crystal Lighting
Windsor Art
Yanigan's (also Xmas)

ACRYLICS
Plexi-Craft Quality Products

ANTIQUES AND REPRODUCTIONS
Baker
Berkeley Upholstering
Borkholder
Bradco
Burton Reproductions
Casa Stradivari
Cedar Rock Home Furnishings
Chapman
Consignment Galleries
Craftique
Drexel Heritage
EJ Victor
Elliott's Designs
Frederick Edwards
Furniture Guild
Hickory Chair
Hickory Furniture Mart
Holton Furniture Co.
House Dressing
Jamestown Sterling
Karges
Kimball
Lane Upholstery
Lifestyles Collection
Old Hickory Tannery
Passport Furniture
Rosalco
Sarreid
Sligh
Southwood Furniture

Statton

ANTIQUE REPRODUCTIONS, FRENCH/ ANTIQUE
AA Laun
Arbek
Baker
Berkeley
Borkholder
Boussac
Bradco
Chapman
Drexel Heritage
EJ Victor
French Heritage
Hickory Chair
House of France
Karges
Kimball
Southwood
Statton
Tradition France
Union City

ARMOIRES
Arbek
Baker
Bernhardt
Drexel Heritage
Habersham Plantation
Henredon
Lane
Lexington
Milling Road
National Mt Airy
Platt Collections
Stein World
Union City

BAKERS RACKS
Koch Originals
Johnston Casuals
Southern Enterprises

BEDDING, LINENS, HOME FURNISHINGS
American Pacific
Harris Levy
Park B. Smith
P & J Fabrics

BEDROOMS, TRADITIONAL
American Drew
Bernhardt
Cochrane
Councill Craftsmen

DMI
Drexel
Henredon
Hooker
Kincaid
Lane
Lexington
Link-Taylor
Nathan Hale
Pennsylvania House
Thomasville Cabinet
Universal

BEDROOMS, GENERAL
Acacia
Accent
Allusions
American Drew
American of Martinsville
Amisco
Amish Country Collection
Arbek
Ardley Hall
Artisans
Ashley
Aspen
Athens
Baker
Barn Door
Bassett
Bemco
Benicia
Berkshire
Bernards
Bernhardt
Bestar
Blackhawk
Bob Timberlake
Borkholder
Boyd
Brady
Brass Bed Shop
Brill
Brown Jordan
Brown Street
Broyhill
Bush
Bushline
Canwood
Capris
Carolina Furniture Works
Carson's
Casa Bique
Casa Stradivari
Catalina
Century
Childcraft
Cisco Brothers

Classic Rattan
Cochrane
Collingwood
Colonial
Corolla Classics
Corsican
Council Companies
Councill Craftsmen
Cox
Craftique
Crate in Motion
Crawford
Creative Elegance
Creative Furniture
Cresent
Cumberland Crown
D & F Wicker/Rattan
D-Scan
Design Institute America
Designer Wicker & Rattan
Dillon
Dino-Mark Anthony
Directions
Dixie
DMI
Dresher
Drexel Heritage
Dubois
Durham
EJ Victor
Ekornes
Elliott's Designs
Ellman's
Englander
Fairchild of California
Fancher
Fashion Bed Group
Florida Furniture
Fortune Rattan
Frisco
Furniture Guild
General
Giorgio Collection
Global Furniture
GMS Imports
Guy Chaddock
Habersham Plantation
Harden
Hart
Henkel-Harris
Henredon
Henry-Link
Hickory Chair
Hickory White
Hood
Hooker
Hyundai
IBC

Ideal
Impact
Imperial
JB Ross
Jamestown Sterling
John Turano
John Widdicomb
Johnston Tombigbee
Karges
Keller
Kessler
Kettler
Kincaid
King Koil
Kingsdown
Knob Creek
Lane
Largo Intl
Laurier
Lea Inds
Leda Furniture
Leggett & Platt
Lehigh
Lexington
Lincoln-Gerard USA
Lineage
Link Taylor
Maitland-Smith
Marge Carson
Martex
Meadowcraft
Millenium
Milling Road
Moosehead
Murphy
Najarian
Nathan Hale
National Mt Airy
Nautilus Bedding
Oakwood Interiors
Orderest Mattress
Orleans
Orman Grubb Co
Palliser
Park Place
Pennsylvania Classics
Pennsylvania House
Pilliod
Pine-Tique
Platt Collections
Progressive
Pulaski
Quality
Restonic
Richardson Bros
Riverside
Rock City
Romweber

Rosalco
Rynone Design
S Bent
Sauder Woodworking
Sealy
Serta
Sharut
Shermag
Simmons
Singer
Sleep Works
Somma
Southern Enterprises
Southern Furniture
Southern Furniture
Reproductions
Spring Air
Springwall
St Martin's Lane
Stanley
Statton
Stearns & Foster
Stevens Inds/ID Home
Stickley
Sumter Cabinet
Swan
Symbol Mattress
Taylor Woodcraft
Tech Designs
Tell City
The Furniture Guild
Thomasville
Through the Barn Door
Traditions France
Transpacific
Trillium Lifestyle Inds
Trouvailles
Union City Imports
Union-National
Unique Originals
Universal
Vanguard
Vaughan
VB Williams
Vermont Precision
Vermont Tubbs
Villageous
Virginia House
Wambold
Warren
Webb
Wellington Hall
Wesley Allen
Wesley Allen
Whitecraft Ratten
Wolf
Workspace
Wright Table

Yesteryear Wicker
Yield House

BEDROOM, NURSERY, BABY AND YOUTH
Albert M Lock
Amisco
Bassett
Child Craft
Colgate Baby Mattress
Crate in Motion
Design Horizons
DMI
Dutailier
Generations
Harden
Lea
Lexington
Michael Showalter
Palliser
Powell
Rooms to Grow
(Lexington)
Rosalco
Sauder Woodworking
Stanley
The Little Ones
Vermont Tubbs

BEDS, IRON/METAL/BRASS
Amisco
Benicia
Bernards
Brass Bed Shop
Cochrane
Comfort Designs
Elliott's Designs
Elm Creek
Fashion Bed Group
Gold Key
Hart
Hickory White
Largo
Powell
Rosalco
Swan/Corsican
Tempo
Wesley Allen

BILLIARD TABLE
Hippopotamus

CARPETING AND RUGS
Aladdin Mills
American Carpet Mills
Amiran

Armstrong Carpet Mills
Asmara
Balta
Barrett
Bashian & Sons
Bashian Bros
Beaver Carpets
Beaulieu of America
Bigelow
Blue Ridge
Burlington Mills
Burtco Ent.
Cabin Craft
Caladium
Callaway
Capel Mill OUtlet
Capel Mills
Carousel
Carpet Express
Carpet Outlet, The
Carpeton Mills
Cascade Carpet Mills
Challenger Industries
Charles Warehouse
Charles W Jacobsen
Charleston Carpets
Citation Carpets
Classic Oriental Rugs
Colonial Mills
Columbia Carpets
Columbus
Conquest
Consolidated Textiles
Coronet
Couristan
Criterion
Cumberland
Customweave
Dalton Paradise Carpet
Davis & Davis
Dejon Contract Collection
Designweave
Diamond Mills
Dimension Carpet
Discount Carpet
Evans & Black
Floorways
Focus
Foreign Accents
Fritz & LaRue
Galaxy Carpets
Gibraltar
Gold Label Carpe
Grassmore
Helios
Hollytex
Horizon Industries
Image Carpets

Instant Turf Industries
International Carpet
Johnson's Carpets
Karastan
Karastan Rug & Carpet Center
Kentile
Kraus Carpet Mills
Lees
Lees Carpet Showcase
Len-Dal Carpets & Rugs
Mair Astley Carpets
Masland
Miles
Mohawk
Monticello
Network Floorcovering
Northwest Carpets
Nourison
Pande Cameron Orientals
Paradise Carpet
Parket's Carpet
Philadelphia
Porter
Porter Carpet Mills
Princeton
Queen
RD Stallion Carpets
Richmond Carpet Mills
Rosecore
Royal Dutch Carpets
Rug Store, The
S & S Mills
Salem Carpet Mills
Shaheen
Shaw Industries
Sheffield Carpets
Sina Oriental Rug
Stark
Stellar Carpet Industries
Statton Industries
Sun Flooring
Sun Mills
Sunrise Carpet
Supreme
Sutton
Tower
Tuftex Industries
Village Carpet
Warehouse Carpet
Wellco
Whitecrest Carpet Mills
World Carpets
Wundaweave

CASEGOODS
American Drew
American of Martinsville

Arbek
Ardley Hall
Armstrong
Ashley
Athens
Athol
Baker
Bassett
Bentwood Furniture
Bernards
Bernhardt
Bob Timberlake
Boyd
Brady
Broyhill
Cal-Style
Canadel
Casa Bique
Century
Childcraft
Cochrane
Collingwood
Councill Craftsman
Craftique
Custom Style
Dino-Mark Anthony
DMI Furniture
Douglas
Drexel Heritage
DSF
Ello
Essex Chair
Fairmont Design
Ficks Reed
Florida
French Heritage
Frisco
Furniture Guild
Garcia Imports
Giorgio
Glass Arts
Guy Chaddock
H & H
Harden
Hekman
Henredon
Hickory Chair
Hickory White
Hickorycraft
Higdon
Hood Furniture
Hooker
Hyundai
ID Kids
Impact
Imperial
John Widdicomb
Kincaid

Kittinger
Koch Originals
Lane
Lea
Leda
Lehigh
Lexington
Lifestyle California
Lineage
Master Design
Milling Road
Moosehead
Murphy
Nathan Hale
Oak Craft
Oakwood Interiors
Pennsylvania House
Pilliod
Premier
Progressive
Reed Furniture
Rex
Richardson Bros
Riverside
Robinson
Ron Fisher
Saloom
Sauder
Sharut
Sidex
Singer
SK Furniture
Southern Furniture
Reproduction
Standard
Stanley
Statton
Stein World
Stickley
Stoneville
Tell City
Thomasville
Timeless Design
Traditions France
Universal
Vargas
Vaughan
Vermont Precision
Vermont Tubbs
Virginia House
Workspace

CEDAR CHESTS
Lane
Murphy

CHAIRS/BARSTOOLS
Best Chairs

Blacksmith Shop
Builtright Chair
Lyon Shaw
Sam Moore
Stein World
Uwharrie

CHAIRS, WOOD
American Drew
Baker
Barlow Tyrie
Bernhardt
Boling
Bradco
Brady
Broyhill
Builtrightt Chair
Century
Chapman
Chatham County
Child Craft
Cochrane
Craftique
Crawford
Curry
DMI Furniture
Daystrom
Dinaire
Drexel Heritage
Dutailier
Flexsteel
General Furniture
Habersham Plantation
Harden
Hekman
Henkel-Harris
Hickory Furniture
Hickory White
Johnston Tombigbee
Karges
Keller
Kettler
Kincaid
Knob Creek
LaBarge
Lakewood
Manchester Wood
Martinsville Novelty
Master Design
Moosehead
Nichols & Stone
North Hickory
P & P Chair
Pawleys Island
Pine-Tique
Pulaski
Richardson Bros
Riverside

Sam Moore Chairs
Singer
Stout
Summer Classics
Taylor Woodcraft
Telescope
Thayer Coggin
Through the Barn Door
Tomlinson/Erwin-Lambeth
Union City
Union Natitonal
US Furniture Industries
Universal Furnitture
Virginnia House
Webb
Windsor Designs

CLOCKS
Ansonia
Chapman
Colonial
D & F Wicker/Rattan
Imports
Dayva Industries
Drexel Heritage
General Furniture
Habersham Plantation
Hall Clock
Hamilton
Howard Miller
Linden
New England Clock Co.
Old Town Clock Co.
Pine-Tique
Pulaski
Ridgeway
Seth Thomas
Sligh
Thayer Coggin
Time Gallery, The
Trend

COMPUTER
Baker
Bernhardt
Boling
Bush
Butler Specialty
Creative Ideas
DMI Furniture
Drexel Heritage
Hekman
Hooker
Klingler
Martin
Master Design
Riverside
Sligh

Stanley
Vaughan
Wambold
Winners Only
Wisconsin Furniture Inds

CONTRACT/COMMERCIAL
(See Home Office also)
Alexvale
Allibert
American of Martinsville
Baker
Barlow Tyrie
Bassett Contract
Basta Sole
Beachley
Berkeley Upholstering
Bernhardt
Boling
Brady
Brown Jordan
Broyhill
Buildright
Butler Specialty
Cabot Wrenn
Century
Chapman
Clark Casual
Classic Rattan
CM Furniture
Collingwood
Conover Chair
Councill Business Furniture
CR Laine
Curran
Dapha
Davis Furniture
Directional
Emerson Leather
Fairfield
Fancher
Flexsteel
Gordon Intl
Grahl
Grosfillex
Halcyon
Harden
Henredon
Hickory Business Furniture
Hickory Chair
Hickory Hill
High Point Woodworking
Intrex
Jackson of Danville
Jasper Desk
Kettler
Key City
KI

Koch
Kusch
L & B Ind
LaBarge
Lane
Lazar
Leathercraft
Lowenstein
Mohawk
Molla
OFS
Paoli
Park Place Furniture
Pearson
Rex
Sam Moore Chairs
Samsonite
Silver
Stout Chair Company
Taylor Woodcraft
Thayer Coggin
Tomlinson/Erwin-Lambeth
Virco
Windsor Designs
Woodard

CURIOS
AA Laun
American of Martinsville
Excelsior
Howard Miller
Koch Originals
Philip Reinisch
Powell
Riverside

DAYBEDS
Elm Creek
Largo
Powell
Tempo

DINETTES, CASUAL DINING
Barlow Tyrie
Bassett
Beechbrook
Bernhardt
Blacksmith Shop
Boling Company
Brady
Brown Jordan
Broyhill
Builtright Chair Co
Bush
Cal-Style
Chatham County
Chromcraft

Classic Rattan
Cochrane
Crawford
Cumberland Crown
Curry & Co
Daystrom
Delmar Designs
Dinaire
Drexel Heritage
Empire
Habersham Plantation
Harbour Towne
Jamestown Sterling
Johnston Casuals
Johnston Tombigbee
Keller
Kettler
Kincaid
Koch Originals
Lehigh
Manchester Wood
Martinsville Novelty
Master Design Furniture
Pennsylvania House
Pulaski
Rex
Richardson Bros
Samsonite
Sidex
Southern Enterprises Inc.
Stoneville
Taylor Woodcraft
Tell City Chair Co
Thayer Coggin
Through the Barn Door
Union City Chair Co
Union-National
Universal
US Furniture Industries
Vaughan
Venture
Virginia House
Wambold
Webb
Woodard
Yield House

DINING ROOM, GENERAL
Alexvale
American of Martinsville
American Drew
Ashley
Athol
Baker
Barlow Tyrie
Bernhardt
Blacksmith Shop

Boling
Borkholder
Brady
Brown Jordan
Broyhill
Builtrightt Chair
Cal-Style
Carson's
Casa Bique
Century
Chapman
Chatham County
Chromcraft
Classic Rattan
Cochrane
Collingwood
Colonial Furniture
Council Craftsmen
Craftique
Crawford
Cresent
CTH/Sherrill Occasional
Cumberland Crown
Curry & Co
D & F Wicker/Ratttan
Davis Cabinet
Daystrom
Designmaster
Dinaire
Dixie
Drexel Heritage
EJ Victor
Elements by Grapevine
Fancher
Ficks Reed
Flair
General
Glass Arts
Habersham
Harden
Hekman
Henkel-Harris
Henredon
Hickory Manufacturing
Hickory Chair
Hickory White
Hood
Imperial
International Express
J. Berdou
Jackson of Danville
Jamestown Sterling
John Boos
Johnston Casuals
Johnston Tombigbee
Karges
Keller
Kimball

Kincaid
Knob Creek
Koch
LaBarge
Lakewood
Lane
Lehigh
Lexington
Lineage
Link-Taylor
Master Design Furniture
Moosehead
Nadeau
Nathan Hale
National Mt Airy
Nichols & Stone
Pearson
Pennsylvania Classics
Pennsylvania House
Pine-Tique
Pulaski
Quality Dinettes
Rex
Richardson Bros
Riverside
Robinson
S. Bent
Sandberg
Schnadig
Sidex
Singer
SK Furniture
Southern Enterprises, Inc.
Southwood
Standard
Stanley
Statton
Stein World
Stoneville
Summer Classics
Sumter Cabinet Co
Taylor Woodcraft
Tell City
Thayer Coggin
Thomasville
Through the Barn Door
Tomlinson/Erwin-Lambeth
Tradition House
Union City Chair Co
Union-National
Unique
Universal
US Furniture Industries
Vargas
Vaughan
Virginia House
Woodcraft
Wambold

Webb
Wellington Hall
White
Wright Table

DINING ROOM, CONTEMPORARY
Casa Bique
Ello - extremely contemporary
Giovanni Torino
Lane - ala Carte
Saloom
Singer
Stone International

DINING ROOM, TRADITIONAL
Baker
Bernhardt
Century
Council Craftsmen
Creations in Wood
Harden
Hekman
Henredon
Pearson
Pennsylvania House
Quality Dinettes
Statton
Thomasville
Universal
Wellington Hall

ETEGERES
Bernhardt
Koch Originals
Southern Enterprises Inc.

FABRIC AND WALLCOVERING
American Textile
Ametex
Andrew Dutton
Anju/Woodridge
Artlee
Artmark
Ashbourne
Atlas Wallcoverings
B. Berger
Bailey & Griffin
Barrow
Belle
Berkeley
Birge
Bishops
Bloomcraft

Bolta Tex
Boussac
Brandt
Brewster
Brunschwig & Fils
Burlington
Calico Corners
Capital Asam
Carefree
Carey Lind Designs
Carlton Wallcovering
Carole Fabrics
Charles Barone
Charter House Design
China Seas
Chris Stone
Clarence House
Cohana
Collins & Aikman
Color House
Columbus Coated
Coulter
Country Life Designs
Covington
Cowtan & Tout
Craftex
Crutchfield Wallings
Cyrus Clark
David & Dash
Decorators Walk
Designer Fabrics
Doblin
Douglass
Duralee
Eisenhardt Wallcovering
Elko
Emmess
Encore Wallcovering
Essex
Exeter
Fabric Center
Fabric Outlet
Fabrics & More
Fabrics & Wallpaper Direct
Fabricut
Fabriyaz
Fashion House
Fine Arts
Foremost
Friendship Design
Galaxie Handprints
George Harrington
Glorbal Wallcoverings &
Blinds
Greeff
Hang it Now
Hanover House Wallcovering
Harmony Supply Inc

Hinson
Hoffman Mills
Home Fabric Mills
Home Interiors
Hugh Cochrane
Hunter & Co.
IDS Design Center
Imperial
Impression Handprinters
International
Irwin Allen
Jablan
Jay Yang
John Wolf
Kasmir
Katzenback & Warren
Kenmill
Key
Kinney Wallcovering
Kravet
Lanscot Arlen
Laura Ashley
Lee Joffa
Lloyd's Wallcovering
Louis Bowen
Luxury Fabrics & Interiors
Madison Avenue
Maenline
Manuel Canovas
Marimekko
Mario Buatta
Marlene's Decorator Fabrics
Marshall
Mastercraft
Mayfair
Mayflower
Merrimac Textiles
Michael's Textiles
Midas Fabrics
Milliken
Mirage
Mitchell Designs
Motif
National Blind & Wallpaper
Co
National Decorators
Norman's of Salisbury
Northwood Prints
Norton Blumenthal
Nova Designs
Old World Weavers
P & J
P Collins
P Kaufmann
Paul Barrow
Payne
Peachtree Fabrics
Phillips Mills

Pindler & Pindler
Porter
Printer's Alley Stores
Quadrille
Quaker
Quality House
Ralph Lauren
Redrum
Regency Mills
Richloom
Riverside
Robert Allen
Robinson's Wallcovering
Rockland Industries
S & S Fabrics
S Harris
Sanderson
Sanitas
Scalamandre
Schumacher
Seabrook
Silk Surplus
SM Hexter
Source
Spectrum
Sterling Prints
Stout Brothers
Strahan
Stroheim & Romann
Sunwall of America
Sunworthy
Taylor
The Drapery
Thibaut
Thomas Strahan
Thybony
Tiara Wallcovering
Tiffany Prints
Tioga Mill
Top Srvice
Tressardo Wallcovering
Ultima Wallcovering
Unique Wall Fashions
USA Express
Valdese
Van Luit
Victorius Prints
Village
Vision
Vogue Wallcovering
Vymura
Wall Trends
Walltex
Warner
Warner of London
Waverly
Westco
Westgate

Woodland
York

FUTON
Casual Lifestyle
Spring Air

GRANITE & MARBLE
Granite Center

GUN CABINETS
Athens Furniture
Pulaski

HOME OFFICE
Ambiance Imports
American Drew
Amisco Industries
Aspen
Bassett
Bernhardt
Bestar
Bevan Funnell
Boling Desk
Bradington Young
Brown Street
Broyhill
Bush
Butler
Canwood
Carolina Furniture Works
Cartwright
Century
Classic Leather
Coaster
Collezione Europe
Commonwealth Contract
Corolla Classics
Councill Cos
Councill Craftsmen
Crawford
Creative Ideas
D-Scan
Davis
DMI
Doxey
DSF
Durham
Fremarc
Furniture Guild
Global
GMS Imports
Grosfillex
Hammary
Harden
Hekman
Henredon
Herman Miller

High Point Desk
Hippopotamus
Hooker
Ideal
Impact
Jasper Cabinet
Jasper Desk
JRW
Kimball
Kittinger
Knoll
Kushwood
Lane
Leathercrat
Leda
Leedo
Lehigh
Leopold
Lexington
Lifestyle California
Madison
Maitland-Smith
Marge Carson
Miller Desk
Moosehead
Myrtle
National Mt Airy
Nottingham Antiques
O'Sullivan
OFS
Oggetti
Palliser
Paoli
Passport Furniture
Peters Revington
Pilliod
Pine-tique
PJ Milligan
Powell
Pulaski
Riverside
Rosalco
Rynone Design
Sauder
Sharut Furniture
Shelby Williams
Shermag
Signature
Sligh
Southern Furniture of Conover
Southern Furniture
Reproductions
Southern Office
Southwood
Standard
Stanley
Statton
Stevens Inds/ID Home

Stickley
Stickley
Thayer Coggin
Thomasville
Thonet
Trouvailles
Union National
Vermont Tubbs
Villageois
Wellington Hall
Whitecraft Rattan
Winners Only
Woodcraft
Wright Table

HOME THEATRE, ENTERTAINMENT CENTERS
American Drew
Ardley Hall
Ashley Furniture
Baker
Bassett
Berkline
Bernhardt
Borkholder
Boyd
Broyhill
Bush
Century
Clark Casual
Classic Rattan
Councill Craftsmam
Crawford
D & F Wicker/Rattan
Design South
Drexel Heritage
EJ Victor
Ello
Emerson et Cie
Florida Furniture
Habersham Plantation
Hammary
Harden
Hekman
Henredon
Hickory White
Hood
Hooker
Hudson River
Jamestown Sterling
Jasper Cabinet
Kacey Fine Furniture
Kincaid
Knob Creek
LaBarge

Lakewood
Lane
Lea Industries
Lexington
Lifestyle California
Manchester Wood
Martin
Members Only
Mohawk
Moosehead
Nichols & Stone
North Hickory
Palliser
Pennsylvania House
Peoploungers
Peters Revington
Pilliod
Pine-Tique
Powell
Progressive
Riverside
Romweber
San Diego Design
Sauder
Schweiger
Sharut
Sligh
Southern
Standard
Stanley
Statton
Stickley
Stuarts
Sumter
Superior
Thayer Coggin
Thomasville
Tradition House
Union National
Universal
Vaughan
Virginia House
Visions
Wambold
Webb
Wisconsin
Yield House

JUVENILE/INFANT FURNITURE
Albert Lock
Amisco
Barlow Tyrie
Bassett
Brady
Builtright
Child Craft
D & F Wicker/Rattan Imports

DMI Furniture
Drexel Heritage
Fancher
Hart
Kettler
Lea Industries
Lee Industries
Moosehead
Palliser
Pennsylvania House
Singer
Stanley
Stout
Union City
Vaughan
Virginia House

LAMPS, LIGHTING
Action Industries
American Lightsource
Basic Concepts - juvenile
Bauer
Bauer Lamp - wrought iron
Butler Specialty
Cambridge Lamp
Casual Lamps
Chapman
Classic Rattan
Crystal Clear
Curry & Co
DAC Lighting
D & F Wicker/Rattan
Dale Tiffany
Drexel Heritage
Flute
Forecast
Fredrick Ramond
Garden Source Furnishings
General Furniture Corp
George Kovacs
Golden Valley Lighting
Gortron
Hardware, Bath & More
Harris Marcus
Hart Associates
Herald Wholesale
House of Troy
Italiana Luce
Kenroy International
Kinder-Harris
King Chandelier
Lamp Warehouse
Lineage
Lite Source
Luigi Crystal
Meyda Tiffany
Murray Feiss
Nationwide Lighting

Norman Perry
Nulco
Oriental Accent
Outdoor Lamp Co
PeeGee
Pennsylvania House
Powell
Progressive
Quoizel
Rembrandt
Ron Hainer Lighting
Designs Sedgefield
Shoal Creek
Signature
Stiffel
Studio of Lights
Stylecraft Lamps
Sunset Lamps
Tell City Chair
Thayer Coggin
Tom Thumb
Top Brass
Troy Lighting
Tyndale
Van Teal
Vanguard
Westwood
Wildwood
Windermere

LEATHER FURNITURE
Amisco
Ashley
Barclay
Benchcraft
Bernhardt
Bradington Young
Broyhill
Century
Chairworks
Classic Leather
CR Laine
Craftwork Guild
Dansen/Motion Only
Dapha
Distinction
Elite
Emerson
Executive
Fairfield
Flexsteel
Gaines Mfg.
Giovanni Turano
Glenncraft
Hickory International
Hickorycraft
HTB-Lane
J Royale

Jaymar
King Hickory
Klaussner
La-Z-Boy
Leather Tech
Leathercraft
Leathermen's Guild
Marlow
Maxim
McKinley Leather
Michael Thomas
Natuzzi
North Hickory
Pearson
Pennsylvania House
Premier Furniture
Pulaski
Reproductions
Saloom
Sharut
Sheffield
Southmark
Southwood St. Timothy
Stratolounger
Tell City
Thomasville
Woodmark
Yorkshire

LEATHER, CONTEMPORARY
Emerson Leather
Harden
Hickory White
Thayer Coggin

LINENS, HOME FURNISHINGS
Harris Levy, Inc.
Wamsutta

MATTRESSES/BEDDING
King Koil
Restonic
Sealy
Serta
Simmons
Spring Air

MIRRORS/GLASS PRODUCTS
American Mirror
Baker
Bassett
Borkholder
Brady
Butler
Carolina Mirror

Carvers Guild
Century
Chapman
Child Craft
Classic Rattan
Colonial Furniture
Craftique
Crawford
CTH/Sherrill
Cumberland Crown
D & F Wicker/Rattan
Drexel Herittage
EJ Victor
Elements by Grapevine
Fancher
Friedman Brothers
General
Habersham Plantation
Harden
Hart
Hekman
Henkel-Harris
Hickory Chair
Jamestown Sterling
Karges
Knob Creek
Koch Originals
LaBarge
Lane
Lineage
Martinsville Novelty
Master Design
Moosehead
Pennsylvania House
Pine-Tique
Powell
Pulaski
Riverside
Southern Enterprises Inc.
Southwood
Stroupe Mirror Co
Through the Barn Door
Universal
Vaughan
Wambold
Yield House

MISCELLANEOUS - THEIR OWN LINE
Hunt Galleries
King Chandelier
Queen Anne Furniture Co.
Rattan & Wicker Furniture
        Factory Outlet

MOTION UPHOLSTERY
Action Industries
Barcalounger

Bassett
Bean Station
Bench Craft
Berkline
Bernhardt
Best Chairs
Broyhill
Carson's
Catnapper
Coja
Classic Ratttan
Conover Chair
England/Corsair
Flexsteel
Franklin
Gentry
Imperial of Morristown
Lane
North Hickory
Pennsylvania House
Peoploungers
Rowe
Shenandoah
Southwood
Stanton

OCCASIONAL FURNITURE
AA Laun
Allusions
American Drew
American of Martinsville
Armstrong
Ashley
Aspen
Athens
Baker
Banks, Coldstone
Bassett
Bean Station
Beaufurn
Belle Orleans
Bentwood
Bernards
Bernhardt
Borkholder
Bradco Wood Products
Brady Furniture
Brown Jordan
Broyhill
Bush
Butler Specialty
Carlton
Carolina Furniture Works
Carson's
Casa Bique
Casa Stradivari
Century

Chapman
Chatham
Child Craft
Classic Rattann
CM Furniture
Cochrane
Collingwood
Colonial
Comfort Designs
Conestoga Wood
Conover Chair
Councill
Councill Craftsmen
Craft Mark
Craftique
Crawford
Cresent
CTH/Sherrill Occasional
Curry & Co
D & F Wicker/Rattan Imports
Dayva
Delmar Designs
Dinaire Corporation
Directional
DMI
Drexel Heritage
Ecco
EJ Victor
Elements by Grapevine
Ello
Empire
England Corsair
Fairfield
Florida Furniture
Fox Fire
Furniture Guild
General
Habersham Plantation
Hammary
Harbour Towne
Harden
Hart
Hekman
Henredon
Hickory White
Hickory Chair
Hickorycraft
Hooker
Hyundai
Impact
Jackson of Danville
Jamestown Sterling
Jasper Cabinet
John Widdicomb
Karges
Keller
Ketttler
Kincaid

Knob Creek
Koch Originals
La-Z-Boy
LaBarge
Lane
Leda
Lehigh
Leisters
Lexington
Lifestyle California
Lineage
Lloyd/Flanders
Manchester Wood
Martinsville Novelty
Master Design
Mersman
Milling Road
Mohasco
Mohawk
Moosehead
Nadeau
National Mt Airy
Nichols & Stone
Nathan Hale
Null
Palliser
Passport
Pennsylvania House
Peters/Revington
Philip Reinisch
Pilliod Cabinet Co
Pine-Tique
Powell
Progressive
Pulaski
RR Schiebe
Richardson Bros
Riverside
Romweber
Rosalco
Rose Hill
Rowe Pottery Works
Rush
Salterini
Sauder
Schnadig
Schweiger
Sebago Woodcrafters
Sharut
Silver
Singer
Sligh
South Shore
Southern Enterprises Inc.
Southern Furniture
Reproductions
Southern
Southwood

Standard
Stanley
Statton
Stein World
Stickley
Taylor Woodcraft
Tell City Chair
Thayer Coggin
This End Up
Thomasville
Through the Barn Door
Tomlinson/Erwin-Lambeth
Tradition House
Transpacific Home
Furnishings
Union City
Union-National
Universal
Vaughan
Venture
Virginia House
Wambold
Webb
Weiman
Wellington Hall
Wisconsin Furniture Inds.
Woodard
Wright Table
Yield House

OUTDOOR/SUMMER/ CASUAL
Alexvale
Allibert USA
American Drew
Arlington House
Ayers
Barlow Tyrie
Baroody Spence
Basta Sole
Braxton-Culler
Brown Jordan
Cebu
Charleston Forge
Charter Table
Clark Casual
Classic Rattan
Comfort Designs
Craftwork Guild
Cumberland Crown
Curry & Co
D & F Wicker
Dallas Pillow Co
Daystrom
Delmar Designs
Dinaire
Diversified Overseas
Dixie

Drexel Heritage
Elements by Grapevine
Ellenburg's
European Furniture Industries
Ficks Reed
Finkel
Grosfillex
Halcyon
Harbour Towne
Hatteras Hammocks
Hekman
Homecrest
Hooker
Indigo
Johnston Benchworks
Johnston Tombigbee
Kettler International
Kiani USA
Kingsley-Bate
Laine
Lane Weathermaster
Lane/Venture
Lane Shaker Country
Lane America
Lexington Furniture
Lineal Design
Link-Taylor
Lloyd/Flanders
Lynn Hollyn Collection
Lyon-Shaw
Macon Umbrella
Manchester Wood
Master Design
McGuire
Meadowcraft
Molla
O'Asian
Olympia Outdoor Lighting
OW Lee
P & P Chair Co
Pacific Rattan
Pawleys Island
Pearson Upholstery
Pennsylvania House
Pinnacle
Plantation Comfort
Poly-Wood
Pulaski
Rattan & Wicker Furniture
Factory Outlet
Riverside Mattress
Rosalco
Salterini
Samsonite
Sedgewick Rattan
Shelly's Cushions/Umbrellas
Stanley
Stein World

Summer Classics
Sun-Aire Umbrella
Symbol Mattress
Telescope Casual
Tradewinds
Trafalgar
Transpacific
Triconfort
Tropitone
Typhoon International
Universal
Vance Rattan
Veneman
Venture
Vogue Rattan
Weathercraft
Whitecraft Rattan
Windsor Designs
Winston
Woodard
Yesteryear Wicker
Yield House

PIANOS
Bossendorfer
Cosmopolitan
Kimball
Masson Hamlin

READY TO ASSEMBLE (RTA)
Barlow Tyrie
Bench Craft
Brady
Bush
Butler Specialty
Catnapper
Chatham County
Chicago Furniture
Classic Gallery
Cumberland Crown
D & F Wicker/Rattan Imports
Delmar
Dutailier Virginia
England/Corsair
Flexsteel
Franklin
Gentry
Hart
Hickory Hill
Kettler
Kinglsey-Bate
Ladd
Lloyd/Flanders
Manchester Wood
Martinsville
Master Design
Pawleys Island

Pilliod Cabinet Co
Plantation Comfort
Sauder
Schweiger
Silver
Trendlines
Union City
Yield House

RECLINERS, MOTION FURNITURE, SECTIONALS
Action by Lane
Barcalounger
Bassett Motion
Bean Station
BenchCraft
Berkline
Best Chairs
Bradington Young
Brooks
Burris
Catnapper
Chairworks
Charles Harland
Conover Chair
Craftwork
Dutailier
Executive Leather
Flexsteel
Franklin (small scale)
Gentry
Highland House
Johnston Benchworks
Keystone
La-Z-Boy
Magnussen
Pennsylvania House
Peoploungers
Robinson
Schweiger
Sheffield
Southern Enterprises, Inc.
Stanton
Stratolounger
Town Square
Waynline

RUGS, ORIENTAL
Charles W. Jacobsen
Fritz & LaRue
High POint Oriental Rug
Pande Cameron
Tainjin-Philadelphia Carpet
The World of Clothing-
Oriental Rugs
Zaki

UNFINISHED FURNITURE

AA Laun
Barlow Tyrie
Boling
Borkholder
Brady
Bultright Chair
Chatham County
Furniture Choices
Kingsley-Bate
Leggett and Platt
Mark Sales Co., Inc.
Martinsville Novelty
Nichols & Stone
P & P Chair
Pawleys Island
Rex
Richardson Bros
Stout Chair
Through the Barn Door
Union City Chair
US Furniture Industries
Woodcraaft
Windsor Designs
Wisconsin Furniture
Yield House

UPHOLSTERED GOODS

Accentrics
Action
Alan White
Alexvale
American Drew
American of Ashley Manor
Athens
Baker
Barcalounger
Barclay
Bassett
Beachley
Bean Station
Benchcraft
Berkline
Bernhard
Bob Timberlake
Bradington Young
Brady
Brookwood
Brown Jordan
Broyhill
Carson's
Catnapper
Century
Chapel Hill
Classic Gallery
Classic Rattan
Classic Traditions
Clayton-Marcus

CM Furniture
Cochrane
Comfort Designs
Conover Chair
Councill Craftsmen
Cox
CR Laine
Craft Mark
Craftwork Guild
Curran
D & F Wicker/Rattan
Dapha
Dinaire
Directional
Disque
Distinction Leather
Door
Drexel Heritage
EJ Victor
Emerson
England/Corsair
Executive Leather
Fairfield
Ficks Reed
Flexsteel
Franklin
Frederick Edward
General
Gentry
Greene Bros
Hammary
Harden
Henredon
Hickory Chair
Hickory Craft
Hickory Hill
Hickory International
Hickory Tavern
Hickorycraft
Highland House
Imperial of J Royale
Jackson of Danville
Jamestown Sterling
Jaymar
Johnston Benchworks
Johnston-Tombigbee
Karges
Key City
Kimball
King Hickory
Klaussner
Kroehler
La-Z-Boy
Lakewood
Lane
Lazar
Leathercraft
Lee

Lexington
Lineage
Lloyd/Flanders
Madison
Martinsville
Michael Thomas
Moosehead
Morristown
Motioncraft
North Hickory
Old Hickory Tannery
Palliser
Park Place
Pearson
Pennsylvania House
Peoploungers
Phillips
Pinnacle
Precedent
Preview
Pulaski
Relax-a-Cliner
Riverside
Rowe
Sam Moore
Schnadig
Schweiger
Sedgewick
Shenandoah
Shermag
Sherrill
Simmons
Sleep Works
Smith
Southern Furniture
Southwood
Stanford
Statton
Stratford
Stratolounger
Stylecraft
Swaim
Taylor King
Taylor Woodcraft
Taylorsville
Tell City
Thayer Coggin
Thomasville
Through the Barn Door
Tom Seely
Tomlinson/Erwin-Lambeth
Union City
Venture
Victorian
Waynline
Weiman
Whittemore-Sherrill
William Alan

Woodmark Originals

UPHOLSTERY, CONTEMPORARY
American of Martinsville
Bradington Young
Dansen Contemporary
Ello
Gaines
Harden
HTB Lane
John Charles Designs
Riverside
Stratolounger
Swaim
Thayer Coggin
Weiman

UPHOLSTERY, TRADITIONAL
American Drew
Baker
Barcalounger
Bassett
Benchcraft
Best Chairs
Bradington Young
C.R. Laine
Clayton Marcus
England/Corsair
Flexsteel
Henredon
La-Z-Boy
Kravet
Lane Upholstery
Lexington
Northwood UPS
Pearson
Pennsylvania House
Precedent
Riverside
Schott
Schweiger
Sherrill
Smith
Tradition House

WALL UNITS
Baker
Bernhardt
Borkholder
Broyhill
Bush
Chapman
Classic Ratan
Drexel Heritage
EJ Victor
Hickory Chair

Hickory White
Hooker
Master Design
Pennsylvania House
Pilliod Cabinet Co
Progressive
Stanley
Union-National
Vaughan
Wambold

WINDOW TREATMENTS, SHADES, ETC.
Bali
Delmar
Duette
Graber
Hunter Douglas
Kirsch
Levolor
Louverdrape
Joanna
M & B (Hunter Douglas' own knock-off)

WROUGHT IRON, IRONWORKS
Alexandra Diez
Amisco
Blacksmith Shop
Charleston Forge
Comfort Designs
Elliott's Designs
Johnston Casuals
Pulaski
Reliable
Stein World
US Furniture Industries

MANUFACTURER LISTING

Following are the names, addresses and/or phone numbers of over 500 manufacturers of furniture, along with a short description of the product(s) they carry. Use this information as a resource for contacting manufacturers and/or identifying your furniture needs or to get an idea of what the manufacturer offers.

Many of the Resources do not list **all** manufacturers they carry. Be persistent! You may have to inquire to several resources if you are in search of a manufacturer you don't see listed.

AA IMPORTING CO
7700 Hall St.
St. Louis, MO 63147
(314)383-8800
Antique reproductions.

A.A. LAUN
300 South 6th St., PO Box 68
Kiel, WI, 53042
(920) 894-7441, FAX
(920)894-3292
Quality occasional furniture.

ACACIA FURNITURE
101 Mclin Creek Rd
Conover, NC 28613
(704)465-1700, FAX
(704)465-4205.
Wicker and rattan furniture.

ACCENTS BY GARY PARLIN
5697 Sarah Ave
Sarasora, FL 34233
(813) 922-8497, FAX (813) 925-3695
A collection of transitional and classic solid maple accent tables and mirrors, featuring hand painted designs signed by each artist.

ACCENT FINE ART COLLECTION
4125 North 14th St
Phoenix, AZ 85014
(602)241-1060; FAX
(602)241-5454
Original art work- framed and unframed.

ACCESSORIES INTERNATIONAL
9820 Drysdale
Houston, TX 77041
(713) 895-9292, (800)
669-7449, (713) 895-0189
FAX.
Accessories inspired by ancient Egyptian, Grcek and Etruscan furnishings.

ACCESSORY ART
929 W Barkley Ave
Orange, CA 92668
(714) 633-8902
Accessories.

ACTION INDUSTRIES
PO Box 1627, Highway 45-S
Tupelo, MS 38802
(601) 566-7211
Motion recliners, upholstery.
Division of Lane.

ADESSO LIGHTING
21 Penn Plaza Suite 1001
New York, NY 10001
(212)736-4440, FAX
(212)736-4806.
Lighting and lamps.

ALABAMA FOLK ART
210 W. Commerce
Greenville, AL 36037
(334)382-5430, FAX
(334)382-7123

ALAN WHITE
Hwy 82 East
Stamps, AR 71860

(501) 533-4471, FAX (501)
533-8858
Traditional and some casual upholstery.

ALBERT M. LOCK CO.
PO Box 151
Okolona, MS 38860
(800)321-8247, (601)447-5409
Glider rockers and rockers for children and adults.

ALEXANDRA DIEZ
51 NE 40th Street
Miami, FL 33137
(305) 576-1345, FAX (305)
576-4798
Eclectic collection of iron furniture.

ALEXVALE
PO Box 817
Taylorsville, NC 28681
(704) 632-9774
Upholstery, rattan and wicker wall units, game tables and chairs in styles ranging from traditional to contemporary.

ALLIBERT IND
12200 Herbert Wayne Ct, Po
Box 1558
Huntersville, NC 28078
(704) 948-0440, FAX (704)948-0190

AMERICAN DREW
P.O. Box HP3, One Plaza
Center
High Point, NC 27261

(336) 889-0333, FAX
(336)888-6482
Wood styles to suit any taste at
the mid-range prices. Good
designs, good construction,
good prices; in short,
exceptional value.
•Cadence
•Chadsford Oak
•Cherry Grove
•Churchill Oak
•Concord Cherry
•Inauguration
•Magens Bay
•Magnolia's Secret
•Vineyard Oaks
•Waterbury

AMERICAN FURNITURE CRAFTSMEN
7730 Central Ave
Meadowlands, MN 55765
(218)427-2421, FAX
(218)427-2223.
Casual dining furniture for the
kitchen.

AMERICAN HERITAGE
(706) 886-2884, (706)
886-4033 FAX.
Pine Shaker furniture.

AMERICAN OF HIGH POINT
P. O. Box 7103
High Point, NC 27264
(910) 431-1513, FAX (910)
2717
High standards for furniture
construction, hundreds of
styles and fabrics. Choose from
infinite numbers of custom
options.
Hampton Hall is a division of
the American of High Point
line. The quality of
construction is the same, but
the prices are lower. They
accomplish this by restricting
the options you can choose
from.

AMERICAN OF MARTINSVILLE
A LADD Furniture Company
PO Box 5071, Church Street
Martinsville, VA 24221
(800)893-2931
Over 50 curio cabinets to
choose from. Upper medium
quality bedroom, dining room
and occasional tables.
Contemporary and transitional.
•Dynasty
•Echelon
•LaRochelle
•Eloquence
•Villa- Pecan

AMERICAN MIRROR COMPANY
PO Box 67 Galax
VA 24333
(540) 236-5111
Decorative mirrors and
occasional furniture.

AMERICAN RUG COMPANY
3090 Sugar Valley Road NW
Sugar Valley, GA 30746
(800) 553-1734, FAX (706)
625-3544
Rugs.

AMERIWOOD
202 Spaulding St, Po Box 270
Dowagiac, MI 49047
(800)253-2093
Home theaters, entertainment
centers, occasional, home
office.

AMISCO INDUSTRIES
PO Box 250
Quebec, CANADA G0R 2C0
(418) 247-5025
Metal beds, bunks, futon bases,
dinettes.

AMISH COUNTRY COLLECTION
5 Sunset Valley Rd
New Castle, PA 16105

(412) 458-4811
Hand-crafted woven twig
designs of hickory and oak.

ANDES INT'L INC
619 W. Green Dr
High Point, NC 27260
(910)889-8912, FAX
(910)889-6290.
Rustic iron and wood furniture

ANDRE ORIGINALS
970-4 New Brunswick Ave
Rahway, NJ 07065
(908) 574-2600, FAX (909)
574-2636

ANDREW PEARSON
1 Andrew Pearson Place
Mt. Airy, NC 27030
(910) 786-1800, (800)
969-2156, FAX (910)786-1810
Glass tables and accessories.

ANTHONY CALIFORNIA
14275 Telephone Ave
Chino, CA 91710
(909)627-0351, FAX
(909)627-9159.
Table and floor lamps,
children's lamps and
chandeliers.

ARBEK
4802 Murrieta St
Chino, CA 91710
(909) 590-1629, (800)
274-7235, FAX (909) 590-1634
Contemporary oak furniture for
bedroom, dining room, living
room and home entertainment.

ARDLEY HALL
PO Box 2143
High Point, NC 27261
(910)475-7600, FAX
(910)475-7601
Traditional 18th Century
reproductions as well as lamps
and accessories.

ARLINGTON HOUSE

P.O. Box 135
Birmingham, AL 35201
(205) 853-2224
Wrought iron outdoor
furniture.

ARMSTRONG FURNITURE
Hwy 460 East, PO Box 848
Appamattos, VA 24522
(804)352-7181, FAX
(804)352-4870
Youth bedrooms, entertainment
centers and RTA (Ready To
Assemble) furniture.

A.R.T
Unit 5-7100 Warden Ave
Markham, Ontario, CN l3R
5M7

ART GALLERY
108 Southport Rd
Spartanburg, SC 29301
(803) 574-8175
Original and reproduction art.

ARTE DE MEXICO
5356 Riverton Ave
Hollywood, CA 91601
(818) 508-0993
Lighting and accessories,
authentic and unusual design
ideas. Southwest flair.

ARTISAN HOUSE
1755 Glendale Blvd
Los Angeles, CA 90026
(213) 664-1111, FAX (213)
664-5679
Metal sculptures and wall-
hangings.

ARTISTICA METAL
DESIGNS
1278 Mercantile St., PO Box
51040
Oxnard, CA 93031
(805) 483-1195, FAX
(805)487-1507
Quality hand-forged metal
baker's racks, occasional

tables, plant stands and
accessories you will find.

AS YOU LIKE IT
536 Townsend Avenue
High Point, NC 27263
(910) 431-7123
Lamps and accessories.
Exclusive Licensee for:
Winterthur Museum, Historic
Charleston Foundation,
Historic Natchez Foundation,
Henry Ford Museum, The
Biltmore Estate.

ASHLEY FURNITURE
INDUSTRIES
One Ashley Way
Arcadia, WI 54612
(608) 323-3377, FAX
(800)678-4492
Bedroom, dining room,
occasional tables, wall systems
and RTA (ready to assemble)
furniture.

ASHLEY MANOR
P.O. Box 477, 1010 Surrett Dr.
High Point, NC 27260
(910) 882-813, FAX (910)
889-5532
Upholstery line featuring sofas,
sectionals, chaises, exposed leg
chairs, ottomans, in
contemporary and traditional.

ASPEN FURNITURE
3625 W. Clarendon Ave
Phoenix, AR 85019
(602)233-0224
FAX(602)269-1277
Home office, bedroom and
entertainment centers in oak.
All contemporary styling.

ATHOL TABLE
151 Harrison St. PO Box 940
Athol, MA 01331
(508)249-3264, FAX
(508)249-3042
Major producer of dinettes and
dining room furniture.

AUSTIN SCULPTURE
815 Grundy Avenue
Holbrook, NY 11741
(516) 981-7300, FAX (516)
467-8823
Sculpture to be used in homes,
gardens, and businesses.

AYERS/CHAIRMAKERS
1001 North Third Street
Fort Smith, AR 72901 (501)
785-4411
Rattan and wicker upholstery,
dining and occasional tables.

B BERGER
1608 22nd St
Cleveland, OH 44114
(800) 288-8400

BAILEY & GRIFFIN
1406 Mermaid Lane
Philadelphia, PA 19118
(215) 836-4350
Furniture.

BAKER FURNITURE
1661 Monroe Ave. NW
Grand Rapids, MI 49505
(616) 361-7321 FAX
(616)361-7067
Fine furniture, casegoods and
upholstery. High end.

BALDWIN CLOCKS
22 Wards Corner Road
Loveland, OH 45140
(513) 576-4579
Floor, curio, mantel, table and
wall clocks using fine
hardwoods, veneers and
imported German movements.
Baldwin has been making fine
traditional clocks since 1862.

BALDWIN DINETTES
26801 Railroad Ave, PO Box
647
Loxley, AL 36551. (205)
964-6204
Promotional dinettes.

BALDWIN HARDWARE
841 E. Wyomissing Blvd.
Box 15048
Reading, PA 19612
(215) 777-7811
The brass division carries
lamps and accessories, using
only the finest brass and
forging techniques.

BANKS COLDSTONE
PO Box 2763, 422 South Road
High Point, NC 27261
(910) 889-6529, FAX (910)
889-6351
Furniture designs from the 18th
and early 19th century.
Primarily casegoods, several
accessory items, paintings,
clocks, mirrors and scultpures
available. Authentically
reproduced.

**BARCALOUNGER
FURNITURE**
1450 Atlantic Avenue, P.O.
Box 6157
Rocky Mount, NC 27802.
(919) 977-6395, FAX (919)
977-2864
Upholstery manufacturer
specializing in motion
recliners, gliders, high-leg
loungers, sofas, love seats and
sectionals. Traditional,
contemporary, and wicker
styles many with optional
finishes and nail head trim.

BARCLAY
A LADD Furniture Company
PO Box 208, 6th Ave
Sherman, MS78869
(601) 844-6003 FAX (601)
841-5015
Moderately-priced upholstery
in contemporary and traditional
styles, in both fabric and
leather.

BARLOW TYRIE
1263/230 Glen Ave

Moorestown, NJ 08057
(800)451-7467, FAX
(609)273-9199
Outdoor furniture in teakwood
and cast aluminum.

BARN DOOR
P.O. Box 927
Henderson, NC 27536
(919) 492-9501, FAX (919)
492-5558
A look with what is commonly
called "crate" furniture.
Virtually indestructible,
usually used in college dorms,
kid's bedrooms, hunting cabins,
rec rooms. Sleep sofas, wall
units and computer desks.
Available in two finishes.

BARLOW TYRIE
1263/230 Glen Ave
Moorestown, NJ 08057
(800)451-7467, FAX
(609)273-9199
Outdoor furniture in teakwood
and cast aluminum.

BARONET
234 Baronet St.
Ste-Marie Bce, Quebec, CN
G6D 3B8.
(418)387-5431
Contemporary and traditional
casegoods.

BASHIAN RUGS
100 Park Plaza Dr
Secaucus, NJ 07094
(800) 628-2167, FAX
(201)330-1001
Handmade Oriental rugs.

BASSETT FURNITURE
P.O. Box 626
Bassett, VA 24055
(540) 629-6000, FAX (540)
629-6333
Low price, sturdy construction.
Choose carefully to get the
quality you want. Bassett uses
solid hardwoods in many of

their groups, however, some
groups use what is referred to as
"wood products". That means
plywood, press-board, or other
materials. When properly cared
for though, they will give many,
many years of service.

**BASSETT MIRROR
COMPANY**
P.O. Box 627
Bassett, VA 24055
(540) 629-3341, FAX
(540)629-3709.
Also known as BMC, the
company has several divisions,
Dining Concepts, Mirrors, and
the occasional line.Quality,
price and designcombined.
Contemporary and some
traditional.

BAUHAUS
1 Bauhaus Dr. Rt. 1 Box 25
Salinas, MS 38866
(601)869-2664, FAX
(601)869-5910.

BEACH MANUFACTURING
13872 West St.
Garden Grove, CA 92843
(714)265-3680, FAX
(714)547-0111
Bars and barstool, game and
pool tables.

BEACHLEY FURNITURE
Box 978, 227 N Prospect St
Hagerstown, MD 32741
(301) 733-1910
Sofa beds, contract furniture.

**BEAN STATION
FURNITURE FACTORY**
P.O. Box 70, County Line Road
Bean Station, TN 37708-0070
(615) 993-3433, FAX (615)
993-3438
Upholstered family room
furniture. Rocker-recliners,
swivel gliders, stationary and
inclining sofas and love seats,

sectionals, sleepers, and a few matching occasional tables.

BEECHBROOK
150 Carol Pl
Moonachie, NJ 07074-1300
(201)641-5300, FAX
(201)440-1452.
Casual dining and dinette sets.

BEMCO SLEEP PRODUCTS
PO Box 697, 801 N. Ashe Ave
Dunn, NC 28334
(800) 992-3626, (910)
892-3107, FAX (910)892-
4661
Mattresses andadjustable beds.

**BEMIS CASUAL
FURNITURE**
300 Mills St, Po Box 901
Sheboygan Falls, WI 53085
(920) 467-4621

BENCHCRAFT
P.O. Box 86
Blue Mountain, MS 38610
(601) 685-4711, FAX
(800)446-1292
Motion upholstery. Recliners, sleepers, sectionals in fabric and leather.

BENICIA BED
2995 Bayshore Rd
Benicia, CA 94510
(707) 745-4645, FAX (707)
745-8746
Still standing on a foundry site that dates back to 1853, manufacturers iron and wood beds, cribs, daybeds, accessories, in twelve colors.

BENT S & BROS.
See S. Bent & Bros.

BENTWOOD FURNITURE
310 N.W. Morgan Lane
Grants Pass, OR 97526
(503) 474-0996, FAX (800)
962-4625

Dining room, entertainment centers, roll top desks, occasional tables, bookcases, and oak accessories in traditional and American Country. Chairs and barstools.

BERKELEY MILLS
2830 Seventh St
Berkeley, CA 94710
(510) 549-2854, FAX (510)
548-0865
Custom building shop specializing in Japanese style, traditional solid wood furniture in the Arts & Crafts, Prairie and Shaker designs.

**BERKELEY
UPHOLSTERING**
PO Box 1147
Martinsburg, WV 25401
(304) 267-2975, FAX (304)
267-7841
Upholstered goods.

BERKLINE
One Berkline Drive
Morristown, TN 37813
(423) 585-1500, FAX (423)
585-1760
Motion furniture. Traditional, country and contemporary.

BERKSHIRE
Sec Fashion Bed Group

BERNE FURNITURE CO
PO Box 329
Berne, IN 46711
(219) 589-2173
Upholstered sofas, loveseats, chairs.

**BERNHARDT FURNITURE
CO.**
PO Box 740, 1839 Morganton
Blvd SW
Lenoir, NC 28645
(704) 758-9811
Upholstered and casegoods.
Mid-upper quality.

BEST CHAIRS
Box 158
Ferdinand, IN 47532-0158
(812) 367-1761, FAX (812)
367-2345
Wing chairs, swivel gliders, video rockers, recliners, club chairs and wood glider rockers. Over 25% of the largest furniture retailers in the country sell Best Chairs.

BESTAR INC
3171 Louis Amos
Lachine, Quebec, Canada GN
H8T 1C4
(800) 567-2708, (514)
636-5585, FAX (514) 636-8701
Chests, night stands, and benches, video/audio carts, microwave carts, entertainment centers, and home office furniture.

BETH WEISSMAN
Unit #1, 2855 Southwest Drive,
Sedona, AZ 86336.
Traditional to contemporary lamps, chandeliers, pin-ups, torchieres and accessories.

BEVAN FUNNEL LTD.
P.O. Box 1109, 105 Depot St.
High Point, NC 27260
(800) 334-8349, (910)
889-4800, FAX (910) 889-7037
Traditional English furniture in the United Kingdom. High end.

BLACKHAWK FURNITURE
3016 Kansas Ave
Riverside, CA 92507
(909)788-4265, FAX
(909)788-9082
Contemporary and traditional bedroom furniture.

BLACKSMITH SHOP
U. S. Furniture Industries
1200 Surrett Dr, P.O. Box 2127,
High Point, NC 27261
(910) 885-8026

Kitchen sets, dining room tables and chairs, barstools, and kitchen corner groups.

BOLING COMPANY
Po Box 409, 108 W 3rd S
Siler City, NC 27344
(919) 663-2400
Casegoods/office furniture.

BORKHOLDER CORP
PO Box 5
Nappanee, IN 46550
(219) 773-4083
Amish crafted fuirniture. Country style.

BOYD FURNITURE
6355 Washington Blvd
Los Angeles, CA 90040
(213) 726-6767, FAX (213) 726-6296
Contemporary bedroom, dining room and occasional in solid oaks and veneers. One feature found on Boyd that few companies have is mid-height pier cabinets to make a bed-wall unit. Most of the ones on the market are 6 - 7 feet in height, Boyd makes several in the 4 to 6 foot range.
•Accents
•Preface
•Horizons
•Hunt

BRADINGTON YOUNG
920 East 1st St
Cherryville, NC 28021
(704) 435-5881, FAX (704) 435-4276
Motion and stationary sofas, love seats, and sectionals, recliners and lounge chairs and sleepers. Upper-end quality and styling. Leather and leather/vinyl combination on almost everything.

BRADY FURNITURE CO
P.O. Box 129 Rural Hall

NC 27045
(919) 969-6816 & 969-9365
(800) 277-2723
Living room upholstery, tables, bedroom, dining room and juvenile, in country, traditional, shaker and crate-style contemporary.
•Casual living
•Cherry Hall
•Country Pine
•Old Chatham
•Smoke House

BRAXTON CULLER
P.O. Box 248, 1950 West Green Drive
High Point, NC 27261
(910) 885-9186, FAX (910)885-4292
Wicker and rattan, along with a complete line traditional and contemporary upholstery, as well as etageres, entertainment centers, porch swings and more. They have a line of metal dining room, bedroom and occasional, baker's racks, some canopy beds and a metal daybed.

BRIAR HILL RUSTIC FURNITURE
HC1, Box 23
Leeper, PA 16233
(814) 744-9913
Indoor and outdoor furniture, A-frame swings.

BRILL MANUFACTURING
715 S James, Box 310
Ludington, MI 49431
(616) 843-2430
Juvenile and infant bedroom furniture. Wood chairs, booths, tables.

BROOKWOOD FURNITURE
PO Box 540, 263 Brookwood Dr
Pontotoc, MS 38863

(601) 489-1100
Upholstered goods.

BROWN JORDAN
9860 Gidley, PO Box 5688
El Monte, CA 91731
(818) 443-8971, FAX (818) 575-0126
Outdoor and patio for residential and contract use. High quality.

BROYHILL
One Broyhill Park, US 321 North
Lenoir, NC 28633
(800) 327-6944, (704) 758-3111, FAX (704) 758-3319
Bedroom, dinette, kitchen. Upholstery. Low medium to upper medium price range.

BRUETON INDUSTRIES
145-68 228th St
Springfield Gardens, NY 11413
(800)221-6783
Upholstery and case goods.

BUILTRIGHT CHAIR COMPANY
901 Connor Street
Statesville, NC 28677
(704) 873-6541
Chairs, rockers and stools

BURRIS INDUSTRIES
Lincolnton, NC 28092
Sorry, they went out of business in 1995. They got "acquired" by La-Z-Boy Furniture Co.

BUSH INDUSTRIES
One Mason Drive, Po Box 460
Jamestown, NY 14702-0460
(716) 665-2000, FAX (716) 665-2074
RTA (ready to assemble) furniture includes accessory tables, entertainment centers and office equipment.

BUTLER SPECIALTY

8200 South Chicago Ave
Chicago, IL 60617.
(312) 221-1200, FAX (312)
221-5892
Accent furniture like jewelry
cabinets, costumers, revolving
book tables, clock tables,
consoles and mirrors, wall
accents, floor lamps, benches,
tables, desks & vanities,
globes, and occasional.

CM FURNITURE
See Craftmark Convertibles

C R LAINE
PO Box 2128
Hickory, NC 28603
(828) 328-1831, FAX (828)
328-4523
Upholstery. Traditional,
contemporary and transitional.

CAL-STYLE FURNITURE
P.O. Box 7240
St. Louis, MO 63177
(314) 291-0400
Mirrors, consoles,
entertainment centers, bombe
chests, occasional chairs,
bakers racks, metal occasional.
Traditional to contemporary.

CAMBRIDGE LAMPS
2605 W. 8th Ave
Hialeah, FL 33010
(305) 885-4628
Table and floor lamps,
torchieres. Traditional to
contemporary.

CANADEL
331 St. Marc, PO Box 5
Louiseville, Quebec CN J5V
2L6
(819) 228-8471, FAX (819)
228-8389
Canadian manufacturer of
dinette and dining room
furniture.

CANAL DOVER

Po Box 275
Midvale, OH 44653
(614) 922-0440, FAX (614)
922-5002
Casual dining and kitchen
furniture in a variety of styles.

CANDELLA LIGHTING
Lighting and lamps.

CAPEL RUGS
PO Box 548
Troy, NC 27371
(800) 334-3711. FAX (910)
572-7040
Area rugs.

CAPITOL LEATHER
A Division of ROWE Furniture
1725 Jefferson Davis Hwy,
#809
Arlington, VA 22202
(703) 413-6050, FAX
(703)979-9121
Medium quality and price
sofas, sleepers, chairs and some
chaises. Competing in the
quality and price range of the
Canadian and Italian import
lines.

CARLTON MCLENDON
PO Box 60
Montgomery, AL 36101
(800) 547-5240
Reproduction Victorian and
Louis XV furniture.

**CAROLINA FURNITURE
WORKS**
PO Drawer 1120
Sumter, SC 29151
(803) 775-6381
Bedroom, occasional, desks.

**CAROLINA MIRROR
COMPANY**
PO Box 548
North Wilkesboro, NC 28659
(919) 838-2151, FAX (919)
838-9734

Wide range of styles and sizes
of mirrors.

CAROLINA SEATING
Division of US Furniture
Industries
101 Liberty Dr
Thomasville, NC 27360
(336)884-7375, FAX (336) 472-
2794
Office furniture, tables, side and
revolving chairs.

**CAROLINA TABLES OF
HICKORY (CTH
OCCASIONAL)**
P O Box 2690
Hickory, NC 28603
(704) 328-5241
Mirrors, consoles, entertainment
centers, bombe chests,
occasional chairs, bakers racks,
metal occasional items.
Traditional to contemporary in
wood, metal and stone.

CARSONS
PO Box 150
High Point, NC 27261
(910) 887-3544, (910) 887-5521
Medium priced contemporary
upholstery and occasional
furniture.

CARTER CONTEMPORARY
100 West Long St, PO Box 1869
Salisbury, NC 28144
(800) 849-8614, FAX (704)
637-2851
Traditional to unusual
upholstery.

CARVER'S GUILD
Cannery Row, PO Box 198
W. Groton, MA 01472
(800) 445-3464, (508)
448-3063, FAX (508) 448-6602
Decorative mirrors and
accessories, fine quality and
design.

CASA BIQUE

PO Box 778
Thomasville, NC 27360. (910)
472-7700, FAX (910)
476-3365
Over 550 individual accent,
occasional, and furniture items.

CASA STRADIVARI
221 McKibbin St.
Brooklyn , NY 11206
(718) 386-0048, FAX (718)
497-4511
Hundreds of casegoods,
occasional, and accent pieces.

CASUAL CREATIONS
2044 47th Street
Sarasota, FL 34234
(813) 355-8523
Sturdy, quality outdoor.

CASUAL LAMPS
15000 S. Broadway
Gardena, CA 90247
(800) 824-8228, (310) ,
321-0180,
FAX (310) 538-1221
Lamps, vases, pedestals and
occasional tables in
Southwestern, Native
American, Art Deco, and
contemporary styles.

CATNAPPER
PO Box 159
Cleveland, TN 37311
(615) 476-8544, FAX (800)
627-2729
Motion upholstery. Traditional,
contemporary and country
styles.

CENTURY FURNITURE CO
PO Box 608, 401 11th St NW
Hickory, NC 28603
(828) 328-1851
Bedroom, dining, mirrors,
occasional, etageres,
bookcases, desks, secretaries,
curios, entertainment center,s
upholstered goods, motion.
High quality.

CHAPEL HILL
FURNITUREBox 609, 1799
Kemp St
Claremont, NC 28610
(704)459-7834
Furniture.

CHAPMAN
481 W Main St
Avon, MA 02322
(508) 588-2300, FAX
(508)587-7592
Lamps, chandeliers, wall
sconces, furniture, decorative
accessories. High quality.

CHARLESTON FORGE
200 Industrial Park Dr
Boone, NC 28607
(704) 264-0100, FAX (704)
264-5901
Handmade wrought iron
furniture. Metal are occasional
tables, traditional,
contemporary, and eclectic.
Baker's racks, bookcases and
TV stands. Sleigh beds, canopy
beds and poster beds, Shaker
style barstools with swivel
seats, contemporary dining
chairs, quilt racks, settees,
pedestals and much more.

CHARTER TABLE
COMPANY
PO Box 422
Conover, NC 28613
(704) 464-3600
Occasional table line. Solid
mahogany, solid brass
hardware.

CHELSEA HOUSE
PO Box 399
Gastonia, NC 28052
(704) 867-5926, FAX (704)
868-3005
Furniture.

CHILDCRAFT INDUSTRIES
501 E Market St, PO Box 444
Salem, IN 47167-0444

(812) 883-3111
Juvenile and infant bedroom,
occasional, mirrors, glass
products.

CHROMCRAFT
Division of Mohasco
PO Box 126, Senatobia, MS
38668
(601) 562-8203, FAX
(800)336-1651
Kitchen and casual dining.

CLARENCE HOUSE
211 E 58th St
New York, NY 10022
(212) 752-2890
Fabric.

CLARK CASUAL
214 Industrial Road
Greensburg, KY 42743
(502) 932-4273, FAX (502)
932-4275
Hand crafted line of rattan
furniture including bedroom,
dining room, rockers, recliners,
sleepers, wall units, desks and
bar stools.

CLASSIC GALLERY
PO Box 1030, 2009 Fulton
Place
High Point, NC 27263
(336) 886-4191, FAX (336)
841-7122
Contemporary and traditional
upholstery. Four companies in
one: Classic Gallery, Classic
Traditions, Ecco Design, and
Classic Gallery contract.

CLASSIC LEATHER
PO Box 2404
Hickory, NC 28603
(828) 328-2046, FAX (828)
324-6212
Leather upholstery.
Contemporary to traditional.

CLASSIC RATTAN
900 John C Watts Dr.

Nicholasville, KY 40356
(606) 885-3384, FAX (606)
887-2195
Bedroom, dining room,
occasional and upholstery in
rattan. High quality.

CLAYTON MARCUS
PO Box 1 00
Hickory
NC 28603. (704) 495-2200,
(704) 495-2260 FAX
Medium price traditional,
formal, country and casual
upholstery.

COCHRANE FURNITURE
PO Box 220
Lincolnton, NC 28092
(800) 752-6104, (828)
732-1151, FAX (800)
752-6109
Quality furniture for the dining
room, kitchen and bedroom.

COJA LEATHER
7881 Keele St
Concord, Ontario CN L4K 1Y6
North American competition
for the Italian leather market.
Medium price, medium quality.

COLONIAL FURNITURE
PO Box 117
Freeburg, PA 17827
(717) 374-8091
Colonial American bedroom,
dining room, and occasional.

COMFORT DESIGNS
263 Schuyler Ave, PO Box
3000
Kingston, PA 18704
(717) 288-6657, FAX (717)
283-2746
Bedroom, dining, metal dinette,
occasional, upholstery.

CONANT BALL
Divsion of Shermag,, 2171
King St. West

Sherbrooke, Quebec, CN J1J
2G1
Wood glider rockers with
upholstered cushion seats and
backs.

CONESTOGA WOOD
PO Box 523, 1050 2nd Ave
Mountain Lake, MN 56159
(507) 427-2028, FAX (507)
427-3113
Bedroom, dining RTA (Ready
to Assemble), occasional.

CONOVER CHAIR
COMPANY
PO Box 759
 Conover, NC 28613
(704) 464-0251, FAX (704)
465-4535
Traditional, transitional,
country and 18th century
exposed wood, sofas, loveseats
and sectionals, wing chairs.
Executive chairs.

CORONA DECOR CO
260 39th Avenue East
Seattle, WA 98112
(206) 763-1600
Tapestries.

CORSICAN/ SWAN BRASS
BED
2417 E. 24th St.
Los Angeles, CA 90058
(800)421-6247, FAX (213)
589-2789
Brass, iron beds and
accessories.

COUNCILL CRAFTSMAN
PO Box 398
Denton
NC 27239. (910) 859-2155,
FAX (910) 859-5289
High-end 18th century English
and American antique
reproductions, country French,
and trsitional upholstery and
case goods.

COUNTRY CASUAL
17317 Germantown Road
Germantown, MD 20874-2999
(301) 540-0040
Garden and outdoor leisure.
Direct importer of authentic
English solid teakwood garden
seats. Also architectural trellis
work, wrought iron arches and
gates, benches, chairs, tables,
swings, trash receptacles and
planters and white painted
mahogany furniture.

COURISTAN
2 Executive Dr
Fort Lee, NJ 07024
(800) 223-6168
Rugs, carpeting.

COVINGTON FABRICS
267 5th Ave
New York, NY 10016
(212) 689-2200
Fabrics.

COWTAN & TOUT
979 3rd Ave
New York, NY 10022
(212) 753-4488
Fabrics.

COX MANUFACTURING
PO Box 1208, 220 10th St S.W
Hickory, NC 28602
(704) 327-4123, FAX (704)
327-9556
Upholstery, occasional and
accent pieces. Benches,
ottomans, fabric headboards,
and stools, slipper chairs.

CRAFTIQUE
PO Box 428
Mebane, NC 27302
(919) 563-1212, FAX (919)
563-4082
Solid mahogany 18th century
reproductions. Quality.

CRAFTMARK CONVERTIBLES/ CM OCCASIONAL
PO Box 617
Maiden, NC 28650-0617
(704) 428-9978
Solid wood occasional tables. Country, French, transitional, European, Georgian, traditional cherry, and others. Craftmark Convertibles is a line of sleepers and matching loveseats. Most sleeper styles come as twin, full or queen size, tight, loose, or attached pillow back, and have a matching loveseat with coil spring base construction.

CRAFTWORK GUILD
PO Box 2187
Hickory, NC 28603
(704) 328-5631, FAX (704) 328-9816
Motion. Made well. Contemporary, traditional and transitional.

CRATE IN MOTION
3605 Virginia Beach Blvd.
Va Beach, VA 23452
(804) 431-1333, FAX (804) 340-2071

CRAWFORD
PO Box 688
Jamestown, NY 14702-0668
(716) 661-9100, FAX (716) 661-9157
Bedroom, dining room and occasional. True value.

CREATIVE METAL AND WOOD
112 Todd Court
Thomasville, NC 27360
(910) 475-9400, FAX (910) 475-9445
Custom metal and wood furniture using only the finest quality materials available.

CRESENT
Maple St, PO Box 1438
Gallatin, TN 37066
(615) 452-1671, FAX (615) 451-0332
Bedroom, dining, occasional.

CRYSTAL CLEAR GALLERIES
2 Bergen Turnpike
Ridgefield Park, NJ 07660
(201) 229-0200, FAX (201) 229-4297
Crystal table lamps, night lights, ceiling lights, floor lamps and wall lighting.

CTH/SHERRILL OCCASIONAL
Hwy 70A-E, PO Box 2690
Hickory, NC 28603
(828)328-5241
Occasional furniture. Quality.

CYRUS CLARK FABRICS
267 5th Ave
New York, NY 10016
(212) 684-5312
Fabrics.

D M I FURNITURE CO
101 Bullitt Lane
Louisville, KY 40222
(502) 426-4351

D-SCAN - THE DANWOOD COLLECTION
Hwy 58 West, PO Box 1067
South Boston, VA 24592
(800) 932-2006, (804) 575-0900, FAX (804) 575-0946
Contemporary bedroom, library wall units, bookcases, entertainment centers and home office, teen bedroom, stairstep bookcases, office chairs and multi-purpose carts. Very sturdy furniture with a clean modern design. Popular priced collection of unique library walls, bookcases, entertainment walls, home office and bedroom.

D&F WICKER RATTAN IMPORTS
1050 Route 46
Ledgewood, NJ 07852
(201) 927-8530
Traditional and casual wicker and rattan designs.

DALE TIFFANY INC
6 Willow St
Moonachie, NJ 07074
(201) 473-1900, FAX (201) 507-1842
Exquisite designer lamps in stained glass and hand made designs.

DAR/RAN
2402 Shore Drive, P.O. Box 7614
High Point, NC 27264
800-334-7891, 910-434-8000
Professional office furniture for the workplace.

DAVID EDWARD
1407 Parker Road
Baltimore, MD 21227
(410) 242-2222
Contract and office seating.

DAVIS AND DAVIS
2900 49th St.
Chattanooga, TN 37407
(800) 251-7838, FAX (615) 867-1151
Area rugs.Custom available.

DAWSON FURNITURE
PO Box 111
Webb City, MO 64870
(417) 673-9000
Curved glass curios. Steamer and carpenter trunks.

DAYSTROM FURNITURE
A division of LADD Furniture
Sinai Road, P.O. Box 130
South Boston, VA 24592

(804) 572-3981
Promotional priced line of
kitchen and casual dining sets.

DECORATIVE CRAFTS
50 Chestnut St
Greenwick, CT 06830
(800) 431-4455

DELLAROBBIA
1221 Warner Ave
Santa Ana, CA 92705
(714) 434-7020
Contemporary upholstery.

DENUNZIO, H. A.
PO Box 508
Sommersville, CT 06072
Accessories and wall decor.

DESIGN GUILD
220 Fifth Ave
New York, NY 10001
(212) 532-2888
Lighting and decorative
accessories

DESIGN HORIZONS
PO Box HP-3
High Point, NC 27261
(910) 889-0333
A division of Lea, a Ladd
company. Promotional
bedroom furniture.

DESIGNMASTER
152 19th St, SE
Hickory, NC 28602
(828) 324-7992
Dining room.

DILLON FURNITURE
Box 310
Dillon, SC 29536
(803) 774-4124, FAX (803)
774-5813
Contemporary shaker/mission
mid-priced home entertainment
centers, wall units and
bedroom. Good quality.

DINAIRE CORP

145 Gruner Rd
Buffalo, NY 14427
(716) 894-1201, FAX (8000
724-3463
Kitchen and casual dining in a
variety of styles and finishes.
Unfinished and wood furniture
also.

DIRECTIONAL
PO Box 2005
High Point, NC 27261
(910) 841-3209
Fine quality contemporary
upholstery.

DISTINCTION LEATHER
Po Box 397, I-40 Exit 133
Conover, NC 28613
(800) 624-6316, (704)
464-9240, FAX (704)
464-9240
Great quality leather upholstery
company. They are just below
the high end companies in price
but very close in quality.

DMI FURNITURE
1 Oxmoor Place
101 Bullitt Lane
Louisville, KY 40222
(502) 426-4351
Furniture.

DOUGLAS FURNITURE
4000 Redondo Beach Ave
Redondo Beach, CA 90278
(310) 643-7200, FAX (310)
536-0626
Kitchen and casual dining sets.

DRESHER
(See Fashion Bed Group)

**DREXEL HERITAGE
FURNISHINGS INC.**
101 N Main St
Drexel, NC 28619
(800)916-1986, (704) 433-
3000
Many varieties in style and
price.

The Drexel Studio Collection
▪Marseille

▪Milan
▪Westbury
▪Madison Cherry
▪Astoria
▪Liberty Inn
▪American Tapestry
▪Deer Valley
▪Bridgeport
▪Radiance

The Drexel Heritage Collection
▪Heirlooms
▪Covington Park
▪Chippendale
▪Carleton Cherry
▪Brittany
▪Et Cetera

Casual Collections
▪French Countryside
▪Collector's Mahogany
▪Royal Country Retreats
▪American Themes
▪Sonora
▪Mayfair

Contemporary Collections
▪Cabochon
▪Bel-Aire
▪Classic Statements
▪Transitions
▪Encenada

DSF
PO Box 1067
South Boxton, VA
(800) 776-3064
Furniture.

DUMMY BOOK COMPANY
76 Harbour Lane
West Bay Shore, NY 11706
(516) 968-9002
They make dummy books.

DUNMILLER LTD
320 Dennis Street, P.O. Box
7657
High Point, NC 27264

(910) 434-5603
Upholstery. Custom available.

DUTAILIER
298 Chaput, Ste-Pie
Quebec, Canada JOH 1WO
(514) 772-2403, FAX (514)
772-5055
Glider rockers. Well-made.

ECCO
PO Box 1030, 211 Fraley Rd
High Point, NC 27261
(336) 886-4191
Furniture.

**EISENHART
WALLCOVERING**
(800) 848-5886
Wallcoverings.

EJ VICTOR
110 Wamsutta Mill Rd, Po Box
309
Morganton, NC 28680
(704) 437-1991, (704) 438-
0744
Antique reproductions,
bdroom, dining, occasional,
upholstery.

EKORNES
500 Memorial Dr
Somerset, NJ 08873.
(908)302-0097, FAX (908)
302-0431.
Recliners. Their "Stressless"
design has won numerous
awards and patent.

ELDEN COLLECTION
1170 N. Main
Orange, CA 92667
(714)771-5999
Known as "Elden Country
Affair." Eclectic, traditional,
casual and country pine.

**ELEMENTS BY
GRAPEVINE**
PO Box 1458
Lockeford, CA 95237

(209)727-3711
Occasional and accessories.

ELLIOTT'S DESIGNS
18201 S. Santa Fe Ave,
Rancho Dominque, CA 90221
(301)631-4931
Iron and brass beds.
Contemporary and traditional.

ELLO
1350 Preston St
Rockford, IL 61102
(815)964-8601
Contemporary bedrooms,
occasional, wall units and
home enterntainment.

EMERSON ET CIE
5351 Industrial Way
Benecia, CA 94510
(707) 747-1002
Accessory and occasional.

EMERSON LEATHER
816 13th St NE
Hickory, NC 28601
(704)328-1701, FAX (704)
328-5845
Upper end leather upholstery.

ENGLAND/CORSAIR
402 Old Knoxville Hwy
New Taxzewell, TN 37825
(615) 626-5211
Occasional and upholstery.
Motion.

ERIC MORGAN
Bush Industries, 1 Mason
Drive,
Jamestown, NY 14702
(716)665-2000
Casegoods for the home and
office.

ERWIN LAMBETH
201 E. Holly Hill Road
Thomasville, NC 27360
(910)472-2700, FAX (910)
476-8745

Custom upholstery in traditional
designs.

EXCELSIOR DESIGNS
1980 New Highway
Farmingdale, NY 11735
(800)533-9235, (516)
249-8484, FAX (516) 249-9460
Contemporary Italian furniture.

EXECUTIVE LEATHER
PO Box 2486, 461 19th St. SE
Hickory, NC 28603
(704)324-2907, FAX (704)
327-6111
High end leather upholstery.
Office chairs and traditional
style sofas and chairs.

FAIRFIELD CHAIR
PO Box 1710
Lenoir, NC 28645
(704)758-5571
Traditional upholstery including
specialty chairs, sectionals and
sleepers.

FAME FABRICS
261 5th Ave
New York, NY 10016
(212) 679-6868
Fabrics.

FANCHER
Box 351
Salamanca, NY 14779
(716) 945-5500, FAX (716)
945-5658
Bedroom, dining. Juvenile,
infant. Ready to assemble.

FASHION BED GROUP
5950 West 51st St
 Chicago, IL 60638
(708) 458-1800, FAX
(800)753-0934
Beds, daybeds and accessories
in brass, metal, iron, wicker and
wood. Moderate to high price.

FICKS REED COMPANY
4900 Charlemar Dr

Cincinnati, OH 45227
(513) 561-2100, FAX (513)
561-1135
Ficks Reed went out of
business in 1996. Their
trademark name was purchased
in the hopes of reviving the
company.

FINE ART LAMPS
7215 West 20th Ave
Hialeah, FL 33014
(305)821-3850, FAX (305)
821-8114
Lighting. Traditional and
transitional designs.

FLEXSTEEL INDUSTRIES
Brunswick Industrial Block
Dubuque, IA 52001
(319) 556-7730, FAX (319)
556-8345
Major manufacturer of
stationary and motion
upholstery.

**FLORIDA FURNITURE
INDUSTRIES**
PO Box 610
Palatka, FL 32178
(904) 328-3444
Bedroom.

FRANKLIN CORP
PO Box 569
Houston, MS 38851
(601)456-42863
Upholstery

FREDERICK COOPER
2545 W. Diversey
Chicago, IL 60647
(312)384-0800, FAX (312)
384-7526
Traditional and transitional
designs in lamps and lighting
accessories.

FREDERICK EDWARD
115 Wamsutta Mill Rd
Morganton, NC 28680
(704)433-0881

Upper-medium quality,
reasonably priced upholstery
for the discriminating buyer
looking for good value.
Traditional designs.

**FRIEDMAN BROS /
DECORATIVE ARTS**
9015 NW 105 Way
Mcdley, FL 33178
(305) 887-3170, (305)
885-5331
Mirrors and decorative
accessories. High end quality
and price.

**FRIENDSHIP
UPHOLSTERY**
Rt. 6, PO Box 262
Taylorsville, NC 28681
(704) 632-9836, FAX (704)
632-4071
Little known company with a
great reputation for good value.

FROELICH FURNITURE
PO Box 588
High Point, NC 27261
(910)889-4111
Very exclusive manufacturer of
accent and casegood pieces.
Traditional styles, chosen for
their uniqueness and ability to
stand out for their quality and
design.

FURNITURE GUILD
PO Box 1647, 8 Railroad St
Canton, Ga 30114
(404) 479-4108
Antique reproduction,
bedroom, computer cabinets,
dining, occasional. Unfinished
and hand-painted furniture.

GAINES MFG
PO Box 450
McKenzie, TN 38201
(901)352-3376, FAX (901)
352-3701
Leather upholstery in a
mid-price range.

GAME ROOM
See Michael Durafeev.

GARCIA IMPORTS
PO Box 5066
Redwood City, CA 94063
(415) 367-9600, FAX (415)
366-9390
Importer of furniture, tables,
accessories,wall accessories
lighting.

**GARDEN SOURCE
FURNITURE**
200 Bennett St
Atlanta, GA 30309
(404) 351-6446
Accessories.

**GENERAL FURNITURE
CORPORATION**
Knob Creek - Kling
25 Lake Ave Extension
Danbury, CT 06811
(203) 743-8600
Furniture.

GEORGE KOVACS
67-25 Otto Road
Glendale, NY 11385
(718) 628-5201, FAX (718)
628-5212
Lighting, contemporary, classic.

GEORGIAN FURNISHINGS
5400 Jefferson Highwa
New Orleans, LA 70123
(504) 522-6297, FAX (504)
568-1831

**GEORGIAN
REPRODUCTIONS**
PO Box 7284
High Point, NC 27264
(910) 884-1171

GLASS ARTS BY ICG
780 Cel-River Rd, Rock Hill,
SC 29730. (800)222-1853, FAX
(800) 329-7998
Occasional, dining tables,
etegeres.

GLENNCRAFT
Division of Emerson Leather
5351 Industrial Way
Benecia, CA 94510
(707) 747-1002
Moderate priced upper quality
leather, made to slightly lower
standards than Emerson, but
still better than the average
import.

GRABER
(800) 356-9102
Window treatments.

GREENE BROS
PO Box 698, White Pine St
North Wilkesboro, NC 28659
(910) 838-2091

GROSFILLEX
Old West Penn Ave, PO Box
204
Robesonia, PA 19551
(215) 693-5835
Outdoor, high impact resin
furniture.

GUARDSMAN PRODUCTS
2960 Lucerne Dr SE, PO Box
88010
Grand Rapids, MI 49546. (616)
940-2900
World class producers of
finishing chemicals. Best
known for their fabric and
wood surface protection. They
are sold through retail stores
and can be applied by the store
or by the consumer.

GUILDMASTER
PO Box 10725, Springfield,
MO 65808. (8000 269-9907,
(616)940-2900, FAX (800)
299-0220
Custom accessories, accent and
occasional pieces.

H T B
Division of Lane

PO Box 729, Conover, NC
28613.
(704) 322-9131
Contemporary upholstery side
of Lane.

**HABERSHAM
PLANTATION**
PO Box 1209
Toccoa, GA 30577
(800) 241-0716, (706)
886-1476, FAX (706) 886-91
Custom designs in furniture,
accessories, occasional and
accent pieces. Specialize in a
Country Casual look by
offering custom finishes and
unique looks.

HALCYON
(800) 237-0728
Quality patio and pool
furniture at affordable prices.

HALE OF VERMONT
Maple Street East
Arlington, VT 05252
(802) 375-6511
Traditional solid maple dining
room furniture.

HAMMARY FURNITURE
Division of La-Z-Boy
PO Box 760
Lenoir, NC 28645
(704) 728-3231, FAX (704)
728-5063
Occasional, wall units and
entertainment centers.
Traditional and contemporary.

HARDEN
Mill Pond Way
McConnellsville, NY 13401
(315) 235-1000, FAX (315)
245-2884
Bedroom, dining,
entertainment, home theater,
occasional upholstery.

HARRIS LAMPS
(Division of Harris Marcus)

HART ASSOCIATES
PO Box 1387
Ruston, LA 71270
(318) 255-5757, FAX (318)
255-8328
Lamps.

HART FURNITURE
141 Eastley St, PO Box 760
Collierville, TN 38017
(901) 853-8595, FAX (901)
854-0614
Bedroom, dinette, dining,
occasional.

HATTERAS COLLECTION
PO Box 6101
Charlotte, NC 28207
(704) 377-6649
Summer, casual, hammocks,
accessories.

HEKMAN FURNITURE
1400 Buchanon S.W
Grand Rapids, MI 49507
(616) 452-1411, FAX (616)
452-0688
High end accent furniture,
occasional tables, wall units,
entertainment centers, office
furniture and chairs in
traditional and transitional
looks.

**HEN-FEATHERS AND
COMPANY**
10 Ballygomingo Road
Gulph Mills, PA 19428
(215) 828-1721

HENKEL-HARRIS
PO Box 2170
Winchester, VA 22601
(703) 667-4900, FAX (703)
667-8261
High end quality. Antique
reproducitons, bedroom, dining,
office, occasional.

HENREDON FURNITURE
PO Box 70, 400 Henredon Rd
Morganton, NC 28680

(704) 437-5261
High quality and price range.
Upholstery and casegoods.

HERITAGE HAUS FURNITURE
Route 1, Box 1641A
Demorest, GA
(706)754-2145, FAX
(706)754-3839
Accent pieces, mirrors, lamps, dining and bedroom.

HEYWARD HOUSE-HEYGILL IMPORTS
909 Commerce, PO Drawer 11047
Charleston, SC 29411
(803) 554-6464
Formal and traditional lamps in brass, porcelain.

HICKORY CHAIR
PO Box 2147, Hickory, NC 28603. (800) 462-6278, (704) 328-1801, FAX (704) 328-8954
Fine traditional furniture. Antique reproductions, bedroom, dining, wall unit. Occasional, upholstery, wood chairs.
•The James River Collection
•The European Country Collection
•The American Digest Collection
•The Mark Hampton Collection
•The French Collection
•The Mount Vernon Collection

HICKORY CRAFT
PO Box 1733
Hickory, NC 28603
(704) 322-5995
Furniture.

HICKORY FRY
PO Box 817, Hwy 90E
Taylorsville, NC 28681
(704) 632-9774

Good quality upholstery and occasional

HICKORY HILL
Po Box 40
Valdese, NC 28690
(704) 874-2124, FAX
(704)874-3622
Upholstery.

HICKORY TAVERN
Traditional part of the Lane Furniture Company's upholstery division.

HICKORY WHITE
Casegoods- 300 Oak Street
High Point, NC 27260
(910) 885-1200, FAX (910) 885-1678
Upholstery- 201 Pendleton Rd
High Point, NC 27260
(910) 884-2244, FAX (910) 885-5329

HIGH POINT DESK
Office furniture for home and commercial use. Usually purchased through n office supply store although a growing number of furniture stores also carry it. The advantage of using High Point Desk is their large selection and heavy duty construction.

HIGHLAND HOUSE
PO Box 2467, 207 20th St SE
Hickory, NC 28603
(828) 323-8600
Upholstery.

HITCHCOCK CHAIR
Chairs and cabinets.

HOLLYWOODS
Mid-priced contemporary and country casual dining and kitchen furniture featuring tile tops. Good quality

HOMECREST

PO Box 350
Wadena, MN 56482
(218) 631-1000, FAX (218) 631-2609
Aluminum and steel outdoor furniture.

HOOD
Po Box 55568
Jackson, MS 39216
(601) 981-1551, FAX (601) 987-5717
October 1996 Hood went out of business. It was taken over by Strait's Furniture. Same phone number.

HOOKER
PO Box 4708
Martinsville, VA 24115
(540) 632-2133, FAX (540) 656-3325
Entertainment centers, occasional and home office furniture. Good quality, medium price.

HOWARD MILLER
860 East Main St
Zeeland, MI 49464
(616) 772-9131, FAX (616) 772-5897
Clocks, curios.

HUNTER DOUGLAS
2 Parkway & Route 175
Upper Saddle, NJ 07458
(800) 32-STYLE
Window treatments.

HYUNDAI
3501 Jamac Rd
High Point, NC 27260
(910) 887-8033, FAX (910) 887-8038
Importers of occasional, casual dining, bedroom and dining room furniture. Promotional product.

IDI

"International Designer Imports", A Division of Sofas & Chairs Unlimited
89 NE 27th St, PO Box 370147
Miami, FL 33137
(305)573-0960
Italian tables, chairs and accent pieces. Contract and residential.

IMPACT FURNITURE
Division of Bassett Furniture
PO Box 2189
Hickory, NC 28603
(704) 397-5551
Bedroom, occasional.

IMPERIAL
(800) 251-9994
Wallcoverings.

INTERMOUNTAIN FURNITURE
235 S 600 W
Salt Lake City, UT 84101
(801) 355-1737
Upholstery.

INTERNATIONAL/ KARPEN
111 East Touhy , Suite 500
Des Plaines, IL 60018
(708) 803-6000, FAX (708) 803-6050
Known as International, Karpen or Schnadig. Mid-priced upholstery. Contemporary and transitional.

ITALMOND
5181 W. Adams Blvd
Los Angeles, CA 90016
(213)935-1103, FAX (213)935-1054.
Formal bergere chairs, accent chairs, and tables in Biedermeier, Empire, French and Traditional design. Custom available.

J ROYALE FURNITURE

1610 Deborah Herman Rd, PO Box 490
Conover, NC 28613
(704) 322-1262
Upholstery.

JACKSON OF DANVILLE
Stewarts Lane, PO Box 169
Danville, KY 40422
(606) 236-2604
Contract furniture.

JAMESTOWN STERLING
PO Box 610, allen St Ext
Jamestown, NY 14702
(716) 665-6115
Furniture.

JASPER CABINET
PO Box 190, 905 ½ Main St
Jasper, IN 47547
(812) 482-1666
Occasional, entertainment centers.

JOHNSTON CASUALS
PO Box 668, shaver St
North Wilkesboro, NC 28659
(910) 838-5178
Furniture.

JOHNSTON TOMBIGBEE
PO Box 2128
Columbus, MS 39704
(800) 654-3876, (601) 327-1814
Bedroom, dining, wrought iron. Lamps, occasional. Upholstery.

KAISER KUHN LIGHTING
Lighting and accessories.

KARGES
1501 W. Maryland St.
Evansville, IN 47719
(812) 425-2291, FAX (812) 425-4016
High end. High quality. Formal French. Antique reproductions. Bedroom, dining, occasional, upholstery. Wood chairs.

KELLER
701 N Water St, PO Box 8
Corydon, IN 47112
(812) 738-2222
Bedroom, dining and wood chairs.

KESSLER
8600 Gateway East
El Paso, TX 79907
(915) 591-8161, FAX (915) 598-7353
Metal occasional, baker's racks, bedroom and dining. Classic.

KETTLER INTERNATIONAL
PO Box 2747
Virginia Beach, VA 23450
(804) 427-2400
Juvenile and infant. Occasional. Ready to assemble. Casual wrought iron.

KEY CITY
PO Box 1049, 503 C St
North Wilkesboro, NC 28659
(910) 838-4191
Upholstery, wood chairs.

KINCAID
168 Main St, Po Box 605
Hudson, NC 28638
(828) 728-3261
Bedroom, dinette, kitchen, dining, wall units.

KING HICKORY
PO Box 1179, 1820 Main Street SE
Hickory, NC 28603
(828) 322-6025
Upholstery, traditional, country. Large selection.

KINGS CREEK
PO Box 1748
Hickory, NC
(828) 328-2957.
Upholstery built to very high standards. All traditional.

KINGSDOWN MATTRESS
126 West Holt St
Mebane, NC 27302
(919) 563-3531, (919)
563-4115

KINGSLEY-BATE
5887-B Guinea Road
FairFAX, Va 22032
(703) 978-7200
Hand carved and traditional
garden furniture in solid teak.
Accessories. Ready to
assemble. Unfinished furniture.

KLAUSSNER
Drw. 220, Lewallen St.
Asheboro, NC 27204
(910) 625-6174, (910)
626-0905
Medium to promotional priced
upholstery. Contemporary to
transitional. Hukla division
makes their leather furniture.
Choose from all leather,
leather/vinyl and vinyl.

KNOB CREEK
101 Airpark Dr
Morganton, NC 28665
(704) 437-6392
Bedroom, dining, wall units.
Occasional, entertainment
centers. Look at this line for
some Ethan Allen look-alikes.

KOCH & LOWY
PO Box 304, 487 W. Main St.
Avon, MA 02322-0304
(508)588-4700, FAX
(508)587-7592.
Contemporary and art deco
lighting and accessories.

KOCH ORIGINALS
Po Box 3436
Evansville, IN 47733
(508) 588-4700, FAX (508)
587-7592
Metal dinette, Occasional.

KUSHWOOD

6905 Aragon Circle
Buena Park, CA 90620.
Oak entertainment centers,
bookcases and office furniture,
curio cabinets, occasional
tables and bedroom furniture.

LA BARGE
P.O. Box 1769300 E. 40th St
Holland, MI 49422
(800) 253-3870, (616)
392-4173, FAX (616)392-7387
Upper end brass and metal
occasional, mirror and accent
pieces.

LA-Z-BOY
1284 N. Telegraph Rd
Monroe, MI 48161
(313)242-1444, (313)
241-4422 FAX
Recliners, sleepers, sectionals,
sofas, chaises, accent chairs.
Choose from hundreds of
fabrics.

LADD FURNITURE INC
One Plaza Center, Box HP-3
High Point, NC 27261
(910)889-0333
Ladd is the parent company
that owns several of furniture's
most prestigious names:
American Drew
From traditional legends to
contemporary classics in fine
wood.
American of Martinsville
World leader in hotel,
dormitory, and health care
furniture.
Barclay
Moderately-priced upholstery
in contemporary and traditional
styles, in both fabric and
leather.
Clayton Marcus
Medium-priced traditional,
country, and casual upholstered
furniture.
Lea

Moderately-priced youth and
adult bedroom furniture in a
broad range of styles and
finishes.
Pennsylvania House
Finely-crafted solid wood and
custom upholstered furniture.
Ttraditional and casual.
Pilliod
Promotionally-priced stylesin
adult bedroom furniture, home
entertainment centers,
occasional tables and china
cabinets.

C R LAINE
PO Box 2128
Hickory, NC 28603
(704) 328-1831
Uphollstery. Ttraditional,
contemporary, and transitional
styles in sofas, sleepers, chairs,
rockers, chaises, and sectionals.

LANE ACTION
PO Box 1627
Hwy 45 South, Tupelo, MS
38807
(800) 447-4700, (601)
566-7211, FAX (601)566-3166
Motion upholstery in every
possible combination.

LAURA ASHLEY
1300 MacArthur Blvd
Mahway, NJ 07430

**LAVALLE
MANUFACTURING**
820 Ela Avenue
Waterford, WI 53185
(800)544-8470, (414)534-9801
FAX
Quality accessories. Quilt racks,
wall shelves, benches.

LAZAR INDUSTRIES
620 East Slauson Ave
Los Angeles, CA 90011
(213) 232-6789, FAX (213)
232-6366
Upholstery.

LEATHERCRAFT
P.O. Box 639, Hwy 70-A,
Conover, NC 28613. (800)
627-1561, (704) 322-3305
One of the best quality brands
available at any price.
Traditional and transitional.

LEATHERMAN'S GUILD
P.O. Box 409
Hickory, NC 28603
(704) 322-5330
Upper-end leather upholstery.

LEATHERWORKS
Traditional and transitional
leather upholstery. Leather
barstools and office chairs.

LEE/JOFFA
800 Central Blvd
Carlstadt, NJ 07072
(201) 438-4444
Furniture.

LEE INDUSTRIES
402 West 25th St, PO Box 26
Newton, NC 28658
(704) 464-8318
Upholstery, beds, juvenile and
infant.

LEE CARPETS
(800) LEES-4-U
Carpeting.

LEEDO CABINETRY
3555 Timmons Lane #1440
Houston, TX 77024
(713) 467-7479
Bedroom, home office,
bookcases, entertainment
centers, wall units, occasional
tables and office chairs. Mainly
contemporary, some
traditional.

LEGGETT & PLATT
14090 W. Lambs Lane
Libertyville, IL 60048.

Bedroom, headboards. They
make the parts that make
motion furiture.

LEISTERS FURNITURE
433 Ridge Ave
Hanover, PA 17331
(717)632-8177,
(717)632-8850.
Accent and occasional. Nice
company at a great price.

LENOX
100 Lenox Dr
Lawrenceville, NJ 08648
(609) 896-2800, (609)
896-2715
Elegant china giftware and
lamps.

LEXINGTON FURNITURE
411 S. Salisbury St., PO Box
1008
Lexington, NC 27292
(800) 539-4636,
(704)249-5300
Upholstery and casegoods. All
styles. Many price ranges.
Good quality.
•American Country West
•Art Cetera
•Betsy Cameron's Children
•The World of Bob Timberlake
•Brush Creek
•Chez Michelle
•Classic Cherry
•Cottage Haven
•Country Cottage
•DeCristofaro
•Grand Tour
•Hamilton House
•Heirloom Mahogany
•Homespun Shaker
•Imaginations
•Island Traditions
•Kid's Retrea
•Lexington Cherry
•Liberty Inn
•Locker Room
•Lynn Hollyn at Home
•Marina Oak
•The Old Salem Collection

•Outrigger
•Pacific Overtures
•The Palmer Home Collection
•Recollections
•Smithsonian
•Triumph
•Vestiges
•Victoriana
•Victorian Sampler
•Weekend Retreat
•Wimbledon
•Windjammer II
•Wicker by Henry Link
•"Weather Guard

**LINEAGE HOME
FURNISHINGS**
4000 Lineage Ct
High Point, NC 27265
(910)454-6688
Furniture.

LLOYD/FLANDERS
3010 Tenth St
Menominee, MI 49858
(800) 526-9894, FAX (906)
863-6700
Versatile wicker, aluminum
outdoor furniture.

LOUIS BOWEN
200 Garden City Place
Garden City, NY 11530
(516) 741-9770

LYON SHAW
Division of Winston Furniture
Company
P.O. Box 2069
Salisbury, NC 28145
(704)636-8270
Metal patio furniture, cafe
tables, dinette settings,
occasional, sofas, chairs,
loveseats, and bar tables and bar
stools.

MADISON SQUARE
Box 65
Hanover, PA 17331
(800) 233-4461, (717)
637-2181, FAX (717) 637-7013

Mahogany bedroom and occasional. Quality and price give consumers great value for their money. Well-known for their mahogany, also carry inlays.

MAHOGANY HEIRLOOMS
P.O. Box 19290
Greensboro, NC 27419
(910) 854-0078

MAITLAND-SMITH
481 Tomlinson St
High Point, NC 27261
(910) 812-2420, FAX (910) 887-5505
Importer of some of the most unusual and unique home furnishing items in the world.

MALLIN
2665 Leonis Boulevard
Los Angeles, CA 90058
(213)589-6591, FAX (213)585-2355.
Outdoor furniture.

MANCHESTER WOOD
PO Drawer 180 North St
Granville, NY 12832
(518) 642-9518

MANUAL CANOVAS
D&D Bldg, 979n 3rd Ave
New York, NY 10016
(212)752-9588
Fabrics.

MARBRO LAMP
PO Box 1769
Holland, MI 49422
(616) 392-1473, FAX (616) 392-5001
Imported lighting and accessories..

MARIMEKKO
37 W 57th st
New York, NY 10019
(203) 325-9380
Fabrics.

MARTINSVILLE NOVELTY
900 Rivers Rd
Martinsville, Va 24115
(800) 848-0138
Furniture.

MASSOUD
8208 Moberly Lane Dallas
TX 75227
(214)388-8655, FAX (214)381-3539
Good quality, moderatly priced upholstery.

MASTER DESIGN FURNITURE
308-A Pomona Dr
Greensboro, NC 27407
(910) 854-8121
Dining room, casual dining and occasional. Traditional to contemporary.

MASTERCRAFT
210 Park St
Spindale, NC 28160
Furniture.

McGUIRE
1201 Bryant St
San Francisco, ca
(415) 626-1414
Outdoor furniture.

MCKINLEY LEATHER
209 W. Main St.
Claremont, NC 28610
(704) 459-2884, FAX (704) 459-9738
Genuine top grain leather upholstery. Competitive prices.

MEADOWCRAFT FURNITURE
Division of Sam Blount Co
PO Box 1357
Birmingham, AL 35215
(205) 853-2220
Outdoor.

MERRIMAC
5 Dan Rd

Canton, MA 02021
(617) 828-6750
Fabrics.

MIAMI METAL
Peru, Indiana 46970
(317)472-1630.
Metal baker's racks, wall shelves, mirrors and occasional.

MICHAEL THOMAS FURNITURE
P.O. Box 1275
100 East Newberry, Liberty, NC 27298
(919) 622-3075
Wonderful collection of upper medium upholstery. Many of their pieces look like those carried by Calico Corner.

MIKHAIL DARAFEEV
Also known as Game Room Furniture
13467 Dalewood Avenue
Baldwin Park, CA 91706.
(818)960-1871
Game tables, bars and barstools, popcorn machines, classic automobiles converted to living room sofas. Great quality products.

MILLENIUM
Division of Ashley
One Ashley Way
Arcadia, WI 54612
(608) 323-3377, FAX (800) 678-4492
Mid-price range for contemporary furniture.

MILLER DESK
Contract, commercial and home office.

MINOFF LAMP
7711 E Pleasant Valley Rd
Cleveland, OH 44131
(216) 573-1000, FAX (216) 573-1001
Lighting.

MIRROR FAIR
1495 3rd Ave
New York, NY 10028
(212) 288-5050, (212)
772-7936
Authentic reproduction
mirrors.

**MOHAWK FINISHING
PRODUCTS**
Route 30 North
Amsterdam, NY 12010
(518) 843-1380
This company makes the
chemicals, touch-up sticks,
varnishes, and glues for fixing
furniture.

MOLLA
A Lineal Group Co
16301 NW 15th Ave
Miami, FL 33169
(305) 624-4411
Furniture.

MOOSEHEAD FURNITURE
PO Box 287
Monson, ME 04464-0287
(207) 997-3621, FAX (207)
997-9611
Adult and youth bedroom,
dining room, occasional,
bookcases, desks, rockers and a
deacon's bench.

MOTIONCRAFT
PO Box 9145
Hickory, NC 28603
(704) 437-2255
Motion sofas, loveseats, chairs,
recliners, and complete
modular groupings.

**MURRAY FEISS
INDUSTRIES**
125 Rose Feiss Blvd
Bronx, NY 10454
(718) 292-2024, FAX (718)
402-6084
Medium quality lighting for all
applications.

NATHAN HALE
214 N Franklin St
Red Lion, PA 17356
(717) 244-7657
Bedroom, dining,
entertainment, home theater.

NATIONAL MT AIRY
P.O. Box 669
Bassett, VA 24055
(703) 629-2501
Bedroom and dining room,
executive desks and office
furniture.

NATURAL LIGHT
P.O. Box 16449
Panama City, FL 32406
(904) 265-0800
Contemporary lighting.

NATUZZI
P.O. Box 2438
High Point, NC 27265.
910) 887-8300
Italy. : Industrie Natuzzi S.p.A,
Via iazzitiello, 47, 70029
Santeramo in Colle (Bari)
Italia. Telefono: +39 80
8820111
Leather furniture.

NEW ENGLAND CLOCK
62 Spring Lane, Farmington
Industrial Park
Farmington, CT 06032
(800) 632-5625
Reproduction clocks.

NEW RIVER ARTISANS
P.O. Box 1, Highway 1316
Piney Creek, NC 28663
(919) 359-2216

NICHOLS & STONE
232 Sherman St
Gardner, MA 01440
(508)632-2770
Bedroom, dining, kitchen,
occasional, entertainment,
home theater.

NORMAN PERRY
501 W Green Dr, P.O. Box 269
High Point, NC 27260
(910) 841-5222
Lighting and accessories. Very
elegant designs.

**NORTH HICKORY
FURNITURE**
509 11th St W
Hickory, NC 28603
(828) 328-1841
Upholstery.

NORWALK FURNITURE
100 Furniture Parkway
Norwalk, OH 44857
(419) 668-4461
Upholstery, motion and
stationary furniture.

NULL INDUSTRIES
P.O. Box 8
Maiden, NC 28650
(704) 428-3033
Hundreds of occasional tables.
Good price and value.

OLD HICKORY TANNERY
P.O. Box 3389
Hickory, NC 28601
(704)322-5076
Leather upholstery. Traditional
styles in an upper quality upper
price range.

**ORIENTAL LACQUER
FURNITURE**
635 Regal Row
Dallas, TX 75247
(214) 631-6611

OW LEE
930 N Todd Ave
Azusa, CA 91702
(818) 334-1218
Dinette, dining, outdoor. Metal
and teak wood.

P & P CHAIR COMPANY
532 W Salisbury St
Asheboro, NC 27204

(910) 625-2339
Wood chairs, rockers.
Unfinished products.

PACIFIC RATTAN
5201 S 34th St
Fort Smith, AR 72906
(501) 646-4741
Rattan furniture.

PALECEK
P.O. Box 225
Richmond, CA 94808-0225
(800) 274-7730, FAX (510)
234-7234
Accessory and furniture
company featuring metal,
wicker and woven designs.
Etegeres, president's rockers,
bar stools, tea carts, accent
pieces.

PALLISER FURNITURE
55 Vulcan Ave
Winnipeg, Manitoba, CN R2G
1B9
(204) 988-5600
Bedroom, dining. Juvenile and
infant. Occasional,
entertainment units,
upholstery, leather.

PAOLI
PO Box 30
Paoli, IN 47454
(800) 457-7415, (812)
723-2791, FAX (812)
723-3880
Office, contract and
institutional
furniture.Traditional to
contemporary.

PARK PLACE FURNITURE
104 Shaw St
Greenville, SC 29608
(803) 242-4900
Upholstery.

PAUL HANSON LAMP
610 Commercial Ave
Carlstadt, NJ 07072

(201) 933-4873
Lighting.

**PAWLEY'S ISLAND
COMPANY**
PO Box 9
Pawley's Island, SC 29585
(803) 237-4291
RTA, unfinished. Hammocks,
rocking chairs, swings.

PEARSON COMPANY
Division of Lane
1420 Progress St, P.O. Box
2838
High Point, NC 27261
(910) 882-8135, FAX (910)
885-5508
Upper end upholstery company.
Top quality and design.
Traditional to contemporary.

PENNSYLVANIA CLASSICS
PO Box 1188
Statesville, NC 28677
(704) 873-9717, FAX (704)
873-9722
18th century reproduction.
Upper end, high quality and
reasonable prices. Occasional,
office, conference table, returns
and bookcase.

PENNSYLVANIA HOUSE
137 North 10th St
Lewisburg, PA 17837
(800) 782-9663, (800)
782-2273 in Pennsylvania,
(717) 523-6278.
Fine furniture with high
quality.
•Allegheny Forge
•Cascades
•Discovery
•Hallmark Cherry
•Homecoming
•Maison Provence
•Miller's Crossing
•Pacific Homestead
•Purely Stated

PEOPLELOUNGER

P.O. Box 429
Nettleton, MS 38858
(601) 963-7301
Motion furniture. All styles.
Occasional, entertainment
centers.

PETERS-REVINGTON
1100 North Washington St, P.O.
Box 238
Delphi, IN 46923
(317) 564-2586, FAX (317)
564-3722
Occasional tables, curios,
entertainment centers.
Lower-medium price range.

**PHILADELPHIA
FURNITURE**
Box 351
Salamance, NY 14779
(716) 945-5500
Furniture.

PHILIP REINISCH
1657 Merchandise Mart
Chicago, IL 60654
(312) 644-6776, FAX (312)
644-9803
Curio cabinets.

PHILLIPS FURNITURE
730 21st St SE
Hickory, NC 28603
(828) 326-6100
Upholstery.

PILLIOD
A LADD Furniture Company
1403 Eastchester Dr
High Point, NC 27265
(336) 884-3929, FAX (336)
884-4076
Bedroom, home entertainment,
occasional and china cabinets.
Promotion priced.

PINE-TIQUE
6022 Culligan Way
Minnetonka, MN 55345
(612) 935-9595, FAX (612)
935-9493

Early American, Shaker and country furniture. Hand-crafted quality. Bedroom, dining, clocks, mirrors, occasional, entertainment centers.

PLANT PLANT
500 Lindburgh Dr NE
Atlanta, GA 30324
(800) 634-2709, (404) 237-5504, FAX (404) 237-7028
Plant Plant makes trees, bushes and plants that look like trees, bushes and plants.

PLATT
PO Box 3397, 11119 Rush Street
South El Monte, CA 91733
(818) 444-6149, FAX (818) 444-5482
High-end bedroom, dining room, and occasional furniture emphasizing custom finishes. Custom available.

POMPEII
255 NW 25th Street
Miami, FL 33127
(305) 576-3600, FAX (305) 576- 2339
Metal furniture. Fine, high quality.

POWELL
P.O. Box 1408
Culver City, CA 90232-1408
(800) 622-4456, (310) 204-2224, FAX (310) 837-6223
Occasional and accent pieces.

PRECEDENT
Division of Sherrill
State Road 1884
Newton, NC 28658
(704) 465-0844, FAX (704) 465-4630
Medium priced contemporary upholstery. Fabric and leather.

PREVIEW FURNITURE
300 Fraley Rd
High Point, NC 27261
(910) 887-3024
High-end contemporary upholstery manufacturer.

PRIVATE LABEL
HWY 421 North, P.O. Box 350
Siler City, NC 27344. (919) 742-3596
Medium quality furniture made for stores that want to carry their own brand.

PROGRESSIVE FURNITURE
413 Broadway
Swanton, OH 43558
(419) 826-8010
Bedroom, dining, occasional, entertainment centers.

PROPTRONICS
1175 McCabe
Elk Grove Village, IL 60007
(800) 362-8118
This is the company that supplies fake electronics, computers and gadgets you see in the furniture stores.

PULASKI
One Pulaski Square, P.O. Box 1371
Pulaski, VA 24301
(703) 980-7330, FAX (800) 456-6230
Curios, collectors cabinets, corner cabinets, consoles, mirrors and bedroom, gem chests, hall trees, entertainment centers, armoires, bookcases and home office, screens and hand painted items, accessories and various accent pieces, hall trees, painted furniture, accent pieces. Reasonably priced.

RELIANCE LAMP
125 Laser Ct
Hauppauge, NY 11788

(516) 434-1120

QUALITY DINETTES
PO Box 197
Arley, AL 35541
(800) 223-4041
Dinettes.

RALPH LAUREN
185 Ave of Americas
New York, NY 10036
Fabrics, accessories, furniture.

RATTAN SPECIALTIES
8222 Allport Ave
Santa Fe Springs, CA 90670
(213) 945-3483
Rattan furniture.

RELIANCE LAMP
125 Laser Ct
Hauppauge, NY 11788
(516) 434-1120
Lighting.

REMBRANDT LAMPS
1548 W 38th St
Chicago, IL 60609
(312) 247-7500
Lighting.

REMINGTON LAMP
5000 Paschal Av
Philadelphia, PA 19143
(215) 729-2600
Lighting.

REPROCRAFTERS
22 Forney Ind Park
Forney, TX 75216
(800) 654-8830
Reproduction furniture.

REX FURNITURE
P.O. Box 488
Rex, GA 30273
(404) 474-8701
Lower-medium dining room. French country and American country. Occasional and curios. Barstools, rockers.

RICHARDSON BROTHERS
P.O. Box 90
Sheboygan Falls, WI 53085
(414) 467-4631
Quality dining room, bedroom, barstools. Traditional colonial look and country.

RIDGEWAY CLOCKS
One Pulaski Square
Pulaski, VA 24301
(703) 980-8990
Medium priced clocks in traditional to contemporary styles.

RIDGEWOOD FURNITURE
Division of Broyhill
One Broyhill Park
Lenoir, NC 28633
(704) 758-3779
Solid pine rustic bedroom furniture like "This End Up."

RIVERSIDE FURNITURE
1400 S. 6th St, P.O. Box 1427
Fort Smith, AR 72901
(501) 785-8100
Promotional to medium quality. Home office, desks, computer desks, file cabinets, credenzas, computer work stations and bookcases, curios, home entertainment and bankers chairs.

ROBERT ALLEN FABRICS
55 Cabot Blvd
Mansfield, MA 02048
(508) 339-9151
Fabric by the yard.

ROBINSON
Route 1
Wilson, MI 49896
(906) 639-2151, FAX (800) 236-5532
Promotional to medium priced furniture. Gliders, rockers, dining room, bar stools and chairs.

ROMWEBER FURNITURE
4 S Park Ave
Batesville, IN 47006
(812) 934-3485
Computer, occasional, entertainment centers.

ROWE FURNITURE
1725 Jefferson Davis Hwy #809
Arlington, VA 22202
(703) 413-6050
Upholstery, motion.

ROYAL PATINA
211 Fraley Road
High Point, NC 27263
(336) 889-7367, (336) 889-7359
Importing unique and eclectic furniture from around the world.

ROYCE CORPORATION
Also known as Crate In Motion
2866 Bee Carter Road
Danbridge, TN 37725
(615) 397-9761

RUBBERMAID
1200 Hwy 27 S
Stanley, NC 28164
(704) 263-9155
Furniture.

S. BENT & BROS.
85 Winter St
Gardner, MA 01440
(508) 632-4300, FAX (508) 632-3657
Comfortable, high quality furniture. Dining, bedroom, occasional.

SALEM SQUARE
108 Avondale St
High Point, NC 27260
(910) 887-3416, FAX (910) 887-3493
Occasional and accent pieces in solid mahogany and select premium veneers.

SALTERINI
1401 Meadowcraft Rd
Birmingham, AL 35215
(205) 853-2220
Outdoor, occasional, iron and steel.

SAM MOORE CHAIRS
P.O. Box 339
Bedford, VA 24523
(703) 586-8253, FAX (703) 586-8497
Dependable, consistent quality. Affordable price. Traditional to contemporary styling, hundreds of fabric choices and plenty of optional wood finishes on exposed pieces. Chairs of all types. Leather and fabric.

SAMSONITE FURNITURE
P.O. Box 189
Murfreesboro, TN 37133
(615) 893-0300
High quality, high tech outdoor furniture, designed to last.

SAMUEL LAWRENCE
PO Box 6691
Phoenix, AZ. 85005.
Medium priced bedroom furniture. Traditional and country to contemporary and Mountain lodge look.

SARREID LTD
P.O. Box 3548
Wilson, NC 27895
(919) 291-1414, FAX (919) 237-1592
Hundreds of accessories for the home.

SAUDER WOODWORKING
502 Middle St
Archibold, OH 43502
(419) 446-2711
Furniture.

SAUVAGNAT/ALLIBERT
12200 Herbert Wayne Ct, Suite 180

Huntersville,NC 28078
(704) 948-0440
Furniture.

SCALAMANDRE
37-24 24th St
Long Island, Ny 11101
(212) 980-3888
Fabrics.

SCHNADIG
4820 West Belmont
Chicago, IL 60641
(312) 545-2300
Lower medium to promotional
upholstery and some motion.
Wide variety of styles.

SCHONBECK
4-8 Industrial Blvd
Plattsburgh, NY 12901
Lighting.

SCHUMACHER
79 Madison Ave
New York, NY 10016
(212) 523-1200
Fabrics.

SCHWEIGER
Division of KCS Inc.
351 Collins Rd
Jefferson, WI 53549
(414) 674-2440
Upholstery. Sofas, loveseats,
chairs and sleepers.

SEABROOK
1325 Farmville Rd
Memphis, TN 38122
(901) 458-3301
Wallcoverings.

SEALY OF MARYLAND
201 E Green Dr
High Point, NC 27260
(336)889-9067 FAX (336)889-9069
Upholstery, specializing in
sleepers. Medium priced.

**SEALY BEDDING AND
MATTRESSES**
1228 Euclid Ave
Cleveland, OH 44115
(216) 522-1310

**SEAY FURNITURE
INDUSTRIES**
3455 Empire Blvd
Atlanta, GA 30354
(404) 767-1880, FAX (404)
763-1308
Budget priced dining room and
dinette furniture. Country
casual.

SEDGEFIELD BY ADAMS
216 Woodbine St
High Point, NC 27260
(910) 882-0196
Lighting. They make several
designs for Bob Timberlake.

S E E IMPORTS
23030 Kidder St
Hayward, CA 94545
(510) 782-1763, FAX (510)
782-1764
Eclectic furniture from around
the world.

**SELIG
MANUFACTURING**Division
of Cox Furniture
Hwy 421 N
Siler City, NC 27344
(919) 742-4126
Furniture.

SERTA
2800 River Road, Suite 300
Des Plaines, IL 60018
(708) 699-9300
Mattresses.

**SHELLY'S CUSIONS AND
UMBRELLAS**
3671 NW 52nd St
Miami, FL 33143
(305) 633-1790, FAX (305)
633-3662

Outdoor replacement cusion,
umbrella, protective covers.

SHENANDOAH FURNITURE
PO Box 97
Collingsville, VA 24078
(703) 632-0502
Motion upholstery.

SHERRILL
PO Box 189
Hickory, NC 28603
(828) 322-2640
High quality upholstery. High
price range.

SILVER FURNITURE
2742 Hancock St
Knoxville, TN 37927
(615) 637-4541
Occasional, ready to assemble.

**SIMMONS UPHOLSTERED
FURNITURE**
400 Skokie Blvd, Suite 300
Northbrook, IL 60062
(708) 291-9171
Motion, sofa beds, upholstery.

SINGER
PO Box 5337
Roanoke, VA
(540) 366-0361, FAX (540)
366-0365
Promotional bedroom and
dining room furniture.

SK PRODUCTS
125 Entin Rd
Clifton, NJ 07014
(800) 433-4635, (201)
473-0700, FAX (201) 779-4582
Dining, dinette, rockers, gliders
and barstools. Often sold as a
generic brand. Low/promotional
to medium price range.

SLIGH
1201 Industrial Ave
Holland, MI 49423
(616) 392-7101

High end price and quality ranges. Clocks, casegoods, computer furniture.

SOUTHERN FURNITURE REPRODUCTIONS (SFR)
PO Box 2225
Elizabetown, NC 28337.
Authentic Shaker and Colonial style furniture.

SOUTHWOOD
Po Box 2245
Hickory, NC 28603
(704) 465-1776, FAX (704) 465-0858
High end upholstery. Entertainment centers, home theater, occasional.

SPRING AIR
2980 River Rd
Des Plaines, IL 60018
(847) 297-5577, FAX (847) 299-0196
Mattresses.

ST. TIMOTHY
PO Box 2427
Hickory, NC 28603
(704) 322-7125, FAX (704) 322-9156
Contract upholstery for the office, usable in the home. Heavy duty upholstery in fabric, leather or vinyl.

STAKMORE CO
Elm St.
Owego, NY 13827
(607) 687-1616, FAX (607) 687-0049
Stacking wooden chairs.

STANFORD UPHOLSTERY
150 19th St. Southeast
Hickory, NC 28602
(704) 323-1992, FAX (704) 323-1994
Medium to upper-medium quality upholstery. Well priced. Traditional and transitional.

STANLEY
PO Box 30
Stanleytown, VA 24168
(540) 627-2000, FAX (540) 629-4085
One of the best known companies in the world. Upholstery, casegoods, bedroom, dining, occasional, wall units, office furniture and home entertainment. Contemporary to Shaker.

STATESVILLE CHAIR
Po Box 245, Hightway 90E
Hiddenite, NC 28636
(704) 632-1800, FAX (704) 632-7833
Reproduction chairs. Great value for the money.

STATTON
PO Box 530
Hagerstown, MD 21741
(301) 739-0360, FAX (301) 739-8421
High quality and design. Bedroom, dining room, occasional and wall systems. Reproductions and originals.

STEIN WORLD
1721 Latham St, Po Box 9491
Memphis, TN 38190
(901) 942-2441, FAX (901) 942-5246
Hand-crafted furniture and accessory items collected from around the world.

STICKLEY
One Stickley Dr
manilus, NY 13104
(315) 682-5500
Casegoods and upholstery. High end. Mission style. Arts and Crafts.

STIFFEL LAMPS
700 N. Kingsbury St.
Chicago, IL 60610

(312) 664-9200, FAX (312) 664-3873
Solid brass and brass-plated lamps and lighting. Traditional mostly, some contemporary.

STONE INTERNATIONAL
72 East Oak, Third Floor
Chicago, IL 60611
(312) 751-1161, FAX (312) 751-1165
Stone tables for the eclectic and contemporary home.

STRATFORD
Old Hwy 178 West
New Albany, MS 38652
(601) 534-4762 FAX (601) 534-1781
Medium priced upholstery. Best known for the Stratolounger.

STRATOLOUNGER
New Albany, MS
(800)544-7682
Recliner.

STROHEIM & ROMANN
31-11 Thompson Ave
Long Island City, NY 11101
(708) 706-7000
Fabrics.

STROUPE MIRROR COMPANY
102 E Holly Hill Rd
Thomasville, NC 27630
(910) 475-2181
Mirrors.

STYLE UPHOLSTERY
33 23rd Ave NW
Hickory, NC 28603
(828) 322-4882, FAX (828) 322-3373
Dozens of dining, stack, party and multi-use chairs. Unusual tables and bar stools, office and desk chairs.

STYLECRAFT LAMPS
PO Box 347

Hernanco, MS 38632
(601) 429-5279
Lighting.

SUMTER CABINET COMPANY
187 S Lafayette Blvd
Sumter, SC 29151
(803)778-5444
Casegoods, gun cabinets, bedroom, dining, entertainment centers.

SWAIM
Po Box 4189
High Point, NC 27263
(910) 886-6131, FAX (910) 885-6227
High quality, high priced upholstery and occasional. Transitional and contemporary.

TAYLOR WOODCRAFT
Po Box 24
Malta, OH 43758
(614) 962-3741, FAX (614) 962-2747
High quality, high priced bedroom, dining, butcher block tables, occasional. Contemporary.

TELESCOPE
85 Church St., Po Box 299
Granville, NY 12832
(518) 642-1100, FAX (518) 642-2536
Outdoor furniture Traditional and contemporary.

TELL CITY
Po Box 369
Tell City, IN 47586
(812) 547-3491, FAX (812) 547-6977
Tell City went out of business in 1996.

THAYER COGGIN
230 S Rd., PO Box 5867
High Point, NC 27262

(910) 841-6000, FAX (910) 841-3245
Contemporary. Residential and office, occasional, upholstery, entertainment centers.

THOMASVILLE FURNITURE INDUSTRIES
PO Box 339
Thomasville, NC 27631
(910) 472-4000
Good quality bedroom, dining, wall units, occasional, entertainment centers, upholstery, motion.

TIANJIN-PHILADELPHIA
Chinese carpet weaving. Fine quality.

TOMLINSON/ERWIN-LAMBETH
201 E Holly Hill Rd
Thomasville, NC 27360
(910) 472-5005
Upholstery.

TRADEWINDS
A Lineal Group Company
16301 NW 15th Ave
Miami, FL 33169
(305) 624-4411
Outdoor

TRADITION FRANCE
PO Box 2308
Morganton, NC 28655
(800) 524-5200

TRADITION HOUSE
237 Ridge Ave
Hanover, PA 17331
(717) 632-5482
Furniture.

TRENDLINES
9912 Governor Lane Blvd
Williamsport, MD 21795
(800) 422-1818
Furniture.

TRICONFORT, INC.

12200 Herbert Wayne St
Huntersville, NC 28078
(704) 875-8787
Outdoor.

TROPITONE
PO Box 92717
Los Angeles, CA 90009
(813) 335-2715
Aluminum outdoor furniture. Quality, value and great design.

TYNDALE
2545 West Diversey
Chicago, IL 60647
(312) 384-0800, FAX (312) 384-7526
Lighting.

U.S FURNITURE INDUSTRIES
1200 Surrett Dr, P.O. Box 2127
High Point, NC 27261
(910) 885-8026
Wood and metal dining, kitchen, dinette.

UNION NATIONAL
226 Crescent St
Jamestown, NY 14701
(716) 487-1165
Furniture.

UNION CITY MIRROR AND TABLE
PO Box 794
Union City, NJ 07087
(201) 867-0050
Case goods and mirrors.

UNIVERSAL
2622 Uwharrie Rd
High Point, NC 27263
(910) 861-7200, FAX (910) 434-2124
Bedroom, dinetter, kitchen, dining room, occasional, entertainment centers, upholstery.

UTTERMOST COMPANY
P.O. Box 558

Rocky Mount, VA 24151
(703) 483-5103
Mirrors. Traditional, eclectic.
Screens and pictures.

UWHARRIE CHAIR
Po Box 7626
High Point, NC 27264
(910) 431-2055, FAX (910)
841-8154
Outdoor furniture made from
one inch thick premium grade
kiln-dried pressure treated
pine. Insect and rot resistant,
can be painted or left natural,
made from renewable resources
and is painted in latex enamel.
Used in some Bob Timberlake
collections.

VANGUARD FURNITURE
P.O. Box 2187
Hickory, NC 28501
(704) 328-5631
Great quality upholstery,
occasional. Fabric and leather.

VAUGHN FURNTURE
P.O. Box 1489
Galax, VA 24333
(703) 236-6111
Promotional priced bedroom
furniture in contemporary,
traditional, transitional and
country. Mirrors, occasional,
wall units, entertainment
centers, home office.
Contemporary to country.
Lower priced, lower quality.

VAUGHN-BASSETT
P.O. Box 1549
Galax, VA 24333
(703) 236-6161
Promotional priced bedroom.
Contemporary to country.
Lower quality, lower priced.

VENTURE
A Division of Lane
Po Box 849
Conover, NC 28613

(704) 328-2352 FAX (704)
328-8274
Upholstery, occasional,
outdoor.

VERMONT PRECISION
WOODWORKING
RR #1, Box 930
Morrisville, Vermont 05661
(802) 888-7974
Bedroom for adults and
children in light, contemporary
maple.
Very clean, utilitarian look.
Tots of Vermont offers
down-sized table, chair and
bedroom sets.

VICTORIAN CLASSICS
PO Box 60
Montgomery, AL 36101
(205) 262-0381
Victorian reproduction.
Casegoods and upholstery.

VIEWPOINT LEATHER
WORKS
P.O. Box 981509
Park City, UT 84068
(801) 649-5999

VIRGINIA HOUSE
FURNITURE
P.O. Box 138
Atkins, VA 24311
(703) 783-7217
Bedroom, kitchen, dinette,
occasional, entertainment
centers.

VIRGINIA
METALCRAFTERS
1010 East Main St
Waynesboro, VA 22980
(703) 949-9400
Reproduction and original
products exclusively licensed
from Colonial Williamsburg,
Smithsonian Institution,
Monticello, Hicstoric Newport,
Old Salem, Mount Vernon, Old
Sturbridge Village, Winterthur

Museum, Historic Charleston,
Mystic Seaport and National
Trust for Historic Preservation.
High quality metal products.

WALKER MARLEN
Wilkesboro Rd
Taylorsville, NC
(704) 632-4662, FAX (704)
632-5643

WAMBOLD FURNITURE
6800 Sith Rd
Simi Valley, CA 93063
(805) 526-5200
Furniture.

WATERFORD FURNITURE
MAKERS
PO Box 11888
Lynchburg, VA 24506
(804) 847-4468, FAX (804)
845-8913
High quality, traditional
bedroom, dining and accent
pieces.

WATERFORD CRYSTAL
1330 Campus Parkway
Wall, NJ 08722
(908) 938-5800, FAX (908)
938-6915
Fine crystal and giftware and
lighting.

WAVERLY
79 Madison Ave, 14th Floor
New York, NY 10016. (800)
423-5881
Fabric by the yard.

WEBB FURNITURE
P.O. Box 1277
Galax, VA 24333
(540) 236-2984
Promotional priced bedroom
furniture. Many styles. Also gun
cabinets and entertainment
units.

WEIMAN
Division of Bassett Furn

P.O. Box 670
Basset, VA 24055
(703) 629-7592
Quality accent and occasional furniture. Also has an upholstery line called "Focus," a competitive, medium quality/priced line.

WELLINGTON HALL
P.O. Box 1354
Lexington, NC 27292
(910) 249-4934
Affordable fine furniture. Accent and wall systems, bedroom and dining room available.

WESLEY ALLEN
1001 East 60th St
Los Angeles, CA 90001
(213) 231-4275
Heirloom quality, high end brass and iron beds.

WHITAKER FURNITURE
P.O. Drawer 1468
Searcy, AR 72143
(501) 268-5374
Good quality, contemporary tables, chairs, bar stools.

WHITE OF MEBANE
201 Center St
Mebane, NC 27302
(919) 563-1217

WHITECRAFT RATTAN
7350 NW Miami Ct, P.O. Box 380309
Miami, FL 33238
(305) 757-3407
Great quality bedroom, occasional, bar stools, casual/formal dining and upholstery. Rattan and wicker.

WILDWOOD LAMPS AND ACCESORIES
P.O. Box 672
Rocky Mount, NC 27802
(919) 446-3266

High quality, high priced lamps and lighting. Wide variety of styles and products.

WILLIAM ALLEN INC
2408 Ashford Circle
High Point, NC 27261
(910) 886-6095
Medium priced upholstery. Transitional to eighteenth century.

WINNERS ONLY
4039 Calle Platino, Suite A
Oceanside, CA 92056
(619) 941-9559
Oak office furniture. Rockers, dining room.

WINSTON FURNITURE
No. 1 Independence Plaza #700
Birmingham, AL 35209
(205) 870-0897
Aluminum outdoor furniture. Higher quality furniture designed to compete with the upper end. Contemporary to traditional.

WOODARD
Outdoor furniture in metal and aluminum.

WOODMARK ORIGINALS
1920 Jarrell St
High Point, NC 27261
(910) 841-4900
Upholstery, motion, wood chairs.

WRIGHT TABLE
P.O. Box 518
Morganton, NC 28655
(704) 437-2766
Custom 18th century occasional and dining room furniture.

YIELD HOUSE
PO Box 5000
North Conway, NH 03860
(704) 437-2766

Furniture.

YORKSHIRE LEATHER
931 18th St Place NW
Hickory, NC 28603
(704) 322-5718
Upper end top grain leather. Traditional and contemporary

YOUNG-HINKLE
See Lexington

RESOURCE DIRECTORY

800 CARPETS INC
7013 THIRD AVE
BROOKLYN, NY 11209
Hours: **M-F: 9-5**

Toll-Free	800-CARPETS
Direct	718-748-8600
Fax	718-721-9854
Internet	**website:** carpets800@aol.com

Notes: Established 1932. Braided rugs and orientals, both imported and domestic, shipped anywhere in the USA free. Call for a beautiful color catalog ($7.50 refundable with purchase) 100% satisfaction guaranteed. Also virtually all domestic broadlooms available at wholesale carpets.

Manufacturers: (Many resources do not list all their manufacturers. Be sure to inquire about those you are interested in, but do not see listed here.)

ALADDIN CARPET	HORIZON	SHAW
COLUMBUS	MOHAWK	WORLD

"A" WINDOW TREATMENT CO, INC
525 BRIGHT LEAF BLVD
SMITHFIELD, NC 27577
Hours: **M-F: 9-5**

Toll-Free	800-552-5463
Direct	
Fax	919-934-7100
Internet	

Notes: Blinds, draperies, window treatments

Manufacturers: (Many resources do not list all their manufacturers. Be sure to inquire about those you are interested in, but do not see listed here.)

A & H WAYSIDE FURNITURE
1086 FREEWAY DRIVE, PO BOX 1143
(BUSINESS 29)
REIDSVILLE, NC 27323
Hours: M-F:9-6; S:9-5

Toll-Free	
Direct	336-342-0717
Fax	336-342-6524
Internet	email: Wayside@netmcr.com

Notes: Company established 1973. Deposit can be paid (up to $500 only) on credit card, balance payment in check form only. Shipper information: in-home set-up by contract furniture carriers. One designer, 7 consultants on this staff. Customers can visit their facilities. Over 300 major manufacturers. Specializing in solid wood manufacturers. This company also has a furniture clearance center in Reidsville with tremendous value on showroom samples, factory closeouts, discontinued items and freight-damaged merchandise from major manufacturers. All at wholesale prices or less

Manufacturers: (Many resources do not list all their manufacturers. Be sure to inquire about those you are interested in, but do not see listed here.)

ACTION BY LANE
AL SHAVER
AMERICAN DREW
AMERICAN OF HIGH POINT
AMERICAN OF MARTINSVILLE
AMERICAN REPRODUCTIONS
AMIRAN CARPETS
ARMSTRONG
ASHLEY MANOR
ATHOL TABLE
BARN DOOR FURNITURE
BALDWIN BRASS
BALDWIN CLOCKS
BARCALOUNGER
BASSETT
BASIC FURNITURE STYLES
BEAN STATION
BENCHCRAFT
BENNINGTON PINE
GEORGE BENT
BERKLINE
BERKSHIRE
BEVAN FUNNELL
BLACKSMITH SHOP
BOLING CHAIR
BRADINGTON YOUNG
BRADY FURNITURE
BRASS ROOTS
BRAXTON CULLER
BROYHILL

BROWN JORDAN
BUTLER SPECIALTY
CAL-STYLE
CAMBRIDGE LAMPS
CARLTON McLENDON
CAROLINA MIRROR
CAROLINA TABLES
CARR & CO
CARSON'S & CRESTWOOD
CARTER CHAIR
CASA BIQUE
CASUAL LAMP
CHADWICK LEATHER
CHAIRCRAFT
CHAPMAN
CHARISMA CHAIRS
CHARLESTON FORGE
CHARLTON
CHARTER TABLE
CHATHAM NOVELTY
CHROMCRAFT
CLARIDGE MANOR
CLARK CASUAL
CLASSIC GALLERY
CLASSIC LEATHER
CLASSIC RATTAN
CLAYTON MARCUS
CLEVELAND LAMP
COCHRANE
COJA LEATHER

COLONIAL
COLONY HOUSE
COMFORT DESIGNS
CONANT BALL
CONOVER CHAIR
CORSICAN IRON BEDS
COUNTRY CONCEPTS
COUNTRY MANOR
COUNTY SEAT DINETTES
COX FURNITURE
CRAFTIQUE
CRAFTMASTER
CRAFTWORK GUILD
CRAWFORD
CRESTLINE
CRESTWOOD
CUSSETA WOOD
DANEKER
DANSEN CONTEMPORARY
DAVID THOMAS
DAYSTROM
DEVILLE
DILLON
DISTINCTION LEATHER
DOUGLAS DINETTES
DRESHER
FREDERICK EDWARD
ELLO
EMERSON LEATHER
EMPIRE

ENGLANDER	LANE	SOMMA
EXECUTIVE LEATHER	LEA	SOUTHERN TABLE
FAIRFIELD CHAIR	LEISTERS	SOUTHWOOD
FAIRINGTON	LEXINGTON	REPRODUCTIONS
FANCHER	LIFESTYLES OF CALIFORNIA	SPRING AIR MATTRESS
FICKS REED	LLOYD FLANDERS	STANTON COOPER
FIVE RIVERS	LYON SHAW	STATE OF HICKORY
FLAIR	MADISON SQUARE	STATESVILLE CHAIR
FLEETWOOD FRAMES	MARIO	STATTON
FLEXSTEEL	MARLOW	STEARNS & FOSTER
FLORIDA FURNITURE	MARTINSVILLE NOVELTY	GERALD STEIN
FRANKLIN	MASTERCRAFT	STIFFEL
FREDERICK COOPER	MASTERFIELD	STONEVILLE
FRIENDSHIP	CARLTON McLENDON	STRATFORD
FUTORIAN CORP	MEADOWCRAFT	STREETMAN
GAINES MFG	MERSMAN	STROUPE MIRRORS
GEORGIAN REPRODUCTIONS	MOBEL	STUART
CORTRON LAMPS	MOOSEHEAD	STYLE UPHOLSTERY
MORRIS GREENSPAN LAMPS	NATHAN HALE	SUMTER CABINET
HAMILTON HALL	NATIONAL MT AIRY	SUPERIOR
HAMMARY	NEW CREATIONS	SWAIM
HEIRLOOM	NICHOLS & STONE	SWAN BRASS BED
HEKMAN	NORTH HICKORY	TAYLOR KING
HICKORY CRAFT	NORTHWOOD FURNITURE	TAYLOR WOODCRAFT
HICKORY FRY	NULL INDUSTRIES	TAYLORSVILLE UPHOLSTERY
HICKORY HILL	O'ASIAN	TELESCOPE
HICKORY INTERNATIONAL	OHIO TABLE PADS	TELL CITY
HICKORY MANUFACTURING	OLD HICKORY TANNERY	TEMPLE UPHOLSTERY
HICKORY LEATHER	OLNEY	TRADEWINDS
HICKORY TAVERN	PM MATTRESS	TREND CLOCKS
HIGH POINT WOODWORKING	P & P CHAIR	TREND WEST
HIGHLAND HOUSE	CLYDE PEARSON	TROPITONE
HITCHCOCK CHAIR	PENNSYLVANIA CLASSICS	TYPHOON
HOLIDAY HOUSE	PEOPLOUNGER	UNIVERSAL
HOOD	PETERS-REVINGTON	VANGUARD
HOOKER	PRECEDENT	VAUGHAN
HOWARD MILLER	PULASKI	VAUGHAN-BASSETT
HUNTINGTON HOUSE	REGENCY HOUSE	VENTURE
HYUNDAI FURNITURE	REGENT	VIRGINIA HOUSE
HTB	REMINGTON LAMPS	VIRGINIA METALCRAFTERS
IMPACT FURNITURE	RESTONIC	VOGUE RATTAN
INTERLINE	REX	WATERFORD
INTERNATIONAL	RICHARDSON BROS	WAYNLINE
J ROYALE	RIDGEWAY CLOCKS	WEBB FURNITURE
JB ROSS BRASS BEDS	RIVERSIDE	WEIMAN
JASPER CABINET	ROBERT ABBEY LAMPS	WELLS TABLES
KAY LYN	JB ROSS BRASS BEDS	WESLEY ALLEN
KELLER	SALOOM	WESTWOOD LAMPS
KEY CITY	SCHUMACHER FABRICS	WILDWOOD
KIMBALL	SCHWARTZ	WILLIAM ALLEN
KINCAID	SCHWEIGER	WILSHIRE
KING HICKORY	SEALY	WINSTON
KINGSDOWN	SERTA MATTRESS	WOODCRAFT ORIGINALS
KLAUSSNER	SIMMONS BEDDING	WOODFIELD
KNOB CREEK	SIMMONS HIDE-A-BEDS	WOODLEE
KRAVET FABRICS	SIMPLY SOUTHERN	WOODMARK CHAIRS
LaBARGE	SK PRODUCTS	WRIGHT TABLE
LAINE	SLIGH	

A CLASSIC DESIGN - FURNITURE & ACCESSORIES
1703 MADISON AVE
GREENSBORO, NC 27403
Hours: **M-F: 9:30-6:00; S: 9:30-2**

Toll-Free	
Direct	336-274-2922
Fax	336-274-1611
Internet	

Notes: Three consultants on staff. Personalized service. Staff will help make suggestions and send brochures, info, etc. Check or money order only for payment. Return policy: according to manufacturer, with a 25% restocking fee. Shipping/return policies: through resource if concealed damage, through shipper if damage in shipping occurs.

Manufacturers: **(Many resources do not list all their manufacturers. Be sure to inquire about those you are interested in, but do not see listed here.)**

BALDWIN BRASS	MICHAEL THOMAS	STATESVILLE
CLASSIC LEATHER	PENNSYLVANIA CLASSICS	TRADITION HOUSE
CRAFTIQUE	SOUTHAMPTON	WELLINGTON HALL
FRIEDMAN BROS MIRRORS	SOUTHWOOD	WILDWOOD
LEXINGTON	REPRODUCTIONS	
MADISON SQUARE	SPEER	

ABC DECORATIVE FABRICS
2410 298TH AVE N
CLEARWATER, FL 34621
Hours: **M-S: 9-5:30**

Toll-Free	800-500-9022
Direct	
Fax	813-789-0046
Internet	

Notes: Free shipping. Strictly decorative upholstery and drapery fabric. No guarantee on dye lots. VISA/MC.

Manufacturers: **(Many resources do not list all their manufacturers. Be sure to inquire about those you are interested in, but do not see listed here.)**

ROBERT ALLEN	WAVERLY	ALL MAJOR MANUFACTURERS

ACCESS CARPET
PO BOX 1007
DALTON, GA 30722
Hours: **M-F: 8:30-5:30**

Toll-Free	800-848-7747 X178
Direct	706-277-7785
Fax	706-277-2474
Internet	**email:** Access@dalton.net **website:** http://www.dalton.net/access/

Notes: All brands, but Milliken, Masland and Karastan. Hardwood, vinyl, rugs and carpeting. 1,000 colors. Lowest prices. 12' and 15' widths. Free samples.

Manufacturers: (Many resources do not list all their manufacturers. Be sure to inquire about those you are interested in, but do not see listed here.)

ALAN FERGUSON ASSOCIATES
422 S MAIN STREET, PO BOX 6222
HIGH POINT, NC 27260
Hours: **M-F:9-5; S:10-4**

Toll-Free	
Direct	336-889-3866
Fax	
Internet	

Notes: Specializing in unique and unusual one-of-a-kind pieces. Custom upholstery and cabinetry. Hundreds of fabrics for upholstery and drapery. Drapery workroom specializes in window treatments to specification. Finishers create any faux look or richest wood finishes. Design scenes and interiors completed anywhere in the country. Save money but get expertise. Art collection includes works by Azoulay and Dali; sculptures by Erte. Accessories: cut glass to porcelain; lighting from ultra to unique

Manufacturers: (Many resources do not list all their manufacturers. Be sure to inquire about those you are interested in, but do not see listed here.)

BEVAN FUNNELL	DLP	FURNITURE GUILD
COUNTRY AFFAIRE-ELDEN	FINE ARTS LAMPS	JOHNSTON CASUALS

LANE	MAITLAND SMITH	SPEER LAMPS
LEXINGTON	MARBRO LAMPS	SWAIM
MARGE CARSON	PREVIEW	THAYER COGGIN

ALMAN'S HOME FURNISHINGS
110 E FIRST ST
NEWTON, NC 28658
Hours: **M-F: 9-5**

Toll-Free	
Direct	704-464-3204
Fax	704-464-3208
Internet	

Notes: Family owned since 1946. Near Hickory. Off I-40 (exit #131) take Hwy 16 south five miles to Newton. Turn left at the courthouse. Nationwide home delivery. Most major brands sold. Deep discounts, great service and financing available through a national bank.

Manufacturers: (Many resources do not list all their manufacturers. Be sure to inquire about those you are interested in, but do not see listed here.)

ACTION BY LANE	COCHRANE	LEA
AMERICAN DREW	CRAFTIQUE	LEXINGTON
ASHLEY	ENGLAND CORSAIR	LINK TAYLOR
ATHENS	FAIRFIELD CHAIR	LANE
BARCALOUNGER	FASHION BED	LIGO PRODUCTS
BASSETT	FLEXSTEEL	LLOYD FLANDERS
BASSETT MIRROR	HAMMARY	LYON SHAW
BENCHCRAFT	HENRY LINK	MORGAN STEWART
BERKLINE	HICKORY HILL	MOBEL
BERKSHIRE	HICKORY LEATHER	MORGANTON CHAIR
BLACKSMITH SHOP	HIGHLAND HOUSE	McKAY TABLE PADS
BOB TIMBERLAKE	HOOKER	NATIONAL MT AIRY
BROYHILL	J ROYALE	NATUZZI
CAROLINA MIRROR	KELLER	NICHOLS & STONE
CHARLESTON FORGE	KINCAID	NORTH HICKORY
CHROMCRAFT	KLAUSSNER	NULL INDUSTRIES
CLARK CASUAL	KROEHLER	
CLASSIC LEATHER		

AMERICAN ACCENTS
THE ATRIUM
430 SOUTH MAIN ST
HIGH POINT, NC 27260
Hours: M-F: 9-6; S: 9-5

Toll-Free	
Direct	336-885-7412
Fax	336-884-4171
Internet	email: accents@theatrium.com

Notes: Part of the Atrium complex. Worth visiting, showrooms available. See **Atrium Furniture Showroom** listing for more information. Solid cherry and pine shaker/country reproductions featuring Brown Street among many other lines. Cast Classics 2-day design.

Manufacturers: (Many resources do not list all their manufacturers. Be sure to inquire about those you are interested in, but do not see listed here.)

AMERICAN BLIND AND WALLPAPER FACTORY
909 N SHELDON RD
PLYMOUTH, MI 48170
Hours: M-F: 7am-1am; SS: 8am-mid

Toll-Free	800-735-5300
Direct	313-207-0549 (Customer Service)
Fax	800-391-2293
Internet	website: www.abwf.com

Notes: Established 1987. Call for a free blind kit and wallpaper catalog. You're always welcome to visit our factory showroom outlet in Plymouth, MI. Thousands of blinds on display and over 3,000 wallpaper books. Ask about our 90 days, same as cash program. Payment policies are VISA/MC/AMEX/DISC/DC/TELECHECK. No returns on custom blinds unless defective. Wallpaper can be returned within 30 days. Lifetime guarantee on blinds and wallpaper. Savings of up to 82%.

Manufacturers: (Many resources do not list all their manufacturers. Be sure to inquire about those you are interested in, but do not see listed here.)

BALI	JOANNA	PROFILE
DELMAR	KIRSCH	VEROSOL
GRABER	LEVOLOR	**WALLPAPERS:**
HUNTER DOUGLAS	LOUVERDRAPE	CAREFREE

KINNEY   SEABROOK   WARNER
LAURA ASHLEY   SUNWALL   YORK
RALPH LAUREN   THYBONY   AND MORE
SANITAS

AMERICAN DREW GALLERY
HICKORY FURNITURE MART
2220 HWY 70 SE
HICKORY, NC 28602
Hours: **M-S:9-6**

Toll-Free	
Direct	828-328-8688
Fax	
Internet	

Notes: This resource is part of the Hickory Furniture Mart complex. This showroom is one of over 80 to visit. **See Hickory Furniture Mart listing for more information.** Consolidated shipping can be arranged with other resources in this center, a standard one/third deposit is required on all orders. Most showrooms accept VISA/MC, but not all. Cash, personal or certified checks accepted by all showrooms. If you elect not to pay for your entire purchase at the time of sale, a personal or certified check will be due upon delivery.

Manufacturers: **(Many resources do not list all their manufacturers. Be sure to inquire about those you are interested in, but do not see listed here.)**

AMERICAN LIGHTSOURCE
511D, W MARKET ST, SUITE 803
GREENSBORO, NC 27409
Hours: **M-Th8:30-7; F:8:30-5:30, S: 10-5:30**

Toll-Free	800-741-0571
Direct	
Fax	706-868-5083
Internet	

Notes: Imported lighting fixtures offer solutions to your decorating problems at substantial savings. Many styles available.

Manufacturers: (Many resources do not list all their manufacturers. Be sure to inquire about those you are interested in, but do not see listed here.)

AMERICAN REPRODUCTIONS
THE ATRIUM
430 SOUTH MAIN ST
HIGH POINT, NC 27262
Hours: M-F:9-6; S: 9-5

Toll-Free	
Direct	336-889-8305
Fax	336-889-8302
Internet	email: american@theatrium.com website: http://ncnet.com/ncnw/ar-intro.html

Notes: Part of the Atrium complex. Worth visiting, showrooms available. See **Atrium Furniture Showroom** listing for more information. Specializing in solid wood furniture, custom upholstery and elegant accessories. Bedroom dining room, occasional and office furniture; plus outdoor and wicker furniture.

Manufacturers: (Many resources do not list all their manufacturers. Be sure to inquire about those you are interested in, but do not see listed here.)

AL SHAVER
AA LAUN
ACTION BY LANE
ALBERT LOCK
AMERICAN CHAIR & TABLE
AMERICAN DREW
AMERICAN
OF HIGH POINT
AMERICAN IMPRESSIONS
AMERICAN OF MARTINSVILLE
AMERICAN REPRODUCTIONS
AMINDO
AMIRAN CORPORATION
ANDRE ORIGINALS
ARCADIAN
ARDLEY HALL
ARTHUR & ASSOCIATES
ARTISTICA
ASHLEY
ASHLEY MANOR
ATHOL
AUSTIN PRODUCTS
AYERS CHAIRMAKERS
BARCALOUNGER
BARN DOOR

BASSETT FURNITURE
BASSETT MIRROR
BASSETT MOTION
BASSETT UPHOLSTERY
BEAN STATION
BENCHCRAFT
BENICIA EAST
BERKLINE
BERKSHIRE BRASS
BEVAN FUNNEL
BLACKHAWK
BLACKSMITH SHOP
BRADINGTON YOUNG
BRADSTON HURRICANE
BRADY FURNITURE
BRAXTON CULLER
BRITTISH COLLECTORS
EDITION
BRITISH TRADITIONS
BROWN JORDAN
BROYHILL CASEGOODS
BROYHILL PREMIER
BROYHILL UPHOLSTERY
BRUCE L ROBERTSON
BUILTRIGHT CHAIR

BURRIS
BUTLER SPECIALTY
CACHET
CAL BEAR
CAL-STYLE
CAMBRIDGE FURNITURE
CAMBRIDGE LAMPS
CANAL DOVER
CARLTON McLENDON
CAROL MORRISON'S
CAROLINA HERITAGE
SLEEPERS
CAROLINA MIRROR
CARR & CO
CARSON'S
CARTER CHAIR
CASA BIQUE
CASUAL LAMP
CENTRUM GROUP
CHAPMAN
CHARLES ADRIAN
CHARLESTON FORGE
CHARTER TABLE
CHATHAM COUNTY
CHATHAM REPRODUCTIONS

CHROMCRAFT
CLARIDGE MANOR
CLARK CASUAL
CLASSIC GALLERY
CLASSIC LEATHER
CLASSIC RATTAN
CLAYTON MARCUS
CLEVELAND LAMP
CM FURNITURE
COCHRANE
COJA LEATHER
COLONIAL
COLONY HOUSE
COMFORT DESIGNS
CONESTOGA WOOD
CONANT BALL
CONOVER CHAIR
COOPER CLASSICS
CORSICAN BRASS
COTTAGE PINE
COUNTRY CONCEPTS
COUNTRY MANOR
COUNTY SEAT DINETTES
COX
CRAFTIQUE
CRAFTMASTER
CRAFTMASTER STANDARDS
CRAFTWORK
CRAWFORD
CREATIVE METAL & WOOD
CRESENT
CRESTLINE
CUSTOMCRAFT
CUSSETA WOOD
D & F WICKER
DANSEN CONTEMPORARY
DECURTIS
DESIGN HORIZONS
DESIGN TREELINE
DESIGNER WICKER
DESIGNMASTER
DEVILLE
DFC
DILLON
DISTINCTION
DISTINCTIVE DESIGNS
DOBBS
DOUGLAS DINETTES
DRESHER
EAGLE CRAFT DESKS
EASTERN ECLECTION
EL CONDOR
ELLER
ELLIOTT'S
EMPIRE
ENCORE EFFECTS
EXECUTIVE LEATHER
FAIRFIELD CHAIR
FAIRINGTON

FANCHER
FASHION BED
FASHION HOUSE
FETCO
FINE ARTS
FIVE RIVERS CRAFT
FLEXSTEEL
FLORAL ART
FLORIDA FURNITURE
FRANKLIN
FREDERICK COOPER
FREDERICK EDWARDS
FRICHE
FRIENDSHIP UPHOLSTERY
FROEHLICH
GENERAL FURNITURE
GENERAL STORE
GEORGIAN PINE CRAFTSMAN
GEORGIAN REPRODUCTIONS
GERALD STEIN
GMS IMPORTS
GORTRON
HALE
HALCYON
HAMMARY
HAMMOCK SHOP
HARRIS MARCUS
HARRIS YOUNG
HEARTHSIDE CLASSICS
HEIRLOOM
HEKMAN
HENDERSON
HERITAGE LEATHER
HICKORY HILL
HICKORY INTERNATIONAL
HICKORY LEATHER
HICKORY TAVERN
HICKORY WHITE
HIGH POINT WOODWORKING
HIGHLAND HOUSE
HITCHCOCK CHAIR
HOLIDAY HOUSE
HOMESTEAD COLLECTION
HOOD
HOOKER
HOUSTON HOUSE
HOWARD FURNITURE
HOWARD MILLER CLOCK
HTB CONTEMPORARY
HUKLA LEATHER
HUNTING BOARD
HUNTINGTON HOUSE
HYUNDAI
J ROYALE
JJ HAINES
JASPER CABINET
JAYMAR
JB ROSS
JDI GROUP

JEFFCO ENTERPRISES
JOHN RICHARD COLLECTION
JOHNSTON BENCHWORKS
JOHNSTON CASUALS
KAREL MINTJENS
KELLER
KEN MAC
KESSLER
KEY CITY
KIMBALL
KINCAID
KING HICKORY
KING MANOR
KINGS CREEK
KINGSDOWN
KINGSTON HULL
KLAUSSNER
KRAVET FABRICS
L & S ANTIQUES
LAMARINA ANTIQUES
LAINE
LANE
LANIER
LEE INDUSTRIES
LEE WOODARD
LEGACY LEATHER
LEHIGH
LEISTERS
LEONARD'S OAK WORLD
LEXINGTON
LIBERTY
LIFESTYLES OF CALIFORNIA
LIGO PRODUCTS
LLOYD FLANDERS
LOLA LTD
LYON SHAW
MADISON SQUARE
MARIO INDUSTRIES
MARK THOMAS
MARLOW
MARTINSVILLE NOVELTY
MASTER DESIGN FURNITURE
MASTERFIELD UPHOLSTERY
MASTERPIECE DESIGN
MASTERPIECE
REPRODUCTIONS
McKAY CUSTOM PRODUCTS
McKINLEY LEATHER
MEADOWCRAFT
MENDEL
MERSMAN
MICHAELS CO
MILLENIUM
MOBEL
MOHAWK
MOOSEHEAD
MORGAN STEWART
MT AIRY
MURPHY

NATHAN HALE
NATIONAL MT AIRY
NEW ENGLAND CLOCK
NICHOLS & STONE
NORTH HICKORY
NORTH STAR
NORTHWOOD
NULL INDUSTRIES
O'ASIAN
OAK CRAFT
OAKWOOD INTERIORS
OHIO TABLE PADS
OLD HICKORY TANNERY
P & P CHAIR
PAMA
PACIFIC COAST LIGHTING
PACIFIC RATTAN
PARKER SOUTHERN
PEARSON
PEMBROKE
PENNSYLVANIA CLASSICS
PEOPLOUNGER
PERFECTION
PETERS-REVINGTON
PINE-TIQUE
PINNACLE
PRECEDENT UPHOLSTERY
PULASKI
REFLECTIONS
REGENCY HOUSE
REX
RICHARDSON BROS
RIDGEWAY CLOCKS
RIDGEWOOD
RIVER OAKS
RIVERSIDE
ROCK CITY
ROWE
ROYAL PATINA
SALEM SQUARE
SALOOM
SAM MOORE
SARREID
SAUDER WOODWORKING
SAXON
SCHNADIG

SCHUMACHER FABRICS
SCHWEIGER INDUSTRIES
SEALY
SEDGEFIELD BY ADAMS
SELIG
SERTA MATTRESS
SIMMONS
SIMPLY SOUTHERN
SINGER
SK PRODUCTS
SKILLCRAFT
SLEEPWORKS
SLIGH
SOMMA
SOUTH CONE TRADING
SOUTH SEAS RATTAN
SOUTHERN
SOUTHERN TRADITION
SOUTHWOOD
REPRODUCTIONS
SPECTRA GALLERIES
SPRING AIR MATTRESS
ST TIMOTHY CHAIR
STAKMORE
STANLEY
STANTON COOPER
STATESVILLE CHAIR
STATTON
STEWART
STIFFEL LAMP
STONEVILLE
STRATFORD
STREETMAN
STUART UPHOLSTERY
(KLAUSSNER)
STYLECRAFT
SUMTER CABINET
SUPERIOR
SWAN BRASS
TAYLOR KING
TAYLOR WOODCRAFT
TAYLORSVILLE UPHOLSTERY
TELESCOPE
TELL CITY
TEMPLE

TEMPLE STUART
THAYER COGGIN
THOMASVILLE
TOM SEELY
TRADEWINDS
TRADITIONS FRANCE
TRADITIONAL HEIRLOOMS
TREND HOUSE
TRENDLINE
TREND WEST
TRIAD BUTCHERBLOCK
TROPITONE
TUBB WOODCRAFTERS
TYPHOON INTL
UNIVERSAL BEDROOM
UNIVERSAL DINING
UWHARRIE CHAIR
VAGABOND HOUSE
VANCE
VANGUARD
VAUGHAN
VAUGHAN BASSETT
VENTURE
VIRGINIA HOUSE
VOGUE RATTAN
WALL STREET DESIGNS
WALLBURG
WATERFORD FURNITURE
MAKERS
WAYNLINE
WEBB
WEIMAN
WELLINGTON HALL
WELLS TABLES
WESLEY ALLEN
WESLEY HALL
WHITAKER
WILLIAM ALLEN
WINNERS ONLY
WINSTON
WOODLEE
WOODMARK
WOODMARK ORIGINALS
WRIGHT TABLE
YORKSHIRE LEATHER

AMERICAN WALLCOVERING DISTRIBUTORS
2260 ROUTE 22
UNION, NJ 07083
Hours: **M-F:9-5**

Toll-Free	800-843-6567
Direct	
Fax	908-688-8390
Internet	

Notes: Guaranteed lowest prices. Orders processed same day. All major brands. Free delivery.

Manufacturers: (**Many resources do not list all their manufacturers. Be sure to inquire about those you are interested in, but do not see listed here.**)

ARTS BY ALEXANDER
701 GREENSBORO ROAD
HIGH POINT, NC 27260
Hours: **M-F: 8:30-5; S: 9-4(MAY-AUG: 9-1)**

Toll-Free	
Direct	336-884-8062
Fax	336-884-8064
Internet	

Notes: Family-owned business over 50 years. Staff of five will help customers make decisions, send photocopies, etc. unique pieces from all over the world. 30% deposit required. Shippers are private delivery service. Factory defects will be handled by factory. Shipping damage claims are filed with the shipper by customer and assistance from resource. Returns not accepted without special permission. Customer can visit facilities filled with furniture, accessories, and one-of-a-kind selections. Custom picture framing.

Manufacturers: (**Many resources do not list all their manufacturers. Be sure to inquire about those you are interested in, but do not see listed here.**)

ACCENTRICS BY PULASKI	AS YOU LIKE IT LAMPS	BRASSCRAFTERS
AMERICAN DREW	AUTUMN GUILD	BUTLER SPECIALTY
AMERICAN OF HIGH POINT	BASSETT FURNITURE	CAL BEAR
AMERICAN MIRROR	BASSETT MIRROR	CAL-STYLE
ARQUATI MIRRORS	BOLING CHAIR	CAROLINA MIRROR
ARTISAN HOUSE	BRADBURN	CARTER
ARTISANS GUILD	BRADINGTON YOUNG	CARVER'S GUILD

CASA BIQUE
CASA STRADIVARI
DBK LTD
CEBU IMPORTS
CHAPMAN
CHARLESTON FORGE
CLARK CASUAL
CLASSIC TRADITIONS
THAYER COGGIN
COMFORT DESIGNS
CORONA DECOR
FREDERICK COOPER LAMPS
CRAFTIQUE
CRAWFORD
BRAXTON CULLER
DAVIS & SMALL
DECORATIVE CRAFTS
DIERRAS LAMPS
EASTERN ART ARCADE
ELEMENTS BY GRAPEVINE
EMERSON LEATHER
FASHION BED
FORT STEUBEN
GARCIA IMPORTS
GATCO
GLASS ARTS OF CALIFORNIA
HART ASSOC

HEKMAN
HENRY LINK
HICKORY LEATHER
INTERLUDE
JDI
JOHNSTON CASUALS
KINDER HARRIS
LaBARGE MIRRORS
LANE
LEXINGTON
LINK TAYLOR
LLOYD FLANDERS
LYON SHAW
MARKEL LIGHTING
MARIO LAMPS
MIAMI METAL
MILLENDER
MILLER IMPORTS
McKAY CUSTOM PRODUCTS
NATURAL LIGHT
ORIENTAL ACCENTS
ORIENTAL LACQUER
PARK PLACE
PASSPORT FURNITURE
EDWARD P PAUL
NORMAN PERRY LAMPS
PULASKI

REMINGTON LAMPS
RUG BARN
CHARLES SADEK IMPORTS
SARREID
SCULLINI
SEDGEFIELD LAMP
CHARLES SEROUYA
SIGNATURE LIGHTING
SPEER COLLECTIBLES
STANTON COOPER
STIFFEL LAMPS
SWAN
TAPESTRIES LTD
TELESCOPE CASUAL
TROPITONE
TYNDALE LAMPS
UNIVERSAL
UTTERMOST
VIRGINIA METALCRAFTERS
WARA INTERCONTINENTAL
WEIMAN
WELLINGTON HALL
WILDWOOD LAMPS
WINSTON
WOODARD
WOODMARK

ASHLEY INTERIORS
310 S ELM ST
HIGH POINT, NC 27262
Hours: **M-S: 9-5**

Toll-Free	
Direct	336-889-7573
Fax	336-889-7574
Internet	

Notes: One of the largest wicker/rattan displays in North Carolina. Living, dining, bedroom furnishings. Also upholstered furnishings, sleep-sofas, metal/wood/wicker tables, etageres, baker racks, etc. A wide selection of fabrics and finishes. Nationwide delivery with in-home set up. Discontinued items and showroom samples often available.

Manufacturers: **(Many resources do not list all their manufacturers. Be sure to inquire about those you are interested in, but do not see listed here.)**

ATRIUM FURNITURE SHOWROOMS
THE ATRIUM
430 SOUTH MAIN ST
HIGH POINT, NC 27320
Hours: M-F: 9-6; S: 9-5

Toll-Free	
Direct	336-882-5599
Fax	336-882-6950
Internet	

Notes: One of the largest home furnishings malls in the south with 230,000 square feet, four floors, and over 600 furniture and accessory lines represented. Located on Main Street in High Point, be sure not to miss it if you're there.

Manufacturers: **(Many resources do not list all their manufacturers. Be sure to inquire about those you are interested in, but do not see listed here.)**

SHOWROOMS:
(Please note all area codes are 336, effective 3/98.)
AMERICAN ACCENTS (885-7412)
AMERICAN DREW (KAGAN'S)(885-8568)
AMERICAN REPRODUCTIONS (889-8305)
CONTEMPORARY COLLECTIONS (887-7265)
DECORATOR'S CHOICE (889-6115)
FEFCO FURNITURE (882-0180)
FRENCH HERITAGE (884-0022)
HICKORY PARK (883-3800)
HOUSEWORK HOME INTERIORS (885-2457)
KAGAN'S FURNITURE GALLERIES (885-1333)
KAGAN'S STANLEY GALLERY (885-8300)
KINCAID GALLERY (883-1818)
LA MAISON (887-6766)
LEATHER UNLIMITED (885-4386)
LINCOLN GERARD (889-9505)
MAIN STREET PENNSYLVANIA HOUSE (886-5200)
MEDALLION FURNITURE INDUSTRIES (889-3432)
PALLISER (882-7031)

PENNSYLVANIA HOUSE GALLERIES (883-2611)
REFLECTIONS (885-5180)
SINA ORIENTAL RUG (885-7600)
ST MARTIN'S LANE LTD (887-0421)
WOOD-ARMFIELD FURNITURE CO (889-6522)
ZAGAROLI CLASSICS (882-7385)

MANUFACTURERS
A & J AMAZIN
AA LAUN
ABIGAILS
ACCENTRICS
ACCENTS BY GARY PARLIN
ACCESSORY ART
ACRYLIC FASHION
ACTION BY LANE
ADAM'S MULFORD
ADESSO
ALAN WHITE
ALEXANDER
ALEXANDER JULIAN
ALEXVALE
ALLISON PALMER
ALLUSIONS
AMBIANCE
AMEDEO DESIGNS
AMERICAN CHAIR & TABLE
AMERICAN DREW
AMERICAN HERITAGE
AMERICAN IMPRESSIONS
AMERICAN MIRROR

AMERICAN OF MARTINSVILLE
AMERICAN REPRODUCTIONS
AMERICRAFT
AMINDO
AMIRAN
AMISCO
ANDREW PEARSON
ANDRE'S ORIGINAL
ANICHINI LENEIUS
AQUARIUS
AQUARIUS MIRROR WORKS
ARCHITECTURAL METAL
ARCTECNICA
ARDLEY
ARK, NY
ARNOLD PALMER
ARTISAN HOUSE
ARTISTICA
ARTMASTER
ARTMAX
ASHLEY
ASHTON BRONZES
ASIL
ATHENS
ATHOL
ATLANTA GLASSCRAFTERS
ATLANTIS
AUSTIN
BABY GUESS
BALDWIN CLOCKS
BARCALOUNGER
BARCLAY
BASIC & BASIC 2 CASEGOODS
BASSETT

BAUER LAMP
BAXLEY HEALTH
BDI
BENCHCRAFT
BENICIA
BERKLINE
BERRYHILL
BEST DESIGN
BEVAN FUNNELL
BIG SKY CARVERS
BISCIOTTI DESIGNS
BLACKHAWK
BLACKSMITH SHOP
BLAST
BOB TIMBERLAKE
BONAVITA CRIBS
BOYD
BRADCO CHAIR
BRADINGTON YOUNG
BRADY
BRAXTON CULLER
BRITISH COLLECTORS
BRITISH TRADITIONS
BROWN JORDAN
BROWNSTREET
BROYHILL
BUILTRIGHT CHAIR
BUSBIN LAMP DESIGNS
BUSH
BUTLER SPECIALTY
C&M TABLES
CAL BEAR
CAL-STYLE
CALDWELL CHAIR
CALIFORNIA KIDS
CAMBRIDGE LAMPS
CANADEL
CANAL DOVER
CANE & REED
CANWOOD
CAPE CRAFTSMEN
CAPITOL LEATHER
CARLTON McLENDON
CAROLINA HERITAGE
CAROLINA MIRROR
CARSON'S
CARTER CONTEMPORARY
CASA BIQUE
CASA STRADIVARI
CASSADY
CAST CLASSICS
CATSKILL CRAFTSMEN
CEDANNA GROUP
CENTURY
CHAIR CO
CHAIR DESIGN
CHAIRCRAFT
CHAIRWORKS
CHAPMAN LAMPS

CHAPS IMPORTS
CHARLESTON FORGE
CHARTER TABLE
CHATHAM COUNTY
CHATHAM REPRODUCTION
CHERRY POND DESIGNS
CHICKEN/EGG
CHRISHAWN
CHRISTY'S CHROMECRAFT
CLARK CASUAL
CLASSIC LEATHER
CLASSIC RATTAN
CLAY, METAL, STONE
CLAYTON MARCUS
CLINE QUEST
CLUB8 HOME THEATER
CMI
COCHRANE
COLLECTIONS '85
COLLEZIONE EUROPA
COLONIAL
COMFORT DEISGN
CONESTOGA WOOD
CONOVER CHAIR
CONTAINER MARKETING
CONTEMPO ARTS
COOPER CLASSICS
CORSICAN BRASS
COTTAGE PINE
COUNCILL
COUNTRY ORIGINALS
COX
CR LAINE
CRAFTMASTER/EAGLE CRAFT
CRAFTWORK
CRAWFORD
CREATIVE ELEGANCE
CREATIVE IDEAS
CREATIVE METAL & WOOD
CRESENT
CROSSWINDS COUNTRY CLUB
CROWN CRAFT
CRYSTAL CLEAR
CHANDELIERS
CSI
CTH
CURREY
CURVET
CUSTOM CHERRY
CUSTOM SHOPPE
CX DESIGN
D & F WICKER
DARY/REES
DAVID LANDIS
DAVID LEE DESIGNS
DAVIS CABINET
DDT
DEARAN
DEBOURNAIS

DESIGNER WICKER
DESIGNMASTER
DILLON
DINAIRE
DINO MARK ANTHONY
DIRECTIONAL UPHOLSTERY
DISTINCTION
DJC
DJC
DL RHEIN
DOMAIN
DONOVAN DESIGNS
DOUGLAS DINING
DUCKS UNLIMITED
DUKE CONGLOMERATE
DUKE LONG LOMERTION
DUTAILIER
EAGLE CRAFT
EDEN TOYS
EDWARD ART
EKORNES
EL CONDOR
ELEMENTS BY GRAPEVINE
ELITE
ELLIOTT'S
ELLO
ELM CREEK BEDS
EMERSON LEATHER
ENGLISH IMPORTS
ENOS
ENTREE BY LABARGE
ER BUCK
EUROLEATHER
EVANS
EXCELSIOR
EXECUTIVE LEATHER
FABLES
FABRICOATE
FAIRFIELD CHAIR
FAIRINGTON
FAROY
FASHION BED GOROUP
FE 26
FEFCO
FETCO
FINE ARTS
FINE ARTS LAMPS
FIVE RIVERS
FLAT ROCK
FLEXSTEEL
FLORIDA FURNITURE
FLORITA NOVA
FOXFIRE
FRANKLIN
FREDERICK COOPER
FREMARC
FRENCH FRAMES
FRENCH HERITAGE
FRIEDMAN BROS

FRIENDSHIP UPHOLSTERY
FROEHLICH
GALBRAITH & PAUL
GALERKIN
GARCIA IMPORTS
GARDEN COURT
GARDEN MIRROR
GARGOYLES
GAUGE
GEM-AN-EYE
GENERAL STORE
ACCESSORIES
GENESIS LIGHTING
GENTRY
GEORGE KOVACS
GEORGIO LEONI
GLASS ARTS
GLASS WORKS
GLOBER
GMS IMPORTS
GOODMAN CHARLTON
GRACE
GREAT CITY TRADERS
GUARDSMAN
GUILDMASTER
HABERSSHAM
HALCYON
HAMMARY
HARPER
HARRIS MARCUS
HARRIS STRONG
HARRIS YOUNG
HART INDUSTRIES
HEARTHSIDE CLASSICS
HEKMAN
HENRY LINK
HERITAGE HAUS
HICKORY FRY
HICKORY HILL
HICKORY WHITE
HIGGINGS LTD
HILL
HITCHCOCK CHAIR
HOLLYWOODS
HOLSHOF LEATHER
HOME SWEET HOME
HOOKER
HOWARD MILLER
HTB CONTEMPORARY
HUKLA
HUNTER/COOK COLLECTION
HUNTINGTON HOUSE
HOLSHOF LEATHER
HYUNDAI FURNITURE
IMPRESSIONS
INTERLINE ITALIA
INTERLUDE
INTERNATIONAL BY
SCHNADIG

INTERPORT
ITAL-DESIGN
ITALIANA LUCE
ITALIANISSIMO
IWI
JARU
JASPER CABINET
JAYMAR
JDI
JOHN RICHARD
JOHNSTON CASUALS
JRW
KAISER KUHN LIGHTING
KARPON
KELLER
KENROY LIGHTING
KENT UPHOLSTERY
KESSLER
KIMBALL
KINCAID
KING HICKORY
KING KOIL
KINGS CREEK
KINGSDOWN
KINGSLEY
KINGSLEY-BATES
KLAUSSNER
KNOB CREEK
KOCH ORIGINALS
L & S
LA LACQUER WORKS
LA-Z-BOY
LABARGE
LAMARINA ANTIQUES
LANDMARK
LANE
LAURIER
LAWRENCE UNLIMITED
LAZAR
LEA
LEATHER CENTER
LEATHER CENTER
LEATHER LOUNGERS
LEATHERMAN'S GUILD
LEATHERTREND
LEDA
LEEAZANNE
LEGACY LEATHER
LEISTERS
LEISURE HOUSE
LEXINGTON
LIBERTY
LIEF PETERSON
LIGHT SOURCE
LIGHTS UP
LIGO
LIMILIGHT
LINCOLN GERARD
LINEAGE

LINK TAYLOR
LITE SOURCE
LLOYD FLANDERS
LT MOSES WILLARD
LUMINARIES
LYNDON
LYNN HANEY
LYON SHAW
MADISON SQUARE
MAITLAND
MAPTIME
MARIE ALBERT
MARTIN
MASTER DESIGN
MASTERFIELD
MASTERPIECE DESIGN
MAX HOWARD
MAXTON
McKAY
MEADOWCRAFT
MELINDA TRENT
MICHAEL ARAM
MICHAEL THOMAS
MICHAEL'S
MIKHAIL DARAFEEV
MILES TALBOT
MILLENIUM
MILLER DESK
MOBEL
MOBILIA
MODERN CLASSICS
MODUS
MOHAWK
MONTAGE
MOON COLLECTION
MOOSEHEAD
MORGAN STEWART
MORGANTON CHAIR
MOTIONCRAFT
MUNIZ
MY DOG SPOT BEDDING
MY ROOM
NADEAU
NAJARIAN
NATHAN HALE
NATIONAL MT AIRY
NATURAL LIGHT
NATUZZI
NEIDERMEIER
NEW ENGLAND CLOCK
NEW RIVER ARTISAN
NICHOLS & STONE
NICOLETTI
NORA FENTON
NULL INDUSTRIES
OAK HERITAGE
OAKWOOD
OEM IMPORTS
OFFICE STAR

OHIO TABLE PAD
OMNIA
ONE OF A KIND
ORDEREST BEDDING
ORIENTAL LACQUER
P & P
PACIFIC COAST
PALLISER
PAMA
PARADIGM
PARAGON PICTURES
PARAMOUNT
PARK PLACE
PARKER SOUTHERN
PARLIAMENT
PASTEL
PAUL ROBINSON
PAVILLION
PEACOCK ALLEY
PEARSON
PENNS CREEK
PENNSYLVANIA CLASSICS
PENNSYLVANIA HOUSE
PENTURA
PEOPLOUNGER
PETERS-REVINGTON
PETITE AMIE CHILDREN'S
FURNITURE
PETITES CHOSES
PHILADELPHIA FURNITURE
PHILLIP REINISCH
PHILLIPS FURNITURE
PICTURE SOURCE
PIERI LAMPS
PIETRARTE
PIETRO CONSTANTIANI
PINE QUARTERS
PINE-TIQUE FURNITURE
PLANT
POMPEII
POUNDER DINING
POWELL
PRESIDENTIAL
PRIVATE LABEL
PRO SCAN
PULASKI
PUZZLE CRAFT
RABY
RAJ
RCA HOME THEATRE
REFLECTIONS
REGENCY HOUSE
RELIABLE BEDDING
REMBRANDT LAMPS
RENOIR
REUBENS
REX
RICHARDSON BROS
RIDGEWOOD

RIVERSIDE
RIVERWALK
ROBERT ABBEY LAMPS
ROBERT GRACE
ROCK CITY
ROUND THE HOUSE
CASEGOODS
ROWE
ROXTON
ROY & BENOT CASEGOODS
ROYAL PATINA
RUG BARN
S BENT
SALEM SQUARE
SALTERINI
SALVATORE POLIZZI
SAM MOORE
SARATOGA MARBLE
SARREID
SCHNADIG
SCHWEIGER
SEALY
SEALY FURNITURE OF
MARYLAND
SECOND AVE
SECOND IMPRESSIONS
SEDGEFIELD
SEE IMPORTS
SEPTEMBER WOODS
SERTA BEDDING
SHADOW CATCHER
SHARUT
SHENANDOAH
SHERMAG
SHERRY KLINE
SHOAL CREEK
SHUFORD
SIDNEY ARTHUR
SIERRA ARTS
SITCOM
SK PRODUCTS
SKILLCRAFT
SLEEP WORKS
SLIDE THREE STUDIO
SLIGH
SOFA ART BY G NICOLETTI
SOILSHIELD
SOMEREST PICTURES
SOMERSET
SOUTH CORE TRADING
SOUTHAMPTON
SOUTHERN FURNITURE
SOUTHERN FURNITURE OF
CONOVER
SOUTHWOOD
SPECTRUM
SPIRAL
SPRING AIR MATTRESS
SPRINGWALL MATTRESS

ST MARTIN'S LANE
STANFORD UPHOLSTERY
STANLEY
STAR CHAIRS/TABLES
STATESVILLE CHAIR
STATTON
STEINWORLD
STEVE BUSS
STEWART MAHOGANY
STONE INTL
STONEVILLE
STRAITS FURNITURE
STUBER STONE
STUDIO 84
STYLE UPHOLSTERY
STYLECRAFT
SUN CITY
SUNBURST
SUNNY QUALITY
SUPERIOR
SUTTON REPRODUCTIONS
SWAIM
TAYLOR KING
TAYLORSVILLE
TDU
TECH DESIGN
TEMPLE
TEMPLE STUART
THAYER COGGIN
THEODORE & ALEXANDER
THOMASVILLE
TIMBERLINE
TIMBERWOOD
TIMELESS BEDDING
TIMMERMAN
TOM SEELY
TOUCHTONE FINE ART
TRADITIONAL HEIRLOOMS
TRIAD BUTCHER BLOCK
TRICA
TROIS EQLISE
TROPITONE
TRUNKS BY BARBARA
TURKART
TWO DAY DESIGNS
ULTIMATE LAMPS
UNITED DESIGNS
UNIVERSAL
US FURNITURE IND
UTTERMOST
UWHARRIE CHAIR
VAN TEAL
VANGUARD
VENEMAN
VENTURE
VERMONT FURNITURE
DESIGNS
VERMONT PRECISION
VERMONT TUBBS

VIETRI
VIEWPOINT LEATHER
VILLAGEOUS
WALL STREET
WAMBOLD
WATERFORD FURNITURE
WAYBORN
WEIMAN
WELLINGTON HALL
WENDY LYNN LAMPS
WESLEY ALLEN

WESLEY HALL
WESTNOVA
WILD ZOO FOR KIDS
WILDWOOD
WILLIAM ALLEN
WINNERS ONLY
WINSOME TRADING
WINSTON
WISCONSIN
WOOD WORKS
WOODARD

WOODMARK
XIN YANG
YIELD HOUSE
YORK UPHOLSTERY
YORKSHIRE HOUSE
ZAGAROLI CLASSICS
ZAKI RUGS
ZILO CASEGOODS
ZINISSER
ZIRO DESIGNS
ZODAC

===

BAKER FURNITURE FACTORY STORE
146 WEST AVE
KANNAPOLIS, NC 28081
Hours: **M-S: 10-5:30**

Toll-Free	
Direct	704-938-9191
Fax	
Internet	

Notes: Factory outlet.

Manufacturers: (**Many resources do not list all their manufacturers. Be sure to inquire about those you are interested in, but do not see listed here.**)
BAKER

===

BAKER GALLERY
HICKORY FURNITURE MART
2220 HWY 70 SE
HICKORY, NC 28602
Hours: **M-F: 9-6; S: 9-5; Closed Sundays**

Toll-Free	
Direct	828-326-1740
Fax	
Internet	

Notes: This resource is part of the Hickory Furniture Mart complex. This showroom is one of over 80 to visit. **See Hickory Furniture Mart listing for more information.** Consolidated shipping can be arranged with other resources in this center, a standard one/third deposit is required on all orders. Most showrooms accept VISA/MC, but not all. Cash, personal or certified checks accepted by all showrooms. If you elect not to pay for your entire purchase at the time of sale, a personal or certified check will be due upon delivery.

Manufacturers: (Many resources do not list all their manufacturers. Be sure to inquire about those you are interested in, but do not see listed here.)

BALDWIN BRASS FACTORY OUTLET
HICKORY FURNITURE MART
2220 HWY 70 SE
HICKORY, NC 28602
Hours: **M-F: 9-6; S: 9-5; Closed Sundays**

Toll-Free	
Direct	828-324-2220
Fax	
Internet	

Notes: This resource is part of the Hickory Furniture Mart complex. This showroom is one of over 80 to visit. **See Hickory Furniture Mart listing for more information.** Consolidated shipping can be arranged with other resources in this center, a standard one/third deposit is required on all orders. Most showrooms accept VISA/MC, but not all. Cash, personal or certified checks accepted by all showrooms. If you elect not to pay for your entire purchase at the time of sale, a personal or certified check will be due upon delivery.

Manufacturers: (Many resources do not list all their manufacturers. Be sure to inquire about those you are interested in, but do not see listed here.)

BARCALOUNGER GALLERIES
1010 N WINSTEAD AVE
ROCKY MOUNT, NC 27804
Hours: M-F: 9-5:30; S: 10-4 (Sept-May)

Toll-Free	
Direct	252-937-2067
Fax	
Internet	

Notes: Specializes in Barcalounger recliners and features other fine furniture, carpet, etc. Showroom available. One-third down payment or full order can be paid by personal check upon order. Balance can be paid by certified check, money order, VISA/MC. No returns. Factory problems are dealt with by the resource. In business since 1986, 15 years in interior design work. Payment policies VISA/MC and personal check accepted with ID. 90 days same as cash, 90 day layaway. 1/3 down on special orders with balance due. Barcalounger recliners are shipped direct from factory by common carrier. Barcalounger mechanism has lifetime warranty, backed by factory. Sales and design consultants on staff. Returns: All merchandise sold is backed by factory and they make necessary arrangements to assist the customer. You can visit this facility. Formerly Interior Images

Manufacturers: (Many resources do not list all their manufacturers. Be sure to inquire about those you are interested in, but do not see listed here.)

BARRON'S
PO BOX 994
NOVI, MI 48376
Hours: M-F: 8AM-10PM; S: 9AM-9PM; SUN: 11AM-7PM

Toll-Free	800-538-6340
Direct	
Fax	800-523-4456
Internet	email: barronsdw@aol.com

Notes: Namebrand tabletop, china, stemware, flatware and giftware. In business 20 years. Forty sales consultants. Strictly mail and phone sales. Sales consultants will help with decisions and mail brochures. Returns or exchanges must be made within 30 days. After the customer notifies the carrier of damage we will take care of any problems and replace damaged items. We will match competitors' prices. Computerized nationwide bridal registry. Greatly reduced prices. VISA/MC/DISC/MO/CHECK.

Manufacturers: **(Many resources do not list all their manufacturers. Be sure to inquire about those you are interested in, but do not see listed here.)**

===

BEACON HILL FACTORY OUTLET
HICKORY FURNITURE MART
2220 HWY 70 SE
HICKORY, NC 28602
Hours: **M-F: 9-6; S: 9-5; Closed Sundays**

Toll-Free	
Direct	828-324-2220
Fax	
Internet	

Notes: This resource is part of the Hickory Furniture Mart complex. This showroom is one of over 80 to visit. **See Hickory Furniture Mart listing for more information.** Consolidated shipping can be arranged with other resources in this center, a standard one/third deposit is required on all orders. Most showrooms accept VISA/MC, but not all. Cash, personal or certified checks accepted by all showrooms. If you elect not to pay for your entire purchase at the time of sale, a personal or certified check will be due upon delivery.

Manufacturers: **(Many resources do not list all their manufacturers. Be sure to inquire about those you are interested in, but do not see listed here.)**

===

BEARDEN BROTHERS CARPET AND TEXTILES
4109 S DIXIE RD
DALTON, GA 30720
Hours: **M-F: 8:30-5:30**

Toll-Free	800-433-0074
Direct	706-277-3265
Fax	706-277-1754
Internet	

Notes: Established in 1965. Also sell their own line of flooring and carpets. Reproduction oriental and contemporary, border designs, braided, and accessories. Special discounts to religious institutions and dealers. Satisfaction guaranteed, orders shipped worldwide, quantity discounts

Manufacturers: **(Many resources do not list all their manufacturers. Be sure to inquire about those you are interested in, but do not see listed here.)**

ALADDIN CARPET	EVANS & BLACK	MASLAND
ARMSTRONG	GALAXY	MOHAWK
BEAULIEU CARPET	HORIZON	PHILADELPHIA
BIGELOW CARPETS	INTERLOOM	SALEM
CABIN CRAFT	JP STEVENS	SHAW
CITATION	LD BRINKMAN	WORLD
CUMBERLAND	LEES CARPET	

BEAVER CARPETS
697 VARNELL RD
TUNNEL HILL, GA 30755
Hours: **M-F: 9-5**

Toll-Free	800-633-5238
Direct	
Fax	706-673-4384
Internet	

Notes: Buy wholesale carpet, vinyl, vinyl tile and hardwood flooring. Save 30-60%. Cash/charge

Manufacturers: **(Many resources do not list all their manufacturers. Be sure to inquire about those you are interested in, but do not see listed here.)**

BERNHARDT GALLERY
HICKORY FURNITURE MART
2220 HWY 70 SE
HICKORY, NC 28602
Hours: **M-F: 9-6; S: 9-5; Closed Sundays**

Toll-Free	
Direct	828-326-1735
Fax	
Internet	

Notes: This resource is part of the Hickory Furniture Mart complex. This showroom is one of over 80 to visit. **See Hickory Furniture Mart listing for more information.** Consolidated shipping can be arranged with other resources in this center, a standard one/third deposit is required on all orders.

Most showrooms accept VISA/MC, but not all. Cash, personal or certified checks accepted by all showrooms. If you elect not to pay for your entire purchase at the time of sale, a personal or certified check will be due upon delivery.

Manufacturers: (Many resources do not list all their manufacturers. Be sure to inquire about those you are interested in, but do not see listed here.)

BETTER HOMES FURNITURE OUTLET
248 FIRST AVE NW
HICKORY, NC 28601
Hours: **M-S: 9-5:30; W: 9-5**

Toll-Free	
Direct	828-328-8302
Fax	828-327-6088
Internet	email: julie@interpath.com

Notes:

Manufacturers: (Many resources do not list all their manufacturers. Be sure to inquire about those you are interested in, but do not see listed here.)

BILTMORE FURNITURE GALLERIES
780 HENDERSONVILLE RD (HWY 25-S)
ASHEVILLE, NC 28803
Hours: **M-S: 9:30-6**

Toll-Free	
Direct	828-274-1819
Fax	828-274-0403
Internet	email: bfg@ioa.com

Notes: Located 1.2 miles south on Hwy 25 off I-40 (exit 50a-W and exit 50-E). 20,000 sq ft showroom. All major credit cards accepted. Financing available. ASID design services available. Fully insured furniture carriers for delivery nationwide.

Manufacturers: (Many resources do not list all their manufacturers. Be sure to inquire

about those you are interested in, but do not see listed here.)

AMERICAN DREW	GLEN ALLEN	PLANT PLANT
AUSTIN	HOLLYWOODS	REPROCRAFTERS
BLACKSMITH SHOP	HOOKER	SERTA
BROYHILL	KAISER KUHN LIGHTING	SERTA
CHARLESTON FORGE	LEXINGTON	SKILLCRAFT
CLASSIC LEATHER	LOTUS ARTS	SOUCHER MARIN
COUNCILL CRAFTSMEN	MAJESTIC MIRRORS	STANLEY
COUNTRY ORIGINALS	NATUZZI	STATESVILLE CHAIR
COX	PARK PLACE	STATESVILLE CHAIR
CRAFTWORK	PENNSYLVANIA CLASSICS	VANGUARD
FRANKLIN	PENNSYLVANIA HOUSE	
FRIEDMAN BROS MIRRORS		

BLACK'S FURNITURE COMPANY, INC
2800 WESTCHESTER
HIGH POINT, NC 27262
Hours: **M-F: 8-5; S: 9-5**

Toll-Free	
Direct	336-886-5011
Fax	336-886-4734
Internet	

Notes: Family owned business established in 1964. Design assistance available. For an intimate, personal approach to furniture savings. Credit cards accepted. Most exciting: warehouse every Saturday clearance prices! Open to the public to take home close-outs, samples, discontinued items, etc. Warehouse **only** open from 9-4 each Saturday. Priced to go home with you. Bus tours can arrange a private showing of the warehouse by appointment. One-third deposit required.

Manufacturers: (Many resources do not list all their manufacturers. Be sure to inquire about those you are interested in, but do not see listed here.)

AMERICAN DREW	CARLTON McLENDON	COX
AS YOU LIKE IT LAMPS	CAROLINA GLASS	CRAFTIQUE
ARTISTICA	CARSON'S	CRAFTWORK GUILD
BALDWIN BRASS BEDS	CASA BIQUE	CREATIVE METAL
BARCALOUNGER	CENTURY	CRYSTAL CLEAR
BASSETT	CHAPMAN	CTH-CAROLINA TABLES
BASSETT MIRROR	CHARLESTON FORGE	DAYSTROM
BENICIA FOUNDRY BEDS	CHATHAM COUNTY	DECORATIVE ARTS
BERKLINE	CHRISTIAN MOSSO	DECORATIVE CRAFTS
BEVAN FUNNELL	CHROMCRAFT	DOLBI CASHIER
BLACKSMITH SHOP	CLASSIC GALLERY	DUCKS UNLIMITED
BRADINGTON YOUNG	CLASSIC LEATHER	ELLIOTT'S DESIGNS
BRAXTON CULLER	CLASSIC RATTAN	EMERSON ET CIE
BROWN JORDAN	CLAYTON MARCUS	EMERSON LEATHER
BUCKS COUNTY	COCHRANE	FAIRFIELD CHAIR
CR LAINE	COLGATE BABY MATTRESS	FASHION BED
CAL-STYLE	CORSICAN BRASS	FICKS REED

FINE ARTS LAMPS	LEA	SERTA
FITZ & FLOYD	LEATHERCRAFT	SHADY LADY
FLEXSTEEL	LEXINGTON	SHERRILL OCCASIONAL
FREDERICK COOPER	LIBRARY LAMPS	SWAIM
FRIEDMAN BROS MIRRORS	LINK TAYLOR	SWAN BRASS BED
GARCIA IMPORTS	LLOYD FLANDERS	SLIGH
GEORGE KOVACS	LYON SHAW	SOUTHERN REPRODUCTIONS
GLASS ARTS	MARIO	STANLEY
GRACE	McKAY TABLE PADS	STANTON COOPER
GRANDEUR BEDS	McKINLEY LEATHER	STATESVILLE CHAIR
GREAT CITY TRADERS	MADISON SQUARE	STIFFEL LAMPS
GUILDMASTER	MAITLAND SMITH	SUPERIOR FURNITURE
HAMMARY	MARBRO LAMPS	TAYLOR WOODCRAFT
HART INDUSTRIES	MEADOWCRAFT	TELESCOPE
HEKMAN	MIKHAIL DARAFEEV	TELL CITY
HENRY LINK WICKER	MOOSEHEAD	THAYER COGGIN
HICKORY HILL	NATIONAL MT AIRY	THOMASVILLE
HICKORY LEATHER	NORA FENTON	TRADITIONAL HEIRLOOMS
HICKORY TAVERN	NULL INDUSTRIES	TROPITONE
HICKORY WHITE	OHIO TABLE PADS	TYNDALE LAMPS
HIGH POINT FURNITURE	OLD HICKORY TANNERY	UNIVERSAL
HOOD	ORIENTAL LACQUER	VANGUARD
HOOKER	PASSPORT	VAUGHAN
HOWARD MILLER	PEARSON	VAUGHAN BASSETT
HYUNDAI	PENNSYLVANIA CLASSICS	VICTORIAN CLASSIC
IMPRESSIONS BY	PLANT PLANT	VIRGINIA METALCRAFTERS
THOMASVILLE	PULASKI	WEIMAN
JASPER	QUOIZEL	WESLEY ALLEN
JOHNSTON CASUALS	REX	WESTWOOD LAMPS
KINGSDOWN	RIVERSIDE	WILDWOOD
LaBARGE	SAM MOORE	WINSTON
LA-Z-BOY	SARREID	WOODARD
LAM LEE GROUP	SEDGEFIELD	WOODMARK
LANE	SEDGEWICK RATTAN	
LANE ALA CARTE		

BLACKWELDER INDUSTRIES, INC
294 TURNERSBURG HWY
STATESVILLE, NC 28677
Hours: **M-S: 9:30-6**

Toll-Free	800-438-0201
Direct	
Fax	704-872-4491
Internet	email: jblackwelder@iamerica.com

Notes: In business since 1938. Deposit of 50% upon order. Payment can be made with
VISA/MC/AMEX/DISC. Balance via check or money order at shipment from factory. Primarily
phone sales; international sales

Manufacturers: (Many resources do not list all their manufacturers. Be sure to inquire about those you are interested in, but do not see listed here.)

ACTION BY LANE
AINSLEY LAMPS
ALEXVALE
AMERICAN DREW
AMERICAN OF MARTINSVILLE
AMERICAN VICTORIAN
ARTISTIC LEATHER
ATHENS FURNITURE
BAKER
BARCALOUNGER
BASSETT FURNITURE
BASSETT MIRROR
BENCHCRAFT
BENTLEY DESIGNS OF CALIFORNIA
BERKELEY UPHOLSTERING
BERNHARDT
BLACKSMITH SHOP
BOLING CHAIR
BOSSENDORFER (PIANOS)
BRADINGTON YOUNG
BRADY FURNITURE
BRASS BEDS OF AMERICA
BRAXTON CULLER
BROWN JORDAN
BROYHILL
BURLINGTON
BURRIS CHAIR
BUTLER SPECIALTY
CAPEL MILLS
CARO-CRAFT
CAROLINA COLLECTION
CAROLINA MIRROR
CARSON'S OF HIGH POINT
CASA BIQUE
CEBU IMPORTS
CENTURY
CHADWICK LEATHER
CHAIRCRAFT
CHARLESTON FORGE
CHATHAM COUNTY
CHILDCRAFT
CHROMCRAFT
CLASSIC LEATHER
CLASSIC GALLERY
CLASSIC RATTAN
CLAYTON MARCUS
CLYDE PEARSON
COCHRANE
COLONIAL MILLS
CONANT BALL
CORSICAN IRON BEDS
CONTEMPORARY SHELLS
COUNCILL CRAFTSMEN
COX BOUDOIR CHAIRS
CRAFTIQUE

CRAFTMASTER
CRAWFORD OF JAMESTOWN
CRESTLINE
CRESTWOOD
DMI (OFFICE)
DANSEN CONTEMPORARY
DAVIS CABINET
DAYSTROM
DESIGNMASTER
DILLINGHAM
DILLON
DISTINCTION LEATHER
DIXIE
DRESHER
DREXEL HERITAGE
DUO-SOFA
ELLO
EMERSON LEATHER
FAIRCHILD
FANCHER
FASHIONCRAFT
FOGLE
FAIRFIELD
FANCHER
FICKS REED
FLAIR
FREDERICK COOPER
FREDERICK EDWARD
FRIEDMAN BROS MIRRORS
GILLIAM
GORDON TABLES
HABERSHAM
HAMMARY
HARDEN
CHARLES HARLAND
HEKMAN
HENKEL-HARRIS
HENRY LINK
HENREDON
HIBRITEN
HICKORY CHAIR
HICKORY FRY
HICKORY HILL
HICKORY MANUFACTURING
HICKORY TAVERN
HIGHLAND HOUSE
HIGH POINT WOODWORKING
HILL
HOOD
HOOKER
HTB CONTEMPORARY
HOWARD MILLER CLOCKS
HUNTINGTON HOUSE
HYUNDAI
JASPER CABINET
JB ROSS BRASS BEDS

JEFFCO
JOHNSTON CASUALS
KELLER
KESSLER
KIMBALL (PIANOS)
KIMBALL (OFFICE)
KIMBALL/VICTORIAN
KITTINGER
LaBARGE
LAINE
LANE
LEA
LEATHERCRAFT
LEXINGTON
LINK-TAYLOR
MADDOX
MADISON SQUARE
LYON-SHAW
MARLOW
MARTINSVILLE NOVELTY
MASTERFIELD
MERSMAN
MOBILIA
MONTGOMERY CHAIR
MASSON HAMLIN (PIANOS)
MASTERCRAFT
MILLER DESK
MT AIRY FURNITURE
MYRTLE DESK
NATIONAL MT AIRY
NATHAN HALE
NATHAN LAGIN LAMPS
NULL INDUSTRIES
OLD HICKORY TANNERY
PANDE CAMERON RUGS
PAUL ROBERT CHAIR
PEOPLOUNGER
PERFECTION
PULASKI
RICHARDSON BROS
RIDGEWAY
RIVERSIDE
SCHWEIGER
SEALY BEDDING
SEALY OF CONNECTICUT
SEDGEFIELD LAMP
SELIG
SHERRILL
SHUFORD
SINGER
SLIGH
SOUTHWOOD
REPRODUCTIONS
STANLEY
STATESVILLE/ROSS
STIFFEL LAMPS

STYLE	TROPITONE	WEIMAN
SUGGS & HARDIN	UNION NATIONAL	WELLS
SUNSET LAMPS	UNIQUE	WELLINGTON HALL
SWAN BRASS BED	UNIVERSAL	WHITE OF MEBANE
TAYLOR WOODCRAFT	VAUGHAN	WHITAKER
TAYLORSVILLE	VANGUARD	WILDWOOD LAMPS
TEMPLE STUART	VENTURE	WOODLEE
TELL CITY	VIRGINIA HOUSE	WOODMARK
TEMPLE UPHOLSTERY	VIRGINIA METALCRAFTERS	WOODARD
THAYER COGGIN	VOGUE RATTAN	YOUNG-HINKLE
THOMASVILLE		

BLINDS DIRECT
10858 HARRY HINES BLVD
DALLAS, TX 75220
Hours: **M-F: 8-5**

Toll-Free	
Direct	800-883-5000
Fax	800-899-0265
Internet	

Notes: In business since 1988. Five sales consultants and 3 designers on staff. Strictly phone sales. Mini-blinds, verticals, pleated shades are manufactured by Nova. VISA/MC/AMEX money order, check. 100% payment upon order. 100% satisfaction guaranteed (Formerly Blindbusters).

Manufacturers: (Many resources do not list all their manufacturers. Be sure to inquire about those you are interested in, but do not see listed here.)
THEIR OWN LINE   SYMPHONY

BLOWING ROCK FURNITURE COMPANY
PO BOX 684, HWY 321
HUDSON, NC 28638
Hours: **M-S: 8:30-5:30**

Toll-Free	
Direct	828-396-3186
Fax	828-396-6031
Internet	

Notes:

Manufacturers: (Many resources do not list all their manufacturers. Be sure to inquire
 about those you are interested in, but do not see listed here.)

ACTION LANE	HICKORY WHITE	SERTA
BARCALOUNGER	HOOKER	SIMMONS
BERKLINE	J ROYALE	STANLEY
BROYHILL PREMIER	KINGSDOWN	THOMASVILLE
CLASSIC LEATHER	LADY ENGLANDER	UNIVERSAL
COCHRANE	LANE	VANGUARD
HEKMAN	LEXINGTON	

═══════════════════════════

BONITA FURNITURE GALLERIES
HWY 321, EXIT 123
HICKORY, NC 28603
Hours: **M-S: 9-5**

Toll-Free	
Direct	828-324-1992
Fax	828-324-7972
Internet	

Notes: Located on Hwy 321. Established 1972. Credit cards not taken. Shipping problems will be
handled by us, freight damage and factory defects only. Over 150 manufacturers carried. Showroom
available.

Manufacturers: (Many resources do not list all their manufacturers. Be sure to inquire
 about those you are interested in, but do not see listed here.)

BERNHARDT GALLERY	LEXINGTON	THOMASVILLE GALLERY
CENTURY	SERTA	

═══════════════════════════

BOYLES CLEARANCE CENTER I
739 OLD LENOIR ROAD
(ADJACENT TO BOYLES COUNTRY SHOP
HICKORY, NC 28601
Hours: M-F: 9-6; S: 9-5

Toll-Free	
Direct	828-326-1700
Fax	828-328-5183
Internet	website: www.Boyles.com

Notes: Virtually all of Boyles famous makers are represented at our clearance centers. There are no holds or layaways. New merchandise is added daily. It is impossible to state exactly what will be in the clearance centers on any given day. These stores serve as clearing houses for clearance merchandise from Boyles 12 statewide locations. They are kept full and prices are low!
IMPORTANT CORPORATE NUMBERS: Customer Service: 828-345-5280; Delivery Info: 828-345-5275; Order Status: 828-345-5290; Billing Questions: 828-345-5206

Manufacturers: **(Many resources do not list all their manufacturers. Be sure to inquire about those you are interested in, but do not see listed here.)**

BOYLES CLEARANCE CENTER II
66 HWY 321 NW
(INSIDE THE HICKORY FURNITURE MART FURNITURE CLEARANCE CENTER)
HICKORY, NC 28601
Hours: **M-F: 9-6; S: 9-5; Closed Sundays**

Toll-Free	
Direct	828-322-5688
Fax	
Internet	website: www.Boyles.com

Notes: Virtually all of Boyles famous makers are represented at our clearance centers. There are no holds or layaways. New merchandise is added daily. It is impossible to state exactly what will be in the clearance centers on any given day. These stores serve as clearing houses for clearance merchandise from Boyles 12 statewide locations. They are kept full and prices are low!
IMPORTANT CORPORATE NUMBERS: Customer Service: 828-345-5280; Delivery Info: 828-345-5275; Order Status: 828-345-5290; Billing Questions: 828-345-5206

Manufacturers: (Many resources do not list all their manufacturers. Be sure to inquire about those you are interested in, but do not see listed here.)

BOYLES DISTINCTIVE FURNITURE
7607 NATIONS FORD ROAD
CHARLOTTE, NC 28217
Hours: MTWF: 9:30-6; TH: 9:30-8; S: 9:30-5:30

Toll-Free	
Direct	704-522-8081
Fax	704-527-5438
Internet	website: www.Boyles.com

Notes: A standard one/third deposit is required on all orders. We're pleased to accept cash, personal or certified checks VISA/MC. If you elect not to pay for your entire purchase at the time of sale, a personal or certified check will be due upon delivery. **IMPORTANT CORPORATE NUMBERS: Customer Service: 828-345-5280; Delivery Info: 828-345-5275; Order Status: 828-345-5290; Billing Questions: 828-345-5206**

Manufacturers: (Many resources do not list all their manufacturers. Be sure to inquire about those you are interested in, but do not see listed here.)

MAJOR LINES:
BAKER	HICKORY CHAIR	MOTIONCRAFT
BERNHARDT	HICKORY WHITE	PRECEDENT
BEVAN FUNNELL	HITCHCOCK CHAIR	SEALY
BRADINGTON YOUNG	HOOKER	SHERRILL
COUNCILL	JEFFCO	SLIGH
DREXEL STUDIO	KARGES	SOUTHAMPTON
GUY CHADDOCK	KINCAID	SOUTHWOOD
HABERSHAM PLANTATION	KINGSDOWN	STANLEY
HAMMARY	LaBARGE	STATTON
HANCOCK & MOORE	LANE	THOMASVILLE
HARDEN HEKMAN	LEXINGTON	UNIVERSAL
HENKEL HARRIS	MAITLAND SMITH	WHITTEMORE SHERRILL
HENREDON	MARGE CARSON	

BOYLES DREXEL HERITAGE
2125 SARDIS ROAD NORTH
CHARLOTTE, NC 28227
Hours: MTWF: 9:30-6; TH: 9:30-8; S: 9:30-5:30

Toll-Free	
Direct	704-845-8300
Fax	704-845-8376
Internet	website: www.Boyles.com

Notes: A standard one/third deposit is required on all orders. We're pleased to accept cash, personal or certified checks VISA/MC. If you elect not to pay for your entire purchase at the time of sale, a personal or certified check will be due upon delivery. **IMPORTANT CORPORATE NUMBERS: Customer Service: 828-345-5280; Delivery Info: 828-345-5275; Order Status: 828-345-5290; Billing Questions: 828-345-5206**

Manufacturers: **(Many resources do not list all their manufacturers. Be sure to inquire about those you are interested in, but do not see listed here.)**
MAJOR LINES: KINGSDOWN
DREXEL HERITAGE   LILLIAN AUGUST
DREXEL STUDIO

BOYLES FURNITURE (ON GREENSBORO ROAD)
616 GREENSBORO ROAD
HIGH POINT, NC 27261
Hours: M-W&S: 8:30-5:30; TH-F: 8:30-8:30

Toll-Free	
Direct	336-884-8088
Fax	336-884-1534
Internet	website: www.Boyles.com

Notes: A standard one/third deposit is required on all orders. We're pleased to accept cash, personal or certified checks visa/mc. If you elect not to pay for your entire purchase at the time of sale, a personal or certified check will be due upon delivery. **IMPORTANT CORPORATE NUMBERS: Customer Service: 828-345-5280; Delivery Info: 828-345-5275; Order Status: 828-345-5290; Billing Questions: 828-345-5206**

Manufacturers: **(Many resources do not list all their manufacturers. Be sure to inquire about those you are interested in, but do not see listed here.)**
MAJOR LINES: CENTURY   HEKMAN
BERNHARDT   IIANCOCK & MOORE   HENKEL HARRIS

Resource Directory

HICKORY WHITE	LANE	SLIGH
HOOKER	LEXINGTON	STANLEY
KARGES	MAITLAND SMITH	STATTON
KINGSDOWN	SEALY	THOMASVILLE
LaBARGE		

BOYLES FURNITURE (ON BUSINESS 85)
5700 RIVERDALE DRIVE
JAMESTOWN, NC 27282
Hours: **M-W&S: 8:30-5:30; TH-F: 8:30-8:30**

Toll-Free	
Direct	336-812-2200
Fax	336-812-9024
Internet	website: www.Boyles.com

Notes: A standard one/third deposit is required on all orders. We're pleased to accept cash, personal or certified checks VISA/MC. If you elect not to pay for your entire purchase at the time of sale, a personal or certified check will be due upon delivery. **IMPORTANT CORPORATE NUMBERS: Customer Service: 828-345-5280; Delivery Info: 828-345-5275; Order Status: 828-345-5290; Billing Questions: 828-345-5206**

Manufacturers: **(Many resources do not list all their manufacturers. Be sure to inquire about those you are interested in, but do not see listed here.)**

MAJOR LINES:	HARDEN	PRECEDENT
BAKER	HEKMAN	SEALY
BEVAN FUNNELL	HENKEL HARRIS	SHERRILL
BOYLES CLASSICS	HENREDON	SOUTHAMPTON
BRADINGTON YOUNG	HICKORY CHAIR	SOUTHWOOD
COUNCILL CRAFTSMEN	HOOKER	THOMASVILLE
CLASSIC ORIENTAL RUGS	JEFFCO	TRADITIONS FRANCE
FINE ARTS	JOHN RICHARD	UNIVERSAL
FREDERICK COOPER	KARGES	WAVERLY PLACE
GARCIA	KINGSDOWN	WESLEY ALLEN
GUY CHADDOCK	MAITLAND SMITH	WHITTEMORE SHERRILL
HABERSHAM PLANTATION	MARGE CARSON	WILDWOOD
HANCOCK & MOORE	MOTIONCRAFT	

BOYLES GALLERIES
HICKORY FURNITURE MART
2220 HWY 70 SE
HICKORY, NC 28603
Hours: **M-F: 9-6; S: 9-5; Closed Sundays**

Toll-Free	
Direct	828-326-1740
Fax	828-326-1799
Internet	website: www.Boyles.com

Notes: This resource is part of the Hickory Furniture Mart complex. This showroom is one of over 80 to visit. **See Hickory Furniture Mart listing for more information.** Consolidated shipping can be arranged with other resources in this center, a standard one/third deposit is required on all orders. Most showrooms accept VISA/MC, but not all. Cash, personal or certified checks accepted by all showrooms. If you elect not to pay for your entire purchase at the time of sale, a personal or certified check will be due upon delivery. **IMPORTANT CORPORATE NUMBERS: Customer Service: 828-345-5280; Delivery Info: 828-345-5275; Order Status: 828-345-5290; Billing Questions: 828-345-5206**

Manufacturers: (Many resources do not list all their manufacturers. Be sure to inquire about those you are interested in, but do not see listed here.)

MAJOR LINES:

BAKER	HICKORY CHAIR	SOUTHWOOD
BEVAN FUNNELL	KINGSDOWN	STATTON
BROWN JORDAN	MADISON SQUARE	THOMASVILLE
COUNCILL	MASTERCRAFT	WESLEY ALLEN
DISQUE	SLIGH	
HENKEL HARRIS	SOUTHAMPTON	

BOYLES ORIGINAL COUNTRY SHOP AND CLEARANCE CENTER IN HICKORY
739 OLD LENOIR ROAD
HICKORY, NC 2860
Hours: **M-F: 9-6; S: 9-5**

Toll-Free	
Direct	828-326-1700
Fax	828-328-5183
Internet	website: www.Boyles.com

Notes: A standard one/third deposit is required on all orders. We're pleased to accept cash, personal or certified checks visa/mc. If you elect not to pay for your entire purchase at the time of sale, a personal or certified check will be due upon delivery. **IMPORTANT CORPORATE NUMBERS: Customer Service: 828-345-5280; Delivery Info: 828-345-5275; Order Status: 828-345-5290; Billing Questions: 828-345-5206**

Manufacturers: **(Many resources do not list all their manufacturers. Be sure to inquire about those you are interested in, but do not see listed here.)**

MAJOR LINES:	HANCOCK & MOORE	LEXINGTON
AMERICAN DREW	HARDEN	MAITLAND SMITH
BAKER	HEKMAN	MARGE CARSON
BERNHARDT	HENKEL HARRIS	POMPEII
BEVAN FUNNELL	HENKEL MOORE	SHERRILL
BRADINGTON YOUNG	HENREDON	SOUTHAMPTON
BROWN JORDAN	HICKORY CHAIR	SOUTHWOOD
CASA BIQUE	HICKORY WHITE	STANLEY
CENTURY	JEFFCO	UNIVERSAL
CHARLESTON FORGE	KARGES	WHITTEMORE SHERRILL
COUNCILL CRAFTSMEN	KINGSDOWN	AND MANY MORE
GUY CHADDOCK	LANE	
HABERSHAM PLANTATION		

BOYLES SHOWCASE GALLERY
HICKORY FURNITURE MART
2220 HWY 70 SE
HICKORY, NC 28603
Hours: **M-F: 9-6; S: 9-5; Closed Sundays**

Toll-Free	
Direct	828-326-1735
Fax	828-326-1758
Internet	website: www.Boyles.com

Notes: This resource is part of the Hickory Furniture Mart complex. This showroom is one of over 80 to visit. **See Hickory Furniture Mart listing for more information.** Consolidated shipping can be arranged with other resources in this center, a standard one/third deposit is required on all orders. Most showrooms accept VISA/MC, but not all. Cash, personal or certified checks accepted by all showrooms. If you elect not to pay for your entire purchase at the time of sale, a personal or certified check will be due upon delivery. **IMPORTANT CORPORATE NUMBERS: Customer Service: 828-345-5280; Delivery Info: 828-345-5275; Order Status: 828-345-5290; Billing Questions: 828-345-5206**

Manufacturers: **(Many resources do not list all their manufacturers. Be sure to inquire about those you are interested in, but do not see listed here.)**

MAJOR LINES:	BROWN JORDAN	CLASSIC ORIENTAL RUGS
BERNHARDT	CASA BIQUE	DISQUE CHAIR
BRADINGTON YOUNG	CASA STRADAVARI	DREXEL STUDIO

ENTREE	KARGES	PRECEDENT
GARCIA	KINGSDOWN	RAYMOND WAITES
GUY CHADDOCK	LaBARGE	SHERRILL
HABERSHAM PLANTATION	LANE	STANLEY
HANCOCK & MOORE	MAITLAND SMITH	TRADITIONS FRANCE
HARDEN	MARGE CARSON	WELLINGTON HALL
HENREDON	MOTIONCRAFT	WHITTEMORE SHERRILL
HOOKER	POMPEII	
JEFFCO		

═══════════════════════════

BRADINGTON YOUNG GALLERY
HICKORY FURNITURE MART
2220 HWY 70 SE
HICKORY, NC 28602
Hours: **M-F: 9-6; S: 9-5; Closed Sundays**

Toll-Free	
Direct	828-328-5257
Fax	828-324-4219
Internet	

Notes: Established 1974. We have fine leather furniture at affordable prices. The quality is superb and the service that the customer receives is timely and personable. We offer a wide range of reclining and stationary furniture, tile-top tables and fine leather sofas and chairs. Two sales consultants, 1 designer on staff. VISA/MC/CHECK/MO. 50% deposit required for special orders. Upon notification of damage, we will issue a return for repair or send a qualified repairman to your house. Customer needs to notify us ASAP about any damage that may occur. This resource is part of the Hickory Furniture Mart complex. This showroom is one of over 80 to visit. **See Hickory Furniture Mart listing for more information.** Consolidated shipping can be arranged with other resources in this center, a standard one/third deposit is required on all orders. Most showrooms accept VISA/MC, but not all. Cash, personal or certified checks accepted by all showrooms. If you elect not to pay for your entire purchase at the time of sale, a personal or certified check will be due upon delivery.

Manufacturers: **(Many resources do not list all their manufacturers. Be sure to inquire about those you are interested in, but do not see listed here.)**

BRADINGTON YOUNG	HOLLYWOODS	PETERS-REVINGTON
COLLEZIONE EUROPA		

═══════════════════════════

Resource Directory

BRASCH ASSOCIATES
7216 GREEN FARM ROAD
WEST BLOOMFIELD, MI 48322
Hours: M-F: 9-5

Toll-Free	
Direct	248-788-2987
Fax	248-788-3991
Internet	email: brasch@earthlink.net

Notes: In business since 1956. The owner of this company was formerly the owner of a series of Scandinavian retail stores and now sells discount. Minimum order $1000. We are an import agent. We import direct for the customer from the manufacturers' factories to our customers' door. The customer handles the shipping problem if any occur. However, we assist if possible. No return policy, credit cards taken. Primarily Scandinavian well-known manufacturers

Manufacturers: (Many resources do not list all their manufacturers. Be sure to inquire about those you are interested in, but do not see listed here.)

BRASS BED SHOPPE, A
12421 CEDAR ROAD
CLEVELAND HEIGHTS, OH 44106
Hours: T-S: 12-6

Toll-Free	
Direct	216-229-4900
Fax	216-229-4900
Internet	

Notes: In business since 1977. VISA/MC, layaway. Buy factory direct and save 50% on heirloom quality solid brass and iron beds. Special layaway and payment plans. Color catalog ($1) offers large selection. Nationally known manufacturers

Manufacturers: (Many resources do not list all their manufacturers. Be sure to inquire about those you are interested in, but do not see listed here.)
ALL NATIONALLY KNOWN   BRASS BED SHOPPE
MANUFACTURERS

BRASS LIGHT GALLERY, INC
131 S FIRST ST
MILWAUKEE, WI 53204
Hours: **M-F: 9-5**

Toll-Free	800-243-9595
Direct	414-271-8300
Fax	414-271-7755
Internet	

Notes: All types of fixtures available at discount prices and styles that vary from mission to nouveau to prairie. Catalog available. Pay by VISA/MC check or money order.

Manufacturers: **(Many resources do not list all their manufacturers. Be sure to inquire about those you are interested in, but do not see listed here.)**
THEIR OWN LINE

BRENTWOOD MANOR
317 VIRGINIA AVENUE
CLARKSVILLE, VA 23927
Hours: **M-F: 9-5**

Toll-Free	800-225-6105
Direct	804-374-4297
Fax	804-374-9420
Internet	

Notes: In business since 1986. VISA/MC check, 50% deposit, cashier's check or money order for balance due. Satisfaction guaranteed. Showroom available for browsing. In home delivery services, repair or replace damaged articles. Returns allowed only on stock orders. You can get an additional 2% savings by providing the full payment with your order.

Manufacturers: **(Many resources do not list all their manufacturers. Be sure to inquire about those you are interested in, but do not see listed here.)**

AMERICAN DREW	COCHRANE	DIXIE
BARCALOUNGER	COLLINGWOOD	ELLIOTT'S BEDS
BASSETT	COLONIAL	EMERSON LEATHER
BOB TIMBERLAKE	CONOVER CHAIR	EXCEL DESIGN
BRADINGTON YOUNG	COUNCILL CRAFTSMEN	FAIRFIELD
BROYHILL	COURISTAN RUGS	FLEXSTEEL
BUTLER SPECIALTY	CRAFTIQUE	GLENNCRAFT
CLASSIC LEATHER	DECORATIVE CRAFTS	HARDEN
CLAYTON MARCUS	D & F WICKER	HEKMAN

HENRY LINK
HICKORY INTERNATIONAL
HIGHLAND HOUSE
HITCHCOCK CHAIR
HOOKER
HOWARD MILLER CLOCKS
JASPER
KELLER
KIMBALL
KINGSDOWN
KIRSCH
LANE
LEXINGTON
LINK-TAYLOR
LLOYD FLANDERS
LYON-SHAW
MADISON SQUARE
MOOSEHEAD
NATHAN HALE

NATIONAL MT AIRY
NICHOLS & STONE
NORMAN'S OF SALISBURY
NORTH HICKORY
NORTHWOOD
OHIO TABLE PADS
CLYDE PEARSON
PETERS-REVINGTON
PINE-TIQUE
PULASKI
RESTONIC
RICHARDSON BROS
ROBINSON
SEDGEFIELD
SHERMAG
SIMMONS
SKILLCRAFT
SLIGH
SOMMA MATTRESS

STAKMORE
STANLEY
STANTON COOPER
STATESVILLE CHAIR
STIFFEL
SUMTER CABINET
SUPERIOR
TAYLOR WOODCRAFT
UNIVERSAL
VANGUARD STUDIOS
VAUGHAN-BASSETT
VICTORIUS
VIRGINIA METALCRAFTERS
WESLEY ALLEN
WINSTON
WOODFIELD
WOODMARK
YOUNG-HINKLE

BROOKLINE FURNITURE FACTORY SHOWROOM
667 WEST WARD ST
HIGH POINT, NC 27262
Hours: **M-F: 9-5**

Toll-Free	
Direct	336-885-8643
Fax	
Internet	

Notes:

Manufacturers: **(Many resources do not list all their manufacturers. Be sure to inquire about those you are interested in, but do not see listed here.)**

BROYHILL SHOWCASE GALLERY
HICKORY FURNITURE MART
2220 HWY 70 SE
HICKORY, NC 28602
Hours: **M-F: 9-6; S: 9-5; Closed Sundays**

Toll-Free	
Direct	828-324-9467
Fax	
Internet	

Notes: This resource is part of the Hickory Furniture Mart complex. This showroom is one of over 80 to visit. **See Hickory Furniture Mart listing for more information.** Consolidated shipping can be arranged with other resources in this center, a standard one/third deposit is required on all orders. Most showrooms accept VISA/MC, but not all. Cash, personal or certified checks accepted by all showrooms. If you elect not to pay for your entire purchase at the time of sale, a personal or certified check will be due upon delivery.

Manufacturers: (Many resources do not list all their manufacturers. Be sure to inquire about those you are interested in, but do not see listed here.)

BULLUCK'S
124 S CHURCH STREET
ROCKY MOUNT, NC 27801
Hours: **M-F: 9-5; S: 9-5**

Toll-Free	
Direct	252-446-1138
Fax	252-977-7870
Internet	

Notes: Family business since 1900.

Manufacturers: (Many resources do not list all their manufacturers. Be sure to inquire about those you are interested in, but do not see listed here.)

BARCALOUNGER	HICKORY CHAIR	NICHOLS & STONE
COUNCILL	HOOKER	SOUTHWOOD
CRAFTIQUE	JASPER CABINET	STANLEY
HANCOCK & MOORE	LEXINGTON	STATTON
HENKEL-HARRIS	MADISON SQUARE	

===

BURLINGTON FURNITURE
2629 RAMADA ROAD
BURLINGTON, NC 27215
Hours: **M-S: 9-5**

Toll-Free	
Direct	336-570-3100
Fax	336-226-8468
Internet	

Notes:

Manufacturers: **(Many resources do not list all their manufacturers. Be sure to inquire about those you are interested in, but do not see listed here.)**

AMERICAN DREW	HEKMAN	STANLEY
BARCALOUNGER	LEXINGTON	UNIVERSAL
CRAFTIQUE	PARKER SOUTHERN	WOODMARK
HAMMARY	PENNSYLVANIA HOUSE	

===

CABOT GALLERY
HICKORY FURNITURE MART
2220 HWY 70 SE
HICKORY, NC 28602
Hours: **M-F: 9-6; S: 9-5; Closed Sundays**

Toll-Free	
Direct	828-345-0409
Fax	828-345-0412
Internet	

Notes: This resource is part of the Hickory Furniture Mart complex. This showroom is one of over 80 to visit. **See Hickory Furniture Mart listing for more information.** Consolidated shipping can be arranged with other resources in this center, a standard one/third deposit is required on all orders. Most showrooms accept VISA/MC, but not all. Cash, personal or certified checks accepted by all showrooms. If you elect not to pay for your entire purchase at the time of sale, a personal or certified check will be due upon delivery.

Manufacturers: **(Many resources do not list all their manufacturers. Be sure to inquire about those you are interested in, but do not see listed here.)**

CALDWELL FURNITURE CLEARANCE CENTER
3509 HICKORY BLVD
HUDSON, NC 28638
Hours: **M-S; 10-5**

Toll-Free	
Direct	828-396-1648
Fax	828-396-8034
Internet	

Notes: Located on Hwy 321. Consignment showroom. Available to dealers and factories in the area.

Manufacturers: **(Many resources do not list all their manufacturers. Be sure to inquire about those you are interested in, but do not see listed here.)**

CALICO CORNERS
WALNUT ROAD BUSINESS PARK
203 GALE LANE
KENNETT SQUARE, PA 19348-1735
Hours: **Vary from store to store.**

Toll-Free	800-213-6366
Direct	610-444-9700
Fax	610-444-1221
Internet	

Notes: Calico Corners carries fabrics and accessories for home decorating in stock and on the bolt, including Ralph Lauren. You can save 30-60% on every yard with designer fabrics and seconds. They carry the finest fabrics printed and woven. Many are exclusive to Calico Corners and cannot be found elsewhere. In addition to a wonderful selection of over 2,500 fabrics in stock, most of our stores carry custom upholstered furniture covered in the customer's choice of fabrics. You can get help with service, custom labor and advice. Locations in the following states: Alabama, Arizona, California (14), Colorado, Connecticut (2), Delaware (2) Florida (8), Georgia (3), Illinois (5), Indiana, Kansas, Louisiana, Maryland (4), Massachusetts (4), Michigan (4), Minnesota (2), Missouri, Nevada, New Jersey (6), New York (7), North Carolina, Ohio (2), Oklahoma, Oregon,

Pennsylvania(6), Tennessee(2), Texas (10), Utah, Virginia (7), Washington (2) and Wisconsin. Call 800-213-6366 to find out the location nearest you.

Manufacturers: **(Many resources do not list all their manufacturers. Be sure to inquire about those you are interested in, but do not see listed here.)**

BRAEMORE	P KAUFMANN	AND MORE
CALICO CORNERS EXCLUSIVE	WAVERLY	

==========

CAMPBELL/CRAVEN FURNITURE
UNIVERSITY COMMONS
341 S COLLEGE RD, S#21
WILMINGTON, NC 28403
Hours: **M-F: 9-6**

Toll-Free	800-488-6493
Direct	910-792-9420
Fax	
Internet	

Notes: Over 20 years experience in the furniture business. Home and office furnishings. To place an order you will need to provide the correct manufacturer's name and item number or other pertinent information. A 50% deposit is required, payable by VISA/MC/check. In-home delivery service available at which time the COD balance is payable by certified funds only.

Manufacturers: **(Many resources do not list all their manufacturers. Be sure to inquire about those you are interested in, but do not see listed here.)**

BASSETT	HOOKER	PENNSYLVANIA CLASSICS
CHARLESTON FORGE	HOWARD MILLER	PETERS REVINGTON
CLASSIC LEATHER	KAISER KUHM LAMPS	STANLEY
CHROMECRAFT	KELLER	STATESVILLE CHAIR
FLEXSTEEL	KINCAID	UNIVERSAL
HEKMAN	LANE	VIRGINIA HOUSE
HENRY LINK	LEXINGTON	WHITECRAFT
HICKORY HOUSE	NICHOLS & STONE	

==========

CANADEL GALLERY
HICKORY FURNITURE MART
2220 HWY 70 SE
HICKORY, NC 28602
Hours: **M-F: 9-6; S: 9-5; Closed Sundays**

Toll-Free	
Direct	828-324-7742
Fax	
Internet	

Notes: This resource is part of the Hickory Furniture Mart complex. This showroom is one of over 80 to visit. **See Hickory Furniture Mart listing for more information.** Consolidated shipping can be arranged with other resources in this center, a standard one/third deposit is required on all orders. Most showrooms accept VISA/MC, but not all. Cash, personal or certified checks accepted by all showrooms. If you elect not to pay for your entire purchase at the time of sale, a personal or certified check will be due upon delivery.

Manufacturers: (Many resources do not list all their manufacturers. Be sure to inquire about those you are interested in, but do not see listed here.)

CANNON VILLAGE
200 WEST AVE
KANNAPOLIS, NC 28081
Hours: **M-S: 10-5:30**

Toll-Free	
Direct	704-938-3200
Fax	
Internet	

Notes: Over 250,000 square feet of furniture and accessories throughout six furniture stores. When you visit any of the six different showrooms in Cannon Village you'll discover a fine selection of furniture and accessories available anywhere. Consolidated shipping available. All stores ship worldwide, in-home setup. Surety bonded protected. Professionally certified interior designers on site. Located 30 miles north of Charlotte. Take Kannapolis exits 58 or 63 off I-85 and follow the signs to Cannon Village.

Manufacturers: (Many resources do not list all their manufacturers. Be sure to inquire about those you are interested in, but do not see listed here.)

CAPEL MILL OUTLET
121 E. MAIN ST
TROY, NC 27371
Hours: **M,T,W,TH,S: 10-5; F: 10-8**

Toll-Free	
Direct	910-572-7011
Fax	910-576-0250
Internet	

Notes: Direct savings from the largest rug manufacturer and importer in America. Eleven salespeople on staff. Showroom available. Complete order can be paid via VISA/MC check. Satisfaction guaranteed-two weeks with receipt. Resource and carrier deal with shipping problems

Manufacturers: **(Many resources do not list all their manufacturers. Be sure to inquire about those you are interested in, but do not see listed here.)**
CAPEL MILLS

CAROLINA CARRIERS
1428 OLDE EDEN DR
HIGH POINT, NC 27262
Hours: **M-F: 9-5**

Toll-Free	
Direct	336-869-5405
Fax	
Internet	

Notes:

Manufacturers: **(Many resources do not list all their manufacturers. Be sure to inquire about those you are interested in, but do not see listed here.)**

CAROLINA FURNITURE DIRECT
PO BOX 22516
HILTON HEAD ISLAND, SC 29925
Hours: **M-S:9-6**

Toll-Free	800-838-7647
Direct	803-681-3330
Fax	803-681-3301
Internet	**email:** carolinafurnish@juno.com

Notes: Saving of up to 60%. Top name furniture brands. Direct from manufacturers. Insured, in-home delivery Showroom. Credit cards for deposits only. VISA/MC/DISC/AMEX/OPTIMA. Two designers on staff of eight. Brochure sent upon request. Members of BBB and Chamber of Commerce.

Manufacturers: (Many resources do not list all their manufacturers. Be sure to inquire about those you are interested in, but do not see listed here.)

CAROLINA FURNITURE OF WILLIAMSBURG
5425 RICHMOND ROAD
WILLIAMSBURG, VA 23188
Hours: **M-S: 9-6; FRI: 9-9; SUN: 1-6**

Toll-Free	
Direct	757-565-3000
Fax	757-565-4476
Internet	

Notes: Established 1975. Furniture drawn from international furniture markets, constant participation of sales reps and factory seminars. Shipments by fully insured, furniture carriers only. Two designers, 4 consultants on a staff of 20. Complete order can be paid by VISA/MC/DISC, cash/check/finance. Only damaged goods will be replaced or repaired. We handle all claims, when we have them. Returns are allowed with a 20% restocking fee. Customers may visit this 24,000 square foot facility.

Manufacturers: (Many resources do not list all their manufacturers. Be sure to inquire about those you are interested in, but do not see listed here.)
AMERICAN OF MARTINSVILLE   AMERICAN DREW   ATHOL TABLE

BAILEY & GRIFFIN
BAKER
BALDWIN BRASS
BARCALOUNGER
BANKS COLDSTONE CO
BERKELEY
BERNHARDT
BEVAN FUNNELL
BLACKSMITH SHOP
BRASS BEDS OF AMERICA
BROWN JORDAN
BRUNSCHWIG & FILS
CASA STRADIVARI
CENTURY
CHAIRCRAFT
CHAPMAN
CHARLTON CENTURY 21
CHATHAM COUNTY
CHELSEA HOUSE
CLARENCE HOUSE
CLARK CASUAL
CLASSIC LEATHER
COLLINGWOOD
COLONIAL
CONOVER CHAIR
CONANT BALL
CONTEMPORARY SHELLS
COUNCILL CRAFTSMEN
CRAFTIQUE
CRAWFORD
CRESTWOOD IMPERIAL
CUSTOM AMERICAN
DELLINGER
DILLINGHAM
DRAKE SMITH
DURALEE FABRICS
ELLO
ELLSWORTH CABINET
ERWIN LAMBETH
FAIRINGTON
FICKS REED
FLEXSTEEL
FREDERICK COOPER
FREDERICK EDWARD
FRIEDMAN BROS MIRRORS
FURNITURE GUILD
GEORGE KOVACS
GEORGIAN LIGHTING
GREEFF FABRICS
GREG COPELAND
HABERSHAM
HALE OF VERMONT
HALL CLOCKS
HANCOCK & MOORE
HARDEN SOLID CHERRY
HEIRLOOM
HEKMAN
HEIRLOOM
HEKMAN

HENKEL HARRIS
HENREDON
HENRY LINK
HERSHEDE
HIBRITEN
HICKORY CHAIR
HICKORY WHITE
HICKORY FRY
HITCHCOCK CHAIR
HOOKER
JAMESTOWN LOUNGE
JASPER CABINET
JEFFCO
JOHN BOOS
JOHN WIDDICOMB
JOHNSTON CASUALS
KARASTAN
KARGES
KATZENBACH & WARREN
KIMBALL
KING KOIL
KINGSDOWN
KINGSLEY-BATES
KITTINGER
GEORGE KOVACS
KREISS
LaBARGE
LANE
LAUREL LAMPS
LEE JOFA
LEXINGTON
LLOYD FLANDERS
LYON SHAW
MADDOX DESK CO
MADISON SQUARE
MAITLAND SMITH
MARK THOMAS LAMPS
MARIMONT
MEADOWCRAFT
MEDALLION
MICHAEL THOMAS
MOLLA
MONITOR
MOTION ONLY
MOTIONCRAFT
MT AIRY
MURRAY FEISS LAMPS
NATIONAL MT AIRY
NETTLE CREEK
NICHOLS & STONE
NORMAN'S OF SALISBURY
NORTH HICKORY
PAUL HANSON
PAYNE
PEARSON
PENNSYLVANIA CLASSICS
PENNSYLVANIA HOUSE
PINECREST
PINE-TIQUE

PLATT
POLYWOOD FURNITURE
PRECEDENT
ROBERT ALLEN
ROMWEBER
S BENT
SALTERINI
SARREID
SCALAMANDRE
SCHOONBECK
SCHOTT
SCHUMACHER
SEALY
SEDGEFIELD
SHERRILL
SHUFORD
SIMMONS
SINGER-MANOR HOUSE
SLIGH
SOUTHAMPTON
SOUTHERN BRASS BED
SOUTHWOOD
SPEER
SPRAGUE & CARLTON
STANDARD OF GARDNER
STANLEY
STARK CARPETS
STATTON
STIFFEL
SUGAR HILL PINE
SUPERIOR
SWAIM
SWAN BRASS BED
TELESCOPE
TELL CITY
TEMPLE STUART
THAYER COGGIN
THOMAS OFFICE
THOMASVILLE
TRADITION HOUSE
TREND CLOCKS
TROPITONE
TROSBY
UNION NATIONAL
UNIQUE
VENTURE
VIRGINIA METALCRAFTERS
VIRGINIA GALLERIES
VIRGINIA GALLERIES
VIRGINIA HOUSE
VOGUE RATTAN
WALKER
WARREN LLOYD
WAVERLY
WEIMAN
WELLINGTON HALL
WESTGATE
WHITECRAFT
WILDWOOD LAMPS

WILLIAM ALLEN   WOODARD   WRIGHT TABLE
WINSTON   WOOD & HOGAN

CAROLINA FURNITURE WORLD
PO BOX 4559 (I-77, EXIT 82A)
ROCK HILL, SC 29142
Hours: **M-F: 9-5**

Toll-Free	
Direct	803-328-3005
Fax	803-328-3906
Internet	

Notes: Near Charlotte, NC. 12,000 square foot showroom, over 100 lines of home furnishings.
Plus swatches of fabrics for upholstered and leather goods and many catalogues.

**Manufacturers: (Many resources do not list all their manufacturers. Be sure to inquire
 about those you are interested in, but do not see listed here.)**

CAROLINA INTERIORS'-CANNON VILLAGE
115 OAK AVE
KANNAPOLIS, NC 28081
Hours: **M-S: 9-5**

Toll-Free	
Direct	704-933-1888
Fax	704-932-0434
Internet	

Notes: In business since 1971. Twelve sales consultants are all designers and can help customers
make decorating and design decisions. Cash, check or money orders accepted. Cancellations of
special orders will be accepted only if we are able to cancel the order with the manufacturer.
Extraordinary savings in a charming village setting. We are covered by a surety bond which covers
the customer 100% to either get their furniture or their money back in case of problems with our
company. Off I-85, exit 63. Thirty minutes north of Charlotte. Over 250,000 sq ft of showroom

**Manufacturers: (Many resources do not list all their manufacturers. Be sure to inquire
 about those you are interested in, but do not see listed here.)**

ACCENTRICS BY PULASKI
ACTION BY LANE
ALEXVALE
AMERICAN DREW
AMERICAN OF MARTINSVILLE
AS YOU LIKE IT
ATHOL
AUSTIN
BAKER
BALDWIN BRASS
BARCALOUNGER
BASHIAN CARPETS
BASSETT
BERNHARDT
BEVAN FUNNELL
BLACKSMITH SHOP
BRADINGTON YOUNG
BRAXTON CULLER
BROYHILL PREMIER
BUTLER
CAL-STYLE
CAROLINA MIRROR
CTH/SHERRILL
CARSON'S
CASA BIQUE
CASA STRADIVARI
CENTURY
CHAPMAN LAMPS
CHARLESTON FORGE
CHELSEA HOUSE/PORT ROYAL
CHROMCRAFT
CLARK CASUAL
CLAYTON MARCUS
COLONIAL
COURISTAN
COX
CRAFTWORK GUILD
CR LAINE UPHOLSTERY
COUNCILL CRAFTSMEN
CRAFTIQUE
DAVIS & DAVIS CARPETS
DANSEN
DECORATIVE CRAFTS
DESIGNMASTER
DILLON
DINAIRE
DISTINCTION LEATHER
ELLO
EMERSON LEATHER
FAIRFIELD
FASHION BED
FLEXSTEEL
FREDERICK COOPER
FRIEDMAN BROS MIRRORS
GEORGIAN HOME
FURNISHINGS
GLASS ARTS
GREAT CITY TRADERS
GUILDMASTER

HABERSHAM PLANTATION
HAMMARY
HANCOCK & MOORE
HART LAMPS
HEIRLOOM
HEKMAN
HENRY LINK WICKER
HICKORY CHAIR
HICKORY FRY
HICKORY LEATHER
HICKORY WHITE
HIGH POINT DESK
HIGHLAND HOUSE
HITCHCOCK CHAIR
HOOD
HOOKER
HOWARD MILLER
HOUSE PARTS
HTB LANE
HYUNDAI
J ROYALE
JASPER CABINET
JOHN RICHARD
JOHNSTON TOMBIGBEE
JOHN WIDDICOMB
JOHN BOOS
JOHNSTON CASUALS
KARGES
KELLER
KESSLER
KEY CITY
KIMBALL
KINCAID
KING KOIL
KINGSDOWN
KING HICKORY
KINGSLEY-BATES
KLAUSSNER
KNOB CREEK
LaBARGE
LANE
LEA
LEXINGTON
LLOYD FLANDERS
LYON SHAW
MADISON SQUARE
MAITLAND SMITH
MARBRO LAMPS
MASLAND CARPET
MASSOUD
MASTERCRAFT BY BAKER
McGUIRE
McKINLEY LEATHER
MICHAEL THOMAS
MOOSEHEAD
MOTIONCRAFT
NATIONAL MT AIRY
NICHOLS & STONE
NORTH HICKORY LEATHER

OLD HICKORY TANNERY
PANDE CAMERON RUGS
PAOLI
PARK PLACE
PAUL ROBERT
PEARSON
PENNSYLVANIA CLASSICS
PENNSYLVANIA HOUSE
PINE-TIQUE
POMPEII
PREVIEW
PULASKI
RIDGEWAY CLOCKS
RIVERSIDE
ROWE
ROYAL PATINA
S BENT
SALEM SQUARE
SALOOM
SARREID
SEDGEFIELD LAMP
SELIG
SHUFORD
SK PRODUCTS
SLIGH DESK/CLOCKS
SOUTHAMPTON
SOUTHERN FURNITURE
REPRODUCTIONS
SOUTHERN OF CONOVER
SOUTHWOOD
SPEER LAMPS
STANLEY
STANTON COOPER
STATESVILLE CHAIR
STATTON
STEIN WORLD
STIFFEL
STONELEIGH
SWAIM
TAYLOR WOODCRAFT
TAYLORSVILLE
THAYER COGGIN
TIANJIN PHILADELPHIA
CARPET
TRADITIONS FRANCE
TROPITONE
TROSBY
UNIVERSAL
VANGUARD
VAUGHAN
VAUGHAN BASSETT
VENTURE/LANE
VERMONT TUBBS
VIRGINIA HOUSE
VIRGINIA METALCRAFTERS
WATERFORD FURNITURE
WELLINGTON HALL
WESLEY ALLEN
WESLEY HALL

WILDWOOD LAMPS WOODARD
WINSTON WOODMARK

CAROLINA MATTRESS GUILD FACTORY OUTLET
781 N MAIN ST
HIGH POINT, NC 27262
Hours: **M-S: 10-5**

Toll-Free	
Direct	336-883-1947
Fax	336-885-0325
Internet	

Notes: No national brands. Just their own brand from their own factory. In business since September, 1995. Purchase must be paid in full by cash, check or VISA/MC. No satisfaction guaranteed policy and no return policies established. If there's a problem with shipment, the carrier is responsible. One of the southeast's largest independent bedding manufacturers.

Manufacturers: (Many resources do not list all their manufacturers. Be sure to inquire about those you are interested in, but do not see listed here.)
CAROLINA MATTRESS GUILD POLTROMEC/POLTROARREDO
LEATHER

CAROLINA PATIO WAREHOUSE
58 LARGO DR
STAMFORD, CT 06907
Hours: **M-F: 8:30-5:30; S: 9-2**

Toll-Free	800-672-8466
Direct	
Fax	203-975-7897
Internet	

Notes: Over 75 major brands of high quality patio furniture and more than 1,000 styles of garden and outdoor furniture.

Manufacturers: (Many resources do not list all their manufacturers. Be sure to inquire about those you are interested in, but do not see listed here.)
ALLIBERT   OW LEE   SAMSONITE
LANE   RIVIERA   TELESCOPE

Resource Directory

CARPET EXPRESS
915 MARKET STREET
DALTON, GA 30720
Hours: **M-F: 9-5**

Toll-Free	800-922-5582
Direct	706-278-8507
Fax	706-275-8763
Internet	

Notes: True wholesale prices on carpet, vinyl and hardwood flooring

Manufacturers: **(Many resources do not list all their manufacturers. Be sure to inquire about those you are interested in, but do not see listed here.)**

CARPET OUTLET
BOX 417
MILES CITY, MT 59301
Hours: **M-F: 9-5**

Toll-Free	800-225-4351
Direct	406-232-3084
Fax	406-232-9790
Internet	

Notes: This company has been in business 40 years. They sell every major brand of carpet at one dollar ($1.00) over dealer's cost. (Service problems have been reported with this company.)

Manufacturers: **(Many resources do not list all their manufacturers. Be sure to inquire about those you are interested in, but do not see listed here.)**

CARSONS GALLERY
HICKORY FURNITURE MART
2220 HWY 70 SE
HICKORY, NC 28602
Hours: **M-F: 9-6; S: 9-5; Closed Sundays**

Toll-Free	
Direct	828-322-6602
Fax	
Internet	

Notes: This resource is part of the Hickory Furniture Mart complex. This showroom is one of over 80 to visit. **See Hickory Furniture Mart listing for more information.** Consolidated shipping can be arranged with other resources in this center, a standard one/third deposit is required on all orders. Most showrooms accept VISA/MC, but not all. Cash, personal or certified checks accepted by all showrooms. If you elect not to pay for your entire purchase at the time of sale, a personal or certified check will be due upon delivery.

Manufacturers: (Many resources do not list all their manufacturers. Be sure to inquire about those you are interested in, but do not see listed here.)

CAYTON FURNITURE INC
217 WEST 3RD ST
WASHINGTON, NC 27889
Hours: **M-F: 9-5**

Toll-Free	800-849-8286
Direct	
Fax	252-975-6225
Internet	email: caytonfurniture@coastalnet.com

Notes: Established 1961. Home and office furniture. Special orders and direct shipment.

Manufacturers: (Many resources do not list all their manufacturers. Be sure to inquire about those you are interested in, but do not see listed here.)

CEDAR ROCK HOME FURNISHINGS
PO BOX 515, HWY 321 S
HUDSON, NC 28638
Hours: M-F: 9-5:30; S: 9-6

Toll-Free	
Direct	828-396-2361
Fax	828-396-7800
Internet	

Notes: Located on Hwy 321. Five sales consultants represent some unique lines and will help customers select and decide. VISA/MC can be used for 50% down payment. Money order for remaining balance. Shipping policies are that the customer and carrier deal with the problem. 11,200 sq. ft. showroom available for browsing. This resource also custom-builds upholstery and has access to upholstery fabrics. They offer fine reproductions from about 300 nationally known manufacturers at savings of 40-50% and will ship **anywhere**.

Manufacturers: (Many resources do not list all their manufacturers. Be sure to inquire about those you are interested in, but do not see listed here.)

ACTION LANE	CLAYTON MARCUS	HEKMAN
AMERICAN DREW	CLYDE PEARSON	HENRY LINK
AMERICAN OF HIGH POINT	COASTER	HICKORY CLASSICS
AMERICAN OF MARTINSVILLE	COCHRANE	HICKORY HILL
ARNOLD PARLMER	COLONIAL BRAIDED RUGS	HICKORY LEATHER
ART GALLERY, THE	COLONIAL FURNITURE	HICKORY TAVERN
AS YOU LIKE IT	CONOVER CHAIR	HIGHLAND HOUSE
ATHENS	COSCO BABY FURNITURE	HITCHCOCK CHAIR
ATHOL	COUNCILL CRAFTSMEN	HOOKER
BARCALOUNGER	CRAFTIQUE	HOWARD MILLER
BARD	CRAFTMASTER	HUNTINGTON HOUSE
BASSETT FURNITURE	CRAWFORD	HYUNDAI
BASSETT	CRESENT	INTERNATIONAL KARPEN
BERKLINE	CR LAINE	JASPER CABINET
BEVAN FUNNELL	CROWN ART	JOHNSTON CASUALS
BOB TIMBERLAKE	DENNY LAMPS	J ROYALE
BRADINGTON YOUNG	DESIGN HORIZONS	KELLER
BRADY	DILLON	KEY CITY
BRANDON MANOR	DINAIRE	KIMBALL UPHOLSTERY
BRASSCRAFTERS	DISTINCTION LEATHER	KING HICKORY
BRAXTON CULLER	EDWARD ART	LANE
BROWN STREET	EMERSON LEATHER	LEA
BROYHILL	EXCEL	LEATHER CLASSICS
BROYHILL PREMIERE	FAIRFIELD CHAIR	LEATHERCRAFT
BUILTRIGHT CHAIR	FAIRMONT DESIGNS	LEISTERS
CAMBRIDGE CHAIR	FASHION BED GROUP	LEISURE HOUSE LEATHER
CAROLINA FURNITURE WORKS	FICKS REED	LEXINGTON
CAROLINA MIRROR	FLEXSTEEL	LINK TAYLOR
CAROLINA TABLES	FROELICH	LYN HOLLYN
CARTER	DENUNZIO	LYON SHAW
CHARLESTON FORGE	HAMMARY	MADISON SQUARE
CHROMCRAFT	HAMPTON HALL	MASTER DESIGN
CLASSIC LEATHER	HANOVER HAIRLOOMS	MASTERFIELD

MOBEL
MOOSEHEAD
MORGAN STEWART
MORGANTON CHAIR
NATHAN HALE
NATIONAL MT AIRY
NICHOLS & STONE
NORTH HICKORY
NULL
OAKLAND
OHIO TABLE PADS
OLD HICKORY TANNERY
PALLISER
PARAGON PICTURES
PARK PLACE
PAUL ROBERTS
PENNSYLVANIA CLASSICS
PETERS REVINGTON
PINNACLE
POLCOR BEDDING
PULASKI
QUOIZEL
REPROCRAFTERS
REX

RICHARDSON BROS
RIDGEWAY CLOCKS
RIVERSIDE
ROSALCO
ROWE
SALEM SQUARE
SAM MOORE
SARRIED
SCHWEIGER
SEALY BEDDING
SERTA BEDDING
SIGNATURE LAMPS
SIMMONS BABY/JUVENILE
SINGER
SKILLCRAFT
SOUTHERN GRAPHICS
SOUTHERN OF CONOVER
SOUTHWOOD
REPRODUCTIONS
SPRING WALL BEDDING
STANLEY
STANTON COOPER
STATESVILLE CHAIR
STATTON

STIFFEL
SUMTER CABINETS
SUPERIOR FURNITURE
SYMBOL BEDDING
TAYLORSVILLE
TEMPLE
TEMPLE STUART
TIMELESS BEDDING
TOWN SQUARE
UWHARRIE CHAIR
UNIVERSAL
VANGUARD
VAUGHAN
VAUGHAN BASSETT
VENTURE
VIRGINIA HOUSE
VIRGINIA METALCRAFTERS
WEIMAN TABLES
WELLINGTON HALL
WESLEY ALLEN
WINSTON
WOODMARK
YORKSHIRE LEATHER

CENTRAL WAREHOUSE FURNITURE
2352 ENGLISH RD
HIGH POINT, NC 27262
Hours: **M-S: 9-6; SUN: 12-5**

Toll-Free	
Direct	336-882-9511
Fax	336-882-0212
Internet	

Notes: Two locations; the other is directly across the street

Manufacturers: **(Many resources do not list all their manufacturers. Be sure to inquire about those you are interested in, but do not see listed here.)**

AMERICAN DREW
BASSETT
ALAN WHITE
ENGLAND CORSAIR
BARCALOUNGER
BLACKSMITH SHOP

CHAIR CO
FAIRFIELD CHAIR
GAINES MFG
HOWARD MILLER
LARGO
LEA

MILLENIUM
PHILIP R
RIVERSIDE
SOUTH SEAS RATTAN
UNIVERSAL
WILLOW CREEK

CENTRE COURT FURNITURE MALL
2161 HWY 321
GRANITE FALLS, NC 28630
Hours: **M-F: 9-5**

Toll-Free	
Direct	828-396-4803
Fax	
Internet	

Notes: Located on Hwy 321. Authorized dealer for over 200 lines of home furnishings. Delivery anywhere in US. 20,000 sq. Ft. showroom.

Manufacturers: **(Many resources do not list all their manufacturers. Be sure to inquire about those you are interested in, but do not see listed here.)**

CENTURY FACTORY OUTLET
HICKORY FURNITURE MART
2220 HWY 70 SE
HICKORY, NC 28602
Hours: **M-F: 9-6; S: 9-5; Closed Sundays**

Toll-Free	
Direct	828-324-2442
Fax	828-464-9964
Internet	

Notes: Great outlet.This resource is part of the Hickory Furniture Mart complex. This showroom is one of over 80 to visit. **See Hickory Furniture Mart listing for more information.** Consolidated shipping can be arranged with other resources in this center, a standard one/third deposit is required on all orders. Most showrooms accept VISA/MC, but not all. Cash, personal or certified checks accepted by all showrooms. If you elect not to pay for your entire purchase at the time of sale, a personal or certified check will be due upon delivery.

Manufacturers: **(Many resources do not list all their manufacturers. Be sure to inquire about those you are interested in, but do not see listed here.)**
CENTURY

CENTURY FURNITURE GALLERY
HICKORY FURNITURE MART
2220 HWY 70 SE
HICKORY, NC 28602
Hours: M-F: 9-6; S: 9-5; Closed Sundays

Toll-Free	
Direct	828-322-6602
Fax	
Internet	

Notes: This resource is part of the Hickory Furniture Mart complex. This showroom is one of over 80 to visit. **See Hickory Furniture Mart listing for more information.** Consolidated shipping can be arranged with other resources in this center, a standard one/third deposit is required on all orders. Most showrooms accept VISA/MC, but not all. Cash, personal or certified checks accepted by all showrooms. If you elect not to pay for your entire purchase at the time of sale, a personal or certified check will be due upon delivery.

Manufacturers: **(Many resources do not list all their manufacturers. Be sure to inquire about those you are interested in, but do not see listed here.)**
CENTURY

CENTURY/HICKORY CHAIR OUTLET
1120 HWY 16 N
CONOVER, NC 28613
Hours: M-S: 9-6

Toll-Free	
Direct	704-464-9940
Fax	704-464-9964
Internet	

Notes: Great outlet. 20,000 square foot location in Conover. VISA/MC accepted.

Manufacturers: **(Many resources do not list all their manufacturers. Be sure to inquire about those you are interested in, but do not see listed here.)**
CENTURY   HICKORY CHAIR

CHARLES W JACOBSEN, INC
401 N SALINA ST
SYRACUSE, NY 13202
Hours: **M-S: 9-5; M & TH: 9-8**

Toll-Free	
Direct	315-422-7832
Fax	
Internet	

Notes: In business since 1924. Source for genuine handwoven oriental rugs. They pay shipping - no obligation to buy. Approximately 8,000 rugs in stock - mats to giant carpets. This company will send rugs "on approval" for you to examine. We pay freight both ways. Twelve salespeople-showroom for browsing. Complete order can be paid by VISA/MC/DISC, cash/check. Shipping problems are handled by the resource.

Manufacturers: (Many resources do not list all their manufacturers. Be sure to inquire about those you are interested in, but do not see listed here.)
RUGS

===

CHERRY HILL FURNITURE & INTERIORS
PO BOX 7405, FURNITURELAND STATION
HIGH POINT, NC 27264
Hours: **M-S: 10-6**

Toll-Free	800-888-0933
Direct	
Fax	336-882-0900
Internet	

Notes: Established in 1933, this company calls themselves "the no-show showroom". They have sales consultants and designers on staff. The manufacturers represented prefer that their name not be listed. This company has more than 500 famous name brands. A toll-free call will identify them. Credit cards not accepted. Special orders cannot be returned. Executive delivery service is their shipper. Damaged goods repaired or replaced by carrier. Call 800-666-0933 for free brochure.

Manufacturers: (Many resources do not list all their manufacturers. Be sure to inquire about those you are interested in, but do not see listed here.)

CLASSIC LEATHER GALLERY
HICKORY FURNITURE MART
2220 HWY 70 SE
HICKORY, NC 28602
Hours: **M-F: 9-6; S: 9-5; Closed Sundays**

Toll-Free	
Direct	828-324-1776
Fax	
Internet	

Notes: This resource is part of the Hickory Furniture Mart complex. This showroom is one of over 80 to visit. **See Hickory Furniture Mart listing for more information.** Consolidated shipping can be arranged with other resources in this center, a standard one/third deposit is required on all orders. Most showrooms accept VISA/MC, but not all. Cash, personal or certified checks accepted by all showrooms. If you elect not to pay for your entire purchase at the time of sale, a personal or certified check will be due upon delivery.

Manufacturers: **(Many resources do not list all their manufacturers. Be sure to inquire about those you are interested in, but do not see listed here.)**

CLASSIC ORIENTAL RUGS
HICKORY FURNITURE MART
2220 HWY 70 SE
HICKORY, NC 28602
Hours: **M-F: 9-6; S: 9-5; Closed Sundays**

Toll-Free	
Direct	828-326-1735
Fax	
Internet	

Notes: This resource is part of the Hickory Furniture Mart complex. This showroom is one of over 80 to visit. **See Hickory Furniture Mart listing for more information.** Consolidated shipping can be arranged with other resources in this center, a standard one/third deposit is required on all orders. Most showrooms accept VISA/MC, but not all. Cash, personal or certified checks accepted by all showrooms. If you elect not to pay for your entire purchase at the time of sale, a personal or certified check will be due upon delivery.

Manufacturers: (Many resources do not list all their manufacturers. Be sure to inquire
 about those you are interested in, but do not see listed here.)

═══════════════════════════════════════

CLAYTON MARCUS GALLERY
HICKORY FURNITURE MART
2220 HWY 70 SE
HICKORY, NC 28602
Hours: **M-F: 9-6; S: 9-5; Closed Sundays**

Toll-Free	
Direct	828-328-8688
Fax	
Internet	

Notes: This resource is part of the Hickory Furniture Mart complex. This showroom is one of over
80 to visit. **See Hickory Furniture Mart listing for more information.** Consolidated shipping can
be arranged with other resources in this center, a standard one/third deposit is required on all orders.
Most showrooms accept VISA/MC, but not all. Cash, personal or certified checks accepted by all
showrooms. If you elect not to pay for your entire purchase at the time of sale, a personal or certified
check will be due upon delivery.

Manufacturers: (Many resources do not list all their manufacturers. Be sure to inquire
 about those you are interested in, but do not see listed here.)

═══════════════════════════════════════

COCHRANE GALLERY
HICKORY FURNITURE MART
2220 HWY 70 SE
HICKORY, NC 28602
Hours: **M-F: 9-6; S: 9-5; Closed Sundays**

Toll-Free	
Direct	828-322-6602
Fax	
Internet	

Notes: This resource is part of the Hickory Furniture Mart complex. This showroom is one of over
80 to visit. **See Hickory Furniture Mart listing for more information.** Consolidated shipping can

be arranged with other resources in this center, a standard one/third deposit is required on all orders. Most showrooms accept VISA/MC, but not all. Cash, personal or certified checks accepted by all showrooms. If you elect not to pay for your entire purchase at the time of sale, a personal or certified check will be due upon delivery.

Manufacturers: **(Many resources do not list all their manufacturers. Be sure to inquire about those you are interested in, but do not see listed here.)**

COFFEY DISCOUNT FURNITURE
HWY 321-POOVEY DR
GRANITE FALLS, NC 28630
Hours: **M-F: 9-5**

Toll-Free	
Direct	828-396-2900
Fax	828-396-3050
Internet	

Notes: Located on Hwy 321. 40,000 sq ft. showroom. Major brands, closeouts and distonntined items. Call for pricing and free brochure.

Manufacturers: **(Many resources do not list all their manufacturers. Be sure to inquire about those you are interested in, but do not see listed here.)**
LEXINGTON   SPRING AIR   STANLEY

COLFAX FURNITURE
S HOLDEN ROAD AT I-85
GREENSBORO, NC 27407
Hours: **M-F: 10-9; S: 10-6; SUN: 1-6**

Toll-Free	
Direct	336-855-0498
Fax	336-275-3797
Internet	

Notes: In business since 1968. VISA/MC/AMEX Colfax credit card. All sales are final, no refunds or returns. Customer can visit facilities. Closeouts, photo samples, volume purchases, market samples, canceled orders, insurance claims. Additional location on HWY 421 in Kernersville. Mailing address: 3501 McCuiston Ct., Greensboro, NC 27407

Manufacturers: (Many resources do not list all their manufacturers. Be sure to inquire about those you are interested in, but do not see listed here.)

ACTION BY LANE	CRAFTMASTER	PALLISER
ALAN WHITE	DOUGLAS	PROGRESSIVE
AMERICAN DREW	FRANKLIN	PULASKI
ARIEL OF FRANCE	GENTRY GALLERY	RESTONIC
AUSTIN PRODUCTIONS	HARRIS	ROWE
BARCLAY	HARRIS MARCUS	SAMUEL LAWRENCE
BASSETT	HICKORY HILL	SANDER
BENCHCRAFT	HYUNDAI	SEALY
BERKLINE	LANDMARK	STYLECRAFT
BEST CHAIR	LANE	VAUGHAN
BROYHILL	LEA	VAUGHAN-BASSETT
CLAREMONT DESIGNS	LEXINGTON	WEBB FURNITURE
COLLEZIONE EUROPA	MASTER DESIGN	WINNERS ONLY

COLOREL BLINDS
8200 E PARK MEADOWS DR
LITTLETON, CO 80124
Hours: **M-F: 7am-6pm; S: 8am-5pm**

Toll-Free	800-877-4800
Direct	
Fax	303-792-5846
Internet	

Notes: Every product is fully guaranteed. 100% no fault, Satisfaction guarantee. UPS freight charges are paid. Since they are the factory, your blinds or shades will be shipped one day after you order. Full order can be paid by VISA/MC/DISC.

Manufacturers: (Many resources do not list all their manufacturers. Be sure to inquire about those you are interested in, but do not see listed here.)

LEVOLOR	LOUVERDRAPE	THEIR OWN LINE
DELMAR	HUNTER DOUGLAS DUETTE	

COMFORT ZONE
HICKORY FURNITURE MART
2220 HWY 70 SE
HICKORY, NC 28602
Hours: **M-F: 9-6; S: 9-5; Closed Sundays**

Toll-Free	
Direct	828-326-9224
Fax	
Internet	

Notes: This resource is part of the Hickory Furniture Mart complex. This showroom is one of over 80 to visit. **See Hickory Furniture Mart listing for more information.** Consolidated shipping can be arranged with other resources in this center, a standard one/third deposit is required on all orders. Most showrooms accept VISA/MC, but not all. Cash, personal or certified checks accepted by all showrooms. If you elect not to pay for your entire purchase at the time of sale, a personal or certified check will be due upon delivery.

Manufacturers: (Many resources do not list all their manufacturers. Be sure to inquire about those you are interested in, but do not see listed here.)

CONNECTICUT CURTAIN COMPANY
COMMERCE PLAZA, RT. 6
DANBURY, CT 06810
Hours: **T-F:10-6; S: 10-3**

Toll-Free	800-732-4549
Direct	203-798-1850
Fax	
Internet	email: csales@curtainrods.com web site: http://www.curtainrods.com

Notes: Established 1984. This company carries an extensive stock of Kirsch drapery hardware as well as wooden hardware. Their discounts are approximately 24-40% off retail. Payment in full at time of order. VISA/MC, check accepted. No COD's. Orders are generally shipped with 48 hours of order placement. Same day shipping can be arranged for in-stock items. Credit for returns can be made if shipped back in the original cartons with all appropriate pieces in good conditions and the brackets in the original unopened packages. Made to order rods or poles cannot be returned. Send $2 for a catalog and receive a coupon worth $5. Showroom available.

Manufacturers: **(Many resources do not list all their manufacturers. Be sure to inquire
about those you are interested in, but do not see listed here.)**

GRABER   PJ HAMILTON   IRON AND STEEL RODS
KIRSCH   SIERRA

CONTEMPORARY COLLECTIONS
THE ATRIUM
430 SOUTH MAIN ST
HIGH POINT, NC 27262
Hours: **M-F:9-6; S: 9-5**

Toll-Free	
Direct	336-887-7265
Fax	336-887-1405
Internet	

Notes: Part of the Atrium complex. Worth visiting, showrooms available. See **Atrium Furniture
Showroom** listing for more information. Contemporary furniture from some of the top manufacturers
and a large selection of unique accessories.

Manufacturers: **(Many resources do not list all their manufacturers. Be sure to inquire
about those you are interested in, but do not see listed here.)**

CARTER CONTEMPORARY   JAFE   SWAIM
ELLO   STONE INTERNATIONAL

CONTEMPORARY GALLERY
HICKORY FURNITURE MART
2220 HWY 70 SE
HICKORY, NC 28602
Hours: **M-F: 9-6; S: 9-5; Closed Sundays**

Toll-Free	
Direct	828-324-1776
Fax	
Internet	

Notes: This resource is part of the Hickory Furniture Mart complex. This showroom is one of over
80 to visit. **See Hickory Furniture Mart listing for more information.** Consolidated shipping can
be arranged with other resources in this center, a standard one/third deposit is required on all orders.

Most showrooms accept VISA/MC, but not all. Cash, personal or certified checks accepted by all showrooms. If you elect not to pay for your entire purchase at the time of sale, a personal or certified check will be due upon delivery.

Manufacturers: (Many resources do not list all their manufacturers. Be sure to inquire about those you are interested in, but do not see listed here.)

CORNER HUTCH FURNITURE, THE
HWY 21 N. PO BOX 1728
STATESVILLE, NC 28677
Hours: M-F: 9-5:30; S: 9-5

Toll-Free	
Direct	704-873-1773
Fax	704-873-1637
Internet	

Notes: In business since 1972. In house delivery east of Mississippi - damages are taken care of by resource. VISA/MC/DISC personal check - 50% downpayment. Sales and design consultants on staff. Showroom available for browsing. Century gallery. 18th century selections. Return policies are limited - depends on reason to return

Manufacturers: (Many resources do not list all their manufacturers. Be sure to inquire about those you are interested in, but do not see listed here.)

AMERICAN DREW	HIGHLAND HOUSE	RICHARDSON BROS
AMERICAN OF HIGH POINT	HITCHCOCK	S BENT
BALDWIN BRASS	HOOKER	SARREID
BOLING DESK	HOWARD MILLER CLOCKS	SEALY
BARCALOUNGER	JAMESTOWN STERLING	SERTA
BRADINGTON YOUNG	JASPER CABINET	SLIGH
BROWN JORDAN	JEFFCO	SOUTHWOOD
BROYHILL PREMIER	KEY CITY	STANLEY
CENTURY FURNITURE	KING HICKORY	STANTON COOPER
CHAPMAN	KNOB CREEK	STATTON
COCHRANE	LaBARGE	STIFFEL LAMPS
CONOVER CHAIR	LANE	SWAN BRASS BED
COUNCILL CRAFTSMEN	LEXINGTON	TELL CITY
CRAFTIQUE	MADISON SQUARE	TRADITION HOUSE
EMERSON LEATHER	NATHAN HALE	TROPITONE
FREDERICK COOPER	NATIONAL MT AIRY	VIRGINIA METALCRAFTERS
HABERSHAM PLANTATION	NICHOLS & STONE	WEIMAN
HALE	ORIENTAL RUGS BY	WELLINGTON HALL
HEKMAN	PANDE CAMERON RUGS	WILDWOOD
HENRY LINK	PARK PLACE SLEEPERS	WOODMARK CHAIRS
HICKORY CHAIR	PEARSON	YOUNG-HINKLE
HICKORY WHITE		

COURISTAN FACTORY OUTLET
HICKORY FURNITURE MART
2220 HWY 70 SE
HICKORY, NC 28602
Hours: **M-F: 9-6; S: 9-5; Closed Sundays**

Toll-Free	
Direct	828-345-0409
Fax	
Internet	

Notes: This resource is part of the Hickory Furniture Mart complex. This showroom is one of over 80 to visit. **See Hickory Furniture Mart listing for more information.** Consolidated shipping can be arranged with other resources in this center, a standard one/third deposit is required on all orders. Most showrooms accept VISA/MC, but not all. Cash, personal or certified checks accepted by all showrooms. If you elect not to pay for your entire purchase at the time of sale, a personal or certified check will be due upon delivery.

Manufacturers: (Many resources do not list all their manufacturers. Be sure to inquire about those you are interested in, but do not see listed here.)

CR LAINE GALLERY
HICKORY FURNITURE MART
2220 HWY 70 SE
HICKORY, NC 28602
Hours: **M-F: 9-6; S: 9-5; Closed Sundays**

Toll-Free	
Direct	828-322-4440
Fax	
Internet	

Notes: This resource is part of the Hickory Furniture Mart complex. This showroom is one of over 80 to visit. **See Hickory Furniture Mart listing for more information.** Consolidated shipping can be arranged with other resources in this center, a standard one/third deposit is required on all orders. Most showrooms accept VISA/MC, but not all. Cash, personal or certified checks accepted by all showrooms. If you elect not to pay for your entire purchase at the time of sale, a personal or certified check will be due upon delivery.

Manufacturers: **(Many resources do not list all their manufacturers. Be sure to inquire about those you are interested in, but do not see listed here.)**

CUSTOM DRAPERY SHOP & INTERIORS
6122 ALTAMA AVE #2
BRUNSWICK, GA 31525-1807
Hours: **M-F:F 8am-5pm**

Toll-Free	800-982-2146
Direct	912-264-2146
Fax	912-264-9043
Internet	

Notes: In business since 1985. Four sales consultants. Very personal service.

Manufacturers: **(Many resources do not list all their manufacturers. Be sure to inquire about those you are interested in, but do not see listed here.)**
FABRICS

DAC LIGHTING
164 BOWERY
NEW YORK, NY 10012
Hours: **M-SUN; 9-5:30**

Toll-Free	
Direct	212-966-7062
Fax	212-219-1291
Internet	

Notes: Manufacturer and importers of lighting fixtures

Manufacturers: **(Many resources do not list all their manufacturers. Be sure to inquire about those you are interested in, but do not see listed here.)**

DALLAS FURNITURE STORE, INC
215 N. CENTENNIAL
HIGH POINT, NC 27261
Hours: **M-F: 9-5**

Toll-Free	
Direct	336-884-5759
Fax	336-885-0519
Internet	

Notes:

Manufacturers: (Many resources do not list all their manufacturers. Be sure to inquire about those you are interested in, but do not see listed here.)

ACTION BY LANE
AMERICAN DREW
ATHENS FURNITURE
BASSETT
BEECHBROOK
BERKSHIRE
BERNHARDT
BEST CHAIR
BRANDON LAMPS
BRASSCRAFTERS
CAROLINA CHOICE
CAROLINA MIRROR
CASARD
CHARLES WAREHOUSE RUGS
CHATHAM COUNTY
CLIFTON ART
COCHRANE
COOK FURNITURE
CRAFT-TEX
CREATIVE ARTS
CREATIVE EXPRESSIONS
CROSLEY
CRYSTAL CLEAR LAMPS
DR KINCAID
DAVIS FURNITURE
DECORATIVE CRAFTS
DESIGNS UNLIMITED
DEVILLE
DIXIE
EDWARD ART

FASHION BED
FLEXSTEEL
FOREMOST
FRISCO MANUFACTURING
GATCO
GENTRY GALLERY
GERALD STEIN
HENRY LINK
HICKORY SPRINGS
HIGH POINT BEDDING
HOPKINS UPHOLSTERY
HOOKER
HUNTINGTON HOUSE
JAY WILLFRED
KELLER
KEMP FURNITURE
KIMBALL
LAINE
LEA
LEXINGTON
LINK-TAYLOR
MARTHA ASHER
MARTINSVILLE NOVELTY
MARY DALE LAMPS
MURPHY FURNITURE
NORA FENTON
NORTHWOOD
OLD COUNTRY
REPRODUCTIONS

ORDEREST MATTRESS
PARAGON PICTURES
PARAMOUNT
PAUL MARSHALL
PHILCO TV/STEREO
PILLIOD FURNITURE
PULASKI
QUALITY DINETTE
PHILLIP REINISCH
SADEK IMPORTS
SELECT MANUFACTURING
SERTA MATTRESS
SINGER
SPECTRUM UPHOLSTERY
SPEED QUEEN
STONEVILLE
STYLE-MART
TOYO
TURNER
TWIN RIVER UPHOLSTERY
UNIVERSAL
VB WILLIAMS
VAUGHAN
VAUGHAN-BASSETT
WEBB FURNITURE
WILTON
WINDSOR OAK COLLECTION
YOUNG-HINKLE

DALTON PARADISE CARPET
PO BOX 2488
DALTON, GA 30722
Hours: **M-F: 9-5**

Toll-Free	800-338-7811
Direct	
Fax	706-226-9061
Internet	

Notes: Call for an excellent carpet sample kit from this company. Eight salespeople on staff. Complete order can be paid by VISA/MC/DISC. Balance, if any, can be paid by check before delivery. They carry their own line of carpet, along with **custom design rugs**. They offer grades of carpet for every need from heavy commercial for offices to the most elegant plushes for residential. They will deliver to home or job site. Deposit will hold your order with balance due prior to shipment. All of their carpets come with full manufacturers' wear and stain resistance warranties. They offer Dupont Stainmaster, Anso V Worry Free, Monsanto Gold/Silver label, Traffic Control, Xtra Life and others. Defective carpet is refunded or exchanged at no additional cost to the customer as long as it has not been cut or installed. Some products have satisfaction guaranteed. If shipping problems, carrier deals with it. This resource states that they sell mill-direct at wholesale prices, consumers can save up to 80% off retail. (Formerly Paradise Mills, Inc)

Manufacturers: (Many resources do not list all their manufacturers. Be sure to inquire about those you are interested in, but do not see listed here.)
CONCEPTS DESIGNER RUGS   DALTON PARADISE CARPET   PARADISE MILLS CARPET

DAR FURNITURE
517 S HAMILTON ST
HIGH POINT, NC 27262
Hours: **M-F: 9-5**

Toll-Free	
Direct	336-885-9193
Fax	336-885-9103
Internet	

Notes:

Manufacturers: (Many resources do not list all their manufacturers. Be sure to inquire about those you are interested in, but do not see listed here.)

DECORATOR'S CHOICE
THE ATRIUM
430 SOUTH MAIN ST
HIGH POINT, NC 27262
Hours: **M-F: 9-6; S: 9-5**

Toll-Free	
Direct	336-889-6115
Fax	336-889-8656
Internet	email: decorators@theatrium.com

Notes: Part of the Atrium complex. Worth visiting, showrooms available. See **Atrium Furniture Showroom** listing for more information. Furniture and accessories. Custom made sofas, loveseats and chairs and oversized furniture; also a wide selection of occasional tables and wrought iron dining sets, barstools and solid oak dining.

Manufacturers: (Many resources do not list all their manufacturers. Be sure to inquire about those you are interested in, but do not see listed here.)

ARBEK	GENTRY	NULL INDUSTRIES
COLDWELL CHAIR	HUNTINGTON HOUSE	PRESIDENTIAL
COLLEZIONE EUROPA	INTERIOR IMAGES BY SALERNI	
ELM CREEK	LANDMARK	

DECORATOR'S EDGE, THE
509 RANDOLPH STREET
THOMASVILLE, NC 27360
Hours: **M-F:9-5**

Toll-Free	
Direct	336-476-3223
Fax	336-476-8802
Internet	

Notes: In business since 1979. Four sales consultants and 3 designers on staff. VISA/MC check, cash ok for deposit and balance. Custom window treatments, bed coverings and upholstered furniture, balloon cornices, swags, draperies, lambrequin, roman shades, micro/mini blinds, vertical blinds Duettes and more. Bedspreads, dust ruffles, headboards, wallpaper, carpet lamps, prints, furniture and accessories. Designers on staff to help customer with choices. Will travel to out-ofstate locations. No returns on custom items, unless defective. Major lines of wallcoverings carried. 25% restocking fee on others. Satisfaction guaranteed. Shipping problems handled by the resource.

Manufacturers: (Many resources do not list all their manufacturers. Be sure to inquire about those you are interested in, but do not see listed here.)

CHELSEA HOUSE	KRAVET FABRICS	STIFFEL LAMPS
CREATIVE METAL	LOUIS BOWEN	STROHEIM & ROMANN
CUSTOMCRAFT	MASLAND	SWAIM ORIGINALS
DAVID THOMAS LAMPS	PAYNE	VANGUARD
DESIGN MOTIF	PINDLER & PINDLER FABRIC	WAVERLY
DISTINCTION LEATHER	PORT ROYAL	WESTGATE
DURALEE FABRICS	ROBERT ALLEN	WILDWOOD LAMPS
FINE ARTS LAMPS	SM HEXTER	WILLIAM ALLEN
GREEFF FABRICS	SCHUMACHER	SEDGEFIELD LAMP
KOCH ORIGINALS	SHOAL CREEK	

DEEP RIVER TRADING CO, THE
2436-F WILLARD RD
HIGH POINT, NC 27265
Hours: **M-F: 9-5**

Toll-Free	
Direct	336-885-2436
Fax	
Internet	

Notes: Established in 1988. We specialize in assisting the customer in the search for furniture. We send color brochures and price lists on selection of popular as well as unusual manufacturers. Specialize in 18th century reproductions, "country", upholstery and leather. Discounts up to 60% off suggested retail. Seasonal sales. Our sales staff is ready to advise you on choices available. VISA/MC check.

Manufacturers: (Many resources do not list all their manufacturers. Be sure to inquire about those you are interested in, but do not see listed here.)

AMERICAN DREW	CRAFTIQUE	JOHN WIDDICOMB
AMERICAN OF MARTINSVILLE	CRAWFORD	KARGES
ATHOL	EJ VICTOR	KELLER
BAKER	FANCHER	KINCAID
BASSETT	FROELICH	KITTINGER
BROWN JORDAN	GEORGIAN	LANE
BROWN STREET	HABERSHAM	LEXINGTON
BROYHILL	HAMMARY	LINK TAYLOR
CASA BIQUE	HEKMAN	LYON SHAW
CENTURY	HICKORY CHAIR	MADISON SQUARE
CHARLESTON FORGE	HICKORY WHITE	MARYLAND CLASSICS
COCHRANE	HITCHCOCK CHAIR	McGUIRE
COLONIAL	HOOKER	MICHAEL'S
COUNCILL	JASPER CABINET	MILLENDER

MOOSEHEAD
NATHAN HALE
NATIONAL MT AIRY
NICHOLS & STONE
PENNSYLVANIA CLASSICS
PULASKI
REPRODUX
RICHARDSON BROS
RICHELIEU
SALEM SQUARE
SERTA
SLIGH
SOUTHAMPTON
SOUTHWOOD
STANLEY
STATTON
STICKLEY
SUMTER CABINET
TAYLOR WOODCRAFT
TELL CITY
TEMPLE STUART

THOMASVILLE
TOM SEELY
TROUVAILLES
UNIVERSAL
VIRGINIA HOUSE
WATERFORD
WEIMAN
WELLINGTON HALL
WINSTON

UPHOLSTERY & LEATHER
BRADINGTON YOUNG
CLAYTON MARCUS
CONOVER CHAIR
CR LAINE
DANSEN
DISTINCTION LEATHER
EMERSON LEATHER
EXECUTIVE LEATHER
FAIRINGTON
FLEXSTEEL

FREDERICK EDWARD
HICKORY CHAIR
HICKORY WHITE
J ROYALE
ACTION BY LANE
LEATHERCRAFT
LEXINGTON
NORTH HICKORY
PEARSON
SOUTHMARK
SOUTHWOOD
STANTON COOPER
STATESVILLE
SUPERIOR
SWAIM
TOMLINSON
VANGUARD
WEIMAN
WILLIAM ALLEN
WOODMARK

===

DESIGNER FABRICS
42 WELSH ROW
NANTWICH, CHESHIRE, ENGLAND CW5 5EW
Hours: M-F: 9-5 (England time)

Toll-Free	
Direct	011-44-1270-61-00-32
Fax	011-44-1270-62-48-45
Internet	

Notes: Very best prices for the top names in fabrics and wallcoverings. Most suppliers are British and European manufacturers. About a 25% discount on British prices. Minimum order: 20 yards fabric or 20 rolls of wallpaper.

Manufacturers: **(Many resources do not list all their manufacturers. Be sure to inquire about those you are interested in, but do not see listed here.)**

DISCOUNT CARPET
206 N MAIN
BRYAN, TX 77803
Hours: **M-F: 9-5**

Toll-Free	
Direct	409-779-3270
Fax	
Internet	

Notes:

Manufacturers: **(Many resources do not list all their manufacturers. Be sure to inquire about those you are interested in, but do not see listed here.)**
PHILADELPHIA

DON LAMOR
HICKORY FURNITURE MART
2220 HWY 70 SE
HICKORY, NC 28602
Hours: **M-F: 9-6; S: 9-5; Closed Sundays**

Toll-Free	
Direct	828-324-1776
Fax	828-324-1676
Internet	

Notes: This resource is part of the Hickory Furniture Mart complex. This showroom is one of over 80 to visit. **See Hickory Furniture Mart listing for more information.** Consolidated shipping can be arranged with other resources in this center, a standard one/third deposit is required on all orders. Most showrooms accept VISA/MC, but not all. Cash, personal or certified checks accepted by all showrooms. If you elect not to pay for your entire purchase at the time of sale, a personal or certified check will be due upon delivery.

Manufacturers: **(Many resources do not list all their manufacturers. Be sure to inquire about those you are interested in, but do not see listed here.)**

DRAPERY, THE
PO BOX 117
OLNEY, ENGLAND MK4 4ZZ
Hours: **M-F: 10-5; S: 10-NOON (CLOSED WEDNESDAY)**

Toll-Free	
Direct	011-44-990-16-87-09
Fax	
Internet	

Notes: British source for designer fabrics.

Manufacturers: **(Many resources do not list all their manufacturers. Be sure to inquire about those you are interested in, but do not see listed here.)**

═══════════════════════════════

DREXEL HERITAGE FACTORY OUTLET
HICKORY FURNITURE MART
2220 HWY 70 SE
HICKORY, NC 28602
Hours: **M-F: 9-6; S: 9-5; Closed Sundays**

Toll-Free	
Direct	828-322-2220
Fax	828-323-8445
Internet	

Notes: This resource is part of the Hickory Furniture Mart complex. This showroom is one of over 80 to visit. **See Hickory Furniture Mart listing for more information.** Consolidated shipping can be arranged with other resources in this center, a standard one/third deposit is required on all orders. Most showrooms accept VISA/MC, but not all. Cash, personal or certified checks accepted by all showrooms. If you elect not to pay for your entire purchase at the time of sale, a personal or certified check will be due upon delivery.

Manufacturers: **(Many resources do not list all their manufacturers. Be sure to inquire about those you are interested in, but do not see listed here.)**

═══════════════════════════════

DREXEL HERITAGE GALLERY
HICKORY FURNITURE MART
2220 HWY 70 SE
HICKORY, NC 28603
Hours: **M-F: 9-6; S: 9-5; Closed Sundays**

Toll-Free	
Direct	828-326-1060
Fax	828-326-1097
Internet	website: www.Boyles.com

Notes: This resource is part of the Hickory Furniture Mart complex. This showroom is one of over 80 to visit. **See Hickory Furniture Mart listing for more information.** Consolidated shipping can be arranged with other resources in this center, a standard one/third deposit is required on all orders. Most showrooms accept VISA/MC, but not all. Cash, personal or certified checks accepted by all showrooms. If you elect not to pay for your entire purchase at the time of sale, a personal or certified check will be due upon delivery. **IMPORTANT CORPORATE NUMBERS: Customer Service: 828-345-5280; Delivery Info: 828-345-5275; Order Status: 828-345-5290; Billing Questions: 828-345-5206**

Manufacturers: **(Many resources do not list all their manufacturers. Be sure to inquire about those you are interested in, but do not see listed here.)**

MAJOR LINES:	KINGSDOWN	GENTLEMAN'S QUARTERS
DREXEL HERITAGE	LILLIAN AUGUST	
DREXEL STUDIO		

DREXEL STUDIO
HICKORY FURNITURE MART
2220 HWY 70 SE
HICKORY, NC 28603
Hours: **M-F: 9-6; S: 9-5; Closed Sundays**

Toll-Free	
Direct	828-326-1735
Fax	
Internet	

Notes: This resource is part of the Hickory Furniture Mart complex. This showroom is one of over 80 to visit. **See Hickory Furniture Mart listing for more information.** Consolidated shipping can be arranged with other resources in this center, a standard one/third deposit is required on all orders. Most showrooms accept VISA/MC, but not all. Cash, personal or certified checks accepted by all

showrooms. If you elect not to pay for your entire purchase at the time of sale, a personal or certified check will be due upon delivery. **IMPORTANT CORPORATE NUMBERS: Customer Service: 828-345-5280; Delivery Info: 828-345-5275; Order Status: 828-345-5290; Billing Questions: 828-345-5206**

Manufacturers: **(Many resources do not list all their manufacturers. Be sure to inquire about those you are interested in, but do not see listed here.)**
Drexel Studio

════════════════════════════

EAST CAROLINA WALLPAPER MARKET, INC
1106 PINK HILL RD
KINSTON, NC 28501
Hours: **M-S: 8:30-5:30**

Toll-Free	800-848-7283
Direct	252-522-3226
Fax	252-522-0590
Internet	web site: ecwallpaper.com

Notes: Wallpaper and fabrics. Call for a brochure. Located 1 1/2 hours east of Raleigh

Manufacturers: **(Many resources do not list all their manufacturers. Be sure to inquire about those you are interested in, but do not see listed here.)**

BREWSTER	IMPERIAL	WARNER
FOREMOST/WESTMOUNT	SEABROOK	
HUNTER/YORK	SUNWORTHY	

════════════════════════════

EKLECTIC INTERIORS, LTD
401 N. FRANKLIN ST, 4TH FL
CHICAGO, IL 60610
Hours: **M-F:9-4:30; S: 9-3**

Toll-Free	
Direct	312-527-1570
Fax	312-670-4414(FAX)
Internet	

Notes: In business since 1969. VISA/MC. Complete interior design service available. Executive delivery service and Berger Transfer used to handle in-home set-up for out of state delivery. If damaged upon receipt, item would need to be refused and replacement would have to be ordered. Furniture, bedding and carpeting, lighting. Sales staff would be willing to help make furniture choices. Purchases can be made with credit card, check or cash. They offer very personalized service. Located near the Merchandise Mart enables them to take clients there. **See Zarbin & Associates listing.**

Manufacturers: (Many resources do not list all their manufacturers. Be sure to inquire about those you are interested in, but do not see listed here.)

ELLENBURG'S FURNITURE
I-40 & STAMEY FARM ROAD/PO BOX 5638
STATESVILLE, NC 28687
Hours: **M-S: 9:30-5:30; S: 9:30-5**

Toll-Free	
Direct	704-873-2900
Fax	704-873-6002
Internet	**web site:** http://www.ellenburg.com

Notes: In business since 1977. Family owned and operated. Four sales consultants on staff. Complete order can be paid via VISA/MC check. 25% down payment when placing an order. Balance due before shipment. COD possible in some cases. Two types of shipping: Roadway (common carrier) can have items delivered in three to ten working days based on geographic location. Most wicker, rattan and lighter products travel this way. Heavy items (wood and upholstery) travel via North Carolina Furniture Carriers. This type of delivery will uncrate and bring items into the home. For both types of delivery, damaged items should be refused. The carrier will return items and it will be reordered. Consultants on staff can help customer with choices. Customers can visit facility. $6 catalog - established customers can request free updates.

Manufacturers: (Many resources do not list all their manufacturers. Be sure to inquire about those you are interested in, but do not see listed here.)

ALLIBERT	EUROPEAN FURNITURE	LLOYD FLANDERS
AMERICAN COUNTRY WEST	INDUSTRIES	LO BROS
AMERICAN DREW	FICKS REED	LYNN HOLLYN
BENCHCRAFT	GEORGIAN REPRODUCTIONS	LYON SHAW
BERKSHIRE/DRESHER	HENRY LINK	MICHAEL THOMAS
BIG SKY	HIGHLAND HOUSE	MIRROR CRAFT
BOB TIMBERLAKE	HOOKER	NATIONAL MT AIRY
BRAXTON CULLER	KELLER	O'ASIAN
CANE & REED IMPORT	KINGSLEY-BATES	PACIFIC RATTAN
CEBU IMPORTS	LANE	PAWLEY'S ISLAND HAMMOCK
CHARLESTON FORGE	LANE SHAKER COUNTRY	PEARSON UPHOLSTERY
CLARK CASUAL	LANE WEATHERMASTER	PULASKI
CLASSIC RATTAN	LANE AMERICA	RATTAN SPECIALTIES
D & F WICKER	LEXINGTON	RIVERSIDE MATTRESS
DRESHER	LINK-TAYLOR	SAMSONITE

SYMBOL MATTRESS   VERANDA   WINSTON FURNITURE
TROPITONE   VOGUE RATTAN   WOODARD
UNIVERSAL   WEATHERCRAFT   YORKSHIRE LEATHER
VENTURE   WHITECRAFT

EPHRAIM MARSH CO
PO BOX 266
CONCORD, NC 28026-0266
Hours: **M-F: 9-5**

Toll-Free	
Direct	704-782-0814
Fax	704-782-0436
Internet	

Notes: In business since 1956. This company offers made-to-order products from a number of manufacturers and sells them under their own name. They offer a 130 catalog ($5 refundable). Home and office furniture. VISA/MC money orders accepted. Full payment required with order. Any item can be returned for refund or replacement. Customer pays shipping charges if returning an item they didn't like. Satisfaction guaranteed. Customers can ask for finish wood chips, fabrics, etc. All personnel are familiar with each piece of furniture and can make recommendations of its use. We describe each piece: solid, veneer, finish, joinery, 8-way hand tied, etc. worldwide shipping. Returns can be made if authorized and in original condition (except COM).

Manufacturers: (Many resources do not list all their manufacturers. Be sure to inquire about those you are interested in, but do not see listed here.)

EUROPEAN FURNITURE IMPORTERS
2145 W. GRAND AVE
CHICAGO, IL 60612
Hours: **M-F: 9-5**

Toll-Free	800-283-1955
Direct	312-243-1955
Fax	312-633-9308
Internet	

Notes: Importers to the trade since 1967. Now available directly to your home. 70,000 sq. ft. showroom. Mostly phone orders, but showroom available for browsing. Designer and consultants on staff. Complete order can be paid by VISA/MC/DISC or certified funds. No returns from warehouse. Catalog order items can be returned within 14 days. 14 day satisfaction guaranteed policy. Shipping problems handled by resource. Special services: excellent quality modern classics made to original specifications of the customer. Our collection of modern classics is stocked in Chicago and expands every year. All imported directly from the factories in Italy. Hand-carved chairs, leather, marble tables, iron and contemporary lighting. No minimum orders and no custom fees, guaranteed 12 week delivery and best prices. Modern classics, bombe chests, carved and lacquer chairs, wholesale. Catalog available for $3. Any other info is free.

Manufacturers: **(Many resources do not list all their manufacturers. Be sure to inquire about those you are interested in, but do not see listed here.)**

BREUER	LE CORBUSIER	MIES VAN DER ROHE
EAMES	MACKINTOSH	and more
EILEEN GRAY		

FABRIC CENTER, THE
485 ELECTRIC AVENUE
FITCHBURG, MA 01420
Hours: M-S: 9-5:30;

Toll-Free	
Direct	508-343-4402
Fax	
Internet	

Notes: In business since 1932. Sampling service available for ordering small to large swatches of fabrics (15 cents to $3.95, depending on size). Order can be paid via VISA/MC/money order.

Manufacturers: **(Many resources do not list all their manufacturers. Be sure to inquire about those you are interested in, but do not see listed here.)**

AMERICAN TEXTILE	KRAVET FABRICS	RICHLOOM
COVINGTON	P KAUFMANN	ROBERT ALLEN
GEORGE HARRINGTON	PAUL BARROW	WAVERLY
JOHN WOLF	PEACHTREE	and most major brands

FABRIC OUTLET, THE
30 AIRPORT RD
WEST LEBANON, NH 03784
Hours: **M-F: 9-5; S: 10-5**

Toll-Free	
Direct	800-635-9715
Fax	
Internet	

Notes: Will ship anywhere. Up to 60% off suggested retail. Designers and consultants on staff. Showroom available. Complete purchase can be paid by VISA/MC/MO/check. Fabric guaranteed first quality. Defects/flaws will be picked up and replaced or refunded. Shipping problems will be handled by the resource.

Manufacturers: (Many resources do not list all their manufacturers. Be sure to inquire about those you are interested in, but do not see listed here.)

AMETEX FABRICS	ELKO	NORMAN'S OF SALISBURY
ANDREW DUTTON	EMMESS	NOBAR FABRICS
ARTMARK FABRICS	FABRICUT	PEACHTREE FABRICS
B BERGER	GREEFF	PINDLER & PINDLER FABRIC
BARROW	IRWIN ALLEN	REDRUM
BISHOPS	JD FABRIC & COULTER	ROBERT ALLEN
BRUNSCHWIG & FILS	KRAVET FABRICS	ROCKLAND INDUSTRIES
BURCH	MAENLINE	S & S FABRICS
CAROLE FABRICS	MAYFLOWER	SCHUMACHER
DOUGLAS	METRO MILLS	STOUT
DURALEE FABRICS	MICHAEL'S TEXTILES	WAVERLY
EC CARTER	NEW ENGLAND UPHOLSTERY	

FABRICS & MORE
572 SOUTH MAIN ST
GRANITE FALLS, NC 28630
Hours: **M-F: 9-5**

Toll-Free	
Direct	828-396-4260(Fabric)828-396-4366 (Rugs and accessories)
Fax	828-396-6139
Internet	

Notes: HWY 321. Also carry area rugs. (Formerly Furniture Focus)

Manufacturers: **(Many resources do not list all their manufacturers. Be sure to inquire about those you are interested in, but do not see listed here.)**

══════════════════════════════

FABRICS & WALLPAPERS DIRECT
HOWBECK LODGE, LONDON ROAD
STEPELEY, CHESHIRE, ENGLAND CW5 7JU
Hours: **M-F: 9-5 (England time)**

Toll-Free	
Direct	011-44-1782-62-89-87
Fax	
Internet	

Notes: Extremely competitive prices for English designer fabrics and wallpaper. Also, French, Italian and German fabrics and wallpapers available. Inquiries welcome. Shipping available for US. VISA/ACCESS.Minimum 6 roll order, plus postage.

Manufacturers: **(Many resources do not list all their manufacturers. Be sure to inquire about those you are interested in, but do not see listed here.)**
Most popular brands

══════════════════════════════

FACTORY DIRECT TABLE PAD CO
1501 W MARKET ST
INDIANAPOLIS, IN 46208
Hours: **M-F: 8-6**

Toll-Free	800-428-4567
Direct	317-631-2577
Fax	317-631-2584
Internet	

Notes: Began in 1997. Solid fiberboard table pads. Light-weight. VISA/MC/DISC, 50% downpayment. Delivery is by UPS. If damage occurs, customer is to call UPS for pick-up and return to resource. Table pad will be remade at no charge. Items are custom-made. No return policy but items will be remade at no cost if resource erred. 20 year workmanship guarantee. Customer can visit facility.

Manufacturers: **(Many resources do not list all their manufacturers. Be sure to inquire**

about those you are interested in, but do not see listed here.)

FARM HOUSE FURNISHINGS
1432 1ST AVE SW
HICKORY, NC 28602-2401
Hours: **M-S: 9-6**

Toll-Free	
Direct	828-324-459-
Fax	
Internet	

Notes: Located on Hwy 321-N. Home furnishings, antiques, calligraphy, children and adult rockers, collectibles, country crafts and gifts, recliner "lift chair" systems, wicker all at discount prices. In business since 1983. Showroom. VISA/MC/DISC (in person only). Travelers checks/certified checks accepted. "The Red House on the Hill".

Manufacturers: **(Many resources do not list all their manufacturers. Be sure to inquire about those you are interested in, but do not see listed here.)**

AMYX
ATHOL TABLE
BARFIELD RECLINERS
BEECHBROOK
BLACK FOREST CLOCKS
BOLING CHAIR
BUILTRIGHT CHAIR
CAROLINA COUNTRY
CAROLINA ROCKERS
CARSON WIND CHIMES
COUNTRY REPRODUCTIONS
FASHION
HERITAGE HAUS
HICKORY LEATHER
HOOKER

HOWARD MILLER CLOCKS
LEXINGTON
DOWN INC
JH CRAVER
JOHNSTON BENCHWORKS
KENNEDY ROCKERS
KEVIN CHRISTIAN
LEA
MARTINSVILLE NOVELTY
MURPHY
OXFORD LEATHER
PINE-TIQUE
REGENCY HOUSE
RELAX-A-CLINER

RIVERSIDE BEDDING
RUG BARN
SIDEX
SK PRODUCTS
SOUTHERN CRAFTSMEN GUILD
LANE
STANLEY
THOMAS MOSER
TIMMERMAN
TOP NOTCH WOODWORK
UNIVERSAL
VAUGHAN OF VIRGINIA
WESLEY ALLEN

FAUCET OUTLET
PO BOX 547
MIDDLETOWN, NY 10940
Hours: **M-F: 8am-6pm**

Toll-Free	800-4445783
Direct	800-444-5783
Fax	914-343-1617
Internet	**email:** faucet@faucet.com **web site:** http:\\www.faucet.com

Notes: In business since 1992. We discount namebrand faucets, sinks, toilets, whirlpools, clawfoot tubs, built-in home products and accessories. Sales consultants and customer service reps can assist in coordinating products, answer questions and point out code requirements and product features. Payment by VISA/MC/CHECK/MO in full prior to shipping.

Manufacturers: (Many resources do not list all their manufacturers. Be sure to inquire about those you are interested in, but do not see listed here.)

AMERICAN STANDARD	JACUZZI	ONDINE
AMERICAN WHIRLPOOL	JADO	PRICE PFISTER
DELTA	JEARDON	SIGN OF THE CRAB
ELKAY	KOHLER	ST THOMAS CREATIONS
FRANKLIN BRASS	KWC DOMO	STERLING
GROHE	MELARD	SWANSTONE
HANSGROHE	MOEN	ULTIMA
HDI	NUTONE	
INSINKERATOR		

FEFCO
THE ATRIUM
430 SOUTH MAIN ST
HIGH POINT, NC 27262
Hours: **M-F: 9-6; S: 9-5**

Toll-Free	
Direct	336-882-0180
Fax	
Internet	

Notes: Part of the Atrium complex. Worth visiting, showrooms available. See **Atrium Furniture Showroom** listing for more information. Chinese furniture and furnishings

Manufacturers: (Many resources do not list all their manufacturers. Be sure to inquire about those you are interested in, but do not see listed here.)

===

FIELDS FURNITURE CO
2700 RANDLEMAN ROAD
GREENSBORO, NC 27406
Hours: **M-F: 10-6; S: 9-5**

Toll-Free	800-222-4809
Direct	336-273-7629
Fax	336-273-5605
Internet	

Notes: Established 1947. VISA/MC/DISC 20% downpayment, balance with certified check at delivery. In-home set-up by shippers. Shipper returns any damaged merchandise for repairs or replacement at no charge to the customer. Customer is responsible for supplying correct style numbers, etc. Resource and shipper will correct any damaged merchandise as a result of factory defect or freight damage. Customer can visit facilities. Brochures and procedures available by mail

Manufacturers: (Many resources do not list all their manufacturers. Be sure to inquire about those you are interested in, but do not see listed here.)

ACTION BY LANE
AMERICAN DREW
AMERICAN OF MARTINSVILLE
BARCALOUNGER
BASSETT FURNITURE
BASSETT MIRROR
BASSETT TABLES
BEMCO MATTRESS
BERKLINE
BLACKSMITH SHOP
BOLING CHAIR
BRADY FURNITURE
BRANDT
BRASS BEDS OF AMERICA
BRAXTON CULLER
BROYHILL
CARLTON McLENDON
CAROLINA FURNITURE
CAROLINA MIRROR
CARSON'S
CHARISMA CHAIRS
CHATHAM COUNTY
CHATHAM NOVELTY
CLASSIC LEATHER
CLASSIC RATTAN
CLAYTON MARCUS
CLYDE PEARSON

COCHRANE
COLONIAL
CRAFTIQUE
CRAWFORD
DANSEN CONTEMPORARY
DAYSTROM
DINAIRE
DISTINCTION LEATHER
DIXIE
ELLER
ERWIN-LAMBERT
FICKS REED
FIVE RIVERS
FLEXSTEEL
FLEXSTEEL
FLORIDA FURNITURE
FRIENDSHIP UPHOLSTERY
GUARDSMAN POLISH
HALE
HAMMARY TABLES
HARRIS LAMPS
HEKMAN
HENRY LINK
HICKORY TAVERN
HIGH POINT FURNITURE
HIGH POINT WOODWORKING
HITCHCOCK CHAIR

HOLIDAY HOUSE
HOOKER
HTB
INTERNATIONAL
JASPER CABINET
KELLER
KING HICKORY
LAINE
LANE
LEA
LEATHERCRAFT
LENOIR HOUSE
LEXINGTON
LYON-SHAW
MADISON SQUARE
MARTINSVILLE NOVELTY
McKAY CUSTOM PRODUCTS
MERSMAN TABLES
MOBEL
MYRTLE DESK
NATIONAL MT AIRY
NICHOLS & STONE
NULL INDUSTRIES
P & P CHAIR
PULASKI
RELIABLE MATTRESS
RIVERSIDE

REX	STRATOLOUNGER	UTTERMOST
ROWE	STREETMAN	VAUGHAN
SAN-DON	STUART	VAUGHAN-BASSETT
SCHWEIGER	SWAN BRASS BED	VENTURE
SEALY MATTRESS	TAYLORSVILLE UPHOLSTERY	VIRGINIA HOUSE
SINGER	TELL CITY	WEBB FURNITURE
SPRING AIR	TEMPLE UPHOLSTERY	WEIMAN
STANLEY	TERRYCRAFT	WILLIAM ALLEN
STANTON COOPER	THAYER COGGIN	WOODCRAFT ORIGINALS
STIFFEL LAMPS	TROUTMAN CHAIR	YOUNG-HINKLE
STRATFORD	UNIVERSAL	

FLEMING DECORATIVE FABRICS
2998 HICKORY BLVD
HUDSON, NC 28638
Hours: M-S; 10-5

Toll-Free	
Direct	828-728-7891
Fax	
Internet	

Notes: Fabrics, wallpaper, trims. Two sales consultants on staff. VISA/MC/CHECK can be used for deposit, check for balance. There is no return policy since fabrics are not guaranteed to us. Carrier is responsible for shipping problems.

Manufacturers: (Many resources do not list all their manufacturers. Be sure to inquire
 about those you are interested in, but do not see listed here.)

AMETEX FABRICS	P KAUFMANN	WAVERLY
CONSO	ROBERT ALLEN	
KRAVET		

FLEXSTEEL GALLERY
HICKORY FURNITURE MART
2220 HWY 70 SE
HICKORY, NC 28602
Hours: **M-F: 9-6; S: 9-5; Closed Sundays**

Toll-Free	
Direct	828-322-6602
Fax	
Internet	

Notes: This resource is part of the Hickory Furniture Mart complex. This showroom is one of over 80 to visit. **See Hickory Furniture Mart listing for more information.** Consolidated shipping can be arranged with other resources in this center, a standard one/third deposit is required on all orders. Most showrooms accept VISA/MC, but not all. Cash, personal or certified checks accepted by all showrooms. If you elect not to pay for your entire purchase at the time of sale, a personal or certified check will be due upon delivery.

Manufacturers: (Many resources do not list all their manufacturers. Be sure to inquire about those you are interested in, but do not see listed here.)

FLOORWAYS
5755 DUPREE DR SUITE 200
ATLANTA, GA 30327
Hours: **M-F: 9-5**

Toll-Free	800-989-5573
Direct	
Fax	
Internet	website: www.floorways.com

Notes: Carpeting and flooring.

Manufacturers: (Many resources do not list all their manufacturers. Be sure to inquire about those you are interested in, but do not see listed here.)
Private Label.

FOUR SEASONS FURNITURE GALLERY
4560 HICKORY BLVD
GRANITE FALLS, NC 28630
Hours: **M-F: 9-5**

Toll-Free	800-496-0090
Direct	828-496-1010
Fax	828-496-2271
Internet	Coming soon

Notes: Located on Hwy 321. Showroom. Living room, family room, sofas, tables, curio cabinets, leather, recliners, entertainment centers and solid oak dining.

Manufacturers: (Many resources do not list all their manufacturers. Be sure to inquire about those you are interested in, but do not see listed here.)

ACACIA	FORTRESS	ROWE
BASSETT	KING KOIL MATTRESSES	SALTERINI
BENTWOOD	OLD HICKORY TANNERY	SCHNADIG
EMERALD CRAFT	PHILLIP REINISCH	

FRAN'S WICKER AND RATTAN
295 ROUTE 10
SUCCASUNNA, NJ 07876
Hours: **M-F: 9-5**

Toll-Free	800-531-1511
Direct	201-584-2230
Fax	
Internet	

Notes: Highest quality, guaranteed lowest price, prompt delivery, large selection.

Manufacturers: (Many resources do not list all their manufacturers. Be sure to inquire about those you are interested in, but do not see listed here.)

BRAXTON	HENRY LINK	MANY MORE

FRANKLIN FURNITURE
3650 HICKORY BLVD
HUDSON, NC 28638-9027
Hours: **M-S: 9-5**

Toll-Free	
Direct	828-728-7369
Fax	828-396-5781
Internet	

Notes: Located on Hwy 321

Manufacturers: (Many resources do not list all their manufacturers. Be sure to inquire about those you are interested in, but do not see listed here.)

FRANKLIN PLACE
HICKORY FURNITURE MART
2220 HWY 70 SE
HICKORY, NC 28602
Hours: **M-F: 9-6; S: 9-5; Closed Sundays**

Toll-Free	
Direct	828-322-5539
Fax	828-322-5339
Internet	

Notes: This resource is part of the Hickory Furniture Mart complex. This showroom is one of over 80 to visit. **See Hickory Furniture Mart listing for more information.** Consolidated shipping can be arranged with other resources in this center, a standard one/third deposit is required on all orders. Most showrooms accept VISA/MC, but not all. Cash, personal or certified checks accepted by all showrooms. If you elect not to pay for your entire purchase at the time of sale, a personal or certified check will be due upon delivery.

Manufacturers: (Many resources do not list all their manufacturers. Be sure to inquire about those you are interested in, but do not see listed here.)

FRENCH HERITAGE FACTORY
THE ATRIUM
430 SOUTH MAIN ST
HIGH POINT, NC 27260
Hours: **M-F: 9-5**

Toll-Free	
Direct	336-884-0022
Fax	336-837-0020
Internet	**email:** french@thcatrium.com

Notes: Part of the Atrium complex. Worth visiting, showrooms available. See **Atrium Furniture Showroom** listing for more information. Offering country French reproductions, hand carved from solid ash. Dining, occasional and bedroom groups, including their best selling "Love Bird" armoire available in eight different finishes. Also featured: Crosswinds Country Club line of casual English country styles, great for decorating around a golfing motif, includes game table, entertainment center and upholstery collection

Manufacturers: (Many resources do not list all their manufacturers. Be sure to inquire about those you are interested in, but do not see listed here.)
CROSSWINDS COUNTRY CLUB   FRENCH HERITAGE

FURNITURE CHOICES
2501 PETERS CREEK PARKWAY
GREENSBORO, NC 27107
Hours: **M-F: 10-8**

Toll-Free	
Direct	336-294-0071
Fax	
Internet	

Notes: Import finished furniture from Mexico, Indonesia, etc. Established 1976. Payments can be made with VISA/MC/DISC/layaway, financing. Returns allowed within 30 days except special orders. **This company handles all unfinished furniture lines.** They have finishes to match any piece. 1250 items from over 200 vendors.

Manufacturers: (Many resources do not list all their manufacturers. Be sure to inquire about those you are interested in, but do not see listed here.)
WOODLAND   KHOURY   WHITEWOOD

FURNITURE CLEARANCE CENTER
1107 TATE ST
HIGH POINT, NC 27260
Hours: **M-F: 9-5**

Toll-Free	
Direct	336-882-1688
Fax	
Internet	

Notes: The clearance center carries a variety of manufacturers. The best way to shop here is to visit High Point. They buy market samples, factory closeouts, etc so most of the time you won't see the very same item repeated.

Manufacturers: **(Many resources do not list all their manufacturers. Be sure to inquire about those you are interested in, but do not see listed here.)**

FURNITURE DEALERS CLEARANCE CENTER OF NC
HWY 321 N
HUDSON, NC 28638
Hours: **M-S: 9-5:30**

Toll-Free	
Direct	828-396-1648
Fax	
Internet	

Notes: Located on Hwy 321. A unique consignment showroom. Major brands 50-80% off. Delivery anywhere in us. First line quality in showroom settings arriving weekly. Designers welcome.

Manufacturers: **(Many resources do not list all their manufacturers. Be sure to inquire about those you are interested in, but do not see listed here.)**

FURNITURE DIRECT
1280 S POWERLINE RD, #189
POMPANO BEACH, FL 33069
Hours: **M-F: 9-5**

Toll-Free	800-444-4154
Direct	
Fax	954-958-9966
Internet	website: www.furnituredir.com

Notes: This company believes in competitive pricing. They do not have a showroom. It is an office with catalogues, fabric and finish samples from the best known manufacturers. Savings up to 65%. They will send you fabric samples and catalogues from a leading manufacturer.
VISA/MC/AMEX

Manufacturers: (Many resources do not list all their manufacturers. Be sure to inquire about those you are interested in, but do not see listed here.)

ALADDIN	GARCIA IMPORTS	MILES TALBOT
AMERICAN DREW	GORDON INTL	MODERN CLASSICS
AMERICAN OF MARTINSVILLE	GRAHL	MOON COLLECTION
ARTIFACTS	GREYSEN	NATIONAL MT AIRY
ARTISTICA METAL	HABERSHAM	NATURAL LIGHT
ASTON GARRETT	HART	ORIENTAL LACQUER
B BERGER	HEKMAN	ORIGINALS 22
BAMBOO ODYSSEY	HELIOS	PACIFIC COAST
BARCALOUNGER	HENRY LINK	PAOLI
BEACHLEY	HICKORY BUSINESS	PARK PLACE
BONART LAMPS	FURNITURE	PEARSON
CABOT WRENN	HICKORY TAVERN	PREVIEW
CAROUSEL	HICKORY WHITE	PULASKI
CARSONS	HOOKER	ROBERT ALLEN
CASA BIQUE	HTB LANE	ROMWEBER
CASUAL OF CALIFORNIA	INTREX	RON FISHER
CEBU IMPORTS	JASPER DESK	SAM MOORE
CHAIR DESIGN	JOHNSTON CASUALS	SAN MIGUEL
CHARLESTON FORGE	JORDI MERE	SARRIED
COOPER DALYN	JSF INDUSTRIES	SEABROOK
DAVIS & DAVIS	KESSLER	SEALY
DINAIRE	KI	SERTA
DISTINCTION LEATHER	KINCAID	SIGNATURE
DURALEE	KRAVET	SK PRODUCTS
ELDEN	KUSCH	SPRINGAIR
ELEMENTS OF GRAPEVINE	L & B INDUSTRIES	STANLEY
EXCELSIOR	LANE	STONE COLLECTION
FABRICUT	LANE WEATHERMASTER	STONE INTERNATIONAL
FASHION BED GROUP	LAZAR IND	TROPITONE WOODARD
FINE ART LAMPS	LEA	TROY WESTNIDGE
FLAT ROCK	LEXINGTON	UNIVERSAL
FLEXSTEEL	LFS	VIRCO
FLEXSTEEL	LORTS	WELLESLEY GUILD
FREMARC	LOWENSTEIN	WELLINGTON HALL

FURNITURE EXPRESS
220 MT CROSS ROAD
DANVILLE, VA 24541
Hours: **M-S: 9-5**

Toll-Free	
Direct	804-792-1818
Fax	804-797-1050
Internet	

Notes: Furniture Express is a division of **A & H Wayside**. See their listing for more information.

Manufacturers: (Many resources do not list all their manufacturers. Be sure to inquire about those you are interested in, but do not see listed here.)

FURNITURE MARKET CLEARANCE CENTER
2200 S MAIN
HIGH POINT, NC 27262
Hours: **M-S; 8:30a-5:30p**

Toll-Free	
Direct	336-841-8599
Fax	336-841-8599
Internet	

Notes: All different manufacturers are sold here. Call or visit to find out more

Manufacturers: (Many resources do not list all their manufacturers. Be sure to inquire about those you are interested in, but do not see listed here.)

FURNITURE PATCH OF CALABASH, THE
10283 BEACH DRIVE SW
PO BOX 4970
CALABASH, NC 28467
Hours: M-S: 9-5:30

Toll-Free	
Direct	910-579-2001
Fax	
Internet	

Notes: Designer and sales consultants on staff can assist customer with choices. Customer can visit this facility. Brochures and procedures available by mail. 25% down payment can be paid with VISA/MC. Balance paid in check/cash/mo. 30% restocking charge for items ordered correctly but customer dissatisfied. Customer service will handle product problems. Located in a beautiful resort area at the beach. Customers can vacation and furniture shop on the same trip. Over 100 golf courses in the area. Furniture, accessories, fabric, wallcoverings, lamps.

Manufacturers: (Many resources do not list all their manufacturers. Be sure to inquire about those you are interested in, but do not see listed here.)

ACTION BY LANE
AMERICAN DREW
AMERICAN OF MARTINSVILLE
ARTMARK FABRICS
ASMARA RUGS
BAKER
BALDWIN BRASS
BARCALOUNGER
BASSETT MIRROR
BERNHARDT
BETH WEISSMAN
BEVAN FUNNELL
BLACKSMITH SHOP
BRADINGTON YOUNG
BRASS BEDS OF VIRGINIA
BRAXTON CULLER
CAROLINA MIRROR
CARSON'S
CASA BIQUE
CASA STRADIVARI
CENTURY
CHAIRCRAFT
CHAPMAN LAMPS
CHELSEA HOUSE
CHROMCRAFT
CLARK CASUAL
CLASSIC LEATHER
CLASSIC RATTAN
COLONIAL FURNITURE
CONANT BALL
COUNCILL CRAFTSMEN
COX

CRAFTIQUE
CRAFTWORK GUILD
DANSEN CONTEMPORARY
DAVID THOMAS LAMPS
DRESHER BRASS BEDS
ELLO
EMERSON LEATHER
ERWIN LAMBETH
FAIRINGTON
FICKS REED
FINE ARTS LAMPS
FLEXSTEEL
FREDERICK COOPER
FREDERICK EDWARD
FRIEDMAN BROS MIRRORS
FRITZ & LaRUE RUGS
GARCIA IMPORTS
GEORGIAN REPRODUCTIONS
GLASS ARTS
GRAPEVINE TABLES
GREEFF FABRICS
HABERSHAM PLANTATION
HAMMARY
PAUL HANSON LAMPS
HART COUNTRY SHOP
HEKMAN
HENRY LINK
HEXTER
HICKORY CHAIR
HICKORY WHITE
HITCHCOCK CHAIR
HOOKER

HOWARD MILLER CLOCKS
JASPER CABINET
JEFFCO
JOHNSTON CASUALS
KAISER KUHN LIGHTING
KARGES
KELLER
KINCAID
KNOB CREEK
KOCH & LOWY LAMPS
KRAVET FABRICS
LaBARGE
LANE
LEXINGTON
LLOYD FLANDERS
LYON-SHAW
McGUIRE
McKAY TABLE PADS
MADISON SQUARE
MAITLAND SMITH
MARBRO LAMPS
MASLAND CARPET & RUGS
MASTERCRAFT
MICHAEL THOMAS
MOTIONCRAFT
MURRAY FEISS LAMPS
NATIONAL MT AIRY
NICHOLS & STONE
NOBAR FABRICS
NORMAN PERRY LAMPS
OHIO TABLE PADS
PANDE CAMERON RUGS

CLYDE PEARSON
PLATT
PULASKI
REPRODUX
RIVERSIDE
ROBERT ALLEN FABRICS
SAMSONITE
SARREID
SCHOTT
SCHUMACHER/WAVERLY
SEABROOK WALLCOVERING
SEALY
SEALY MATTRESS
SERTA MATTRESS
SHERRILL OCCASIONAL
SHOAL CREEK LAMP

SHUFORD
SLIGH
SOUTHMARK LEATHER
SOUTHWOOD
SPEER
STANLEY
STANTON COOPER
STATTON
STIFFEL
STONE INTL
STROHEIM & ROMANN
SUPERIOR
SWAIM
SWAN BRASS BED
TAYLORSVILLE
TAYLOR WOODCRAFT

THAYER COGGIN
THOMASVILLE
TROPITONE
VANGUARD
VENTURE
VIRGINIA METALCRAFTERS
WATERFORD FURNITURE
WEDGEWOOD/WATERFORD
WEIMAN
WELLESLEY GUILD
WELLINGTON HALL
WESLEY ALLEN
WESLEY HALL
WILDWOOD
WOODARD
WOODMARK

FURNITURE SHOPPE, THE
1903 E 24TH ST PL
CHATTANOOGA, TN 37404
Hours: M-S: 10-6

Toll-Free	
Direct	423-493-7630
Fax	
Internet	

Notes: A family tradition since 1888. Full service, discount showroom representing only quality manufacturers. All major credit cards accepted. Due to distribution policies, certain restrictions may apply.

Manufacturers: (Many resources do not list all their manufacturers. Be sure to inquire about those you are interested in, but do not see listed here.)

BAKER	MAITLAND SMITH	STATTON
CENTURY	SLIGH	STICKLEY
CLASSIC LEATHER	SOUTHWOOD	
LEXINGTON	STANFORD	

FURNITURE SHOPPE, THE
PO Box 703, 3351 HICKORY BLVD
HUDSON, NC 28638
Hours: **M-S:9-5**

Toll-Free	800-861-6756
Direct	828-396-1942
Fax	828-396-2376
Internet	

Notes: Located on Hwy 321. Established 1977. We specialize in solid wood furniture. Fifty percent deposit required. Can be paid by VISA/MC/DISC/AMEX, but full amount must be paid at time of order. 25% restocking fee is charged if returns are made. Showroom available for shopping. Methods of shipment are in-home delivery (recommended) or common carrier(not normally recommended)

Manufacturers: (Many resources do not list all their manufacturers. Be sure to inquire about those you are interested in, but do not see listed here.)

ACTION BY LANE
AMERICAN DREW
AMERICAN OF MARTINSVILLE
BASSETT
BASSETT MIRROR
BLACKSMITH SHOP
BOB TIMBERLAKE
BROYHILL
CAL-STYLE
CANAL DOVER
CAROLINA MIRROR
CHATHAM COUNTY
CHROMCRAFT
CLAYTON MARCUS
CM FURNITURE
COCHRANE
CORSICAN CRAFTIQUE
DAYSTROM
DECORATIVE CRAFTS
DINAIRE
DIXIE
EMERSON LEATHER
FAIRFIELD
FLEXSTEEL

GLENNCRAFT
HAMMARY
HEKMAN
HENRY LINK
HICKORY TAVERN
HICKORY WHITE
HOMECREST
HOOKER
HTB
IRON CLASSIC
JASPER CABINET
JOHNSTON CASUALS
KIMBALL
KINCAID
LANE
LANE UPHOLSTERY
LEA
LEXINGTON
LINK TAYLOR
LLOYD FLANDERS
LYON SHAW
MACON UMBRELLA
M & M NAUTICAL

NATIONAL MT AIRY
O'ASIAN
PINNACLE
PULASKI
RIVERSIDE
SEALY
SERTA
SOUTHERN OFFICE
STANLEY
STRATFORD
STRATOLOUNGER
SWAN BRASS BED
TAPESTRIES LTD
TAYLORSVILLE UPHOLSTERY
TELESCOPE
TELL CITY CHAIR
TROPITONE
UNIVERSAL
VOGUE RATTAN
WEIMAN
WESLEY ALLEN
WINSTON
YOUNG-HINKLE

FURNITURELAND SOUTH
BUSINESS I-85 at RIVERDALE RD
JAMESTOWN, NC 27282
Hours: MTWS: 8:30-5:30; TH,F: 8:30-8:30

Toll-Free	
Direct	336-841-4328
Fax	336-841-8745
Internet	

Notes: In business since 1968. This place is one of the best locations to see and shop for furniture in the High Point area. 350,000 sq ft of showrooms. A restaurant is part of the facilities, serving breakfast and lunch. Your purchase can be paid by cash or check, with a one-third deposit. **No credit cards accepted.** Balance paid by certified check at time of delivery. They do not order on approval and cannot accept cancellations after manufacturing process has begun. Damaged or defective goods may be returned for repair or replacement at the resource's discretion. Guarantees are those of the manufacturer's quality, not the pleasure of customer's choice. Shipping problems are handled by the resource. Damages must be noted at time of delivery. Delivery anywhere in us. Free video available. A new showroom scheduled to open mid-1998.

Manufacturers: (Many resources do not list all their manufacturers. Be sure to inquire about those you are interested in, but do not see listed here.)

AA LAUN	BROYHILL	CRAFTWORK GUILD
ART	BUTLER SPECIALTY	CRAWFORD
ACTION BY LANE	C-STYLE	DESIGN SOUTH
AMERICAN CHAIR & TABLE	CAL-STYLE	DESIGN HORIZONS
AMERICAN DREW	CAROLINA MIRROR	DILLON
ANDREW PEARSON	CARRIER	DINAIRE
AMP	CARSON'S	DIRECTIONAL
ARDLEY HALL	CARTER UPHOLSTERY	DISCOVERY RATTAN
ARTISTICA	CASA BIQUE	DISTINCTION LEATHER
ASHLEY MANOR	CASA STRADIVARI	DREXEL HERITAGE
ATHOL TABLE	CENTURY	DUTAILIER
ATLANTA GLASSCRAFTER	CHARTER TABLE	EKORNES
BALDWIN	CHATHAM COUNTY	ELEMENTS BY GRAPEVINE
BARCALOUNGER	CHROMCRAFT	ELLIOTT'S DESIGNS
BARN DOOR FURNITURE	CLARK CASUAL	ELLO
BASSETT	CLASSIC GALLERY	EMERSON LEATHER
BEAN STATION	CLASSIC LEATHER	ENTREE
BEAUFURN	CLASSIC RATTAN	ERIC MORGAN
BENCHCRAFT	CLAYTON MARCUS	EXCELSIOR
BENICIA	COCHRANE	FAIRFIELD CHAIR
BERNHARDT	COJA LEATHER	FASHION BED
BERKLINE	COLONIAL FURNITURE	FICKS REED
BERKSHIRE	COMFORT DESIGNS	FLEXSTEEL
BESTAR	CONANT BALL	FOCUS
BLACKSMITH SHOP	CONOVER CHAIR	FORMA DESIGN
BOB TIMBERLAKE	COURTLEIGH	FRIEDMAN BROS MIRRORS
BOLING	COX MANUFACTURING	GEORGIAN FURNISHINGS
BRAXTON CULLER	CRAFT-TEX	GLASS ARTS
BROWN JORDAN	CRAFTIQUE	GLOSTER

GRACE MANUFACTURING
GUARDSMAN
HAMMARY
HEKMAN
HENRY LINK
HICKORY HILL
HICKORY HOUSE
HICKORY WHITE
HIGH POINT FURNITURE
HIGHLAND HOUSE
HINKLE CHAIR
HITCHCOCK CHAIR
HOLLYWOODS
HOOD
HOOKER
HOWARD MILLER
HYUNDAI
JACKSON OF DANVILLE
JAMES R COOPER
JASPER CABINET
JJ HYDE
JOHNSTON BENCHWORKS
JOHNSTON CASUALS
JSF INDUSTRIES
KARGES
KELLER
KESSLER
KEY CITY
KIMBALL REPRODUCTIONS
KING HICKORY
KOCH ORIGINALS
LaBARGE
LANE
LEA INDUSTRIES
LEATHERCRAFT
LEATHERTREND
LEEDO
LEXINGTON
LINK TAYLOR
LORRAINE HEADBOARDS
LLOYD FLANDERS
LYON SHAW
MADISON SQUARE
MAGNUSSEN RESIDENTIAL
MAITLAND SMITH
MARLOW
MARVEL

MARYLAND CLASSICS
MASLAND CARPETS
MASTERLOOMS
McKAY TABLE PADS
MEADOWCRAFT
MIKHAIL DARAFEEV
MILLENDER
MILLER DESK
MOHAWK
NATUZZI
NICHOLS & STONE
NORTH HICKORY
NULL INDUSTRIES
OFS
OLD HICKORY TANNERY
PARKER SOUTHERN
PEARSON
PENNSYLVANIA CLASSICS
PEOPLOUNGER
PETERS-REVINGTON
POWELL
PREVIEW
PRIVILEGE HOUSE
PULASKI
REFLECTIONS
REGENCY HOUSE
RICHARDSON BROS
RIDGEWAY
RIDGEWOOD
RIVERSIDE
ROBERT ALLEN FABRICS
SK PRODUCTS
SAGEFIELD LEATHER
SALEM SQUARE
SALOOM
SAM MOORE
SAMSONITE
SARREID
SCHNADIG
SCHOTT FURNITURE
SCHWEIGER INDUSTRIES
SEDGEFIELD BY ADAMS
SERTA
SHUFORD
SIDNEY ARTHUR
SILVER

SIMMONS
SLIGH
SOUTHERN CRAFTSMEN GUILD
SOUTHERN FURNITURE
REPRODUCTIONS
SPRING AIR
STAKMORE
STANLEY
STATESVILLE CHAIR
STATTON
STIFFEL
STONE INTL
STONEVILLE
STRATFORD/STRATOLOUNGER
SUMTER CABINET
SUPERIOR FURNITURE
SWAIM
SWAN BRASS BED
TELESCOPE
TELL CITY
TEMPLE UPHOLSTERY
THAYER COGGIN
TIMMERMAN
TRADITIONS BY KIMBALL
TRADITION HOUSE
TRANS PACIFIC
TRIAD BUTCHER BLOCK
TROPITONE
TUBB WOODCRAFTERS
UNIVERSAL
UNIQUE ORIGINALS
UWHARRIE CHAIR
VANGUARD
VAUGHAN
VAUGHAN BASSETT
VENTURE BY LANE
VIRGINIA HOUSE
WEIMAN
WAVERLY FABRICS
WELLINGTON HALL
WESLEY ALLEN
WHITECRAFT
WINNERS ONLY
WINSTON OUTDOOR
WOODARD
WOODMARK

Resource Directory

GALLERY OF LIGHTS
HICKORY FURNITURE MART
2220 HWY 70 SE
HICKORY, NC 28602
Hours: **M-F: 9-6; S: 9-5; Closed Sundays**

Toll-Free	
Direct	828-324-6337
Fax	828-327-9894
Internet	

Notes: This resource is part of the Hickory Furniture Mart complex. This showroom is one of over 80 to visit. **See Hickory Furniture Mart listing for more information.** Consolidated shipping can be arranged with other resources in this center, a standard one/third deposit is required on all orders. Most showrooms accept VISA/MC, but not all. Cash, personal or certified checks accepted by all showrooms. If you elect not to pay for your entire purchase at the time of sale, a personal or certified check will be due upon delivery.

Manufacturers: **(Many resources do not list all their manufacturers. Be sure to inquire about those you are interested in, but do not see listed here.)**

GENADA IMPORTS
PO BOX 204, DEPT R1
TEANECK, NJ 07666
Hours: **M-S: 9-5**

Toll-Free	
Direct	201-790-7522
Fax	201-790-7522
Internet	

Notes: Direct importer of Danish and modern furniture. Imports from western Europe of Scandanavian knock-offs. In business since 1968. Most shipping is UPS. VISA/MC/CHECK/MO accepted. 48 catalog ($1). Money back guarantee policy. Returns can be made for any reason, freight prepaid by customer. If shipping problems, customer must file claim.

Manufacturers: **(Many resources do not list all their manufacturers. Be sure to inquire about those you are interested in, but do not see listed here.)**

GENERATIONS
HICKORY FURNITURE MART
2220 HWY 70 SE
HICKORY, NC 28602
Hours: **M-F: 9-6; S: 9-5; Closed Sundays**

Toll-Free	
Direct	828-322-7275
Fax	828-322-1454
Internet	

Notes: In business since 1992. Three sales consultants, three designers on staff. 25% deposit can be made with VISA/MC/DISC/CASH/CHECK. Children are our only business. We have everything to complete a child's bedroom, from the furniture, mattresses, bedding/comforters, lamps, pictures and accessories. This resource is part of the Hickory Furniture Mart complex. This showroom is one of over 80 to visit. **See Hickory Furniture Mart listing for more information.** Consolidated shipping can be arranged with other resources in this center, a standard one/third deposit is required on all orders. Most showrooms accept VISA/MC, but not all. Cash, personal or certified checks accepted by all showrooms. If you elect not to pay for your entire purchase at the time of sale, a personal or certified check will be due upon delivery.

Manufacturers: (Many resources do not list all their manufacturers. Be sure to inquire about those you are interested in, but do not see listed here.)

GIBSON INTERIORS
1628 S MAIN ST
HIGH POINT, NC 27260
Hours: **M-S: 9-6**

Toll-Free	800-247-5460
Direct	336-883-4444
Fax	336-883-0417
Internet	

Notes: A very unique discount store. Antique, vintage and antique reproduction furniture. Specialists in lamps, leather furniture and decorative accessories. In business since 1983. VISA/MC/DISC/CHECK. 30% downpayment. Consumer generally should know model numbers, styles, etc, but staff members can help and make suggestions. In home delivery or UPS. Generally, resource handles shipping problems, although customer's assistance is required in some circumstances. Customer can visit facilities

Manufacturers: (Many resources do not list all their manufacturers. Be sure to inquire about those you are interested in, but do not see listed here.)

ARTEMIDE	GATCO	RELIANCE
AS YOU LIKE IT LAMPS	GEORGE KOVACS	REMBRANDT
BALDWIN BRASS	HOUSE OF TROY	REMINGTON LAMPS
BAUER LAMP	HOWARD MILLER CLOCKS	ROSS
BRASSCRAFTERS	HYUNDAI	RUSTIC CRAFTS
CAMBRIDGE LAMPS	JAYMAR	SALEM SQUARE
CAROLINA MIRROR	LEATHERTREND	SEDGEFIELD
CASTILLIAN IMPORTS	LENOX LIGHTING	STIFFEL
CASUAL LAMP	MARKEL LIGHTING	STYLECRAFT LAMPS
CHAPMAN	MARIO	TOP BRASS
CHARLES SADEK IMPORTS	NATURAL LIGHT	TOYO
CRAFT-TEX	OKLAHOMA CASTING	UPPER DECK
CRAIG NORMAN	ORIENTAL ACCENTS	UTTERMOST
CRYSTAL CLEAR	PACIFIC COAST	VANGUARD STUDIOS
DALE TIFFANY	PARAGON PICTURES	VIRGINIA METALCRAFTERS
DECORATIVE CRAFTS	PASSPORT	WILDWOOD
EMERSON LEATHER	PHILLIP REINISCH	WILLOW CREEK
FINE ARTS LAMPS	QUOIZEL	WINDSOR ART
FREDERICK COOPER	REGENCY HOUSE TABLES	

GLOBAL WALLCOVERINGS AND BLINDS
3359 WEST MAIN ST
SKOKIE, IL 60067
Hours: **M-F: 7-mid; S: 8:30-7; SUN: 10-7**

Toll-Free	800-220-7610
Direct	
Fax	847-763-2111
Internet	

Notes: Free ordering kit for blinds. Special wallpaper case discounts. All major credit cards accepted. Verticals, duettes, pleated shades, horizontals, woods. All major credit cards accepted.

Manufacturers: (Many resources do not list all their manufacturers. Be sure to inquire about those you are interested in, but do not see listed here.)

BALI	HUNTER DOUGLAS	LEVOLOR
DELMAR	KIRSCH	LOUVERDRAPE
GRABER		

GLOBE FURNITURE
910 US HWY 321 NW, #100
HICKORY, NC 28601
Hours: **M-F: 9-5**

Toll-Free	800-258-3273
Direct	828-323-1580
Fax	828-345-5007
Internet	

Notes: In business since 1991. Parent company has been in business 35 years. No showroom. Mail or phone orders only. Deposit required: 20% down in cashiers check or certified funds. Balance and freight charges due upon shipping.

Manufacturers: (Many resources do not list all their manufacturers. Be sure to inquire about those you are interested in, but do not see listed here.)

ALEXVALE	HENRY LINK	OHIO TABLE PADS
AMERICAN DREW	HICKORY FRY	OLD HICKORY TANNERY
ATHENS FURNITURE	IIICKORY MANUFACTURING	OAKWOOD
ATHOL TABLE	HICKORY TAVERN	PULASKI
AMERICAN OF MARTINSVILLE	HOOKER	PINE-TIQUE
ACTION BY LANE	HICKORY WHITE	PEOPLOUNGER
BROYHILL	HIGHLAND HOUSE	PARK PLACE
BALDWIN BRASS	HUNTINGTON HOUSE	PENNSYLVANIA CLASSICS
BERKLINE	HICKORY INTERNATIONAL	REX
BASSETT	HOWARD MILLER	RIVERSIDE
BRADINGTON YOUNG	HAMMARY	RICHARDSON BROS
BARCALOUNGER	HALE	ROBINSON
CHAIRCRAFT	HERMAN MILLER	J ROYALE
CLAYTON MARCUS	HOOD	JB ROSS BRASS BEDS
CLASSIC LEATHER	JAMESTOWN STERLING	STANLEY
CRAFTWORK GUILD	JASPER	SERTA MATTRESS
COCHRANE	JETTON	SEALY MATTRESS
COUNCILL CRAFTSMEN	KEY CITY	ST TIMOTHY CHAIR
CRAFTIQUE	KIMBALL	STYLE UPHOLSTERY
CUSTOM DESIGNS	KINCAID	SEDGEFIELD LEATHER
CRESENT	KING HICKORY	SOUTHERN FURNITURE OF
DISTINCTION LEATHER	LANE	CONOVER
DILLON	LEXINGTON	SLIGH
DAYSTROM	LINK TAYLOR	SIMPLY SOUTHERN
DRESHER	CR LAINE	SINGER
DIXIE	MOBEL	SUMTER
EMERSON	MONTGOMERY CHAIR	TAYLOR KING
ELLO	MASTERFIELD	TELL CITY
FAIRFIELD CHAIR	MERSMAN	TAYLOR CLASSICS
FLEXSTEEL	MILLER DESK	TEMPLE
FREDERICK COOPER	NATIONAL MT AIRY	TIMMERMAN
FICKS REED	NULL INDUSTRIES	TROPITONE
FLORIDA FURNITURE	NATHAN HALE	TAYLORSVILLE UPHOLSTERY
FRANKLIN FURNITURE	NICHOLS & STONE	UNIVERSAL
GLENNCRAFT	NORTH HICKORY	VAUGHAN
GEORGIAN REPRODUCTIONS	NORA FENTON	VIRGINIA HOUSE

VENTURE   WHITAKER   WEIMAN
VANGUARD   WELLINGTON HALL YOUNG HINKLE
VAUGHAN-BASSETT WESLEY ALLEN   YORKSHIRE LEATHER

GOLD LABEL CARPETS
PO BOX 3876
DALTON, GA 30721
Hours: **M-F: 9-5**

Toll-Free	800-346-4531
Direct	706-278-7919
Fax	706-278-7741
Internet	

Notes: In business since 1980. Major credit cards or check can be used for full payment before delivery. Shippers are major interstate trucking companies. Shipping policies: They will handle problems. Return policies: Defective or damaged items can be returned for full credit. Various guarantees apply from each manufacturer. Sales and design consultants on staff. Customer can visit this facility. This company can purchase direct from all major mills for their customers at wholesale prices. Call for manufacturers and prices.

Manufacturers: (Many resources do not list all their manufacturers. Be sure to inquire about those you are interested in, but do not see listed here.)

ALADDIN CARPET	DIAMOND	QUEEN
CASUAL CARPET	DYNAMIC	SALEM
CONQUEST	IMAGE CARPET	SUTTON CARPETS
CUMBERLAND MILLS	INTERLOOM	

GOLDEN VALLEY LIGHTING
274 EASTCHESTER DRIVE, SUITE 117a
HIGH POINT, NC 27262
Hours: **M-F: 10-6;**

Toll-Free	800-735-3377
Direct	336-882-7330
Fax	336-882-2262
Internet	website: http://www.gvlight.com

Notes: Established in 1989. Family owned and operated. Ceiling fans, floor and table lamps and lighting fixtures. Call or send $2 for complete color catalog, refundable with first purchase.

Payment policies are VISA/MC/CHECK. We ship via UPS mainly. Sales and design consultants on staff. Return policies - defective or damaged goods may be returned. Customers cannot visit this facility. Certain manufacturers will not allow their names to be printed. Over 200 manufacturers represented. Please ask. Special deals for Japanese customers.

Manufacturers: (Many resources do not list all their manufacturers. Be sure to inquire about those you are interested in, but do not see listed here.)

GORDON'S FURNITURE STORES
214 N. CENTER ST
STATESVILLE, NC 28677-1192
Hours: **M-F: 9-6; S: 9-5**

Toll-Free	
Direct	704-873-4329
Fax	704-873-4397
Internet	

Notes: In business since 1917. We maintain our own warehouse and delivery. Most merchandise in our showroom is ready for immediate shipment. Our credit rating is the highest granted by Dun and Bradstreet. All merchandise must be paid in full via VISA/MC/DISC. Catalogs and samples are readily available. Special orders require a 30% deposit upon order and balance upon notification that it is ready. Balance paid by personal check, cash, or certified funds. Shipping problems are handled by customer by filing claim with the carrier. Ask about their lodging advantage with purchase.

Manufacturers: (Many resources do not list all their manufacturers. Be sure to inquire about those you are interested in, but do not see listed here.)

ACACIA	CHROMCRAFT	LIGO
ALEXANDER JULIAN COLLECTION	CLARK CASUAL	LLOYD FLANDERS
	CLAYTON MARCUS	LYON SHAW
AMERICAN OF MARTINSVILLE	COUNCILL	MASLAND CARPET
ARTMARK	CRAFT MARK	McKAY TABLE PADS
AMERICAN DREW	CUSTOM RUGS	MINOFF LAMPS
ARNOLD PALMER COLLECTION	DENNY LAMP	NORA FENTON
ATHENS	DISTINCTION LEATHER	OHIO TABLE PADS
BASSETT	FAIRFIELD CHAIR	PENNSYLVANIA HOUSE
BEST CHAIR	FASHION BED	PHILADELPHIA CARPET
BLACKSMITH SHOP	HAMMARY	PULASKI
BOB TIMBERLAKE	HEKMAN	RIVERSIDE
BROYHILL	HENRY LINK	SARREID
BUILTRIGHT CHAIR	HOOKER	SEDGEFIELD LAMP
CABIN CRAFT CARPET	J ROYALE	SIMMONS
CAROLINA MIRROR	KINCAID	STANLEY
CHAIR CO	LA-Z-BOY	STONEVILLE
CHARLESTON FORGE	LANE	STRATOLOUNGER
CHATHAM COUNTY	LEES CARPET	TELESCOPE
CHINA TRADERS LAMPS	LEXINGTON	TIMELESS BEDDING

UMBRELLA FACTORY   VIRGINIA HOUSE   WINSTON
UNIVERSAL   VIRGINIA METALCRAFTERS
VANGUARD STUDIOS

====

GRANIT DESIGN
PO BOX 130
WATERTOWN, SD 57201
Hours: **M-F: 8-4:30**

Toll-Free	800-843-3305
Direct	605-886-6942
Fax	605-886-6943
Internet	**email:** granite@icontrol.net **website:** www.granitecenter.com

Notes: Established in 1882. This company can provide custom-made granite or marble for kitchen counter tops, bathroom vanities, accent islands, bar tops, tiles, custom furniture, buildings and monuments. Savings of often 50% or more below suggested retail. 1/3 deposit required upon order, 1/3 upon receipt, net 30 days. VISA/MC/DISC accepted. Returns allowed for defects in materials and workmanship. Carrier is responsible for any damage in shipping. Shop by mail or phone. Free brochure, nationwide service.

Manufacturers: (Many resources do not list all their manufacturers. Be sure to inquire about those you are interested in, but do not see listed here.)

====

GREENHILL FURNITURE COMPANY
1308 HWY 70 W
HICKORY, NC 28602
Hours: **M-S: 9-5**

Toll-Free	
Direct	828-327-2024
Fax	828-327-2106
Internet	

Notes: Nationwide in-home delivery.

Manufacturers: (Many resources do not list all their manufacturers. Be sure to inquire

about those you are interested in, but do not see listed here.)

BROYHILL   LEXINGTON   and more
KELLER   STANLEY

GREEN FRONT FURNITURE STORE
316 N MAIN STREET
FARMVILLE, VA 23901
Hours: M-S: 9am-5pm

Toll-Free	
Direct	804-392-5943
Fax	804-392-8552
Internet	

Notes: More than 500,000 square feet spread in ten buildings. Factory-direct carpeting and linoleum, too. Don't miss the northern Virginia location at 1304-A Sevrin Way, Sterling, Va. 20166; 703-406-0761

Manufacturers: (Many resources do not list all their manufacturers. Be sure to inquire about those you are interested in, but do not see listed here.)

UPHOLSTERY
BARCALOUNGER
BRADINGTON YOUNG
CONNOISSEUR
EJ VICTOR
FREDERICK EDWARD
HENREDON
JOHNSTON TOMBIGBEE
JON ELLIOTT
KING HICKORY
MICHAEL THOMAS
MILES TALBOT
MOTIONCRAFT
PRECEDENT
SHERRILL
SOUTHWOOD
STANFORD
STANLEY
THOMASVILLE

IMPORTED
CHINESE ANTIQUES
FRENCH HERITAGE
GIEMME
MAITLAND SMITH
ROYAL PATINA
TRADITIONS FRANCE

LEATHER

BLUE RIDGE
BRADINGTON YOUNG
DISTINCTION
HANCOCK & MOORE
HENREDON
LEATHERCRAFT
MONTGOMERY
OLD HICKORY TANNERY
SOUTHWOOD
WHITTEMORE SHERRILL

KILIMS
AFGHANISTAN
CHINESE
TURKISH

OUTDOOR
BASTA SOLE
KINGSLEY-BATES
LLOYD FLANDERS
LYON SHAW
MEADOWCRAFT
PAWLEY'S ISLAND HAMMOCK
PINEHURST
TELESCOPE
TROPITONE
VENEMAN
WINSTON
WOODARD

CASEGOODS
AMERICAN DREW
BERNHARDT
BROWN STREET
BUCKS COUNTY
BUILTRIGHT
COCHRANE
COLONIAL
COUNCILL CRAFTSMEN
CRAFTIQUE
CRAWFORD
DURHAM
EJ VICTOR
ELDRED WHEELER
GUILDMASTER
HENKEL HARRIS
HENREDON
HOOKER
JASPER
KELLER
KEYSTONE
KNOB CREEK
LANE
LEISTERS
LEXINGTON
MADISON SQUARE
NATIONAL MT AIRY
NICHOLS & STONE
SALOOM

Resource Directory

SIMPLY SOUTHERN
SOUTHERN OF CONOVER
STANLEY
STATTON
THOMASVILLE
TRADITION HOUSE
UNIVERSAL
WELLINGTON HALL
WESLEY ALLEN
WICKER
CLARK CASUAL
FICKS REED
HENRY LINK
JOHNSTON TOMBIGBEE
LANE-VENTURE

OFFICE
BOLING
COUNCILL CRAFTSMEN
HANCOCK & MOORE
HENKEL MOORE
MILLER DESK
NATIONAL MT AIRY
SLIGH

ACCESSORIES
ANTIQUITIES PORCELAINS
CHARLESTON FORGE

FETCO
GREAT CITY TRADERS
HEN FEATHERS
LaBARGE
MAITLAND SMITH
PALECEK BASKETS
PIMPERNEL
SADEK IMPORTS
SHERRILL OCCASIONAL
SOUTHAMPTON
ARTHUR COURT

IMPORTS
CHINESE HOOK RUGS
CHINESE NEEDLEPOINT RUGS
GRIFONI MIRRORS
INDIAN DHURRIES
INDIAN TUFTED RUGS
ITALIAN CERAMICS
STONEWASH DHURRIES

LAMPS
BALDWIN
JOHN RICHARD LAMPS
NATURAL LIGHT
RELIANCE
SPEER
WILDWOOD

PICTURES
BIG FISH
JOHN RICHARD
OIL PAINTINGS
PARAGON PICTURES
W KING AMBLER
AND MORE

MIRRORS
CARVER'S GUILD
FRIEDMAN BROS MIRRORS
LaBARGE
SNOW CATCHERS

LINENS
DEWOOLFSON DOWN
MALABAR GROVE
PEACOCK ALLEY

RUGS
BALTA RUGS
CAPEL BRAIDED
COLONIAL MILLS
FEIZY IMPORTS
MARCELLA

GREEN FRONT FURNITURE STORE
1304 A SEVRIN WAY
STERLING, VA 20166
Hours: **M-S: 10-6;SUN: 12-5**

Toll-Free	
Direct	703-406-0761
Fax	703-406-0762
Internet	

Notes: Imported rugs, American made furniture, some accessories in 38,000 square feet of space. This store has been in business since 1995. Don't forget to visit their big store in Farmville, VA.

Manufacturers: (Many resources do not list all their manufacturers. Be sure to inquire about those you are interested in, but do not see listed here.)
HENKEL HARRIS   LANE
HENREDON   THOMASVILLE

GRINDSTAFF'S INTERIORS
1007 W MAIN
FOREST CITY, NC 28043
Hours: **M-F: 9-5**

Toll-Free	
Direct	704-245-4263
Fax	704-245-7758
Internet	

Notes:

Manufacturers: **(Many resources do not list all their manufacturers. Be sure to inquire about those you are interested in, but do not see listed here.)**

HAMILTON'S
506 LIVE OAK STREET
BEAUFORT, NC 28516
Hours: **M-S; 9am-5:30pm**

Toll-Free	800-488-4720
Direct	252-728-4720
Fax	
Internet	**web site**: www.clis.com/hamfurn

Notes: In business since 1946 Payment accepted for purchases by VISA/MC/DISC/AMEX/CHECK.

Manufacturers: **(Many resources do not list all their manufacturers. Be sure to inquire about those you are interested in, but do not see listed here.)**

ACTION BY LANE	CAL-STYLE	D & F WICKER IMPORTS
BARCALOUNGER	CAMBRIDGE CHAIR CO	DR KINCAID
BARN DOOR	CARLTON McLENDON	DESIGN HORIZONS
BASSETT	CASUAL CRATES	DISTINCTION
BEECHBROOK	CHARISMA CHAIRS	DIXIE
BEMCO MATTRESS	CHARTER HOUSE	FAIRFIELD CHAIR
BRAXTON CULLER	CHATHAM NOVELTY CO	FLEXSTEEL INDUSTRIES
BROOKWOOD	CLASSIC LEATHER	FORTRESS
BROYHILL	COCHRANE	FORTUNE RATTAN
BUILTRIGHT CHAIR	COUNTY SEAT	H & H
BUTLER	COUNTRY EXPRESSIONS	HALCYON

HENRY LINK	NATIONAL MT AIRY	SUMTER CABINET
HOOD	NULL INDUSTRIES	TELESCOPE
HOOKER	OHIO TABLE PADS	TEMPLE FURNITURE
HYUNDAI	P & P CHAIR	BLACKSMITH SHOP
JASPER CABINET	PENNSYLVANIA	TINSLEY-CLARK
KELLER	PULASKI	TROUTMAN CHAIR
KEY CITY	RIDGEWOOD	UNIVERSAL
KINCAID	RIVERSIDE	UTTERMOST
KLAUSSNER	ROOMS TO GROW	VAUGHAN-BASSETT
KNOB CREEK	SAMSONITE	VICTORIAN CLASSIC
LANE	SERTA MATTRESS	VIRGINIA HOUSE
LEA	SK PRODUCTS	WEBB
LEXINGTON	SLEEP MASTER	WEIMAN
LINEAL DESIGN	SOMMA MATTRESS	WINSTON
LINEAL GROUP	STANLEY	YOUNG AMERICAN
MARTINSVILLE NOVELTY	STATESVILLE	YOUNG HINKLE
MURPHY BEDS BY SICO		

HANCOCK & MOORE GALLERY
HICKORY FURNITURE MART
2220 HWY 70 SE
HICKORY, NC 28602
Hours: **M-F: 9-6; S: 9-5; Closed Sundays**

Toll-Free	
Direct	828-326-1735
Fax	
Internet	

Notes: This resource is part of the Hickory Furniture Mart complex. This showroom is one of over 80 to visit. **See Hickory Furniture Mart listing for more information.** Consolidated shipping can be arranged with other resources in this center, a standard one/third deposit is required on all orders. Most showrooms accept VISA/MC, but not all. Cash, personal or certified checks accepted by all showrooms. If you elect not to pay for your entire purchase at the time of sale, a personal or certified check will be due upon delivery.

Manufacturers: **(Many resources do not list all their manufacturers. Be sure to inquire about those you are interested in, but do not see listed here.)**

HANG-IT-NOW WALLPAPER STORES
304 TRINDALE RD
ARCHDALE, NC 27263
Hours: M-F:9-6; S:9-3

Toll-Free	800-325-9494
Direct	336-431-6341
Fax	336-431-0449
Internet	

Notes: Family owned business established in 1981. Six sales consultants on staff. Wall coverings and decorator fabrics can be purchased via VISA/MC/AMEX/MO. String and grasscloth available, as well as borders. We go out of our way to find hard to find items. No minimum order. Returns allowed with a 25% restocking charge. Satisfaction guaranteed.

Manufacturers: (Many resources do not list all their manufacturers. Be sure to inquire about those you are interested in, but do not see listed here.)

COLOR HOUSE	KATZENBACH & WARREN	SUNWALL
CRUTCHFIELD	CAREY LIND DESIGNS	UNITED
EISENHART WALLCOVERINGS	SANITAS	VAN LUIT
IMPERIAL		

HARDEE'S FURNITURE WAREHOUSE
4603 S US 301
ROCKY MOUNT, NC 27806
Hours: MTThF:9-9; WS:9-5

Toll-Free	We accept collect calls.
Direct	252-977-2325
Fax	252-977-2326
Internet	

Notes: Opened in 1981. 23,000 square foot warehouse.

Manufacturers: (Many resources do not list all their manufacturers. Be sure to inquire about those you are interested in, but do not see listed here.)

AMERICAN DREW	CAROLINA FURNITURE	HUNTINGTON HOUSE
ASHLEY	CHROMCRAFT	KIMBALL
ATHENS	CRAFTMASTER	LANE
BASSETT	ENGLAND	LEA
BEECHBROOK	FAIRFIELD	LEISTERS
BEMCO	GREENE BROS	LEXINGTON
BROYHILL	HOOKER	MASTERFIELD

MOBEL
MURPHY
PETERS-REVINGTON
PULASKI
RIVERSIDE

SEALY
STANLEY
STONEVILLE
UNIVERSAL

VAUGHAN
VAUGHAN BASSETT
VENTURE
WEBB

HARDEN GALLERY
HICKORY FURNITURE MART
2220 HWY 70 SE
HICKORY, NC 28602
Hours: **M-F: 9-6; S: 9-5; Closed Sundays**

Toll-Free	
Direct	828-326-1735
Fax	
Internet	

Notes: This resource is part of the Hickory Furniture Mart complex. This showroom is one of over 80 to visit. **See Hickory Furniture Mart listing for more information.** Consolidated shipping can be arranged with other resources in this center, a standard one/third deposit is required on all orders. Most showrooms accept VISA/MC, but not all. Cash, personal or certified checks accepted by all showrooms. If you elect not to pay for your entire purchase at the time of sale, a personal or certified check will be due upon delivery.

Manufacturers: (Many resources do not list all their manufacturers. Be sure to inquire about those you are interested in, but do not see listed here.)

HARDWARE BATH & MORE
20830 COOLIDGE HWY
OAK PARK, MI 48237
Hours: **M-F:8-5:30pm**

Toll-Free	800-760-3278
Direct	
Fax	248-546-2328
Internet	email: magazine@h-b-m.com website: www.h-b-m.com

Notes: This company sells unique and high-end plumbing fixtures, hardware and lighting. It is the catalog division of Herald Wholesale, located in Oak Park, MI (see listing). Residents outside of Michigan can call and request free literature. Michigan residents are asked to call or visit their discount showroom at the same address listed above.

Manufacturers: (Many resources do not list all their manufacturers. Be sure to inquire about those you are interested in, but do not see listed here.)

ABBAKA
ACRYMET
ADIA
ALLIBERT
ALNO
AFTMANS FAUCETS
AMERICAN ART LIGHTING
AMERICAN CHINA
AMERICAN LANTERN
AMERICAN STANDARD
AMERICH
ANDRE COLLECTION
ANNE AT HOME
AQUA BRASS
AQUATIC
AQUAWARE
ARAM HARDWARE
ARROW LOCK
ARTCRAFT LIGHTING
ARTISTIC BRASS
B&W HARDWARE
BACI MIRRORS
BALDWIN HARDWARE &
ACCESSORIES
BARCLAY PLUMBING
BATES & BATES SINKS
BESA LIGHTING
BLANCO PLUMBING
BOUVET HARDWARE
BROADWAY COLLECTION
BROAN BATH CABINETS &
RANGE HOODS
CALCRYSTAL HARDWARE
CALIFORNIA FAUCETS
CASABLANCA FANS
CHAPMAN LIGHTING
CHERRY CREEK GLASS SINKS
CIFIAL FAUCETS
COLONIAL BRONZE
COLONY METALSMITH
CONCINNITY FAUCETS
CONCORD FANS
CORBETT LIGHTING
CROPUSA
DOMUS ACCESSORIES
DORNBRACHT FAUCETS
DURAVIT
ELKAY
ELK LIGHTING
EMCO HARDWARE
ESQUEMA ACCESSORIES

EUROBATH
EUROFASE LIGHTING
EUROTECH PLUMBING &
HARDWARE
EVERPURE WATER FILTERS
EVOLUTIONS LIGHTING
FRANKE PLUMBING
FREDERICK-RAMOND
LIGHTING
FRENCH REFLECTIONS
MIRRORS
FRIEDLAND CHIMES
GAINSBOROUGH
GET-A-GRIP HARDWARE
GINGER ACCESSORIES
GREENSTREET DETAILS
GROHE PLUMBING
HAFELE
HANSA AMERICA
HANSGROHE
HARRINGTON BRASS
HASTINGS COLLECTION
HYDRO SYSTEMS
WHIRLPOOLS
SAMUEL HEATH & SONS
MAURICE HERBEAU
HEWI
ILOOMINATING EXPERIENCE
LIGHTING
IN-SINK-ERATOR
ITAL BRASS
ITALIANA
LUCE LIGHTING
JACUZZI TUBS
JADO PLUMBING &
HARDWARE
JANZER MAILBOXES
JUNO LIGHTING
JUST SINKS
KALCO LIGHTING
KALLISTA
KENROY LIGHTING
KICHLER LIGHTING
KINDRED SINKS
KLUDI FAUCETS
KOCH & LOWY LIGHTING
KOHLER PLUMBING
GEORGE KOVACS
KROIN FAUCETS
KWC FAUCETS

KWIKSET DOOR HARDWARE-
TITAN
LAUFEN
LCN DOOR CLOSERS
LEBIJOU SINKS
MASTER LOCK
MAXIM LIGHTING
MILLS CUSTOM HOUSE
NUMBERS
MINKA LIGHTING
MONET
MR STEAM
MRS H'S HANDLES
MURRAY FEISS LIGHTING
MYSON TOWEL WARMERS
NEWPORT BRASS
NORSTAD POTTERY SINKS
NORWELL LIGHTING
NULCO LIGHTING
NUTONE
OASIS WHIRLPOOLS
OMNIA HARDWARE
PAUL
DECORATIVE/GREENWICH
COLLECTION
PERIOD BRASS HARDWARE
PERRIN & ROWE
PHYLRICH FAUCENTS, SINKS,
ETC
PORCHER CHINA SINKS &
WATERCLOSETS
PROGRESS LIGHTING
QUINTESSENTIALS-QII
QUOIZEL LIGHTING
ROBERO BATH CABINETS
ST THOMAS CHINA
SCHLAGE DOOR HARDWARE
SCHONBEK CRYSTAL
CHANDELIERS
SIBES ACCESSORIES
SMIDBO ACCESSORIES
SPEAKMAN
STARFIRE LIGHTING
STEAMIST
SUGATSUNE
TAYMOR ACCESSORIES
TECH LIGHTING
TEVIS & DUNLAP
THOMAS LIGHTING
THC
TON JON MIRRORS

TOTO
TOWEL WARMERS
TRIARCH INDUSTRIES
TRI-LIGHT LIGHTING
VALLI & VALLI HARDWARE
VANCE STAINLESS SINKS

VAN TEAL LIGHTING
VAXCEL LIGHTING
VITA BATH WHIRLPOOLS
VUE LIGHTING

WATERFORD CRYSTAL
LIGHTING
REID WATSON PLUMBING
WESAUNARD
WHITEHAUS
WILSHIRE LIGHTING

HARMONY SUPPLY INC
PO BOX 313
MEDFORD, MA 02155
Hours: MTWFS: 9-5; THURS: 8:00am-9:00pm

Toll-Free	
Direct	617-395-2600
Fax	617-396-8218
Internet	

Notes: In business since 1949. Wallpaper and window treatments. Designer and consultants on staff will help assist and advise customer with choices. People-oriented sales result in most customers placing additional orders and recommending them to their friends. They will go out of their way to locate items for their customers. They also manufacture their own unconditionally guaranteed line of vertical blinds and can usually ship within 24 hours. Shipping problems handled by carrier or resource. Returns within 30 day, subject to handling charge if not defective. No charge if defective. Complete order can be paid via VISA/MC. Showroom available for browsing. Can usually get any wallcovering. Over 100,000 rolls of wallpaper in stock including grass cloth and strings.

Manufacturers: (Many resources do not list all their manufacturers. Be sure to inquire about those you are interested in, but do not see listed here.)

WALLCOVERINGS:
IMPERIAL
KATZENBACH & WARREN
LAURA ASHLEY
SCHUMACHER
VAN LUIT
WALLTEX

WAVERLY

WINDOWS:
BALI
CRYSTAL PLEAT
DUETTE

HUNTER DOUGLAS
GRABER
KIRSCH
LEVOLOR
LOUVERDRAPE
VEROSOL

HARRIS LEVY, INC
278 GRAND STREET
NEW YORK, NY 10002
Hours: M-TH: 9-5; F: 9-4; SUN:9-4:30

Toll-Free	800-221-7750
Direct	212-226-3102
Fax	212-334-9360
Internet	email: harrislevy@aol.com

Notes: Established in 1894. Owner operated by the fourth generation of the founder. New York's premier discount linen shop. We specialize in the finest bed and table linens, bath and kitchen accessories, closet shop, pillows, mattress pads, down comforters and much more. Twelve consultants, 4 designers on staff. You can visit the store or call for a great catalog. Complete order can be paid by VISA/MC/DISC/AMEX/OPTIMA/CHECK/CASH/MO. Returns must be unopened in the original packaging with all tags and inserts attached, within 30 days. Satisfaction guaranteed by resource and manufacturer. Shipping is always insured and carrier is responsible for any damage.

Manufacturers: (Many resources do not list all their manufacturers. Be sure to inquire about those you are interested in, but do not see listed here.)

CANNON	MARTEX	STEVENS
CROWN CRAFT	PALAIS ROYAL	WAMSUTTA
FIELDCREST		

HEKMAN GALLERY
HICKORY FURNITURE MART
2220 HWY 70 SE
HICKORY, NC 28602
Hours: M-F: 9-6; S: 9-5; Closed Sundays

Toll-Free	
Direct	828-322-4440
Fax	
Internet	

Notes: This resource is part of the Hickory Furniture Mart complex. This showroom is one of over 80 to visit. **See Hickory Furniture Mart listing for more information.** Consolidated shipping can be arranged with other resources in this center, a standard one/third deposit is required on all orders. Most showrooms accept VISA/MC, but not all. Cash, personal or certified checks accepted by all showrooms. If you elect not to pay for your entire purchase at the time of sale, a personal or certified check will be due upon delivery.

Manufacturers: (Many resources do not list all their manufacturers. Be sure to inquire about those you are interested in, but do not see listed here.)

======

HENDRICKS FURNITURE (OWNED BY BOYLES FURNITURE)
I-40 AND FARMINGTON ROAD
MOCKSVILLE, NC 27082
Hours: **M-F: 9-6; S: 9-5**

Toll-Free	
Direct	336-998-7712
Fax	336-998-9598
Internet	website: www.Boyles.com

Notes: A standard one/third deposit is required on all orders. We're pleased to accept cash, personal or certified checks VISA/MC. If you elect not to pay for your entire purchase at the time of sale, a personal or certified check will be due upon delivery. **IMPORTANT CORPORATE NUMBERS: Customer Service: 828-345-5280; Delivery Info: 828-345-5275; Order Status: 828-345-5290; Billing Questions: 828-345-5206**

Manufacturers: (Many resources do not list all their manufacturers. Be sure to inquire about those you are interested in, but do not see listed here.)

MAJOR LINES:
AMERICAN DREW
BAKER
BERNHARDT
BEVAN FUNNELL
BRADINGTON YOUNG
BROYHILL
CENTURY
COUNCILL
HARDEN
HEKMAN
HENKEL HARRIS
HENKEL MOORE

HENREDON
HICKORY CHAIR
HICKORY WHITE
HOOKER
JEFFCO
KARGES
KINCAID
KINGSDOWN
LaBARGE
LANE
LEATHERCRAFT
LEXINGTON

MAITLAND SMITH
MARGE CARSON
MOTIONCRAFT
PENNSYLVANIA HOUSE
RIVERSIDE
SEALY
SLIGH
SOUTHWOOD
STANLEY
THOMASVILLE
UNIVERSAL

HENKEL HARRIS GALLERY
HICKORY FURNITURE MART
2220 HWY 70 SE
HICKORY, NC 28602
Hours: **M-F: 9-6; S: 9-5; Closed Sundays**

Toll-Free	
Direct	828-326-1740
Fax	
Internet	

Notes: This resource is part of the Hickory Furniture Mart complex. This showroom is one of over 80 to visit. **See Hickory Furniture Mart listing for more information.** Consolidated shipping can be arranged with other resources in this center, a standard one/third deposit is required on all orders. Most showrooms accept VISA/MC, but not all. Cash, personal or certified checks accepted by all showrooms. If you elect not to pay for your entire purchase at the time of sale, a personal or certified check will be due upon delivery.

Manufacturers: (Many resources do not list all their manufacturers. Be sure to inquire about those you are interested in, but do not see listed here.)

HENREDON FACTORY OUTLET
3943 NEW BERN AVE
RALEIGH, NC 27610-1332
Hours: **M-S: 10-6; Sun: 1-6**

Toll-Free	
Direct	919-212-8250
Fax	919-212-8249
Internet	

Notes: Manufacturer outlet. Look for good deals here, in person especially.

Manufacturers: (Many resources do not list all their manufacturers. Be sure to inquire about those you are interested in, but do not see listed here.)
HENREDON

HENREDON FACTORY OUTLET
HICKORY FURNITURE MART
2220 HWY 70 SE
HICKORY, NC 28602
Hours: **M-F: 9-6; S: 9-5; Closed Sundays**

Toll-Free	
Direct	828-322-7111
Fax	828-322-6839
Internet	

Notes: Great finds available here if you can visit. Salespeople will try to help out over the phone. This resource is part of the Hickory Furniture Mart complex. This showroom is one of over 80 to visit. **See Hickory Furniture Mart listing for more information.** Consolidated shipping can be arranged with other resources in this center, a standard one/third deposit is required on all orders. Most showrooms accept VISA/MC, but not all. Cash, personal or certified checks accepted by all showrooms. If you elect not to pay for your entire purchase at the time of sale, a personal or certified check will be due upon delivery.

Manufacturers: **(Many resources do not list all their manufacturers. Be sure to inquire about those you are interested in, but do not see listed here.)**

HENREDON FURNITURE CLEARANCE
ROUTE 3, BOX 379
SPRUCE PINE, NC 28777-8603
Hours: **M-S: 10-6; Closed Sunday**

Toll-Free	
Direct	704-765-1320
Fax	704-765-4811
Internet	

Notes: Manufacturer outlet.

Manufacturers: **(Many resources do not list all their manufacturers. Be sure to inquire about those you are interested in, but do not see listed here.)**
HENREDON

HENREDON/DREXEL HERITAGE FACTORY OUTLET
3004A PARQUET DR
DALTON, GA 30720
Hours: **M-S: 9-5**

Toll-Free	
Direct	706-270-8250
Fax	706-270-8560
Internet	

Notes: Manufacturer outlet.

Manufacturers: (Many resources do not list all their manufacturers. Be sure to inquire about those you are interested in, but do not see listed here.)
DREXEL HERITAGE   HENREDON

HENREDON GALLERY
HICKORY FURNITURE MART
2220 HWY 70 SE
HICKORY, NC 28602
Hours: **M-F: 9-6; S: 9-5; Closed Sundays**

Toll-Free	
Direct	828-326-1740
Fax	
Internet	

Notes: This resource is part of the Hickory Furniture Mart complex. This showroom is one of over 80 to visit. **See Hickory Furniture Mart listing for more information.** Consolidated shipping can be arranged with other resources in this center, a standard one/third deposit is required on all orders. Most showrooms accept VISA/MC, but not all. Cash, personal or certified checks accepted by all showrooms. If you elect not to pay for your entire purchase at the time of sale, a personal or certified check will be due upon delivery.

Manufacturers: (Many resources do not list all their manufacturers. Be sure to inquire about those you are interested in, but do not see listed here.)

Resource Directory

HERALD WHOLESALE
20830 COOLIDGE HWY
OAK PARK, MI 48237
Hours: **M-F:8-5:30pm**

Toll-Free	800-760-3278
Direct	248-398-4560
Fax	248-546-2328
Internet	**email:** magazine@h-b-m.com **website:** www.h-b-m.com

Notes: This company sells unique and high-end plumbing fixtures, hardware and lighting. Residents outside of Michigan can call and request free literature through their discount catalog division, Hardware, Bath and More (see listing).

Manufacturers: (Many resources do not list all their manufacturers. Be sure to inquire about those you are interested in, but do not see listed here.)

ABBAKA
ACRYMET
ADIA
ALLIBERT
ALNO
AFTMANS FAUCETS
AMERICAN ART LIGHTING
AMERICAN CHINA
AMERICAN LANTERN
AMERICAN STANDARD
AMERICH
ANDRE COLLECTION
ANNE AT HOME
AQUA BRASS
AQUATIC
AQUAWARE
ARAM HARDWARE
ARROW LOCK
ARTCRAFT LIGHTING
ARTISTIC BRASS
B&W HARDWARE
BACI MIRRORS
BALDWIN HARDWARE &
ACCESSORIES
BARCLAY PLUMBING
BATES & BATES SINKS
BESA LIGHTING
BLANCO PLUMBING
BOUVET HARDWARE
BROADWAY COLLECTION
BROAN BATH CABINETS &
RANGE HOODS
CALCRYSTAL HARDWARE
CALIFORNIA FAUCETS
CASABLANCA FANS

CHAPMAN LIGHTING
CHERRY CREEK GLASS SINKS
CIFIAL FAUCETS
COLONIAL BRONZE
COLONY METALSMITH
CONCINNITY FAUCETS
CONCORD FANS
CORBETT LIGHTING
CROPUSA
DOMUS ACCESSORIES
DORNBRACHT FAUCETS
DURAVIT
ELKAY
ELK LIGHTING
EMCO HARDWARE
ESQUEMA ACCESSORIES
EUROBATH
EUROFASE LIGHTING
EUROTECH PLUMBING &
HARDWARE
EVERPURE WATER FILTERS
EVOLUTIONS LIGHTING
FRANKE PLUMBING
FREDERICK-RAMOND
LIGHTING
FRENCH REFLECTIONS
MIRRORS
FRIEDLAND CHIMES
GAINSBOROUGH
GET-A-GRIP HARDWARE
GINGER ACCESSORIES
GREENSTREET DETAILS
GROHE PLUMBING
HAFELE
HANSA AMERICA

HANSGROHE
HARRINGTON BRASS
HASTINGS COLLECTION
HYDRO SYSTEMS
WHIRLPOOLS
SAMUEL HEATH & SONS
MAURICE HERBEAU
HEWI
ILOOMINATING EXPERIENCE
LIGHTING
IN-SINK-ERATOR
ITAL BRASS
ITALIANA
LUCE LIGHTING
JACUZZI TUBS
JADO PLUMBING &
HARDWARE
JANZER MAILBOXES
JUNO LIGHTING
JUST SINKS
KALCO LIGHTING
KALLISTA
KENROY LIGHTING
KICHLER LIGHTING
KINDRED SINKS
KLUDI FAUCETS
KOCH & LOWY LIGHTING
KOHLER PLUMBING
GEORGE KOVACS
KROIN FAUCETS
KWC FAUCETS
KWIKSET DOOR HARDWARE-
TITAN
LAUFEN
LCN DOOR CLOSERS

LEBIJOU SINKS
MASTER LOCK
MAXIM LIGHTING
MILLS CUSTOM HOUSE
NUMBERS
MINKA LIGHTING
MONET
MR STEAM
MRS H'S HANDLES
MURRAY FEISS LIGHTING
MYSON TOWEL WARMERS
NEWPORT BRASS
NORSTAD POTTERY SINKS
NORWELL LIGHTING
NULCO LIGHTING
NUTONE
OASIS WHIRLPOOLS
OMNIA HARDWARE
PAUL
DECORATIVE/GREENWICH
COLLECTION

PERIOD BRASS HARDWARE
PERRIN & ROWE
PHYLRICH FAUCENTS, SINKS,
ETC
PORCHER CHINA SINKS &
WATERCLOSETS
PROGRESS LIGHTING
QUINTESSENTIALS-QII
QUOIZEL LIGHTING
ROBERO BATH CABINETS
ST THOMAS CHINA
SCHLAGE DOOR HARDWARE
SCHONBEK CRYSTAL
CHANDELIERS
SIBES ACCESSORIES
SMIDBO ACCESSORIES
SPEAKMAN
STARFIRE LIGHTING
STEAMIST
SUGATSUNE
TAYMOR ACCESSORIES

TECH LIGHTING
TEVIS & DUNLAP
THOMAS LIGHTING
THC
TON JON MIRRORS
TOTO
TOWEL WARMERS
TRIARCH INDUSTRIES
TRI-LIGHT LIGHTING
VALLI & VALLI HARDWARE
VANCE STAINLESS SINKS
VAN TEAL LIGHTING
VAXCEL LIGHTING
VITA BATH WHIRLPOOLS
VUE LIGHTING
WATERFORD CRYSTAL
LIGHTING
REID WATSON PLUMBING
WESAUNARD
WHITEHAUS
WILSHIRE LIGHTING

HERITAGE HOUSE FURNITURE
917 LIBERTY RD
HIGH POINT, NC 27262
Hours: **M-F: 9-5**

Toll-Free	
Direct	336-431-5926
Fax	
Internet	

Notes:

Manufacturers: **(Many resources do not list all their manufacturers. Be sure to inquire about those you are interested in, but do not see listed here.)**

HICKORY CHAIR FACTORY OUTLET
HICKORY FURNITURE MART
2220 HWY 70 SE
HICKORY, NC 28602
Hours: **M-F: 9-6; S: 9-5; Closed Sundays**

Toll-Free	
Direct	828-324-2442
Fax	828-464-9964
Internet	

Notes: This resource is part of the Hickory Furniture Mart complex. This showroom is one of over 80 to visit. **See Hickory Furniture Mart listing for more information.** Consolidated shipping can be arranged with other resources in this center, a standard one/third deposit is required on all orders. Most showrooms accept VISA/MC, but not all. Cash, personal or certified checks accepted by all showrooms. If you elect not to pay for your entire purchase at the time of sale, a personal or certified check will be due upon delivery.

Manufacturers: (Many resources do not list all their manufacturers. Be sure to inquire about those you are interested in, but do not see listed here.)
HICKORY CHAIR

HICKORY CHAIR GALLERY
HICKORY FURNITURE MART
2220 HWY 70 SE
HICKORY, NC 28602
Hours: **M-F: 9-6; S: 9-5; Closed Sundays**

Toll-Free	
Direct	828-326-1740
Fax	
Internet	

Notes: This resource is part of the Hickory Furniture Mart complex. This showroom is one of over 80 to visit. **See Hickory Furniture Mart listing for more information.** Consolidated shipping can be arranged with other resources in this center, a standard one/third deposit is required on all orders. Most showrooms accept VISA/MC, but not all. Cash, personal or certified checks accepted by all showrooms. If you elect not to pay for your entire purchase at the time of sale, a personal or certified check will be due upon delivery.

Manufacturers: (Many resources do not list all their manufacturers. Be sure to inquire

about those you are interested in, but do not see listed here.)

═══════════════════════

HICKORY FURNITURE MART FURNITURE CLEARANCE CENTER
66 HWY 321 NW
HICKORY, NC 28601
Hours: **M-F: 9-6; S: 9-5; Closed Sundays**

Toll-Free	
Direct	828-323-1558
Fax	
Internet	

Notes: Many, many manufacturers. This is the clearance center for the Hickory Furniture Mart. It changes all the time and has a great deal of "finds". Large warehouse. You can consolidate purchases from the Hickory Furniture Mart with the clearance center also.

Manufacturers: **(Many resources do not list all their manufacturers. Be sure to inquire about those you are interested in, but do not see listed here.)**

═══════════════════════

HICKORY FURNITURE MART
2220 US 70 SE
HICKORY, NC 28602
Hours: **M-F: 9-6; S: 9-5; Closed Sundays**

Toll-Free	800-462-MART (462-6278)
Direct	828-322-3510
Fax	828-322-1132
Internet	**email:** www.hickoryfurniture.com **web site:** http://www.webcom.com~hickory/

Notes: Hickory Furniture Mart is the largest furniture complex of its kind open to the public in the nation. Factory outlets for some of the most prestigious names offer deeply discounted prices. Over eighty galleries and factory outlets operate in this 17-acre center, which also has a hotel on the property. Elegantly appointed showrooms carry more than 700 lines of furniture, accessories, bedding, linens, original art, gifts, imports, wicker, lighting, floor and wall coverings and bath fixtures, plus antiques and collectibles. Stores primarily use three reputable carriers who do in-home set-up. Damaged goods are worked out by shipper and stores at no cost to the customer. Payment for delivery is due at the time of delivery by cash or cashier's check. Every store has sales consultants and designers on staff. Customers can and should visit this facility. Thomasville, Drexel Heritage, Bernhardt and Pennsylvania House can be purchased in person. If you have a day or two to spend in North Carolina, this is the place. You can consolidate shipments from all resources for best cost and the Hickory Furniture Mart stands behind each showroom.

Manufacturers: **(Many resources do not list all their manufacturers. Be sure to inquire about those you are interested in, but do not see listed here.)**

RESOURCES REPRESENTED
(Please note that all area codes are 828, effective 3/22/98)

AMERICAN DREW GALLERY
328-8688

BAKER GALLERY
326-1740

BEACON HILL FACTORY OUTLET
324-2220

BERNHARDT GALLERY
326-1735

BOYLES GALLERY
326-1740

BOYLES SHOWCASE
326-1735

BRADINGTON YOUNG
328-5257

BROYHILL SHOWCASE GALLERY
324-9467

CR LAINE GALLERY
322-4440

CABOT GALLERY
345-0409

CANADEL GALLERY
324-7742

CARSONS GALLERY
322-6602

CENTURY FACTORY OUTLET
324-2442

CENTURY FURNITURE GALLERY
322-6602

CLASSIC LEATHER GALLERY
324-1776

CLASSIC ORIENTAL RUGS
326-1735

CLAYTON MARCUS GALLERY
328-8688

COCHRANE GALLERY
322-6602

COMFORT ZONE
326-9224

CONTEMPORARY GALLERY
324-1776

COURISTAN FACTORY OUTLET
345-0409

DESIGNING WOMEN
328-5200

COUNCILL

CRAFTSMEN/BOYLES
326-1740

DON LAMOR, INC
324-1776

DREXEL HERITAGE
326-1060

DREXEL HERITAGE FACTORY OUTLET
324-2220

DREXEL STUDIO
326-1735

FLEXSTEEL GALLERY
322-6602

FRANKLIN PLACE
322-5539

GALLERY OF LIGHTS
324-6337

GENERATIONS
322-7275

HANCOCK & MOORE GALLERY
326-1735

HARDEN GALLERY
326-1735

HEKMAN GALLERY
322-4440

HENKEL HARRIS GALLERY
326-1740

HENREDON FACTORY OUTLET
322-7111

HENREDON GALLERY
326-1735

HICKORY CHAIR FACTORY OUTLET
324-2442

HICKORY CHAIR GALLERY
326-1740

HICKORY PARK FURNITURE GALLERIES
322-4440

HICKORY FRY
322-4440

HICKORY WHITE GALLERY
326-1740

HIGHLAND HOUSE GALLERY
322-6602

HOME FOCUS BY PALLISER
324-7742

HOOKER GALLERY
326-1735

HOUSE OF MIRRORS BY HICKORY HOME ACCENTS
323-8893

J ROYALE GALLERY
324-7742

JEFFCO
326-1735

KARGES GALLERY
326-1735

KIMBALL GALLERY
324-7742

KINCAID GALLERY
322-4440

LaBARGE FACTORY OUTLET
324-2220

LANE GALLERY
326-1735

LEXINGTON GALLERY
326-1709

MAITLAND SMITH FACTORY OUTLET
324-2220

MARGE CARSON GALLERY
326-1735

MART SHIPPING ASSOCIATION
800-874-6486

MORGAN STEWART GALLERY
324-4040

MOTIONCRAFT GALLERY
326-1735

NATIONAL ART GALLERY
324-9400

NATIONAL CLOCK GALLERY
324-9400

NOSTALGIA GALLERY
345-0409

PALLISER
324-7742

PEARSON GALLERY
322-6602

PENNSYLVANIA HOUSE GALLERY
324-1776

PRECEDENT GALLERY
326-1735

REFLECTIONS
327-8485

RESOURCE DESIGN
322-3161

RHONEY FURNITURE HOUSE

328-8688
ROBERT BERGELIN
345-1500
ROWE GALLERY
322-4440
SAM MOORE GALLERY
322-6602
SEASONS OUTDOOR GALLERY
322-9445
SHERRILL GALLERY
326-1735
SOUTHERN DESIGNS
328-8855
STANLEY GALLERY
326-1735
THE RUG ROOM
324-1776
THE WORK STATION
322-4440
THOMASVILLE GALLERY
326-1740
UNIVERSAL GALLERY
322-6602
VANGUARD GALLERY
324-1776
VIRGINIA HOUSE GALLERY
328-8855
WAVERLY
322-3161
WEIMAN GALLERY
324-1776
WILDERMERE
322-6602
ZAGAROLI CLASSICS
328-3373
SHOPS AT THE MART:
HOLIDAY PATIO
345-0882

MANUFACTURERS
AA IMPORTS
AA LAUN
ACACIA
ACCENT FINE ARTS
ACCENTRICS BY PULASKI
ACCESS
ACCESSORIES ABROAD
ACRYLIC FASHION
ACTION BY LANE
ADJUSTA-POST
ALACARTE
ALADDIN LIGHT LIFTS
ALAN CAMPBELL
ALAN WHITE
ALEXANDER JULIAN
ALEXVALE
ALLIBERT

ALLUSIONS
AMBIANCE LIGHTING &
ACCESSORIES
AMERICAN BRONZE
AMERICAN DECOR
AMERICAN DREW
AMERICAN OF MARTINSVILLE
ANDRE BON
ANDRE ORIGINALS
ANDREA
ANDREW PEARSON
ANTLER DESIGN
ARBEK
ARCHIPED
ARCHITECTURAL
MASTERWORKS
ARDLEY HALL
ARIEL OF FRANCE
ART & COMMERCE
ART & FRAME
ART CRAFT
ART DE GALI
ART GALLERY
ART HORIZONS
ARTE DE MEXICO
ARTIMMAGE
ARTISAN HOUSE
ARTISAN LAMPS
ARTISTICA
ARTMASTER STUDIOS
ARTMAX
AS YOU LIKE IT
ASHLEY
ASHTON
ASIART
ASSEMBLAAGE
ATHOL
ATILLA'S BAYSHORE
AUSTIN
AXI DESIGNS
BAKER
BALDWIN BATH ACCESSORIES
BALDWIN BRASS
BARCALOUNGER
BARCLAY
BARLOW TYRIE
BASIC SOURCE
BASSETT MCNAB
BASTA SOLE UMBRELLAS
BDI
BEACH
BEACON HILL SHOWROOM
BEAUCHAMP
BEKA CASTING
BENCHCRAFT (LEATHER)
BENCHCRAFT (RATTAN)
BENICIA DAYBEDS
BENNETT & CO
BERKELEY

BERKLINE
BERKSHIRE
BERNHARDT
BETH WEISSMAN LAMPS
BETTIS BROOKE CO
BEVAN FUNNELL
BIBI CONTINENTAL
BIG FISH, INC
BIG SKY CARVERS
BLACKSMITH SHOP
BOB TIMBERLAKE
BOBBO
BOSTON ROCKER
BOUSSAC
BOYD
BRADBURN GALLERY
BRADINGTON YOUNG
BRADY
BRASSCRAFTERS
BRETT AUSTIN
BRITISH COLLECTORS
BRITISH TRADITIONS
BROWN JORDAN
BROWN STREET
BROYHILL
BROYHILL PREMIER
BRUNSCHWIG & FILS
BUTLER
CAL-BEAR
CAL-STYLE
CAMBRIDGE LAMPS
CANADEL
CANDILES TA
CAROLINA MIRROR
CARSON'S
CARTER
CARVER'S GUILD
CASA BIQUE
CASA RUSTICA
CASA STRADIVARI
CASAFINA
CASEY COLLECTION
CAST CLASSICS
CASTILLIAN
CASUAL LAMP
CBS IMPORTS
CCM
CEBU
CENTURY
CENTURY OUTLET
CHAIRWORKS
CHAPMAN
CHARLES ADRIAN
CHARLES SADEK
CHARLESTON FORGE
CHATHAM COUNTY
CHATHAM REPRODUCTIONS
CHELSEA HOUSE
CHERRY POND

CHILDCRAFT
CHRISTOPHER HYLAN
CHROMCRAFT
CJC
CLARENCE HOUSE
CLARK CASUAL
CLASSIC ART
CLASSIC GEORGIAN
CLASSIC LEATHER
CLASSIC LIGHTING
CLASSIC ORIENTAL RUGS
CLAYTON & CO
CLAYTON MARCUS
CLOVER
CLYDE PEARSON
COCHRANE
COLLECTIONS '85
COLLEZIONE EUROPA
COMFORT DESIGNS
CONOVER CHAIR
CONSO
CONTEMPO ARTS
COOPER CLASSICS
COPPER CANYON
CORBETT
CORONA
CORSICAN BEDS
COUNCILL CRAFTSMEN
COUNTRY TRADITIONS
COURISTAN
COURTLEIGH
COWTAN & TOUT
COX MANUFACTURING
CR LAINE
CRAFT-TEX
CRAFTIQUE
CRAFTWORK GUILD
CRAWFORD OF JAMESTOWN
CREATIONS ACRYLICS
CREATIONS AT DALLAS
CREATIVE ELEGANCE
CREATIVE FINE ARTS
CREATIVE LIGHTING
CREATIVE METAL & WOOD
CRISTAL
CROSSWINDS
CRYSTAL CLEAR
CRYSTALROMA
CTH
CURRY & CO
D & F WICKER
DALE TIFFANY
DANSEN
DAPHNE TYSON
DAUPHINE MIRROR CO
DAVID WINTERS COTTAGES
DAVIS & DAVIS RUGS
DAYVA COVERS
DEBOURNAIS

DECORATIVE ARTS
DECORATIVE CRAFTS
DECORATOR'S WALK
DECOY
DELTA
DENNY LAMP
DENUNZIO
DESIGN GUILD
DESIGN LIGHTING
DESIGN MATERIALS
DESIGN PRINTERY
DESIGN SOUTH
DESIGNER FOUNTAIN
DESIGN MASTER
DESIGNS UNLIMITED
DEWOOLFSON DOWN
DIA
DIANE LAMP SHADES
DILLON
DINAIRE
DINICO
DIRECTIONAL
DISQUE CHAIR
DISTINCTION LEATHER
DOLBY CASHIER
DOUGLAS
DREAMWEAVERS
DRESHER
DREXEL
DREXEL HERITAGE
DUCKS UNLIMITED
DUMMY BOOK
DURA WICKER
DUTAILIER
EAGLE CRAFT
EKORNES
ELDEN COLLECTIONS
ELDRED WHEELER
ELEMENTS BY GRAPEVINE
ELGEEWEST
ELITE MANUFACTURING
ELK LIGHTING
ELLO
EMERSON ET CIE
EMERSON LEATHER
ENESCO
ENGLISH IMPORTS
ENTREE BY LaBARGE
EPOCH COLLECTION
ERNEST STOECKLIN
EUROFASE
EVANS DESIGNS
EXCELSIOR
EXECUTIVE IMPORTS
FABRICUT
FAIRFIELD
FASCO
FASHION BED
FATTORI STAR

FAUSTIG
FEIZY RUGS
FETCO
FINE ARTS LAMPS
FINE ARTS LTD
FLEXSTEEL
FLORAL ART
FLORITA NOVA
FONTHILL LTD
FORECAST
FOREIGN ACCENTS
FOXFIRE
FRAMES & ARTS
FRANBURG
FRANKLIN PLACE
FREDERICK COOPER
FREDERICK EDWARD
FREDRICK-RAMOND
FREMARC DESIGNS
FRENCH HERITAGE
FRIEDMAN BROS MIRRORS
FROELICH
FURNITURE GUILD
GARCIA IMPORTS
GATCO
GENTLEMAN'S QUARTERS
GEORGE KOVACS LIGHTING
GEORGIAN ART
GEORGIAN FURNISHINGS
GEORGIO LEONI
GILLIS COMPANY
GIORGIO COLLECTION
GLASS ARTS
GLOBAL FURNITURE
GLOBER/REFLECTIONS
GLOSTER
GMS IMPORTS
GRAY WATKINS
GREAT CITY TRADERS
GREEFF WALLPAPERS &
FABRICS
GREG SHEZ
GROSFILLEX
GUARDSMAN
GUILDMASTER
GUY CHADDOCK
HABERSHAM PLANTATION
HAMMARY
HAMPSTEAD
HANCOCK & MOORE
HANCOCK FURNITURE
HANOVER
HARBOUR LIGHTS
HARDEN
HART
HEKMAN
HEN FEATHERS & CO
HENKEL HARRIS
HENKEL MOORE

HENREDON
HENRY LINK
HERITAGE
HERSCHELL'S
HI-LITE
HICKORY CHAIR
HICKORY CHAIR OUTLET
HICKORY FRY
HICKORY LEATHER
HICKORY WHITE
HIDE COMPANY
HIGH POINT
HIGHLAND HOUSE
HIGHLIGHT
HINES & CO
HINKLEY LIGHTING
HITCHCOCK CHAIR
HOLLY GREEN
HOLLYWOODS
HOMECREST
HOOD
HOOKER
HORIZONS INTERNATIONAL
HOUSE PARTS
HOWARD MILLER CLOCKS
HUDSON RIVER
HUGH COCHRAN
HUNTING BOARD
HUNTINGTON HOUSE
HYUNDAI FURNITURE
ID KIDS
ILOOMINATING EXPERIENCE
INTERLUDE
ITAL DESIGN
ITALIANA LUCE
J ROYALE
JAB
JAC DEY
JACK LENOR LARSEN
JAGUAR DESIGNS
JAMES R MOTOR
JAMES STEWART & SONS
JASPER CABINET
JAYMAR
JDI
JEFFCO
JENE'S COLLECTION
JENSEN JARRAH
JOE COGGINS
JOHN CHARLES DESIGNS
JOHN MCGILL LAMPS
JOHN RICHARD COLLECTION
JOHN WIDDICOMB
JOHNSTON CASUALS
JONDY SOIL SHIELD
JRW
JSF INDUSTRIES
JW STANNARD CHIMES
KAISER KUHN LIGHTING

KALCO
KARGES
KAS ORIENTAL RUGS
KATCO DESIGN INC
KATZENBACH & WARREN
KELLER
KENROY
KEY CITY
KIMBALL
KIMBALL/VICTORIAN
KINCAID
KINDER HARRIS
KING HICKORY
KINGSDOWN
KINGSLEY-BATES
KITCHLER
KNF DESIGNS
KNOB CREEK
KOCH
KOCH & LOWY LAMPS
KRAVET FABRICS
KRISTOLINA
KROEHLER
KRUPNICK BROS
LaBARGE
LAMONTAGE
LAMPCRAFTERS, INC
LANE
LANE VENTURE
LAURA LEE DESIGNS
LAZAR
LEA
LEATHERMARK
LEATHERTREND
LEATHERWORKS
LEDA
LEE INDUSTRIES
LEE JOFA
LEEAZANNE
LEGRAND
LENOX LAMPS
LEXINGTON
LIBRARY LAMPS
LIGHTING ENTERPRISES
LILLIAN AUGUST
LINA'S INTERIORS
LINEAGE
LINK TAYLOR
LITTLE BRIDGE LANE
LLOYD FLANDERS
LONG COAST LAMPS
LORTS
LOTFY & SONS
LOTUS ARTS
LOUIS DE POORTERE
LOUIS W BOWEN
LT MOSES WILLARD
LUCIA DESIGNS
LUNAR

LUX ART SILKS
LYON SHAW
MAC SCULPTURE
MADISON AVENUE
MADISON SQUARE
MAITLAND SMITH
MAOR LIGHTING
MARBRO LAMPS
MARGE CARSON
MARLOW
MASSOUD UPHOLSTERY
MASTERCRAFT
MASTERLOOMS
MATTEO
MAX HOWARD
MAXIM
MAXTON
McFARLINS
McKAY TABLE PADS
McKINLEY LEATHER
MEADOWCRAFT
MER CORPORATION
METROPOLITAN LIGHTING
MEYDA TIFFANY
MICHAEL THOMAS
MICHAELIAN & KOHLBERG
MICHAELS CO
MIKHAIL DARAFEEV
MILLENDER
MILLENIUM
MILLER DESK
MILLER IMPORTS
MILLIKEN RUGS
MINKA-LAVERY
MOBEL
MODA LIGHTING
MOHAWK
MOLLA
MONTAGE
MOONLIGHT TIFFANY LAMP &
FIXTURES
MOONLIGHTING
MOOSEHEAD
MORGAN STEWART
MOTIONCRAFT
MOTTAHEDEH
MP IMPORTS
MUROBELLO
NAGYKERY IMPORTS
NAPTIME
NATHAN HALE
NATIONAL MT AIRY
NATURAL DECORATIONS
NATUZZI
NICHOLS & STONE
NOBILLIS-FONTAN
NOJO
NORA FENTON
NORBERT ROESSLER

NORTHEAST LANTERN, LTD
NOSTALGIA
NOURY & SONS
NULCO
NULL INDUSTRIES
NUTONE
OGGETTI
OHIO TABLE PADS
OLD HICKORY TANNERY
OLD WORLD WEAVERS
OLYMPIA LIGHTING
ONE OF A KIND
ORDEREST
ORIENTAL ACCENTS
ORIENTAL LACQUER
ORIENTAL PRODUCTS
ORIENTAL WEAVERS RUGS
ORIENTAL WEAVERS USA
ORIGO DESIGNS
OUTDOOR LIFESTYLE
P COLLINS
PACIFIC COAST LIGHTING
PALLISER
PALMER HOME COLLECTION
PANDE CAMERON RUGS
PARAGON DECORS
PARK AVENUE
PARK IMPORTS
PARKER SOUTHERN
PASTEL
PAUL ROBERT
PAWLEY'S ISLAND
HAMMOCKS
PAYNE FABRICS
PAYNE STREET IMPORTS
PENDULES CLOCKS
PENNSYLVANIA CLASSICS
PENNSYLVANIA HOUSE
PENTURA
PETERS-REVINGTON
PHILIP WHITNEY
PHILLIPS LEATHER
PHOENIX ART
PHOENIX GALLERIES
PIEFA ART STONE
PIERI
PINDLER & PINDLER
PLATT
POLOMA PICASSO
POLYWOOD
POMEROY COLLECTION
POMPEII
PORT ROYAL
POWELL
PRECEDENT
PROGRESS LIGHTING
PULASKI
QUADRILLE
QUALITY LAMP

QUEEN'S VIEW
QUINTESSA ART
QUOIZEL
QUORUM
RAJ
RALPH LAUREN FABRICS
RALPH LAUREN WALLPAPERS
RAYMOND WAITES
REGENCY HOUSE
RELAX-R
RELIANCE LAMPS
REMBRANDT LAMPS
REPROCRAFTERS
RESTONIC
REX
RICHARDSON BROS
RIVERSIDE
RIVERWALK
ROBERT ALLEN
ROBERT BERGELIN CO
ROBERT GRACE
RON FISHER
ROSE CUMMINGS
ROWE
ROYAL DESIGNS
ROYAL PATINA
RUG HOLD
RUG MARKET
S. HARRIS & CO
SADEK
SAGEFIELD LEATHER
SALEM SQUARE
SAM MOORE
SAMAD BROS
SAMARCAND
SAMSONITE
SANDERSON
SARATOGA
SARREID LTD
SCALAMANDRE
SCHOLTE TABLE
SCHONBEK
SCHUMACHER
SEALY FURNITURE
SEALY LEATHER
SECOND AVE GREAT STUFF
SEDGEFIELD LAMP
SERTA
SHADY LADY
SHALOM BROS
SHELLY'S CUSHIONS &
UMBRELLAS
SHERIDAN
SHERMAG
SHERRILL
SHUFORD BY CENTURY
SIGNATURE RUGS
SIMMONS
SIMMONS MATTRESS

SINOUS
SK PRODUCTS
SKILLCRAFT
SLEEP WORKS
SLIGH
SOICHER-MARIN FINE ARTS
SOMERSET
SOUTH SEAS RATTAN
SOUTHAMPTON
SOUTHERN OF CONOVER
SOUTHWESTERN IMPORTS
SOUTHWOOD
REPRODUCTIONS
SPEER LIGHTING
SPINNING WHEEL RUGS
SPRING AIR
STAKMORE
STANFORD
STANLEY
STANTON COOPER
STATESVILLE CHAIR
STATTON
STIFFEL
STONE ART
STONE COUNTRY IRONWORKS
STONELEIGH
STOTTER
STRATOLOUNGER
STROHEIM & ROMANN
STYLE UPHOLSTERY
SUMMER CLASSICS
SUPERIOR
SUSTAINABLE LIFESTYLES
SWAIM DESIGNS
TAPESTRIES LTD
TAYLOR KING UPHOLSTERY &
LEATHER
TELESCOPE
TEMPLE
TEXTILLERY
TEXTRA
THAYER COGGIN
THIEF RIVER LINEN
THOMAS BLAKEMORE
THOMAS LIGHTING
THOMASVILLE
THOMASVILLE ACCESSORIES
THREE COINS IMPORTS
TIFFANY
TIMBERLAKE
TIMELESS BEDDING
TIMMERMAN
TODAY'S HOME UPHOLSTERY
TOEPPERWEINS
TOLTEC
TOM SEELY
TOM THUMB LIGHTING
TOMLIN DESIGNS
TOP BRASS

TOUCHSTONE FINE ARTS
TRADITION HOUSE
TRADITIONAL HEIRLOOMS
TRADITION FRANCE
TRANSGLOBE
TRESSARD
TRI-ARC
TRICOMFORT
TROPITONE
TROSBY
TROY LIGHTING
TRYMAR LAMPS
TUCKER DESIGNS
TUSCANA
TWO DAY DESIGNS
UNIQUE ORIGINALS
UNITED DESIGN
UNIVERSAL
URBAN WOODS
UTTERMOST MIRRORS
VAN LUIT
VAN PATTEN CURIOS
VAN TEAL
VANGUARD

VANGUARD STUDIOS
VAUGHAN
VELCO
VENEMAN
VENETIAN TRADERS
VENTURE
VINEYARD
VIRGINIA HOUSE
VIRGINIA METALCRAFTERS
WALKER MARLEN
WAMBOLD
WARA
WATERFORD CRYSTAL
WATERFORD FURNITURE
WAVERLY
WAVERLY & SCHUMACHER
WEATHERCRAFT
WEATHERMASTER
WEIMAN CO
WEINSTOCK
WEISS & BIHELLER
WELLINGTON HALL
WESLEY ALLEN
WESLEY BOBER

WESTGATE
WHITECRAFT
WHITTEMORE SHERRILL
WILDWOOD
WILDWOOD LAMPS
WILLOW CREEK
WILSHIRE
WINDSOR DESIGN
WINNERS ONLY
WINSTON
WISCONSIN FURNITURE
WOODARD
WOODMARK
WORLD GLASS IMPORTS
WORLD IMPORTS
WRIGHT TABLE CO
YORKSHIRE HOUSE INC
YOUNG AMERICA BY STANLEY
ZAGAROLI CLASSICS
ZINNISSER

====================

HICKORY PARK FURNITURE GALLERIES
THE ATRIUM
430 SOUTH MAIN ST
HIGH POINT, NC 27262
Hours: M-F:9-6; S: 9-5

Toll-Free	
Direct	336-883-8300
Fax	336-883-9047
Internet	

Notes: Part of the Atrium complex. Worth visiting, showrooms available. See **Atrium Furniture Showroom** listing for more information. Transitional, traditional and contemporary furniture. Lane action motion furniture with a large selection of recliners and motion sofas, love seats and sectionals. Hammary upholstery and occasional tables, bar stools by Style, Timmerman and Dinaire. Lea bedrooms, Daystrom dinettes and a large selection of children's furniture.

Manufacturers: (Many resources do not list all their manufacturers. Be sure to inquire about those you are interested in, but do not see listed here.)

DAYSTROM	HOOD	STYLE
DINAIRE	LANE	TIMMERMAN
HAMMARY	LEA	

HICKORY PARK FURNITURE GALLERIES
HICKORY FURNITURE MART
2220 HWY 70 SE
HICKORY, NC 28602
Hours: M-F: 9-6; S: 9-5; Closed Sundays

Toll-Free	
Direct	828-322-4440
Fax	828-322-1454
Internet	**email:** hparksales@hickorypark.com **web site:** www.hickorypark.com

Notes: Established 1983. Four members of staff of eight have design degrees. 25% deposit, balance when complete, freight upon delivery. VISA/MC/CHECK. Returns are handled on a case by case basis, but usually a 25% restocking charge. In case of damage, small repairs can be coordinated through us, returns are coordinated by us too. This resource is part of the Hickory Furniture Mart complex. This showroom is one of over 80 to visit. **See Hickory Furniture Mart listing for more information.** Consolidated shipping can be arranged with other resources in this center, a standard one/third deposit is required on all orders. Most showrooms accept VISA/MC, but not all. Cash, personal or certified checks accepted by all showrooms. If you elect not to pay for your entire purchase at the time of sale, a personal or certified check will be due upon delivery.

Manufacturers: (Many resources do not list all their manufacturers. Be sure to inquire about those you are interested in, but do not see listed here.)

HICKORY PARK:
ALEXVALE
CHARLESTON FORGE
CR LAINE
DINAIRE
DUCKS UNLIMITED
GLOBER/REFLECTIONS
GMS IMPORTS
HAMMARY
HEKMAN
HICKORY FRY
HIGH POINT FURNITURE
JSF
KINCAID
KINGSDOWN
McKINLEY LEATHER
OHIO TABLE PADS
PARKER SOUTHERN
REGENCY HOUSE
RIVERSIDE
RON FISHER

ROWE
SK PRODUCTS
SPRING AIR
STAINSAFE
STYLE UPHOLSTERY
TIMMERMAN
WAMBOLD
WINNERS ONLY
WOODARD

COMFORT ZONE (MOTION)
ACTION BY LANE
ALEXVALE
BARCALOUNGER
BERK
DUTAILIER
HAMMARY
RIVERSIDE
STRATOLOUNGER
WAMBOLD

SEASONS (OUTDOOR AND RATTAN)
BENCHCRAFT
CEBU
CEBU BEDROOM
JENSEN JARRAH
KNF
SIDNEY ARTHUR
WHITECRAFT
WOODARD

GENERATIONS (CHILDREN'S)
ACCESSORIES
CHILDCRAFT
ID KIDS
KINGSDOWN
LEA
LITTLE MISS LIBERTY
SIMMONS
SPRING AIR

HICKORY WHITE GALLERY
HICKORY FURNITURE MART
2220 HWY 70 SE
HICKORY, NC 28602
Hours: **M-F: 9-6; S: 9-5; Closed Sundays**

Toll-Free	
Direct	828-326-1740
Fax	
Internet	

Notes: This resource is part of the Hickory Furniture Mart complex. This showroom is one of over 80 to visit. **See Hickory Furniture Mart listing for more information.** Consolidated shipping can be arranged with other resources in this center, a standard one/third deposit is required on all orders. Most showrooms accept VISA/MC, but not all. Cash, personal or certified checks accepted by all showrooms. If you elect not to pay for your entire purchase at the time of sale, a personal or certified check will be due upon delivery.

Manufacturers: (Many resources do not list all their manufacturers. Be sure to inquire about those you are interested in, but do not see listed here.)

HIGH POINT FURNITURE SALES, INC
2000 BAKER ROAD
HIGH POINT, NC 27260
Hours: **M-F: 9-5**

Toll-Free	800-334-1875
Direct	
Fax	336-841-5664
Internet	

Notes: In business since 1983. 30% deposit can be paid with VISA/MC/CHECK. Balance due upon delivery with personal check if you use their trucks. Certified funds if delivered by in home delivery service. No credit card on balances. If there are any problems with shipment, claims are filed by the resource.

Manufacturers: (Many resources do not list all their manufacturers. Be sure to inquire about those you are interested in, but do not see listed here.)

ACE CRYSTAL	AMERICAN MIRROR	ARMSTRONG
ACTION BY LANE	AMERICAN OF MARTINSVILLE	ATHENS FURNITURE
AMERICAN DREW	ARLINGTON HOUSE	AUSTIN PRODUCTIONS

BALDWIN BRASS
BARCALOUNGER
BASSETT
BASSETT MIRROR
BEAN STATION
BENICIA BEDS
BERKLINE
BERKSHIRE
BERNHARDT
BESTAR
BLACKSMITH SHOP
BRADINGTON YOUNG
BRASS CRAFT
BRASSCRAFTERS
BRAXTON CULLER
BROWN JORDAN
BROYHILL
CM FURNITURE
CALIFORNIA UMBRELLA
CAL-STYLE
CAROLINA MIRROR
CARSON'S
CARTER
CASARD
CASA BIQUE
CASTILLIAN IMPORTS
CASUAL LAMP
CHAIRCRAFT
CHALLENGER LAMPS
CHARISMA CHAIRS
CHATHAM COUNTY
CHARTER TABLE
CHROMCRAFT
CLARK CASUAL
CLASSIC RATTAN
CLAUDE GABLE
CLAYTON MARCUS
CLOVER LAMPS
CLYDE PEARSON
COCHRANE
COLONIAL HEIRLOOMS
COLONY HOUSE
CONOVER CHAIR
COUNTY SEAT DINETTES
COX
CRAWFORD
CONTEMPORARY SHELLS
CREATIVE ACCENTS
CRYSTAL CLEAR
DANSEN
DAR/RAN
DAYSTROM
DECORATIVE CRAFTS
DESIGN ENVIRONMENT
DESIGNMASTER
DESIGN TREES
DESIGN TRENDS/COCHRANE
DILLON
DINAIRE

DIRECTIONAL OF NORTH
CAROLINA
DISTINCTIVE DESIGNS
DIXIE
DRESHER
ELLO
EMERSON LEATHER
ENGLAND CORSAIR
EVANS DESIGNS
EXCELSIOR
EXECUTIVE LEATHER
FABRICOATE
FAIRFIELD CHAIR
FASHION BED
MURRAY FEISS LAMPS
FICKS REED
FINE ARTS LAMPS
FLEXSTEEL
FLORAL ART
FLORIDA FURNITURE
FORBES LAMPS
FREDERICK COOPER
FRIENDSHIP UPHOLSTERY
FITZ & FLOYD
GEORGE KOVACS
GERALD STEIN
GEORGIA CHAIR
GLASS FASHIONS
GREAT AMERICAN TRADING
GIOVANNE TRAVANO
GREAT CITY TRADERS
HALCYON
HAMMARY
HARBOUR TOWNE
HEKMAN
HENRY LINK
HENDERSON
HEYWARD HOUSE
HEYGILL
HICKORY HILL
HICKORY TAVERN
HICKORY WHITE
HIGH POINT FURNITURE
HIGH POINT WOODWORKING
HOOD
HOOKER
HOWARD MILLER CLOCKS
HTB LANE
HUNTINGTON HOUSE
HYUNDAI
INNOVA
INTERNATIONAL
JAMES R COOPER
JAMESTOWN STERLING
JARU
JASPER CABINET
JEFFCO
JOHNSTON CASUALS
JOHNSTON-TOMBIGBEE

JULIE ART LAMPS
KAY LYN
KELLER
KEMP FURNITURE
KEY CITY
KIMBALL
KINCAID
KINDER HARRIS
KING HICKORY
KINGSDOWN
LAINE
LANE
LEA
LEISTERS
LEXINGTON
LIGHTING MATEGRA
LINK TAYLOR
LITELINE LTD LAMPS
LLOYD FLANDERS
LUBKE
LYON-SHAW
MARLOW
MARSH CABINETS
MARTINSVILLE NOVELTY
MARY DALE LAMPS
MASTER DESIGN
MASTERFIELD
MERSMAN TABLES
MH & H SEATING
MILLER DESK
MILLENDER
MINT HILL LAMPS
MIRROR CRAFT
MOBEL
MODULAR CONCEPTS
MYRTLE DESK
NATHAN HALE
NATIONAL MT AIRY
NEW CREATIONS
NICHOLS & STONE
NORMAN'S
NORTH HICKORY
NORTH STAR
NULL INDUSTRIES
O'ASIAN
ORDEREST MATTRESS
OHIO TABLE PADS
OLD HICKORY TANNERY
ORIENTAL LACQUER
PARAGON PICTURES
PARK AVENUE
PARK PLACE
PEE GEE LAMPS
PEOPLOUNGER
PERFECTION
PETERS-REVINGTON
PINNACLE
PLANT PLANT
POULIOT

PREVIEW
PULASKI
REGENCY HOUSE
REID LEATHER
REMINGTON LAMPS
REPLOGLE
REX FURNITURE
RICHARDSON BROS
RICHLIGHT LAMP CO
RIDGEWAY
RIVERSIDE
ROSALCO
JB ROSS BRASS BEDS
ROWE
SALOOM
SAN-DON
SIMMONS
SAMSONITE
SK PRODUCTS
SCHNADIG
SCHWEIGER
SEALY MATTRESS
SEDGEFIELD LAMP
SELIG
SETH THOMAS
SERTA MATTRESS

SHOAL CREEK
SILVESTRI
SINGER
SKILLCRAFT
SHAFER SEATING
SHERRILL OCCASIONAL
SOUTHWOOD
SPRAGUE & CARLTON
STANLEY
GERALD STEIN
STIFFEL LAMPS
STRATOLOUNGER
STRATFORD
SUGGS & HARDIN
STANTON COOPER
SWAIM
SWAN BRASS BED
TAYLORSVILLE UPHOLSTERY
TELESCOPE
TELL CITY
TEMPLE STUART
THAYER COGGIN
THOMASVILLE CABINET
TIMELESS BEDDING
TOYO

TROPITONE
TYPHOON
UNIVERSAL
US FURNITURE
UNION NATIONAL
VAN TEAL
VANGUARD
VAUGHAN-BASSETT
VAUGHAN FURNITURE
VENTURE
VIRGINIA HOUSE
VOGUE RATTAN
WEATHER WICKER
WEBB FURNITURE
WEIMAN
BETH WEISSMAN LAMPS
WESLEY ALLEN
WESTCHESTER LEATHER
WESTWOOD LAMPS
WHITE
WINSTON
WOODARD
WILLIAM ALLEN
WOODFIELD
YOUNG-HINKLE

=========================

HIGHLAND HOUSE GALLERY
HICKORY FURNITURE MART
2220 HWY 70 SE
HICKORY, NC 28602
Hours: M-F: 9-6; S: 9-5; Closed Sundays

Toll-Free	
Direct	828-322-6602
Fax	
Internet	

Resource Directory

HOLIDAY PATIO
HICKORY FURNITURE MART
2220 HWY 70 SE
HICKORY, NC 28602
Hours: **M-F: 9-6; S: 9-5; Closed Sundays**

Toll-Free	
Direct	828-345-0882
Fax	
Internet	

·**Notes:**   Located at "Shoppes at the Mart". This resource is part of the Hickory Furniture Mart complex. This showroom is one of over 80 to visit. **See Hickory Furniture Mart listing for more information.** Consolidated shipping can be arranged with other resources in this center, a standard one/third deposit is required on all orders. Most showrooms accept VISA/MC, but not all. Cash, personal or certified checks accepted by all showrooms. If you elect not to pay for your entire purchase at the time of sale, a personal or certified check will be due upon delivery.

Manufacturers: **(Many resources do not list all their manufacturers. Be sure to inquire about those you are interested in, but do not see listed here.)**

HOLIDAY PATIO SHOWCASE
PO BOX 767, 3318 HICKORY BLVD
HUDSON, NC 28638
Hours: **M-S: 9-5**

Toll-Free	800-808-8819
Direct	828-728-2664
Fax	828-728-1545
Internet	email: hps1@twave.net

Notes: Established in 1976. We accept VISA/MC/DISC. Located on Hwy 321. Featuring patio furniture, wicker and rattan.

Manufacturers: **(Many resources do not list all their manufacturers. Be sure to inquire about those you are interested in, but do not see listed here.)**

ACACIA	BENCHCRAFT	CAST CLASSICS
ALLIBERT	BROWN JORDAN	DURA WICKER

HALCYON	MEADOWCRAFT	THREE COINS
HOMECREST	SAMSONITE	TRICOMFORT
LANE VENTURE	SHELLY'S CUSHIONS	TROPITONE
LLOYD FLANDERS	SUMMER CLASSICS	WINSTON
LYON SHAW	TELESCOPE	WOODARD

HOLTON FURNITURE CO
805 RANDOLPH ST
THOMASVILLE, NC 27360
Hours: **M-F: 8:30-5:30; S: 9-5**

Toll-Free	800-334-3183
Direct	336-472-0400
Fax	
Internet	email: holtonfurn@aol.com

Notes: In business since 1927. They offer dedicated service before and after the sale. Sales consultants on staff. Payment policies - 50% deposit by check or money order to start orders, balance due prior to shipping. Shipping policies spelled out in company brochure. Returns when authorized by manufacturer. Showroom available. They will correct any errors in shipment made by Holton or the manufacturer. Customer can visit their facility. Brochures and procedures available by mail.

Manufacturers: (Many resources do not list all their manufacturers. Be sure to inquire about those you are interested in, but do not see listed here.)

A & W TABLE MATS	BROYHILL	CREATIVE EXPRESSIONS
A CRYSTAL COUNTRY	BUTLER SPECIALTY	CRYSTAL CLEAR
AINSLEY LAMPS	C & M FURNITURE	CUSTOM DECOR
AMERICAN DREW	CAMBRIDGE LAMPS	CRAFT-TEX
AMERICAN FURNITURE GALLERY	CARLTON McLENDON	CRAFTIQUE
	CAROLINA MIRROR	DECORATIVE ARTS
AMERICAN OF MARTINSVILLE	CAROLINA TABLES	DECORATIVE CRAFTS
AMERICAN MIRROR	CASA BIQUE	DENNY LAMP
ATHOL TABLE	CASTILLIAN IMPORTS	DFC
BARCALOUNGER	CASUAL LAMP	DISTINCTIVE DESIGNS
BALDWIN CLOCKS	CHATHAM COUNTY	DISTINCTION LEATHER
BASSETT FURNITURE	CHARLES W JACOBSEN	DRESHER
BASSETT MIRROR	CLARIDGE MANOR	EXECUTIVE LEATHER
BASSETT TABLES	CLARK CASUAL	FAIRFIELD CHAIR
BASSETT UPHOLSTERY	CLASSIC GALLERY	FICKS REED
BENCHCRAFT	CLASSIC LEATHER	FINE ARTS LAMPS
BENICIA BEDS	CLASSIC RATTAN	FITZ & FLOYD
BERKLINE	CLASSIC TRADITIONS	FLEXSTEEL
BERKSHIRE	CLYDE PEARSON	FREDERICK COOPER
BEVAN FUNNELL	COCHRANE	FROELICH
BUILTRIGHT CHAIR	CORONA DECOR	GEORGIAN FURNISHINGS
BLACKSMITH SHOP	CORONET IRON BEDS	GERALD STEIN
BOLING CHAIR	CORSICAN IRON BEDS	GREAT CITY TRADERS
BRANDT	COX	HAMILTON CLOCKS
BRASSCRAFTERS	CRAWFORD	HAMMARY

HICKORY CHAIR
HOGAN CHAIR CO
HOLIDAY UMBRELLA
HOOKER
HOWARD MILLER CLOCKS
INTERNATIONAL IMAGE
MAKERS
IRON MOUNTAIN STONEWARE
JB ROSS BRASS BEDS
JACK THORN IMPORTS
JAMES R COOPER
JAMESTOWN STERLING
JASPER CABINET
JEFFCO
KARGES
KIMBALL/VICTORIAN
KINDER-HARRIS
KING HICKORY
KINGSDOWN
KOCH METALCRAFT
L & S ANTIQUES
LANE
LEA
LEATHERCRAFT
LYON-SHAW
LEXINGTON
LaBARGE
MARIO INDUSTRIES
MARTINSVILLE NOVELTY
McKAY TABLE PADS
MEADOWCRAFT
MILLER DESK
MORRIS GREENSPAN LAMPS

MOTIONCRAFT
MURRAY FEISS LAMPS
MURPHY
NATIONAL MT AIRY
NAUTILUS IMPORTS
NEW ENGLAND CLOCK
NICHOLS & STONE
NORTH HICKORY
NULL INDUSTRIES
OHIO TABLE PADS
OLD COUNTRY
REPRODUCTIONS
OLD HICKORY TANNERY
PALECEK
P & P CHAIR
PEE GEE LAMPS
PEOPLOUNGER
PETERS-REVINGTON
PULASKI
QUOIZEL
REMARK MFG
REMINGTON LAMPS
REPLOGLE GLOBES
RIDGEWAY CLOCKS
RIVERSIDE
ROSE TRUNKS
SAN DIEGO DESIGNS
SEALY MATTRESS
SERTA MATTRESS
SETH THOMAS CLOCKS
SILVESTRI
SK FURNITURE
STAKMORE

STANICK
STANTON COOPER
STANLEY
STIFFEL
SUPERIOR
SWAN BRASS BED
TAYLORSVILLE UPHOLSTERY
TELESCOPE
THAYER COGGIN
THE CHAIR CO, INC
TRADERS LEAGUE
TRADEWINDS
TRAFALGAR GARDEN
TROPITONE
TROUTMAN CHAIR
TROUVAILLES
UNIVERSAL
VANGUARD
VAUGHAN
VAUGHAN-BASSETT
VIRGINIA HOUSE
WEIMAN
WESLEY ALLEN
WESTWOOD
WHITECRAFT
WILDWOOD
WILDWOOD TABLES
WILLIAM ALLEN
WINSTON FURNITURE
WOODARD
WOODMARK ORIGINALS
YORKSHIRE LEATHER

HOME FABRIC MILLS
882 S MAIN ST
CHESHIRE, CT 06410
Hours: M-W: 10-9; TH-S: 10-5

Toll-Free	
Direct	203-272-3529
Fax	203-272-6686
Internet	

Notes: In business since 1968. This company has three locations in New England. You can order by mail or fax. All fabric sales are final. Swatches are available upon request and they have a helpful catalog.

Manufacturers: (Many resources do not list all their manufacturers. Be sure to inquire

about those you are interested in, but do not see listed here.)

AMETEX FABRICS	GRABER	ROSSVILLE
BARTSON	JB MARTIN	SUNBURY
BELLE	JOHN WOLF	TFA
BLOOMCRAFT	P KAUFMANN	VALDESE WEAVERS
BURLINGTON	KIRSCH	WAVERLY
CONSO	LANSCOT ARLEN	WEAVE CORP
COVINGTON	MERRIMAC	WOLF
FABRIYAZ	RICHLOOM	and many more

HOME FOCUS BY PALLISER
HICKORY FURNITURE MART
2220 HWY 70 SE
HICKORY, NC 28602
Hours: **M-F: 9-6; S: 9-5; Closed Sundays**

Toll-Free	
Direct	828-324-7742
Fax	
Internet	

Notes: This resource is part of the Hickory Furniture Mart complex. This showroom is one of over 80 to visit. **See Hickory Furniture Mart listing for more information.** Consolidated shipping can be arranged with other resources in this center, a standard one/third deposit is required on all orders. Most showrooms accept VISA/MC, but not all. Cash, personal or certified checks accepted by all showrooms. If you elect not to pay for your entire purchase at the time of sale, a personal or certified check will be due upon delivery.

Manufacturers: **(Many resources do not list all their manufacturers. Be sure to inquire about those you are interested in, but do not see listed here.)**

Resource Directory

HOME INTERIORS
PO BOX 97
HULL, EAST YORKSHIRE ENGLAND
Hours: **M-F: 9-5 (England time)**

Toll-Free	All the top British fabrics!
Direct	011-44-990-23-99-55
Fax	011-44-1482-21-60-18
Internet	**email:**mail@homeinteriors.com.uk

Notes: The fabrics available are the more popular manufacturers of this British company. All inquiries welcome. Name brands are not listed here due to concern about manufacturers reaction, but very nice lines carried. Samples are supplied at a small charge. They will also custom-make most home furnishings, curtains, etc. Designers given additional discount (upon presentation of tax id number).

Manufacturers: (Many resources do not list all their manufacturers. Be sure to inquire about those you are interested in, but do not see listed here.)

BLENDWORTH	JOHN WILMAN	And many more.
CROWSONS	SANDERSONS	
HARLEQUIN		

HOMEWAY FURNITURE CO OF MT AIRY, INC
121 W. LEBANON STREET
MT AIRY, NC 27030
Hours: **M-F: 9-5:30; S: 9-5; Closed Sundays**

Toll-Free	800-334-9094
Direct	336-786-6151
Fax	336-786-1822
Internet	website: http://web.infoave.net/~esystems/homeway.html

Notes: In business since 1976. They accept VISA/MC 50% downpayment. Balance due can be paid by cashier's check, money order or COD. Specialized custom home deliveries. Sales and design consultants on staff. Customer satisfaction guaranteed. Shipping policies: customer, carrier and resource all work together. Return policy: if damaged, repair or replace 100%. Customer can visit facilities. **Customer service number: 336-786-6151.**

Manufacturers: (Many resources do not list all their manufacturers. Be sure to inquire about those you are interested in, but do not see listed here.)

AA LAUN	ACTION/LANE	AMERICAN CHAIR & TABLE
ACACIA	ALEXVALE	AMERICAN DREW

AMERICAN MIRROR	CRESENT	JOHNSTON TOMBIGBEE
AMERICAN OF HIGH POINT	CRYSTAL CLEAR LAMPS	JON ELLIOTT
AMERICAN OF MARTINSVILLE	D SCAN	KAISER KHUN LIGHTING
ANDREW PEARSON	D & F WICKER	KELLER
AS YOU LIKE IT LAMPS	DAYSTROM	KETTLER
ATHENS FURNITURE	DECORATIVE CRAFTS	KESSLER
ATHOL TABLE	DENNY LAMP	KEY CITY
BALDWIN BRASS	DESIGN CONNECTION	KIMBALL
BARCALOUNGER	DESIGN MASTER	KINCAID
BARN DOOR	DILLON	KING HICKORY
BASSETT FURNITURE	DINAIRE	KINGCRAFT
BASSETT	DISTINCTION LEATHER	KINGSDOWN
BEAN STATION	DUTAILIER	KINGSLEY
BEECHBROOK	EAGLE CRAFT	KLAUSSNER
BENCHCRAFT	ELLIOTT'S DESIGNS	KOCH ORIGINALS
BENICIA	EMERALD CRAFT	LANE
BENTWOOD	EMERSON LEATHER	LARGO
BERKLINE	EXECUTIVE LEATHER	LEA
BEST CHAIR	FAIRFIELD CHAIR	LEATHER TRENDS/LEATHER
BEVAN FUNNELL	FAIRMONT DESIGNS	MART
BLACKSMITH SHOP	FASHION BED GROUP	LEISTERS
BOYD	FASHION BEDDING	LEXINGTON
BRADY	FICKS REED	LLOYD FLANDERS
BRAXTON CULLER	FLEXSTEEL	LYON SHAW
BROWN JORDAN	FREDERICK COOPER	LaBARGE
BROWNWOOD	FRIENDSHIP UPHOLSTERY	LIFESTYLES OF CALIFORNIA
BROYHILL	FROELICH	MADISON SQUARE
BRUNSCHWIG & FILS	GARDNER MIRROR	MAITLAND SMITH
BUTLER SPECIALTY	GENTRY UPHOLSTERY	MARLOW/LOWMAR
CANAL DOVER	GEORGIAN FURNISHING	MASTER DESIGN
CANADEL	GLENNCRAFT	MASTERFIELD
CAPEL RUGS	GREENE BROS	MEADOWCRAFT
CAROLINA COMFORT	GREYSTONE VICTORIAN	MILLER DESK
CAROLINA MIRROR	HABERSHAM PLANTATION	MOBEL
CARSON'S	HALCYON	MOHAWK
CARTER	HAMMARY	MOOSEHEAD
CASA BIQUE	HARRIS MARCUS	MORGAN STEWART
CATALINA	HEKMAN	MURPHY
CATNAPPER	HICKORY CHAIR	MURRAY IRON WORKS
CHAPMAN	HICKORY HILL	NATHAN HALE
CHARISMA CHAIRS	HICKORY INTERNATIONAL	NATIONAL MT AIRY
CHARLESTON FORGE	HICKORY MARK	NICHOLS & STONE
CHATHAM COUNTY	HIGH POINT	NULL
CHATHAM NOVELTY	HIGHLAND HOUSE	OAKWOOD INTERIORS
CHROMCRAFT	HIPPOPOTAMUS	OHIO TABLE PAD
CLARK CASUAL	HITCHCOCK CHAIR	OLD HICKORY TANNERY
CLASSIC GALLERY	HOMECREST	ORIENTAL ACCENT
CLASSIC LEATHER	HOOKER	OVERNIGHT SLEEPERS
CLASSIC RATTAN	HOWARD MILLER CLOCK	PALLISER
CLAYTON MARCUS	HUNTINGTON HOUSE	PARAGON PICTURE
COCHRANE	HYUNDAI	PARKER SOUTHERN
COLONIAL	INTERNATIONAL	PAUL ROBERT
CONOVER CHAIR	J ROYALE	PEARSON
COUNCILL CRAFTSMEN	JSF ORIENTAL	PENNSYLVANIA CLASSICS
COUNTY SEAT	JAMES DAVID JDI	PENNSYLVANIA HOUSE
COX	JASPER CABINET	PEOPLOUNGER
CRAFTIQUE	JETTON	PETERS REVINGTON
CRAFTMASTER	JOHNSTON BENCHWORKS	PHILIP REINISCH
CRAWFORD	JOHNSTON CAUALS	PINNACLE

POWELL
PREVIEW
PULASKI
REGENCY HOUSE
RELIANCE LAMP
REMBRANDT LAMP
REMINGTON LAMP
RESTONIC CAROLINAS
REX
RICHARDSON BROS
RIDGEWOOD
RIVERSIDE
ROBERT ALLEN
ROBINSON
ROSALCO
ROSS ACCESSORIES
SALOOM
SAM MOORE
SAMSONITE/HARBOR TOWNE
SARRIED
SCHNADIG
SCHUMACHER/WAVERLY
SCHWEIGER
SEALY
SEALY MATTRESS
SEAY
SEDGEFIELD
SERTA MATTRESS
SHENANDOAH

SHERRILL
SIMPLY SOUTHERN
SIMMONS
SK PRODUCTS
SKILLCRAFT
SOUTHAMPTONSOUTH SEA
RATTAN
SOUTHWOOD
SPRING AIR
ST TIMOTHY
STATESVILLE CHAIR
STATTON
STEIN WORLD
STEWART
STIFFEL
STONEVILLE
STRATFORD/STRATOLOUNGER
STROUPE MIRROR
STYLE
STYLECRAFT LAMPS
SUPERIOR
SWAIM
TAYLOR WOODCRAFT
TAYLORCRAFT
TAYLORSVILLE UPHOLSTERY
TEMPLE
TEMPLE STUART
THAYER COGGIN
THREE COINS

TOWNE SQUARE
TRADITION FRANCE
TROPITONE
TYNDALE
US FURNITURE
UNION CITY CHAIR CO
UNIVERSAL
VARGAS
VAUGHAN BASSETT
VAUGHAN
VENTURE
VICTORIAN CLASSICS
VIEWPOINT LEATHER
WALKER MARLEN
WAMBOLD
WEBB
WEIMAN
WELLINGTON HALL
WESLEY ALLEN
WESLEY HALL
WESTWOOD
WHITAKER
WILDWOOD LAMPS
WINNERS ONLY
WINSTON
WOODARD
WOODMARK ORIGINALS

===

HOOKER GALLERY
HICKORY FURNITURE MART
2220 HWY 70 SE
HICKORY, NC 28602
Hours: **M-F: 9-6; S: 9-5; Closed Sundays**

Toll-Free	
Direct	828-326-1735
Fax	
Internet	

Notes: This resource is part of the Hickory Furniture Mart complex. This showroom is one of over 80 to visit. **See Hickory Furniture Mart listing for more information.** Consolidated shipping can be arranged with other resources in this center, a standard one/third deposit is required on all orders. Most showrooms accept VISA/MC, but not all. Cash, personal or certified checks accepted by all showrooms. If you elect not to pay for your entire purchase at the time of sale, a personal or certified check will be due upon delivery.

Manufacturers: **(Many resources do not list all their manufacturers. Be sure to inquire about those you are interested in, but do not see listed here.)**

═══════════════════════════

HOTEL RESERVATIONS NETWORK
8140 WALNUT HILL LANE #203
DALLAS, TX 75231
Hours: **M-F: 6a-10p; S: 9-6; Sun:10-6**

Toll-Free	800-96-HOTEL
Direct	
Fax	
Internet	

Notes: This isn't a home furnishings or furniture resource, but I think it's a very helpful number to know about. This company owns hotel properties all over the US and offers available rooms at substantial discounts. No membership fee. Just call and try it.

Manufacturers: **(Many resources do not list all their manufacturers. Be sure to inquire about those you are interested in, but do not see listed here.)**

═══════════════════════════

HOUSE DRESSING INTERNATIONAL FURNITURE
3608 W WENDOVER
GREENSBORO, NC 27407
Hours: **M-F: 8:30-5:30; S: 10:00-2:00**

Toll-Free	800-322-5850
Direct	336-294-3900
Fax	336-294-0004
Internet	

Notes: Free brochure. In business since 1986, their motto is "We specialize in special orders". One-half or one-third deposit on orders can be paid with VISA/MC. Balance with check. Use their own trucks for shipping in most cases. Shipping problems handled by the resource. Sales and design consultants on staff can help and advise customers. No returns unless factory defective or damages. Customers can visit this large facility. Direct British and continental imported antiques, oriental imports and accessories on display along with a wide variety of the most unique one of a kind manufacturers' reproductions available.

Manufacturers: **(Many resources do not list all their manufacturers. Be sure to inquire about those you are interested in, but do not see listed here.)**

A LOCK	CASUAL CRATES	FINE ARTS
ALEXANDER JULIAN	CELLINI	FLEXSTEEL
ALEXVALE	CHAPEL HILL	FREEMAN & CO
ALLIBERT	CHARLESTON FORGE	FRIEDMAN BROS MIRRORS
ALLMARK	CHILDCRAFT	FROELICH
ALPA PLUS	CHROMCRAFT	GALBRAITH
AMERICAN DREW	CHROMCRAFT	GEORGE KOVACS
AMERICAN MIRROR	CLARIDGE MANOR	GEORGE KOVACS
AMERICAN OF MARTINSVILLE	CLARK CASUAL	GEORGIA FURNISHINGS
AMYX	CLASSIC GALLERY	GEORGIAN REPRODUCTIONS
ANDRE ORIGINALS	CLASSIC TRADITIONS	GLASS ARTS
ANDREW PEARSON	CLAYTON MARCUS	GLASS MIRRORCRAFTS
ARLINGTON HOUSE	CM FURNITURE	GMS IMPORTS
ARTISAN HOUSE	COCHRANE	GRAND MANOR
ARTISTICA	COJA LEATHER	GREAT CITY TRADERS
AS YOU LIKE IT LAMPS	COLLINGWOOD	GROSFILLEX
ASHLEY	COMFORT DESIGNS	GULDEN GALLERY
ASHLEY MANOR	CONTEMPORARY FURNITURE	HALCYON
ATHOL TABLE	DESIGNS	HAMMARY
AVANTI	CORONA DECOR	HARRIS MARCUS
BAKER	COX	HEKMAN
BAMBOO ODYSSEY	CR LAINE	HENDERSON WALL UNITS
BARCALOUNGER	CRAFTIQUE	HENRY LINK
BASSETT	CRAWFORD	HERCO LIGHTING
BASSETT MIRROR	CRYSTAL CLEAR	HICKORY FRY
BAUER LIGHTING	CUSTOMCRAFT	HICKORY HILL
BEACHLEY UPHOLSTERY	D SCAN	HICKORY LEATHER
BEAN STATION	DAVID THOMAS	HIGH POINT WOODWORKING
BENICIA BEDS	DAVIS CABINET	HIGHLAND HOUSE
BERKSHIRE	DECORATIVE ARTS	HOOD
BESTAR	DECORATIVE CRAFTS	HOOKER
BETH WEISSMAN LAMPS	DESIGNED IMPORTS	HOUSEMAN CHANDELIERS
BEVAN FUNNELL	DILLON	HOWARD MILLER
BLACKSMITH SHOP	DINAIRE	HYUNDAI
BOB TIMBERLAKE	DIRECTIONAL	INTERNATIONAL
BRADINGTON YOUNG	DISTINCTION LEATHER	ITALIA CRYSTAL
BRASS ROOTS	DISTINCTIVE DESIGNS	J BERDOU
BRASSCRAFTERS	DIXIE	J STRASBORG
BRAXTON CULLER	DOUGLAS & MARSHALL	JOHN TURANO
BROOKWOOD	DRESHER	JACK HOUSMAN
BROWN JORDAN	DURALEE FABRICS	JASPER CABINET
BROWN STREET	DUTAILIER	JB ROSS
BROYHILL	EAGLE CRAFT	JB ROSS
BUTLER SPECIALTY	ECCO	JOHN BOOS
CAL-STYLE	EDWARD FERRELL	JOHN BOOS
CAMBRIDGE	EKORNES	JOHN BOOS
CANAL DOVER	ELEMENTS OF GRAPEVINE	JOHN WIDDICOMB
CARLTON McLENDON	ELLIOTT'S DESIGNS	JOHN WIDDICOMB
CAROLE FABRICS	ELLO	JOHNSTON BENCHWORKS
CAROLE FABRICS	EMERSON LEATHER	JOHNSTON CASUALS
CAROLINA CRAFTSMEN	ERIC MORGAN	JRW CONTEMPORARY
CAROLINA MIRROR	ERWIN LAMBETH	KAISER KUHN LIGHTING
CAROLINA TABLES	EXCELSIOR	KELLER
CARSON'S CONTEMPORARY	FAIRFIELD CHAIR	KESSLER
CARTER	FANCHER	KEY CITY
CASTILLIAN IMPORTS	FASHION BED	KIMBALL

KINCAID
KINGSLEY
KIRSCH
KLAUSSNER
KOCH & LOWY LAMPS
KOCH ORIGINALS
LANE
LANE DINING ALA CARTE
LEA
LEATHERTREND
LEATHERMAN'S GUILD
LEXINGTON
LIFESTYLES OF CALIFORNIA
LINK TAYLOR
LLOYD FLANDERS
LOUIS J SOLOMON
LOWENSTEIN
LYNN HOLLYN
LYON SHAW
MADISON SQUARE
MAHOGANY REPRODUCTIONS
MALLIN
MARIO LAMPS
MARK THOMAS
MARYLAND CLASSICS
MASLAND CARPET
MASTER DESIGN
McENROE
McKAY TABLE PADS
MERSMAN
MICHAEL THOMAS
MILLENIUM
MOOSEHEAD
MORGANTON CHAIR
MORRIS GREENSPAN
MOTIF
MURRAY FEISS
NATHAN HALE
NATIONAL MT AIRY
NATURAL LIGHT
NOBAR FABRICS
NORTH HICKORY
NORTH STAR GAME TABLES
NULL INDUSTRIES
OHIO TABLE PADS
OLD HICKORY TANNERY
OLD WAVERLY
ORIENTAL LACQUER
PACIFIC RATTAN
PAOLI
PARK AVENUE
PAUL HANSON

PEARSON
PEE GEE LAMPS
PENNSBURG WOODCRAFT
PENNSYLVANIA CLASSICS
PENNSYLVANIA HOUSE
PETERS-REVINGTON
PHILLIP REINISCH
PLANT PLANT
POULIOT DESIGNS
PRECEDENT
PRESTIGE
PREVIEW
PROVIDENCE RUGS
PULASKI
REGENCY HOUSE
RELIANCE LAMPS
REMINGTON LAMPS
REPRODUX
REUBENS
REX
RICHARDSON BROS
RIDGEWAY CLOCKS
RIVERSIDE
ROBERT ALLEN FABRICS
ROSENTHAL NETTER
ROUGIER
SALEM SQUARE
SALOOM
SAM MOORE
SARREID
SCHNADIG
SCHUMACHER
SCHWEIGER
SEALY MATTRESS
SEDGEFIELD LAMP
SELIG
SERTA MATTRESS
SHENANDOAH LEATHER
SHERRILL OCCASIONAL
SILVER
SIMMONS MATTRESS
SINGER
SK FURNITURE
SLIGH DESK
SOMMA MATTRESS
SOUTH SEAS RATTAN
SPRING AIR MATTRESS
STAKMORE
STANLEY
STANTON COOPER
STATESVILLE CHAIR
STEIN WORLD

STIFFEL
STONE INTL
STONELEIGH
STOUT CHAIR
STRATFORD
STRATOLOUNGER
STYLECRAFT
SUGGS & HARDIN
SUPERIOR
SWAIM
SWAN
TAYLOR WOODCRAFT
TEMPLE STUART
THAYER COGGIN
THAYER COGGIN
THOMASVILLE CABINET CO
TIMMERMAN
TOM SEELY
TRADITIONS FRANCE
TROPITONE
TUBB
UNIQUE
UNIVERSAL
UWHARRIE CHAIR
VAN TEAL
VARGUS
VAUGHAN
VAUGHAN-BASSETT
VENTURE
VERMONT PRECISION
VIETRI
VIRGINIA HOUSE
VIRGINIA METALCRAFTERS
VOGUE RATTAN
WALBURG
WATSON OF TAYLORSVILLE
WAVERLY
WEIMAN
WELLESLEY GUILD
WHITAKER
WHITECRAFT
WHITTIER
WILDWOOD LAMPS
WILLIAM ALLEN
WINSTON
WOODARD
WOODMARK ORIGINALS
WORKSPACE
YORKSHIRE LEATHER
YOUNG-HINKLE

HOUSE OF MIRRORS BY HICKORY HOME ACCENTS
HICKORY FURNITURE MART
2220 HWY 70 SE
HICKORY, NC 28602
Hours: M-F: 9-6; S: 9-5; Closed Sundays

Toll-Free	
Direct	828-323-8893
Fax	
Internet	

Notes: This resource is part of the Hickory Furniture Mart complex. This showroom is one of over 80 to visit. **See Hickory Furniture Mart listing for more information.** Consolidated shipping can be arranged with other resources in this center, a standard one/third deposit is required on all orders. Most showrooms accept VISA/MC, but not all. Cash, personal or certified checks accepted by all showrooms. If you elect not to pay for your entire purchase at the time of sale, a personal or certified check will be due upon delivery.

Manufacturers: **(Many resources do not list all their manufacturers. Be sure to inquire about those you are interested in, but do not see listed here.)**

HOUSEWORKS HOME INTERIORS
THE ATRIUM
430 SOUTH MAIN ST
HIGH POINT, NC 27260
Hours: M-F: 9-6; S:9-5

Toll-Free	
Direct	336-885-2457
Fax	336-885-1867
Internet	**email:** houseworks@theatrium.com

Notes: Part of the Atrium complex. Worth visiting, showrooms available. See **Atrium Furniture Showroom** listing for more information. Transitional lifestyle - clean, pure, natural simple and uncomplicated in ash, maple, cherry, oak, pine and metal.

Manufacturers: **(Many resources do not list all their manufacturers. Be sure to inquire about those you are interested in, but do not see listed here.)**

CANWOOD	NADEAU	TECH LINE
LYNDON	SHENANDOAH	VERMONT TUBBS

HUDSON DISCOUNT FURNITURE
940 HIGHLAND AVE, NE (PO BOX 2547)
HICKORY, NC 28601
Hours: **M-S: 8:30-5**

Toll-Free	
Direct	828-322-4996
Fax	828-322-6953
Internet	

Notes: Family owned and operated since 1922. 30,000 sq ft showroom

Manufacturers: **(Many resources do not list all their manufacturers. Be sure to inquire**
 about those you are interested in, but do not see listed here.)
SEALY

HUNT GALLERIES, INC
2920 HWY 127 N., PO BOX 2324
HICKORY, NC 28603
Hours: **M-F: 9-5**

Toll-Free	800-248-3876
Direct	
Fax	828-324-9921
Internet	

Notes: This company manufactures their own fine quality custom upholstered furniture, including
sofas, love seats, chaise lounges, wing chairs, bedroom chairs, ottomans, benches and more. In
business since 1944. Small, family owned and operated. Orders usually ship in 6-8 weeks. 50%
deposit on order, can be paid VISA/MC/CHECK/MO, remaining balance due in 30 days.
Satisfaction guaranteed with workmanship and quality. Specialize in COM orders, or select from our
numerous fabrics or leather. With shrinkwrap packaging and reinforced cartons, damage in shipment
is rare. Shipments are fully insured and carrier is responsible but we will assist with any damage
claims. Worldwide shipping available. 60 color catalog includes manufacturer's price list is $10
(deductible on first order). We also offer upholstered headboards, mirrors and sofa tables.

Manufacturers: **(Many resources do not list all their manufacturers. Be sure to inquire**
 about those you are interested in, but do not see listed here.)

IDS DESIGN CENTER
50 EAST HOUSTON ST
NEW YORK, NY 10012
Hours: **MTWF: 9-6; Th:9-8; S: 10-6; Sun:10-5**

Toll-Free	
Direct	212-925-6171; 212-226-0313
Fax	212-925-2273
Internet	

Notes: Decorator fabrics and wallcoverings. Custom made furniture (send us a sketch). Custom made comforters, bedspreads, draperies and other decorative accessories. Formerly Rubin & Green.

Manufacturers: (Many resources do not list all their manufacturers. Be sure to inquire about those you are interested in, but do not see listed here.)

BRUNSCHWIG & FILS	KRAVET FABRICS	SCHUMACHER
DAVID & DASH	PAYNE	STROHEIM & ROMANN
DURALEE	ROBERT ALLEN	WAVERLY
JAY YANG		

INTERIOR FURNISHINGS, ETC
PO BOX 1644
HICKORY, NC 28603
Hours: **M-F: 8:30-5;S: 9-3**

Toll-Free	
Direct	828-328-5683
Fax	828-327-2106
Internet	

Notes: Family owned and run since 1976. When you call, you are sent a questionnaire asking about your preferences and what type of furniture you're looking for. Then, this resource can best serve your needs and send you appropriate information. Cash, personal check, money order or certified check are accepted for the 30% required deposit. Sales and design consultants on staff. In-house set-up. Delivery personnel are specially trained and equipped to handle new furniture. This virtually eliminates the possibility of transit damage. Each item should be inspected before you sign the delivery receipt. If a problem is found, make a notation on the receipt. There is a showroom to browse and their sales staff is very willing to give advice and help the customer make choices. All orders are special-no returns. Satisfaction guaranteed policy is one year manufacturer's warranty. Carrier and resource deal with shipping problems.

Manufacturers: (Many resources do not list all their manufacturers. Be sure to inquire about those you are interested in, but do not see listed here.)

ACTION BY LANE	DINAIRE	LEA
AMERICAN DREW	EMERSON LEATHER	LEXINGTON
AMERICAN OF MARTINSVILLE	FAIRFIELD CHAIR	LINK-TAYLOR
ARNOLD PALMER	FUTURISTIC	NATHAN HALE
ARTISTRY DESIGN	GLASS FASHIONS	OHIO TABLE PADS
BASSETT	GREENE BROS	PULASKI
BASSETT MIRROR	HEKMAN	REX FURNITURE
BLACKSMITH SHOP	HENRY LINK	RIVERSIDE
BOB TIMBERLAKE	HIGHLAND HOUSE	SERTA
BMC FURNITURE	HOME LAMP CO	SKILLCRAFT
BROYHILL	HOOKER	STANLEY
CAMBRIDGE LAMPS	HOWARD MILLER CLOCKS	TROPITONE
CAROLINA CHOICE	JASPER CABINET	UNIVERSAL
CAROLINA MIRROR	KINGSDOWN BEDDING	VAUGHAN
CARSON'S	L & S IMPORTS	VENTURE
CHARTER TABLE	CR LAINE	VIRGINIA HOUSE
CHATHAM COUNTY	LANE	
COCHRANE		

INTERNATIONAL CARPET
1384 CONEY ISLAND AVE
BROOKLYN, NY 11230
Hours: M-W: 9-6; TH: 9-8;
FRI: 9-4; SUN 10:30-5

Toll-Free	
Direct	718-253-5700
Fax	718-692-2363
Internet	

Notes: Huge selection of wool imports. In business 72 years. VISA/MC/AMEX/CHECK. Customer arranges own shipping or trucking. No return policy. Customers can visit this facility.

Manufacturers: (Many resources do not list all their manufacturers. Be sure to inquire about those you are interested in, but do not see listed here.)

CABIN CRAFT	PHILADELPHIA	ROBBINS BROS
COLONIAL MILLS	CARPET FAX	TUFTEX
CONCEPTS	GALAXY	MOHAWK
COURISTAN	CAROUSEL CARPET	ALEX SMITH
KARASTAN		

J ROYALE GALLERY
HICKORY FURNITURE MART
2220 HWY 70 SE
HICKORY, NC 28602
Hours: **M-F: 9-6; S: 9-5; Closed Sundays**

Toll-Free	
Direct	828-324-7742
Fax	
Internet	

Notes: This resource is part of the Hickory Furniture Mart complex. This showroom is one of over 80 to visit. **See Hickory Furniture Mart listing for more information.** Consolidated shipping can be arranged with other resources in this center, a standard one/third deposit is required on all orders. Most showrooms accept VISA/MC, but not all. Cash, personal or certified checks accepted by all showrooms. If you elect not to pay for your entire purchase at the time of sale, a personal or certified check will be due upon delivery.

Manufacturers: (Many resources do not list all their manufacturers. Be sure to inquire about those you are interested in, but do not see listed here.)

JEFFCO GALLERY
HICKORY FURNITURE MART
2220 HWY 70 SE
HICKORY, NC 28602
Hours: **M-F: 9-6; S: 9-5; Closed Sundays**

Toll-Free	
Direct	828-326-1735
Fax	
Internet	

Notes: This resource is part of the Hickory Furniture Mart complex. This showroom is one of over 80 to visit. **See Hickory Furniture Mart listing for more information.** Consolidated shipping can be arranged with other resources in this center, a standard one/third deposit is required on all orders. Most showrooms accept VISA/MC, but not all. Cash, personal or certified checks accepted by all showrooms. If you elect not to pay for your entire purchase at the time of sale, a personal or certified check will be due upon delivery.

Manufacturers: (**Many resources do not list all their manufacturers. Be sure to inquire about those you are interested in, but do not see listed here.**)

===============

JOHNSON'S CARPETS
3519 CORPORATE DR
DALTON, GA 30721
Hours: **M-F: 8-7;**

Toll-Free	800-235-1079
Direct	706-277-9835
Fax	706-277-9835
Internet	

Notes: In business since 1976. Twelve sales consultants. Savings up to 80% on brand name carpet, vinyl, vinyl tile, hardwood flooring, pad and custom area rugs. Their own styles, plus most major mills. Free quotes, samples, brochures, rug patterns. Residential, commercial. Direct shipping. No minimums. Pay by VISA/MC/AMEX/DISC/MO, in full at time of order. Vinyl flooring, area rugs also available. Returns must be authorized. Your order will be right or they will make it right at no cost to you. They will handle shipping problems if notified of damages by customer. Showroom available. Send for brochure for more info.

Manufacturers: (**Many resources do not list all their manufacturers. Be sure to inquire about those you are interested in, but do not see listed here.**)

ALADDIN CARPET
AMERICAN CARPET MILLS
ARMSTRONG
ATLAS-CREATIVE IND, INC
BALTA
BARRETT
BIGELOW CARPETS
BLUE RIDGE
BRUCE WOOD
BURLINGTON
BURTCO
CABIN CRAFT
CALADIUM
CALLAWAY
CAPITOL VICTORIAN
CARPETON MILLS, INC
CASCADE
CEDAR CARPETS
CHALLENGER INDUSTRIES
CHARLESTON CARPETS
CITATION
COLUMBIA
COLUMBUS
CONGOLEUM

CONSOLIDATED TEXTILES
CONQUEST
CORONET
CRITERION CARPET
CUMBERLAND
CUSTOMWEAVE
DeJON CONTRACT
COLLECTION
DESIGNWEAVE
DIAMOND
DIMENSION
DORSETT CARPET
DOWNS CARPET
EVANS & BLACK
FOCUS
GALAXY
GRASSMORE
HARRIS-TARKETT
HELIOS
HOLLYTEX
HORIZON INDUSTRIES
IMAGE CARPET
INSTANT TURF
INTERLOOM

KRAUS
LEES CARPET
LEN-DAL CARPETS & RUGS
MAIR ASTLEY
MANNINGTON
MASLAND
MILES
MOHAWK
MONTICELLO
NORTHWEST
PATCRAFT
PHILADELPHIA CARPET
PORTER
PRINCETON, INC
QUEEN CARPET
RD STALLION
RICHMOND
ROYAL DUTCH CARPETS
SALEM
SHAHEEN
SHAW
SHEFFIELD
RA SIEGEL
STELLAR CARPET

Resource Directory

JP STEVENS	SUPREME CARPET	WELLCO
STATTON IND	SUTTON CARPETS	WHITECREST
SUN FLOORING	TARKETT	WORLD CARPETS
SUN MILLS	TOWER	WUNDAWEAVE
SUNRISE CARPET	TUFTEX	

JONES BROTHERS
PO BOX 991, HWY 301 N
SMITHFIELD, NC 27577
Hours: **M&F:9-9; TWThS:9-5:30**

Toll-Free	
Direct	919-934-4162
Fax	919-989-7500
Internet	

Notes: In business since 1946. Located 2 minutes off I-95 at exit #97. Showroom available and sales representatives with years of experience will provide full assistance and serve you efficiently at no cost. Carry collections of English, French, 18th Century, American, Italian, Oriental and contemporary. 25% deposit, balance due before shipment made. Changes and/or cancellations accepted as long as manufacturer accepts them.

Manufacturers: (Many resources do not list all their manufacturers. Be sure to inquire about those you are interested in, but do not see listed here.)

ACTION	HAMMARY	NATHAN HALE
AMERICAN DREW	HANCOCK AND MOORE	PEARSON
AMERICAN OF MARTINSVILLE	HEKMAN	PULASKI
ATHOL	HENKEL HARRIS	REX
BEVAN FUNNELL	HENKEL MOORE	RIVERSIDE
BLACKSMITH SHOP	HENRY LINK	SEALY
BOB TIMBERLAKE	HICKORY CHAIR	SLIGH
BRADINGTON YOUNG	HOOKER	STANLEY
BROYHILL	JASPER CABINET	STIFFEL LAMPS
CASA BIQUE	JOHN RICHARD	SUMTER CABINET
CHARLESTON FORGE	KIMBALL	TAYLOR KING
CLASSIC RATTAN	LABARGE	THOMASVILLE
COCHRANE	LAINE	TRADITION HOUSE
COLONIAQL	LANE	UNIVERSAL
COX	LEXINGTON	VENTURE
CRAFTIQUE	LINK TAYLOR	WATERFORD
DISQUE	MADISON SQUARE	WELLINGTON HALL
DIXIE	MAITLAND SMITH	WILDWOOD LAMPS
FAIRFIELD CHAIR	MICHAEL THOMAS	WOODMARK
FREDERICK COOPER LAMPS	MILES TALBOT	YOUNG HINKLE

KAGAN'S AMERICAN DREW
THE ATRIUM
430 SOUTH MAIN ST
HIGH POINT, NC 27260
Hours: **M-F: 9-6; S: 9-5**

Toll-Free	
Direct	336-885-8568
Fax	336-885-8566
Internet	email: kagans@theatrium.com

Notes: Part of the Atrium complex. Worth visiting, showrooms available. See **Atrium Furniture Showroom** listing for more information. American Drew and other lines showing dining rooms, bedrooms, kitchen furniture and home theaters in cherry, oak, maple and pecan. All available in solid and wood veneers.

Manufacturers: **(Many resources do not list all their manufacturers. Be sure to inquire about those you are interested in, but do not see listed here.)**

KAGAN'S FURNITURE GALLERIES
THE ATRIUM
430 SOUTH MAIN ST
HIGH POINT, NC 27262
Hours: **M-F: 9-6; S: 9-5**

Toll-Free	
Direct	336-885-1333
Fax	336-889-9316
Internet	email: kagansfurniture@theatrium.com

Notes: Part of the Atrium complex. Worth visiting, showrooms available. See **Atrium Furniture Showroom** listing for more information. Furniture for every room. White-washed transitional to exotic contemporary.

Manufacturers: **(Many resources do not list all their manufacturers. Be sure to inquire about those you are interested in, but do not see listed here.)**

AMERICAN DREW	EXCELSIOR	PULASKI
AMERICAN OF MARTINSVILLE	FLEXSTEEL	SCHWEIGER
BERKLINE	HOOKER	UNIVERSAL
CLAYTON MARCUS	MILLENIUM	WEIMAN

KAGAN'S STANLEY GALLERY
THE ATRIUM
430 SOUTH MAIN ST
HIGH POINT, NC 27262
Hours: **M-F: 9-6; S: 9-5**

Toll-Free	
Direct	336-885-8300
Fax	
Internet	email: kagansgallery@theatrium.com

Notes: Part of the Atrium complex. Worth visiting, showrooms available. See **Atrium Furniture Showroom** listing for more information. Large selections of dining room furniture, bedroom furniture, occasional tables and entertainment centers. Other manufacturers also shown.

Manufacturers: **(Many resources do not list all their manufacturers. Be sure to inquire about those you are interested in, but do not see listed here.)**
STANLEY

KARASTAN CARPET & RUG CENTER
4309 WILEY DAVIS RD
GREENSBORO, NC 27407
Hours: **M-F:9-5; S: 10-4:30**

Toll-Free	800-877-1955
Direct	
Fax	336-852-9573
Internet	

Notes: Established 1933. Three sales consultants. Substantial discounts (40-50%) on all sizes and styles. Plus handmades. Very nice color brochure sent upon request of customer. Carry broadloom also. VISA/MC/CHECK. Rugs can be sent "on approval" - 30 day return policy. Customer pays shipping both ways, via UPS. If you're not satisfied, you can return it.

Manufacturers: **(Many resources do not list all their manufacturers. Be sure to inquire about those you are interested in, but do not see listed here.)**

| KARASTAN BROADLOOM | ORIENTAL WEAVERS | 828 TRADING CO |
| KARASTAN ORIENTALS | | |

KARGES GALLERY
HICKORY FURNITURE MART
2220 HWY 70 SE
HICKORY, NC 28602
Hours: **M-F: 9-6; S: 9-5; Closed Sundays**

Toll-Free	
Direct	828-326-1735
Fax	
Internet	

Notes: This resource is part of the Hickory Furniture Mart complex. This showroom is one of over 80 to visit. **See Hickory Furniture Mart listing for more information.** Consolidated shipping can be arranged with other resources in this center, a standard one/third deposit is required on all orders. Most showrooms accept VISA/MC, but not all. Cash, personal or certified checks accepted by all showrooms. If you elect not to pay for your entire purchase at the time of sale, a personal or certified check will be due upon delivery.

Manufacturers: **(Many resources do not list all their manufacturers. Be sure to inquire about those you are interested in, but do not see listed here.)**

KATHRYN'S COLLECTION
781 N. MAIN STREET
HIGH POINT, NC 27262
Hours: **M-S: 10-5**

Toll-Free	
Direct	336-841-7474
Fax	
Internet	

Notes: No phone sales. Pre-owned and new furnishings, accessories and gifts arriving daily from the area's finest manufacturers, interior designers and private homes. Accessories including antique silver, china, crystal, art porcelain, oriental rugs and lamps. VISA/MC accepted for full payment. No returns. Wide selection of estate and costume jewelry. Hard-to-find decorator items such as tassels, plate stands and hangers, lamp finials and picture bows. Gourmet foods gallery.

Manufacturers: **(Many resources do not list all their manufacturers. Be sure to inquire**

about those you are interested in, but do not see listed here.)

====================

KIMBALL GALLERY
HICKORY FURNITURE MART
2220 HWY 70 SE
HICKORY, NC 28602
Hours: **M-F: 9-6; S: 9-5; Closed Sundays**

Toll-Free	
Direct	828-324-7742
Fax	
Internet	

Notes: This resource is part of the Hickory Furniture Mart complex. This showroom is one of over 80 to visit. **See Hickory Furniture Mart listing for more information.** Consolidated shipping can be arranged with other resources in this center, a standard one/third deposit is required on all orders. Most showrooms accept VISA/MC, but not all. Cash, personal or certified checks accepted by all showrooms. If you elect not to pay for your entire purchase at the time of sale, a personal or certified check will be due upon delivery.

Manufacturers**: (Many resources do not list all their manufacturers. Be sure to inquire about those you are interested in, but do not see listed here.)**

====================

KINCAID GALLERY
THE ATRIUM
430 SOUTH MAIN ST
HIGH POINT, NC 27262
Hours: **M-F: 9-6; S: 9-6**

Toll-Free	
Direct	336-883-1818
Fax	336-883-1850
Internet	email: kincaid@theatrium.com

Notes: Part of the Atrium complex. Worth visiting, showrooms available. See **Atrium Furniture Showroom** listing for more information. The complete home furnishings store by Kincaid, America's largest manufacturer of solid wood furniture. Living room, dining room, bedroom and wicker furniture.

Manufacturers: (Many resources do not list all their manufacturers. Be sure to inquire about those you are interested in, but do not see listed here.)

KINCAID GALLERY
HICKORY FURNITURE MART
2220 HWY 70 SE
HICKORY, NC 28602
Hours: **M-F: 9-6; S: 9-5; Closed Sundays**

Toll-Free	
Direct	828-322-4440
Fax	
Internet	

Notes: This resource is part of the Hickory Furniture Mart complex. This showroom is one of over 80 to visit. **See Hickory Furniture Mart listing for more information.** Consolidated shipping can be arranged with other resources in this center, a standard one/third deposit is required on all orders. Most showrooms accept VISA/MC, but not all. Cash, personal or certified checks accepted by all showrooms. If you elect not to pay for your entire purchase at the time of sale, a personal or certified check will be due upon delivery.

Manufacturers: (Many resources do not list all their manufacturers. Be sure to inquire about those you are interested in, but do not see listed here.)

KING'S CHANDELIER COMPANY
729 SOUTH VAN BUREN RD
EDEN , NC 27289
Hours: **M-S: 10-4:30**

Toll-Free	
Direct	336-623-6188
Fax	336-627-9935
Internet	**email:**crystal@vnet.net **web site:** www.chandelier.com

Notes: Family owned and operated since 1936. This company produces original crystal and Victorian designs comparable to wholesale prices of other fixtures. They promise 48 hour delivery on any broken part whether it was ordered 30 years ago, or a part was broken in transit. Two designers on this staff of five can help customers with ideas and designs. Showroom available. Many designs and price ranges. Complete order can be paid by VISA/MC/MO. Satisfaction guaranteed. Refund, less shipping cost, if returned within 5 days. Showroom contains over 200 models that can be modified to suit customer. Catalog available for $4. Videotape of up to six models will be sent for a $25 deposit, refundable with purchase. Orders shipped worldwide.

Manufacturers: (Many resources do not list all their manufacturers. Be sure to inquire about those you are interested in, but do not see listed here.)
Kin'gs Chandelier - Their own line.

KJ'S FURNITURE OUTLET
400 UNDERHILL ST
HIGH POINT, NC 27262
Hours: **M-F: 8-8; S: By appt**

Toll-Free	
Direct	336-885-4911
Fax	336-885-9994
Internet	Coming soon.

Notes: Personalized shopping. Catalog service. Warehouse holds market samples that customers can view. Interior design. Residential and commercial.

Manufacturers: (Many resources do not list all their manufacturers. Be sure to inquire about those you are interested in, but do not see listed here.)
Most popular lines.

KNIGHT GALLERIES INC
835 CREEKWAY DR NW
LENOIR, NC 28645
Hours: **M-F: 9-5**

Toll-Free	800-334-4721
Direct	704-758-8422
Fax	704-754-1592
Internet	

Notes: Featuring over 75 lines. They will ship anywhere.

Manufacturers: (Many resources do not list all their manufacturers. Be sure to inquire about those you are interested in, but do not see listed here.)
BOB TIMBERLAKE   SERTA

LaBARGE FACTORY OUTLET
HICKORY FURNITURE MART
2220 HWY 70 SE
HICKORY, NC 28602
Hours: **M-F: 9-6; S: 9-5; Closed Sundays**

Toll-Free	
Direct	828-324-2220
Fax	
Internet	

Notes: This resource is part of the Hickory Furniture Mart complex. This showroom is one of over 80 to visit. **See Hickory Furniture Mart listing for more information.** Consolidated shipping can be arranged with other resources in this center, a standard one/third deposit is required on all orders. Most showrooms accept VISA/MC, but not all. Cash, personal or certified checks accepted by all showrooms. If you elect not to pay for your entire purchase at the time of sale, a personal or certified check will be due upon delivery.

Manufacturers: (Many resources do not list all their manufacturers. Be sure to inquire about those you are interested in, but do not see listed here.)

LAKE HICKORY FURNITURE
4360 HICKORY BLVD
GRANITE FALLS, NC 28630
Hours: **M-S: 9-5**

Toll-Free	
Direct	828-396-2194
Fax	828-396-1226
Internet	

Notes: Located on Hwy 321. In business since 1983. Two sales consultants on staff. No credit cards honored. No returns. No satisfaction guaranteed policy. If damaged in shipping, customer deals with carrier. If manufacturer defect, customer deals with us. Factory outlet pieces available. Located on Hwy 321. In-stock and special orders can be purchased. Shipping just about anywhere. Showroom for browsing.

Manufacturers: (Many resources do not list all their manufacturers. Be sure to inquire about those you are interested in, but do not see listed here.)

AMERICAN DREW
AMERICAN OF MARTINSVILLE
ANDREA BY SADEK
ARTMASTER STUDIOS
ASHTON PICTURES
BOB TIMBERLAKE
BROWN STREET
CAMBRIDGE GLIDERS
CARSON'S
CAROLINA MIRROR
CASUAL LAMP
CONOVER CHAIR
COOPER CLASSICS
COUNTY SEAT COPIES
COLLECTION
COX
CRAFT-TEX ACCESSORIES
CRAWFORD OF JAMESTOWN
CRYSTAL CLEAR LAMPS
DISTINCTION LEATHER
HABERSHAM PLANTATION

HAMMARY
HENRY LINK
HITCHCOCK CHAIR
HOOKER
HUNTINGTON HOUSE
JASPER CABINET
JOHNSTON CASUALS
KAISER KUHN LIGHTING
KEY CITY
LANE
LEXINGTON
LINK TAYLOR
LT MOSES WILLARD
McKAY TABLE PADS
MARLOW
MOBEL
MOHAWK
NATHAN HALE
NULL INDUSTRIES
PETERS-REVINGTON

PULASKI
SIGNATURE LIGHTING
SIMPLY SOUTHERN
SLEEPWORKS
SOUTHERN FURNITURE OF CONOVER
SOUTHERN FURNITURE REPRODUCTIONS
SPEER
STANLEY
STONE COUNTRY IRONWORKS
SUPERIOR
TELL CITY
TIMELESS BEDDING
UNIVERSAL
UTTERMOST
VENTURE
VIRGINIA HOUSE
WINSOME WOOD
WISCONSIN FURNITURE

LA MAISON
THE ATRIUM
430 SOUTH MAIN ST
HIGH POINT, NC 27260
Hours: **M-F: 9-6; S: 9-5**

Toll-Free	
Direct	336-887-6766
Fax	336-887-1405
Internet	email: hptcc@bellsouth.net

Notes: Part of the Atrium complex. Worth visiting, showrooms available. See **Atrium Furniture Showroom** listing for more information. Unique casegoods, screens, art, accessories and lighting fixtures.

Manufacturers: (Many resources do not list all their manufacturers. Be sure to inquire about those you are interested in, but do not see listed here.)
DILLON   PIETRARTE   VAN TEAL
JOHNSTON CASUALS

LAMP WAREHOUSE
1073 39TH STREET
BROOKLYN, NY 11219
Hours: **M-F: 9-5:30; TH: 9-8; S,S: 10-5:00; CLOSED WEDNESDAYS**

Toll-Free	800-52-LITES
Direct	
Fax	718-438-6836
Internet	

Notes: In business since 1952.(formerly Lamp Warehouse/New York Ceiling Fan Center) specializing in better brands of merchandise at discount prices, we can also give you immediate quotes on almost any lighting fixture, table lamp or ceiling fan you may have seen. Orders are placed by phone, fax or mail. Complete orders can be paid with VISA/MC/DISC. Most goods are shipped via UPS, RPS or common carrier. Damaged merchandise is replaced and call tags are issued to pick up defective goods. Please select carefully as any returns which were ordered in error may be subject to restocking charges. Sales and design consultants on staff to help with selections.

Manufacturers: (Many resources do not list all their manufacturers. Be sure to inquire about those you are interested in, but do not see listed here.)
ARROYO CRAFTSMAN   CHAPMAN LAMPS   CORBETT
CASABLANCA FAN   CLASSIC LIGHTING   FRAMBURG

FREDERICK COOPER	LENOX LAMPS	REMINGTON LAMPS
GEORGE KOVACS	NULCO LIGHTING	STIFFEL
GEORGIAN ART	REMBRANDT LAMPS	WORLD IMPORTS
HART		

LANE GALLERY
HICKORY FURNITURE MART
2220 HWY 70 SE
HICKORY, NC 28602
Hours: **M-F: 9-6; S: 9-5; Closed Sundays**

Toll-Free	
Direct	828-326-1735
Fax	
Internet	

Notes: This resource is part of the Hickory Furniture Mart complex. This showroom is one of over 80 to visit. **See Hickory Furniture Mart listing for more information.** Consolidated shipping can be arranged with other resources in this center, a standard one/third deposit is required on all orders. Most showrooms accept VISA/MC, but not all. Cash, personal or certified checks accepted by all showrooms. If you elect not to pay for your entire purchase at the time of sale, a personal or certified check will be due upon delivery.

Manufacturers: (Many resources do not list all their manufacturers. Be sure to inquire about those you are interested in, but do not see listed here.)

LAWINGS FURNITURE
2636 HICKORY BLVD
HUDSON, NC 28638
Hours: **M-S:9-5**

Toll-Free	800-637-1292
Direct	828-728-4292
Fax	
Internet	

Notes: Located on Hwy 321. 10,000 sq. ft. showroom.

Manufacturers: (Many resources do not list all their manufacturers. Be sure to inquire about those you are interested in, but do not see listed here.)

ARNOLD PALMER   BOB TIMBERLAKE

LEATHER SHOP, THE
ROUTE 12, BOX 57
HICKORY, NC 23101
Hours: M-S: 10-5

Toll-Free	
Direct	828-396-6294
Fax	828-396-1272
Internet	email: wsvb@vvi.net www: theleathershop@twave.net

Notes: Custom made furniture. Located on Hwy 321. Showroom. Fine leather furniture. Residential, commercial, office recliners.

Manufacturers: (Many resources do not list all their manufacturers. Be sure to inquire about those you are interested in, but do not see listed here.)

LEATHER UNLIMITED
THE ATRIUM
430 SOUTH MAIN ST
HIGH POINT, NC 27260
Hours: M-F: 9-6; S:9-5

Toll-Free	
Direct	336-885-4386
Fax	336-885-4362
Internet	email: leather@theatrium.com

Notes: Part of the Atrium complex. Worth visiting, showrooms available. See **Atrium Furniture Showroom** listing for more information. Shopping here is a unique experience. One may sink down into a comfortable leather sofa, stretch out on a sectional to test the comfort before deciding to order. We will educate the customer on the desirability of top grain leather.

Manufacturers: (Many resources do not list all their manufacturers. Be sure to inquire

about those you are interested in, but do not see listed here.)

LEE'S CARPET SHOWCASE
3068 NORTH DUG GAP ROAD
DALTON, GA 30722-0481
Hours: **M-F: 9-5**

Toll-Free	800-433-8479
Direct	
Fax	706-277-9896
Internet	email: Leescarp@catt.com

Notes: Carpeting, vinyl, hardwood and oriental rugs. Showroom available and free samples mailed directly to your home or office.

Manufacturers: (Many resources do not list all their manufacturers. Be sure to inquire about those you are interested in, but do not see listed here.)

BRUCE	LEES	PERGO
COURISTAN	MANNINGTON	SHAW
GALAXY	MOHAWK	TARKETT

LEXINGTON GALLERY (BOYLES)
HICKORY FURNITURE MART
2220 HWY 70 SE
HICKORY, NC 28603
Hours: **M-F: 9-6; S: 9-5; Closed Sundays**

Toll-Free	
Direct	828-326-1709
Fax	
Internet	website: www.Boyles.com

Notes: This resource is part of the Hickory Furniture Mart complex. This showroom is one of over 80 to visit. **See Hickory Furniture Mart listing for more information.** Consolidated shipping can be arranged with other resources in this center, a standard one/third deposit is required on all orders. Most showrooms accept VISA/MC, but not all. Cash, personal or certified checks accepted by all showrooms. If you elect not to pay for your entire purchase at the time of sale, a personal or certified check will be due upon delivery.**IMPORTANT CORPORATE NUMBERS: Customer Service:**

828-345-5280; Delivery Info: 828-345-5275; Order Status: 828-345-5290; Billing Questions: 828-345-5206

Manufacturers: (Many resources do not list all their manufacturers. Be sure to inquire about those you are interested in, but do not see listed here.)

MAJOR LINES: LEXINGTON
BOB TIMBERLAKE   PALMER HOME COLLECTION

LINCOLN GERARD USA INC
THE ATRIUM
430 SOUTH MAIN ST
HIGH POINT, NC 27260
Hours: M-F: 9-6; S:9-5

Toll-Free	
Direct	336-889-9505
Fax	336-889-0559
Internet	email: lincolngerard@theatrium.com

Notes: Part of the Atrium complex. Worth visiting, showrooms available. See **Atrium Furniture Showroom** listing for more information. This is the US gallery of the specialist international furniture maker exclusively of 18th century mahogany antique reproductions. Acclaimed as one of the finest and largest collections in the world, every piece is crafted by hand from beautiful mahogany solids to the finest detail by master craftsmen.

Manufacturers: (Many resources do not list all their manufacturers. Be sure to inquire about those you are interested in, but do not see listed here.)

LINDY'S FURNITURE COMPANY
233 FIRST AVE NW
HICKORY, NC 28601
Hours: M-S; 8:30a-5:15p (Closed Wednesday)

Toll-Free	
Direct	828-327-8986
Fax	828-327-6088
Internet	**email**: julie@interpath.com **website**:http://www.bhdf.com

Notes: Operated by third generation family. Ten salespersons staff showroom and telephones. Telephone quotes will be followed by a written quote. No VISA/MC on out of state orders. No returns.150,000 sq ft showroom.

Manufacturers: (Many resources do not list all their manufacturers. Be sure to inquire about those you are interested in, but do not see listed here.)

AMERICAN DREW
AMERICAN FURNITURE
GALLERY
BASSETT
BROYHILL
HENRY LINK
HENRY LINK

HIGHLAND HOUSE
KINCAID
KINGSDOWN BEDDING
KROEHLER
LANE
LEXINGTON

LINK TAYLOR
SINGER
STONEVILLE
UNIVERSAL
YOUNG HINKLE

LJ BEST FURNITURE
PO BOX 489
THOMASVILLE, NC 27360
Hours: M-F: 9-5

Toll-Free	800-334-8000
Direct	
Fax	
Internet	

Notes:

Manufacturers: (Many resources do not list all their manufacturers. Be sure to inquire about those you are interested in, but do not see listed here.)

LOFTIN-BLACK FURNITURE COMPANY
111 SEDGEHILL DR
THOMASVILLE, NC 27360
Hours: M-F: 8:30-5:30; S: 8:30-4:30; Closed Sundays

Toll-Free	800-334-7398 or 800-745-FURN
Direct	
Fax	336-472-2052
Internet	

Notes: Note second location at 214 North Main St, High Point, NC 27261; 336-883-4711.
Established in 1948. Ten consultants on staff. Fifty percent deposit can be paid via
VISA/MC/DISC/MO and balance due upon delivery as cashiers check, money order or cash. You can
visit their 14,000 square foot showroom. Home furnishings, bedding and accessories.

Manufacturers: (Many resources do not list all their manufacturers. Be sure to inquire
about those you are interested in, but do not see listed here.)

AA LAUN	CLASSIC GEORGIAN REPROD	FLEXSTEEL
ACCENTRICS	CLASSIC LEATHER	FLORAL ART
ACTION BY LANE	CLASSIC RATTAN	FRANKLIN CHAIR
ALEXVALE	CLAYTON MARCUS	FREDERICK COOPER LAMPS
ALVA	COCHRANE	FROELICH
AMERICAN DREW	COLONIAL	FUTURISTIC RECLINERS
AMERICAN OF HIGH POINT	COMFORT DESIGNS	GLASS ARTS
AMERICAN OF MARTINSVILLE	CONOVER CHAIR	GOODWIN WEAVERS
BALDWIN BRASS	CONTINENTAL ACCENTS	HALE OF VERMONT
BARCALOUNGER	CORSICAN BEDS	HAMMARY
BARN DOOR	COUNCILL CRAFTSMEN	HEKMAN
BASSETT	COX	HENRY LINK
BEACHLEY UPHOLSTERY	CRAFTIQUE	HICKORY HILL
BENCHCRAFT	CRAWFORD	HICKORY MARK
BEST CHAIRS	CRYSTAL CLEAR	HICKORY TAVERN
BLACKSMITH SHOP	DANSEN	HICKORY HOUSE
BOB TIMBERLAKE	DAYSTROM	HIGHLAND HOUSE
BRADINGTON YOUNG	DILLON	HITCHCOCK CHAIR
BRAXTON CULLER	DINAIRE	HOOKER
BROWN STREET	DIRECTIONAL	HOWARD MILLER CLOCKS
BROYHILL	DISTINCTION LEATHER	HTB CONTEMPORARY
BUTLER SPECIALTY	DUTAILIER	JASPER
CAL-STYLE	EAGLECRAFT DESKS	JETTON UPHOLSTERY
CAPE CRAFTSMAN	EDWARD ART	JOHNSTON CASUALS
CAROLINA MIRROR	ELLIOTT'S DESIGNS	KELLER
CARSON'S	EMERSON LEATHER	KIMBALL 18TH CENTURY
CARTER	EMISSARY	KINCAID
CASA BIQUE	EXCELSIOR	KING HICKORY
CENTURY	EXECUTIVE LEATHER	KINGSDOWN
CHARLESTON FORGE	FAIRFIELD CHAIR	KNF DESIGNS
CHATHAM FURNITURE	FASHION BED GROUP	KNOB CREEK
CHATHAM COUNTY	FEATHERMADE MATTRESS	LaBARGE
CHROMCRAFT	FICKS REED	LAINE UPHOLSTERY
CLASSIC GALLERY	FINE ART LAMPS	LANE

LEA
LEISTERS
LEXINGTON
LILLIAN AUGUST
LINK TAYLOR
LLOYD FLANDERS
LYON SHAW
MADISON SQUARE
MARK THOMAS LAMPS
MARLOW
MARYLAND CLASSICS
MILLENDER
MCKINLEY LEATHER
MOOSEHEAD
NAJARIAN
NATHAN HALE
NATIONAL MT AIRY
NICHOLS & STONE
NORTH FRANKLIN
NORTH HICKORY
NULL INDUSTRIES
O'ASIAN
OHIO TABLE PADS
PALECEK
PALMER COLLECTION
PEARSON UPHOLSTERY

PENNSYLVANIA CLASSICS
PEOPLOUNGER
PETERS-REVINGTON
PULASKI
REX
RICHARDSON BROS
RIDGEWAY CLOCKS
RIVERSIDE
JOHN ROCHELLE
ROCK CITY
ROWE
SAM MOORE
SAMSONITE
SARREID
SCHUMACHER
SEALY
SEALY OF MARYLAND
SEDGEFIELD LAMP
SELIG UPHOLSTERY
SERTA MATTRESS
SKILLCRAFT
SLIGH
SOUTHERN
SOUTHWOOD
STANLEY

STANTON COOPER
STATESVILLE CHAIR
STIFFEL LAMP
STRATFORD
STRATOLOUNGER
SUPERIOR
SWAIM DESIGNS
SWAN BRASS BED
TAYLOR WOODCRAFT
THAYER COGGIN
THROUGH BARN DOOR
UNIVERSAL
UWHARRIE CHAIR
VENTURE
VICTORIAN CLASSICS
VIRGINIA HOUSE
VIRGINIA METALCRAFTERS
WEIMAN
WESLEY ALLEN
WESTWOOD LAMPS
WILDWOOD LAMPS
WINSTON
WOODARD
WOODMARK
YORKSHIRE LEATHER

LOUNGE SHOP, THE
2222-E PATTERSON STREET
GREENSBORO, NC 27260
Hours: **M-F: 9:30-8; S: 9:30-6; SUN: 1-6**

Toll-Free	
Direct	336-852-3088
Fax	336-852-3088
Internet	

Notes: High Point market samples and more. Financing available.

Manufacturers: (Many resources do not list all their manufacturers. Be sure to inquire about those you are interested in, but do not see listed here.)

BASSETT
CRAWFORD
FASHION HOUSE
FLEXSTEEL
HOOKER

KROEHLER
LEISTERS OF HANOVER
MARTINSVILLE NOVELTY
MORGAN STEWART

SINGER
UNIVERSAL
US FURNITURE
VIRGINIA HOUSE

LUIGI CRYSTAL
7332 FRANKFORD AVE
PHILADELPHIA, PA 19136
Hours: **M-S: 9-5:30; F:9-8**

Toll-Free	800-952-9204
Direct	215-338-2978
Fax	
Internet	

Notes: In business since 1935. 44-catalog shows each fixture. Replacement parts available. Pay by VISA/MC/AMEX/MO.

Manufacturers: (Many resources do not list all their manufacturers. Be sure to inquire about those you are interested in, but do not see listed here.)

LUXURY FABRICS AND INTERIORS
PO BOX 250
GASTONIA, NC 28053
Hours: **M-S: 9-5**

Toll-Free	800-292-0003
Direct	704-867-5313
Fax	704-853-3018
Internet	

Notes: Great fabric source selling exclusive fabrics from leading design houses all over the world. We can help you identify just about any fabric by name, magazine ad, photograph, sample or description and save you big dollars. Customized window and bed treatments and headboards. We also manufacture and ship our own line of upholstered pieces. Located near the junction of I-85 and HWY 321, as you head from Charlotte to Hickory. Great place to stop and visit.**Other locations at: 9715 Kingston Pike, Knoxville, TN 37922 (615-693-7021) and 7813 Two Notch Road, Columbia, SC 29223 (803-788-3743).**

Manufacturers: (Many resources do not list all their manufacturers. Be sure to inquire about those you are interested in, but do not see listed here.)
HERITAGE HOUSE   WAVERLY   and much more

MACKIE FURNITURE CO, INC
13 N MAIN ST, PO DRAWER 70
GRANITE FALLS, NC 28630
Hours: **M-F: 9-5**

Toll-Free	
Direct	828-396-3313
Fax	828-396-3314
Internet	email: mackie@abts.net website:www/MackieFurniture.com

Notes: Located on Hwy 321. Founded in 1916. Nationwide delivery. Showroom available. Fifty percent deposit required. Cancellation is allowable as long as manufacturer approves it.

Manufacturers: (Many resources do not list all their manufacturers. Be sure to inquire about those you are interested in, but do not see listed here.)

ACTION BY LANE
AMERICAN DREW
ASHLEY
BASSETT
BLACKSMITH SHOP
BRADINGTON YOUNG
BROYHILL
CAROLINA MIRROR
CHATHAM COUNTY
CLAYTON MARCUS
COCHRANE
DUCKS UNLIMITED
EMERSON LEATHER

FAIRFIELD
FASHION BED GROUP
FLORIDA FURNITURE
HAMMARY
HENRY LINK
HOOKER
JASPER CABINET
KELLER
KINCAID
KINGSDOWN
LANE
LEA

LEXINGTON
LINK TAYLOR
LLOYD FLANDERS
MCKAY TABLE PADS
MORGANTON CHAIR
MORGAN STEWART
PULASKI
RIVERSIDE
THER-A-PEDIC
TELESCOPE
UNIVERSAL
VAUGHAN

MAIN STREET PENNSYLVANIA HOUSE
THE ATRIUM
430 SOUTH MAIN ST
HIGH POINT, NC 27262
Hours: **M-F: 9-6; S: 9-5**

Toll-Free	
Direct	336-886-5200
Fax	336-886-5204
Internet	email: mainstreetpa@theatrium.com

Notes: Part of the Atrium complex. Worth visiting, showrooms available. See **Atrium Furniture Showroom** listing for more information. American, traditional furniture in cherry, oak, mahogany, pine or maple. Bedroom, dining room, and living room furniture. Due to some manufacturer requirements, some lines cannot be sold outside of North Carolina. Out of state customers must be physically present at the Atrium to make a purchase.

Manufacturers: (Many resources do not list all their manufacturers. Be sure to inquire about those you are interested in, but do not see listed here.)
PENNSYLVANIA HOUSE

MAITLAND SMITH FACTORY OUTLET
HICKORY FURNITURE MART
2220 HWY 70 SE
HICKORY, NC 28602
Hours: **M-F: 9-6; S: 9-5; Closed Sundays**

Toll-Free	
Direct	828-324-2220
Fax	
Internet	

Notes: This resource is part of the Hickory Furniture Mart complex. This showroom is one of over 80 to visit. **See Hickory Furniture Mart listing for more information.** Consolidated shipping can be arranged with other resources in this center, a standard one/third deposit is required on all orders. Most showrooms accept VISA/MC, but not all. Cash, personal or certified checks accepted by all showrooms. If you elect not to pay for your entire purchase at the time of sale, a personal or certified check will be due upon delivery.

Manufacturers: (Many resources do not list all their manufacturers. Be sure to inquire about those you are interested in, but do not see listed here.)

MAITLAND SMITH FURNITURE OUTLET
411 TOMLINSON ST
HIGH POINT, NC 27260
Hours: **M-F: 9-5; S: 10-3**

Toll-Free	
Direct	336-812-2441
Fax	336-812-2625
Internet	

Notes: Closed for two weeks in April and October for furniture markets

Manufacturers: (Many resources do not list all their manufacturers. Be sure to inquire about those you are interested in, but do not see listed here.)
MAITLAND SMITH

MALLORY'S FINE FURNITURE
2153 LEJEUNE BLVD
JACKSONVILLE, NC 28540
Hours: **M-F: 9-6**

Toll-Free	
Direct	910-353-1828
Fax	910-353-3348
Internet	mallorys@onslowonline.net

Notes: In business since 1947. VISA/MC 40% down payment. Shippers used are van lines. Brochures and procedures available by mail.

Manufacturers: (Many resources do not list all their manufacturers. Be sure to inquire about those you are interested in, but do not see listed here.)

ACACIA
ACCENTRICS BY PULASKI
ACTION BY LANE
ALEXANDER JULIAN BY UNIVERSAL
AMERICAN DREW
AMERICAN OF MARTINSVILLE
ATHOL
BALDWIN BRASS
BASSETT
BASSETTT MIRROR
BERNHARDT
BETSY CAMERON
BLACKSMITH SHOP
BRAXTON CULLER
BROWN JORDAN
BROYHILL
CAROLINA MIRROR
CARSON'S
CASA BIQUE
CEBU IMPORTS
CENTURY
CHAPMAN LAMPS
CHARLESTON FORGE
CHROMCRAFT
CLASSIC LEATHER
CLAYTON MARCUS
COCHRANE
COLONIAL FURNITURE CO
COUNCILL CRAFTSMEN
COX
CRAFTIQUE
CRAFTWORK GUILD
CRAWFORD
CTH/SHERRILL
DECORATIVE CRAFTS

DECRISTOFARO
DINAIRE
DINING ALA CARTE BY LANE
EMERSON
ENTREE BY LaBARGE
FAIRFIELD CHAIR
FICKS REED
FLEXSTEEL
FREDERICK COOPER LAMPS
FREDERICK EDWARD
FRIEDMAN BROS MIRRORS
FROELICH
HABERSHAM PLANTATION
HAMMARY
HANCOCK & MOORE
HEKMAN
HENKEL HARRIS
HENKEL MOORE
HENRY LINK
HICKORY CHAIR
HICKORY WHITE
HICKORY TAVERN BY LANE
HIGHLAND HOUSE
HOOKER
HOWARD MILLER
HTB BY LANE
J ROYALE
JASPER CABINET
JOHNSTON CASUALS
KAISER KUHN LIGHTING
KARGES
KESSLER
KIMBALL
KINCAID

KNOB CREEK
KOCH
LaBARGE
LANE
LEA
LEXINGTON
LILLIAN AUGUST
LINK TAYLOR
LLOYD FLANDERS
LYON SHAW
LYNN HOLLYN
MADISON SQUARE
MAITLAND SMITH
MARBRO LAMPS
McKAY TABLE PADS
MICHAEL THOMAS
MILLENDER
MOTIONCRAFT BY SHERRILL
NATIONAL MT AIRY
NORMAN ROCKWELL BY
STANLEY
OHIO TABLE PADS
OLD SALEM BY LEXINGTON
OLD WAVERLY BY JTB
PARK PLACE
PEARSON
PETERS-REVINGTON
POMPEII
PULASKI
RICHARDSON BROS
RIDGEWAY CLOCKS
RIVERSIDE
ROBERT ALLEN FABRICS
SAM MOORE

SARREID
SEDGEFIELD BY ADAMS
SHOAL CREEK LAMP
SIMMONS
SIMPLY SOUTHERN
SOUTHERN REPRODUCTIONS
SOUTHAMPTON
SOUTHMARK LEATHER
SOUTHWOOD
REPRODUCTIONS
SPEER
STANFORD
STANLEY
STIFFEL LAMP
TAYLOR WOODCRAFT
TELL CITY
THOMASVILLE CABINET
TRADITION HOUSE
UNIVERSAL
VANGUARD
VENTURE BY LANE
VIRGINIA METALCRAFTERS
WATERFORD FURNITURE
WEIMAN
WELLINGTON HALL
WESLEY ALLEN
WESLEY HALL
WHITECRAFT
WILDWOOD LAMPS
WINSTON
WOODARD
WOODMARK ORIGINALS

MARGE CARSON GALLERY
HICKORY FURNITURE MART
2220 HWY 70 SE
HICKORY, NC 28602
Hours: **M-F: 9-6; S: 9-5; Closed Sundays**

Toll-Free	
Direct	828-326-1735
Fax	
Internet	

Notes: This resource is part of the Hickory Furniture Mart complex. This showroom is one of over 80 to visit. **See Hickory Furniture Mart listing for more information.** Consolidated shipping can be arranged with other resources in this center, a standard one/third deposit is required on all orders.

Most showrooms accept VISA/MC, but not all. Cash, personal or certified checks accepted by all showrooms. If you elect not to pay for your entire purchase at the time of sale, a personal or certified check will be due upon delivery.

Manufacturers: **(Many resources do not list all their manufacturers. Be sure to inquire about those you are interested in, but do not see listed here.)**

MARION TRAVIS
PO BOX 929 OR 1041
STATESVILLE, NC 28687
Hours: **M-T: 8-3:30; FRI: 8-NOON**

Toll-Free	
Direct	704-528-4424
Fax	
Internet	

Notes: Established in 1968. Country chairs, ladderback chairs, barstools, swings and tables. Complete order can be paid by VISA/MC/CHECK. Showroom available for browsing. Staff of four can help customer with selections. Satisfaction guaranteed. Shipping problems are handled by customer and carrier.

Manufacturers: **(Many resources do not list all their manufacturers. Be sure to inquire about those you are interested in, but do not see listed here.)**

MARK SALES CO, INC
151-20 88TH ST, DEPT 2G
QUEENS, NY 11414
Hours: **M-F:9-5**

Toll-Free	
Direct	718-835-9319
Fax	
Internet	

Notes: Imported unfinished furniture can be viewed in the 62 catalog ($3). Completely assembled hand-carved chairs and furniture come ready to paint, stain or varnish. French provincial, country

French or Italian. No credit cards accepted, satisfaction guaranteed, authorized returns accepted within 20 days. We are the only unfinished antique reproduction furniture company that sells wholesale to the public.

Manufacturers: (Many resources do not list all their manufacturers. Be sure to inquire about those you are interested in, but do not see listed here.)

MARKET SAMPLE FURNITURE OUTLET
2850 S MAIN ST
HIGH POINT, NC 27262
Hours: **TH-S: 10-6**

Toll-Free	
Direct	336-434-5185
Fax	
Internet	

Notes: Samples from recent markets are available for sale Thursdays through Saturdays. Open year round. Part of Colfax Furniture store.

Manufacturers: (Many resources do not list all their manufacturers. Be sure to inquire about those you are interested in, but do not see listed here.)

MARLENE'S DECORATOR FABRICS
301 BEECH STREET, DEPT 2J
HACKENSACK, NJ 07601
Hours: **M-F: 9:30-6**

Toll-Free	
Direct	201-843-0844
Fax	
Internet	

Notes: In business since 1951. Mail order only for upholstery, slipcover and drapery fabrics. Designers and consultants on this staff. First quality decorator fabrics at 34-50% off retail complete order can be paid by VISA/MC/AMEX/MO. Shipped UPS, received within 2-3 weeks, unless otherwise stated. We can never guarantee dyelots. No refunds, returns or cancellations except merchandise damaged by manufacturer or ups. Shipping problems are handled by resource.

Manufacturers: (Many resources do not list all their manufacturers. Be sure to inquire about those you are interested in, but do not see listed here.)

MINIMUM 10 YARDS:

ADO	PIERRE DEUX	COLLINS & AIKMAN
AMETEX FABRICS	PINDLER & PINDLER	COVINGTON
ARTMARK	R&M/COCO	CYRUS CLARK
ASHBOURNE	RALPH LAUREN	DOBLIN
B BERGER	ROBERT ALLEN	EDGAR
BARROW	ROSE CUMMINGS	FAME
BLAUTEX	S HARRIS	HAMPTON MILLS
BOUSSAC	SANDERSON	HOFFMAN MILLS
BRUNSCHWIG & FILS	SCALAMANDRE	HOME TEXTILES
CARLETON V	SCHUMACHER	JB MARTIN
CLARENCE HOUSE	STOUT	KENMILL
COLEFAX & FOWLER	STROHEIM & ROMANN	LANSCOT ARLEN
DURALEE	WAVERLY	MASTERCRAFT
ELCO	WESCO	MERRIMAC/J NASH
FABRICUT	WESTGATE	MILL CREEK/SWAVELLE
JAB		P KAUFMANN
KASMIR	**DIRECT MANUFACTURERS;**	PORTFOLIO
KRAVET	**15-30 YARD MINIMUM:**	RICHLOOM
KRUPNICK BROS	AMERICAN SILK	SANDOWN & BOURNE
LEE JOFA	AMETEX FABRICS	SPECTRUM
MAENLINE	ANJU WOODRIDGE	SUNBRELLA
MANUEL CANOVAS	BRAEMORE	VALDESE WEAVERS
P COLLINS	BLOOMCRAFT	WEAVE
PACIFIC WEAVERS	CHRIS STONE	WESTERN TEXTILE
PAYNE	COHAMA RIVERDALE	JOHN WOLF
	COLLAGE/KALEIDOSCOPE	

═══════════════════════════

MARTY RAE OF LEXINGTON
5108 SUNSET BLVD
LEXINGTON, SC 29072
Hours: **M-F: 9-5**

Toll-Free	
Direct	803-957-7999
Fax	803-957-7557
Internet	email: martyrae@microbyte.net

Notes: Showroom available.

Manufacturers: (Many resources do not list all their manufacturers. Be sure to inquire about those you are interested in, but do not see listed here.)

COUNCILL CRAFTSMEN	LANE	PULASKI
HICKORY CHAIR	LEXINGTON	SOUTHWOOD

MAYFIELD LEATHER
340 9TH ST SE
HICKORY, NC 28603
Hours: **M-F: 9-5**

Toll-Free	800-342-7729
Direct	
Fax	828-324-5127
Internet	

Notes: Choose from more than 100 unique accent chairs, bar chairs, sofas/loveseats, chairs/ottomans in rich leathers. Custom order, all at reasonable pricing.

Manufacturers: **(Many resources do not list all their manufacturers. Be sure to inquire about those you are interested in, but do not see listed here.)**

MDC DIRECT, INC
PO BOX 569
MARIETTA, GA 30061
Hours: **M-S: 8-8**

Toll-Free	800-892-2083
Direct	
Fax	770-324-3399
Internet	

Notes: Great little sample package of window treatment samples.

Manufacturers: **(Many resources do not list all their manufacturers. Be sure to inquire about those you are interested in, but do not see listed here.)**

BALI/GRABER	HUNTER DOUGLAS	M & B
COMFORTEX	LEVOLOR	Their own line

MECKLENBURG FURNITURE
520 PROVIDENCE ROAD
CHARLOTTE, NC 28207
Hours: M-S: 9-5:30; Th: 9-8

Toll-Free	
Direct	704-376-8401
Fax	704-347-0499
Internet	

Notes: Fourteen designers on staff. 50,000 square foot showroom available to browse. Staff will help customers make decisions, send photocopies, etc. Check or money order only. Worldwide shipping. One-third down payment required. Full service. Brochure and procedures available by mail

Manufacturers: (**Many resources do not list all their manufacturers. Be sure to inquire about those you are interested in, but do not see listed here.**)

A LOCK	CHARLESTON FORGE	FITZ & FLOYD
ACTION BY LANE	CHELSEA HOUSE/PORT ROYAL	FREDERICK COOPER
AMERICAN DREW	CHROMCRAFT	FREDERICK EDWARD
AMERICAN OF MARTINSVILLE	CLARENCE HOUSE	FRIEDMAN BROS MIRRORS
ARTLEE FABRICS	CLASSIC GALLERY	GARCIA IMPORTS
ARTMARK FABRICS	CLASSIC RATTAN	GEORGE KOVACS
AS YOU LIKE IT LAMPS	CLAYTON MARCUS	GEORGE KOVACS
BAILEY & GRIFFIN	CORSICAN IRON BEDS	GEORGIAN LIGHTING
BAKER	COUNCILL CRAFTSMEN	GORDON'S
BARCALOUNGER	COWTAN & TOUT	GREEFF
BASSETT	COX	GROSFILLEX
BASSETT MIRROR	CRAFTIQUE	GROW & CUTTLE
BATES FABRICS	CRAFTWORK GUILD	HABERSHAM PLANTATION
BERKSHIRE	CRYSTAL CLEAR	HALE CO
BETH WEISSMAN LAMPS	CTH/SHERRILL	HAMMARY
BETH WEISSMAN LAMPS	D & F WICKER	HEKMAN FURNITURE
BEVAN FUNNELL	DANSEN	HEYGILL IMPORTS
BIGGS	DAPHA	HEYWARD HOUSE
BLONDER	DAVID MORGAN	HICKORY CHAIR
BORKHOLDER	DAVID MORGAN	HICKORY FRY
BRADINGTON YOUNG	DAVID THOMAS LAMPS	HICKORY WHITE
BRASS BEDS OF AMERICA	DAVIS & DAVIS	HIGH POINT FURNITURE
BRAXTON CULLER	DESIGNMASTER	HIGH POINT WOODWORKING
BROWN JORDAN	DINAIRE	HIGHLAND HOUSE
BROYHILL PREMIER	DRESHER	HILL
BRUNSCHWIG & FILS	DURALEE FABRICS	HITCHCOCK CHAIR
BUILTRIGHT CHAIR	ELEMENTS BY GRAPEVINE	HOOKER
CAL-STYLE	ELLO	HTB LANE
CAPITAL ASAM	EMERSON LEATHER	INTERNATIONAL WROUGHT
CAROLINA MIRROR	ERWIN-LAMBETH	IRON
CASA BIQUE	FABRICADE	J ROYALE
CASA STRADIVARI	FAIRFIELD CHAIR	JASPER CABINET
CENTURY	FAIRINGTON	JEFFCO
CENTURY CHAIR	FASHION BED	JOHN BOOS
CHAIRCRAFT	FICKS REED	JOHN WIDDICOMB
CHAPMAN	FINKEL OUTDOOR	JOHN WIDDICOMB

JOHNSTON CASUALS
KARASTAN
KARGES
KATZENBACH & WARREN
KEY CITY
KIMBALL
KING KOIL
KINGSDOWN
KIRK STIEFF
KITTINGER
KNOB CREEK
L & S IMPORTS
LaBARGE
LAINE
LANE
LEA
LEATHER LINING
LEE JOFA
LEXINGTON
LLOYD FLANDERS
LYON-SHAW
MADISON SQUARE
MAITLAND SMITH
MASLAND CARPET
MASTERCRAFT
McGUIRE
McKAY TABLE PADS
MEADOWCRAFT
MILLENDER
MILLER DESK
MOTTAHEDEH
MURRAY FEISS LAMPS
NEW CREATIONS
NICHOLS & STONE
NORMAN PERRY LAMPS

O'ASIAN
OHIO TABLE PADS
OLD HICKORY TANNERY
PALECEK
PANDE CAMERON RUGS
PAUL HANSON CO
PAYNE FABRICS
PEARSON
PENNSYLVANIA CLASSICS
PENNSYLVANIA HOUSE
PINNACLE
PULASKI
REMINGTON LAMPS
RIDGEWAY CLOCKS
SALEM SQUARE
SCALAMANDRE
SCHOONBECK
SCHOTT FURNITURE
SCHUMACHER/WAVERLY
SEALY
SEDGEFIELD LAMP
SELIG
SERTA
SHOAL CREEK LIGHTING
SHUFORD
SLIGH FURNITURE
SOUTHAMPTON
SOUTHWOOD
REPRODUCTIONS
STANLEY FURNITURE
STATESVILLE CHAIR
STATTON
STIFFEL
STROHEIM & ROMANN

SWAIM ORIGINALS
SWAN BRASS BED
TAYLORSVILLE UPHOLSTERY
TELL CITY
TEMPLE
THONET
TOUCH OF BRASS
TRADEWINDS
TRADITIONS FRANCE
TRADITION HOUSE
TROPITONE
UNION NATIONAL
UNIQUE
UNIVERSAL
VANGUARD
VENTURE
VIRGINIA HOUSE
VIRGINIA METALCRAFTERS
VIRGINIA METALCRAFTERS
VOGUE RATTAN
WATERFORD
WEIMAN
WELLINGTON HALL
WESLEY ALLEN
WESTCHESTER LEATHER
WHITECRAFT
WILDWOOD LAMPS
WINSTON OUTDOOR
FURNITURE
WOODARD
WOODLEE
WOODMARK ORIGINALS
WRIGHT TABLE

Resource Directory

MEDALLION FURNITURE
THE ATRIUM
430 SOUTH MAIN ST
HIGH POINT, NC 27260
Hours: M-F: 9-6; S:9-5

Toll-Free	
Direct	336-889-3432
Fax	336-889-3433
Internet	email: medallion@theatrium.com

Notes: Part of the Atrium complex. Worth visiting, showrooms available. See **Atrium Furniture Showroom** listing for more information. Hundreds of fabic selections allow you to go from a tropical environment to a northern atmosphere. Top quality fossil stone and faux stone, rattan, wicker and high-end upholstery

Manufacturers: (Many resources do not list all their manufacturers. Be sure to inquire about those you are interested in, but do not see listed here.)

═══════════════════════════════════

MIDAS FABRIC
4813 W MARKET ST
GREENSBORO, NC 27407
Hours: **M-S: 9AM-5PM**

Toll-Free	
Direct	336-294-9000
Fax	336-294-9001
Internet	

Notes: In business since 1971. VISA/MC/DISC accepted. Discount drapery & upholstery fabrics/trims and patterns

Manufacturers: (Many resources do not list all their manufacturers. Be sure to inquire about those you are interested in, but do not see listed here.)

AMETEX FABRICS	GREENHOUSE	RICHLOOM
ADO	GREEFF	REGAL
ANJU WOODRIDGE	HAMILTON	RAPIER
AWARD	HOFFMAN	ROTHSCHILD
BARROW	HAZZARD	STOUT
BURLINGTON	JABLAN	STEVENS
BRAEMORE	KASMIR	SPECTRUM
BLOOMCRAFT	KAUFMANN	SANDOWN
CONCORD	LATIMER	SL
CYRUS CLARK	LANSCOT	T & E
COVINGTON	MILL CREEK	TRI TEX
CHRIS STONE	MAGNOLIA	UPS
CAMBRIDGE	MERRIMAC	WAVERLY
CAROLE	PREMIER	SCHUMACHER
P COLLINS	PEACHTREE	WESTGATE
EDGAR	PORTFOLIO	WESTERN
FMA	QUAKER	WOLF
FABRICUT		

═══════════════════════════════════

MIDAS FABRIC
7912 GLENWOOD AVE
RALEIGH, NC 27612
Hours: **M-S: 9AM-5PM**

Toll-Free	
Direct	919-782-5500
Fax	919-781-3588
Internet	

Notes: In business since 1971. VISA/MC/DISC accepted. Discount drapery & upholstery fabrics/trims and patterns

Manufacturers: (Many resources do not list all their manufacturers. Be sure to inquire about those you are interested in, but do not see listed here.)

AMETEX FABRICS	GREENHOUSE	RICHLOOM
ADO	GREEFF	REGAL
ANJU WOODRIDGE	HAMILTON	RAPIER
AWARD	HOFFMAN	ROTHSCHILD
BARROW	HAZZARD	STOUT
BURLINGTON	JABLAN	STEVENS
BRAEMORE	KASMIR	SPECTRUM
BLOOMCRAFT	KAUFMANN	SANDOWN
CONCORD	LATIMER	SL
CYRUS CLARK	LANSCOT	T & E
COVINGTON	MILL CREEK	TRI TEX
CHRIS STONE	MAGNOLIA	UPS
CAMBRIDGE	MERRIMAC	WAVERLY
CAROLE	PREMIER	SCHUMACHER
P COLLINS	PEACHTREE	WESTGATE
EDGAR	PORTFOLIO	WESTERN
FMA	QUAKER	WOLF
FABRICUT		

MIDAS FABRIC
3120 N SHARON AMITY RD
CHARLOTTE, NC 28205
Hours: **M-S: 9AM-5PM**

Toll-Free	
Direct	704-537-7600
Fax	704-537-7632
Internet	

Notes: In business since 1971. VISA/MC/DISC accepted. Discount drapery & upholstery fabrics/trims and patterns

Manufacturers: (Many resources do not list all their manufacturers. Be sure to inquire about those you are interested in, but do not see listed here.)

AMETEX FABRICS	GREENHOUSE	RICHLOOM
ADO	GREEFF	REGAL
ANJU WOODRIDGE	HAMILTON	RAPIER
AWARD	HOFFMAN	ROTHSCHILD
BARROW	HAZZARD	STOUT
BURLINGTON	JABLAN	STEVENS
BRAEMORE	KASMIR	SPECTRUM
BLOOMCRAFT	KAUFMANN	SANDOWN
CONCORD	LATIMER	SL
CYRUS CLARK	LANSCOT	T & E
COVINGTON	MILL CREEK	TRI TEX
CHRIS STONE	MAGNOLIA	UPS
CAMBRIDGE	MERRIMAC	WAVERLY
CAROLE	PREMIER	SCHUMACHER
P COLLINS	PEACHTREE	WESTGATE
EDGAR	PORTFOLIO	WESTERN
FMA	QUAKER	WOLF
FABRICUT		

MILLER'S - THE WINDOW DECOR STORE
201 INDUSTRY PARKWAY
NICHOLASVILLE, KY 40356
Hours: **M-F: 9-6**

Toll-Free	
Direct	606-272-8199
Fax	606-887-4778
Internet	

Notes: In business since 1981. Window treatments, storage and closet systems, storage ideas. Sales and design consultants on staff. All orders are custom. VISA/MC/CHECK accepted. Four sales consultants on staff. Mail order payments require full payment at time of purchase. Custom made products are warranted by manufacturer and no return allowed.

Manufacturers: (Many resources do not list all their manufacturers. Be sure to inquire about those you are interested in, but do not see listed here.)

ARQUATI	HUNTER DOUGLAS	LEE/ROWAN
DELMAR	KIRSCH	

MINCEY'S INC
600 SUGAR CREEK ROAD W.
CHARLOTTE, NC 28213
Hours: **M-F: 10-6; S: 10-5**

Toll-Free	
Direct	704-596-2341
Fax	704-596-1675
Internet	

Notes: In business since 1922. Three sales consultants. VISA/MC accepted for down payment, same for balance. Only authorized return accepted. Factory warranties honored.

Manufacturers: (Many resources do not list all their manufacturers. Be sure to inquire about those you are interested in, but do not see listed here.)

AMERICAN DREW	HUNTINGTON HOUSE	PULASKI
BLACKSMITH SHOP	KELLER	RIVERSIDE
BROYHILL	LA-Z-BOY	SEALY
CHROMCRAFT	LEXINGTON	SUMTER
CRAFTIQUE	LINK-TAYLOR	TELL CITY
HENRY LINK	PETERS-REVINGTON	VICTORIAN CLASSIC
HOOKER		

MODERN UPHOLSTERY CO
1101 GREENSBORO RD
HIGH POINT, NC 27262
Hours: **M-F: 10-5**

Toll-Free	
Direct	336-454-5988
Fax	
Internet	

Notes: In business since 1940.

Manufacturers: (Many resources do not list all their manufacturers. Be sure to inquire about those you are interested in, but do not see listed here.)
BASSETT   STANLEY

MONROE'S FURNITURE
100 RIGBY ST, PO BOX 38
REEVESVILLE, SC 29471
Hours: **M-F: 9am-5pm**

Toll-Free	
Direct	803-563-6300
Fax	803-563-3160
Internet	

Notes: Located just off I-95 (exit 77). Experienced staff. Shipment is made by a home delivery carrier who will deliver and place the furniture inside your home. Shipping rates are based on the weight and distance. Estimated freight charge will be quoted. 30% deposit required. Cancellations or changes can be made as long as manufacturer accepts them. 25% restocking fee will be charged on orders we are unable to stop. We will handle serious freight damage. At our discretion, we will replace only those items that cannot be repaired properly. (Formerly National Carolina Interiors).

Manufacturers: (Many resources do not list all their manufacturers. Be sure to inquire about those you are interested in, but do not see listed here.)

ACACIA	AMERICAN HERITAGE	ASHLEY
ACCENTRICS BY PULASKI	AMERICAN IMPRESSIONS	ATHOL
ACTION BY LANE	AMERICAN MIRROR	ATLANTA GLASSCRAFTER
AMERICAN DREW	ANDRE ORIGINALS	BALDWIN BRASS

BASSETT
BAUER LAMP
BENICIA
BERNARD'S
BERNHARDT
BERRYHILL PRINTS
BEST CHAIR
BLACKSMITH SHOP
BOB TIMBERLAKE
BRADINGTON YOUNG
BROWN STREET
BROYHILL
BUILTRIGHT CHAIR
BUTLER
CALDWELL CHAIR
CAMBRIDGE
CARLTON McLENDON
CAROLINA FURNITURE
CAROLINA MIRROR
CARSON'S
CEBU
CHAPMAN
CHARLES SADEK
CHARLESTON FORGE
CHROMCRAFT
CLASSIC ART
CLASSIC LEATHER
COCHRANE
COLONIAL
COROLLA
COUNCILL CRAFTSMEN
COX
CRAFTIQUE
CRAFTMASTERS
CRAWFORD OF JAMESTOWN
D & F WICKER
DAVID KENT
DAVIS CABINET
DINAIRE
DISTINCTION LEATHER
ENTREE
FAIRFIELD CHAIR
FASHION BED
FASHION HOUSE
FITZ & FLOYD
FURNITURE CLASSICS
GEORGIA CHAIR
GLASS ARTS

GRACE MANUFACTURING
GREENE BROS
HABERSHAM PLANTATION
HAMMARY
HANCOCK & MOORE
HARDEN
HEKMAN
HENKEL MOORE
HENKEL HARRIS
HENRY LINK
HICKORY BRANCH LAMPS
HICKORY WHITE
HOMECREST
HON
HOOKER
HOWARD MILLER
HUNT COUNTRY
JASPER CABINET
JAY WILLFRED
JENE'S COLLECTION
JETTON
JOHNSTON CASUALS
KARGES
KIMBALL
KINCAID
KOCH ORIGINALS LaBARGE
LANE
LEA
LEATHERCRAFT
LEE TABLE PAD
LEISTERS
LEXINGTON
LIGO
LLOYD FLANDERS
LYON SHAW
MADISON SQUARE
MILLER DESK
MOBEL
MOOSEHEAD
NICHOLS & STONE
NULL INDUSTRIES
QEW
OHIO TABLE PADS
P & P CHAIR
PARKER SOUTHERN
PANASONIC
PETERS-REVINGTON

PULASKI
REFLECTIONS
REX
RIVERSIDE
ROCK CITY
SALEM SQUARE
SAM MOORE
SARREID
SEALY
SEDGEFIELD LAMP
SERTA BEDDING
SHERIDAN
SHERRILL
SKILLCRAFT
SLIGH
SOUTH CONE TRADING
SOUTHERN CRAFTSMEN GUILD
SPRING AIR BEDDING
STANLEY
STATESVILLE CHAIR
STATTON
STIFFEL LAMP
SUMTER CABINET
SUPERIOR
TAHOE
TAYLOR KING
TEMPLE
TRADITIONAL HEIRLOOMS
TRADITIONS FRANCE
TROPITONE
US FURNITURE
UNIVERSAL
VANGUARD
VAUGHAN BASSET
VENEMAN
VENTURE
VICTORIAN CLASSIC
VIRGINIA HOUSE
VIRGINIA METALCRAFTERS
WATERFORD
WEBB
WEIMAN
WESLEY ALLEN
WILDWOOD
WINSTON
WOODARD

MORGAN STEWART GALLERY
HICKORY FURNITURE MART
2220 HWY 70 SE
HICKORY, NC 28602
Hours: **M-F: 9-6; S: 9-5; Closed Sundays**

Toll-Free	
Direct	828-324-4040
Fax	
Internet	

Notes: This resource is part of the Hickory Furniture Mart complex. This showroom is one of over 80 to visit. **See Hickory Furniture Mart listing for more information.** Consolidated shipping can be arranged with other resources in this center, a standard one/third deposit is required on all orders. Most showrooms accept VISA/MC, but not all. Cash, personal or certified checks accepted by all showrooms. If you elect not to pay for your entire purchase at the time of sale, a personal or certified check will be due upon delivery.

Manufacturers: **(Many resources do not list all their manufacturers. Be sure to inquire about those you are interested in, but do not see listed here.)**

MOTIONCRAFT GALLERY
HICKORY FURNITURE MART
2220 HWY 70 SE
HICKORY, NC 28602
Hours: **M-F: 9-6; S: 9-5; Closed Sundays**

Toll-Free	
Direct	828-326-1735
Fax	
Internet	

Notes: This resource is part of the Hickory Furniture Mart complex. This showroom is one of over 80 to visit. **See Hickory Furniture Mart listing for more information.** Consolidated shipping can be arranged with other resources in this center, a standard one/third deposit is required on all orders. Most showrooms accept VISA/MC, but not all. Cash, personal or certified checks accepted by all showrooms. If you elect not to pay for your entire purchase at the time of sale, a personal or certified check will be due upon delivery.

Manufacturers: **(Many resources do not list all their manufacturers. Be sure to inquire**

about those you are interested in, but do not see listed here.)

MURROW FURNITURE GALLERIES
3514 S COLLEGE ROAD
PO BOX 4337
WILMINGTON, NC 28406
Hours: **M-F: 8:30-5:30; S: 9-5:30**

Toll-Free	
Direct	910-799-4010
Fax	910-791-2791
Internet	

Notes: In business since 1979. Designer and sales consultants on staff can assist customer with choices. Customer can visit this facility. Brochures and procedures available by mail. 50% down payment can be paid with check. Balance paid in check/cash/mo. 30% restocking charge for items ordered correctly but customer dissatisfied. Customer service will handle product problems. Located in a beautiful resort area at the beach. Customers can vacation and furniture shop on the same trip. Over 100 golf courses in the area. Furniture, accessories, fabric, wallcoverings, lamps.

Manufacturers: (Many resources do not list all their manufacturers. Be sure to inquire about those you are interested in, but do not see listed here.)

A LOCK	CANADEL	CLYDE PEARSON
AMBIANCE	CANTERBURY	DANSEN CONTEMPORARY
AMERICAN DREW	CAROLINA MIRROR	DECORATIVE CRAFTS
AMERICAN HERITAGE	CARSON'S	DILLON
AMERICAN OF MARTINSVILLE	CARVER'S GUILD	DISTINCTIVE LEATHER
AMISCO	CASA BIQUE	DSF (SCANDANAVIAN)
ARTE DE MEXICO	CASA STRADIVARI	DURALEE FABRICS
ARTISTICA	CENTURY	DUTAILIER
ARTMARK	CHARLESTON FORGE	EKORNES
ASMARA RUGS	CHAPMAN LAMPS	ELLO
BAKER	CHELSEA HOUSE	ELEMENTS BY GRAPEVINE
BALDWIN BRASS	CHROMCRAFT	EMERSON ET CIE
BARCALOUNGER	CLARK CASUAL	EMERSON LEATHER
BASSETT CASEGOODS	CLASSIC LEATHER	EXCELSIOR
BASSETT MIRROR	CLASSIC RATTAN	FAIRFIELD CHAIR
BERNHARDT	COLONIAL FURNITURE	FASHION BED
BEVAN FUNNELL	COUNCILL CRAFTSMEN	FICKS REED
BLACKSMITH SHOP	COOPER CLASSICS	FINE ARTS LAMPS
BRADINGTON YOUNG	COUNTRY AFFAIR/ELDEN	FORBES BROS LAMPS
BRASS BEDS OF VIRGINIA	COX	FREDERICK COOPER
BRAXTON CULLER	CRAFTIQUE	FREDERICK EDWARD
BROYHILL	CRAFTMARK	FRIEDMAN BROS MIRRORS
BURTON REPRODUCTIONS	CRAFTWORK GUILD	FRITZ & LaRUE RUGS
BUTLER	CRAWFORD OF JAMESTOWN	GAINES
CAMBRIDGE	CRYSTAL CLEAR LIGHTING	GARCIA IMPORTS

Resource Directory

GEORGIAN
GLASS ARTS
GLOBER
GRACE
GREEFF FABRICS
GUILDMASTER
HABERSHAM PLANTATION
HAMMARY
HANCOCK & MOORE
HART COUNTRY SHOP
HEKMAN
HEN FEATHERS
HENRY LINK
HICKORY CHAIR
HICKORY WHITE
HILL
HITCHCOCK CHAIR
HOOD
HOOKER
HOWARD MILLER
HYUNDAI
JASPER CABINET
JEFFCO
JOHN WIDDICOMB
JOHNSTON CASUALS
JON ELLIOTT
J ROYALE
KAISER KUHN LIGHTING
KARGES
KELLER
KIMBALL
KINCAID
KING HICKORY
KNOB CREEK
KOCH ORIGINALS
KOCH & LOWY LAMPS
KRAVET FABRICS
LaBARGE
LANE
ACTION BY LANE
LARGO
LEA INDUSTRIES
LEATHERMAN'S GUILD
LEXINGTON
LILLIAN AUGUST
LLOYD FLANDERS
LYON SHAW
McGUIRE
McKAY TABLE PADS

MADISON SQUARE
MAITLAND SMITH
MARBRO LAMPS
MARYLAND CLASSICS
MASLAND CARPET & RUGS
MASTERCRAFT
MICHAEL THOMAS
MOTIONCRAFT
MURRAY FEISS LAMPS
NATIONAL MT AIRY
NATURAL LIGHT
NATHAN HALE
NICHOLS & STONE
NOBAR FABRICS
NORMAN PERRY LAMPS
OHIO TABLE PADS
OLD HICKORY TANNERY
OLD WAVERLY BY JTB
PANDE CAMERON RUGS
PAUL HANSON
PAUL ROBERT
PLATT
PULASKI
REFLECTIONS
RELIANCE LAMPS
REX
RIDGEWOOD FURNITURE
RIVERSIDE
ROBERT ALLEN FABRICS
SALEM SQUARE
SALOOM
SAM MOORE
SARREID
S BENT
SCHOTT
SCHUMACHER
SEABROOK WALLCOVERING
SEALY OF MARYLAND
SEDGEFIELD LAMP
SERTA MATTRESS
SHERRILL OCCASIONAL
SHUFORD
SLIGH
SIMPLY SOUTHERN
SOUTHERN FURNITURE
SOUTHAMPTON
SOUTHWOOD
SPEER
STANLEY

STANTON COOPER
STATESVILLE CHAIR
STATTON
STIFFEL
STONELEIGH
STROHEIM & ROMANN
SUPERIOR
SWAIM
TAYLORSVILLE
TAYLOR WOODCRAFT
TELL CITY
TEMPLE STUART
THAYER COGGIN
THOMASVILLE
TIANJIN PHILADELPHIA
CARPET
TIMBERLAKE COLLECTION
TRADITIONS FRANCE
TRADITION HOUSE
TRANSPACIFIC
TROPITONE
TROSBY
UNIVERSAL
VANGUARD
VAUGHAN
VENTURE
VERMONT TUBBS
VIRGINIA HOUSE
VIRGINIA METALCRAFTERS
WATERFORD FURNITURE
WATERFORD
WAVERLY
WEDGEWOOD
WEIMAN
WELLESLEY GUILD
WELLINGTON HALL
WESLEY ALLEN BRASS
WESLEY HALL
WESTGATE FABRICS
WISCONSIN
WILDWOOD
WILLIAM ALLEN
WINSTON FURNITURE
WOODARD
WOODMARK
WRIGHT TABLE
YORKSHIRE

NATIONAL ART GALLERY
HICKORY FURNITURE MART
2220 HWY 70 SE
HICKORY, NC 28602
Hours: **M-F: 9-6; S: 9-5; Closed Sundays**

Toll-Free	
Direct	828-324-9400
Fax	828-464-9964
Internet	

Notes: This store carries reproductions, sculptures, final furniture, estate furniture, European style paintings, artwork, antiques and collectibles. Quite an eyeful. This resource is part of the Hickory Furniture Mart complex. This showroom is one of over 80 to visit. **See Hickory Furniture Mart listing for more information.** Consolidated shipping can be arranged with other resources in this center, a standard one/third deposit is required on all orders. Most showrooms accept VISA/MC, but not all. Cash, personal or certified checks accepted by all showrooms. If you elect not to pay for your entire purchase at the time of sale, a personal or certified check will be due upon delivery.

Manufacturers: (**Many resources do not list all their manufacturers. Be sure to inquire about those you are interested in, but do not see listed here.**)

ANTIQUES
COLLECTIBLES

EUROPEAN STYLE PAINTINGS
FINAL FURNITURE

HOWARD MILLER
SLIGH

NATIONAL BLIND AND WALLPAPER FACTORY
400 GALLERIA-OFFICE CENTRAL #400
SOUTHFIELD, MI 48034
Hours: **M-F: 7-MIDNIGHT; S-S: 8a-10P**

Toll-Free	800-477-8000
Direct	800-521-3393
Fax	800-858-4550
Internet	

Notes: This company merged with Mary's Wallcovering and Style Wallcovering in 1997. Most well-known major brands carried. Some of this company's discounts are as high as 80% off suggested manufacturers' retail prices. All products can be ordered and paid for with VISA/MC/DISC, certified check or money order. Delivery takes approximately 10-15 working days and is free of charge. Strictly phone sales. Defective merchandise will be replaced.

Manufacturers: (**Many resources do not list all their manufacturers. Be sure to inquire about those you are interested in, but do not see listed here.**)

WALLCOVERINGS	
EISENHART WALLCOVERINGS	SEABROOK
ESSEX	SUNWORTHY
FASHION	UNITED
IMPERIAL	VAN LUIT
LAURA ASHLEY	VILLAGE
LOUIS BOWEN	VYMURA
MIRAGE	WALL TRENDS
RALPH LAUREN	WALLTEX
SANITAS	WARNER
	YORK

AND MORE

WINDOW TREATMENTS
HUNTER DOUGLAS
LEVOLOR
DELMAR
KIRSCH
BALI
GRABER
AND MORE

NATIONAL CAROLINA INTERIORS
PO BOX 7
REEVESVILLE, SC 29471
Hours: **M-F: 9-5**

Toll-Free	
Direct	803-563-8300
Fax	803-563-6888
Internet	**email:** monroes@colum.mindspring.com **website:** ncnet.com\ncnw\nci.html

Notes: Catalog orders. Sister company of Monroe's Furniture.

Manufacturers: **(Many resources do not list all their manufacturers. Be sure to inquire about those you are interested in, but do not see listed here.)**

ACACIA	BUILTRIGHT CHAIR	D & F WICKER
ACCENTRICS BY PULASKI	BUTLER	DAVID KENT
ACTION BY LANE	CALDWELL CHAIR	DAVIS CABINET
AMERICAN DREW	CAMBRIDGE	DINAIRE
AMERICAN HERITAGE	CARLTON McLENDON	DISTINCTION LEATHER
AMERICAN IMPRESSIONS	CAROLINA FURNITURE	ENTREE
AMERICAN MIRROR	CAROLINA MIRROR	FAIRFIELD CHAIR
ANDRE ORIGINALS	CARSON'S	FASHION BED
ASHLEY	CEBU	FASHION HOUSE
ATHOL	CHAPMAN	FITZ & FLOYD
ATLANTA GLASSCRAFTER	CHARLES SADEK	FURNITURE CLASSICS
BALDWIN BRASS	CHARLESTON FORGE	GEORGIA CHAIR
BASSETT	CHROMCRAFT	GLASS ARTS
BAUER LAMP	CLASSIC ART	GRACE MANUFACTURING
BENICIA	CLASSIC LEATHER	GREENE BROS
BERNARD'S	COCHRANE	HABERSHAM PLANTATION
BERRYHILL PRINTS	COLONIAL	HAMMARY
BEST CHAIR	COROLLA	HANCOCK & MOORE
BLACKSMITH SHOP	COUNCILL CRAFTSMEN	HARDEN
BOB TIMBERLAKE	COX	HEKMAN
BRADINGTON YOUNG	CRAFTIQUE	HENKEL MOORE
BROWN STREET	CRAFTMASTERS	HENKEL HARRIS
BROYHILL	CRAWFORD OF JAMESTOWN	HENRY LINK

HICKORY BRANCH LAMPS
HICKORY WHITE
HOMECREST
HON
HOOKER
HOWARD MILLER
HUNT COUNTRY
JASPER CABINET
JAY WILLFRED
JENE'S COLLECTION
JETTON
JOHNSTON CASUALS
KARGES
KIMBALL
KINCAID
KOCH ORIGINALS LaBARGE
LANE
LEA
LEATHERCRAFT
LEE TABLE PAD
LEISTERS
LEXINGTON
LIGO
LLOYD FLANDERS
LYON SHAW
MADISON SQUARE
MILLER DESK
MOBEL

MOOSEHEAD
NICHOLS & STONE
NULL INDUSTRIES
QEW
OHIO TABLE PADS
P & P CHAIR
PARKER SOUTHERN
PANASONIC
PETERS-REVINGTON
PULASKI
REFLECTIONS
REX
RIVERSIDE
ROCK CITY
SALEM SQUARE
SAM MOORE
SARREID
SEALY
SEDGEFIELD LAMP
SERTA BEDDING
SHERIDAN
SHERRILL
SKILLCRAFT
SLIGH
SOUTH CONE TRADING
SOUTHERN CRAFTSMEN GUILD
SPRING AIR BEDDING
STANLEY

STATESVILLE CHAIR
STATTON
STIFFEL LAMP
SUMTER CABINET
SUPERIOR
TAHOE
TAYLOR KING
TEMPLE
TRADITIONAL HEIRLOOMS
TRADITIONS FRANCE
TROPITONE
US FURNITURE
UNIVERSAL
VANGUARD
VAUGHAN BASSET
VENEMAN
VENTURE
VICTORIAN CLASSIC
VIRGINIA HOUSE
VIRGINIA METALCRAFTERS
WATERFORD
WEBB
WEIMAN
WESLEY ALLEN
WILDWOOD
WINSTON
WOODARD

NATIONAL CLOCK GALLERY
HICKORY FURNITURE MART
2220 HWY 70 SE
HICKORY, NC 28602
Hours: **M-F: 9-6; S: 9-5; Closed Sundays**

Toll-Free	
Direct	828-324-9400
Fax	
Internet	

Notes: This resource is part of the Hickory Furniture Mart complex. This showroom is one of over 80 to visit. **See Hickory Furniture Mart listing for more information.** Consolidated shipping can be arranged with other resources in this center, a standard one/third deposit is required on all orders. Most showrooms accept VISA/MC, but not all. Cash, personal or certified checks accepted by all showrooms. If you elect not to pay for your entire purchase at the time of sale, a personal or certified check will be due upon delivery.

Manufacturers: **(Many resources do not list all their manufacturers. Be sure to inquire**

about those you are interested in, but do not see listed here.)

NATIONAL DECORATORS
20467 OLD CUTLER RD
MIAMI, FL 33189
Hours: **M-F: 8-9; SS: 9-6**

Toll-Free	800-862-2424
Direct	
Fax	
Internet	website: www.blinds.com

Notes: All first quality fabric, wallcovering and blinds. Most orders shipped within three days. Real wood blinds, pleated shades, vertical blinds and mini blinds. Call with book name, pattern or number.

Manufacturers: **(Many resources do not list all their manufacturers. Be sure to inquire about those you are interested in, but do not see listed here.)**

FABRIC:	SCHUMACHER	HUNTER DOUGLAS
ROBERT ALLEN	VILLAGE	JOANNA
KRAVET		KIRSCH
WESTGATE	**BLINDS:**	LEVOLOR
DURALEE	BALI	LOUVERDRAPE
FABRICUT	DELMAR	VEROSOL
STROHEIM & ROMANN	DUETTE	
WAVERLY	GRABER	

NATIONAL FURNITURE
5598 YORK RD
GRANITE FALLS, NC 28630
Hours: **M-F: 9-5**

Toll-Free	
Direct	828-396-9400
Fax	
Internet	

Notes: Located on Hwy 321.

Manufacturers: **(Many resources do not list all their manufacturers. Be sure to inquire about those you are interested in, but do not see listed here.)**

NETWORK FLOOR COVERING
3200 DUG GAP RD
DALTON, GA 30720
Hours: **M-F: 9-5**

Toll-Free	800-442-2013
Direct	706-277-3091
Fax	706-277-2709
Internet	

Notes: VISA/MC/AMEX/DISCOVER. All brands, all warranties, all first quality. Up to 80% off. Call for price quote, free brochure or free samples.

Manufacturers: **(Many resources do not list all their manufacturers. Be sure to inquire about those you are interested in, but do not see listed here.)**
ALL BRANDS

NEW ENGLAND BLINDS
7013 3RD AVE
BROOKLYN, NY 11209
Hours: **M-F: 8:30-5:30; S: 9-5**

Toll-Free	800-859-5958
Direct	
Fax	718-921-9854
Internet	website: www.HAGGAR-IND.com

Notes: Now part of Haggar Industries. 100% satisfaction guaranteed. Top quality and service. VISA/MC/DISC.

Manufacturers: **(Many resources do not list all their manufacturers. Be sure to inquire about those you are interested in, but do not see listed here.)**

DELMAR	LOUVERDRAPE	CRYSTAL PLEAT
GRABER	MINI-BLINDS	DUETTE
M & B	WOOD BLINDS	AND MORE
HUNTER DOUGLAS	VERTICAL	

NORTH CAROLINA FURNITURE CLEARANCE
1813 S MAIN ST
HIGH POINT, NC 27260
Hours: **M-F: 9-5**

Toll-Free	
Direct	336-886-8525
Fax	336-884-8290
Internet	

Notes: This is one of two clearance centers for Rose Furniture. This one carries quality market samples, discontinued products, over-runs, bedroom, dining room, entertainment centers, etc. They take VISA/MC/AMEX/DISC.

Manufacturers: (Many resources do not list all their manufacturers. Be sure to inquire about those you are interested in, but do not see listed here.)

NORTH CAROLINA FURNITURE CLEARANCE
2017 COLLEGE ROAD
HIGH POINT, NC 27260
Hours: **M-F: 9-5**

Toll-Free	
Direct	336-886-6092
Fax	336-886-4912
Internet	

Notes: This is one of two clearance centers for Rose Furniture. This one carries quality market samples, discontinued products, over-runs, bedroom, dining room, entertainment centers, etc. They take VISA/MC/AMEX/DISC.

Manufacturers: (Many resources do not list all their manufacturers. Be sure to inquire about those you are interested in, but do not see listed here.)

OFFICE IMAGES
1638 WESTCHESTER DR
HIGH POINT, NC 27262
Hours: M-F: 9-6; S: 9-5

Toll-Free	
Direct	336-841-6665
Fax	336-841-7402
Internet	officeimag@aol.com

Notes: Good selection of contemporary, traditional and transitional office furniture for the home office, business office motel/hotel, healthcare and the corporate offices from many manufacturers. No project too small or too large. Designer available.

Manufacturers: (Many resources do not list all their manufacturers. Be sure to inquire about those you are interested in, but do not see listed here.)

A&R
ADDEN
ADJUSTABLE BOOKCASES
AGI
ALLIBERT
ALLSEATING
AMCO
AMERICAN OF MARTINSVILLE
AMOTEK/USA
ARNOLD GROUP
AVENUE
BASSETT
BASSETT
BERCO
BERNHARDT
BLACKSMITH SHOP
BOLING
BURROUGHS
BRUETON
CAROLINA BUSINESS
CASAMANIA HOME OFFICE
GEIGER BRICKEL
CHARLOTTE COLLECTION
CONTINUUM INC
GORDON INTL
COUNCILL CRAFTSMEN
CURRAN
CUSTOMCRAFT
DAR/RAN
DAVIS FURNITURE
DIMENSIONS STORAGE
DMI
DURAFORM
ECKADAMS
EF EXPRESSIONS
EGAN VISUAL

EMCO/METWOOD
ERGO MED SOLUTIONS
ERGOSPEC
EXECUTIVE FURNITURE
EXECUTIVE OFFICE CONCEPTS
FALCON
FIXTURES
FLEX-Y-PLAN
FREDERICK COOPER
GARDEN CONCEPTS
GIANNI
GILBERT INTL
GIRSBERGER
GLARO ACCESSORIES
GLOBE
GREGOR
GREGSON
GROLEN
HALCYON
HALE
HASKELL
HICKORY LEATHER
HICKORY MANOR
HLF
HYDE PARK PANELING
INDIAN DESK
INTERIOR CONCEPTS
INVINCIBLE
JASPER SEATING
JOHNSON TABLES
JSI
KI
KING CONTRACT
KING HICKORY
KRUEGER
KRUG

KWIK-FILE
L & B EMPIRE
LA-Z-BOY CONTRACT
LACASSE
LEATHERCRAFT
LEEDO
LITE SOURCE
LOWENSTEIN
MARVEL
MILLER DESK
NEVERS
NOVA
OFS
OUTDOOR LIFESTYLE
PANEL CONCEPTS
PAOLI
PENNSYLVANIA CLASSICS
PETER PEPPER
PHOENIX DESIGNS
PLAN HOLD
PLANT PLANT
REGENCY HOUSE
REMINGTON
ROSE JOHNSON
RUDD LIGHTING
SAMSONITE
SCHWAB
SMITH SYSTEMS
SOURCE INTERNATIONAL
SOUTH SEAS RATTAN
STIFFEL LIGHTING
STOUT CHAIR
TELLUS
TIFFANY
TOUHY
TRIUNE BUSINESS

TROSBY
TYPHOON
ULTRUM

UNICOR
UNIVERSAL CONTRACT
VERSTEEL

WILKHAHN

OLD TOWN CLOCK SHOP
3738 REYNOLDA RD
WINSTON-SALEM, NC 27106
Hours: **M-F:9:30-5:30; S: 9:30-5**

Toll-Free	
Direct	336-924-8807
Fax	
Internet	

Notes: Established 1977. Two sales consultants on staff will assist customer with choices and selections. Showroom available for browsing. VISA/MC/CHECK accepted for orders. 30-day refund policy. We deal with shipping problems. Clocks of all styles available - grandfather, wall, mantel and small brass clocks. Complete clock repair.

Manufacturers: (Many resources do not list all their manufacturers. Be sure to inquire about those you are interested in, but do not see listed here.)
HARRINGTON HOUSE
HOWARD MILLER

NEW ENGLAND CLOCK
RIDGEWAY

SLIGH

P & J HOME FURNISHINGS AND FABRIC OUTLET
4114 HWY 70 WEST
HICKORY, NC 28602
Hours: **M-F: 9-5; S: 9-4**

Toll-Free	
Direct	828-326-9755
Fax	828-397-3703
Internet	

Notes: This resource carries plenty of Laura Ashley and Ralph Lauren popular fabrics (bolt ends, discontinued, etc.) They carry designer comforters, shams, ruffles, sheets, lace. They do custom sewing, curtains, fabric by the pound, roll fabric, etc. Will try to help identify and find fabrics, in person or over the phone. It's worth a stop if you're there visiting. Carry sheeting-width fabrics.

Manufacturers: (Many resources do not list all their manufacturers. Be sure to inquire
 about those you are interested in, but do not see listed here.)
LAURA ASHLEY   WAVERLY   Many others.
RALPH LAUREN

PALLISER
HICKORY FURNITURE MART
2220 HWY 70 SE
HICKORY, NC 28602
Hours: **M-F: 9-6; S: 9-5; Closed Sundays**

Toll-Free	
Direct	828-324-7742
Fax	828-327-3825
Internet	

Notes: In business since 1944. Palliser is expanding its lifestyle and casual home furnishings and
unique accessories with a 24,000 square foot store. You will find both traditional and contemporary
lines here. Please join them for a cup of gourmet coffee and a snack in the new bistro area.
Cash/credit card/check/financing available. All sales final unless otherwise approved at time of
purchase. Custom orders are non-cancellable. Warranties apply on all purchases. We deal with
shipping problems and damages are worked out immediately to the customer's satisfaction. Styles
are classic to contemporary in a price range that accommodates most any budget. Our collections of
bedrooms, youth rooms, home office, leather upholstery, rugs, accessories and occasional tables
offer a great selection and quality. This resource is part of the Hickory Furniture Mart complex. This
showroom is one of over 80 to visit. **See Hickory Furniture Mart listing for more information.**
Consolidated shipping can be arranged with other resources in this center, a standard one/third
deposit is required on all orders. Most showrooms accept VISA/MC, but not all. Cash, personal or
certified checks accepted by all showrooms. If you elect not to pay for your entire purchase at the
time of sale, a personal or certified check will be due upon delivery.

**Manufacturers: (Many resources do not list all their manufacturers. Be sure to inquire
 about those you are interested in, but do not see listed here.)**

ALAN WHITE	ERGOSCAPES	PALLISER
ASHLEY	J ROYALE UPHOLSTERY	WOODCRAFT
BOYD	KIMBALL	
DOUGLAS	MARTIN	

PALLISER
THE ATRIUM
430 SOUTH MAIN ST
HIGH POINT, NC 27260
Hours: **M-F: 9-6; S: 9-5**

Toll-Free	
Direct	336-882-7031
Fax	336-886-7607
Internet	**email:** palliser@theatrium.com

Notes: Part of the Atrium complex. Worth visiting, showrooms available. See **Atrium Furniture Showroom** listing for more information. Room by room, Palliser offers you all the options. Whatever your lifestyle, the collection of bedrooms, youth rooms, home office, upholstery, rugs, accessories and tables offer you the best selection and quality at great prices. Casual, comfortable and timeless.

Manufacturers: (Many resources do not list all their manufacturers. Be sure to inquire about those you are interested in, but do not see listed here.)

PARAMOUNT FURNITURE CO INC
1100 N MAIN
HIGH POINT, NC 27262
Hours: **MTThFS:9-5, Closed Wed**

Toll-Free	
Direct	336-884-0132
Fax	
Internet	

Notes: Showroom available. No credit cards. Ship anywhere in the US. Four salesperson.

Manufacturers: (Many resources do not list all their manufacturers. Be sure to inquire about those you are interested in, but do not see listed here.)
LEXINGTON

PARKER'S CARPET
3200 DUG GAP ROAD
DALTON, GA 30720
Hours: **M-F: 9-5**

Toll-Free	800-442-2013
Direct	
Fax	706-277-2709
Internet	

Notes: Established in 1963. Large selection of commercial products. Special discounts for carpet stores, churches, volume purchases, contractors, realtors. Free samples. Nation wide home and to-site delivery. Special products, drop style and discontinued items. Free technical support. First quality.

Manufacturers: (Many resources do not list all their manufacturers. Be sure to inquire about those you are interested in, but do not see listed here.)

CARPET PRODUCTS:	DOWNS	STYLECRAFT
ALADDIN	DORSETT	SHAW
BALTA	DURKAN	SALEM
BEAULIEU	EVANS & BLACK	RICHMOND
BIGELOW	FAIRFAX	RD STALLION
BURLINGTON	GALAXY	VICTOR & BISHOP
BLUE RIDGE	GENERAL FELT	SUPREME
BURTCO	GIBRALTAR	TOWER
CASCADE	HELIOS	WIMBLEDON
CABIN CRAFT	HORIZON	WORLD
CASUAL	HARBINGER	WELLCO
CEDAR	INTERLOOM	WELLINGTON
CRITERION	IMAGE	WHITECREST
CUSTOMWEAVE	HOLLYTEX	**VINYL FLOORING:**
CONQUEST	INSTANT TURF	ARMSTRONG
CITATION	J & L	ACROOT
CORONET	LEN-DAL	MERCER
CONCORD	LEES	JOHNSONITE
CREATIVE	MATTEO	CONGOLEUM
CRAFTER	MANNINGTON	NAFCO
CALADIUM	MASLAND	DOMCO
CALAIS	MOHAWK	MANNINGTON
CROWN CRAFT	MARGLEN	PIRELLI RUBBER FLOORS
CUMBERLAND	MONTICELLO	TARKETT
DAN RIVER	PATCRAFT	APACHEE
DANUBE	PHILADELPHIA	TOWER
DIMENSION	QUEEN	AZROCK
DIAMOND	JP STEVENS	ROPPE
DYNAMIC	J & P CARPET	MERCER

Resource Directory

PEARSON GALLERY
HICKORY FURNITURE MART
2220 HWY 70 SE
HICKORY, NC 28602
Hours: **M-F: 9-6; S: 9-5; Closed Sundays**

Toll-Free	
Direct	828-322-6602
Fax	
Internet	

Notes: This resource is part of the Hickory Furniture Mart complex. This showroom is one of over 80 to visit. **See Hickory Furniture Mart listing for more information.** Consolidated shipping can be arranged with other resources in this center, a standard one/third deposit is required on all orders. Most showrooms accept VISA/MC, but not all. Cash, personal or certified checks accepted by all showrooms. If you elect not to pay for your entire purchase at the time of sale, a personal or certified check will be due upon delivery.

Manufacturers: **(Many resources do not list all their manufacturers. Be sure to inquire about those you are interested in, but do not see listed here.)**

═══════════════════════════════════

PENNSYLVANIA HOUSE COLLECTOR'S GALLERY
1300 N MAIN
HIGH POINT, NC 27262
Hours: **M-F: 9-5:30; S: 9-5**

Toll-Free	
Direct	336-887-3000
Fax	336-887-0329
Internet	

Notes:

Manufacturers: **(Many resources do not list all their manufacturers. Be sure to inquire about those you are interested in, but do not see listed here.)**
AMERICAN DREW   LEXINGTON   PENNSYLVANIA HOUSE

═══════════════════════════════════

PENNSYLVANIA HOUSE GALLERY
HICKORY FURNITURE MART
2220 HWY 70 SE
HICKORY, NC 28602
Hours: **M-F: 9-6; S: 9-5; Closed Sundays**

Toll-Free	
Direct	828-324-1776
Fax	
Internet	

Notes: This resource is part of the Hickory Furniture Mart complex. This showroom is one of over 80 to visit. **See Hickory Furniture Mart listing for more information.** Consolidated shipping can be arranged with other resources in this center, a standard one/third deposit is required on all orders. Most showrooms accept VISA/MC, but not all. Cash, personal or certified checks accepted by all showrooms. If you elect not to pay for your entire purchase at the time of sale, a personal or certified check will be due upon delivery.

Manufacturers: (Many resources do not list all their manufacturers. Be sure to inquire about those you are interested in, but do not see listed here.)

PHILLIPS FURNITURE
116 W MARKET CENTER DR
HIGH POINT, NC 27262
Hours: **M-F: 9-5**

Toll-Free	
Direct	336-885-4216
Fax	
Internet	

Notes: Mainly glass and brass tables, dining rooms, etegeres

Manufacturers: (Many resources do not list all their manufacturers. Be sure to inquire about those you are interested in, but do not see listed here.)
CARSON

PIEDMONT DESIGN
HICKORY FURNITURE MART
2220 HWY 70 SE
HICKORY, NC 28602
Hours: **M-F: 9-6; S: 9-5; Closed Sundays**

Toll-Free	
Direct	828-324-4546
Fax	828-324-2461
Internet	email: piedmontdesigns@conninc.com

Notes: This resource is part of the Hickory Furniture Mart complex. This showroom is one of over 80 to visit. **See Hickory Furniture Mart listing for more information.** Consolidated shipping can be arranged with other resources in this center, a standard one/third deposit is required on all orders. Most showrooms accept VISA/MC, but not all. Cash, personal or certified checks accepted by all showrooms. If you elect not to pay for your entire purchase at the time of sale, a personal or certified check will be due upon delivery.

Manufacturers: (Many resources do not list all their manufacturers. Be sure to inquire about those you are interested in, but do not see listed here.)

PINTCHIK HOMEWORKS
478 BERGEN ST
BROOKLYN, NY 11217
Hours: **M-F:9-6**

Toll-Free	800-847-4199
Direct	718-996-5580
Fax	718-783-4646
Internet	

Notes: Custom window treatments since 1912. Full payment can be made with VISA/MC/CHECK/MO. Sales and design consultants on staff. No returns on custom orders. Shipping problems will be handled by resource. We have six stores in the New York city area. Glossy brochure and price lists available upon request.

Manufacturers: (Many resources do not list all their manufacturers. Be sure to inquire about those you are interested in, but do not see listed here.)

BALI	HUNTER DOUGLAS	LOUVERDRAPE
DELMAR	LAFONT	VEROSOL
GRABER	LEVOLOR	

PLAZA FURNITURE GALLERY
HWY 321 AT TIMBERBROOK LANE
GRANITE FALLS, NC 28630
Hours: **M-S: 10-5**

Toll-Free	
Direct	828-396-8150
Fax	828-396-8151
Internet	

Notes: Located on Hwy 321. In business since 1988. In-home set up and delivery. Returns are accepted if damaged or defective merchandise. Carrier is responsible for shipping problems. Carry unique accessories. Visit their showroom.

Manufacturers: (Many resources do not list all their manufacturers. Be sure to inquire about those you are interested in, but do not see listed here.)

AMERICAN DREW	UNIVERSAL	WEIMAN
HAMMARY	VAUGHAN	
LEXINGTON	VAUGHAN BASSETT	

PLAZA FURNITURE INC
PO BOX 7640
MYRTLE BEACH, SC 29577
Hours: **M-F: 9-5**

Toll-Free	800-262-9898
Direct	803-449-8636
Fax	803-497-5887
Internet	

Notes: Fifty percent deposit required. Can be paid VISA/MC/DISC. (They also have their own credit card). Balance due when furniture is received at their distribution center. Delivered nationwide with in-home setup. A damaged or defective item will be repaired or replaced, if necessary.

Manufacturers: (Many resources do not list all their manufacturers. Be sure to inquire about those you are interested in, but do not see listed here.)

ACTION	AMERICAN DREW	BASSETT
ALEXVALE	BARCALOUNGER	BENCHCRAFT

BENICIA	HICKORY WHITE	REX
BERKLINE	HIGHLAND HOUSE	RICHARDSON BROTHERS
BEVAN FUNNELL	HOOKER	SALEM SQUARE
BRADINGTON YOUNG	JASPER CABINET	SAM MOORE
BRAXTON CULLER	JOHNSTON CASUALS	SEDGEFIELD
BROWN JORDAN	KAISER KUHN	SERTA
BROYHILL	KESSLER	SK PRODUCTS
CAPEL	KEY CITY	SOUTHERN FURNITURE
CASA BIQUE	KIMBALL	STATESVILLE CHAIR
CHARLESTON FORGE	KIMBALL-HARMONY WOODS	STATTON
CLASSIC LEATHER	KIMBALL VICTORIAN	STIFFEL
CLAYTON MARCUS	KINCAID	SUMTER CABINET
COCHRANE	LABARGE	SWAIM
COUNCILL	LANE	TAYLOR KING
CR LAINE	LEA	UNIVERSAL
CRAFTIQUE	LEXINGTON	VANGUARD
CRAFTWORK	LLOYD FLANDERS	VAUGHAN
CRAWFORD	LYON SHAW	VAUGHAN BASSETT
CTH/SHERRILL	MADISON SQUARE	VENTURE
DESIGN SOUTH	MARBRO	VIRGINIA HOUSE
DISTINCTION LEATHER	MOTIONCRAFT	WEIMAN
ENTREE	NICHOLS & STONE	WELLINGTON HALL
FAIRFIELD CHAIR	OHIO TABLE PAD	WESLEY ALLEN
FASHION BED GROUP	PEARSON	WHITTEMORE
HABERSHAM	PENNSYLVANIA CLASSICS	WILDWOOD
HAMMARY	PRECEDENT	WINSTON
HEKMAN	PULASKI	WOODARD

PLEXI-CRAFT QUALITY PRODUCTS CORP
514 W. 24TH ST
NEW YORK, NY 10011-1179
Hours: M-F: 9:30-5

Toll-Free	
Direct	212-924-3244
Fax	212-924-3508
Internet	email: plexi@escape.com website: www.escape.com/plexi

Notes: In business since 1972. Acrylic furnishings and accessories, TV stands, tables, chairs, custom orders from drawings, photos or specs. Turn-around time usually less than four weeks. VISA/MC/CASH/CHECKS for 50% down payment. Shipping is done via UPS insured. Shipping problems handled by customer. No returns on custom orders, unless damaged. On stock items, if in saleable condition, store credit or exchange only is issued. Customer can visit this facility.$2 catalog available upon request.

Manufacturers: **(Many resources do not list all their manufacturers. Be sure to inquire about those you are interested in, but do not see listed here.)**

PRECEDENT GALLERY
HICKORY FURNITURE MART
2220 HWY 70 SE
HICKORY, NC 28602
Hours: M-F: 9-6; S: 9-5; Closed Sundays

Toll-Free	
Direct	828-326-1735
Fax	
Internet	

Notes: This resource is part of the Hickory Furniture Mart complex. This showroom is one of over 80 to visit. **See Hickory Furniture Mart listing for more information.** Consolidated shipping can be arranged with other resources in this center, a standard one/third deposit is required on all orders. Most showrooms accept VISA/MC, but not all. Cash, personal or certified checks accepted by all showrooms. If you elect not to pay for your entire purchase at the time of sale, a personal or certified check will be due upon delivery.

Manufacturers: **(Many resources do not list all their manufacturers. Be sure to inquire about those you are interested in, but do not see listed here.)**

PRIBA FURNITURE SALES AND INTERIORS
PO BOX 13295
GREENSBORO, NC 27415
Hours: **M-F: 9-5:30; S: 9-5; AND BY APPOINTMENT**

Toll-Free	
Direct	336-855-9034
Fax	336-855-1370
Internet	email: pribafurniture@worldnet.att.net website: www.pribafurniture.com

Notes: In business since 1972. 30% deposit payable by VISA/MC/CHECK. Balance payable by check, money order, cashier's check. Shipping is done by an in-home delivery service. Transit damages are handled by the carrier. Freight charges are paid by money order or certified check at time of delivery. Sales and design consultants on staff and can assist customer with choices. Customer can visit facility. Repairs or returns allowed in case of factory defect after a factory representative inspects. Over 300 lines of furniture discounted accessories, lamps, wallcoverings, fabrics, carpets. Fliers are sent out to those customers on their mailing list announcing sales and specials.

Manufacturers: (Many resources do not list all their manufacturers. Be sure to inquire about those you are interested in, but do not see listed here.)

AMERICAN DREW	GERVAIS	PEARSON
AMERICAN OF HIGH POINT	GLASS ARTS	PETERS-REVINGTON
ARTLEE FABRICS	GUY CHADDOCK	PINDLER & PINDLER FABRIC
AS YOU LIKE IT LAMPS	GREEFF	PLANT PLANT
BARCALOUNGER	HAMILTON HALL	POULIOT DESIGNS
BASSETT	HAMMARY	PORT ROYAL
B BERGER	HEKMAN	PULASKI
BERNHARDT	HENRY LINK	REMINGTON LAMPS
BLACKSMITH SHOP	HICKORY CHAIR	REPRODUX
BOUSSAC OF FRANCE	HICKORY WHITE	RICHARDSON BROS
BRADINGTON YOUNG	HOOD	ROBERT ALLEN
BRAXTON CULLER	HOOKER	ROSECORE CARPETS
BROWN JORDAN	JOHNSTON CASUALS	SALEM SQUARE
BROYHILL	JOHN WIDDICOMB	SAM MOORE
BRUNSCHWIG & FILS	J ROYALE	SAMSONITE
CAL-STYLE	KAISER KUHN LIGHTING	SARREID
CAPITAL ASAM	KARGES	SCALAMANDRE
CAROLINA TABLES	KATZENBACH & WARREN	SCHUMACHER
CAROUSEL CARPET	KESSLER	SEABROOK
CARSON'S	KINCAID	SEALY
CARTER	KINGSDOWN	SERTA
CASA STRADIVARI	KRAVET FABRICS	SHERRILL METAL
CHAPMAN LAMPS	KREISS	SLIGH DESK
CHARLESTON FORGE	LaBARGE	SOUTHAMPTON
CHATHAM COUNTY	LANE	SOUTHWOOD
CHELSEA HOUSE	LEATHERCRAFT	REPRODUCTIONS
CHROMCRAFT	LEATHERMAN'S GUILD	SPRING AIR
CLARENCE HOUSE	LEATHER SHOP	STANLEY
CLARK CASUAL	LEE INDUSTRIES	STANTON COOPER
CLASSIC GALLERY	LEE JOFA	STARK CARPETS
CLASSIC LEATHER	LEXINGTON	STATTON
CONOVER CHAIR	LLOYD FLANDERS	STIFFEL
CORSICAN IRON BEDS	LOWENSTEIN	STROHEIM & ROMANN
COUNCILL CRAFTSMEN	LYON-SHAW	SWAIM
COX	MADISON SQUARE	THAYER COGGIN
CRAFTIQUE	MAITLAND SMITH	THOMASVILLE
CRAFTWORK GUILD	MARBRO LAMPS	TOMLINSON
DAVIS & DAVIS	MARYLAND CLASSICS	TRADITIONS FRANCE
DECORATOR'S WALK	MASLAND CARPET	TROPITONE
DFC	McGUIRE	TROSBY
DILLON	McKAY TABLE PADS	TROUVAILLES
DINAIRE	MEADOWCRAFT	UNIVERSAL
DIRECTIONAL	MOTTAHEDEH	VANGUARD
DISTINCTION LEATHER	MURRAY FEISS LAMPS	VAN LUIT
DURALEE FABRICS	NATHAN HALE	VENTURE
ELLO	NICHOLS & STONE	VIRGINIA HOUSE
EMERSON LEATHER	NORMAN PERRY	VIRGINIA METALCRAFTERS
FICKS REED	NORTH HICKORY	VOGUE RATTAN
FITZ & FLOYD	OHIO TABLE PADS	WAVERLY
FREDERICK COOPER	OLD HICKORY TANNERY	WELLINGTON HALL
FRIEDMAN BROS MIRRORS	PAUL HANSON	WESLEY ALLEN
FROELICH	PAYNE	WESTGATE
GEORGIAN FURNISHINGS	P COLLINS	WEIMAN

WILDWOOD LAMPS　　　　　WOODARD　　　　　　　YORKSHIRE LEATHER
WILLIAM ALLEN　　　　　　WOODLEE
WINSTON　　　　　　　　　WOODMARK

═══

PRINTER'S ALLEY STORES
1324-104 WESTOVER TERRACE
GREENSBORO, NC 27408
Hours:　M-F: 9-5

Toll-Free	
Direct	336-272-4227
Fax	
Internet	

Notes:　This company has a total of five locations, and most fabrics are seconds. It's best to visit these places in person. Their talented and experienced sales staff is very helpful with customers in fabric selection and window designs. They also carry custom-ordered upholstered furniture, bed coverings, decorative trims and unique accessories. Other locations include: **5910-111 Duraleigh Rd, Raleigh, NC 27612** (919-781-1777); **5478 West Broad St, Richmond, VA 23230** (804-285-9591); **4369 Starkey Rd SW, Roanoke, VA 24014** (703-774-0966); and **2133 Coliseum Dr, Hampton, VA 23666** (804-827-1404).

Manufacturers: (Many resources do not list all their manufacturers. Be sure to inquire about those you are interested in, but do not see listed here.)
BLOOMCRAFT　　　　　　　　BRAEMORE　　　　　　　P KAUFMANN

═══

QUALITY FURNITURE MARKET OF LENOIR, INC
2034 HICKORY BLVD SW
LENOIR, NC 28645
Hours:　M-S: 8:30-5

Toll-Free	
Direct	704-728-2946
Fax	704-726-0226
Internet	

Notes:　Located on HWY 321. In business since 1955. Family owned and operated. 40,000 square foot showroom. 100% payment at time of order with VISA/MC/DISC/ CHECK/MO. In home delivery services nationwide. Freight collect. No returns unless we ordered incorrectly. Customer receives only the warranty the factories offer. Shipping problems handled by our customer service department. Sales and design consultants on staff. Customer can visit this 40,000 sq.ft. facilities. Home furnishings, outdoor furniture, bedding and unique accessories

Manufacturers: (Many resources do not list all their manufacturers. Be sure to inquire about those you are interested in, but do not see listed here.)

ACTION BY LANE
ALEXANDER JULIAN BY UNIVERSAL
ALLUSIONS
AMBIANCE IMPORTS
AMERICAN DREW
AMERICAN OF MARTINSVILLE
ANDREW PEARSON DESIGNS
ARDLEY HALL
ARNOLD PALMER COLLECTION
ARTMAX
ARTISAN HOUSE
ARTMARK FABRICS
BAILEY & GRIFFIN
BALDWIN BRASS
BARCALOUNGER
BASSETT
BEACON HILL FABRICS
BEAN STATION
BERNHARDT
BLACKSMITH SHOP
BOB TIMBERLAKE
BOLING CHAIR
BRADBURN GALLERY
BRITISH TRADITIONS
BROYHILL
BRUNSCHWIG & FILS
BUILTRIGHT
BUTLER
CAMBRIDGE LAMPS
CARLTON McLENDON
CAROLINA MIRROR
CAROLINA TABLES
CARSON'S OF HIGH POINT
CARVER'S GUILD
CASA BIQUE
CASA RUSTICA
CASUAL LAMP
CHAPMAN LAMPS/ACCESSORIES
CHARLESTON FORGE
CHATHAM COUNTY
CHROMCRAFT
CLARK CASUAL
CLASSIC LEATHER
CLAYTON MARCUS
CLYDE PEARSON
COCHRANE
COMFORT DESIGNS
CONOVER CHAIR
COX
CRAFTIQUE

CRAWFORD OF JAMESTOWN
CRYSTAL CLEAR
CUSTOMCRAFT
D & F WICKER
TIFFANY LAMPS
DAVIS & DAVIS RUGS
DECORATIVE ARTS
DECORATIVE CRAFTS
DESIGN GUILD
DESIGN SOUTH
DINAIRE
DINING ALA CARTE
DISTINCTIVE DESIGNS
DILLON
EKORNES STRESSLESS CHAIR
ELEMENTS BY GRAPEVINE
EMERSON ET CIE
EMERSON LEATHER
FAIRFIELD CHAIR
FASHION BED
FIAM
FINE ARTS LAMPS
FITZ & FLOYD CHINA
FREDERICK COOPER
FUR DESIGNS
GEORGIA ART LIGHTING
GLASS ARTS
GREAT CITY TRADERS
GUILDMASTER
HTB CONTEMPORARY
HART ASSOC
HAMMARY
HEKMAN
HENRY LINK
HICKORY FRY
HIGHLAND HOUSE
HITCHCOCK CHAIR
HOMECREST
HOOKER
HOWARD MILLER CLOCKS
IMPERIAL/KINNEY WALLPAPER
JG HOOK
JSF INDUSTRIES
J ROYALE
JACKSON OF DANVILLE
JAMES R COOPER
JAMESTOWN MANOR BY STATTON
JASPER CABINET
JEFFCO
JOHN RICHARD COLLECTION

KIMBALL
KINDER HARRIS
KING HICKORY
KOCH & LOWY LAMPS
KRAVET FABRICS
LANE
LANE UPHOLSTERY
LaBARGE
LEXINGTON
LINK TAYLOR
LLOYD FLANDERS
LYON SHAW
M&H SEATING
MER RUGS
MIKHAIL DARAFEEV
MILLER DESK
MURRAY FEISS
NDI
NATIONAL MT AIRY
NATURAL LIGHT LAMPS
NEW RIVER ARTISAN
NORMAN ROCKWELL BY STANLEY
OKLAHOMA IMPORTING
OHIO TABLE PADS
ORIENTAL LACQUER
OSBORNE & LITTLE
PALECEK
PANDE CAMERON RUGS
PAPER WHITE
PENNSYLVANIA CLASSICS
PENNSYLVANIA HOUSE
PETERS-REVINGTON
PHILLIP JEFFRIES
PLANT PLANT
POMPEII
PULASKI
RAYMOND WAITES BY LANE
RELIANCE LAMPS
REX
RIDGEWAY CLOCKS
RIVERSIDE
ROBERT ALLEN FABRICS
SEE IMPORTS
SAGEFIELD LEATHER
SARREID
ST TIMOTHY
SCHUMACHER
SEABROOK WALLCOVERING
SECOND AVE
SEDGEFIELD LAMP
SERTA BEDDING

SHERRILL TABLES
SKILLCRAFT
SLIGH
SOUTH SEAS RATTAN
SPINNING WHEEL RUGS
SPRING AIR BEDDING
STANLEY
STATESVILLE CHAIR
STIFFEL LAMP
STROHEIM & ROMANN
STYLE SEATING
TAPESTRIES LTD
TAYLOR WOODCRAFT
THAYER COGGIN

THIEF RIVER LINEN
ROMLIN LAMPS
TRICA
TROPITONE
TYPHOON
UNIVERSAL
UTTERMOST
VANGUARD
VELCO
VENTURE
VIRGINIA METALCRAFTERS
VISIONS
WARNER WALLPAPER

WAVERLY
WEIMAN
WELLINGTON HALL
WESLEY ALLEN BRASS BEDS
WESTGATE FABRICS/TRIMS
WHITNEY RUGS
WILDWOOD
WINNERS ONLY
WINSTON
WOODARD
WOODMARK
YOUNG HINKLE
YOUNGER

REFLECTIONS
HICKORY FURNITURE MART
2220 HWY 70 SE
HICKORY, NC 28602
Hours: **M-F: 9-6; S: 9-5; Closed Sundays**

Toll-Free	
Direct	828-327-8485
Fax	
Internet	email: reflections@twave.net

Notes: This resource is part of the Hickory Furniture Mart complex. This showroom is one of over 80 to visit. **See Hickory Furniture Mart listing for more information.** Consolidated shipping can be arranged with other resources in this center, a standard one/third deposit is required on all orders. Most showrooms accept VISA/MC, but not all. Cash, personal or certified checks accepted by all showrooms. If you elect not to pay for your entire purchase at the time of sale, a personal or certified check will be due upon delivery.

Manufacturers: (Many resources do not list all their manufacturers. Be sure to inquire about those you are interested in, but do not see listed here.)

REFLECTIONS
THE ATRIUM
430 SOUTH MAIN ST
HIGH POINT, NC 27262
Hours: M-F: 9-6; S: 9-5

Toll-Free	
Direct	336-885-5180
Fax	336-885-5188
Internet	

Notes: Part of the Atrium complex. Worth visiting, showrooms available. See **Atrium Furniture Showroom** listing for more information. Contemporary living room, dining room and bedroom furniture; occasional pieces and accessories, large leather selection,

Manufacturers: **(Many resources do not list all their manufacturers. Be sure to inquire about those you are interested in, but do not see listed here.)**

JAYMAR	NATUZZI	SARATOGA MARBLE
JRW GLASS	REUBENS	SHARUT

REPLACEMENTS, LTD
1089 KNOX ROAD POB 26029
GREENSBORO, NC 27420
Hours: M-S: 9-5

Toll-Free	
Direct	336-697-3000
Fax	336-697-3100
Internet	**email:** replaceltd@aol.com

Notes: Tabletop - china, crystal, flatware - obsolete, inactive and active

Manufacturers: **(Many resources do not list all their manufacturers. Be sure to inquire about those you are interested in, but do not see listed here.)**

RESOURCE DESIGN
HICKORY FURNITURE MART
2220 HWY 70 SE
HICKORY, NC 28602
Hours: **M-F: 9-6; S: 9-5; Closed Sundays**

Toll-Free	
Direct	828-322-3161
Fax	
Internet	

Notes: Expanded showroom includes a conference room and designer alcoves to sit and work undisturbed. If you're pressed for time when you come to visit, our sales staff will organize information in advance and prepare samples for your arrival. This resource is part of the Hickory Furniture Mart complex. This showroom is one of over 80 to visit. **See Hickory Furniture Mart listing for more information.** Consolidated shipping can be arranged with other resources in this center, a standard one/third deposit is required on all orders. Most showrooms accept VISA/MC, but not all. Cash, personal or certified checks accepted by all showrooms. If you elect not to pay for your entire purchase at the time of sale, a personal or certified check will be due upon delivery.

Manufacturers: (Many resources do not list all their manufacturers. Be sure to inquire about those you are interested in, but do not see listed here.)

BOUSSAC	NOBILIS	STROHEIM & ROMANN
BRUNSCHWIG & FILS	PINDLER & PINDLER	THIBAUT
CLARENCE HOUSE	ROBERT ALLEN	Decorator/Designer Fabrics
COWTAN & TOUT	SCALAMANDRE	

RHONEY FURNITURE HOUSE
2401 HWY 70 SW
HICKORY, NC 28602
Hours: **M-S: 9-5**

Toll-Free	
Direct	828-328-2034
Fax	828-328-2036
Internet	

Notes:

Manufacturers: (Many resources do not list all their manufacturers. Be sure to inquire about those you are interested in, but do not see listed here.)

ACCENTRICS BY PULASKI	ACTION BY LANE	AMERICAN DREW

AMERICAN OF MARTINSVILLE
ARTMASTER STUDIOS
ARTISANS BRASS
AS YOU LIKE IT
AUSTIN PRODUCTIONS
BARCALOUNGER
BASSETT UPHOLSTERY
BERKSHIRE
BETH WEISSMAN
BLACKSMITH SHOP
BOB TIMBERLAKE
BRASS BEDS OF AMERICA
CAROLINA MIRROR
CASA BIQUE
CASTILLIAN
CHATHAM COUNTY
CHROMCRAFT
CLAYTON MARCUS
CLOVER LAMPS
CLYDE PEARSON
COMFORT DESIGNS
COX
CRAFTIQUE
CRAFTWORK GUILD
CREATIVE ACCENTS
DECORATIVE CRAFTS
DIXIE
DRESHER
EMERSON LEATHER
ENTREE BY LaBARGE

FINE ARTS
FLORAL ART
FREEMEN
GERALD STEIN
GEORGIAN FURNISHINGS
HEKMAN
HTB CONTEMPORARY
HENRY LINK
HICKORY TAVERN
HITCHCOCK
HOOKER
HOWARD MILLER CLOCKS
INTERLUDE
JASPER
KELLER
KIMBALL/VICTORIAN
KING HICKORY
LANE
LEA
LEISTERS
LENOX LAMPS
LEXINGTON FURNITURE
LYON SHAW
MADDOX
MADISON SQUARE
MERSMAN
MORGAN STEWART
MORRIS GREENSPAN
McKAY TABLE PADS
OHIO TABLE PADS

PULASKI
REMINGTON
RIVERSIDE
ROSENTHAL NETTER
SARREID LTD
SERTA
SIERRA ARTS
STAKMORE
STANLEY
STANTON COOPER
STIFFEL LAMP
STONEVILLE
STYLE UPHOLSTERY
SWAN BRASS
TEMPLE
THAYER COGGIN
TIMMERMAN
TOYO
TROPITONE
UNIVERSAL
VANGUARD STUDIOS
VAUGHAN
VENTURE
VIRGINIA HOUSE
WELLINGTON HALL
WESLEY ALLEN
WINDSOR ART
WOODMARK
YOUNG-HINKLE

RHONEY FURNITURE HOUSE
HICKORY FURNITURE MART
2220 HWY 70 SE
HICKORY, NC 28602
Hours: **M-F: 9-6; S: 9-5; Closed Sundays**

Toll-Free	
Direct	828-328-8688
Fax	828-328-8710
Internet	

Notes: This resource is part of the Hickory Furniture Mart complex. This showroom is one of over 80 to visit. **See Hickory Furniture Mart listing for more information.** Consolidated shipping can be arranged with other resources in this center, a standard one/third deposit is required on all orders. Most showrooms accept VISA/MC, but not all. Cash, personal or certified checks accepted by all showrooms. If you elect not to pay for your entire purchase at the time of sale, a personal or certified check will be due upon delivery.

Manufacturers: **(Many resources do not list all their manufacturers. Be sure to inquire about those you are interested in, but do not see listed here.)**

ACCENTRICS BY PULASKI
ACTION BY LANE
AMERICAN DREW
AMERICAN OF MARTINSVILLE
ARTMASTER
ARTISANS BRASS
AS YOU LIKE IT
AUSTIN PRODUCTIONS
BARCALOUNGER
BASSETT UPHOLSTERY
BERKSHIRE
BETH WEISSMAN
BLACKSMITH SHOP
BOB TIMBERLAKE
BRASS BEDS OF AMERICA
CAROLINA MIRROR
CASA BIQUE
CASTILLIAN
CHATHAM COUNTY
CHROMCRAFT
CLAYTON MARCUS
CLOVER LAMPS
CLYDE PEARSON
COMFORT DESIGNS
COX
CRAFTIQUE
CRAFTWORK GUILD
CREATIVE ACCENTS
DECORATIVE CRAFTS
DIXIE
DRESHER

EMERSON LEATHER
ENTREE BY LaBARGE
FINE ARTS
FLORAL ART
FREEMEN
GERALD STEIN
GEORGIAN FURNISHINGS
HEKMAN
HTB CONTEMPORARY
HENRY LINK
HICKORY TAVERN
HITCHCOCK
HOOKER
HOWARD MILLER CLOCKS
INTERLUDE
JASPER
KELLER
KIMBALL/VICTORIAN
KING HICKORY
LANE
LEA
LEISTERS
LENOX LAMPS
LEXINGTON FURNITURE
LYON SHAW
MADDOX
MADISON SQUARE
MERSMAN
MORGAN STEWART
MORRIS GREENSPAN
McKAY TABLE PADS

OHIO TABLE PADS
PULASKI
REMINGTON
RIVERSIDE
ROSENTHAL NETTER
SARREID LTD
SERTA
SIERRA ARTS
STAKMORE
STANLEY
STANTON COOPER
STIFFEL LAMP
STONEVILLE
STYLE UPHOLSTERY
SWAN BRASS
TEMPLE
THAYER COGGIN
TIMMERMAN
TOYO
TROPITONE
UNIVERSAL
VANGUARD STUDIOS
VAUGHAN
VENTURE
VIRGINIA HOUSE
WELLINGTON HALL
WESLEY ALLEN
WINDSOR ART
WOODMARK
YOUNG-HINKLE

ROBERT BERGELIN
HICKORY FURNITURE MART
2220 HWY 70 SE
HICKORY, NC 28602
Hours: **M-F: 9-6; S: 9-5; Closed Sundays**

Toll-Free	
Direct	828-345-1500
Fax	
Internet	

Notes: This resource is part of the Hickory Furniture Mart complex. This showroom is one of over 80 to visit. **See Hickory Furniture Mart listing for more information.** Consolidated shipping can be arranged with other resources in this center, a standard one/third deposit is required on all orders. Most showrooms accept VISA/MC, but not all. Cash, personal or certified checks accepted by all

showrooms. If you elect not to pay for your entire purchase at the time of sale, a personal or certified check will be due upon delivery.

Manufacturers: (Many resources do not list all their manufacturers. Be sure to inquire about those you are interested in, but do not see listed here.)

ROBINSON'S WALLCOVERINGS
225 W. SPRING ST
TITUSVILLE, PA 16354-0427
Hours: **M-F: 9-6;S: 9-4**

Toll-Free	800-458-2426
Direct	800-458-2426
Fax	814-827-1693
Internet	email: RWALLCOVER@MAIL.USACHOICE.NET

Notes: In business since 1919. Telephone representatives available. Complete payment can be made by VISA/MC/AMEX/DISC/CHECK MO. Catalog and mail orders ship via UPS. Sales and design consultants on staff. 30 day money back guarantee. This company has 3 retail stores located in PA. $2 catalog sent out upon request. Mailing list catalog sent out yearly. This company has a very nice catalog with color samples available for over 300 in-stock wallcoverings and borders. Ideas for decorating, sewing, using fabrics, borders and wallcoverings. Very thorough.

Manufacturers: (Many resources do not list all their manufacturers. Be sure to inquire about those you are interested in, but do not see listed here.)

BIRGE	GENCORP	SCHUMACHER
CAREY LIND	IMPERIAL WALLCOVERINGS	SUNWORTHY
COLOR HOUSE	MAYFAIR	WALLCOVERINGS
EISENHART	QUALITY HOUSE	YORK WALLCOVERINGS

RON HAINER LIGHTING DESIGNS, INC
3556 VINEWOOD AVE SE
GRAND RAPIDS, MI 48546
Hours: **M-F: 9-5**

Toll-Free	
Direct	616-956-6896
Fax	
Internet	

Notes: Phone orders only. Claims he will beat any price. Everything is cost-plus. Furniture, lighting. One consultant and one lighting designer on staff. Only checks accepted as deposit. Balance due upon shipping. Drop shipped from manufacturer. Defective products only returned. Satisfaction guaranteed only to the extent that the product will be what it was purported to be. Shipments are responsibility of consignee, but will interact in every way possible. We do not advertise, display or warehouse so our overhead is very low. We specialize in lighting, particularly upscale, including contemporary and period.

Manufacturers: (Many resources do not list all their manufacturers. Be sure to inquire about those you are interested in, but do not see listed here.)

ROSE FURNITURE
916 FINCH AVENUE, PO BOX 1829
HIGH POINT, NC 27261
Hours: **M-F: 8:30-5; S: 8:30-4**

Toll-Free	
Direct	336-886-6050
Fax	336-886-5055
Internet	**website:** www.rosefurniture.com (Password: rosegarden)

Notes: Company founded in 1925. Over 163,000 square feet in one building. Visit their clearance store at 1830 S Main St. (336-886-8525). Over 300 major furniture manufacturers and lamp and accessory manufacturers. Payment policies are cash or bank check with a 30% deposit. Fifty sales consultants and designers on staff.

Manufacturers: (Many resources do not list all their manufacturers. Be sure to inquire about those you are interested in, but do not see listed here.)

AA LAUN	AKKO	ACCENT GRAPHICS
AGI INDUSTRIES	ART	ACCENTS BY GARY PARLIN

ACCESSORIES INTL
ACTION BY LANE
ALA (BAMMA) FOLK ART
ALAN WHITE
ALEXANDER DIEZ
ROBERT ALLEN FABRICS
WESLEY ALLEN BRASS BEDS
ALEXVALE
ALLIBERT
ALLISON DIZE
AMERICAN DREW
AMERICAN FURNITURE
GALLERY
AMERICAN HERITAGE
AMERICAN OF HIGH POINT
AMERICAN OF MARTINSVILLE
AMERICAN TEXTILES
AMISCO
AMISH COUNTRY COLLECTION
ANDRE ORIGINALS
ANDREW KNOB & SON
ANDREW PEARSON
ARBEK
ARCADIA LIGHTING
ARDLEY HALL
ARLINGTON HOUSE
ART FLO
ART GALLERY
ARTE DE MEXICO
ARTE LORE
ARTISAN HOUSE
ARTISTICA METAL DESIGNS
ARTMARK FABRICS
AS YOU LIKE IT LAMPS
ASHLEY
ASHLEY MANOR
AUSTINS ACCENTS
AUTUMN GUILD
B & D DESIGNS
BDT FURNITURE
B BERGER
BALDWIN BRASS
BALDWIN CLOCKS
BAMBOO ODYSSEY
BANKS COLDSTONE
BARCALOUNGER
BARN DOOR
BARROW
BASHIAN RUGS
BASSETT CASEGOODS
BASSETT UPHOLSTERY
BASSETT MIRROR
BASTA SOLE
BAUER LAMP
BEAN STATION
BENCHCRAFT RATTAN
BENCHCRAFT
BENICIA BEDS
BENTWOOD

BERKLINE
BERKSHIRE
BERNHARDT
BEST CHAIR
BESTAR
BEVAN FUNNELL
BLACKSMITH SHOP
BOB TIMBERLAKE
BOLING
BOYD
BRADBURN GALLERY
BRADINGTON COURT
BRADINGTON YOUNG
BRADY
BRASSCRAFTERS
BRAXTON CULLER
BRETT AUSTIN
BROWN JORDAN
BROYHILL
BRUNSCHWIG & FILS
BUILTRIGHT
BUTLER
CM FURNITURE
CSD FURNITURE
CTH/SHERRILL OCCASIONAL
C-STYLE
CAL BEAR
CAL-STYLE
CAMBRIDGE LAMPS
CANADEL
CANDELLA LIGHTING
CANTERBURY
CAPE CRAFTSMEN
CAPEL RUGS
CAPITOL LEATHER
CAROLINA MIRROR
CAROLINA TABLE OF HICKORY
CAROLINA'S CHOICE
CARSON'S
CARTER
CARVER'S GUILD
CASA BIQUE
CASA STRADIVARI
CASUAL CREATIONS
CASUAL LAMP
CATNAPPER
CENTURY
CHAIRWORKS
CHAPMAN
CHARLESTON FORGE
CHART HOUSE IMPORTS
CHATHAM COUNTY
CHATHAM REPRODUCTIONS
CHELSEA CLOCK
CHERRY POND DESIGNS
CHRISHAWN DISTINCTIVE ART
CHROMCRAFT
CLAIRE MURRAY
CLARK CASUAL

CLASSIC GALLERY
CLASSIC GEORGIAN
CLASSIC LEATHER
CLASSIC RATTAN
CLASSIC TRADITIONS
CLAYTON MARCUS
CLOVERHURST
COCHRANE & COCHRANE
UPHOLSTERY
COCO ISLAND
THAYER COGGIN
COJA LEATHER
COLLECTIONS '85
COLLEZIONE EUROPA
COLONIAL FURNITURE
COMFORT DESIGNS
CONANT BALL
CONOVER
COOPER CLASSICS
FREDERICK COOPER
CORSICAN
COULTER
COUNCILL CRAFTSMEN
COUNTY LINE
COWTAN & TOUT
COX
CRATE IN MOTION
CRAFTIQUE
CRAFTMARK
CRAFTWORK GUILD
CRAWFORD
CREATIONS BY HILL
CREATIVE EXPRESSIONS
CREATIVE FURNITURE
CREATIVE METAL & WOOD
CREATIVE OFFICE SEATING
CRYSTAL CLEAR
CUSTOM STYLE
DFC
D & F WICKER RATTAN
IMPORTS
DIA
DMI FURNITURE
D SCAN/DANWOOD
TIFFANY
DANSEN CONTEMPORARY
DAR/RAN
DAVID KENT
DAVIS CONFERENCE GROUP
DAVIS & DAVIS
DAYSTROM
DECORATIVE ARTS
DECORATIVE CRAFTS
DENUNZIO
DESIGN GUILD LAMPS
DESIGN INSTITUTE OF
AMERICA
DESIGNMASTER
DESIGN SYSTEMS

DILLON
DINAIRE
DIRECTIONAL
DISTINCTION
DIXIE
DOLBI CASHIER
DOUBLE R LEATHER
DOUGLAS
DREAMWEAVERS RUGS
DURALEE FABRICS
DURA WICKER
DUTAILIER
ER BUCK
EAGLE CRAFT
ECCO
EKORNES
ELDEN COLLECTIONS
ELEMENTS BY GRAPEVINE
ELLO
EMERSON ET CIE
EMERSON LEATHER
ENTREE
ERIC MORGAN
EXCEL OFFICE
EXCELSIOR
EXECUTIVE FURNITURE
EXECUTIVE LEATHER
FAIRFIELD CHAIR
FASHION BED
FEIZY
MURRAY FEISS
FIAM/FORMA DESIGN
FICKS REED
FINE ARTS LAMPS
FITZ & FLOYD
FLEXSTEEL
FLORAL ART
FLORITA NOVA
FORBES BROS
FOXFIRE
FRANK & SON
FRANKLIN CHAIRS
FREDERICK COOPER
FRIEDMAN BROS MIRRORS
FRIENDSHIP UPHOLSTERY
FROELICH
FROM THE EARTH
FUN WITH FURS
FUTURISTIC
GMS IMPORTS
GABY'S SHOPPE
GAINES MFG
GALBRAITH
GAME ROOM
GARCIA IMPORTS
GATCO BRASS
GENERAL STORE
GEORGE KOVACS
GEORGIAN FURNISHINGS

GIOVANNI TORINO
GLENNCRAFT
GREAT CITY TRADERS
GREAT WOODS
GREEFF FABRICS
GROSFILLEX
GUILDMASTER
GUILDMASTER ART
H & H FURNITURE
HTB CONTEMPORARY
HZD COLLECTIONS
HABERSHAM PLANTATION
HALCYON
HALE
HALE OF VERMONT
HAMMARY
HARRIS STRONG
HART
HATTERAS HAMMOCKS
HEARTHSIDE CLASSICS
HEKMAN
HENDERSON
HEN FEATHERS
HENKEL HARRIS
HENKEL MOORE
HENRY LINK
HERITAGE HAUS FURNITURE
HICKORY CHAIR
HICKORY FRY
HICKORY HILL
HICKORY LEATHER
HICKORY MANUFACTURING
HICKORY TAVERN
HICKORY WHITE
HIGH POINT DESK
HIGHBORN MANOR
HINKLE CHAIR
YOUNG HINKLE
HOBE SOUND
HOLLYWOODS
HOMECREST ALUMINUM
HOOD
HOOKER
HOWARD MILLER
HUNTER DOUGLAS
HYUNDAI
IDEAL IMPORTS
IMAGES OF AMERICA
INTERNATIONAL
INTERNATIONAL DESIGNER
IMPORTS
INTERNATIONAL GLASS
NJ ROSS
JDI
JSF
JAMES R COOPER
JAMES STEWART & SONS
JARU
JASPER CABINET

JASPER DESK
JAY WILLFRED
JOFFCO
JOHN BOOS
JOHN MCGILL
JOHN RICHARD COLLECTION
JOHNSTON CASUALS
JOHNSTON TOMBIGBEE
JOHN ELLIOTT
JK REED
J ROYALE
J SIDNEY SMITH
J WILLIAMS
JRW CONTEMPORARY
KAISER KUHN LIGHTING
KAREL MINTJENS
KARGES
KAY LYN
KENNEBUNK WEAVERS
KESSLER
KIMBALL HARMONY WOODS
KIMERS FURNITURE
KINDER HARRIS
KING HICKORY
W KING AMBLER
KINGS ANTIQUE
KINGS CREEK
KINGSDOWN
KINGSLEY-BATES
KINGSTON HULL
KINNEY WALLCOVERING
KLAUSSNER
KOCH & LOWY LAMPS
GEORGE KOVACS
KRAVET FABRICS
KUSHWOOD
LaBARGE
LAFALEGNAMI
LAMONTAGE
CR LAINE
LAMBERT
ACTION BY LANE
LANE CASEGOODS
LANE UPHOLSTERY
LANE VENTURE
LAWRENCE UNLIMITED
LEA
LEATHERMAN'S GUILD
LEE JOFFA FABRICS
LEEAZANNE LAMPS
LEEDO
LEGACY DESIGNS
LEISTERS
LENNOX
LEXINGTON
LIGO
LINEAL
LINK TAYLOR
LIGON IMPORTS

LINRENE
LISTER BY GEEBRO
LOTUS ARTS
LUI
LUMINART PICTURES
LYNN HOLLYN
LYON SHAW
MP IMPORTS
MADISON FURNITURE
MADISON SQUARE
MAHOGANY HEIRLOOMS
MAITLAND SMITH
MALLIN
MANCHESTER WOOD
MANOR TRADITIONS
MARBLEWORKS
MARBRO LAMPS
MARKEL LIGHTING
MARSHALL JAMES
MARTINSVILLE NOVELTY
MARYLAND CLASSICS
MASTER DESIGN
MASTERFIELD
McENROE
McGUIRE
McKINLEY LEATHER
MEADOWCRAFT
MERSMAN
MAIMI METAL
MICHAEL SHOWALTER
MICHAEL THOMAS (MANOR
TRADITIONS)
MIKHAIL DARAFEEV
MILA INTERNATIONAL
MILLENIUM
MILLER DESK
MILLIKEN
MINOFF LAMPS
MIRROR FAIR
MOLLA
MONTAGE
MOON COLLECTION
MOOSEHEAD
MORGAN STEWART
MOTIONCRAFT
MOTTAHEDEH
MURRAY FEISS
MYRTLE DESK
MYSTIC VALLEY TRADERS
NDI
NAGYKERY IMPORTS
NATHAN HALE
NATIONAL MT AIRY
NATURAL LIGHT
NATUZZI
NESSEN
NEW RIVER ARTISAN
NICHOLAS JAMES
NICHOLS & STONE

NORA FENTON
NORMAN PERRY LAMPS
NORTH HICKORY
NULL INDUSTRIES
OAK CRAFT
OGGETTI
OHIO TABLE PADS
OKLAHOMA IMPORTING
OLD HICKORY FURNITURE
OLD HICKORY TANNERY
OLD WAVERLY
ORIENTAL LACQUER
OTTO ZENKE
P COLLINS
PACE
PACE-STONE
PACIFIC COAST LIGHTING
PACIFIC RATTAN
PALAZETTI
PALECEK
PALLISER
PAPER WHITE
PARLIAMENT
P & P CHAIR
PAOLI
PARAGON PICTURES
PAUL ROBERT
PAUL ROBINSON
PAWLEY'S ISLAND HAMMOCK
PAYNE FABRICS
PAYNE STREET
PEACOCK ALLEY
PEARSON
PEM KAY
PENNSYLVANIA CLASSICS
PEOPLOUNGER
PETERS-REVINGTON
PHILLIP REINISCH
PHILLIPS COLLECTION
PHILLIPS FURNITURE
PHOENIX ART PRESS
PINE-TIQUE
PINNACLE
PLANT PLANT
PLANTATION COMFORT
PLATT COLLECTION
POMPEII
POWELL COLLECTIONS
PRECEDENT
PRESIDENTIAL
PREVIEW
PRIVILEGE HOUSE
PULASKI
REGENCY FURNITURE
RELIANCE LAMPS
REMBRANDT LAMPS
REMINGTON LAMPS
REPROCRAFTERS
REPRODUX

REX
RICHARDSON BROS
RIDGEWAY CLOCKS
RIDGEWOOD
RIVERSIDE
ROBERT ALLEN FABRICS
ROBINSON FURNITURE
ROBINSON IRON
ROSALCO
ROSENBAUM FINE ARTS
ROYAL PATINA
ROYCE CORPORATION
ROWE
SEE IMPORTS
SK PRODUCTS
SALEM SQUARE
SAM MOORE
SAMSONITE
SAMUEL LAWRENCE
SAN DIEGO DESIGNS
SAN MIGUEL TRADING
SANDERSON
SARREID
SCALAMANDRE
SCHEIBE
SCHNADIG
SCHUMACHER
SCHWEIGER
SEALY
SEALY FURNITURE OF
MARYLAND
SEALY FURNITURE
SEDGEFIELD BY ADAMS
SEDGEWICK RATTAN
SERTA
SHUFORD
SIGLA
SIGNATURE RUGS
SILVESTRI
SINGER
SKILLCRAFT
SLIGH
SOICHER-MARIN FINE ARTS
SOMMA
SOUTH SEAS RATTAN
SOUTHAMPTON
SOUTHERN CRAFTSMEN GUILD
SOUTHERN OF CONOVER
SOUTHERN TABLE
SOUTHWEST CO
SOUTHWEST DESIGNS
SOUTHWOOD
REPRODUCTIONS
SOVA & SOVA
SPEER COLLECTIBLES
SPRING AIR
ST TIMOTHY
STAKMORE
STANFORD FURNITURE

STANLEY
STANTON COOPER
STATEMENTS
STATESVILLE CHAIR
STATTON
STEIN WORLD
STEWART FURNITURE
STIFFEL
STONE ART
STONE COUNTRY IRONWORKS
STONE INTL
STONEVILLE
STRATFORD
STRATOLOUNGER
STROHEIM & ROMANN
FABRICS
STYLE UPHOLSTERY
SUMMER CLASSICS
SUPERIOR
SWAIM CLASSICS
SWAIM DESIGNS
SWAIM ORIGINALS
SWAN BRASS PRODUCTS
TAPESTRIES LTD
TAYLOR WOODCRAFT
TAYLORSVILLE UPHOLSTERY
TELESCOPE
TELL CITY
TEMPLE STUART
THAYER COGGIN
MICHAEL THOMAS
THOMASVILLE LAMP
TIANJIN PHILADELPHIA

TIMMERMAN
TOMLIN
TOU LEMONDE BOCHART
TOWN SQUARE
TRADITIONS FRANCE
TRADITIONAL HEIRLOOMS
TRANSPACIFIC
TRIUNE
TROPITONE
TUFENKIAN TIBETAN CARPETS
TYNDALE
US FURNITURE
ULTIMATE LAMPS
UNION CITY CHAIR
UNIQUE ORIGINALS
UNIVERSAL
UTTERMOST
UWHARRIE CHAIR
VAN TEAL
VAUGHAN
VANGUARD
VANGUARD STUDIOS
VAUGHAN BASSETT
VENEMAN
VENTURE
VICTORIAN CLASSIC
VIETRI
VIRGINIA GALLERIES
VIRGINIA HOUSE
VIRGINIA METALCRAFTERS
VISUAL COMFORT
W KING AMBLER

WAMBOLD
WATERFORD CRYSTAL LAMPS
WATERFORD FURNITURE
WATSON CHAIR
WAVERLY
WAVERLY HOME FASHIONS
WEIMAN
WELLESLEY GUILD
WELLINGTON HALL
WESLEY ALLEN
WESTGATE FABRICS
WHITAKER FURNITURE
WHITE OF MEBANE
WHITECRAFT
WILDWOOD LAMPS AND
ACCESSORIES
WILLIAM ALLEN
WILSONART
WILTON ARMATALE
WINDSONG
WINDSOR DESIGN
WINNERS ONLY
WINSTON
WOOD CLASSICS
WOOD & HOGAN
WOODARD
WOODMARK ORIGINALS
WRIGHT TABLES
YESTERYEAR WICKER
YORKSHIRE LEATHER
YOUNG HINKLE

ROWE GALLERY
HICKORY FURNITURE MART
2220 HWY 70 SE
HICKORY, NC 28602
Hours: **M-F: 9-6; S: 9-5; Closed Sundays**

Toll-Free	
Direct	828-322-4400
Fax	
Internet	

Notes: This resource is part of the Hickory Furniture Mart complex. This showroom is one of over 80 to visit. **See Hickory Furniture Mart listing for more information.** Consolidated shipping can be arranged with other resources in this center, a standard one/third deposit is required on all orders. Most showrooms accept VISA/MC, but not all. Cash, personal or certified checks accepted by all

showrooms. If you elect not to pay for your entire purchase at the time of sale, a personal or certified check will be due upon delivery.

Manufacturers: (Many resources do not list all their manufacturers. Be sure to inquire about those you are interested in, but do not see listed here.)

═══════════════════════

RUG ROOM, THE
HICKORY FURNITURE MART
2220 HWY 70 SE
HICKORY, NC 28602
Hours: **M-F: 9-6; S: 9-5; Closed Sundays**

Toll-Free	
Direct	828-324-1776
Fax	
Internet	

Notes: This resource is part of the Hickory Furniture Mart complex. This showroom is one of over 80 to visit. **See Hickory Furniture Mart listing for more information.** Consolidated shipping can be arranged with other resources in this center, a standard one/third deposit is required on all orders. Most showrooms accept VISA/MC, but not all. Cash, personal or certified checks accepted by all showrooms. If you elect not to pay for your entire purchase at the time of sale, a personal or certified check will be due upon delivery.

Manufacturers: (Many resources do not list all their manufacturers. Be sure to inquire about those you are interested in, but do not see listed here.)

═══════════════════════

RUG STORE, THE
2201 CROWNPOINT EXEC DR
CHARLOTTE, NC 28227
Hours: **M-F: 9-5**

Toll-Free	
Direct	800-257-5078
Fax	704-845-8591
Internet	

Notes: Area rugs. Pay by VISA/MC/MO. Satisfaction guaranteed. Returns accepted within seven days for exchange, refund or credit. Shipments worldwide.

Manufacturers: (Many resources do not list all their manufacturers. Be sure to inquire about those you are interested in, but do not see listed here.)

S & S MILLS, INC
PO BOX 1568
DALTON, GA 30722
Hours: **M-F: 9-5**

Toll-Free	800-651-2916
Direct	800-241-4013
Fax	706-277-3922
Internet	**email:** ssmills@alltel.net **website:** www.ssmills.com

Notes: This company carries an excellent array of carpet and hardwood at discount prices. They will send a great sample box of carpets and pads, prices, etc. Very reliable.

Manufacturers: (Many resources do not list all their manufacturers. Be sure to inquire about those you are interested in, but do not see listed here.)
S & S MILLS

SALLY STOWE INERIORS
4100 WILKINSON BLVD
GASTONIA, NC 28056
Hours: **M-S: 9-5;**

Toll-Free	
Direct	704-824-2129
Fax	704-824-7980
Internet	

Notes: In business since 1943. Retail furniture store and design studio. All sales consultants on staff are designer. 50% deposit required, balance when merchandise arrives at warehouse. VISA/MC/AMEX accepted. Heirloom delivery service is their shipper - 100% guaranteed to be put in your home in good condition. Sales and design consultants on staff. Damaged goods will be returned or replaced at their expense. Defective merchandise will be replaced or returned also. Customer can visit this facility. Formerly Craig Furniture.

Manufacturers: (Many resources do not list all their manufacturers. Be sure to inquire about those you are interested in, but do not see listed here.)

AMERICAN DREW	HENRY LINK	PETERS-REVINGTON
BARCALOUNGER	HICKORY CHAIR	PULASKI
BERKLINE	HICKORY TAVERN	REX
BLACKSMITH SHOP	HITCHCOCK	STANTON COOPER
BRADINGTON YOUNG	HOOKER	STATTON
COUNCILL CRAFTSMEN	JASPER	STIFFEL
CRAFTIQUE	KEY CITY	SUMTER CABINET
CRESENT	KINGSDOWN	TAYLORSVILLE
DIXIE	LANE	TRADITION HOUSE
EMERSON LEATHER	LEXINGTON	WELLINGTON HALL
FASHION BED	LINK-TAYLOR	WESLEY HALL
FRIEDMAN BROS MIRRORS	MADISON SQUARE	WINNERS ONLY
HANCOCK & MOORE	MOBEL	WOODMARK
HEKMAN	PEOPLOUNGER	YOUNG-HINKLE
HENKEL-HARRIS		

SAM MOORE GALLERY
HICKORY FURNITURE MART
2220 HWY 70 SE
HICKORY, NC 28602
Hours: **M-F: 9-6; S: 9-5; Closed Sundays**

Toll-Free	
Direct	828-322-6602
Fax	
Internet	

Notes: This resource is part of the Hickory Furniture Mart complex. This showroom is one of over 80 to visit. **See Hickory Furniture Mart listing for more information.** Consolidated shipping can be arranged with other resources in this center, a standard one/third deposit is required on all orders. Most showrooms accept VISA/MC, but not all. Cash, personal or certified checks accepted by all showrooms. If you elect not to pay for your entire purchase at the time of sale, a personal or certified check will be due upon delivery.

Manufacturers: (Many resources do not list all their manufacturers. Be sure to inquire about those you are interested in, but do not see listed here.)

SEASONS OUTDOOR GALLERY
HICKORY FURNITURE MART
2220 HWY 70 SE
HICKORY, NC 28602
Hours: **M-F: 9-6; S: 9-5; Closed Sundays**

Toll-Free	
Direct	828-322-9445
Fax	828-322-1454
Internet	**email**: hparksales@hickorypark.com **website**: www.hickorypark.com

Notes: This resource is part of the Hickory Furniture Mart complex. This showroom is one of over 80 to visit. **See Hickory Furniture Mart listing for more information.** Consolidated shipping can be arranged with other resources in this center, a standard one/third deposit is required on all orders. Most showrooms accept VISA/MC, but not all. Cash, personal or certified checks accepted by all showrooms. If you elect not to pay for your entire purchase at the time of sale, a personal or certified check will be due upon delivery.

Manufacturers: (Many resources do not list all their manufacturers. Be sure to inquire about those you are interested in, but do not see listed here.)

SHAW FURNITURE GALLERIES
131 W. ACADEMY STREET
RANDLEMAN, NC 27317
Hours: **M-F: 9-5:30; S: 9-5**

Toll-Free	
Direct	336-498-2628
Fax	336-498-7889
Internet	

Notes: In business since 1940. 30% downpayment with VISA/MC. Balance paid by certified funds. Shipping done by Superior Delivery Service (75% owned by Shaw). Customers deal with Shaw if any problems arise. If any damages occur in shipping, local repair person will be consulted. If it cannot be repaired easily, the item will be returned to Shaw's facility where professionally trained personnel repair it to the customer's satisfaction-or it will be replaced. Customer can visit this facility. Over 2 acres of showroom. Designers and consultants on staff will assist customers with choices. Some major manufacturers do not want their name listed. If you don't see the factory whose goods you want, please call for verification. If you want to visit this showroom, Shaw will pay for your lodging, based upon a minimum purchase. Established customers receive postcard notices of sales.

Manufacturers: (Many resources do not list all their manufacturers. Be sure to inquire about those you are interested in, but do not see listed here.)

ACTION BY LANE	CASTILLIAN IMPORTS	FLEXSTEEL
ALEXVALE	CBK LTD	FORBES LAMPS
ALLUSIONS	CENTURY	FOSS CREEK CERAMICS
ALL CONTINENTAL	CHARLESTON FORGE	FRAME ONE STUDIOS
AMERICAN DREW	CHATHAM COUNTY	FRANKLIN PICTURES
AMERICAN HERITAGE	CHROMCRAFT	FRIEDMAN BROS MIRRORS
AMERICAN OF HIGH POINT	CL LIGHTING	FREDERICK COOPER
AMERICAN OF MARTINSVILLE	CLARK CASUAL	FROM THE EARTH
ARTAGRAPH REPRODUCTIONS	CLASSIC GEORGIAN	GEORGIAN FURNISHINGS
ART FLO	CLASSIC LEATHER	GLASS ARTS
ARTISTRY DESIGNS	CLASSIC RATTAN	GLENNCRAFT
ARTMASTER STUDIOS	CLASSICO	GLOBER
AS YOU LIKE IT LAMPS	CLAYTON MARCUS	GOOD SHIP
ASHLEY	CLOVERHURST	GROSFILLEX OUTDOOR
ATHENS WOODCRAFTERS	CM FURNITURE	GUARDSMAN PRODUCTS
ATHOL	COCHRANE	HABERSHAM PLANTATION
ATLANTA GLASSCRAFTER	COLLECTIONS '85	HAEGER POTTERIES
AUSTIN PRODUCTS	COLLEZIONE EUROPA	HAMILTON COLLECTION
BARCALOUNGER	COLONIAL	HAMMARY
BARN DOOR	COMFORT DESIGNS	J HARRINGTON/BURTON
BASSETT INDUSTRIES	COOPER CLASSICS	REPRO
BAUER LAMP	CORHAM	HART
BDT	CORNELISON SILK TREE	HEKMAN
BENICIA IRON BEDS	CORSICAN IRON BEDS	HEN FEATHERS
BERKLINE	COUNCILL CRAFTSMEN	HERITAGE HAUS
BLACKSMITH SHOP	COUNTRY ORIGINALS	HICKORY CHAIR
BRADINGTON YOUNG	COX	HICKORY FRY
BRADY	CRAFTIQUE	HICKORY HILL
BRASSCRAFTERS	CRAWFORD	HICKORY INTERNATIONAL
BRAXTON CULLER	CREATIVE LIGHTING	HICKORY WHITE
BROWN JORDAN	CRYSTAL CLEAR	HIGH POINT FURNITURE
BROYHILL	D SCAN (DSF)	HILL
BROYHILL PREMIER	DAYSTROM	HITCHCOCK CHAIR
BURNS	DECORATIVE ARTS	HOOKER
BUSH	DECORATIVE CRAFTS	HOUSE OF FRANCE
BUTLER TABLES	DESIGNMASTER	HOWARD MILLER
BUYING & DESIGN	DESIGN TREELINE	HYUNDAI
CADWELL	DILLON	INWOOD OFFICE FURNITURE
CAL-STYLE	DINAIRE	JH BOONE
CANAL DOVER	DISTINCTION LEATHER	JH CRAVER & SON
CANADEL	DISTINCTIVE DESIGNS	JSF INDUSTRIES
CANE & REED	DUTAILIER	JARU
CAPEL	EAGLE CRAFT	JASPER CABINET
CARLTON McLENDON	EKORNES	JAY WILLFRED
CARTER CONTEMPORARY	ELLO	JOHNSTON CASUALS
CAROLINA MIRROR	EMERSON ET CIE	JOHNSTON TOMBIGBEE
CAROLINA TABLES	EMERSON LEATHER	KAISER KUHN LIGHTING
CTH/SHERRILL	EVANS CERAMICS	KELLER
CARSON'S OF HIGH POINT	EXCELSIOR DESIGN	KEYNOTE BY CRAFTWORK
CARVER'S GUILD	FAIRFIELD CHAIR	KIMBALL
CASA BIQUE	FASHION BED	KIM ORIGINALS
CASA STRADIVARI	FICKS REED	KINDER HARRIS
CASE CASARD	FINE ARTS LAMPS	KLAUSSNER

KOFABCO
LaBARGE
LANE
CR LAINE
LEA INDUSTRIES
LEATHERCRAFT
LEEDO
LEGGETT & PLATT
LEISTERS
LENOX
LEXINGTON
LIFELINE
LLOYD FLANDERS
LYON SHAW
MADISON SQUARE
MARIO
MARYLAND CLASSICS
MASTER DESIGN
MAXTON
McKAY TABLE PADS
McKINLEY LEATHER
MERSMAN TABLES
MICHAELS CO
MIKHAIL DARAFEEV
MILLENIUM
MILLER OFFICE DESKS
MOBY DICK
MOON/MONTAGE
MOTIONCRAFT BY SHERRILL
MURRAY FEISS LAMPS
NAPP DEADY
NATHAN HALE
NATIONAL MT AIRY
NATURAL LIGHT
NEW CENTURY PICTURE
NICHOLS & STONE
NORA FENTON
NORTH HICKORY FURNITURE
NULL INDUSTRIES
OHIO TABLE PADS
OKLAHOMA IMPORTING
OLD HICKORY TANNERY
OLD WAVERLY
OLDE BRICKYARD COOPER
O & P CHAIR
PALECEK
PARAGON PICTURES
PARK PLACE
PENNSYLVANIA CLASSICS
CLYDE PEARSON
PEOPLOUNGER
PHASE IV
PILGRIM GLASS
PINE-TIQUE

POULIOT DESIGNS
PULASKI
QUALITY DINETTES
JK REED
RAVENWOOD
RELIANCE LAMPS
REX
RICHARDSON BROS
RIDGEWAY CLOCKS
RIDGEWOOD FURNITURE
RIVERSIDE
ROSALCO
ROWE
ROXTON
J ROYALE
ROYAL PATINA
ROYCE
RUPPERSBURG
S & K PRODUCTS
SADEK IMPORTS
SALEM SQUARE
SAM MOORE
SARREID
SCHNADIG
SCHWEIGER
SEALY BEDDING
SEDGEFIELD BY ADAMS
SERTA BEDDING
SHADOW CATCHER
SHELLY'S CUSHIONS &
UMBRELLAS
SHOAL CREEK LAMP
SHUFORD
SIGNATURE RUGS
SILK TREE FACTORY
SLEEPWORKS
SLIGH
SOUTHERN FURNITURE OF
CONOVER
SOUTHERN FURNITURE
REPRODUCTIONS
SOUTHAMPTON
SOICHER MARIN
SOUTHWOOD
SPEER COLLECTIBLES
SPRING AIR MATTRESS
STANLEY
STANTON COOPER
STATESVILLE CHAIR
STIFFEL LAMP
STONE COLLECTION
STONE COUNTRY IRONWORKS
STONE INTL
STONEVILLE

STRATOLOUNGER
STYLECRAFT LAMPS
SUNBEAM OUTDOOR
SUPERIOR TABLES
SWAIM OCCASIONAL
TAPESTRIES LTD
TAYLOR WOODCRAFT
TAYLORSVILLE
TELESCOPE
THAYER COGGIN
BOLING CO
GENERAL STORE
PLANT PLANT
TEMPLE STUART
THREE WEAVERS
THOMASVILLE CABINET
TIANJIN PHILADELPHIA
CARPET
TOP BRASS LAMPS
TOYO TRADING
TRADITION HEIRLOOMS
TRADITION HOUSE
TRADITIONS FRANCE
TRIUNE BUSINESS
TROPITONE OUTDOOR
TUBB WOODCRAFTERS
TURKART
US FURNITURE
UNIVERSAL
UNIVERSAL STATUARY
UTTERMOST
VAN TEAL
VANGUARD FURNITURE
VANGUARD STUDIOS
VAUGHAN
VAUGHAN BASSETT
VENEMAN COLLECTION
VENTURE
VIETRI
VIRGINIA HOUSE
VIRGINIA METALCRAFTERS
WATERLOO
WEBB
WEIMAN
WELLESLEY GUILD
WELLINGTON HALL
WESLEY ALLEN
WILDWOOD LAMPS
WILLIAM ALLEN
WINDSOR ART
WINSTON CASUAL
WOODMARC
WOODMARK ORIGINALS

SHEPHERDS DISCOUNT FURNITURE
10609-C MAIN STREET
ARCHDALE, NC 27263
Hours: **M-F: 9-5; S: 9-4**

Toll-Free	800-431-7209
Direct	336-431-7209
Fax	
Internet	Coming soon.

Notes: Nationwide in-home delivery. VISA/MC accepted. Five salespeople. Showroom available.

Manufacturers: (Many resources do not list all their manufacturers. Be sure to inquire about those you are interested in, but do not see listed here.)

AMERICAN DREW	HENRY LINK	QUEEN ANNE
BASSETT	LEXINGTON	YOUNG-HINKLE
CRAWFORD	LINK TAYLOR	VAUGHAN-BASSETT
FLEXSTEEL	LYNN HOLLYN	UNIVERSAL

SHERRILL GALLERY
HICKORY FURNITURE MART
2220 HWY 70 SE
HICKORY, NC 28602
Hours: **M-F: 9-6; S: 9-5; Closed Sundays**

Toll-Free	
Direct	828-326-1735
Fax	
Internet	

Notes: This resource is part of the Hickory Furniture Mart complex. This showroom is one of over 80 to visit. **See Hickory Furniture Mart listing for more information.** Consolidated shipping can be arranged with other resources in this center, a standard one/third deposit is required on all orders. Most showrooms accept VISA/MC, but not all. Cash, personal or certified checks accepted by all showrooms. If you elect not to pay for your entire purchase at the time of sale, a personal or certified check will be due upon delivery.

Manufacturers: (Many resources do not list all their manufacturers. Be sure to inquire about those you are interested in, but do not see listed here.)

SHUTTER DEPOT
RT 2, BOX 157
GREENVILLE, GA 30222
Hours: **M-F: 9-5**

Toll-Free	
Direct	706-672-1214
Fax	706-672-1122
Internet	

Notes: Custom interior and exterior shutters wholesale to the public. Two and one-half inch moveable louver, raised panel and fixed louver shutters. Custom finished or unfinished. Complete selection of hardware. $2 brochure.

Manufacturers: (Many resources do not list all their manufacturers. Be sure to inquire about those you are interested in, but do not see listed here.)

SILK SURPLUS
235 EAST 58TH ST
NEW YORK, NY 10022
Hours: **M-S: 10-5:30**

Toll-Free	
Direct	212-753-6511
Fax	212-753-0463
Internet	

Notes: Established in 1962. Closeouts of Scalamandre and other fabrics. Fabrics and trims available via VISA/MC/MO. If you buy by mail, you must know exactly what you want. Better to visit in person. Sample cuttings are free. All sales final.

Manufacturers: (Many resources do not list all their manufacturers. Be sure to inquire about those you are interested in, but do not see listed here.)
SCALAMANDRE

SILVER QUEEN, THE
730 N INDIAN ROCKS RD
BELLEAIRE BLUFFS, FL 33770
Hours: **M-F: 9-5; S: 10-4**

Toll-Free	800-262-3134
Direct	813-581-6827
Fax	813-586-0822
Internet	

Notes: Tabletop, china, stemware, flatware and giftware. In business since 1974. Over 1500 patterns of active and discontinued sterling patterns. VISA/MC/DISCOVER. Also buy sterling.

Manufacturers: (Many resources do not list all their manufacturers. Be sure to inquire about those you are interested in, but do not see listed here.)

===

SILVER SHOP
3164 PEACHTREE RD NE
ATLANTA, GA 30305
Hours: **M-S: 10-5**

Toll-Free	
Direct	404-261-4009
Fax	404-261-9708
Internet	**email:**sterlingsilver@worldnet.att.net **website:** www.beverlybremer.com

Notes: Tabletop, china, stemware, flatware and giftware. Replace pieces or add to your sterling silver at up to 75% off retail. We specialize in new and used flatware and hollow-ware. Over 1200 patterns in stock. Call or write for a free inventory of your sterling pattern. We buy sterling silver, with a careful appraisal for maximum value.

Manufacturers: (Many resources do not list all their manufacturers. Be sure to inquire about those you are interested in, but do not see listed here.)

===

SINA ORIENTAL RUG
THE ATRIUM
430 SOUTH MAIN ST
HIGH POINT, NC 27260
Hours: **M-F: 9-6; S: 9-5**

Toll-Free	
Direct	336-885-7600
Fax	
Internet	**email:** sina@theatrium.com

Notes: Part of the Atrium complex. Worth visiting, showrooms available. See **Atrium Furniture Showroom** listing for more information. Importers of fine handmade oriental rugs featuring a large selection of contemporary traditional and transitional style rugs from different corners of the world.

Manufacturers: (Many resources do not list all their manufacturers. Be sure to inquire about those you are interested in, but do not see listed here.)

SKYLAND FURNITURE SHOP
HWY 321 N, PO BOX 10
PATTERSON, NC 28661
Hours: **M-S: 9-5**

Toll-Free	
Direct	704-758-4580
Fax	
Internet	

Notes: Located on Hwy 321 in the foothills of the NC mountains. Showroom available for browsing and buying. Fifty percent deposit required. This deposit is held in an escrow account. Full refunds will be made on any order cancelled providing they can cancel order with manufacturer. If they are unable to cancel the order and customer so desires, they will place the item in their showroom and sell it for customer. Nationwide shipping.

Manufacturers: (Many resources do not list all their manufacturers. Be sure to inquire about those you are interested in, but do not see listed here.)

AUSTIN	AMERICAN HERITAGE	BERKLINE
ACTION RECLINERS	AMERICAN OF MARTINSVILLE	BERNHARDT
AMERICAN DREW	ATHOL	BOB TIMBERLAKE
AMERICAN FURNITURE	BASSETT	BROWN STREET
GALLERIES	BENICIA BEDS	BROYHILL

BUILTRIGHT CHAIR
CR LAINE
CARLTON MCLENDON
CAPITOL VICTORIAN
CAROLINA MIRROR
CASA BIQUE
CASTILIAN IMPORTS
CHARLESTON FORGE
CHROMECRAT
CLASSIC RATTAN
CLAYTON MARCUS
CLYDE PEARSON
COCHRANE
CRAFTIQUE
DENNY LAMPS
DINAIRE
DISTINCTIVE DESIGNS
DRESHER BRASS
EAGLE CRAFT
EMERSON LEATHER
FAIRFIELD
FASHION BED
FLEXSTEEL
FREDERICK COOPER
GENESIS LAMPS
GEORGIAN FURNISHINGS
HTB CONTEMPORARY
HAMMARY
HANOVER CHERRY TABLES
HANOVER CRAFTSMEN
HEKMAN
HENRY LINK
HICKORY INTERNATIONAL
LEATHER
HICKORY HILL
HICKORY LEATHER

HICKORY TAVERY
HIGHLAND HOUSE
HIGH POINT FURNITURE CO
HIGH POINT WOODWORKING
HOOD
HOOKER
INTERLINE
JASPER CABINET
JOHNSTON BENCHWORKS
KELLER
KING HICKORY
KINGSDOWN
LAINE UPHOLSTERY
LANE
LEA
LEATHER SHOP
LEATHERMAN'S GUILD
LEISTER FURNITURE
LEXINGTON
LINK TAYLOR
LLOYD FLANDERS
LYNN HOLLAND
MARKEL LIGHTING
MASTERFIELD UPHOLSTERY
MOOSEHEAD
NATHAN HALE
NATIONAL MT AIRY
NICHOLS & STONE
NORTHWOOD
NULL
OHIO TABLE PAD
OLD HICKORY TANNERY
OLD SALEM
PARK PLACE
PAUL ROBERTS CHAIR
PEARSON UPHOLSTERY

PINNACLE
PLYMOUTH HARLEE LAMPS
POULIOT
PULASKI
REX
SK PRODUCTS
SARRIED
SEALY BEDDING SEAY
SERTA
SHELBY WILLIAMS
SKILLCRAFT
SPEER LIGHTING
STAKMORE
STANLEY
STANTON COOPER
TAYLORSVILLE
TEMPLE STUART
TIMBERLAKE
TRADITION HOUSE
TROPITONE
UNIVERSAL
VAUGHAN BASSETT
VAUGHAN
VENTURE
VICTORIAN CLASSICS
VIRGINIA HOUSE
VIRGINIA METALCRAFTERS
WEATHERCRAFT
WEATHERMASTER
WEEKEND RETREAT
WELLINGTON HALL
WESLEY ALLEN
WOODMARK
YESTERYEAR WICKER
YOUNG HINKLE

===

SLEEP SHOP
3136 HICKORY BLVD (US 321 S)
HUDSON, NC 28638
Hours: **M-S: 9-5:30**

Toll-Free	800-905-6252
Direct	828-728-7002
Fax	828-728-6685
Internet	Coming soon.

Notes: Hwy 321. In business since 1977. We carry several lines of bedroom furniture, including linens, waterbeds, mattresses. VISA/MC/AMEX/DISC/MO.

Manufacturers: **(Many resources do not list all their manufacturers. Be sure to inquire about those you are interested in, but do not see listed here.)**

ARBEK

ACCENT

BEAUTYREST BY SIMMONS

BLACKHAWK

ELLIOTT'S DESIGNS

SPRINGWALL MATTRESS CO

===============================

SLEEP SHOP
2407 NORWOOD ST
LENOIR, NC 28645
Hours: **M-S: 9-5:30**

Toll-Free	800-664-4229
Direct	704-728-1161
Fax	704-728-0187
Internet	

Notes: Hwy 321. In business since 1977. We carry several lines of bedroom furniture, including linens, waterbeds, mattresses. VISA/MC/AMEX/DISC/MO all accepted.

Manufacturers: **(Many resources do not list all their manufacturers. Be sure to inquire about those you are interested in, but do not see listed here.)**

ACCENT

BEAUTYREST BY SIMMONS

SAMUEL LAWRENCE

FRISCO

FORTUNE RATTAN & WICKER

ELLIOTT'S DESIGNS

SPRINGWALL MATTRESS CO

===============================

SMOKEY MOUNTAIN FURNITURE OUTLET
3281 HICKORY BLVD (HWY 321)
HUDSON, NC 28638
Hours: **M-F: 9-5**

Toll-Free	
Direct	704-726-1434
Fax	704-726-1152
Internet	

Notes: Located on Hwy 321. In stock furniture for immediate delivery nationwide.

Manufacturers: **(Many resources do not list all their manufacturers. Be sure to inquire about those you are interested in, but do not see listed here.)**

ACTION BY LANE

KINGSDOWN

SOBOL HOUSE OF FURNISHINGS
RICHARDSON BLVD
BLACK MOUNTAIN, NC 28711
Hours: **M-F: 9-5; S: 9-5:30**

Toll-Free	
Direct	704-669-8031
Fax	704-669-7969
Internet	

Notes: Established 1970. Traditional, contemporary, 18th century and country styles are their specialty. Consultants on staff can help customers with advice on choices. Credit cards. Worldwide shipping.

Manufacturers: **(Many resources do not list all their manufacturers. Be sure to inquire about those you are interested in, but do not see listed here.)**

SOUTH SEAS RATTAN
1708 FAIRFAX ROAD
GREENSBORO, NC 27407
Hours: **M-F: 9-5:00; S: 10-4**

Toll-Free	800-233-7133(FAX)
Direct	336-294-4100
Fax	336-294-4125
Internet	

Notes: This company is the manufacturer and also has a showroom open to the public. Visiting their showroom is the best idea. Savings direct from the manufacturer to you. Area's largest selection of rattan and wicker furniture

Manufacturers: **(Many resources do not list all their manufacturers. Be sure to inquire about those you are interested in, but do not see listed here.)**
Their own line.

SOUTHEAST WHOLESALERS
3637 FORT ST N, SUITE 290
ST PETERS BURG, FL 33704
Hours: **M-F: 9-10;S:10-6; SUN: NOON-6**

Toll-Free	800-894-1957
Direct	
Fax	813-898-7200
Internet	email: se@msn.com or southeastwholesalers@msn.com website: www.southeastwholesalers.com;

Notes: Free shipping. Woods, mini blinds, Duettes, pleated shades.

Manufacturers: (Many resources do not list all their manufacturers. Be sure to inquire about those you are interested in, but do not see listed here.)

BALI	JOANNA	LOUVERDRAPE
GRABER	KIRSCH	M & B
HUNTER DOUGLAS	LEVOLOR	VEROSOL

SOUTHERN DESIGNS
HICKORY FURNITURE MART
2220 HWY 70 SE
HICKORY, NC 28602
Hours: **M-F: 9-6; S: 9-5; Closed Sundays**

Toll-Free	
Direct	828-328-8855
Fax	828-328-1806
Internet	

Notes: Specialize in solid wood furniture (no particle board)This resource is part of the Hickory Furniture Mart complex. This showroom is one of over 80 to visit. **See Hickory Furniture Mart listing for more information.** Consolidated shipping can be arranged with other resources in this center, a standard one/third deposit is required on all orders. Most showrooms accept VISA/MC, but not all. Cash, personal or certified checks accepted by all showrooms. If you elect not to pay for your entire purchase at the time of sale, a personal or certified check will be due upon delivery.

Manufacturers: (Many resources do not list all their manufacturers. Be sure to inquire about those you are interested in, but do not see listed here.)

BROWN STREET	HABERSHAM	JASPER
CHATHAM	HITCHCOCK	MOBEL
DISTINCTION LEATHER	HOOKER	NATHAN HALE

PETERS-REVINGTON
RICHARDSON BROS
STONE COUNTRY IRON WORKS

SUPERIOR
VIRGINIA HOUSE

WISCONSIN FURNITURE
INDUSTRIES

===

SOUTHLAND FURNITURE GALLERIES
1244 HWY 17, PO BOX 1837
LITTLE RIVER, SC 29566
Hours: **M-S: 9-5:30**

Toll-Free	
Direct	843-280-9342
Fax	843-249-4527
Internet	Coming soon!

Notes: 30,000 sq ft showroom. Located near Myrtle Beach, we offer a unique shopping experience near the Grand Strand. Ship anywhere.

Manufacturers: (Many resources do not list all their manufacturers. Be sure to inquire about those you are interested in, but do not see listed here.)

AMBIANCE
AMERICAN DREW
BAKER
BERNHARDT
BLACKSMITH SHOP
CANADEL
CASA BIQUE
CASA STRADIVARI
CENTURY
CHARLESTON FORGE
CLASSIC LEATHER
CLYDE PEARSON
COLONIAL FURNITURE
COUNCILL CRAFTSMEN
CRAFTIQUE
CRAFTWORK GUILD
CRAWFORD
DISTINCTION LEATHER
ELLO
EMERSON LEATHER
FAIRFIELD CHAIR
FICKS REED
FINE ARTS LAMPS
FREDERICK COOPER
HABERSHAM PLANTATION
HAMMARY
HANCOCK & MOORE
HEKMAN
HICKORY WHITE
HITCHCOCK CHAIR

HOOKER
HOWARD MILLER
JASPER CABINET
JEFFCO
JOHN WIDDICOMB
JOHNSTON CASUALS
JON ELLIOTT
KARGES
KELLER
KING HICKORY
KNOB CREEK
KRAVET FABRICS
LaBARGE
LANE
LARGO
LEXINGTON
LILLIAN AUGUST
LLOYD FLANDERS
MAITLAND SMITH
MICHAEL THOMAS
MOTIONCRAFT
NATHAN HALE
NATHAN HALE
NATIONAL MT AIRY
NICHOLS & STONE
PANDE CAMERON RUGS
PENNSYLVANIA HOUSE
PULASKI
REX
RIVERSIDE

ROBERT ALLEN FABRICS
SALEM SQUARE
SALOOM
SAM MOORE
SARREID
SERTA MATTRESS
SHERRILL OCCASIONAL
SHUFORD
SLIGH
SOUTHAMPTON
SOUTHERN FURNITURE
SOUTHWOOD
STANLEY
STATTON
STIFFEL
TAYLOR WOODCRAFT
TEMPLE STUART
TIMBERLAKE COLLECTION
TRADITIONS FRANCE
TRADITION HOUSE
TROPITONE
UNIVERSAL
VANGUARD
VAUGHAN
VENTURE
VIRGINIA HOUSE
VIRGINIA METALCRAFTERS
WEIMAN
WELLINGTON HALL
WESLEY ALLEN BRASS

WESLEY HALL   WINSTON   WOODMARK
WILDWOOD   WISCONSIN
WILLIAM ALLEN   WOODARD

SPRING VALLEY DISCOUNT FURNITURE
429 W. MEADOWVIEW RD
GREENSBORO, NC 27406
Hours: **M-F: 10-8; S: 10-6**

Toll-Free	
Direct	336-272-9655
Fax	336-272-9655
Internet	

Notes:

Manufacturers: **(Many resources do not list all their manufacturers. Be sure to inquire about those you are interested in, but do not see listed here.)**

BASSETT   STYLECRAFT   VAUGHAN
KLAUSSNER   UNIVERSAL   WEBB
PHILLIP REINISCH

ST MARTIN'S LANE LTD
THE ATRIUM
430 SOUTH MAIN ST
HIGH POINT, NC 27262
Hours: **M-F: 9-6; S: 9-5**

Toll-Free	
Direct	336-887-0421
Fax	336-889-9555
Internet	

Notes: Part of the Atrium complex. Worth visiting, showrooms available. See **Atrium Furniture Showroom** listing for more information. A magnificent collection of 18th century English and French design antique reproductions. Complete settings for bedroom, dining, living, entrance and executive suite. Hand-carved and hand-finished mahogany.

Manufacturers: **(Many resources do not list all their manufacturers. Be sure to inquire**

about those you are interested in, but do not see listed here.)

STANLEY GALLERY
HICKORY FURNITURE MART
2220 HWY 70 SE
HICKORY, NC 28602
Hours: **M-F: 9-6; S: 9-5; Closed Sundays**

Toll-Free	
Direct	828-326-1735
Fax	
Internet	

Notes: This resource is part of the Hickory Furniture Mart complex. This showroom is one of over 80 to visit. **See Hickory Furniture Mart listing for more information.** Consolidated shipping can be arranged with other resources in this center, a standard one/third deposit is required on all orders. Most showrooms accept VISA/MC, but not all. Cash, personal or certified checks accepted by all showrooms. If you elect not to pay for your entire purchase at the time of sale, a personal or certified check will be due upon delivery.

Manufacturers: **(Many resources do not list all their manufacturers. Be sure to inquire about those you are interested in, but do not see listed here.)**

STAR CARPET BLIND & WALLCOVERINGS
7013 THIRD AVE
BROOKLYN, NY 11209
Hours: **M-F: 9-5**

Toll-Free	800-782-7800
Direct	718-748-8600
Fax	888-924-7811
Internet	website: www.haggar-ind.com

Notes: Established 1932. Free ups shipping. Free sample kit.

Manufacturers: **(Many resources do not list all their manufacturers. Be sure to inquire about those you are interested in, but do not see listed here.)**

WINDOW:	FABRICS:	KRUPNICK BROS
BALI	ARTMARK	MAENLINE
DELMAR	ASHBOURNE	MITCHELL
GRABER	B BERGER	PEACHTREE
LEVOLOR	BARROW	R & M COCO
M & B	BENNISON	RALPH LAUREN
DUETTE	BRUNSCHWIG & FILS	ROBERT ALLEN
HUNTER DOUGLAS	CAROLE FABRICS	S & S FABRICS
SYMPHONY	COULTER	SANDERSON
WALLPAPER:	DAVIS	STOUT BROS
CAREY LIND	FABRICADE	STROHEIM & ROMANN
IMPERIAL	FABRICUT	SYDNEY DAVIS
MIRAGE	GREEFF	WESCO
SANITAS	HINSON	WESTGATE
SEABROOK	JD FABRIC	WHITTAKER & WOODS
SUNWORTHY	KRAVET	
YORK		

STEVENS FURNITURE COMPANY, INC
1258 HICKORY BLVD, PO BOX 270, 2-H
LENOIR, NC 28645
Hours: **M-S: 9-5:30**

Toll-Free	
Direct	704-728-5511
Fax	704-728-5518
Internet	

Notes: Located on Hwy 321. In business since 1962. 26,000 sq. ft. showroom.Representing 150 distinctive manufacturers. One-half deposit required. VISA/MC accepted.

Manufacturers: (Many resources do not list all their manufacturers. Be sure to inquire about those you are interested in, but do not see listed here.)

ACTION/LANE	CANADEL	FASHION BED
ART FORMS	CAROLINA MIROR	FREDERICK COOPER
AINSLEY LAMPS	CARVERS MIRRORS	GARCIA IMPORTS
AMERICAN DREW	CASA BIQUE	HAMMARY
AMERICAN OF HIGH POINT	CHARLESTON FORGE	HEKMAN
AMERICAN OF MARTINSVILLE	CHELSEA HOUSE	HENRY LINK
ARNOLD PALMER	CLARK CASUAL	HICKORY CHAIR
BALDWIN BRASS	CLASSIC LEATHER	HICKORY HILL
BARCALOUNGER	COOPER CLASSICS	HICKORY TAVERN
BASSETT	CORSICAN	HICKORY WHITE
BERNHARDT	COX	HIGH POINT DESK
BEVAN FUNNELL	CRAFTWORK GUILD	HOWARD MILLER
BOB TIMBERLAKE	CRYSTAL CLEAR	JEFFCO
BRADY	DECORATIVE CRAFTS	JERAL INC
BROYHILL	DISTINCTIVE DESIGNS	JOHN RICHARD COLLECTION
BROYHILL PREMIER	ENTREE	KAISER KUHN

Resource Directory

KELLER	NATIONAL MT AIRY	STANLEY
KIMBALL	PEARSON	STANFORD
KING HICKORY	PENNSYLVANIA CLASSICS	STATESVILLE CHAIR
KOCH TABLES	PHILIP REINISCH	STATTON
LaBARGE	PORT ROYAL	STIFFEL
LANE	PULASKI	SWAN BRASS BEDS
LEA	REFLECTIONS	THAYER COGGIN
LEXINGTON	REPRODUX	HITCHCOCK CHAIR
LINK TAYLOR	REX	TRADITION HOUSE
LLOYD FLANDERS	RIDGEWAY	TROPITONE
LYON SHAW	RIVERSIDE	TYNDALE
MCKAY TABLE PADS	SALEM SQUARE	UNIVERSAL
MADISON SQUARE	SARRIED	VANGUARD
MAITLAND SMITH	SCHOTT	VIRGINIA METALCRAFTERS
MARK HAMPTON BY HICKORY	SEDGEFIELD	WAVERLY WEIMAN
CHAIR	SERTA BEDDING	WELLINGTON HALL
MARYLAND CLASSICS	SIMMONS	WESLEY ALLEN
MEADOWCRAFT	SKILLCRAFT	WILDWOOD
MICHAEL THOMAS	SOUTHERN FURNITURE	WINNERS ONLY
MILLENDER	REPRODUCTIONS	WINSTON
MORGANTON CHAIR	SPEER COLLECTIBLES	WOODARD
NATHAN HALE	ST TIMOTHY	

STEVENS OF BOONE
PO BOX 2450, HWY 105 SOUTH
BOONE, NC 28607
Hours: **M-S: 8-5; Closed Wednesdays**

Toll-Free	
Direct	704-264-3993
Fax	704-262-3530
Internet	

Notes: 50% deposit required. VISA/MC accepted. Cancellations will be accepted subject to their ability to cancel with the manufacturer. No cancellations will be accepted if fabric is cut or shipment made by manufacturer. Deposit will be refunded in case of an allowable cancellation, less a $25 special handling charge. This company is **unable** to service drawer and door adjustments, touch-up or leveling of piece, but will help customer in minor damage claims. They are willing to assist in every possible manner in collecting claims for loss or damage but will not be responsible for filing or collecting claims or replacing merchandise. Formerly Parkway Furniture.

Manufacturers: (Many resources do not list all their manufacturers. Be sure to inquire about those you are interested in, but do not see listed here.)

ACTION BY LANE	ATLANTA GLASSCRAFTER	BEDROOM BOUTIQUES
AINSLEY LAMPS	AUSTIN PRODUCTIONS	BENCHCRAFT
ALVA MUSEUM REPLICAS	BALDWIN BRASS	BENICIA BEDS
AMERICAN DREW	BARCALOUNGER	BERKSHIRE
AMERICAN OF MARTINSVILLE	BASSETT	BLACKSMITH SHOP
ARMONIE ESSEBI	BASSETT MIRROR	BOLING CHAIR

BROWN JORDAN
BROWN STREET
BROYHILL
BROYHILL PREMIER
CAL-STYLE
CAPEL CARPET
CAROLINA MIRROR
CARTER CONTEMPORARY
CASA BIQUE
CHAIRCRAFT
CHARLES HARLAND
CHARLESTON FORGE
CHATHAM COUNTY
CHILDCRAFT
CHROMCRAFT
CLARK CASUAL
CLASSIC LEATHER
CLASSIC RATTAN
CLAYTON MARCUS
CM FURNITURE
COCHRANE
COLONIAL CANDLE OF CAPE
COD
COLONIAL FURNITURE
COOPER CLASSICS
CORONA DECOR
COSMOPOLITAN PIANOS
COUNCILL
COX MANUFACTURING
CRAFTIQUE
CRAFTWORK GUILD
CRYSTAL CLEAR
DAVID THOMAS
DAYSTROM
DECORATIVE CRAFTS
DENUNZIO
DINAIRE
DISTINCTIVE DESIGNS
DIXIE
DRESHER BRASS BEDS
ELLIOTT'S DESIGNS
EMERSON LEATHER
FAIRFIELD
FITZ & FLOYD
FLEXSTEEL
FLUTE
FOREST OF ADRIAN
FREDERICK COOPER
GENESIS LIGHTING
GLASS ARTS
GRANDEUR BRASS
GREAT CITY TRADERS
HAMMARY
HANOVER HEIRLOOMS
HEKMAN
HENRY LINK

HICKORY MANUFACTURING
HICKORY TAVERN
HICKORY WHITE
HIGH POINT DESK
HITCHCOCK CHAIR
HOLIDAY HOUSE
HOOD
HOOKER
HOWARD MILLER
HTB
IMAGE MAKERS
JB ROSS BRASS BEDS
J ROYALE
JASPER CABINET
JEFFCO
JOHNSON BENCHWORKS
KAY LYN
KELLER
KIMBALL
KINCAID
KINGSTON HULL
LaBARGE
LAINE
LANE
LEA
LEATHERMAN'S GUILD
LEXINGTON
LINK TAYLOR
LLOYD FLANDERS
LOCK
LYON SHAW
MADISON SQUARE
McKAY TABLE PADS
MEADOWCRAFT
MERSMAN
MICHAEL THOMAS
MIKASA
MILLENDER
MILLER DESK
MODULUS
NATIONAL MT AIRY
NICHOLS & STONE
O'ASIAN
OHIO TABLE PADS
PALECEK
PARAGON PICTURES
PAUL HANSON LAMPS
PENNSYLVANIA HOUSE
PEARSON
PETERS-REVINGTON
PINE-TIQUE
PLANT PLANT
PLYCRAFT
POULIOT
PULASKI

RALEIGH ROAD
REPLOGLE
REX
RICHARDSON BROS
RIDGEWAY CLOCKS
RIVERSIDE
ROYAL HAEGER LAMPS
SADEK
SALEM SQUARE
SAMSONITE
SARREID
S BENT
SCHOTT
SCHUMACHER
SERTA BEDDING
SEVEN SEAS OF KEY WEST
SHOAL CREEK
SKILLCRAFT
SK PRODUCTS
SLIGH
SOMMA
STAKMORE
ST TIMOTHY CHAIR
STANLEY FURNITURE
STANTON COOPER
STATESVILLE CHAIR
STATTON
STIFFEL LAMP
STONE POINT DECOYS
TAYLOR WOODCRAFT
TAYLORSVILLE
TELL CITY
TEMPLE
TOYO
TROPITONE
TUBB
UNION NATIONAL
UNIVERSAL
UNIVERSAL
VANGUARD
VENTURE
VICTORIUS
VIRGINIA HOUSE
VIRGINIA METALCRAFTERS
VOGUE RATTAN
WABON
WAMBOLD
WESLEY ALLEN
WESTWOOD LAMPS
WHITE
WILDWOOD LAMPS
WINSTON
WOODARD
WOODMARK
YOUNG-HINKLE

STUCKEY BROTHERS FURNITURE CO, INC
RTE 1, BOX 527
STUCKEY, SC 29554
Hours: M-F: 9-6; S: 9-5

Toll-Free	
Direct	803-558-2591
Fax	803-558-9229
Internet	

Notes: In business since 1946. Over 300 manufacturers. Indoor and outdoor furnishings, nursery, accessories, clocks, lamps, mirrors, bedding

Manufacturers: (Many resources do not list all their manufacturers. Be sure to inquire about those you are interested in, but do not see listed here.)

ALLIBERT	DAYSTROM	LANE
AS YOU LIKE IT LAMPS	DIXIE	LA-Z-BOY
ACTION BY LANE	FAIRFIELD	LEA
AMERICAN DREW	FAIRINGTON	LEXINGTON
AMERICAN OF MARTINSVILLE	FICKS REED	LINK-TAYLOR
ARTISANS GUILD	FINKEL OUTDOOR	LULLABYE
BASSETT	FLEXSTEEL	LYON-SHAW
BARCALOUNGER	FREDERICK COOPER	MADISON SQUARE
BENICIA BEDS	FRIEDMAN BROS MIRRORS	MARK THOMAS LAMPS
S BENT	GEORGIAN	MEADOWCRAFT
BERKLINE	HABERSHAM PLANTATION	MERSMAN
BERNHARDT/FLAIR	HAMMARY	MICHAEL THOMAS
BLACKSMITH SHOP	HANCOCK & MOORE	MOBEL
BOLING CHAIR	HARDEN	MOOSEHEAD
BRADINGTON YOUNG	HENKEL HARRIS	MORRIS GREENSPAN LAMPS
BROWN JORDAN	HENRY LINK	MURRAY FEISS LAMPS
BROYHILL	HEKMAN	NATIONAL MT AIRY
CARLTON McLENDON	HEYWARD HOUSE	NICHOLS & STONE
CAROLINA MILLS	HICKORY CHAIR	OLD HICKORY TANNERY
CAROLINA/SHERRILL TABLES	HICKORY MANUFACTURING	PAUL HANSON
CASUSALCRAFT	HICKORY TAVERN	PEARSON
CENTURY	HIGHLAND HOUSE	PULASKI
CHATHAM COUNTY	HITCHCOCK CHAIR	REMINGTON LAMPS
CHILDCRAFT	HOLIDAY HOUSE	REX
CHAIRCRAFT	HOOKER	RIDGEWAY CLOCKS
CHROMCRAFT	HOWARD MILLER CLOCKS	RIVERSIDE
CLARK CASUAL	JB ROSS BRASS BEDS	SAMSONITE
CLASSIC LEATHER	JASPER CABINET	SEALY
CONOVER CHAIR	KELLER	SELIG
CORSICAN IRON BEDS	KEYSTONE	SERTA
COUNCILL CRAFTSMEN	KEY CITY	SHUFORD
COX	KIMBALL	SLIGH DESK
CRAFTIQUE	KINCAID	SINGER
CRAWFORD	KINGSDOWN	SOUTHWOOD
CRESENT	LaBARGE	REPRODUCTIONS
DANSEN CONTEMPORARY	LAINE	STANLEY

STANTON COOPER
STATESVILLE/ROSS
STATTON
STRATFORD
STIFFEL
SUMTER CABINET
SWAN
TAYLORSVILLE
TELL CITY
TEMPLE STUART

TROPITONE
TYNDALE
VANGUARD
VAUGHAN-BASSETT
VENTURE
VIRGINIA HOUSE
VOGUE RATTAN
WEIMAN
WESTWOOD

WHITE
WHITECRAFT
WILDWOOD
WINSTON
WILLIAM ALLEN
WOODARD
WOODMARK
WOODFIELD
YOUNG-HINKLE

STUDIO OF LIGHTS
2418 S MAIN ST
HIGH POINT, NC 27263
Hours: **M-F:8-5; S:9-1**

Toll-Free	
Direct	336-882-6854
Fax	336-885-3365
Internet	

Notes: Residential lighting specialist. All major lighting fixtures, ceiling fans. VISA/MC/DISC. Sales consultants/no designers on staff. Satisfaction guaranteed. Return of damaged items only. Customer can visit these facilities.

Manufacturers: (Many resources do not list all their manufacturers. Be sure to inquire about those you are interested in, but do not see listed here.)

CASABLANCA CEILING FANS
EMERSON
QUOIZEL

WORLD IMPORTS
HINKLEY
FRAMBURG

MURRAY FEISS LAMPS
SCHONBEK
SEIGEL LIGHTING

STYLE CRAFT INTERIORS
102 E FRONT STREET
BURLINGTON, NC 27216
Hours: **MTThF: 9-5; WS: 9:30-1**

Toll-Free	800-822-1849
Direct	336-228-1346
Fax	336-228-9901
Internet	email: MNEWTON@NETPATH.NET

Notes: Family owned and operated since 1968. 12,500 sq. ft. showroom. Quality furniture, customer service and outstanding value are well-known characteristics. Sales consultants are available to help you. 50% deposit required on all furniture orders. Can be paid by mo/check. No credit cards.

Manufacturers: (Many resources do not list all their manufacturers. Be sure to inquire about those you are interested in, but do not see listed here.)

ALEXVALE	GUARDSMAN POLISHES	PULASKI
AMERICAN DREW	HENRY LINK	REMINGTON LAMPS
ATLANTIC BENCH CO	HOOKER	RIVERSIDE
ARTISTRY DESIGNS	HOWARD MILLER CLOCK	J ROYALE
BARCALOUNGER	KETTLER	SALEM SQUARE
BLACKSMITH SHOP	KEY CITY	SALTERINI
BRASS BARON	KOCH ORIGINALS	SAM MOORE
CAPEL RUGS	LANE CEDAR	SARREID
COUNCILL CRAFTSMEN	CHESTS/CASEGOODS	SEDGEFIELD BY ADAMS
COVENT GARDEN	LENOX LIGHTING	SIMMONS BEAUTYREST
CRAFTIQUE	LEXINGTON UPHOLSTERY	SOUTHERN OFFICE
CRAFT-TEX ACCESSORIES	LINK TAYLOR	SPEER COLLECTIBLES
CROWN CRAFT	LOWENSTEIN	STAKMORE
DARAFEEV	LEXINGTON	STANLEY
DECORATIVE CRAFTS	MACON UMBRELLA	TREES INTERNATIONAL
DENNY LAMP	MEADOWCRAFT WROUGHT	TROPITONE
DINAIRE	IRON	VIRGINIA HOUSE
DISTINCTIVE DESIGNS	OHIO TABLE PADS	VIRGINIA METALCRAFTERS
EKORNES	OKLAHOMA IMPORTING	UNIVERSAL
GARDEN SOURCE	PASSPORT	WELLINGTON HALL
GOODWIN WEAVERS	PINEHURST UMBRELLA	WILLIAM ALLEN

SUTTON-COUNCIL FURNITURE COMPANY
421 S COLLEGE ROAD, PO BOX 3288
WILMINGTON, NC 28406
Hours: **M-F: 9-6; S:10-5**

Toll-Free	
Direct	910-799-9000
Fax	910-791-8242
Internet	

Notes: In business since 1924. 50% down payment by VISA/MC/DISC/CHECK. Balance due before shipping. Shipping paid by customer. Shipping can be arranged by customer, or sent by Executive Delivery Service which is insured for damages. Returns are based on damages or defects only. Sales and design consultants on staff. Customer can visit facilities - 40,000 sq.ft. store.

Manufacturers: (Many resources do not list all their manufacturers. Be sure to inquire about those you are interested in, but do not see listed here.)

ACTION BY LANE	COLONIAL	HOOKER
ALEXCRAFT	COMFORT DESIGNS	HTB
ALEXVALE	CONOVER CHAIR	JB ROSS BRASS BEDS
AMERICAN OF MARTINSVILLE	COUNCILL	JACK THORN IMPORTS
AMERICAN DREW	CRAFTIQUE	JACKSON OF DANVILLE
ANDRE ORIGINALS	CRAWFORD	JAMES RIVER
ARMSTRONG	CRYSTAL CLEAR LAMPS	JASPER CABINET
AYERS	DAN RIVER	JEFFCO
BARN DOOR FURNITURE	DANSEN	JOHNSTON CASUALS
BARCALOUNGER	DAVID THOMAS	KARASTAN
BENICIA BEDS	DAVIS & DAVIS RUGS	KARGES
BERKSHIRE	DESIGN SYSTEMS	KELLER
BETH WEISSMAN LAMPS	DIRECTIONAL	KEY CITY
BIGELOW CARPETS	DIXIE	KING HICKORY
BOB TIMBERLAKE	ELLO	KINGSDOWN
BRADINGTON YOUNG	ENCORE WALLCOVERING	KITTINGER
BRAXTON CULLER	FAIRFIELD	LaBARGE
BROWN STREET	FICKS REED	LAINE
BROWN JORDAN	FLEXSTEEL	LANE
BROYHILL	FREDERICK COOPER	LEA
BURRIS CHAIR	GEORGIAN FURNISHINGS	LEATHERCRAFT
CAL-STYLE	GLASS ARTS	LEXINGTON
CAPEL RUGS	HAMMARY	LINK-TAYLOR
CAPRI FURNITURE	HANCOCK & MOORE	LLOYD FLANDERS
CARSON'S	HEKMAN	LYNN HOLLYN
CARTER	HENREDON	LYON-SHAW
CASA STRADIVARI	HENRY LINK	MARBRO LAMPS
CASA BIQUE	HICKORY WHITE	MADISON SQUARE
CATNAPPER	HICKORY CHAIR	MAITLAND SMITH
CHAIRCRAFT	HICKORY INTERNATIONAL	MARYLAND CLASSICS
CHAPMAN	HICKORY TAVERN	MARK THOMAS LAMPS
CLARK CASUAL	HICKORY FRY	MARK THOMAS LAMPS
CLASSIC RATTAN	HILL	MASLAND
CLOVER LAMPS	HITCHCOCK CHAIR	McKAY TABLE PADS
CLYDE PEARSON	HOOD	McKINLEY LEATHER

MEADOWCRAFT	SCHOONBECK	TELESCOPE
MICHAEL THOMAS	SEDGEFIELD	TELL CITY
MT AIRY	SHELBY WILLIAMS	THAYER COGGIN
NATIONAL MT AIRY	SHOAL CREEK	UNIVERSAL
NATURAL LIGHT	SIMMONS	VANCE
NICHOLS & STONE	SLIGH	VENTURE
NULL INDUSTRIES	SOUTHERN MANOR	VIRGINIA METALCRAFTERS
O'ASIAN	SOUTHERN FURNITURE OF	VOGUE
PACIFIC RATTAN	CONOVER	WATERFORD
PANDE CAMERON RUGS	SOUTHMARK LEATHER	WEIMAN
PAOLI	SOUTHWOOD	WELLINGTON HALL
PARK AVENUE	SOVEREIGN COLLECTION	WESTON HALL
PEACHTREE	STAKMORE	WHITE OF MEBANE
PENNSYLVANIA HOUSE	STANLEY	WHITECRAFT
PERFECTION	STATESVILLE CHAIR	WILDWOOD TABLES
PHILADELPHIA CARPET	STATTON	WILDWOOD LAMPS
PINNACLE	STATTON	WINSTON
POULIOT DESIGNS	STIFFEL	WOODARD
PULASKI	STONE INTL	WOODFIELD
ROSALCO	STRATHROY	WOODSTOCK
REMINGTON LAMPS	STRATOLOUNGER	WUNDAWEAVE
RIDGEWAY	SUGGS & HARDIN	YORKSHIRE LEATHER
RIDGEWOOD	SUPERIOR FURNITURE	YOUNG-HINKLE
SALEM SQUARE	SUPERIOR REED & RATTAN	

THOMAS HOME FURNISHINGS
4346 HICKORY BLVD
GRANITE FALLS, NC 28630
Hours: **M-S: 9-5**

Toll-Free	
Direct	828-396-2147
Fax	828-396-6179
Internet	

Notes: Located on Hwy 321. In business since 1980. 50% downpayment required. VISA/MC credit cards accepted. Company handles any damage problems for the customer. No returns except on defective goods which are repaired or replaced. Customer can visit facility. Six sales consultants on staff. Galleries by Century, La-Z-Boy, Leathercraft, Knob Creek, Pennsylvania House. Designers and consultants on staff.

Manufacturers: (Many resources do not list all their manufacturers. Be sure to inquire about those you are interested in, but do not see listed here.)

LIVING ROOM:	BRADINGTON YOUNG	CLASSIC GEORGIAN
AMERICAN DREW	BUCKS COUNTY	CLAYTON MARCUS
ARNOLD PALMER	CARSON'S	CONOVER CHAIR
BASSETT	CASA BIQUE	COUNCILL
BERNHARDT	CENTURY	COX
BOB TIMBERLAKE	CHARLESTON FORGE	DUCKS UNLIMITED

HAMMARY
HEKMAN
HENRY LINK
HIGHLAND HOUSE
HOOKER
JASPER
KIMBALL
KNOB CREEK
LANE
LA-Z-BOY
LEATHERCRAFT
LEXINGTON
MADISON SQUARE
MICHAELS
NICHOLS & STONE
PENNSYLVANIA HOUSE
SAM MOORE
SOUTHAMPTON
SHUFORD
SOUTHWOOD
STANFORD
STANLEY
TIMBERLAKE
UNIVERSAL
VENTURE
WATERFORD
WEIMAN
WOODMARK
WELLINGTON HALL

DINING ROOM:
AMERICAN DREW
AMERICAN OF MARTINSVILLE
ARNOLD PALMER
ATHOL TABLE
BASSETT
S BENT
BERNHARDT
BOB TIMBERLAKE
BLACKSMITH SHOP
BUCKS COUNTY
CARSON'S
CENTURY
CLASSIC GEORGIAN
COUNCILL

COCHRANE
CRAFTIQUE
DESIGNMASTER
HEKMAN
HENRY LINK
HITCHCOCK
KELLER
KNOB CREEK
LANE
LEXINGTON
MICHAELS
MOOSEHEAD
NATIONAL MT AIRY
NICHOLS & STONE
PENNSYLVANIA HOUSE
PULASKI
STANLEY
TIMBERLAKE
UNIVERSAL
VENTURE
WATERFORD
WELLNGTON HALL

BEDROOM:
AMERICAN DREW
AMERICAN OF MARTINSVILLE
ARNOLD PALMER
BASSETT
BERNHARDT
BOB TIMBERLAKE
BUCKS COUNTY
CENTURY
CHARLESTON FORGE
COCHRANE
COX
COUNCILL
CRAFTIQUE
ELLIOTT'S DESIGNS
HENRY LINK
HITCHCOCK
HOOKER
KELLER
KNOB CREEK
LANE

LEA
LEXINGTON
MADISON SQUARE
MICHAELS
MOOSEHEAD
NATIONAL MT AIRY
NICHOLS & STONE
ORIGO
PENNSYLVANIA HOUSE
PULASKI
SERTA
STANLEY
TIMBERLAKE
UNIVERSAL
WATERFORD
WESLEY ALLEN
WELLINGTON HALL

OFFICE FURNITURE:
COUNCILL
HEKMAN
LEATHERCRAFT
SOUTHWOOD

OUTDOOR:
LLOYD FLANDERS
TROPITONE
VENEMAN
WINSTON

ACCESSORIES:
AUSTIN
BALDWIN BRASS
CAROLINA MIRROR
CHAPMAN
FRIEDMAN BROS
GREAT CITY TRADERS
KINDER HARRIS
SEDGEFIELD
STEWART CLOCKS
STIFFEL
VIRGINIA METALCRAFTERS
WILDWOOD

Resource Directory

THOMASVILLE GALLERY
HICKORY FURNITURE MART
2220 HWY 70 SE
HICKORY, NC 28602
Hours: **M-F: 9-6; S: 9-5; Closed Sundays**

Toll-Free	
Direct	828-326-1740
Fax	
Internet	

Notes: This resource is part of the Hickory Furniture Mart complex. This showroom is one of over 80 to visit. **See Hickory Furniture Mart listing for more information.** Consolidated shipping can be arranged with other resources in this center, a standard one/third deposit is required on all orders. Most showrooms accept VISA/MC, but not all. Cash, personal or certified checks accepted by all showrooms. If you elect not to pay for your entire purchase at the time of sale, a personal or certified check will be due upon delivery.

Manufacturers: **(Many resources do not list all their manufacturers. Be sure to inquire about those you are interested in, but do not see listed here.)**

TIME GALLERY
3121 BATTLEGROUND AVE
GREENSBORO, NC 27408
Hours: **M-F: 10-5:30; S: 10-4**

Toll-Free	800-683-8463
Direct	336-282-5132
Fax	336-288-8669
Internet	

Notes: Established 1984. Family owned and operated. Clocks at discount prices. Sales consultants on staff. Showroom available. Company will make suggestions, send photocopies upon request. Complete order can be paid by VISA/MC/DISC/CHECK/CASH. No returns except on damaged merchandise.

Manufacturers: **(Many resources do not list all their manufacturers. Be sure to inquire about those you are interested in, but do not see listed here.)**

ANSONIA	LINDEN CLOCKS	RIDGEWAY
BALDWIN BRASS	NEW ENGLAND CLOCK	SLIGH
HOWARD MILLER		

TIOGA MILL OUTLET STORES, INC
200 S HARTMAN ST.
YORK, PA 17403
Hours: **M-TH: 9:30-6; FRI: 9:30-8; S: 9-5**

Toll-Free	
Direct	717-843-5139
Fax	717-854-9223
Internet	

Notes: In business since 1970. Large in-house selection of drapery and upholstery fabrics. Mail order available through brochure. Full payment by VISA/MC/DISC/CHECK. UPS is shipper. Only their first quality fabrics are guaranteed. Fabric with flaws will be accepted for return. Sales and design consultants on staff. Customer can visit facility

Manufacturers: (Many resources do not list all their manufacturers. Be sure to inquire about those you are interested in, but do not see listed here.)

BARROW	JOHN WOLF	ROBERT ALLEN
BLOOMCRAFT	KRAVET	WAVERLY
COVINGTON	LANSCOT ARLEN	WESTERN TEXTILE
FABRICUT		

TOP SERVICE
CHURCH END HOUSE, WHICHFORD
SHIPSTON ON STOUR, WARKSHIRE, ENGLAND CV36 5PG
Hours: **M-F: 9-5(England time)**

Toll-Free	
Direct	011-44-1608-68-48-29
Fax	011-44-1608-68-43-00
Internet	

Notes: British source for fabrics and wallpaper. Direct from manufacturers. Most designer brands.VISA. Ship to US.

Manufacturers: (Many resources do not list all their manufacturers. Be sure to inquire about those you are interested in, but do not see listed here.)

BAKER	SANDERSON

TRIAD FURNITURE DISCOUNTERS
9770 N KINGS HWY; MAGNOLIA PLAZA
MYRTLE BEACH, SC 29572
Hours: **M-F:9-6; S: 10-5**

Toll-Free	800-323-8469
Direct	803-497-6400
Fax	803-497-5887
Internet	

Notes: Your order can be initiated with a 50% deposit payable by VISA/MC/CHECK. All orders are confirmed in writing. 30% restocking fee charged on cancelled or changed orders. Shipping policies say they will work with shipper and customer in fixing any problems. Call for brochure.

Manufacturers: **(Many resources do not list all their manufacturers. Be sure to inquire about those you are interested in, but do not see listed here.)**

ACTION BY LANE	GEORGIAN FURNISHINGS	PEARSON
AMERICAN DREW	GLASS ARTS	PETERS-REVINGTON
ARBEK	HAMMARY	PULASKI
BASSETT	HANOVER HEIRLOOM	RICHARDSON BROS
BENCHCRAFT	HABERSHAM	SK PRODUCTS
BENICIA BEDS	HEKMAN	SCHWEIGER
BLACKSMITH SHOP	HICKORY LEATHER	SERTA
BOWEN	HICKORY WHITE	SEDGEFIELD
BRAXTON CULLER	HOOD	SOUTHWOOD
CAROLINA CLASSICS	HOOKER	STANLEY
CAROLINA MIRROR	HYUNDAI	STANTON COOPER
CASA BIQUE	JASPER CABINET	STIFFEL
CHARLESTON FORGE	KAISER KUHN LIGHTING	SUPERIOR
COLONIAL FURNITURE	KESSLER	TAYLOR WOODCRAFT
DR KINCAID	KEY CITY	TROPITONE
DANSEN	KIMBALL	UNIVERSAL
DECORATIVE CRAFTS	KINCAID	US FURNITURE
DESIGN SYSTEMS	LANE	VANGUARD PICTURES
DILLON	LANE DINING ALA CARTE	VENTURE
DISTINCTION LEATHER	LANE UPHOLSTERY	VIRGINIA HOUSE
ELLIOTT'S BEDS	LEA	WEBB FURNITURE
ELLO	LEXINGTON	WELLINGTON HALL
EMERSON LEATHER	LLOYD FLANDERS	WESLEY ALLEN
FAIRFIELD	MADISON SQUARE	WHITECRAFT
FICKS REED	MARYLAND CLASSICS	WOODARD
FLEXSTEEL	NATIONAL MT AIRY	WOODMARK
FREDERICK EDWARD	NICHOLS & STONE	YORKSHIRE LEATHER

TRIPLETT'S FURNITURE FASHION
2084 HICKORY BLVD SW
LENOIR, NC 28645
Hours: M-S: 8:30-5

Toll-Free	
Direct	704-728-8211
Fax	704-726-0171
Internet	

Notes: Located on Hwy 321Established 1963. Family owned and operated. Five sales consultants and one designer on staff. One-half deposit is required when placing an order, payment can be made by VISA/MC/CASH CHECK. Balance by credit card or check. Only items that are freight damaged or factory defective can be returned at the time of delivery. Specializing in solid wood galleries, casegoods, upholstery, pictures and accessories.

Manufacturers: (Many resources do not list all their manufacturers. Be sure to inquire about those you are interested in, but do not see listed here.)

ACTION BY LANE
AMERICAN DREW
AMERICAN OF MARTINSVILLE
ARNOLD PALMER
AS YOU LIKE IT
ATHOL
AUSTIN PRODUCTIONS
BARCALOUNGER
BERKLINE
BETSY CAMERON
BLACKSMITH SHOP
BOB TIMBERLAKE
BOSTON ROCKERS
BUILTRIGHT ROCKERS
CALDWELL CHAIR
CAROLINA MIRROR
CHARLESTON FORGE
CHATHAM COUNTY
CHROMCRAFT
CLAYTON MARCUS
COCHRANE
COLONIAL FURNITURE
COOPER CLASSICS
COX
CRYSTAL CLEAR
DENNY LAMP
DESIGNMASTER

DILLON
FASHION BED
FASHION HOUSE
FREDERICK COOPER
HAMMARY
HEKMAN
HENRY LINK
HOLLYWOODS
HOOKER
JASPER
JOHNSTON CASUALS
KELLER
KIMBALL
LANE
LANE VENTURE
LEA
LEATHER TECH
LEXINGTON
LEXINGTON YOUTH
LEXINGTON UPHOLSTERY
LEISTERS
LINK TAYLOR
MEADOWCRAFT
NATIONAL MT AIRY
NICHOLS & STONE
NORMAN ROCKWELL
NULL INDUSTRIES

OHIO TABLE PADS
OLD SALEM
P & P CHAIR
PENNSYLVANIA CLASSICS
PULASKI
RIVERSIDE
SARREID
SCHOTT
SERTA
SKILLCRAFT
STANLEY
STANLEY YOUTH
STANLEY UPHOLSTERY
STATESVILLE CHAIR
SUMTER CABINET
TEMPLE
TRADITIONAL HEIRLOOMS
UNION CITY CHAIR
UNIVERSAL
UWHARRIE CHAIR
WALKER MARLEN
WEATHERCRAFT
WEATHERMASTER
WEEKEND RETREAT
WESLEY ALLEN
WEIMAN TABLES

TROTT FURNITURE CO
PO BOX 7, DEPT. F.
RICHLANDS, NC 28574
Hours: **M-F: 10-6**

Toll-Free	
Direct	910-324-1119
Fax	910-324-2515
Internet	

Notes: In business since 1964. This company specializes in 18th century and colonial styles in solid wood and quality veneer. 30% deposit required by VISA/MC/CHECK. Balance by CHECK/MO. Returns by store approval only. Shipping problems handled by customer and shipper with help of resource. Main emphasis is quality customer service. Sales and design consultants on staff. Customer can visit facility. $5 catalog sent on request only.

Manufacturers: (Many resources do not list all their manufacturers. Be sure to inquire about those you are interested in, but do not see listed here.)

AMERICAN DREW	LANE	ROBINSON
BRADINGTON YOUNG	LEXINGTON	SEDGEFIELD
CHARTER TABLE	LINK TAYLOR	SERTA
CRAFTIQUE	MADISON SQUARE	SKILLCRAFT
CRAFTMARK	MARIO	SLIGH
DISTINCTION LEATHER	McKINLEY LEATHER	SOMMA
FRITZ & LaRUE RUGS	NICHOLS & STONE	STIFFEL
HENRY LINK	NULL INDUSTRIES	STATTON
HOOKER	OHIO TABLE PADS	SUMTER
JASPER	PANDE CAMERON RUGS	TIMBERLAKE
KAREL MINTJENS	PARKER SOUTHERN	UNIVERSAL
KELLER	PETERS-REVINGTON	WESLEY ALLEN
LAINE	PULASKI	

TYSON FURNITURE COMPANY, INC
109 BROADWAY
BLACK MOUNTAIN, NC 28711
Hours: **M-S: 9-5:30**

Toll-Free	
Direct	704-669-5000
Fax	704-669-8292
Internet	

Notes: In business since 1946. This company has a 70,000 square foot showroom consisting of old store buildings dating from the 1920's in a small western north Carolina resort town - 15 miles east of Asheville. VISA/MC payments of 25% down required. Balance can be paid with credit card also. 15% percent restocking charge on returned items, unless defective. Furniture is shipped by their own trucks or specialized furniture delivery services. All shipments prepaid. Sales consultants on staff. Defective or damaged merchandise is repaired or replaced at no cost to consumer (within 30 days). Shipping problems must be reported to carrier. Resource will assist in resolving problems.

Manufacturers: (Many resources do not list all their manufacturers. Be sure to inquire about those you are interested in, but do not see listed here.)

AA LAUN	CANE & REED IMPORT	FASHION BED
ACTION BY LANE	CAPEL CARPET	FICKS REED
AINSLEY LAMPS	CAROLINA CHOICE	FINE ARTS LAMPS
ALADDIN CARPET	CAROLINA FURNITURE	FITZ & FLOYD
ALVA MUSEUM REPLICAS	CAROLINA MIRROR	FLAT ROCK
AMERICAN CUT CRYSTAL	CASA BIQUE	FLORAL ART
AMERICAN DREW	CASUAL LAMP	FREDERICK COOPER
AMERICAN OF MARTINSVILLE	CHAIRCRAFT	FREDERICK EDWARD
ANDREW PEARSON	CHATHAM COUNTY	FRITZ & LaRUE
ANGELO BROS	CHINA SEA TRADER	FROELICH
ARMSTRONG	CHROMCRAFT	GEORGE KOCH
ART GALLERY	CLASSIC GEORGIAN	GEORGE KOVACS
ARTAGRAPH REPRODUCTIONS	CLASSIC LEATHER	GLASS ARTS
ARTISAN HOUSE	CLAYTON MARCUS	GLOBER
ASPEN	CM FURNITURE	GOODWIN WEAVERS
ATHENS	COCHRANE	GOLD MEDAL
AUSTIN PRODUCTIONS	COMMONWEALTH CONTRACT	GREAT CITY TRADERS
BALDWIN BRASS	CONGOLEUM	GROSFILLEX
BARCALOUNGER	CONTEMPO ARTS	GUILDMASTER
BARLOW TYRIE	COUNTY SEAT	HABERSHAM PLANTATION
BASSETT FURNITURE	COX	HALE OF VERMONT
BASSETT MIRROR	CRAFTIQUE	HAMMARY
BEAULIEU CARPET	CRESENT	HANCOCK & MOORE
BENICIA BEDS	CRITERION CARPET	HARTCO WOOD
BERKSHIRE	CROWN CRAFT	HEKMAN
BERNHARDT	CROWNFORD	HENKEL-HARRIS
BEVAN FUNNELL	CRYSTAL CLEAR	HENKEL-MOORE
BLACKSMITH SHOP	CUMBERLAND CARPET	HENRY LINK
BLUFF CITY	D & F WICKER	HICKORY CHAIR
BOLING CHAIR	D SCAN	HICKORY WHITE
BORKHOLDER	DAVIS & DAVIS RUGS	HIGHLAND HOUSE
BOYD	DAYSTROM	HITCHCOCK CHAIR
BRADCO CHAIR	DECORATIVE CRAFTS	HOOD
BRADINGTON YOUNG	DENUNZIO	HOOKER
BRADY FURNITURE	DEPARTMENT 56	HOUSE PARTS
BRASSCRAFTERS	DSF	HOWARD MILLER
BROOKS	DINAIRE	INSTANT TURF
BROWN JORDAN	DISTINCTION LEATHER	JACK THORN IMPORTS
BROWN STREET	DOLBI CASHIER	JASPER CABINET
BROYHILL	DRESHER	JB ROSS BRASS BEDS
BUDORR CLASSIC FURNITURE	EKORNES	JOHN BOOS
BUILTRIGHT CHAIR	ELDRED WHEELER	JOHNSTON CASUALS
BURRIS CHAIR	EMERSON ET CIE	JSF INDUSTRIES
BUTLER SPECIALTY	EMERSON LEATHER	KAISER KUHN LIGHTING
CABIN CRAFT	EVANS & BLACK	KARASTAN
CAL-STYLE	EXECUTIVE LEATHER	KELLER
CALIFORNIA UMBRELLA	FAIRFIELD CHAIR	KENTILE

KESSLER
KIANI
KINCAID
KINDER-HARRIS
KINGSLEY-BATES
KNOB CREEK
LA-Z-BOY
LaBARGE
LANE
LEA
LEATHERCRAFT
LEEDO CABINETRY
LEES CARPET
LEISTERS
LENOX LAMPS
LEXINGTON
LIGHT & SIGHT
LINK-TAYLOR
LLOYD FLANDERS
LOTUS ARTS
LYON-SHAW
MADE IN THE SHADE
MADISON SQUARE
MAITLAND SMITH
MANCHESTER WOOD
MANNINGTON
MARKEL LIGHTING
MARBRO LAMPS
MARTINSVILLE NOVELTY
MARYLAND CLASSICS
MASLAND
McENROE
McKAY TABLE PADS
MEADOWCRAFT
MICHAELS CO
MILLIKEN
MINOFF LAMPS
MOBEL
MOOSEHEAD
MOTIONCRAFT
MURPHY BED COMPANY
MURPHY FURNITURE
NAFCO
NATHAN HALE
NATIONAL MT AIRY
NATURAL DECORATIONS
NATURAL LIGHT
NEW ENGLAND CLOCK
NEWPORT CABINET
NICHOLS & STONE
NORA FENTON
NS GUSTIN

OLD WAVERLY BY JTB
OHIO TABLE PADS
OLD HICKORY
OLYMPIA LIGHTING
ORIENTAL LACQUER
P & P CHAIR
PALECEK
PANDE CAMERON RUGS
PAOLI
PAWLEY'S ISLAND HAMMOCK
PENNSYLVANIA HOUSE
PETERS-REVINGTON
PHILADELPHIA CARPET
PLANT PLANT
POLYWOOD
PORT MERION
POULIOT
POWELL
PULASKI
QUEEN CARPET
REGENCY HOUSE
REMINGTON LAMPS
REX FURNITURE
RICHARDSON BROS
RIVERSIDE
ROCK CITY
ROSALCO
ROYAL HAEGAR LAMPS
ROYAL WORCESTER/SPODE
RR SCHIEBE
S BENT
SADEK IMPORTS
SAM MOORE
SARREID
SEALY
SEALY FURNITURE OF
MARYLAND
SEDGEFIELD
SHELLY'S CUSHIONS
CTH/SHERRILL OCCASIONAL
SILVESTRI
SIMMONS
SIMMONS UPHOLSTERY
SIMPLY SOUTHERN
SK PRODUCTS
SKILLCRAFT
SLEEPWORKS
SLIGH
SOUTHAMPTON
SOUTHERN FURNITURE
REPRODUCTIONS
STAKMORE

STANFORD
STANLEY FURNITURE
STANTON COOPER
STATESVILLE CHAIR
STATTON
STEVENS CARPET
STEVENS/GULISTAN CARPET
STIFFEL
STRATFORD
STATTON
STYLE UPHOLSTERY
SUGAR CREEK
SUMMER CLASSICS
SUMTER CABINET
SUPERIOR
TARKETT
TAYLOR WOODCRAFT
TELESCOPE
TELL CITY
TEMPLE
TEMPLE-STUART
THOMASVILLE
TRADITIONS FRANCE
TRADITIONAL HEIRLOOMS
TROPITONE
TROUTMAN CHAIR
UNIVERSAL
UWHARRIE CHAIR
VALRITE LEATHER
VAUGHAN
VENEMAN
VENTURE
VICTORIAN CLASSIC
VIEWPOINT LEATHERWORKS
VINTAGE FURNITURE
VIRGINIA HOUSE
VOGUE
WATERFORD-WEDGEWOOD
WAVERLY
WELLINGTON HALL
WESLEY ALLEN
WESTWOOD
WHITAKER
WILDWOOD
WILLSBORO WOOD PRODUCTS
WINDEMERE LAMPS
WINNERS ONLY
WINSTON
WOODARD
WOODMARK
WUNDAWEAVE

UNIVERSAL GALLERY
HICKORY FURNITURE MART
2220 HWY 70 SE
HICKORY, NC 28602
Hours: **M-F: 9-6; S: 9-5; Closed Sundays**

Toll-Free	
Direct	828-322-6602
Fax	
Internet	

Notes: This resource is part of the Hickory Furniture Mart complex. This showroom is one of over 80 to visit. **See Hickory Furniture Mart listing for more information.** Consolidated shipping can be arranged with other resources in this center, a standard one/third deposit is required on all orders. Most showrooms accept VISA/MC, but not all. Cash, personal or certified checks accepted by all showrooms. If you elect not to pay for your entire purchase at the time of sale, a personal or certified check will be due upon delivery.

Manufacturers: (Many resources do not list all their manufacturers. Be sure to inquire about those you are interested in, but do not see listed here.)

USA BLIND FACTORY
1312 LIVE OAK
HOUSTON, TX 77003
Hours: **M-F: 9-5**

Toll-Free	800-275-9416
Direct	
Fax	713-227-4011
Internet	

Notes: Special discounts on USA woods, minis, micros, pleated and cellular shades, verticals, vinyls and true wood blinds. They carry their own private label window coverings, too. Free sample kit.

Manufacturers: (Many resources do not list all their manufacturers. Be sure to inquire about those you are interested in, but do not see listed here.)

BALI	GRABER	LEVOLOR
COUNTRY WOODS	HUNTER DOUGLAS	M & B
DEL MAR	JOANNA	MICROS
DUETTE	KIRSCH	MINIS

NU WOODS	SYMPHONY	WOODS
PVC BUDGET	USA WOODS	WOODWINDS
SYMPHONY	VERTICALS	

USA EXPRESS
2260C ROUTE 22
UNION, NJ 07083
Hours: **M-F: 9-5**

Toll-Free	800-965-5678
Direct	
Fax	908-688-8390
Internet	

Notes: Fabric and wallcovering. VISA/MC/DISC.

Manufacturers: (Many resources do not list all their manufacturers. Be sure to inquire about those you are interested in, but do not see listed here.)

UTILITY CRAFT
2630 EASTCHESTER
HIGH POINT, NC 27265
Hours: **M-F: 9:30; S: 9-5**

Toll-Free	
Direct	336-454-6153
Fax	336-454-5065
Internet	

Notes: Over 40 years of service. Designers and consultants on staff can help customer with selections. Showroom available for browsing. Check/cash/money order only. 33% restocking fee for returns. Three year protection plan and one year warranty available. Specializes in 18th century traditional wood furniture. In home delivery and set-up.

Manufacturers: (Many resources do not list all their manufacturers. Be sure to inquire about those you are interested in, but do not see listed here.)

ACTION BY LANE	AS YOU LIKE IT LAMPS	BASSETT
AMERICAN DREW	BALDWIN BRASS	BENICIA BEDS
AMERICAN OF MARTINSVILLE	BARCALOUNGER	BLACKSMITH SHOP

BRADINGTON YOUNG
BROYHILL
CAROLINA MIRROR
CARSON'S
CASA BIQUE
CENTURY
CLARK CASUAL
CLASSIC LEATHER
CLASSIC RATTAN
CLAYTON MARCUS
COCHRANE
COX
CRAFTWORK
CRESENT
DANSEN CONTEMPORARY
FICKS REED
FREDERICK COOPER
HABERSHAM PLANTATION
HADLEY POTTERY
HAMMARY
HEKMAN
HICKORY WHITE
HIGH POINT WOODWORKING
HITCHCOCK
HOOKER
JAMESTOWN STERLING
JASPER CABINET
KELLER
KINGSDOWN
KNOB CREEK

LAINE
LANE
LA-Z-BOY
LEXINGTON
LLOYD FLANDERS
LYON-SHAW
MADISON SQUARE
McKAY TABLE PADS
MILLER DESK
MOOSEHEAD
NATHAN HALE
NATIONAL MT AIRY
O'ASIAN
OHIO TABLE PADS
PEARSON
PULASKI
RIVERSIDE
SALEM SQUARE
SARREID
SEALY
SEDGEFIELD/WOODCRAFT
LAMPS
SELIG
SERTA
SHERRILL TABLES
SHOAL CREEK LAMP
SHUFORD
SLIGH
SOMMA

SOUTHAMPTON
SOUTHWOOD
STANLEY
STANTON COOPER
STATESVILLE CHAIR
STATTON
STIFFEL LAMP
SUPERIOR
SWAN
TELL CITY
TEMPLE STUART
THAYER COGGIN
TRADITION HOUSE
TROPITONE
UNIVERSAL
VANGUARD
VENTURE
VIRGINIA HOUSE
VIRGINIA METALCRAFTERS
WATERFORD
WELLINGTON HALL
WEIMAN
WELLINGTON HALL
WESLEY ALLEN
WESLEY HALL
WILDWOOD
WINSTON
WOODMARK ORIGINALS

VALERIE MAKSTELL INTERIORS
1050 MEHRING WAY
CINCINNATI, OHIO 45203
Hours: M-S: 10-5; SUN: 12-4

Toll-Free	
Direct	513-241-1050
Fax	513-241-9691
Internet	

Notes: Established 1985. Company ships to local receiving docks where possible, then delivers by local carrier to customer. Freight and delivery are additional. Up to 50% off manufacturers' suggested retail price. Prices subject to change depending on size of order. We offer complete design service and workroom facilities for wallpaper, fabrics, carpeting, window treatments, upholstery, slipcovers and accessories. No returns on custom orders.

Manufacturers: (Many resources do not list all their manufacturers. Be sure to inquire about those you are interested in, but do not see listed here.)

ALLUSIONS	EMERSON ET CIE	MAITLAND SMITH
AMERICAN DREW	EXECUTIVE LEATHER	MASLAND
ANDRE ORIGINALS	FAIRFIELD CHAIR	MASTERCRAFT
BALDWIN BRASS	FASHION BED	MIAMI METAL
BARLOW TYRIE	FINE ARTS LAMPS	MOTIONCRAFT
BASSETT	FREDERICK COOPER	ORIENTAL LACQUER
BEVAN FUNNELL	GARCIA IMPORTS	PAYNE
BOUSSAC OF FRANCE	GUILDMASTER	PHILADELPHIA
BRASS COLLECTION	HABERSHAM PLANTATION	PLATT
BRUNSCHWIG & FILS	HART	PULASKI
CAMBRIDGE LAMPS	HEKMAN	PREVIEW
CARLTON	HICKORY CHAIR	ROBERT ALLEN
CASA STRADIVARI	HICKORY WHITE	RYNONE
CASA BIQUE	HOOKER	SAM MOORE
CASUAL LAMP	JEFFCO	SARREID
CENTURY	JOHN RICHARD COLLECTION	SCALAMANDRE
CHELSEA HOUSE	JOHNSTON CASUALS	SCHUMACHER
CHAPMAN	KARGES	SPEER
CHARLESTON FORGE	KESSLER	STANLEY
CLASSIC LEATHER	KIMBALL	STARK CARPETS
COLONIAL	LaBARGE	SWAIM
COMFORT DESIGNS	LANE	TYNDALE
COURTLEIGH	LAZAR	WAVERLY
CREATIVE METAL	LEXINGTON	DIA
ELLO		

VANGUARD GALLERY
HICKORY FURNITURE MART
2220 HWY 70 SE
HICKORY, NC 28602
Hours: M-F: 9-6; S: 9-5; Closed Sundays

Toll-Free	
Direct	828-324-1776
Fax	
Internet	

Notes: This resource is part of the Hickory Furniture Mart complex. This showroom is one of over 80 to visit. **See Hickory Furniture Mart listing for more information.** Consolidated shipping can be arranged with other resources in this center, a standard one/third deposit is required on all orders. Most showrooms accept VISA/MC, but not all. Cash, personal or certified checks accepted by all showrooms. If you elect not to pay for your entire purchase at the time of sale, a personal or certified check will be due upon delivery.

Manufacturers: (Many resources do not list all their manufacturers. Be sure to inquire about those you are interested in, but do not see listed here.)

VILLAGE CARPET
3203 US HWY 70 SE
NEWTON, NC 28613
Hours: **M-F: 8:30-5**

Toll-Free	
Direct	704-465-6818
Fax	704-465-1864
Internet	

Notes: In business since 1989. 100% advance payment required - check or money order. Shipping is common carrier, collect. Transit damage handled by consumer, defective goods handled by resource. Custom rugs available. Located in heart of discount furniture shopping area. Brochure available. Satisfaction guaranteed. One designer on staff of four. Mohawk color center and magic carpet can only be purchased in person.

Manufacturers: **(Many resources do not list all their manufacturers. Be sure to inquire about those you are interested in, but do not see listed here.)**

ALADDIN CARPET	EVANS & BLACK	NAFCO VINYL
ARMSTRONG	GALAXY	NEW VISION
BEAULIEU	HARTCO WOOD	PATCRAFT
BRUCE WOOD	HORIZON	PHILADELPHIA
CABIN CRAFT	MANNINGTON CERAMIC	QUEEN
CITATION	MANNINGTON VINYL	SALEM
CONGOLEUM	MANNINGTON WOOD	SUTTON CARPETS
CUMBERLAND	MASLAND	TARKETT VINYL
DIAMOND	MILLIKEN PATTERN CARPET	WUNDAWEAVE
DIMENSION	MOHAWK	
DOMCO VINYL		

VILLAGE FURNITURE HOUSE
146 WEST AVE
KANNAPOLIS, NC 28081
Hours: **M-S: 9-6**

Toll-Free	
Direct	704-938-9171
Fax	704-932-2503
Internet	

Notes: Located in beautiful Cannon Village, North Carolina's only Baker factory store is part of this operation. Also, Century factory clearance center offers savings of up to 80% off retail, along with a Maitland Smith Factory Outlet. Complete security on your financial investment. When you place your order it is backed by a sealed bond which insures 100% of your money. Located 30 minutes north of Charlotte off I-85. Designers and sales consultants on staff.

Manufacturers: (Many resources do not list all their manufacturers. Be sure to inquire about those you are interested in, but do not see listed here.)

ACTION BY LANE	FLEXSTEEL	NICHOLS & STONE
ALEXVALE	FREDERICK COOPER	NORMAN ROCKWELL
AMERICAN OF MARTINSVILLE	FREDERICK EDWARD	OLD HICKORY TANNERY
AMERICAN DREW	FRIEDMAN BROS MIRRORS	PARK PLACE
ASHLEY	HABERSHAM PLANTATION	PEARSON
BAKER FACTORY STORE	HAMMARY	PENNSYLVANIA CLASSICS
BALDWIN BRASS	HEKMAN	PULASKI
BARCALOUNGER	HENRY LINK WICKER	RIDGEWAY CLOCKS
BASSETT	HICKORY FRY	RIVERSIDE
BERKLINE	HICKORY HILL	ROWE
BEVAN FUNNELL	HICKORY WHITE	SALEM SQUARE
BOB TIMBERLAKE	HIGHLAND HOUSE	SEALY
BRADINGTON YOUNG	HITCHCOCK CHAIR	SHUFORD
BRAXTON CULLER	HOOKER	SIMPLY SOUTHERN
BROWN STREET	J ROYALE	SINGER
BROYHILL	JASPER CABINET	SLIGH DESK/CLOCKS
CAPITOL LEATHER	KELLER	SK DINETTES
CAROLINA MIRROR	KEY CITY	SOUTHERN FURNITURE
CASA BIQUE	KESSLER	SOUTHWOOD
CASA STRADIVARI	KIMBALL	STANLEY
CENTURY FACTORY	KINCAID	STATTON
CLEARANCE CENTER	KING HICKORY	STIFFEL
CHAPMAN LAMPS	KINGSDOWN BEDDING	TRADITIONS FRANCE
CHELSEA HOUSE	KNOB CREEK	TRADITION HOUSE
CHARLESTON FORGE	LEA	TROPITONE
CHROMCRAFT	LaBARGE	VANGUARD
CLASSIC LEATHER	LANE	VENTURE
CLAYTON MARCUS	CR LAINE	VIRGINIA HOUSE
COLONIAL SOLID CHERRY	LEXINGTON	VIRGINIA METALCRAFTERS
COUNCILL CRAFTSMEN	LINK TAYLOR	WATERFORD FURNITURE
CRAFTIQUE	LLOYD FLANDERS	WEIMAN
CRAFTWORK GUILD	LYON SHAW	WELLINGTON HALL
DESIGN HORIZONS	MAITLAND SMITH FACTORY	WESLEY ALLEN
DINAIRE	OUTLET	WILDWOOD LAMPS
DRESHER	MADISON SQUARE	WOODARD
ELLO	MICHAEL THOMAS	WOODMARK
EMERSON LEATHER	MILLENIUM	YIELD HOUSE
FAIRFIELD	MOOSEHEAD	AND MANY MORE
FASHION BED	NATIONAL MT AIRY	

VIRGINIA HOUSE GALLERY
HICKORY FURNITURE MART
2220 HWY 70 SE
HICKORY, NC 28602
Hours: **M-F: 9-6; S: 9-5; Closed Sundays**

Toll-Free	
Direct	828-328-8855
Fax	
Internet	

Notes: This resource is part of the Hickory Furniture Mart complex. This showroom is one of over 80 to visit. **See Hickory Furniture Mart listing for more information.** Consolidated shipping can be arranged with other resources in this center, a standard one/third deposit is required on all orders. Most showrooms accept VISA/MC, but not all. Cash, personal or certified checks accepted by all showrooms. If you elect not to pay for your entire purchase at the time of sale, a personal or certified check will be due upon delivery.

Manufacturers: (Many resources do not list all their manufacturers. Be sure to inquire about those you arc interested in, but do not see listed here.)

WAREHOUSE CARPETS, INC
PO BOX 3233
DALTON, GA 30719
Hours: **M-F: 8-5**

Toll-Free	800-526-2229
Direct	
Fax	706-278-1008
Internet	

Notes: In business since 1977. Savings on name brand carpets, vinyl flooring and padding. All first quality. All manufacturer and fiber warranties apply. Shipping problems are handled by the shipper and customer with help of the resource. Check, money order or wire transfer only.

Manufacturers: (Many resources do not list all their manufacturers. Be sure to inquire about those you are interested in, but do not see listed here.)

ALADDIN CARPET	CORONET	GALAXY
ARMSTRONG	DIAMOND	HORIZON
CABIN CRAFT	DOMCO	MANNINGTON
CONGOLEUM	EVANS & BLACK	PHILADELPHIA

QUEEN CARPET TARKETT WORLD
SUTTON CARPETS WELLINGTON

═══════════════════════════════════

WEAVER WAYSIDE FURNITURE
2031 W. MAIN STREET
DANVILLE, VA 24541
Hours: **T-F: 11-9; S: 10-6**

Toll-Free	800-832-8225
Direct	
Fax	804-792-3638
Internet	

Notes: Custom draperies, hand-crafted clocks, hand-made oriental carpets

Manufacturers: (Many resources do not list all their manufacturers. Be sure to inquire about those you are interested in, but do not see listed here.)

BAKER HICKORY MANUFACTURING SOUTHWOOD
BERNHARDT HITCHCOCK REPRODUCTIONS
CHELSEA HOUSE KITTINGER STATTON
CLASSIC LEATHER LaBARGE VANGUARD
EMERSON LEATHER LEXINGTON VIRGINIA METALCRAFTERS
FICKS REED LINK-TAYLOR WILDWOOD
HARDEN PORT ROYAL
HEYGILL SLIGH

═══════════════════════════════════

WEIMAN GALLERY
HICKORY FURNITURE MART
2220 HWY 70 SE
HICKORY, NC 28602
Hours: **M-F: 9-6; S: 9-5; Closed Sundays**

Toll-Free	
Direct	828-324-1776
Fax	
Internet	

Notes: This resource is part of the Hickory Furniture Mart complex. This showroom is one of over 80 to visit. **See Hickory Furniture Mart listing for more information.** Consolidated shipping can be arranged with other resources in this center, a standard one/third deposit is required on all orders.

Most showrooms accept VISA/MC, but not all. Cash, personal or certified checks accepted by all showrooms. If you elect not to pay for your entire purchase at the time of sale, a personal or certified check will be due upon delivery.

Manufacturers: **(Many resources do not list all their manufacturers. Be sure to inquire about those you are interested in, but do not see listed here.)**

WELLINGTONS FINE LEATHER FURNITURE
7771 VALLEY BLVD, PO BOX 1849
BLOWING ROCK, NC 28605
Hours: **M-S: 9-6**

Toll-Free	800-262-1049
Direct	704-295-0491
Fax	704-295-0495
Internet	

Notes: Established 1982. Specializing in leather furniture. Traditional, contemporary, southwestern and more. For home or office. 50% down payment required via VISA/MC/CHECK. Nationwide in-home delivery. Customer satisfaction guaranteed 100% through manufacturers warranties and store reputation. Through our 70-color catalog we bring to you the look and feel of our showroom. $5 refundable.

Manufacturers: **(Many resources do not list all their manufacturers. Be sure to inquire about those you are interested in, but do not see listed here.)**

DISTINCTION LEATHER	LEATHERCRAFT	PALLISER
EMERSON	McKINLEY LEATHER	WELLINGTON'S COLLECTION

WELLS INTERIORS INC
7171 AMADOR PLAZA DO
DUBLIN, CA 94568
Hours: **M-F: 6-6 PST**
S: 10-5; SUN: 12PST

Toll-Free	800-547-8982
Direct	
Fax	
Internet	

Notes: In business since 1980. Window treatments, blinds, shades and accessories. Check-payment with order. No charge for shipping via UPS in the continental USA. Sales consultants and window covering experts on staff. Brochures/written materials. No returns unless defective. Facilities can be visited by customer. 20 retail stores.

Manufacturers: (Many resources do not list all their manufacturers. Be sure to inquire about those you are interested in, but do not see listed here.)

BALI	KIRSCH	M & B (Hunter Douglas's own
DELMAR	LEVOLOR	knock-off)
GRABER	LOUVERDRAPE	
HUNTER DOUGLAS		

WICKER GALLERY, THE
8009 RALEIGH-DURHAM HWY
RALEIGH, NC 27612
Hours:

Toll-Free	
Direct	919-781-2215
Fax	919-781-3520
Internet	

Notes: We specialize in only medium and upper end wicker and rattan furniture. Well trained staff to help select appropriate product and company to deal with to meet needs. VISA/MC/CHECK accepted. No returns on special orders. Any defective product problem will be resolved. Customer must acknowledge shipping damage at delivery. Store will take care of problem

Manufacturers: (Many resources do not list all their manufacturers. Be sure to inquire about those you are interested in, but do not see listed here.)

WICKER WAREHOUSE INC
195 S RIVER ST
HACKENSACK, NJ 07601
Hours: **M-F: 9-5**

Toll-Free	800-989-4253
Direct	201-342-6709
Fax	201-342-1495
Internet	**website:** http://www.wickerwarehouse.com

Notes: We carry current styles by well-known names, including those lines treated to withstand rain and weather. Plus our own hand-picked imports of bedrooms, bathrooms, children's furniture, wrought iron and teak. Even doll carriages. Nation-wide shipping. 112-color catalog available ($6 refundable) satisfaction guaranteed. Pay by VISA/MC/CHECK/MO.

Manufacturers: (Many resources do not list all their manufacturers. Be sure to inquire about those you are interested in, but do not see listed here.)

ACACIA	LANE	SOUTH SEAS
BRAXTON	LINK	WHITECRAFT
CEBU	LLOYD	WINDSOR
KIANI	MEADOWCRAFT	

WILDERMERE
HICKORY FURNITURE MART
2220 HWY 70 SE
HICKORY, NC 28602
Hours: **M-F: 9-6; S: 9-5; Closed Sundays**

Toll-Free	
Direct	828-322-6602
Fax	828-322-6433
Internet	

Notes: Twelve designers on staff here. Deposits can be paid via VISA/MC/CHECK/CASH. We provide in store free design services. No satisfaction guaranteed policy. No returns if furniture is correct. This resource is part of the Hickory Furniture Mart complex. This showroom is one of over 80 to visit. **See Hickory Furniture Mart listing for more information.** Consolidated shipping can be arranged with other resources in this center, a standard one/third deposit is required on all orders. Most showrooms accept VISA/MC, but not all. Cash, personal or certified checks accepted by all

showrooms. If you elect not to pay for your entire purchase at the time of sale, a personal or certified check will be due upon delivery.

Manufacturers: (Many resources do not list all their manufacturers. Be sure to inquire about those you are interested in, but do not see listed here.)

WINDOWARE CATALOG-SMITH & NOBLE
PO BOX 1838
CORONA, CA 91718
Hours: **M-Sat: 6-6 (PST)**

Toll-Free	800-248-8888
Direct	
Fax	800-426-7780
Internet	

Notes: A great window treatment catalog. Extensive collection of wood blinds, Duette shades, roller shades Roman shades, cornices, soft shades, vertical blinds, metal blinds, Duraflex blinds, etc. Swatches available for a small fee. Free shipping and handling.

Manufacturers: (Many resources do not list all their manufacturers. Be sure to inquire about those you are interested in, but do not see listed here.)

WOOD-ARMFIELD FURNITURE COMPANY
THE ATRIUM
430 SOUTH MAIN ST
HIGH POINT, NC 27260
Hours: **M-F:9-6; S: 9-5**

Toll-Free	
Direct	336-889-6522
Fax	336-889-5381
Internet	email: woodarmfield@theatrium.com

Notes: Part of the Atrium complex. Worth visiting, showrooms available. See **Atrium Furniture Showroom** listing for more information. Medium to high end manufacturers all displayed in gallery settings. Dining room, bedroom, occasional, youth, contemporary, leather, wicker and upholstery. Additional large showroom located next door at 460 South Main St.

Manufacturers: (Many resources do not list all their manufacturers. Be sure to inquire about those you are interested in, but do not see listed here.)

ARNOLD PALMER COLLECTION	JASPER	SOUTHWOOD
BOB TIMBERLAKE	KNOB CREEK	REPRODUCTIONS
CALSSIC LEATHER	LABARGE	STANFORD
CASA STRADIVARI	LANE	STATESVILLE CHAIR
CENTURY	LEXINGTON	STATTON
HABERSHAM PLANTATION	MICHAEL THOMAS	THOMASVILLE IPRESSIONS
HEKMAN	MILES TALBOT	VANGUARD
HENRY LINK WICKER	NATIONAL MT AIRY	VIEWPOINT LEATHER
HICKORY WHITE	PENNSYLVANIA CLASSICS	WEIMAN
HOLLYWOODS	BROYHILL	WESLEY HALL
J ROYALE		

WOOD-ARMFIELD FURNITURE COMPANY
460 S MAIN ST
HIGH POINT, NC 27261
Hours: **M-F: 9-6; S: 9-5**

Toll-Free	
Direct	336-889-6522
Fax	336-889-5381
Internet	

Notes: Established 1939. Five-story 160,000 sq ft showroom. Clearance center. Designer assistance available. This company will notify customers on its mailing list of sales and specials throughout the year. In-home delivery and set up by company-owned trucks. Additional location located in **Atrium Furniture Showroom.**

Manufacturers: (Many resources do not list all their manufacturers. Be sure to inquire about those you are interested in, but do not see listed here.)

ACTION BY LANE	BROYHILL	COLONIAL
ALLUSIONS	CANADEL	COMFORT DESIGNS
AMERICAN DREW	CARSON'S	CONOVER
ANDREW PEARSON	CASA BIQUE	COOPER CLASSICS
ARDLEY HALL	CASA STRADIVARI	CORSICAN
ARTISTICA	CENTURY	COUNCILL
BASSETT	CHAIRWORKS	COX
BERKLINE	CHARLESTON FORGE	CR LAINE
BERNHARDT	CHROMCRAFT	CRAFTWORK
BLACKSMITH SHOP	CLARK CASUAL	CRAWFORD
BOB TIMBERLAKE	CLASSIC LEATHER	CRESENT
BRADINGTON YOUNG	CLASSIC RATTAN	CTH/SHERRILL
BRAXTON CULLER	CLAYTON MARCUS	CUSTOMCRAFT
BRITISH TRADITIONS	COCHRANE	DAVIS CABINET

DAR/RAN
DESIGNMASTER
DILLON
DINO MARK ANTHONY
DISTINCTION LEATHER
ELEMENTS BY GRAPEVINE
ELLIOTT'S
ELLO
EMERSON ET CIE
EMERSON LEATHER
EXCELSIOR
FABLES
FAIRFIELD CHAIR
FASHION BED
FICKS REED
FLAT ROCK
FLEXSTEEL
FREMARC
GARCIA IMPORTS
GRACE
HABERSHAM
HAMMARY
HEKMAN
HENRY LINK
HICKORY WHITE
HOLLYWOODS
HOOKER
HOWARD MILLER
HTB LANE
HUDSON RIVER VALLEY
JASPER CABINET
JDI
JOHNSTON CASUALS
J ROYALE
JSF
KIMBALL
KING HICKORY
KNOB CREEK
KOCH
LaBARGE
LANE
LA-Z-BOY
LEA
LEXINGTON
LIGNE

LLOYD FLANDERS
LYON SHAW
MADISON SQUARE
MAITLAND SMITH
MICHAEL THOMAS
MIKHAIL DARAFEEV
MILES TALBOT
MILLENIUM
MOOSEHEAD
MOTIONCRAFT
NATUZZI
NICHOLS & STONE
OEM IMPORTS
ONE OF A KIND
PALMER HOME COLLECTION
PARKER SOUTHERN
PAVILLION
PEARSON
PENNSYLVANIA CLASSICS
PENTURA
PETERS-REVINGTON
PHILLIP REINISCH
POMPEII
PULASKI
REX
RICHARDSON BROS
RIVERSIDE
ROWE
ROYAL PATINA
SALEM SQUARE
SAM MOORE
S BENT
SEALY
SERTA SHUFORD
SK PRODUCTS
SLIGH
SOUTH CONE
SOUTHERN REPRODUCTIONS
SOUTHWOOD
SOUTHAMPTON
STANLEY
STANFORD UPHOLSTERY
STATESVILLE CHAIR
STATTON
SUPERIOR

SWAIM
THEODORE ALEXANDER
THOMASVILLE
TIMBERWOOD
TROPITONE
UNIVERSAL
VANGUARD
VENTURE
WATERFORD
WEIMAN
WELLINGTON HALL
WESLEY ALLEN
WESLEY HALL
WINSTON
WOODARD
WOODMARK
YORKSHIRE HOUSE

ACCESSORIES
AMBIANCE
CAMBRIDGE
CAPE CRAFTSMEN
CAPEL
CHAPMAN
FINE ARTS
FLORITA NOVA
FREDERICK COOPER
FRIEDMAN BROS MIRRORS
GARCIA IMPORTS
GREAT CITY TRADERS
GUILDMASTER
HART
HILDA FLACK
JOHN RICHARD
KINDER HARRIS
MAITLAND SMITH
NORA FENTON
PALECEK
PHOENIX ART
PHILLIPS COLLECTION
SARREID
SEDGEFIELD
SHADOW CATCHER
SOICHER MARIN
WILDWOOD

WORK STATION, THE
HICKORY FURNITURE MART
2220 HWY 70 SE
HICKORY, NC 28602
Hours: **M-F: 9-6; S: 9-5; Closed Sundays**

Toll-Free	
Direct	828-322-4440
Fax	
Internet	

Notes: This resource is part of the Hickory Furniture Mart complex. This showroom is one of over 80 to visit. **See Hickory Furniture Mart listing for more information.** Consolidated shipping can be arranged with other resources in this center, a standard one/third deposit is required on all orders. Most showrooms accept VISA/MC, but not all. Cash, personal or certified checks accepted by all showrooms. If you elect not to pay for your entire purchase at the time of sale, a personal or certified check will be due upon delivery.

Manufacturers: (Many resources do not list all their manufacturers. Be sure to inquire about those you are interested in, but do not see listed here.)

WORLD OF LEATHER
1209 GREENSBORO ROAD
HIGH POINT, NC 27260
Hours: **M-F: 9-5**

Toll-Free	
Direct	336-454-2212
Fax	336-454-6829
Internet	

Notes:

Manufacturers: (Many resources do not list all their manufacturers. Be sure to inquire about those you are interested in, but do not see listed here.)
KLAUSSNER

WORTHINGTON FURNITURE GALLERY
5002 HICKORY BLVD
HICKORY, NC 28601
Hours: **M-S: 9:30-5:30**

Toll-Free	
Direct	828-396-6343
Fax	828-396-6345
Internet	

Notes: Located on HWY 321

Manufacturers: (Many resources do not list all their manufacturers. Be sure to inquire about those you are interested in, but do not see listed here.)
LEXINGTON

======================================

YOUNG'S FURNITURE & RUG COMPANY
PO BOX 5005,1706 N. MAIN
HIGH POINT, NC 27262
Hours: **M-S: 9-5:30**

Toll-Free	
Direct	336-883-4111
Fax	
Internet	

Notes: Young's specializes in the finest home furnishings available. Their entire staff of nine all have interior design backgrounds. They highly recommend visiting their beautiful showroom and working with their fine sales/design staff. One-third deposit required. In-store purchases can be paid by VISA/MC. Phone orders must be paid by personal check/certified funds. Special order items cannot be returned. No satisfaction guaranteed policy, but their sales staff works hard to make sure you make the right purchase. Showroom maintains the highest inventory per square foot. Problems with shipping are handled by the shipper and young's customer service personnel

Manufacturers: (Many resources do not list all their manufacturers. Be sure to inquire about those you are interested in, but do not see listed here.)

AMERICAN DREW	BROWN JORDAN	COUNCILL CRAFTSMEN
AMERICAN OF MARTINSVILLE	CASA BIQUE	DANSEN
AS YOU LIKE IT LAMPS	CASA STRADIVARI	DAVIS & DAVIS RUGS
BETH WEISSMAN LAMPS	CENTURY	FICKS REED
BEVAN FUNNELL	CHAPMAN	FINE ARTS LAMPS
BRADINGTON YOUNG	CLARK CASUAL	FREDERICK COOPER

FRIEDMAN BROS MIRRORS	LANE	SOVA & SOVA
GARCIA IMPORTS	LEXINGTON	SPEER
GEORGE KOVACS	MADISON SQUARE	STANTON COOPER
HANCOCK & MOORE	MAITLAND SMITH	STIFFEL
HART	MARBRO LAMPS	STUBBERON
HEKMAN	MASLAND CARPET	TROPITONE
HENKEL-HARRIS	MOTTAHEDEH	VIRGINIA METALCRAFTERS
HENKEL MOORE	NATIONAL MT AIRY	WATERFORD
HENREDON	NEW MARBRO	WEIMAN
HENRY LINK	NORMAN PERRY	WELLINGTON HALL
HICKORY CHAIR	O'ASIAN	WILDWOOD
JASPER	PLANT PLANT	WINSTON
JEFFCO	SARREID	WOODARD
JOHN WIDDICOMB	SEALY	WOODMARK
KARGES	SOUTHAMPTON	WRIGHT TABLE
LaBARGE	SOUTHWOOD	

ZAGAROLI CLASSICS
THE ATRIUM
430 SOUTH MAIN ST
HIGH POINT, NC 27260
Hours: **M-F: 9-6; S: 9-5**

Toll-Free	800-887-2424
Direct	336-882-7386
Fax	336-882-7386
Internet	**website:** http:\\zagarolileather.com

Notes: Part of the Atrium. Worth visiting, showrooms available. See **Atrium Furniture Showroom** listing for more information. Manufacturer of highest quality leather furnishings since 1993, all custom built with a kiln-dried hardwood frame, 8-way hand-tied springs and top-grain fully aniline dyed leathers. Our showrooms have a great assortment of our luxurious fine leather furnishings along with unusual accessories from other small custom-oriented manufacturers. We take VISA/MC/DISC/CHECK and can usually ship your furniture within four weeks. A 20-full color catalog is available.

Manufacturers: (Many resources do not list all their manufacturers. Be sure to inquire about those you are interested in, but do not see listed here.)

ZAGAROLI CLASSICS
HICKORY FURNITURE MART
2220 HWY 70 SE
HICKORY, NC 28601
Hours: **M-F: 9-6; S: 9-5; Closed Sundays**

Toll-Free	800-887-2424
Direct	828-328-3373
Fax	828-345-1176
Internet	**email:** zagaroli@twave.net **website:** http:\\zagarolileather.com

Notes: Located in "Shoppes at the Mart". Manufacturer of highest quality leather furnishings since 1993, all custom built with a kiln-dried hardwood frame, 8-way hand-tied springs and top-grain fully aniline dyed leathers. Our showrooms have a great assortment of our luxurious fine leather furnishings along with unusual accessories from other small custom-oriented manufacturers. We take VISA/MC/DISC/CHECK and can usually ship your furniture within four weeks. A 20-full color catalog is available. This resource is part of the Hickory Furniture Mart complex. This showroom is one of over 80 to visit. **See Hickory Furniture Mart listing for more information.** Consolidated shipping can be arranged with other resources in this center, a standard one/third deposit is required on all orders. Most showrooms accept VISA/MC, but not all. Cash, personal or certified checks accepted by all showrooms. If you elect not to pay for your entire purchase at the time of sale, a personal or certified check will be due upon delivery.

Manufacturers: (Many resources do not list all their manufacturers. Be sure to inquire about those you are interested in, but do not see listed here.)

ZAKI ORIENTAL RUGS
600 S MAIN STREET
HIGH POINT, NC 27260
Hours: **M-S: 9-6**

Toll-Free	
Direct	336-884-4407
Fax	336-884-5987
Internet	

Notes: Eight sales consultants on staff. New in 1997, 100,000 square foot showroom available for browsing/shopping. Purchases in check or cash form. Rugs can be returned for a full refund if they are not soiled or damaged if returned within 10 days of receipt. Customer pays freight bill both ways, if returned. Resource deals with any shipping problems or damage. A large selection of quality rugs from Pakistan, India, China, Iran, Afghanistan, dhurries from India and kilims from China, Romania and Turkey. Needlepoint china and chainstitch from india. Over 12,000 rugs in stock. Sizes up to 16'x27'

Manufacturers: (Many resources do not list all their manufacturers. Be sure to inquire about those you are interested in, but do not see listed here.)

ZARBIN & ASSOCIATES
401 N FRANKLIN-FOURTH FLOOR
CHICAGO, IL 60610
Hours: **M-F: 9-4:30; S: 9-3**

Toll-Free	
Direct	312-527-1570
Fax	312-670-4414
Internet	

Notes: See Eklectic Interiors, Ltd. Listing

Manufacturers: (Many resources do not list all their manufacturers. Be sure to inquire about those you are interested in, but do not see listed here.)
OVER 150 MANUFACTURERS

GEOGRAPHIC LISTING

This listing is sorted alphabetically by **state** and then alphabetically by **city**. You can use the previous **Resource Listing** section to find phone numbers, hours of operation, manufacturers carried, etc.

CALIFORNIA
WELLS INTERIORS INC
7171 AMADOR PLAZA DO
DUBLIN, CA 94568

COLORADO
COLOREL BLINDS
8200 E PARK MEADOWS DR
LITTLETON, CO 80124

CONNECTICUT
HOME FABRIC MILLS
882 S MAIN ST
CHESHIRE, CT 06410

CONNECTICUT CURTAIN
COMPANY
COMMERCE PLAZA, RT. 6
DANBURY, CT 06810

CAROLINA PATIO WAREHOUSE
58 LARGO DR
STAMFORD, CT 06907

FLORIDA
SILVER QUEEN, THE
730 N INDIAN ROCKS RD
BELLEAIRE BLUFFS, FL 33770

ABC DECORATIVE FABRICS
2410 298TH AVE N
CLEARWATER, FL 34621

NATIONAL DECORATORS
20467 OLD CUTLER RD
MIAMI, FL 33189

FURNITURE DIRECT
1280 S POWERLINE RD, #189
POMPANO BEACH, FL 33069

SOUTHEAST WHOLESALERS
3637 FORT ST N, SUITE 290
ST PETERS BURG, FL 33704

GEORGIA
FLOORWAYS
5755 DUPREE DR SUITE 200
ATLANTA, GA 30327

SILVER SHOP
3164 PEACHTREE RD NE
ATLANTA, GA 30305

CUSTOM DRAPERY SHOP &
INTERIORS
6122 ALTAMA AVE #2
BRUNSWICK, GA 31525-1807

ACCESS CARPET
PO BOX 1007
DALTON, GA 30722

BEARDEN BROTHERS CARPET
AND TEXTILES
4109 S DIXIE RD
DALTON, GA 30720

CARPET EXPRESS
915 MARKET STREET
DALTON, GA 30720

DALTON PARADISE CARPET
PO BOX 2488
DALTON, GA 30722

GOLD LABEL CARPETS
PO BOX 3876
DALTON, GA 30721

HENREDON/DREXEL
HERITAGE FACTORY OUTLET
3004A PARQUET DR
DALTON, GA 30720

JOHNSON'S CARPETS
3519 CORPORATE DR
DALTON, GA 30721

LEE'S CARPET SHOWCASE
3068 NORTH DUG GAP ROAD
DALTON, GA 30722-0481

NETWORK FLOOR COVERING
3200 DUG GAP RD
DALTON, GA 30720

PARKER'S CARPET
3200 DUG GAP ROAD
DALTON, GA 30720

S & S MILLS, INC
PO BOX 1568
DALTON, GA 30722

WAREHOUSE CARPETS, INC
PO BOX 3233
DALTON, GA 30719

SHUTTER DEPOT
RT 2, BOX 157
GREENVILLE, GA 30222

MDC DIRECT, INC
PO BOX 569
MARIETTA, GA 30061

BEAVER CARPETS
697 VARNELL RD
TUNNEL HILL, GA 30755

ILLINOIS
EKLECTIC INTERIORS, LTD
401 N. FRANKLIN ST, 4TH FL
CHICAGO, IL 60610

ZARBIN & ASSOCIATES
401 N FRANKLIN-FOURTH
FLOOR
CHICAGO, IL 60610

GLOBAL WALLCOVERINGS
AND BLINDS
3359 WEST MAIN ST
SKOKIE, IL 60067

EUROPEAN FURNITURE
IMPORTERS
2145 W. GRAND AVE
CHICAGO, ILL 60612

INDIANA
FACTORY DIRECT TABLE PAD
CO
1501 W MARKET ST
INDIANAPOLIS, IN 46208

KENTUCKY
MILLER'S - WINDOW DECOR
201 INDUSTRY PARKWAY
NICHOLASVILLE, KY 40356

MASSACHUSETTS

FABRIC CENTER, THE
485 ELECTRIC AVENUE
FITCHBURG, MA 01420

HARMONY SUPPLY INC
PO BOX 313
MEDFORD, MA 02155

MICHIGAN

RON HAINER LIGHTING
DESIGNS, INC
3556 VINEWOOD AVE SE
GRAND RAPIDS, MI 48546

BARRON'S
PO BOX 994
NOVI, MI 48376

HARDWARE BATH & MORE
20830 COOLIDGE HWY
OAK PARK, MI 48237

HERALD WHOLESALE
20830 COOLIDGE HWY
OAK PARK, MI 48237

AMERICAN BLIND AND
WALLPAPER FACTORY
909 N SHELDON RD
PLYMOUTH, MI 48170

NATIONAL BLIND AND
WALLPAPER FACTORY
400 GALLERIA-OFFICE
CENTRAL #400
SOUTHFIELD, MI 48034

BRASCH ASSOCIATES
7216 GREEN FARM ROAD
WEST BLOOMFIELD, MI 48322

MONTANA

CARPET OUTLET
BOX 417
MILES CITY, MT 59301

NORTH CAROLINA

HANG-IT-NOW WALLPAPER
STORES
304 TRINDALE RD
ARCHDALE, NC 27263

SHEPHERDS DISCOUNT
FURNITURE
10609-C MAIN STREET
ARCHDALE, NC 27263

BILTMORE FURNITURE
GALLERIES
780 HENDERSONVILLE RD
ASHEVILLE, NC 28803

HAMILTON'S
506 LIVE OAK STREET
BEAUFORT, NC 28516

SOBOL HOUSE OF
FURNISHINGS
RICHARDSON BLVD
BLACK MOUNTAIN, NC 28711

TYSON FURNITURE COMPANY
109 BROADWAY
BLACK MOUNTAIN, NC 28711

WELLINGTONS FINE LEATHER
FURNITURE
7771 VALLEY BLVD, PO BOX
1849
BLOWING ROCK, NC 28605

STEVENS OF BOONE
PO BOX 2450, HWY 105 SOUTH
BOONE, NC 28607

BURLINGTON FURNITURE
2629 RAMADA ROAD
BURLINGTON, NC 27215

STYLE CRAFT INTERIORS
102 E FRONT STREET
BURLINGTON, NC 27216

FURNITURE PATCH OF
CALABASH, THE
10283 BEACH DRIVE SW
PO BOX 4970
CALABASH, NC 28467

BOYLES DISTINCTIVE
FURNITURE
7607 NATIONS FORD ROAD
CHARLOTTE, NC 28217

BOYLES DREXEL HERITAGE
2125 SARDIS ROAD NORTH
CHARLOTTE, NC 28227

MECKLENBURG FURNITURE
520 PROVIDENCE ROAD
CHARLOTTE, NC 28207

MIDAS FABRIC
3120 N SHARON AMITY RD
CHARLOTTE, NC 28205

MINCEY'S INC
600 SUGAR CREEK ROAD W.
CHARLOTTE, NC 28213

RUG STORE, THE
2201 CROWNPOINT EXEC DR
CHARLOTTE, NC 28227

EPHRAIM MARSH CO
PO BOX 266
CONCORD, NC 28026-0266

CENTURY/HICKORY CHAIR
OUTLET
1120 HWY 16 N
CONOVER, NC 28613

KING'S CHANDELIER
COMPANY
729 SOUTH VAN BUREN RD
EDEN , NC 27289

GRINDSTAFF'S INTERIORS
1007 W MAIN
FOREST CITY, NC 28043

LUXURY FABRICS AND
INTERIORS
PO BOX 250
GASTONIA, NC 28053

SALLY STOWE INERIORS
4100 WILKINSON BLVD
GASTONIA, NC 28056

CENTRE COURT FURNITURE
MALL
2161 HWY 321
GRANITE FALLS, NC 28630

COFFEY DISCOUNT
FURNITURE
HWY 321-POOVEY DR
GRANITE FALLS, NC 28630

FABRICS & MORE
572 SOUTH MAIN ST
GRANITE FALLS, NC 28630

FOUR SEASONS FURNITURE
GALLERY
4560 HICKORY BLVD
GRANITE FALLS, NC 28630

LAKE HICKORY FURNITURE
4360 HICKORY BLVD
GRANITE FALLS, NC 28630

MACKIE FURNITURE CO, INC
13 N MAIN ST, PO DRAWER 70
GRANITE FALLS, NC 28630

NATIONAL FURNITURE
5598 YORK RD
GRANITE FALLS, NC 28630

PLAZA FURNITURE GALLERY
HWY 321 AT TIMBERBROOK
GRANITE FALLS, NC 28630

THOMAS HOME FURNISHINGS
4346 HICKORY BLVD
GRANITE FALLS, NC 28630

A CLASSIC DESIGN -
1703 MADISON AVE
GREENSBORO, NC 27403

AMERICAN LIGHTSOURCE
511D, W MARKET ST, SUITE 803
GREENSBORO, NC 27409

COLFAX FURNITURE
S HOLDEN ROAD AT I-85
GREENSBORO, NC 27407

FIELDS FURNITURE CO
2700 RANDLEMAN ROAD
GREENSBORO, NC 27406

FURNITURE CHOICES
2501 PETERS CREEK PARKWAY
GREENSBORO, NC 27107

HOUSE DRESSING
INTERNATIONAL FURNITURE
3608 W WENDOVER
GREENSBORO, NC 27407

KARASTAN CARPET & RUG
CENTER
4309 WILEY DAVIS RD
GREENSBORO, NC 27407

LOUNGE SHOP, THE
2222-E PATTERSON STREET
GREENSBORO, NC 27260

MIDAS FABRIC
4813 W MARKET ST
GREENSBORO, NC 27407

PRIBA FURNITURE SALES AND
INTERIORS
PO BOX 13295
GREENSBORO, NC 27415

PRINTER'S ALLEY STORES
1324-104 WESTOVER TERRACE
GREENSBORO, NC 27408

REPLACEMENTS, LTD
1089 KNOX ROAD POB 26029
GREENSBORO, NC 27420

SOUTH SEAS RATTAN
1708 FAIRFAX ROAD
GREENSBORO, NC 27407

SPRING VALLEY DISCOUNT
FURNITURE
429 W. MEADOWVIEW RD
GREENSBORO, NC 27406

TIME GALLERY
3121 BATTLEGROUND AVE
GREENSBORO, NC 27408

AMERICAN DREW GALLERY
HICKORY FURNITURE MART
2220 HWY 70 SE
HICKORY, NC 28602

BAKER GALLERY
HICKORY FURNITURE MART
2220 HWY 70 SE
HICKORY, NC 28602

BALDWIN BRASS FACTORY
OUTLET
HICKORY FURNITURE MART
2220 HWY 70 SE
HICKORY, NC 28602

BEACON HILL FACTORY
OUTLET
HICKORY FURNITURE MART
2220 HWY 70 SE
HICKORY, NC 28602

BERNHARDT GALLERY
HICKORY FURNITURE MART
2220 HWY 70 SE
HICKORY, NC 28602

BETTER HOMES FURNITURE
OUTLET
248 FIRST AVE NW
HICKORY, NC 28601

BONITA FURNITURE
GALLERIES
HWY 321, EXIT 123
HICKORY, NC 28603

BOYLES CLEARANCE CENTER
II
66 HWY 321 NW
HICKORY, NC 28601

BOYLES CLEARANCE CENTER I
739 OLD LENOIR ROAD
HICKORY, NC 28601

BOYLES GALLERIES
HICKORY FURNITURE MART
2220 HWY 70 SE
HICKORY, NC 28603

BOYLES ORIGINAL COUNTRY
SHOP AND CLEARANCE
CENTER IN HICKORY
739 OLD LENOIR ROAD
HICKORY, NC 2860

BOYLES SHOWCASE GALLERY
HICKORY FURNITURE MART
2220 HWY 70 SE
HICKORY, NC 28603

BRADINGTON YOUNG
GALLERY
HICKORY FURNITURE MART
2220 HWY 70 SE
HICKORY, NC 28602

BROYHILL SHOWCASE
GALLERY
HICKORY FURNITURE MART
2220 HWY 70 SE
HICKORY, NC 28602

CABOT GALLERY
HICKORY FURNITURE MART
2220 HWY 70 SE
HICKORY, NC 28602

CANADEL GALLERY
HICKORY FURNITURE MART
2220 HWY 70 SE
HICKORY, NC 28602

CARSONS GALLERY
HICKORY FURNITURE MART
2220 HWY 70 SE
HICKORY, NC 28602

CENTURY FACTORY OUTLET
HICKORY FURNITURE MART
2220 HWY 70 SE
HICKORY, NC 28602

CENTURY FURNITURE
HICKORY FURNITURE MART
2220 HWY 70 SE
HICKORY, NC 28602

CLASSIC LEATHER GALLERY
HICKORY FURNITURE MART
2220 HWY 70 SE
HICKORY, NC 28602

CLASSIC ORIENTAL RUGS
HICKORY FURNITURE MART
2220 HWY 70 SE
HICKORY, NC 28602

CLAYTON MARCUS GALLERY
HICKORY FURNITURE MART
2220 HWY 70 SE
HICKORY, NC 28602

COCHRANE GALLERY
HICKORY FURNITURE MART
2220 HWY 70 SE
HICKORY, NC 28602

COMFORT ZONE
HICKORY FURNITURE MART
2220 HWY 70 SE
HICKORY, NC 28602

CONTEMPORARY GALLERY
HICKORY FURNITURE MART
2220 HWY 70 SE
HICKORY, NC 28602

COURISTAN FACTORY OUTLET
HICKORY FURNITURE MART
2220 HWY 70 SE
HICKORY, NC 28602

CR LAINE GALLERY
HICKORY FURNITURE MART
2220 HWY 70 SE
HICKORY, NC 28602

DON LAMOR
HICKORY FURNITURE MART
2220 HWY 70 SE
HICKORY, NC 28602

DREXEL HERITAGE FACTORY
OUTLET
HICKORY FURNITURE MART
2220 HWY 70 SE
HICKORY, NC 28602

DREXEL HERITAGE GALLERY
HICKORY FURNITURE MART
2220 HWY 70 SE
HICKORY, NC 28603

DREXEL STUDIO
HICKORY FURNITURE MART
2220 HWY 70 SE
HICKORY, NC 28603

FARM HOUSE FURNISHINGS
1432 1ST AVE SW
HICKORY, NC 28602-2401

FLEXSTEEL GALLERY
HICKORY FURNITURE MART
2220 HWY 70 SE
HICKORY, NC 28602

FRANKLIN PLACE
HICKORY FURNITURE MART
2220 HWY 70 SE
HICKORY, NC 28602

GALLERY OF LIGHTS
HICKORY FURNITURE MART
2220 HWY 70 SE
HICKORY, NC 28602

GENERATIONS
HICKORY FURNITURE MART
2220 HWY 70 SE
HICKORY, NC 28602

GLOBE FURNITURE
910 US HWY 321 NW, #100
HICKORY, NC 28601

GREENHILL FURNITURE
COMPANY
1308 HWY 70 W
HICKORY, NC 28602

HANCOCK & MOORE GALLERY
HICKORY FURNITURE MART
2220 HWY 70 SE
HICKORY, NC 28602

HARDEN GALLERY
HICKORY FURNITURE MART
2220 HWY 70 SE
HICKORY, NC 28602

HEKMAN GALLERY
HICKORY FURNITURE MART
2220 HWY 70 SE
HICKORY, NC 28602

HENKEL HARRIS GALLERY
HICKORY FURNITURE MART
2220 HWY 70 SE
HICKORY, NC 28602

HENREDON FACTORY OUTLET
HICKORY FURNITURE MART
2220 HWY 70 SE
HICKORY, NC 28602

HENREDON GALLERY
HICKORY FURNITURE MART
2220 HWY 70 SE
HICKORY, NC 28602

HICKORY CHAIR GALLERY
HICKORY FURNITURE MART
2220 HWY 70 SE
HICKORY, NC 28602

HICKORY CHAIR FACTORY
OUTLET
HICKORY FURNITURE MART
2220 HWY 70 SE
HICKORY, NC 28602

HICKORY FURNITURE MART
2220 US 70 SE
HICKORY, NC 28602

HICKORY FURNITURE MART
FURNITURE CLEARANCE
CENTER
66 HWY 321 NW
HICKORY, NC 28601

HICKORY PARK FURNITURE
GALLERIES
HICKORY FURNITURE MART
2220 HWY 70 SE
HICKORY, NC 28602

HICKORY WHITE GALLERY
HICKORY FURNITURE MART
2220 HWY 70 SE
HICKORY, NC 28602

HIGHLAND HOUSE GALLERY
HICKORY FURNITURE MART
2220 HWY 70 SE
HICKORY, NC 28602

HOLIDAY PATIO
HICKORY FURNITURE MART
2220 HWY 70 SE
HICKORY, NC 28602

HOME FOCUS BY PALLISER
HICKORY FURNITURE MART
2220 HWY 70 SE
HICKORY, NC 28602

HOOKER GALLERY
HICKORY FURNITURE MART
2220 HWY 70 SE
HICKORY, NC 28602

HOUSE OF MIRRORS
HICKORY FURNITURE MART
2220 HWY 70 SE
HICKORY, NC 28602

HUDSON DISCOUNT
FURNITURE
940 HIGHLAND AVE, NE (PO
BOX 2547)
HICKORY, NC 28601

HUNT GALLERIES, INC
2920 HWY 127 N., PO BOX 2324
HICKORY, NC 28603

INTERIOR FURNISHINGS, ETC
PO BOX 1644
HICKORY, NC 28603

J ROYALE GALLERY
HICKORY FURNITURE MART
2220 HWY 70 SE
HICKORY, NC 28602

JEFFCO GALLERY
HICKORY FURNITURE MART
2220 HWY 70 SE
HICKORY, NC 28602

KARGES GALLERY
HICKORY FURNITURE MART
2220 HWY 70 SE
HICKORY, NC 28602

KIMBALL GALLERY
HICKORY FURNITURE MART
2220 HWY 70 SE
HICKORY, NC 28602

KINCAID GALLERY
HICKORY FURNITURE MART
2220 HWY 70 SE
HICKORY, NC 28602

LaBARGE FACTORY OUTLET
HICKORY FURNITURE MART
2220 HWY 70 SE
HICKORY, NC 28602

LANE GALLERY
HICKORY FURNITURE MART
2220 HWY 70 SE
HICKORY, NC 28602

LEATHER SHOP, THE
ROUTE 12, BOX 57
HICKORY, NC 23101

LEXINGTON GALLERY
(BOYLES)
HICKORY FURNITURE MART
2220 HWY 70 SE
HICKORY, NC 28603

LINDY'S FURNITURE CO
233 FIRST AVE NW
HICKORY, NC 28601

MAITLAND SMITH FACTORY
OUTLET
HICKORY FURNITURE MART
2220 HWY 70 SE
HICKORY, NC 28602

MARGE CARSON GALLERY
HICKORY FURNITURE MART
2220 HWY 70 SE
HICKORY, NC 28602

MAYFIELD LEATHER
340 9TH ST SE
HICKORY, NC 28603

MORGAN STEWART GALLERY
HICKORY FURNITURE MART
2220 HWY 70 SE
HICKORY, NC 28602

MOTIONCRAFT GALLERY
HICKORY FURNITURE MART
2220 HWY 70 SE
HICKORY, NC 28602

NATIONAL ART GALLERY
HICKORY FURNITURE MART
2220 HWY 70 SE
HICKORY, NC 28602

NATIONAL CLOCK GALLERY
HICKORY FURNITURE MART
2220 HWY 70 SE
HICKORY, NC 28602

P & J HOME AND FABRICS
4114 HWY 70 WEST
HICKORY, NC 28602

PALLISER
HICKORY FURNITURE MART
2220 HWY 70 SE
HICKORY, NC 28602

PEARSON GALLERY
HICKORY FURNITURE MART
2220 HWY 70 SE
HICKORY, NC 28602

PENNSYLVANIA HOUSE
HICKORY FURNITURE MART
2220 HWY 70 SE
HICKORY, NC 28602

PIEDMONT DESIGN
HICKORY FURNITURE MART
2220 HWY 70 SE
HICKORY, NC 28602

PRECEDENT GALLERY
HICKORY FURNITURE MART
2220 HWY 70 SE
HICKORY, NC 28602

REFLECTIONS
HICKORY FURNITURE MART
2220 HWY 70 SE
HICKORY, NC 28602

RESOURCE DESIGN
HICKORY FURNITURE MART
2220 HWY 70 SE
HICKORY, NC 28602

RHONEY FURNITURE HOUSE
2401 HWY 70 SW
HICKORY, NC 28602

RHONEY FURNITURE HOUSE
HICKORY FURNITURE MART
2220 HWY 70 SE
HICKORY, NC 28602

ROBERT BERGELIN
HICKORY FURNITURE MART
2220 HWY 70 SE
HICKORY, NC 28602

ROWE GALLERY
HICKORY FURNITURE MART
2220 HWY 70 SE
HICKORY, NC 28602

RUG ROOM, THE
HICKORY FURNITURE MART
2220 HWY 70 SE
HICKORY, NC 28602

SAM MOORE GALLERY
HICKORY FURNITURE MART
2220 HWY 70 SE
HICKORY, NC 28602

SEASONS OUTDOOR GALLERY
HICKORY FURNITURE MART
2220 HWY 70 SE
HICKORY, NC 28602

SHERRILL GALLERY
HICKORY FURNITURE MART
2220 HWY 70 SE
HICKORY, NC 28602

SOUTHERN DESIGNS
HICKORY FURNITURE MART
2220 HWY 70 SE
HICKORY, NC 28602

STANLEY GALLERY
HICKORY FURNITURE MART
2220 HWY 70 SE
HICKORY, NC 28602

THOMASVILLE GALLERY
HICKORY FURNITURE MART
2220 HWY 70 SE
HICKORY, NC 28602

UNIVERSAL GALLERY
HICKORY FURNITURE MART
2220 HWY 70 SE
HICKORY, NC 28602

VANGUARD GALLERY
HICKORY FURNITURE MART
2220 HWY 70 SE
HICKORY, NC 28602

VIRGINIA HOUSE GALLERY
HICKORY FURNITURE MART
2220 HWY 70 SE
HICKORY, NC 28602

WEIMAN GALLERY
HICKORY FURNITURE MART
2220 HWY 70 SE
HICKORY, NC 28602

WILDERMERE
HICKORY FURNITURE MART
2220 HWY 70 SE
HICKORY, NC 28602

WORK STATION, THE
HICKORY FURNITURE MART
2220 HWY 70 SE
HICKORY, NC 28602

WORTHINGTON FURNITURE
GALLERY
5002 HICKORY BLVD
HICKORY, NC 28601

ZAGAROLI CLASSICS
HICKORY FURNITURE MART
2220 HWY 70 SE
HICKORY, NC 28601

ALAN FERGUSON ASSOCIATES
422 S MAIN STREET
HIGH POINT, NC 27260

AMERICAN ACCENTS
THE ATRIUM
430 SOUTH MAIN ST
HIGH POINT, NC 27260

AMERICAN REPRODUCTIONS
THE ATRIUM
430 SOUTH MAIN ST
HIGH POINT, NC 27262

ARTS BY ALEXANDER
701 GREENSBORO ROAD
HIGH POINT, NC 27260

ASHLEY INTERIORS
310 S ELM ST
HIGH POINT, NC 27262

ATRIUM FURNITURE
SHOWROOMS
THE ATRIUM
430 SOUTH MAIN ST
HIGH POINT, NC 27320

BLACK'S FURNITURE
COMPANY, INC
2800 WESTCHESTER
HIGH POINT, NC 27262

BOYLES FURNITURE (ON
GREENSBORO ROAD)
616 GREENSBORO ROAD
HIGH POINT, NC 27261

BROOKLINE FURNITURE
FACTORY SHOWROOM
667 WEST WARD ST
HIGH POINT, NC 27262

CAROLINA CARRIERS
1428 OLDE EDEN DR
HIGH POINT, NC 27262

CAROLINA MATTRESS GUILD
FACTORY OUTLET
781 N MAIN ST
HIGH POINT, NC 27262

CENTRAL WAREHOUSE
FURNITURE
2352 ENGLISH RD
HIGH POINT, NC 27262

CHERRY HILL FURNITURE &
INTERIORS
PO BOX 7405, FURNITURELAND
STATION
HIGH POINT, NC 27264

CONTEMPORARY
COLLECTIONS
THE ATRIUM
430 SOUTH MAIN ST
HIGH POINT, NC 27262

DALLAS FURNITURE STORE,
INC
215 N. CENTENNIAL
HIGH POINT, NC 27261

DAR FURNITURE
517 S HAMILTON ST
HIGH POINT, NC 27262

DECORATOR'S CHOICE
THE ATRIUM
430 SOUTH MAIN ST
HIGH POINT, NC 27262

DEEP RIVER TRADING CO, THE
2436-F WILLARD RD
HIGH POINT, NC 27265

FEFCO
THE ATRIUM
430 SOUTH MAIN ST
HIGH POINT, NC 27262

FRENCH HERITAGE FACTORY
THE ATRIUM
430 SOUTH MAIN ST
HIGH POINT, NC 27260

FURNITURE CLEARANCE
CENTER
1107 TATE ST
HIGH POINT, NC 27260

FURNITURE MARKET
CLEARANCE CENTER
2200 S MAIN
HIGH POINT, NC 27262

GIBSON INTERIORS
1628 S MAIN ST
HIGH POINT, NC 27260

GOLDEN VALLEY LIGHTING
274 EASTCHESTER DRIVE
HIGH POINT, NC 27262

HERITAGE HOUSE FURNITURE
917 LIBERTY RD
HIGH POINT, NC 27262

HICKORY PARK FURNITURE
GALLERIES
THE ATRIUM
430 SOUTH MAIN ST
HIGH POINT, NC 27262

HIGH POINT FURNITURE
SALES, INC
2000 BAKER ROAD
HIGH POINT, NC 27260

HOUSEWORKS HOME
INTERIORS
THE ATRIUM
430 SOUTH MAIN ST
HIGH POINT, NC 27260

KAGAN'S AMERICAN DREW
THE ATRIUM
430 SOUTH MAIN ST
HIGH POINT, NC 27260

KAGAN'S FURNITURE
GALLERIES
THE ATRIUM
430 SOUTH MAIN ST
HIGH POINT, NC 27262

KAGAN'S STANLEY GALLERY
THE ATRIUM
430 SOUTH MAIN ST
HIGH POINT, NC 27262

KATHRYN'S COLLECTION
781 N. MAIN STREET
HIGH POINT, NC 27262

KINCAID GALLERY
THE ATRIUM
430 SOUTH MAIN ST
HIGH POINT, NC 27262

KJ'S FURNITURE OUTLET
400 UNDERHILL ST
HIGH POINT, NC 27262

LA MAISON
THE ATRIUM
430 SOUTH MAIN ST
HIGH POINT, NC 27260

LEATHER UNLIMITED
THE ATRIUM
430 SOUTH MAIN ST
HIGH POINT, NC 27260

LINCOLN GERARD USA INC
THE ATRIUM
430 SOUTH MAIN ST
HIGH POINT, NC 27260

MAIN STREET PENNSYLVANIA
HOUSE
THE ATRIUM
430 SOUTH MAIN ST
HIGH POINT, NC 27262

MAITLAND SMITH FURNITURE
OUTLET
411 TOMLINSON ST
HIGH POINT, NC 27260

MARKET SAMPLE FURNITURE
OUTLET
2850 S MAIN ST
HIGH POINT, NC 27262

MEDALLION FURNITURE
THE ATRIUM
430 SOUTH MAIN ST
HIGH POINT, NC 27260

MODERN UPHOLSTERY CO
1101 GREENSBORO RD
HIGH POINT, NC 27262

NORTH CAROLINA FURNITURE
CLEARANCE
1813 S MAIN ST
HIGH POINT, NC 27260

NORTH CAROLINA FURNITURE
CLEARANCE
2017 COLLEGE ROAD
HIGH POINT, NC 27260

OFFICE IMAGES
1638 WESTCHESTER DR
HIGH POINT, NC 27262

PALLISER
THE ATRIUM
430 SOUTH MAIN ST
HIGH POINT, NC 27260

PARAMOUNT FURNITURE CO
INC
1100 N MAIN
HIGH POINT, NC 27262

PENNSYLVANIA HOUSE
COLLECTOR'S GALLERY
1300 N MAIN
HIGH POINT, NC 27262

PHILLIPS FURNITURE
116 W MARKET CENTER DR
HIGH POINT, NC 27262

REFLECTIONS
THE ATRIUM
430 SOUTH MAIN ST
HIGH POINT, NC 27262

ROSE FURNITURE
916 FINCH AVENUE, PO BOX
1829
HIGH POINT, NC 27261

SINA ORIENTAL RUG
THE ATRIUM
430 SOUTH MAIN ST
HIGH POINT, NC 27260

ST MARTIN'S LANE LTD
THE ATRIUM
430 SOUTH MAIN ST
HIGH POINT, NC 27262

STUDIO OF LIGHTS
2418 S MAIN ST
HIGH POINT, NC 27263

UTILITY CRAFT
2630 EASTCHESTER
HIGH POINT, NC 27265

WOOD-ARMFIELD FURNITURE
COMPANY
460 S MAIN ST
HIGH POINT, NC 27261

WOOD-ARMFIELD FURNITURE
COMPANY
THE ATRIUM
430 SOUTH MAIN ST
HIGH POINT, NC 27260

WORLD OF LEATHER
1209 GREENSBORO ROAD
HIGH POINT, NC 27260

YOUNG'S FURNITURE & RUG
COMPANY
PO BOX 5005,1706 N. MAIN
HIGH POINT, NC 27262

ZAGAROLI CLASSICS
THE ATRIUM
430 SOUTH MAIN ST
HIGH POINT, NC 27260

ZAKI ORIENTAL RUGS
600 S MAIN STREET
HIGH POINT, NC 27260

BLOWING ROCK FURNITURE
COMPANY
PO BOX 684, HWY 321
HUDSON, NC 28638

CALDWELL FURNITURE
CLEARANCE CENTER
3509 HICKORY BLVD
HUDSON, NC 28638

CEDAR ROCK HOME
PO BOX 515, HWY 321 S
HUDSON, NC 28638

FLEMING DECORATIVE
FABRICS
2998 HICKORY BLVD
HUDSON, NC 28638

FRANKLIN FURNITURE
3650 HICKORY BLVD
HUDSON, NC 28638-9027

FURNITURE DEALERS
CLEARANCE CENTER OF NC
HWY 321 N
HUDSON, NC 28638

FURNITURE SHOPPE, THE
3351 HICKORY BLVD
HUDSON, NC 28638

HOLIDAY PATIO SHOWCASE
PO BOX 767, 3318 HICKORY
BLVD
HUDSON, NC 28638

LAWINGS FURNITURE
2636 HICKORY BLVD
HUDSON, NC 28638

SLEEP SHOP
3136 HICKORY BLVD (US 321 S)
HUDSON, NC 28638

SMOKEY MOUNTAIN
FURNITURE OUTLET
3281 HICKORY BLVD (HWY 321)
HUDSON, NC 28638

MALLORY'S FINE FURNITURE
2153 LEJEUNE BLVD
JACKSONVILLE, NC 28540

BOYLES FURNITURE (ON
BUSINESS 85)
5700 RIVERDALE DRIVE
JAMESTOWN, NC 27282

FURNITURELAND SOUTH
BUSINESS I-85 at RIVERDALE
RD
JAMESTOWN, NC 27282

BAKER FURNITURE FACTORY
STORE
146 WEST AVE
KANNAPOLIS, NC 28081

CANNON VILLAGE
200 WEST AVE
KANNAPOLIS, NC 28081

CAROLINA INTERIORS'-
CANNON VILLAGE
115 OAK AVE
KANNAPOLIS, NC 28081

VILLAGE FURNITURE HOUSE
146 WEST AVE
KANNAPOLIS, NC 28081

EAST CAROLINA WALLPAPER
MARKET, INC
1106 PINK HILL RD
KINSTON, NC 28501

KNIGHT GALLERIES INC
835 CREEKWAY DR NW
LENOIR, NC 28645

QUALITY FURNITURE MARKET
OF LENOIR, INC
2034 HICKORY BLVD SW
LENOIR, NC 28645

SLEEP SHOP
2407 NORWOOD ST
LENOIR, NC 28645

STEVENS FURNITURE
COMPANY, INC
1258 HICKORY BLVD
LENOIR, NC 28645

TRIPLETT'S FURNITURE
FASHION
2084 HICKORY BLVD SW
LENOIR, NC 28645

HENDRICKS FURNITURE
(OWNED BY BOYLES
FURNITURE)
I-40 AND FARMINGTON ROAD
MACKSVILLE, NC 27082

HOMEWAY FURNITURE CO OF
MT AIRY, INC
121 W. LEBANON STREET
MT AIRY, NC 27030

ALMAN'S HOME FURNISHINGS
110 E FIRST ST
NEWTON, NC 28658

VILLAGE CARPET
3203 US HWY 70 SE
NEWTON, NC 28613

SKYLAND FURNITURE SHOP
HWY 321 N, PO BOX 10
PATTERSON, NC 28661

HENREDON FACTORY OUTLET
3943 NEW BERN AVE
RALEIGH, NC 27610-1332

MIDAS FABRIC
7912 GLENWOOD AVE
RALEIGH, NC 27612

WICKER GALLERY, THE
8009 RALEIGH-DURHAM HWY
RALEIGH, NC 27612

SHAW FURNITURE GALLERIES
131 W. ACADEMY STREET
RANDLEMAN, NC 27317

A & H WAYSIDE FURNITURE
1086 FREEWAY DRIVE, PO BOX
1143
(BUSINESS 29)
REIDSVILLE, NC 27323

TROTT FURNITURE CO
PO BOX 7, DEPT. F.
RICHLANDS, NC 28574

BARCALOUNGER GALLERIES
1010 N WINSTEAD AVE
ROCKY MOUNT, NC 27804

BULLUCK'S
124 S CHURCH STREET
ROCKY MOUNT, NC 27801

HARDEE'S FURNITURE
WAREHOUSE
4603 S US 301
ROCKY MOUNT, NC 27806

"A" WINDOW TREATMENT CO,
INC
525 BRIGHT LEAF BLVD
SMITHFIELD, NC 27577

JONES BROTHERS
PO BOX 991, HWY 301 N
SMITHFIELD, NC 27577

HENREDON FURNITURE
CLEARANCE
ALTAPASS HWY
SPRUCE PINE, NC 28777-8603

HENREDON FURNITURE
CLEARANCE
ROUTE 3, BOX 379
SPRUCE PINE, NC 28777-8603

BLACKWELDER INDUSTRIES,
INC
294 TURNERSBURG HWY
STATESVILLE, NC 28677

CORNER HUTCH FURNITURE,
THE
HWY 21 N. PO BOX 1728
STATESVILLE, NC 28677

ELLENBURG'S FURNITURE
I-40 & STAMEY FARM ROAD/PO
BOX 5638
STATESVILLE, NC 28687

GORDON'S FURNITURE STORES
214 N. CENTER ST
STATESVILLE, NC 28677-1192

MARION TRAVIS
PO BOX 929 OR 1041
STATESVILLE, NC 28687

DECORATOR'S EDGE, THE
509 RANDOLPH STREET
THOMASVILLE, NC 27360

HOLTON FURNITURE CO
805 RANDOLPH ST
THOMASVILLE, NC 27360

LJ BEST FURNITURE
PO BOX 489
THOMASVILLE, NC 27360

LOFTIN-BLACK FURNITURE
COMPANY
111 SEDGEHILL DR
THOMASVILLE, NC 27360

CAPEL MILL OUTLET
121 E. MAIN ST
TROY, NC 27371

CAYTON FURNITURE INC
217 WEST 3RD ST
WASHINGTON, NC 27889

CAMPBELL/CRAVEN
FURNITURE
UNIVERSITY COMMONS
341 S COLLEGE RD, S#21
WILMINGTON, NC 28403

MURROW FURNITURE
GALLERIES
3514 S COLLEGE ROAD
PO BOX 4337
WILMINGTON, NC 28406

SUTTON-COUNCIL FURNITURE
COMPANY
421 S COLLEGE ROAD, PO BOX
3288
WILMINGTON, NC 28406

OLD TOWN CLOCK SHOP
3738 REYNOLDA RD
WINSTON-SALEM, NC 27106

NEW HAMPSHIRE
FABRIC OUTLET, THE
30 AIRPORT RD
WEST LEBANON, NH 03784

NEW JERSEY
MARLENE'S DECORATOR
FABRICS
301 BEECH STREET, DEPT 2J
HACKENSACK, NJ 07601

WICKER WAREHOUSE INC
195 S RIVER ST
HACKENSACK, NJ 07601

FRAN'S WICKER AND RATTAN
295 ROUTE 10
SUCCASUNNA, NJ 07876

GENADA IMPORTS
PO BOX 204, DEPT R1
TEANECK, NJ 07666

AMERICAN WALLCOVERING
DISTRIBUTORS
2260 ROUTE 22
UNION, NJ 07083

USA EXPRESS
2260C ROUTE 22
UNION, NJ 07083

NEW YORK
800 CARPETS INC
7013 THIRD AVE
BROOKLYN, NY 11209

INTERNATIONAL CARPET
1384 CONEY ISLAND AVE
BROOKLYN, NY 11230

LAMP WAREHOUSE
1073 39TH STREET
BROOKLYN, NY 11219

NEW ENGLAND BLINDS
7013 3RD AVE
BROOKLYN, NY 11209

PINTCHIK HOMEWORKS
478 BERGEN ST
BROOKLYN, NY 11217

STAR CARPET BLIND &
WALLCOVERINGS
7013 THIRD AVE
BROOKLYN, NY 11209

FAUCET OUTLET
PO BOX 547
MIDDLETOWN, NY 10940

DAC LIGHTING
164 BOWERY
NEW YORK, NY 10012

HARRIS LEVY, INC
278 GRAND STREET
NEW YORK, NY 10002

IDS DESIGN CENTER
50 EAST HOUSTON ST
NEW YORK, NY 10012

PLEXI-CRAFT QUALITY
PRODUCTS CORP
514 W. 24TH ST
NEW YORK, NY 10011-1179

SILK SURPLUS
235 EAST 58TH ST
NEW YORK, NY 10022

MARK SALES CO, INC
151-20 88TH ST, DEPT 2G
QUEENS, NY 11414

CHARLES W JACOBSEN, INC
401 N SALINA ST
SYRACUSE, NY 13202

OHIO
BRASS BED SHOPPE, A
12421 CEDAR ROAD
CLEVELAND HTS, OH 44106

VALERIE MAKSTELL
1050 MEHRING WAY
CINCINNATI, OH 45203

PENNSYLVANIA
CALICO CORNERS
WALNUT ROAD
203 GALE LANE
KENNETT SQUARE, PA 19348

LUIGI CRYSTAL
7332 FRANKFORD AVE
PHILADELPHIA, PA 19136

ROBINSON'S WALLCOVERINGS
225 W. SPRING ST
TITUSVILLE, PA 16354-0427

TIOGA MILL OUTLET STORES,
200 S HARTMAN ST.
YORK, PA 17403

SOUTH CAROLINA
CAROLINA FURNITURE DIRECT
PO BOX 22516
HILTON HEAD, SC 29925

MARTY RAE OF LEXINGTON
5108 SUNSET BLVD
LEXINGTON, SC 29072

SOUTHLAND FURNITURE
1244 HWY 17, PO BOX 1837
LITTLE RIVER, SC 29566

PLAZA FURNITURE INC
PO BOX 7640
MYRTLE BEACH, SC 29577

TRIAD FURNITURE
DISCOUNTERS
9770 N KINGS HWY
MYRTLE BEACH, SC 29572

MONROE'S FURNITURE
100 RIGBY ST, PO BOX 38
REEVESVILLE, SC 29471

NATIONAL CAROLINA
INTERIORS
REEVESVILLE, SC 29471

CAROLINA FURNITURE WORLD
PO BOX 4559 (I-77, EXIT 82A)
ROCK HILL, SC 29142

STUCKEY BROTHERS
FURNITURE CO, INC
RTE 1, BOX 527
STUCKEY, SC 29554

SOUTH DAKOTA
GRANIT DESIGN
PO BOX 130
WATERTOWN, SD 57201

TENNESSEE
FURNITURE SHOPPE, THE
1903 E 24TH ST PL
CHATTANOOGA, TN 37404

TEXAS
DISCOUNT CARPET
206 N MAIN
BRYAN, TX 77803

BLINDS DIRECT
10858 HARRY HINES BLVD
DALLAS, TX 75220

HOTEL RESERVATIONS
NETWORK
8140 WALNUT HILL LANE #203
DALLAS, TX 75231

USA BLIND FACTORY
1312 LIVE OAK
HOUSTON, TX 77003

VIRGINIA
BRENTWOOD MANOR
317 VIRGINIA AVENUE

CLARKSVILLE, VA 23927

FURNITURE EXPRESS
220 MT CROSS ROAD
DANVILLE, VA 24541

WEAVER WAYSIDE FURNITURE
2031 W. MAIN STREET
DANVILLE, VA 24541

GREEN FRONT FURNITURE
316 N MAIN STREET
FARMVILLE, VA 23901

GREEN FRONT FURNITURE
STORE
1304 A SEVRIN WAY
STERLING, VA 20166

CAROLINA FURNITURE OF
WILLIAMSBURG
5425 RICHMOND ROAD
WILLIAMSBURG, VA 23188

WISCONSIN
BRASS LIGHT GALLERY, INC
131 S FIRST ST
MILWAUKEE, WI 53204

GREAT BRITAIN
HOME INTERIORS
PO BOX 97
HULL, EAST YORKSHIRE
ENGLAND

DESIGNER FABRICS
42 WELSH ROW
NANTWICH, CHESHIRE,
ENGLAND CW5 5EW

DRAPERY, THE
PO BOX 117
OLNEY, ENGLAND MK4 4ZZ

TOP SERVICE
CHURCH END HOUSE,
WHICHFORD
**SHIPSTON ON STOUR,
WARKSHIRE**, ENGLAND CV36
5PG

FABRICS & WALLPAPERS
DIRECT
HOWBECK LODGE, LONDON
ROAD
STEPELEY, CHESHIRE,
ENGLAND CW5 7JU

INDEX

"A" WINDOW TREATMENT CO, INC, 69, 342

800 CARPETS INC, 69, 342

828 TRADING CO, 216

A & H WAYSIDE FURNITURE, 70, 341

A & J AMAZIN, 82

A CLASSIC DESIGN - FURNITURE & ACCESSORIES, 72

A CRYSTAL COUNTRY, 199

A LOCK, 206, 240, 249

AA IMPORTS, 189

AA LAUN, 26, 30, 35, 38, 77, 82, 162, 189, 202, 229, 277, 313

ABBAKA, 177, 184

ABC DECORATIVE FABRICS, 72, 334

ABIGAILS, 82

ACACIA, 26, 41, 153, 169, 189, 198, 202, 234, 246, 252, 325

ACCENT, 26, 34, 47- 49, 53, 58, 61- 63, 67-68, 170, 189, 203, 239, 277

ACCENT FINE ART, 41

ACCENT GRAPHICS, 277

ACCENTRICS, 38, 80, 82, 116, 189, 229, 234, 246, 252, 273, 275

ACCENTS BY GARY PARLIN, 41, 82, 277

ACCESS, 24, 73, 120, 147, 189, 334

ACCESS CARPET, 73, 334

ACCESSORIES, 5, 19, 25, 41, 43, 45, 47-49, 53-54, 56-57, 59, 60, 63, 72, 73, 77, 80, 84, 89, 109, 130, 146, 149, 159, 177, 179, 185, 187, 189, 192, 194, 204, 205, 210, 222, 223, 229, 249, 257, 260, 265-267, 269-270, 272, 278, 281, 302, 304, 307, 311, 317, 324, 328, 331, 332

ACCESSORIES ABROAD, 189

ACCESSORIES INTL, 278

ACCESSORY ART, 25, 41, 82

ACE CRYSTAL, 195

ACROOT, 261

ACRYLIC FASHION, 82, 189

ACRYMET, 177, 184

ACTION BY LANE, 37, 70, 74, 77, 82, 94, 116, 128, 134, 138, 150, 159, 161, 162, 167, 173, 189, 194, 195, 211, 229, 232, 234, 240, 246, 250, 252, 270, 273, 275, 278, 279, 286, 293, 300, 302, 305, 310, 311, 313, 316, 320, 327

ADAM'S MULFORD, 82

ADDEN, 257

ADESSO, 41, 82

ADIA, 177, 184

ADJUSTABLE BOOKCASES, 257

ADJUSTA-POST, 189

ADO, 238, 242-244

AFGHANISTAN, 171, 333

AFTMANS FAUCETS, 177, 184

AGI, 257, 277

AGI INDUSTRIES, 277

AINSLEY LAMPS, 94, 199, 299, 300, 313

AKKO, 277

AL SHAVER, 70, 77

ALA (BAMMA) FOLK ART, 278

ALACARTE, 189

ALADDIN CARPET, 69, 90, 168, 213, 313, 319, 321

ALADDIN LIGHT LIFTS, 189

ALAN CAMPBELL, 189

ALAN FERGUSON ASSOCIATES, 73, 339

ALAN WHITE, 38, 41, 82, 121, 128, 189, 259, 278

ALBERT LOCK, 34, 77

ALEX SMITH, 211

ALEXANDER, 80, 85, 169, 189, 206, 234, 270, 278, 328, 339

ALEXANDER DIEZ, 278

ALEXANDER JULIAN, 82, 169, 189, 206, 234, 270

ALEXCRAFT, 305

ALEXVALE, 30, 30, 36, 38, 41, 82, 94, 116, 167, 189, 202, 206, 229, 265, 278, 286, 304, 305, 320

ALL CONTINENTAL, 286

ALLIBERT, 30, 36, 41, 63, 117, 143, 177, 184, 189, 198, 206, 257, 278, 302

ALLISON DIZE, 278

ALLISON PALMER, 82

ALLMARK, 206

ALLSEATING, 257

ALLUSIONS, 26, 35, 82, 189, 270, 286, 318, 327

ALMAN'S HOME FURNISHINGS, 74, 341

ALNO, 177, 184

ALPA PLUS, 206

ALVA MUSEUM REPLICAS, 300, 313

AMBIANCE, 33, 82, 189, 249, 270, 296, 328

AMCO, 257

AMEDEO DESIGNS, 82

AMERICAN ACCENTS, 74, 74

AMERICAN ART LIGHTING, 177, 184

AMERICAN BLIND AND WALLPAPER FACTORY, 75, 335

AMERICAN BRONZE, 189

AMERICAN CARPET MILLS, 27, 213

AMERICAN CHAIR & TABLE, 77, 82, 162, 202

AMERICAN CHINA, 177, 184

AMERICAN COUNTRY WEST, 143

AMERICAN CUT CRYSTAL, 313

AMERICAN DECOR, 189

AMERICAN DREW, 26, 26, 28-30, 35, 36, 38, 39, 41, 57, 70, 74, 76, 77, 80, 94, 102, 105, 108, 113, 116, 120, 121, 128, 131, 134, 137, 143, 150, 157, 159, 161, 162, 167, 169, 171, 175, 180, 188, 189, 195, 199, 202, 206, 211, 214-215, 222, 228, 229, 232, 234, 240, 245, 246, 249, 252, 262, 268, 270, 273, 275,

278, 284, 286, 288, 291,
296, 299, 300, 302, 304,
310-313, 316, 318, 320,
327, 330, 336, 340
AMERICAN DREW GALLERY,
76, 76
AMERICAN FURNITURE
GALLERY, 199, 228,
278
AMERICAN HERITAGE, 42, 82,
246, 249, 252, 278, 286,
291
AMERICAN IMPRESSIONS, 77,
82, 246, 252
AMERICAN LANTERN, 177, 184
AMERICAN LIGHTSOURCE, 34,
76, 336
AMERICAN MIRROR, 35, 42, 80,
82, 195, 199, 203, 206,
246, 252
AMERICAN OF HIGH POINT, 42,
42, 70, 80, 120, 131, 203,
229, 268, 278, 286, 299
AMERICAN OF MARTINSVILLE,
26, 28, 30, 35, 39, 42, 57,
70, 77, 82, 94, 113, 116,
120, 137, 150, 157, 159,
161, 167, 169, 189, 195,
199, 203, 206, 211, 214,
215, 222, 229, 234, 240,
249, 257, 270, 274, 275,
278, 286, 291, 299, 300,
302, 305, 311, 313, 316,
320, 330
AMERICAN REPRODUCTIONS,
70, 70
AMERICAN SILK, 238
AMERICAN STANDARD, 149,
177, 184
AMERICAN TEXTILES, 278
AMERICAN VICTORIAN, 94
AMERICAN WALLCOVERING
DISTRIBUTORS, 79,
342
AMERICAN WHIRLPOOL, 149
AMERICH, 177, 184
AMERICRAFT, 82
AMETEX FABRICS, 146, 151,
201, 242-244
AMINDO, 77, 82
AMIRAN, 27, 70, 77, 82
AMISCO, 26-27, 33-34, 39, 42, 82,
249, 278
AMISH COUNTRY
COLLECTION, 26, 42,
278
AMOTEK/USA, 257
AMP, 162
AMYX, 148, 206

ANDRE, 42, 77, 177, 184, 206,
246, 252, 278, 305, 318
ANDRE COLLECTION, 177, 184
ANDREA, 189, 222
ANDREW DUTTON, 31, 146
ANDREW KNOB & SON, 278
ANDREW PEARSON, 42, 42, 82,
162, 189, 203, 206, 270,
278, 313, 327
ANGELO BROS, 313
ANICHINI LENEIUS, 82
ANJU WOODRIDGE, 238,
242-244
ANNE AT HOME, 177, 184
ANSONIA, 29, 308
ANTIQUES, 25, 33, 84, 148, 171,
187, 200, 205
ANTIQUITIES PORCELAINS, 172
ANTLER DESIGN, 189
APACHEE, 261
AQUA BRASS, 177, 184
AQUARIUS MIRROR WORKS, 82
AQUATIC, 177, 184
AQUAWARE, 177, 184
ARAM HARDWARE, 177, 184
ARBEK, 26-26, 28, 42, 136, 189,
278, 293, 310
ARCADIA LIGHTING, 278
ARCADIAN, 77
ARCHIPED, 189
ARCHITECTURAL
MASTERWORKS, 189
ARCHITECTURAL METAL, 82
ARCTECNICA, 82
ARDLEY HALL, 26, 28, 33, 42, 77,
162, 189, 270, 278, 327
ARIEL OF FRANCE, 128, 189
ARLINGTON HOUSE, 36, 42, 195,
206, 278
ARMONIE ESSEBI, 300
ARMSTRONG, 28, 28, 35, 43, 70,
90, 195, 213, 261, 305,
313, 319, 321
ARNOLD GROUP, 257
ARNOLD PALMER, 82, 169, 211,
225, 270, 299, 306-307,
311, 327
ARQUATI, 80, 245
ARROW LOCK, 177, 184
ARROYO CRAFTSMAN, 223
ART, 5, 1, 25, 48, 53, 57, 73, 78,
81-83, 120, 157, 162,
166, 177, 184, 187, 190,
217, 223, 224, 229, 247,
251, 252, 270, 277, 280,
281, 286, 287, 299, 328,
338
ART & COMMERCE, 189
ART & FRAME, 189

ART CRAFT, 189
ART DE GALI, 189
ART FLO, 278, 286
ART GALLERY, 43, 120, 188, 189,
251, 278, 313, 338
ART HORIZONS, 189
ARTAGRAPH REPRODUCTIONS,
286, 313
ARTCRAFT LIGHTING, 177, 184
ARTE DE MEXICO, 43, 189, 249,
278
ARTE LORE, 278
ARTEMIDE, 166
ARTHUR & ASSOCIATES, 77
ARTIFACTS, 157
ARTISAN HOUSE, 25, 43, 80, 82,
189, 206, 270, 278, 313
ARTISAN LAMPS, 189
ARTISANS BRASS, 274, 275
ARTISANS GUILD, 80, 302
ARTISTIC BRASS, 177, 184
ARTISTIC LEATHER, 94
ARTISTICA, 43, 77, 82, 92, 157,
162, 189, 206, 249, 278,
327
ARTISTRY DESIGN, 211
ARTLEE FABRICS, 240, 268
ARTMARK, 31, 146, 159, 169,
238, 240, 249, 270, 278,
299
ARTMASTER STUDIOS, 25, 189,
222, 274, 286
ARTMAX, 82, 189, 270
ARTS BY ALEXANDER, 80, 339
AS YOU LIKE IT, 25, 43, 80, 92,
116, 120, 166, 189, 203,
206, 240, 268, 274, 275,
278, 286, 302, 311, 316,
330
ASHBOURNE, 31, 238, 299
ASHLEY, 26, 28, 30, 32-35, 38, 43,
57, 70, 74, 76-77, 81, 82,
162, 175, 178, 189, 232,
246, 258-259, 286, 320,
339
ASHLEY INTERIORS, 81, 339
ASHLEY MANOR, 38, 43, 70, 77,
162, 206, 278
ASHTON, 82, 189, 222
ASIART, 189
ASIL, 82
ASMARA RUGS, 159, 249
ASPEN, 26, 33, 35, 43, 313
ASTON GARRETT, 157
ATHENS, 26, 28, 33, 35, 38, 74,
82, 94, 120, 134, 167,
169, 175, 195, 203, 286,
313

ATHOL, 28, 30, 70, 77, 82, 113, 116, 120, 137, 148, 162, 167, 189, 199, 203, 206, 214, 234, 246, 252, 286, 291, 307, 311

ATHOL TABLE, 43, 70, 113, 148, 162, 167, 199, 203, 206, 307

ATILLA'S BAYSHORE, 189

ATLANTA GLASSCRAFTER, 162, 246, 252, 286, 300

ATLANTIC BENCH CO, 304

ATLANTIS, 11, 82

ATRIUM FURNITURE SHOWROOMS, 82, 339

AUSTIN, 25, 43, 77, 82, 92, 116, 128, 195, 274, 275, 278, 286, 291, 300, 307, 311, 313

AUTUMN GUILD, 80, 278

AVANTI, 206

AVENUE, 9-9, 32, 44, 49, 57, 59, 105, 145, 191, 192, 196, 207, 257, 277, 306, 335, 340, 343

AWARD, 242-244

AXI DESIGNS, 189

AYERS, 36, 43, 77, 305

AZROCK, 261

B & D DESIGNS, 278

B BERGER, 43, 146, 157, 238, 268, 278, 299

B&W HARDWARE, 177, 184

BABY GUESS, 82

BACI MIRRORS, 177, 184

BAILEY & GRIFFIN, 31, 43, 114, 240, 270

BAKER, 5, 1, 25-26, 28, 31, 33, 38-39, 43, 81, 86, 94, 98, 100-102, 112, 114, 137, 159, 160, 180, 188, 189, 195, 206, 240, 249, 296, 309, 322, 336, 340, 341

BAKER FURNITURE FACTORY STORE, 86, 341

BAKER GALLERY, 86, 188, 336

BALDWIN, 25, 43, 44, 59, 72, 82, 87, 92, 114, 116, 131, 159, 162, 166, 167, 172, 177, 184, 196, 199, 203, 229, 234, 246, 249, 252, 270, 299, 300, 307, 308, 313, 316, 318, 320, 336

BALDWIN BRASS, 70, 72, 87, 92, 114, 116, 131, 159, 166, 167, 189, 196, 203, 229, 234, 246, 249, 252, 270, 278, 299, 300, 307, 308, 313, 316, 318, 320, 336

BALDWIN BRASS FACTORY OUTLET, 87, 336

BALDWIN CLOCKS, 43, 70, 82, 199, 278

BALDWIN HARDWARE & ACCESSORIES, 177, 184

BALI, 39, 75, 166, 178, 239, 252, 254, 264, 295, 299, 315, 324

BALTA, 28, 172, 213, 261

BAMBOO ODYSSEY, 157, 206, 278

BANKS COLDSTONE, 44, 114, 278

BARCALOUNGER, 35, 37-39, 44, 70, 74, 77, 82, 87-88, 92, 94, 96, 105, 107, 108, 114, 116, 120, 121, 131, 150, 157, 159, 162, 167, 171, 173, 189, 194, 196, 199, 203, 206, 229, 240, 249, 265, 268, 270, 274, 275, 278, 284, 286, 299, 300, 302, 304, 305, 311, 313, 316, 320, 342

BARCALOUNGER GALLERIES, 87, 342

BARCLAY, 34, 38, 44, 57, 82, 128, 177, 184, 189

BARCLAY PLUMBING, 177, 184

BARFIELD RECLINERS, 148

BARLOW TYRIE, 29-30, 34, 36-38, 189, 313, 318

BARN DOOR, 26, 27, 29-31, 35, 36, 44, 70, 77, 162, 173, 203, 229, 230, 278, 286, 305

BAROODY SPENCE, 36

BARRETT, 28, 213

BARRON'S, 88, 335

BARROW, 31, 32, 145, 146, 238, 242-244, 278, 299, 309

BARTSON, 201

BASHIAN CARPETS, 116

BASHIAN RUGS, 44, 278

BASIC, 5, 1, 2, 15, 34, 70, 189

BASIC FURNITURE STYLES, 70

BASIC SOURCE, 189

BASSETT, 25-28, 34-35, 37-39, 44, 56, 60, 70, 71, 79-80, 82, 93-94, 105, 106, 110, 137, 150, 151, 153, 159, 162, 163, 167-169, 173-176, 189, 197, 200, 204, 207, 228-230, 232, 234, 246, 247, 252, 266, 268, 270, 274, 275, 278, 281, 286, 291, 292, 297, 299-300, 302, 303, 306-307, 310, 316, 318, 320, 327

BASTA SOLE, 30, 36, 171, 189, 278

BATES & BATES SINKS, 177, 184

BATES FABRICS, 240

BAUER LAMP, 34, 83, 166, 247, 252, 278, 286

BAUER LIGHTING, 206

BDI, 83, 189

BDT, 278, 286

BEACH, 44, 56, 157, 189, 249, 265, 296, 310, 334, 335

BEACHLEY UPHOLSTERY, 206, 229

BEACON HILL, 89, 188, 189, 270, 336

BEACON HILL FACTORY OUTLET, 89, 188, 336

BEAN STATION, 35, 35, 37, 38, 70, 77, 162, 196, 203, 206, 270, 278

BEARDEN BROTHERS CARPET AND TEXTILES, 89, 334

BEAUCHAMP, 189

BEAUFURN, 35, 162

BEAULIEU, 28, 90, 261, 313, 319

BEAUTYREST BY SIMMONS, 293, 293

BEAVER CARPETS, 28, 90, 334

BEDROOM BOUTIQUES, 300

BEECHBROOK, 30, 45, 134, 148, 173, 175, 203

BEKA CASTING, 189

BELLE, 31, 35, 201

BEMCO, 26, 45, 150, 173, 175

BENCHCRAFT, 34, 37-39, 45, 70, 74, 77, 83, 94, 128, 143, 162, 194, 198, 199, 203, 229, 265, 300, 310

BENICIA, 26, 27, 77, 83, 92, 162, 189, 196, 199, 203, 206, 247, 252, 266, 278, 286, 291, 300, 302, 305, 310, 313, 316

BENNETT & CO, 189

BENNINGTON PINE, 70

BENNISON, 299

BENTLEY DESIGNS OF CALIFORNIA, 94

BENTWOOD, 28, 35, 45, 153, 203, 278

BERCO, 257

BERK, 194

BERKELEY, 25, 26, 30, 31, 45, 94, 114, 189

BERKLINE, 33, 35, 37, 38, 70, 74, 77, 83, 92, 96, 120, 128,

150, 162, 167, 189, 196, 199, 203, 215, 266, 278, 284, 286, 291, 302, 311, 320, 327

BERKSHIRE BRASS, 77

BERKSHIRE/DRESHER, 143

BERNARD'S, 247, 252

BERNHARDT, 26-26, 28, 30-31, 34-35, 39, 45, 90, 94, 96, 98, 99, 114, 116, 134, 159, 162, 171, 180, 189, 196, 234, 247, 249, 257, 268, 270, 278, 291, 296, 299, 302, 306-307, 313, 322, 327, 336

BERNHARDT GALLERY, 90, 96, 188, 336

BERRYHILL PRINTS, 247, 252

BESA LIGHTING, 177, 184

BEST CHAIR, 128, 134, 169, 203, 247, 252, 278

BEST DESIGN, 83

BESTAR, 26, 33, 45, 162, 196, 206, 278

BETH WEISSMAN, 45, 159, 189, 197, 206, 274, 275, 305, 330

BETSY CAMERON, 234, 311

BETTER HOMES FURNITURE OUTLET, 91, 336

BETTIS BROOKE CO, 189

BEVAN FUNNEL, 45, 77

BIBI CONTINENTAL, 189

BIG FISH, 172, 189

BIG SKY, 83, 143, 189

BIGELOW, 28, 90, 213, 261, 305

BIGGS, 240

BILTMORE FURNITURE GALLERIES, 91, 335

BIRGE, 31, 276

BISCIOTTI DESIGNS, 83

BISHOPS, 31, 146

BLACK FOREST CLOCKS, 148

BLACK'S FURNITURE COMPANY, INC, 92, 339

BLACKHAWK, 26, 45, 77, 83, 293

BLACKSMITH SHOP, 29-30, 39, 45, 70, 74, 77, 83, 94, 114, 116, 121, 150, 159, 161, 162, 169, 174, 189, 196, 199, 203, 206, 211, 214, 229, 232, 234, 245, 247, 249, 252, 257, 268, 270, 274, 275, 278, 284, 286, 296, 300, 302, 304, 307, 310, 311, 313, 316, 327

BLACKWELDER INDUSTRIES, INC, 93, 342

BLANCO PLUMBING, 177, 184

BLAST, 83

BLAUTEX, 238

BLINDS DIRECT, 95, 343

BLONDER, 240

BLOOMCRAFT, 31, 201, 238, 242-244, 269, 309

BLOWING ROCK FURNITURE COMPANY, 95, 341

BLUE RIDGE, 28, 171, 213, 261

BLUFF CITY, 313

BMC FURNITURE, 211

BOB TIMBERLAKE, 25, 26, 28, 38, 58, 64, 67, 74, 83, 105, 120, 143, 161, 162, 169, 189, 206, 211, 214, 221, 222, 225, 227, 229, 247, 252, 270, 274, 275, 278, 291, 299, 305, 311, 320

BOBBO, 189

BOLING, 29, 29-31, 33, 38, 46, 70, 80, 94, 131, 148, 150, 162, 172, 199, 257, 270, 278, 287, 300, 302, 313

BONART, 157

BONAVITA CRIBS, 83

BONITA FURNITURE GALLERIES, 96, 336

BORKHOLDER, 25-26, 31, 33, 38, 39, 46, 240, 313

BOSSENDORFER (PIANOS), 37, 94

BOSTON ROCKER, 189

BOUSSAC, 26, 32, 189, 238, 268, 273, 318

BOUVET HARDWARE, 177, 184

BOWEN, 32, 58, 137, 191, 252, 310

BOYD, 26, 28, 33, 46, 83, 189, 203, 259, 278, 313

BOYLES, 8, 97, 99, 101-102, 141, 188, 336, 338, 339

BOYLES CLEARANCE CENTER I, 96, 336

BOYLES CLEARANCE CENTER II, 97, 336

BOYLES DISTINCTIVE FURNITURE, 98, 335

BOYLES DREXEL HERITAGE, 98, 335

BOYLES FURNITURE (ON BUSINESS 85), 100, 100

BOYLES FURNITURE (ON GREENSBORO ROAD), 99, 99

BOYLES GALLERIES, 100, 336

BOYLES ORIGINAL COUNTRY SHOP AND CLEARANCE CENTER IN HICKORY, 101, 336

BOYLES SHOWCASE GALLERY, 102, 336

BRADBURN, 80, 189, 270, 278

BRADCO CHAIR, 83, 313

BRADINGTON COURT, 278

BRADINGTON YOUNG, 33, 34, 37, 46, 70, 77, 80, 83, 92, 94, 98, 100, 105, 116, 120, 131, 138, 159, 167, 180, 188, 189, 196, 206, 214, 229, 232, 240, 247, 249, 252, 266, 268, 278, 284, 286, 302, 305, 306, 312, 313, 317, 320, 327, 330, 336

BRADINGTON YOUNG GALLERY, 103, 336

BRADSTON HURRICANE, 77

BRADY, 26, 28, 31, 34-35, 37-38, 46, 70, 77, 83, 94, 120, 150, 189, 203, 278, 286, 299, 313

BRAEMORE, 110, 238, 242-244, 269

BRANDON LAMPS, 134

BRANDT, 32, 150, 199

BRASCH ASSOCIATES, 104, 335

BRASS BARON, 304

BRASS BED SHOPPE, 104, 104, 343

BRASS BED SHOPPE, A, 104, 343

BRASS BEDS OF AMERICA, 94, 114, 150, 240, 274, 275

BRASS BEDS OF VIRGINIA, 159, 249

BRASS COLLECTION, 318

BRASS CRAFT, 196

BRASS LIGHT GALLERY, INC, 105, 343

BRASS ROOTS, 70, 206

BRASSCRAFTERS, 25, 80, 120, 134, 166, 189, 196, 199, 206, 278, 286, 313

BRAXTON, 36, 46, 70, 77, 81, 83, 92, 94, 116, 120, 143, 150, 153, 159, 162, 173, 196, 203, 206, 229, 234, 240, 249, 266, 268, 278, 286, 305, 310, 320, 325, 327

BRAXTON CULLER, 46, 70, 77, 81, 83, 92, 94, 116, 120, 143, 150, 159, 162, 173, 196, 203, 206, 229, 234,

240, 249, 266, 268, 278, 286, 305, 310, 320, 327
BRENTWOOD MANOR, 105, 343
BRETT AUSTIN, 189, 278
BREWSTER, 32, 142
BRITISH COLLECTORS, 83, 189
BRITISH TRADITIONS, 77, 83, 189, 270, 327
BROADWAY COLLECTION, 177, 184
BROAN BATH CABINETS & RANGE HOODS, 177, 184
BROOKLINE FURNITURE FACTORY SHOWROOM, 106, 339
BROOKS, 37, 313
BROOKWOOD, 38, 173, 206
BROWN JORDAN, 26, 31, 35, 36, 38, 46, 70, 77, 83, 92, 94, 101-102, 114, 131, 137, 162, 189, 196, 198, 203, 206, 234, 240, 266, 268, 278, 286, 301, 302, 305, 313, 330
BROWN STREET, 26, 33, 75, 120, 137, 171, 189, 206, 222, 229, 247, 252, 291, 295, 301, 305, 313, 320
BROYHILL, 1, 26, 28, 31, 34-35, 38, 39, 70, 74, 77, 83, 92, 94, 96, 105, 106, 116, 128, 131, 137, 150, 161, 162, 167, 169, 171, 173, 175, 180, 188-189, 196, 199, 203, 206, 211, 214, 228, 229, 232, 234, 240, 245, 247, 249, 252, 266, 268, 270, 278, 291, 302, 305, 313, 317, 320, 336
BROYHILL SHOWCASE GALLERY, 106, 188, 336
BRUCE L ROBERTSON, 77
BRUCE WOOD, 213, 319
BRUETON, 46, 257
BRUNSCHWIG & FILS, 32, 114, 146, 189, 203, 210, 238, 240, 268, 270, 273, 278, 299, 318
BUCKS COUNTY, 92, 171, 306-307
BUDORR CLASSIC FURNITURE, 313
BUILTRIGHT, 29, 30, 34, 46, 77, 83, 120, 148, 169, 171, 173, 199, 240, 247, 252, 270, 278, 292, 311, 313
BULLUCK'S, 107, 342

BURCH, 146
BURLINGTON, 28, 32, 94, 201, 213, 242-244, 261, 304, 335
BURLINGTON FURNITURE, 108, 335
BURNS, 286
BURRIS, 37, 46, 77, 94, 305, 313
BURROUGHS, 257
BURTCO, 28, 213, 261
BURTON REPRODUCTIONS, 25, 249
BUSBIN LAMP, 83
BUSH, 26, 29, 30, 35, 37, 39, 46, 52, 83, 286
BUTLER, 29, 30, 33, 37, 46, 70, 77, 80, 83, 94, 105, 116, 162, 173, 189, 199, 203, 206, 229, 247, 249, 252, 270, 278, 286, 313
BUYING & DESIGN, 286
C & M FURNITURE, 199
C&M TABLES, 83
CABIN CRAFT, 28, 90, 169, 211, 213, 261, 313, 319, 321
CABOT GALLERY, 108, 108
CABOT WRENN, 30, 157
CACHET, 77
CADWELL, 286
CAL BEAR, 77, 80, 83, 278
CALADIUM, 28, 213, 261
CALAIS, 261
CALCRYSTAL HARDWARE, 177, 184
CALDWELL CHAIR, 83, 247, 252, 311
CALDWELL FURNITURE CLEARANCE CENTER, 109, 341
CALICO CORNERS, 32, 109, 110, 343
CALICO CORNERS EXCLUSIVE, 110
CALIFORNIA FAUCETS, 177, 184
CALIFORNIA KIDS, 83
CALIFORNIA UMBRELLA, 196, 313
CALLAWAY, 28, 213
CAL-STYLE, 28, 30, 31, 70, 77, 80, 83, 92, 116, 161, 162, 173, 189, 229, 278, 286, 301
CAMBRIDGE, 34, 47, 70, 83, 120, 166, 173, 189, 199, 206, 211, 222, 242-244, 247, 249, 252, 270, 278, 318, 328

CAMBRIDGE LAMPS, 47, 70, 77, 83, 166, 189, 199, 211, 270, 278, 318
CAMPBELL/CRAVEN FURNITURE, 110, 342
CANADEL, 28, 47, 83, 110, 188, 189, 203, 249, 278, 286, 296, 299, 327, 336
CANADEL GALLERY, 110, 188, 336
CANAL DOVER, 47, 77, 83, 161, 203, 206, 286
CANDELLA LIGHTING, 47, 278
CANDILES TA, 189
CANE & REED, 83, 143, 286, 313
CANNON, 111-111, 115, 179, 320
CANNON VILLAGE, 111-111, 115, 320
CANTERBURY, 249, 278
CANWOOD, 26, 33, 83, 208
CAPE CRAFTSMEN, 83, 278, 328
CAPEL, 28, 28, 47, 94, 172, 203, 266, 278, 286, 301, 304, 305, 313, 328, 342
CAPEL MILL OUTLET, 28, 112, 342
CAPITAL ASAM, 32, 240, 268
CAPITOL LEATHER, 47, 83, 278, 320
CAPITOL VICTORIAN, 213, 292
CAPRI FURNITURE, 305
CAPRIS, 26
CAREFREE, 32, 75
CAREY LIND, 32, 175, 276, 299
CARLETON V, 238
CARLTON, 32, 35, 47, 70, 71, 77, 83, 92, 114, 150, 173, 197, 199, 206, 247, 252, 270, 286, 292, 302, 318
CARLTON McLENDON, 47, 70, 71, 77, 83, 92, 150, 173, 199, 206, 247, 252, 270, 286, 292, 302
CAROL MORRISON'S, 77
CAROLE, 32, 146, 242-244, 299
CAROLINA BUSINESS, 257
CAROLINA CARRIERS, 112, 339
CAROLINA CHOICE, 134, 211, 313
CAROLINA CLASSICS, 310
CAROLINA COLLECTION, 94
CAROLINA COUNTRY, 148
CAROLINA CRAFTSMEN, 206
CAROLINA FURNITURE, 26, 33, 35, 47, 115, 120, 143, 150, 175, 247, 252, 313, 343
CAROLINA FURNITURE DIRECT, 113, 343

Index

CAROLINA FURNITURE OF
WILLIAMSBURG, 113,
343
CAROLINA FURNITURE
WORLD, 115, 343
CAROLINA GLASS, 92
CAROLINA HERITAGE, 77, 83
CAROLINA INTERIORS'-
CANNON VILLAGE,
115
CAROLINA MATTRESS GUILD,
117, 117, 339
CAROLINA MATTRESS GUILD
FACTORY OUTLET,
117, 339
CAROLINA MILLS, 302
CAROLINA MIRROR, 25, 35, 47,
70, 74, 77, 80, 83, 94,
116, 120, 134, 150, 159,
161, 162, 166, 169, 189,
196, 199, 203, 206, 211,
222, 229, 232, 234, 240,
247, 249, 252, 270, 274,
275, 278, 286, 292, 301,
307, 310, 311, 313, 317,
320
CAROLINA PATIO
WAREHOUSE, 117, 334
CAROLINA ROCKERS, 148
CAROLINA TABLE OF
HICKORY, 278
CAROLINA TABLES, 47, 70, 92,
120, 199, 206, 268, 270,
286
CAROLINA'S CHOICE, 278
CAROLINA/SHERRILL TABLES,
302
CAROUSEL CARPET, 211, 268
CARPET EXPRESS, 28, 118, 334
CARPET FAX, 211
CARPET OUTLET, 28, 118, 335
CARR & CO, 70, 77
CARRIER, 12, 12, 112, 117, 120,
124, 135, 151, 161, 162,
169, 170, 178, 179, 202,
209, 211, 222, 223, 236,
246, 265, 267, 313, 317,
319
CARSON WIND CHIMES, 148
CARSON'S, 26, 31, 38, 70, 77, 83,
92, 94, 116, 150, 159,
162, 189, 196, 203, 206,
211, 222, 229, 234, 247,
249, 252, 268, 270, 278,
286, 305-307, 317, 327
CARSONS GALLERY, 119, 188,
336
CARTER, 47, 63, 70, 77, 80, 83,
120, 130, 146, 162, 189,

196, 203, 206, 229, 268,
278, 286, 301, 305
CARTER CONTEMPORARY, 47,
83, 130, 286, 301
CARTWRIGHT, 33
CARVER'S GUILD, 47, 80, 172,
189, 249, 270, 278, 286
CASA BIQUE, 26, 28, 35, 47, 70,
77, 81, 83, 92, 94, 116,
137, 157, 159, 162, 189,
196, 199, 203, 214, 229,
234, 240, 249, 266, 270,
274, 275, 278, 286, 292,
296, 299, 301, 305, 306,
310, 313, 317, 318, 320,
327, 330
CASA RUSTICA, 189, 270
CASA STRADAVARI, 102
CASABLANCA FAN, 223
CASAFINA, 189
CASAMANIA HOME OFFICE,
257
CASARD, 134, 196, 286
CASCADE, 28, 213, 261
CASE CASARD, 286
CASEY COLLECTION, 189
CASSADY, 83
CAST CLASSICS, 75, 83, 189, 198
CASTILLIAN, 166, 189, 196, 199,
206, 274, 275, 286
CASUAL, 8, 34, 37, 41, 42, 47,
50-52, 56-57, 59, 64, 68,
74, 77, 78, 83, 114, 116,
143, 155, 157, 159, 162,
166, 168, 169, 172, 173,
189, 190, 203, 222, 249,
259-261, 268, 278, 286,
287, 299, 301, 302, 305,
313, 317, 318, 327, 330
CASUAL CARPET, 168
CASUAL CRATES, 173, 206
CASUAL CREATIONS, 48, 278
CASUAL LAMP, 70, 77, 166, 189,
196, 199, 222, 270, 278,
313, 318
CASUSALCRAFT, 302
CATNAPPER, 35, 38, 48, 203, 278,
305
CATSKILL CRAFTSMEN, 83
CAYTON FURNITURE INC, 119,
342
CBK LTD, 286
CBS IMPORTS, 189
CCM, 189
CEBU, 36, 81, 94, 143, 157, 189,
234, 247, 252, 325
CEDANNA GROUP, 83
CEDAR, 20, 25, 29, 104, 120, 213,
261, 304, 341, 343

CEDAR ROCK HOME
FURNISHINGS, 25, 120
CELLINI, 206
CENTRAL WAREHOUSE
FURNITURE, 121, 339
CENTRE COURT FURNITURE
MALL, 122, 335
CENTRUM GROUP, 77
CENTURY, 26, 28, 34-35, 38, 42,
44, 48-49, 61, 83, 92, 94,
96, 99, 102, 112, 116,
131, 159, 160, 162, 180,
192, 214, 227, 234, 249,
278, 286, 287, 294, 296,
297, 302, 312, 316-318,
330, 335-337
CENTURY FACTORY OUTLET,
122, 188, 336
CENTURY FURNITURE
GALLERY, 123, 188
CENTURY/HICKORY CHAIR
OUTLET, 123, 335
CHADWICK LEATHER, 70, 94
CHAIR, 1, 5, 6, 17, 20, 25-26, 29,
31, 34, 36, 39, 46, 49, 52,
60, 65, 70-71, 77, 80, 82,
92, 94, 100, 105-107,
110, 114, 116, 120-121,
128, 134, 136, 148, 150,
151, 157, 161, 167,
173-174, 180, 185-186,
191, 192, 196, 199-200,
202, 206-207, 211, 232,
238, 240, 241, 247,
249-250, 252-253, 257,
270, 271, 278, 284,
286-287, 299, 301-302,
311, 313-314, 317-318,
320, 327-328, 331, 335
CHAIR CO, 30-31, 37, 83, 121,
169, 173, 204
CHAIR DESIGN, 83, 157
CHAIRCRAFT, 70, 83, 94, 114,
159, 167, 196, 240, 301,
302, 305, 313
CHAIRWORKS, 34, 37, 83, 189,
278, 327
CHALLENGER INDUSTRIES, 28,
213
CHALLENGER LAMPS, 196
CHANDELIERS, 42, 45, 48, 83,
177, 185, 206
CHAPEL HILL, 38, 48, 206
CHAPMAN, 25, 26, 30, 31, 34-36,
39, 48, 70, 77, 81, 83, 92,
114, 116, 131, 159, 166,
177, 184, 189, 203, 223,
234, 240, 247, 249, 252,

268, 270, 278, 305, 307, 318, 320, 328, 330
CHARISMA CHAIRS, 70, 150, 173, 196, 203
CHARLES ADRIAN, 77, 189
CHARLES BARONE, 32
CHARLES HARLAND, 37, 94, 301
CHARLES SADEK, 81, 166, 189, 247, 252
CHARLES SEROUYA, 81
CHARLES W JACOBSEN, 28, 124, 199, 343
CHARLES W JACOBSEN, INC, 124, 343
CHARLES WAREHOUSE RUGS, 134
CHARLESTON CARPETS, 28, 213
CHARLESTON FORGE, 36, 39, 48, 70, 74, 77, 81, 83, 94, 102, 110, 116, 120, 137, 143, 157, 169, 172, 189, 194, 203, 206, 214, 229, 234, 240, 247, 249, 252, 266, 268, 270, 278, 286, 292, 296, 299, 301, 306, 307, 310, 311, 318, 320, 327
CHARLOTTE COLLECTION, 257
CHARLTON, 70, 84, 114
CHART HOUSE IMPORTS, 278
CHARTER HOUSE, 32, 173
CHARTER TABLE, 36, 48, 70, 77, 83, 162, 196, 211, 312
CHATHAM, 29-31, 36-38, 46, 70, 92, 94, 114, 134, 161, 162, 169, 173, 196, 199, 211, 232, 268, 270, 274, 275, 286, 295, 301, 302, 311, 313
CHATHAM COUNTY, 29-31, 37, 38, 77, 83, 92, 94, 114, 134, 150, 161, 162, 169, 189, 196, 199, 203, 211, 229, 232, 268, 270, 274, 275, 278, 286, 301, 302, 311, 313
CHATHAM NOVELTY, 70, 150, 173, 203
CHATHAM REPRODUCTIONS, 77, 189, 278
CHELSEA CLOCK, 278
CHELSEA HOUSE, 48, 114, 116, 137, 159, 189, 240, 249, 268, 299, 318, 320, 322
CHERRY CREEK GLASS SINKS, 177, 184
CHERRY HILL FURNITURE & INTERIORS, 124, 339
CHERRY POND, 83, 189, 278

CHICKEN/EGG, 83
CHILDCRAFT, 26, 28, 48, 94, 190, 194, 206, 301, 302
CHINA SEA TRADER, 313
CHINA TRADERS LAMPS, 169
CHINESE, 11, 66, 149
CHINESE ANTIQUES, 171
CHINESE HOOK RUGS, 172
CHINESE NEEDLEPOINT RUGS, 172
CHRIS STONE, 32, 238, 242-244
CHRISHAWN, 83, 278
CHRISTIAN MOSSO, 92
CHRISTOPHER HYLAN, 190
CHROMCRAFT, 30, 31, 48, 70, 74, 78, 92, 94, 116, 120, 159, 161, 162, 169, 175, 190, 196, 203, 229, 234, 240, 245, 247, 249, 252, 268, 270, 274, 275, 278, 286, 301, 302, 311, 313, 320, 327
CIFIAL FAUCETS, 177, 184
CITATION, 28, 90, 213, 261, 319
CJC, 190
CL LIGHTING, 286
CLAIRE MURRAY, 278
CLAREMONT DESIGNS, 128
CLARENCE HOUSE, 32, 48, 114, 190, 238, 240, 268, 273
CLARIDGE MANOR, 70, 78, 199, 206
CLARK CASUAL, 30, 33, 36, 48, 70, 74, 78, 81, 83, 114, 116, 143, 159, 162, 169, 172, 190, 196, 199, 203, 206, 249, 268, 270, 278, 286, 299, 301, 302, 305, 317, 327, 330
CLASSIC ART, 190, 247, 252
CLASSIC GALLERY, 37, 38, 48, 70, 78, 92, 94, 162, 199, 203, 206, 229, 240, 268, 278
CLASSIC GEORGIAN, 190, 229, 278, 286, 306, 307, 313
CLASSIC LEATHER, 33, 34, 48, 70, 72, 74, 78, 83, 94, 96, 105, 110, 114, 120, 125, 150, 159, 160, 162, 167, 173, 188, 190, 199, 203, 229, 234, 247, 249, 252, 266, 268, 270, 278, 286, 296, 299, 301, 302, 313, 317, 318, 320, 322, 327, 337
CLASSIC LEATHER GALLERY, 125, 188, 337
CLASSIC LIGHTING, 190, 223

CLASSIC ORIENTAL RUGS, 28, 28
CLASSIC RATTAN, 26, 31, 33-36, 38, 48, 70, 78, 83, 92, 94, 143, 150, 159, 162, 196, 199, 203, 214, 229, 240, 249, 278, 286, 292, 301, 305, 317, 327
CLASSIC TRADITIONS, 38, 48, 81, 199, 206, 278
CLASSICO, 286
CLAUDE GABLE, 196
CLAYTON & CO, 190
CLAYTON MARCUS, 39, 49, 57, 70, 78, 83, 92, 94, 105, 116, 120, 126, 138, 150, 161, 162, 167, 169, 188, 190, 196, 203, 206, 215, 229, 232, 234, 240, 266, 270, 274, 275, 278, 286, 292, 301, 306, 311, 313, 317, 320, 327, 337
CLAYTON MARCUS GALLERY, 126, 188, 337
CLEVELAND LAMP, 70, 78
CLIFTON ART, 134
CLINE QUEST, 83
CLOVER, 190, 196, 274, 275, 305
CLOVERHURST, 278, 286
CLYDE PEARSON, 71, 94, 106, 120, 150, 160, 190, 196, 199, 249, 270, 274, 275, 287, 292, 296, 305
CM FURNITURE, 30, 36, 38, 47, 78, 161, 196, 206, 278, 286, 301, 313
CMI, 83
COCHRANE, 26, 26-32, 36, 38, 49, 70, 74, 78, 83, 92, 94, 96, 105, 120, 126, 131, 134, 137, 150, 161, 162, 167, 171, 173, 188, 190, 199, 203, 206, 211, 214, 229, 232, 234, 247, 252, 266, 270, 286, 292, 301, 311, 313, 317, 327, 337
COCHRANE GALLERY, 126, 188, 337
COCO ISLAND, 278
COFFEY DISCOUNT FURNITURE, 127, 335
COHAMA RIVERDALE, 238
COJA LEATHER, 49, 70, 78, 162, 206, 278
COLDWELL CHAIR, 136
COLEFAX & FOWLER, 238
COLFAX FURNITURE, 127, 237, 336

Index

COLGATE BABY MATTRESS, 27, 92
COLLAGE/KALEIDOSCOPE, 238
COLLECTIBLES, 81, 148, 187, 280, 287, 300, 304
COLLECTIONS '85, 190
COLLEZIONE EUROPA, 83, 103, 128, 136, 190, 278, 286
COLLINGWOOD, 26, 28, 30, 31, 36, 105, 114, 206
COLLINS & AIKMAN, 32, 238
COLONIAL, 26, 28, 29, 31, 35, 36, 63, 65, 67, 70, 78, 83, 94, 105, 114, 116, 137, 150, 159, 162, 171, 172, 177, 184, 196, 203, 211, 229, 234, 247, 249, 252, 278, 286, 296, 305, 310-312, 318, 320, 327
COLONIAL BRONZE, 177, 184
COLONIAL CANDLE OF CAPE COD, 301
COLONIAL FURNITURE, 31, 35, 49, 120, 159, 162, 234, 249, 278, 296, 301, 310, 311
COLONIAL HEIRLOOMS, 196
COLONIAL MILLS, 28, 94, 172, 211
COLONIAL SOLID CHERRY, 320
COLONY HOUSE, 70, 78, 196
COLONY METALSMITH, 177, 184
COLOR HOUSE, 32, 175, 276
COLOREL BLINDS, 128, 334
COLUMBIA, 14, 28, 213, 231
COLUMBUS, 28, 32, 56, 69, 213
COMFORT DESIGNS, 27, 38, 39, 49, 70, 78, 81, 162, 190, 206, 229, 270, 274, 275, 278, 286, 305, 318, 327
COMFORT ZONE, 128, 128
COMFORTEX, 239
COMMONWEALTH CONTRACT, 33, 313
CONANT BALL, 49, 70, 78, 94, 114, 159, 162, 278
CONCEPTS, 34, 44, 70, 78, 135, 196, 211
CONCEPTS DESIGNER RUGS, 135
CONCINNITY FAUCETS, 177, 184
CONCORD, 49, 144, 177, 184, 242-244, 261, 335
CONCORD FANS, 177, 184
CONESTOGA WOOD, 36, 49, 78, 83

CONGOLEUM, 213, 261, 313, 319, 321
CONNECTICUT CURTAIN COMPANY, 129, 334
CONNOISSEUR, 171
CONOVER, 30, 33, 35-38, 41, 48-49, 51, 54, 56, 58, 67, 70, 78, 83, 85, 105, 114, 116, 120, 121, 131, 138, 162, 167, 172, 190, 192, 196, 203, 229, 268, 270, 278, 280, 287, 302, 305-306, 327, 335
CONQUEST, 28, 168, 213, 261
CONSO, 151, 190, 201
CONSOLIDATED TEXTILES, 28, 213
CONTAINER MARKETING, 83
CONTEMPO ARTS, 83, 190, 313
CONTEMPORARY COLLECTIONS, 51, 51
CONTEMPORARY FURNITURE DESIGNS, 206
CONTEMPORARY GALLERY, 130, 130
CONTEMPORARY SHELLS, 94, 114, 196
CONTINENTAL ACCENTS, 229
CONTINUUM, 257
COOK FURNITURE, 134
COOPER CLASSICS, 78, 83, 190, 222, 249, 278, 286, 299, 301, 311, 327
COPPER CANYON, 190
CORBETT, 177, 184, 190, 223
CORBETT LIGHTING, 177, 184
CORHAM, 286
CORNELISON SILK TREE, 286
CORNER HUTCH FURNITURE, THE, 131, 342
COROLLA, 26, 33, 247, 252
CORONA, 49, 81, 190, 199, 206, 301, 326
CORONET, 28, 199, 213, 261, 321
CORSICAN, 26, 27, 49, 70, 78, 83, 92, 94, 161, 190, 199, 229, 240, 268, 278, 286, 299, 302, 327
CORTRON LAMPS, 71
COSMOPOLITAN PIANOS, 301
COTTAGE PINE, 78, 83
COULTER, 32, 146, 278, 299
COUNCILL, 26-26, 28, 30-31, 33, 38, 49, 83, 92, 94, 98, 100-102, 105, 107, 114, 116, 120, 131, 137, 159, 167, 169, 171, 172, 180, 188, 190, 203, 229, 234, 238, 240, 247, 249, 252,

257, 266, 268, 278, 284, 286, 296, 301, 302, 304, 307, 320, 327, 330
COUNCILL CRAFTSMEN, 26, 26, 33, 36, 38, 92, 94, 100, 102, 105, 114, 116, 120, 131, 159, 167, 171, 172, 188, 190, 203, 229, 234, 238, 240, 247, 249, 252, 257, 268, 278, 284, 286, 296, 302, 304, 320, 330
COUNTRY AFFAIR/ELDEN, 249
COUNTRY CONCEPTS, 70, 78
COUNTRY EXPRESSIONS, 173
COUNTRY LIFE DESIGNS, 32
COUNTRY MANOR, 70, 78
COUNTRY ORIGINALS, 83, 92, 286
COUNTRY REPRODUCTIONS, 75, 134, 148, 200
COUNTRY TRADITIONS, 190
COUNTRY WOODS, 315
COUNTY LINE, 44, 278
COUNTY SEAT, 70, 78, 173, 196, 203, 222, 313
COUNTY SEAT COPIES COLLECTION, 222
COURISTAN, 28, 49, 105, 116, 132, 188, 190, 211, 226, 337
COURISTAN FACTORY OUTLET, 132, 188, 337
COURTLEIGH, 162, 190, 318
COVENT GARDEN, 304
COVINGTON, 32, 49, 145, 201, 238, 242-244, 309
COWTAN & TOUT, 32, 49, 190, 240, 273, 278
COX, 26, 38, 49, 64, 70, 78, 83, 94, 116, 159, 162, 190, 196, 199, 203, 206, 214, 222, 229, 234, 240, 247, 249, 252, 268, 270, 274, 275, 278, 286, 299, 301, 302, 306, 307, 311, 313, 317, 327
COX BOUDOIR CHAIRS, 94
CR LAINE, 30, 34, 38, 83, 92, 116, 120, 132, 138, 167, 188, 190, 194, 206, 211, 266, 279, 287, 292, 320, 327, 337
CR LAINE GALLERY, 132, 188, 337
CRAFT MARK, 36, 38, 169
CRAFTED, 42, 46, 48, 57, 62, 65, 227, 322
CRAFTER, 261

CRAFTIQUE, 25, 26, 28, 29, 31, 35, 36, 49, 70, 72, 74, 78, 81, 92, 94, 105, 107, 108, 114, 116, 120, 131, 137, 150, 159, 161, 162, 167, 171, 190, 199, 203, 206, 214, 229, 234, 240, 245, 247, 249, 252, 266, 268, 270, 274, 275, 278, 284, 286, 292, 296, 301, 302, 304, 305, 312, 313, 320

CRAFTMASTER, 70, 83, 94, 120, 128, 175, 203

CRAFTWORK GUILD, 34, 36, 38, 50, 70, 92, 116, 159, 162, 167, 190, 234, 240, 249, 268, 274, 275, 278, 296, 299, 301, 320

CRAFT-TEX, 162, 190, 222, 304

CRAIG NORMAN, 166

CRATE IN MOTION, 26, 27, 50, 63, 278

CRAWFORD, 26, 29-31, 35, 36, 50, 70, 78, 81, 83, 94, 114, 120, 137, 150, 162, 171, 190, 196, 199, 203, 206, 222, 229, 230, 234, 247, 249, 252, 266, 270, 278, 286, 288, 296, 302, 305, 327

CREATIONS ACRYLICS, 190

CREATIONS AT DALLAS, 190

CREATIONS BY HILL, 278

CREATIVE, 25-26, 29, 33, 50, 78, 83, 92, 137, 196, 199, 213, 261, 274, 275, 286, 318

CREATIVE ACCENTS, 25, 196, 274, 275

CREATIVE ARTS, 134

CREATIVE ELEGANCE, 26, 83, 190

CREATIVE EXPRESSIONS, 134, 199, 278

CREATIVE FINE ARTS, 190

CREATIVE FURNITURE, 26, 278

CREATIVE IDEAS, 29, 33, 83

CREATIVE LIGHTING, 190, 286

CREATIVE METAL, 50, 78, 83, 92, 137, 190, 278, 318

CREATIVE METAL & WOOD, 78, 83, 190, 278

CREATIVE OFFICE SEATING, 278

CRESENT, 26, 31, 36, 50, 78, 83, 120, 167, 203, 284, 302, 313, 317, 327

CRESTLINE, 70, 78, 94

CRESTWOOD, 70, 70, 94, 114

CRITERION, 28, 213, 261, 313

CROPUSA, 177, 184

CROSLEY, 134

CROSSWINDS, 83, 190

CROWN CRAFT, 83, 179, 261, 304, 313

CROWNFORD, 313

CRUTCHFIELD, 32, 175

CRYSTAL CLEAR, 34, 50, 83, 92, 134, 166, 190, 196, 199, 203, 206, 222, 229, 240, 249, 270, 278, 286, 299, 301, 305, 311, 313

CRYSTAL PLEAT, 178, 255

CRYSTALROMA, 190

CSD FURNITURE, 278

CSI, 83

CTH, 31, 35, 36, 47, 50, 83, 92, 116, 190, 234, 240, 266, 278, 286, 314, 327

CTH/SHERRILL, 31, 35, 36, 50, 116, 234, 240, 266, 278, 286, 314, 327

CTH-CAROLINA TABLES, 92

CUMBERLAND, 26, 28, 30, 31, 35-37, 90, 168, 213, 261, 313, 319

CURRAN, 30, 38, 257

CURREY, 83

CURRY & CO, 30, 31, 34, 190

CURVET, 83

CUSSETA WOOD, 70, 78

CUSTOM AMERICAN, 114

CUSTOM CHERRY, 83

CUSTOM DECOR, 199

CUSTOM DESIGNS, 54, 167

CUSTOM DRAPERY SHOP & INTERIORS, 133, 334

CUSTOM RUGS, 169, 319

CUSTOM SHOPPE, 83

CUSTOM STYLE, 28, 278

CUSTOMCRAFT, 78, 137, 206, 257, 270, 327

CUSTOMWEAVE, 28, 213, 261

CX DESIGN, 83

CYRUS CLARK, 32, 50, 238, 242-244

C-STYLE, 162, 278

D & F WICKER, 26, 29, 31, 33, 37, 38, 78, 83, 105, 143, 173, 190, 203, 240, 247, 252, 270, 313

D SCAN, 203, 206, 278, 286, 313

DAC LIGHTING, 34, 133, 342

DAKOTA, 14, 15, 343

DALLAS FURNITURE STORE, INC, 134, 339

DALTON PARADISE CARPET, 28, 28

DAN RIVER, 261, 305

DANEKER, 70

DANSEN, 34, 39, 70, 78, 94, 116, 138, 150, 159, 190, 196, 229, 240, 249, 278, 302, 305, 310, 317, 330

DANSEN CONTEMPORARY, 39, 70, 78, 94, 150, 159, 249, 278, 302, 317

DANUBE, 261

DANWOOD, 50, 278

DAPHA, 30, 34, 38, 240

DAPHNE TYSON, 190

DAR FURNITURE, 135, 339

DAR/RAN, 50, 196, 257, 278, 328

DARAFEEV, 59, 84, 93, 163, 191, 270, 280, 287, 304, 328

DARY/REES, 83

DAUPHINE MIRROR CO, 190

DAVID & DASH, 32, 210

DAVID KENT, 247, 252, 278

DAVID LANDIS, 83

DAVID LEE, 83

DAVID MORGAN, 240, 240

DAVID THOMAS, 70, 137, 159, 206, 240, 301, 305

DAVID WINTERS COTTAGES, 190

DAVIS, 28, 28, 30, 31, 33, 47, 63, 81, 83, 94, 134, 206, 216, 247, 252, 257, 278, 327, 336

DAVIS & DAVIS, 28, 116, 157, 190, 240, 268, 270, 278, 305, 313, 330

DAVIS & SMALL, 81

DAVIS CABINET, 31, 83, 94, 206, 247, 252, 327

DAVIS CONFERENCE GROUP, 278

DAVIS FURNITURE, 30, 134, 257

DAYSTROM, 29-31, 36, 50, 70, 92, 94, 150, 161, 167, 196, 203, 229, 278, 286, 301, 302, 313

DAYVA COVERS, 190

DBK LTD, 81

DDT, 83

DEARAN, 83

DEBOURNAIS, 83, 190

DECORATIVE ARTS, 25, 53, 92, 190, 199, 206, 270, 278, 286

DECORATIVE CRAFTS, 25, 51, 81, 92, 105, 116, 134, 161, 166, 190, 196, 199, 203, 206, 234, 249, 270, 274, 275, 278, 286, 299, 301, 304, 310, 313

DECORATOR'S CHOICE, 82, 82
DECORATOR'S EDGE, THE, 136, 342
DECORATOR/DESIGNER FABRICS, 273
DECORATOR'S WALK, 190
DECOY, 190
DECRISTOFARO, 235
DECURTIS, 78
DEEP RIVER TRADING CO, THE, 137, 339
DeJON CONTRACT COLLECTION, 28, 213
DELLINGER, 114
DELMAR, 30, 37, 39, 75, 128, 166, 245, 252, 254, 255, 264, 299, 324
DELTA, 8, 149, 190
DENNY LAMP, 169, 190, 199, 203, 304, 311
DENUNZIO, 51, 120, 190, 278, 301, 313
DEPARTMENT 56, 25, 313
DESIGN ENVIRONMENT, 196
DESIGN GUILD, 51, 190, 270, 278
DESIGN HORIZONS, 27, 51, 78, 120, 162, 173, 320
DESIGN INSTITUTE OF AMERICA, 278
DESIGN LIGHTING, 190
DESIGN MATERIALS, 190
DESIGN MOTIF, 137
DESIGN PRINTERY, 190
DESIGN SOUTH, 33, 162, 190, 266, 270
DESIGN SYSTEMS, 278, 305, 310
DESIGN TREELINE, 78, 286
DESIGN TREES, 196
DESIGN TRENDS/COCHRANE, 196
DESIGNED IMPORTS, 206
DESIGNER FABRICS, 32, 109, 138, 140, 147, 273, 343
DESIGNER FOUNTAIN, 190
DESIGNER WICKER, 26, 78, 83
DESIGNING WOMEN, 188
DESIGNMASTER, 31, 51, 78, 83, 94, 116, 196, 240, 278, 286, 307, 311, 328
DESIGNS UNLIMITED, 134, 190
DESIGNWEAVE, 28, 213
DEVILLE, 70, 78, 134
DEWOOLFSON DOWN, 172, 190
DFC, 78, 199, 268, 278
DIA, 190, 278, 318
DIAMOND, 28, 168, 213, 261, 319, 321
DIANE LAMP SHADES, 190
DIERRAS LAMPS, 81

DILLINGHAM, 94, 114
DILLON, 26, 70, 78, 83, 94, 116, 120, 162, 167, 190, 196, 203, 206, 223, 229, 249, 268, 270, 279, 286, 310, 311, 328
DIMENSION, 28, 213, 261, 319
DIMENSIONS STORAGE, 257
DINAIRE, 29-31, 38, 51, 83, 116, 120, 150, 157, 161, 162, 190, 194, 196, 203, 206, 211, 229, 235, 240, 247, 252, 268, 270, 279, 286, 292, 301, 304, 313, 320
DINICO, 190
DINING ALA CARTE, 207, 235, 270, 310
DINO MARK ANTHONY, 83, 328
DIRECTIONAL, 30, 36, 38, 51, 83, 162, 190, 196, 206, 229, 268, 279, 305
DISCOUNT CARPET, 28, 138, 343
DISCOVERY RATTAN, 162
DISQUE, 38, 101, 102, 190, 214
DISTINCTION, 34, 38, 51, 70, 78, 83, 94, 116, 120, 137, 138, 150, 157, 162, 167, 169, 171, 173, 190, 199, 203, 206, 222, 229, 247, 252, 266, 268, 279, 286, 295, 296, 310, 312, 313, 323, 328
DISTINCTIVE LEATHER, 249
DIVERSIFIED, 36
DIXIE, 26, 31, 36, 89, 94, 105, 134, 150, 161, 167, 173, 196, 206, 214, 274, 275, 279, 284, 301, 302, 305, 334
DJC, 83, 83
DL RHEIN, 83
DLP, 73
DMI, 26, 26, 33, 34, 36, 51, 94, 257, 278
DOBBS, 78
DOBLIN, 32, 238
DOLBI CASHIER, 92, 279, 313
DOMAIN, 83
DOMCO, 261, 319, 321
DOMUS ACCESSORIES, 177, 184
DON LAMOR, 139, 139
DONOVAN DESIGNS, 83
DORNBRACHT FAUCETS, 177, 184
DORSETT, 213, 261
DOUBLE R LEATHER, 279
DOUGLAS, 28, 39, 51, 55, 70, 75, 78, 83, 146, 166, 178, 190, 206, 239, 245, 252,

254, 255, 259, 264, 295, 299, 315, 324
DOUGLAS & MARSHALL, 206
DOWN INC, 148
DOWNS, 213, 261
DR KINCAID, 134, 173, 310
DRAKE SMITH, 114
DRAPERY, THE, 140, 343
DREAMWEAVERS, 190, 279
DRESHER, 26, 51, 70, 78, 94, 159, 167, 190, 196, 199, 206, 240, 274, 275, 292, 301, 313, 320
DRESHER BRASS BEDS, 159, 301
DREXEL, 25-26, 28-31, 33-39, 94, 102, 140-142, 162, 334, 335, 337
DREXEL HERITAGE, 25-26, 28-31, 33-34, 36-39, 94, 98, 99, 140-141, 162, 188, 190, 334, 335
DREXEL HERITAGE FACTORY OUTLET, 140, 183, 188, 334, 337
DREXEL HERITAGE GALLERY, 141, 337
DREXEL STUDIO, 51, 51
DSF (SCANDANAVIAN), 249, 249
DUCKS UNLIMITED, 83, 92, 190, 194, 232, 306
DUETTE, 39, 128, 178, 254, 255, 299, 315, 326
DUKE CONGLOMERATE, 83
DUKE LONG LOMERTION, 83
DUMMY BOOK, 51, 190
DURA WICKER, 190, 198, 279
DURAFORM, 257
DURALEE, 32, 114, 137, 146, 157, 206, 210, 238, 240, 249, 254, 268, 279
DURALEE FABRICS, 114, 137, 146, 206, 240, 249, 268, 279
DURAVIT, 177, 184
DURHAM, 7, 7, 26, 33, 171, 324, 341
DURKAN, 261
DUTAILIER, 27, 29, 52, 83, 162, 190, 194, 203, 206, 229, 249, 279, 286
DYNAMIC, 168, 261
EAGLE CRAFT, 78, 190, 203, 206, 279, 286, 292
EAMES, 145
EAST CAROLINA WALLPAPER MARKET, INC, 142, 341
EASTERN ART ARCADE, 81

EASTERN ECLECTION, 78
EC CARTER, 146
ECCO, 36, 48, 52, 206, 279
ECKADAMS, 257
EDEN TOYS, 83
EDGAR, 238, 242-244
EDWARD ART, 83, 120, 134, 229
EDWARD FERRELL, 206
EDWARD P PAUL, 81
EF EXPRESSIONS, 257
EGAN VISUAL, 257
EILEEN GRAY, 145
EISENHART, 52, 175, 252, 276
EJ VICTOR, 25-26, 31, 33, 35, 36,
    38, 39, 52, 137
EKLECTIC INTERIORS, LTD,
    142, 333, 334
EKORNES, 26, 52, 83, 162, 190,
    206, 249, 270, 279, 286,
    304, 313
EL CONDOR, 78, 83
ELCO, 238
ELDEN COLLECTIONS, 190, 279
ELDRED WHEELER, 171, 190,
    313
ELEMENTS BY GRAPEVINE, 31,
    35-37, 52, 81, 83, 162,
    190, 240, 249, 270, 279,
    328
ELGEEWEST, 190
ELITE, 34, 83, 190
ELK LIGHTING, 177, 184, 190
ELKAY, 149, 177, 184
ELKO, 32, 146
ELLENBURG'S FURNITURE, 143,
    342
ELLER, 78, 150
ELLIOTT'S, 25, 25-27, 39, 52, 78,
    92, 105, 162, 203, 206,
    229, 301, 307, 310, 328
ELLO, 28, 31, 33, 36, 39, 52, 70,
    83, 94, 114, 116, 130,
    159, 162, 167, 190, 196,
    206, 240, 249, 268, 279,
    286, 296, 305, 310, 318,
    320, 328
ELLSWORTH CABINET, 114
ELM CREEK, 27, 30, 83, 136
EMCO HARDWARE, 177, 184
EMCO/METWOOD, 257
EMERSON, 30, 33-35, 38, 70, 81,
    83, 94, 105, 116, 120,
    131, 138, 159, 161, 162,
    166, 167, 196, 203, 206,
    211, 229, 232, 235, 240,
    268, 274, 275, 284, 292,
    296, 301, 303, 310, 318,
    320, 322, 323

EMERSON ET CIE, 33, 52, 92,
    190, 249, 270, 279, 286,
    313, 318, 328
EMMESS, 32, 146
EMPIRE, 30, 36, 56, 64, 70, 78,
    257
ENCORE EFFECTS, 78
ENCORE WALLCOVERING, 32,
    305
ENESCO, 190
ENGLAND, 29, 35-39, 52, 60, 74,
    79, 84, 121, 140,
    146-147, 175, 196, 255,
    258, 308-309, 314,
    342-343
ENGLAND CORSAIR, 36, 74, 121,
    196
ENGLANDER, 26, 71, 96
ENGLISH IMPORTS, 83, 190
ENOS, 83
ENTREE, 83, 103, 162, 190, 235,
    247, 252, 266, 274, 275,
    279, 299
EPHRAIM MARSH CO, 144, 335
EPOCH COLLECTION, 190
ER BUCK, 83, 279
ERGO MED SOLUTIONS, 257
ERGOSCAPES, 259
ERGOSPEC, 257
ERIC MORGAN, 52, 162, 206, 279
ERNEST STOECKLIN, 190
ERWIN LAMBETH, 52, 114, 159,
    206
ESQUEMA ACCESSORIES, 177,
    184
ESSEX, 28, 32, 252
EUROBATH, 177, 184
EUROFASE, 177, 184, 190
EUROFASE LIGHTING, 177, 184
EUROLEATHER, 83
EUROPEAN FURNITURE
    IMPORTERS, 144, 334
EUROPEAN STYLE PAINTINGS,
    251, 251
EUROTECH PLUMBING &
    HARDWARE, 177, 184
EVANS, 28, 83, 90, 190, 196, 213,
    261, 286, 313, 319, 321
EVANS & BLACK, 28, 90, 213,
    261, 313, 319, 321
EVERPURE WATER FILTERS,
    177, 184
EVOLUTIONS LIGHTING, 177,
    184
EXCEL DESIGN, 105
EXCEL OFFICE, 279
EXCELSIOR, 30, 52, 83, 157, 162,
    190, 196, 206, 215, 229,
    249, 279, 286, 328

EXECUTIVE FURNITURE, 257,
    279
EXECUTIVE IMPORTS, 190
EXECUTIVE LEATHER, 37, 38,
    52, 71, 78, 83, 138, 196,
    199, 203, 229, 279, 313,
    318
EXECUTIVE OFFICE
    CONCEPTS, 257
EXPRESSIONS, 134, 173, 199,
    257, 278
FABLES, 83, 328
FABRIC CENTER, THE, 145, 335
FABRIC OUTLET, THE, 145, 342
FABRICADE, 240, 299
FABRICOATE, 83, 196
FABRICS & MORE, 32, 146, 335
FABRICS & WALLPAPERS
    DIRECT, 147, 343
FABRICUT, 32, 146, 157, 190,
    238, 242-244, 254, 299,
    309
FABRIYAZ, 32, 201
FACTORY DIRECT TABLE PAD
    CO, 147, 334
FAIRCHILD, 26, 94
FAIRFAX, 57, 261, 294, 336
FAIRFIELD, 9, 10, 30, 34, 36, 38,
    52, 71, 74, 78, 83, 92, 94,
    105, 116, 120, 121, 161,
    162, 167, 169, 173, 175,
    190, 196, 199, 203, 206,
    211, 214, 229, 232, 235,
    240, 247, 249, 252, 266,
    270, 279, 286, 292, 296,
    301, 302, 305, 310, 313,
    318, 320, 328
FAIRINGTON, 71, 78, 83, 114,
    138, 159, 240, 302
FALCON, 257
FAME, 52, 238
FANCHER, 26, 30, 31, 34, 35, 52,
    71, 78, 137, 206
FARM HOUSE FURNISHINGS,
    148, 337
FAROY, 83
FASCO, 190
FASHION, 26, 27, 32, 45, 51, 52,
    74, 81-83, 92, 116, 120,
    134, 148, 157, 162, 169,
    189, 190, 196, 206, 229,
    230, 232, 240, 249, 252,
    266, 270, 279, 284, 286,
    292, 299, 311, 313, 318,
    320, 328, 341
FASHION BED, 26, 27, 45, 51, 52,
    74, 78, 81, 83, 92, 116,
    120, 134, 157, 162, 169,
    190, 196, 203, 206, 229,

232, 240, 247, 249, 252, 266, 270, 279, 284, 286, 292, 299, 311, 313, 318, 320, 328

FASHION HOUSE, 32, 78, 230, 247, 252, 311

FASHIONCRAFT, 94

FATTORI STAR, 190

FAUCET OUTLET, 148, 342

FAUSTIG, 190

FE 26, 83

FEFCO, 82, 82-83

FEIZY, 172, 190, 279

FETCO, 78, 83, 172, 190

FIAM, 270, 279

FICKS REED, 28, 31, 37, 38, 52, 53, 71, 92, 94, 114, 120, 143, 150, 159, 162, 167, 172, 196, 199, 203, 229, 235, 240, 249, 268, 279, 286, 296, 302, 305, 310, 313, 317, 322, 328, 330

FIELDCREST, 179

FIELDS FURNITURE CO, 150, 336

FINAL FURNITURE, 251, 251

FINE ARTS, 32, 73, 78, 93, 100, 137, 159, 166, 189-190, 192, 193, 196, 199, 206, 249, 270, 274, 275, 279-280, 286, 296, 313, 318, 328, 330

FINE ARTS LAMPS, 73, 83, 93, 137, 159, 166, 190, 196, 199, 249, 270, 279, 286, 296, 313, 318, 330

FINKEL OUTDOOR, 240, 302

FITZ & FLOYD, 93, 196, 199, 240, 247, 252, 268, 270, 279, 301, 313

FIVE RIVERS, 71, 78, 83, 150

FIXTURES, 5, 76, 105, 133, 168, 177, 184, 187, 191, 220, 223, 257, 303

FLAIR, 31, 43, 71, 94, 302

FLAT ROCK, 83, 157, 313, 328

FLEETWOOD FRAMES, 71

FLEMING DECORATIVE FABRICS, 151, 341

FLEXSTEEL, 29, 30, 34, 35, 38, 39, 53, 71, 74, 78, 83, 93, 105, 110, 114, 116, 120, 134, 138, 151, 159, 161, 162, 167, 173, 188, 190, 196, 199, 203, 206, 215, 229, 235, 279, 286, 288, 292, 301, 302, 305, 310, 320, 328, 337

FLEXSTEEL GALLERY, 151, 188, 337

FLEX-Y-PLAN, 257

FLOORWAYS, 28, 334

FLORAL ART, 78, 190, 196, 229, 274, 275, 279, 313

FLORIDA FURNITURE, 26, 33, 36, 53, 71, 78, 83, 150, 167, 196, 232

FLORITA NOVA, 83, 190, 279, 328

FLUTE, 25, 34, 301

FMA, 242-244

FOCUS, 28, 68, 146, 162, 188, 201, 213, 338

FOGLE, 94

FONTHILL LTD, 190

FORBES, 196, 249, 279, 286

FORECAST, 34, 190

FOREIGN ACCENTS, 28, 190

FOREMOST, 32, 134, 142

FOREMOST/WESTMOUNT, 142

FOREST OF ADRIAN, 301

FORMA DESIGN, 162, 279

FORT STEUBEN, 81

FORTRESS, 153, 173

FORTUNE RATTAN, 26, 173, 293

FOSS CREEK CERAMICS, 286

FOUR SEASONS FURNITURE GALLERY, 153, 335

FOXFIRE, 83, 190, 279

FRAMBURG, 223, 303

FRAME ONE STUDIOS, 286

FRAMES & ARTS, 190

FRAN'S WICKER AND RATTAN, 153, 342

FRANBURG, 190

FRANK & SON, 279

FRANKE PLUMBING, 177, 184

FRANKLIN, 35, 38, 53, 60, 71, 78, 83, 92, 128, 142, 149, 167, 188, 190, 229, 230, 279, 286, 333-334, 337, 341

FRANKLIN BRASS, 149

FRANKLIN CHAIRS, 279

FRANKLIN FURNITURE, 154, 154

FRANKLIN PICTURES, 286

FRANKLIN PLACE, 154, 154

FREDERICK COOPER, 53, 71, 78, 81, 83, 93, 94, 100, 114, 116, 131, 159, 166, 167, 190, 196, 199, 203, 214, 224, 229, 235, 240, 249, 257, 268, 270, 278, 279, 286, 292, 296, 299, 301, 302, 305, 311, 313, 317, 318, 320, 328, 330

FREDERICK EDWARD, 38, 53, 70, 94, 114, 138, 159, 171, 190, 235, 240, 249, 310, 313, 320

FREDRICK-RAMOND, 190

FREEMAN & CO, 206

FREMARC, 33, 83, 157, 190, 328

FRENCH FRAMES, 83

FRENCH HERITAGE, 26, 28, 82, 83, 171, 190, 339

FRENCH HERITAGE FACTORY, 155, 339

FRENCH REFLECTIONS MIRRORS, 177, 184

FRICHE, 78

FRIEDLAND CHIMES, 177, 184

FRIEDMAN BROS MIRRORS, 72, 92-94, 114, 116, 159, 162, 172, 190, 206, 235, 240, 249, 268, 279, 284, 286, 302, 320, 328, 331

FRIENDSHIP, 32, 53, 71, 78, 84, 150, 196, 203, 279

FRISCO, 26, 28, 134, 293

FRITZ & LaRUE, 28, 37, 159, 249, 312, 313

FROEHLICH, 78, 84

FROM THE EARTH, 279, 286

FUN WITH FURS, 279

FUR DESIGNS, 270

FURNITURE CHOICES, 38, 143, 155, 336

FURNITURE CLASSICS, 247, 252

FURNITURE CLEARANCE CENTER, 70, 97, 109, 112, 156, 187, 337, 339, 341

FURNITURE DEALERS CLEARANCE CENTER OF NC, 156, 341

FURNITURE DIRECT, 113, 157, 334, 343

FURNITURE EXPRESS, 158, 158, 343

FURNITURE GUILD, 25-28, 33, 36, 53, 73, 114, 190

FURNITURE MARKET CLEARANCE CENTER, 158, 340

FURNITURE PATCH OF CALABASH, THE, 159, 335

FURNITURE SHOPPE, THE, 160-160

FURNITURELAND SOUTH, 161, 341

FUTORIAN CORP, 71

FUTURISTIC, 211, 229, 279

GABY'S SHOPPE, 279

GAINES, 34, 39, 53, 71, 121, 249, 279
GAINSBOROUGH, 177, 184
GALAXY, 28, 90, 211, 213, 226, 261, 319, 321
GALBRAITH, 84, 206, 279
GALERKIN, 84
GALLERY OF LIGHTS, 163, 163
GAME ROOM, 53, 59, 279
GARCIA, 28, 53, 81, 84, 93, 100, 103, 157, 159, 190, 240, 249, 279, 299, 318, 331
GARDEN CONCEPTS, 257
GARDEN COURT, 84
GARDEN MIRROR, 84
GARDEN SOURCE, 34, 53, 304
GARGOYLES, 84
GATCO, 81, 134, 166, 190, 279
GAUGE, 84
GEM-AN-EYE, 84
GENADA IMPORTS, 164, 342
GENCORP, 276
GENERAL, 5, 20, 23, 25-26, 30, 31, 34-36, 38, 53, 84, 261, 279, 287
GENERAL FELT, 261
GENERAL FURNITURE, 29, 29, 34, 53, 78
GENERAL STORE, 25, 78, 84, 279, 287
GENERAL STORE ACCESSORIES, 84
GENERATIONS, 27, 27
GENESIS LIGHTING, 84, 301
GENTLEMAN'S QUARTERS, 141
GENTRY, 35, 38, 84, 128, 134, 136, 203
GEORGE BENT, 70
GEORGE HARRINGTON, 32, 145
GEORGE KOCH, 313
GEORGE KOVACS, 34, 53, 84, 93, 166, 177, 184, 190, 196, 224, 313, 331
GEORGIA ART LIGHTING, 270
GEORGIA CHAIR, 196, 247, 252
GEORGIA FURNISHINGS, 206
GEORGIAN, 50, 71, 114, 116, 137, 143, 159, 162, 167, 190, 199, 203, 206, 224, 229, 240, 250, 268, 274, 275, 278, 279, 292, 302, 305-307, 310, 313
GEORGIAN ART, 190, 224
GEORGIAN FURNISHINGS, 53, 162, 190, 199, 268, 274, 275, 279, 286, 292, 305, 310
GEORGIAN HOME FURNISHINGS, 116

GEORGIAN LIGHTING, 114, 240
GEORGIAN PINE CRAFTSMAN, 78
GEORGIAN REPRODUCTIONS, 53, 71, 78, 143, 159, 167, 206
GEORGIO LEONI, 84, 190
GERALD STEIN, 71, 78, 134, 196, 197, 199, 274, 275
GERVAIS, 268
GET-A-GRIP HARDWARE, 177, 184
GIANNI, 257
GIBRALTAR, 28, 261
GIBSON INTERIORS, 165, 340
GIEMME, 171
GILBERT, 257
GILLIAM, 94
GINGER ACCESSORIES, 177, 184
GIORGIO COLLECTION, 26, 190
GIOVANNE TRAVANO, 196
GIOVANNI TORINO, 31, 279
GIRSBERGER, 257
GLARO ACCESSORIES, 257
GLASS ARTS, 28, 31, 53, 81, 84, 93, 116, 159, 162, 190, 206, 229, 247, 250, 252, 268, 270, 286, 301, 305, 310, 313
GLASS FASHIONS, 196, 211
GLASS MIRRORCRAFTS, 206
GLASS WORKS, 84
GLEN ALLEN, 92
GLENNCRAFT, 34, 54, 105, 161, 167, 203, 279, 286
GLOBAL FURNITURE, 26, 190
GLOBAL WALLCOVERINGS AND BLINDS, 166, 334
GLOBE, 167, 257, 337
GLOBE FURNITURE, 167, 337
GLOBER, 84, 190, 194, 250, 286, 313
GLOSTER, 162, 190
GMS IMPORTS, 26, 33, 78, 84, 190, 194, 206, 279
GOLD LABEL CARPETS, 168, 334
GOLD MEDAL, 313
GOLDEN VALLEY LIGHTING, 34, 168, 340
GOOD SHIP, 286
GOODMAN CHARLTON, 84
GOODWIN WEAVERS, 229, 304, 313
GORDON TABLES, 94
GORDON'S, 169, 240, 342
GORDON'S FURNITURE STORES, 169, 342
GORTRON, 34, 78

GRABER, 39, 54, 75, 130, 166, 178, 201, 239, 252, 254, 255, 264, 295, 299, 315, 324
GRACE, 84, 85, 93, 163, 192, 247, 250, 252, 328
GRAHL, 30, 157
GRAND MANOR, 206
GRANDEUR BEDS, 93
GRANIT DESIGN, 170, 343
GRAPEVINE TABLES, 159
GRASSMORE, 28, 213
GRAY WATKINS, 190
GREAT AMERICAN TRADING, 196
GREAT CITY TRADERS, 84, 93, 116, 172, 190, 196, 199, 206, 270, 279, 301, 307, 313, 328
GREAT WOODS, 279
GREEFF, 32, 114, 137, 146, 159, 190, 240, 242-244, 250, 268, 279, 299
GREEN FRONT FURNITURE STORE, 171, 171-172
GREENE BROS, 38, 54, 175, 203, 211, 247, 252
GREENHILL FURNITURE COMPANY, 170, 337
GREENHOUSE, 242-244
GREENSTREET DETAILS, 177, 184
GREG COPELAND, 114
GREG SHEZ, 190
GREGOR, 257
GREGSON, 257
GREYSEN, 157
GRIFONI MIRRORS, 172
GRINDSTAFF'S INTERIORS, 173, 335
GROHE, 149, 177, 184
GROLEN, 257
GROSFILLEX, 30, 33, 37, 54, 190, 206, 240, 279, 286, 313
GROW & CUTTLE, 240
GUARDSMAN, 54, 84, 150, 163, 190, 286, 304
GUILDMASTER, 25, 54, 84, 93, 116, 171, 190, 250, 270, 313, 318, 328
GULDEN GALLERY, 206
GUY CHADDOCK, 26, 28, 98, 100, 102, 103, 190, 268
H & H, 28, 173, 279
HABERSHAM, 26, 26, 30, 31, 33, 35, 36, 54, 94, 98, 100, 102, 103, 114, 116, 131, 137, 157, 159, 190, 203, 222, 235, 240, 247, 250,

Index

252, 266, 279, 286, 295, 296, 302, 310, 313, 317, 318, 320, 327, 328

HABERSHAM PLANTATION, 26, 26, 30, 33, 35, 36, 54, 98, 100, 102, 103, 116, 131, 159, 190, 203, 222, 235, 240, 247, 250, 252, 279, 286, 296, 302, 313, 317, 318, 320, 327

HADLEY POTTERY, 317

HAEGER POTTERIES, 286

HAFELE, 177, 184

HALCYON, 30, 37, 54, 78, 84, 173, 196, 199, 203, 206, 257, 279

HALE, 26, 27, 29, 31, 36, 54, 60, 71, 78, 79, 84, 94, 106, 114, 121, 138, 150, 191, 196, 203, 207, 211, 214, 222, 229, 230, 240, 250, 257, 268, 280, 287, 292, 295-296, 300, 313, 314, 317

HALE OF VERMONT, 54, 114, 229, 279, 313

HALL CLOCKS, 114

HAMILTON, 29, 71, 130, 135, 199, 242-244, 268, 286, 339

HAMILTON HALL, 71, 268

HAMILTON'S, 173, 335

HAMMARY, 33, 33, 36, 38, 54, 71, 74, 78, 84, 93, 94, 98, 108, 116, 120, 137, 150, 159, 161, 163, 167, 169, 190, 196, 199, 203, 206, 214, 222, 229, 232, 235, 240, 247, 250, 252, 265, 266, 268, 270, 279, 286, 292, 296, 299, 301, 302, 305, 307, 310, 311, 313, 317, 320, 328

HAMMOCK SHOP, 78

HAMPSTEAD, 190

HAMPTON MILLS, 238

HANCOCK & MOORE, 98-100, 102, 103, 107, 114, 116, 171, 172, 174, 188, 190, 235, 247, 250, 252, 284, 296, 302, 305, 313, 331, 337

HANCOCK & MOORE GALLERY, 174, 188, 337

HANCOCK FURNITURE, 190

HANG-IT-NOW WALLPAPER STORES, 175, 335

HANOVER, 32, 66, 120, 190, 230, 301, 310

HANSA AMERICA, 177, 184

HANSGROHE, 149, 177, 184

HARBINGER, 261

HARBOUR LIGHTS, 190

HARBOUR TOWNE, 30, 36, 37, 196

HARDEE'S FURNITURE WAREHOUSE, 175, 342

HARDEN, 26, 36, 38, 39, 54, 94, 98, 100, 102, 103, 105, 114, 176, 180, 188, 190, 247, 252, 302, 322, 337

HARDEN GALLERY, 176, 188, 337

HARDWARE BATH & MORE, 176, 335

HARMONY SUPPLY INC, 32, 178, 335

HARRINGTON BRASS, 177, 184

HARRINGTON HOUSE, 258

HARRIS, 25, 25-26, 29, 31, 32, 54, 81, 84, 94, 98-102, 107, 114, 150, 171, 172, 178, 188, 190-192, 196, 200, 203, 206, 213, 214, 235, 238, 247, 252, 270, 279, 284, 286, 302, 307, 313, 314, 328, 331, 337, 342

HARRIS LEVY, INC, 35, 178, 342

HARRIS MARCUS, 34, 54, 78, 84, 128, 203, 206

HARRIS STRONG, 84, 279

HARRIS YOUNG, 78, 84

HARRIS-TARKETT, 213

HART, 26, 27, 35-37, 81, 84, 93, 116, 157, 159, 190, 224, 250, 270, 279, 286, 318, 328, 331

HART COUNTRY SHOP, 159, 250

HART INDUSTRIES, 84, 93

HART LAMPS, 116

HARTCO WOOD, 313, 319

HASKELL, 257

HASTINGS COLLECTION, 177, 184

HATTERAS HAMMOCKS, 37, 279

HAZZARD, 242-244

HDI, 149

HEARTHSIDE CLASSICS, 78, 84, 279

HEIRLOOM, 68, 71, 78, 104, 116, 283, 310

HEKMAN, 28-29, 35-37, 54, 71, 78, 81, 84, 93, 94, 96, 98-100, 102, 105, 108, 110, 116, 120, 131, 137, 150, 157, 159, 161, 163, 169, 179, 180, 188, 190, 194, 196, 203, 206, 211,

214, 229, 235, 240, 247, 250, 252, 266, 268, 270, 274, 275, 279, 284, 286, 292, 296, 299, 301, 302, 305, 307, 310, 311, 313, 317, 318, 320, 327, 328, 331, 337

HEKMAN GALLERY, 179, 188, 337

HELIOS, 28, 157, 213, 261

HEN FEATHERS, 25, 172, 190, 250, 279, 286

HENDERSON, 44, 78, 196, 206, 279

HENDERSON WALL UNITS, 206

HENDRICKS FURNITURE (OWNED BY BOYLES FURNITURE), 180, 180

HENKEL HARRIS, 98-102, 114, 171, 172, 188, 190, 214, 235, 247, 252, 279, 302, 337

HENKEL HARRIS GALLERY, 180, 188, 337

HENKEL MOORE, 102, 172, 180, 190, 214, 235, 247, 252, 279, 331

HENREDON, 5, 26, 28, 30-31, 36, 38, 39, 94, 98, 100, 102, 103, 114, 171, 172, 180, 182-183, 191, 305, 331, 334, 341-342

HENREDON FACTORY OUTLET, 181, 181-182

HENREDON FURNITURE CLEARANCE, 182

HENREDON GALLERY, 183, 188, 337

HENREDON/DREXEL HERITAGE FACTORY OUTLET, 183, 334

HENRY LINK, 58, 74, 81, 84, 93, 94, 106, 110, 114, 116, 120, 131, 134, 143, 150, 153, 157, 159, 161, 163, 167, 169, 172, 174, 191, 196, 206, 211, 214, 222, 229, 232, 235, 245, 247, 250, 252, 268, 270, 274, 275, 279, 284, 288, 292, 299, 301, 302, 304, 305, 307, 311-313, 320, 327, 328, 331

HERALD WHOLESALE, 34, 177, 184, 335

HERCO LIGHTING, 206

HERITAGE, 25-26, 29-31, 33-34, 36-39, 42, 55, 77, 78, 94, 98, 99, 140-141, 148,

162, 171, 185, 188, 191, 231, 246, 249, 252, 278, 279, 291, 334, 335, 339, 340

HERITAGE HAUS, 55, 84, 148, 279, 286

HERITAGE HOUSE, 185, 231, 340

HERITAGE HOUSE FURNITURE, 185, 340

HERMAN MILLER, 33, 167

HERSCHELL'S, 191

HERSHEDE, 114

HEWI, 177, 184

HEXTER, 32, 137, 159

HEYGILL, 55, 196, 240, 322

HEYWARD HOUSE, 55, 196, 240, 302

HIBRITEN, 94, 114

HICKORY BRANCH LAMPS, 247, 253

HICKORY BUSINESS FURNITURE, 30, 157

HICKORY CHAIR, 25-26, 28, 30, 31, 35, 36, 38, 39, 55, 94, 98, 100-102, 107, 114, 116, 131, 137, 138, 159, 180, 185-186, 200, 203, 214, 235, 238, 240, 250, 268, 279, 284, 286, 299, 300, 302, 305, 313, 318, 331, 335

HICKORY CHAIR FACTORY OUTLET, 185, 188, 337

HICKORY CHAIR GALLERY, 186, 188, 337

HICKORY CRAFT, 38, 55, 71

HICKORY FRY, 55, 71, 84, 94, 114, 116, 167, 188, 191, 194, 206, 240, 270, 279, 286, 305, 320

HICKORY FURNITURE MART, 7-7, 10, 13, 25, 76, 86-87, 89-90, 97, 100, 102-103, 106, 108, 110-111, 119, 122-123, 128, 130, 139, 151-152, 154, 163, 165, 174, 176, 179, 182-183, 185, 187, 188, 194-195, 197-198, 201, 204, 208, 217, 219, 221, 224, 226, 233, 235, 251, 253, 259, 262, 264, 267, 271, 273, 275, 281-282, 284-285, 288, · 295, 298, 307-308, 315, 318, 321-322, 325, 328-329, 332, 336, 339

HICKORY FURNITURE MART FURNITURE

CLEARANCE CENTER, 97, 187, 337

HICKORY HILL, 30, 37, 38, 55, 71, 74, 78, 84, 93, 94, 120, 128, 163, 196, 203, 206, 229, 279, 286, 292, 299, 320

HICKORY HOUSE, 110, 163, 229

HICKORY INTERNATIONAL, 34, 38, 71, 78, 106, 167, 203, 286, 292, 305

HICKORY LEATHER, 71, 74, 78, 81, 93, 120, 148, 191, 206, 257, 279, 292, 310

HICKORY MANOR, 257

HICKORY MANUFACTURING, 31, 71, 94, 167, 279, 301, 302, 322

HICKORY PARK, 82, 188, 193-194, 337, 340

HICKORY PARK FURNITURE GALLERIES, 188, 188

HICKORY SPRINGS, 134

HICKORY TAVERN, 38, 55, 71, 78, 93, 94, 120, 150, 157, 161, 167, 196, 229, 235, 274, 275, 279, 284, 299, 301, 302, 305

HICKORY WHITE, 26-29, 31, 33, 35, 36, 39, 55, 78, 84, 93, 96, 98, 100, 102, 114, 116, 131, 137, 138, 157, 159, 161, 163, 167, 180, 188, 191, 195, 196, 235, 240, 247, 250, 253, 266, 268, 279, 286, 296, 299, 301, 305, 310, 313, 317, 318, 320, 327, 328, 337

HICKORY WHITE GALLERY, 188, 195, 337

HIGGINGS, 84

HIGH POINT, 7-8, 10-11, 30, 33, 37, 41, 44-48, 50, 55, 57, 62, 67-68, 70, 71, 73, 75, 78, 81-82, 92, 99, 106, 112, 116, 117, 120, 121, 124, 130, 131, 135-137, 149-150, 155-156, 158, 162, 163, 165, 168, 185, 191, 193, 206, 208, 216-218, 220, 223, 225, 227, 230, 232, 234, 237, 241, 246, 257, 262, 263, 268, 270, 272, 277-279, 286, 291-292, 297, 301, 303, 316, 317, 326, 327, 329-332, 339

HIGH POINT BEDDING, 134

HIGH POINT DESK, 33, 116, 279, 299, 301

HIGH POINT FURNITURE, 93, 150, 163, 194-196, 240, 286, 292, 340

HIGH POINT FURNITURE SALES, INC, 195, 340

HIGH POINT WOODWORKING, 30, 71, 78, 94, 150, 196, 206, 240, 292, 317

HIGHBORN MANOR, 279

HIGHLAND HOUSE, 37, 38, 55, 71, 74, 78, 94, 106, 116, 120, 131, 143, 163, 167, 188, 191, 197, 203, 206, 211, 228, 229, 235, 240, 266, 270, 292, 302, 307, 313, 320, 337

HIGHLAND HOUSE GALLERY, 188, 197, 337

HIGHLIGHT, 191

HILDA FLACK, 328

HILL, 30, 36, 46, 48, 52, 53, 55, 65, 66, 71, 74, 78, 89, 90, 93-94, 114, 115, 120, 124, 128, 142, 148, 163, 188, 189, 203, 205-206, 229, 240, 250, 270, 278, 279, 292, 299, 305, 320, 334, 336, 339, 341

HINES & CO, 191

HINKLE CHAIR, 163, 279

HINKLEY, 191, 303

HINSON, 32, 299

HIPPOPOTAMUS, 27, 33, 203

HITCHCOCK, 55, 71, 78, 84, 98, 106, 114, 116, 120, 131, 137, 150, 159, 163, 191, 203, 222, 229, 240, 250, 270, 274, 275, 284, 286, 295, 296, 300-302, 305, 313, 317, 320, 322

HI-LITE, 191

HLF, 257

HOBE SOUND, 279

HOFFMAN, 32, 238, 242-244

HOGAN CHAIR CO, 200

HOLIDAY HOUSE, 71, 78, 150, 301, 302

HOLIDAY PATIO, 189, 189

HOLIDAY PATIO SHOWCASE, 198, 341

HOLIDAY UMBRELLA, 200

HOLLY GREEN, 191

HOLLYTEX, 28, 213, 261

HOLLYWOODS, 55, 84, 92, 103, 163, 191, 279, 311, 327, 328

HOLSHOF LEATHER, 84, 84

HOLTON FURNITURE CO, 25, 199, 342
HOME FABRIC MILLS, 32, 200, 334
HOME FOCUS BY PALLISER, 188, 188
HOME INTERIORS, 32, 82, 201, 208, 340, 343
HOME LAMP CO, 211
HOME SWEET HOME, 84
HOME TEXTILES, 238
HOMECREST, 37, 55, 161, 191, 199, 203, 247, 253, 270, 279
HOMESTEAD, 61, 78
HOMEWAY FURNITURE CO OF MT AIRY, INC, 202, 341
HON, 247, 253
HOOD, 26, 28, 31, 33, 71, 78, 93, 94, 116, 163, 167, 174, 191, 193, 196, 206, 250, 268, 279, 292, 301, 305, 310, 313
HOOKER, 26, 26, 28, 29, 36, 37, 39, 55, 71, 74, 78, 84, 92-94, 96, 98, 103, 106, 107, 110, 114, 116, 120, 131, 134, 137, 143, 148, 150, 157, 159, 161, 163, 167, 169, 171, 174, 175, 180, 188, 191, 196, 200, 203, 204, 206, 211, 214, 215, 222, 229, 230, 232, 235, 240, 245, 247, 250, 253, 266, 268, 270, 274, 275, 279, 284, 286, 292, 295, 296, 301, 302, 304, 305, 310-313, 317, 318, 320, 328, 338
HOOKER GALLERY, 188, 204, 338
HOPKINS UPHOLSTERY, 134
HORIZON INDUSTRIES, 28, 213
HORIZONS INTERNATIONAL, 191
HOTEL RESERVATIONS NETWORK, 205, 343
HOUSE DRESSING INTERNATIONAL FURNITURE, 205, 336
HOUSE OF FRANCE, 26, 286
HOUSE OF MIRRORS BY HICKORY HOME ACCENTS, 188, 208
HOUSE OF TROY, 34, 166
HOUSE PARTS, 116, 191, 313
HOUSEMAN CHANDELIERS, 206
HOUSEWORK HOME INTERIORS, 82

HOUSEWORKS HOME INTERIORS, 208, 340
HOUSTON HOUSE, 78
HOWARD FURNITURE, 78
HOWARD MILLER, 29, 30, 55, 71, 78, 84, 93, 94, 106, 110, 116, 120, 121, 131, 148, 159, 163, 166, 167, 191, 196, 200, 203, 206, 211, 229, 235, 247, 250, 251, 253, 258, 270, 274, 275, 279, 286, 296, 299, 301, 302, 304, 308, 313, 328
HTB, 34, 39, 71, 78, 84, 94, 116, 150, 157, 161, 196, 229, 235, 240, 270, 274, 275, 279, 292, 301, 305, 328
HTB CONTEMPORARY, 78, 84, 94, 229, 270, 274, 275, 279, 292
HUDSON DISCOUNT FURNITURE, 209, 338
HUDSON RIVER, 33, 191, 328
HUGH COCHRAN, 191
HUKLA, 57, 78, 84
HUNT COUNTRY, 247, 253
HUNT GALLERIES, INC, 209, 338
HUNTER, 32, 55, 75, 84, 128, 142, 166, 178, 239, 245, 252, 254, 255, 264, 279, 295, 299, 315
HUNTER DOUGLAS, 39, 55, 75, 128, 166, 178, 239, 245, 252, 254, 255, 264, 279, 295, 299, 315, 324
HUNTER/COOK COLLECTION, 84
HUNTER/YORK, 142
HUNTING BOARD, 78, 191
HUNTINGTON HOUSE, 71, 78, 84, 94, 120, 134, 136, 167, 175, 191, 196, 203, 222, 245
HYDE PARK PANELING, 257
HYDRO SYSTEMS WHIRLPOOLS, 177, 184
HYUNDAI, 26, 28, 36, 55, 71, 78, 84, 93, 94, 116, 120, 128, 163, 166, 174, 191, 196, 203, 206, 250, 279, 286, 310
HZD COLLECTIONS, 279
ID KIDS, 28, 191, 194
IDEAL IMPORTS, 279
IDS DESIGN CENTER, 32, 210, 342
ILOOMINATING EXPERIENCE, 177, 184, 191

IMAGE, 28, 168, 200, 213, 261, 301
IMAGES OF AMERICA, 279
IMPACT FURNITURE, 56, 71
IMPERIAL, 27, 28, 31, 32, 35, 38, 56, 114, 142, 175, 178, 252, 270, 276, 299
IMPERIAL/KINNEY WALLPAPER, 270
IMPRESSIONS, 77, 82, 84, 85, 93, 246, 252
INDEX, 5, 3, 25, 345
INDIAN DESK, 257
INDIAN DHURRIES, 172
INDIAN TUFTED RUGS, 172
INNOVA, 196
INSINKERATOR, 149
INSTANT TURF, 28, 213, 261, 313
INTERIOR CONCEPTS, 257
INTERIOR FURNISHINGS, ETC, 210, 338
INTERLINE, 71, 84, 292
INTERLOOM, 90, 168, 213, 261
INTERLUDE, 25, 81, 84, 191, 274, 275
INTERNATIONAL BY SCHNADIG, 84
INTERNATIONAL CARPET, 28, 211, 342
INTERNATIONAL DESIGNER IMPORTS, 56, 279
INTERNATIONAL GLASS, 279
INTERNATIONAL IMAGE MAKERS, 200
INTERNATIONAL WROUGHT IRON, 240
INTERPORT, 84
INTREX, 30, 157
INVINCIBLE, 257
INWOOD OFFICE FURNITURE, 286
IN-SINK-ERATOR, 177, 184
IRON CLASSIC, 161
IRON MOUNTAIN STONEWARE, 200
IRWIN ALLEN, 32, 146
ITAL BRASS, 177, 184
ITALIA, 60, 84, 206
ITALIAN CERAMICS, 172
ITALIANA, 34, 84, 177, 184, 191
ITALIANA LUCE, 34, 84, 191
ITALIANISSIMO, 84
ITAL-DESIGN, 84
IWI, 84
J & L, 261
J & P CARPET, 261
J BERDOU, 206
J HARRINGTON/BURTON REPRO, 286

J ROYALE, 34, 38, 56, 71, 74, 78, 96, 116, 120, 138, 167, 169, 188, 191, 203, 212, 235, 240, 250, 259, 268, 270, 279, 287, 301, 304, 320, 327, 328, 338

J ROYALE GALLERY, 188, 212, 338

J SIDNEY SMITH, 279

J STRASBORG, 206

J WILLIAMS, 279

JAB, 15, 191, 238

JABLAN, 32, 242-244

JAC DEY, 191

JACK HOUSMAN, 206

JACK LENOR LARSEN, 191

JACK THORN, 200, 305, 313

JACKSON OF DANVILLE, 30, 31, 36, 38, 56, 163, 270, 305

JACUZZI, 149, 177, 184

JADO, 149, 177, 184

JAFE, 130

JAGUAR DESIGNS, 191

JAMES R COOPER, 163, 196, 200, 270, 279

JAMES R MOTOR, 191

JAMES RIVER, 55, 305

JAMES STEWART & SONS, 191, 279

JAMESTOWN LOUNGE, 114

JAMESTOWN MANOR BY STATTON, 270

JAMESTOWN STERLING, 25, 27, 30, 31, 33, 35, 36, 38, 56, 131, 167, 196, 200, 317

JANZER MAILBOXES, 177, 184

JARU, 84, 196, 279, 286

JASPER CABINET, 33, 33, 36, 56, 71, 78, 84, 94, 107, 114, 116, 120, 131, 137, 150, 159, 161, 163, 174, 191, 196, 200, 203, 206, 211, 214, 222, 232, 235, 240, 247, 250, 253, 266, 270, 279, 286, 292, 296, 301, 302, 305, 310, 313, 317, 320, 328

JASPER DESK, 30, 33, 157, 279

JASPER SEATING, 257

JAY WILLFRED, 134, 247, 253, 279, 286

JAY YANG, 32, 210

JAYMAR, 35, 38, 78, 84, 166, 191, 272

JB MARTIN, 201, 238

JB ROSS BRASS BEDS, 71, 71, 94, 167, 197, 200, 301, 302, 305, 313

JD FABRIC, 146, 299

JDI, 78, 81, 84, 191, 203, 279, 328

JEARDON, 149

JEFFCO, 78, 94, 98, 100, 102, 103, 114, 131, 159, 180, 188, 191, 196, 200, 212, 240, 250, 270, 296, 299, 301, 305, 318, 331, 338

JEFFCO GALLERY, 212, 338

JEFFERSON, 47, 53, 63, 64

JENE'S COLLECTION, 247, 253

JENSEN JARRAH, 191, 194

JERAL INC, 299

JETTON, 167, 203, 229, 247, 253

JG HOOK, 270

JH BOONE, 286

JH CRAVER, 148, 286

JJ HAINES, 78

JJ HYDE, 163

JK REED, 279, 287

JOANNA, 39, 75, 254, 295, 315

JOE COGGINS, 191

JOFFCO, 279

JOHN BOOS, 31, 114, 116, 206, 240, 279, 313

JOHN CHARLES DESIGNS, 39, 191

JOHN ELLIOTT, 279

JOHN MCGILL, 191, 279

JOHN RICHARD, 25, 78, 84, 100, 116, 191, 214, 270, 279, 299, 318, 328

JOHN TURANO, 27, 206

JOHN WIDDICOMB, 27, 28, 36, 114, 116, 137, 191, 250, 268, 296, 331

JOHN WOLF, 32, 145, 201, 238, 309

JOHNSON BENCHWORKS, 301

JOHNSON TABLES, 257

JOHNSON'S CARPETS, 28, 213, 334

JOHNSONITE, 261

JOHNSTON BENCHWORKS, 37, 37, 38, 78, 148, 163, 203, 206, 292

JOHNSTON CASUALS, 26, 30, 31, 39, 56, 73, 78, 81, 84, 93, 94, 114, 116, 120, 157, 159, 161, 163, 191, 196, 206, 222, 223, 229, 235, 241, 247, 250, 253, 266, 268, 279, 286, 296, 305, 311, 313, 318, 328

JOHNSTON TOMBIGBEE, 27, 29-31, 37, 56, 116, 171, 172, 203, 279, 286

JON ELLIOTT, 171, 203, 250, 296

JONDY SOIL SHIELD, 191

JONES BROTHERS, 214, 342

JORDI MERE, 157

JP STEVENS, 90, 214, 261

JRW, 33, 84, 191, 206, 272, 279

JSF, 157, 163, 191, 194, 203, 270, 279, 286, 313, 328

JSF INDUSTRIES, 157, 163, 191, 270, 286, 313

JSI, 257

JULIE ART LAMPS, 196

JUNO LIGHTING, 177, 184

JUST SINKS, 177, 184

JW STANNARD CHIMES, 191

KAGAN'S, 82-82, 216, 340

KAGAN'S AMERICAN DREW, 215, 340

KAGAN'S FURNITURE GALLERIES, 82, 215, 340

KAGAN'S STANLEY GALLERY, 82, 216, 340

KAISER KUHN LIGHTING, 56, 84, 92, 159, 191, 206, 222, 235, 250, 268, 279, 286, 310, 313

KALCO, 177, 184, 191

KALCO LIGHTING, 177, 184

KALLISTA, 177, 184

KARASTAN, 28, 28, 73, 114, 211, 216, 241, 305, 313, 336

KARASTAN CARPET & RUG CENTER, 216, 336

KARASTAN ORIENTALS, 216

KAREL MINTJENS, 78, 279, 312

KARGES, 25-27, 29, 31, 35, 36, 38, 56, 98, 102, 103, 114, 116, 137, 159, 163, 180, 188, 191, 200, 217, 235, 241, 247, 250, 253, 268, 279, 296, 305, 318, 331, 338

KARGES GALLERY, 188, 217, 338

KARPON, 84

KAS ORIENTAL RUGS, 191

KASMIR, 32, 238, 242-244

KATCO DESIGN INC, 191

KATHRYN'S COLLECTION, 217, 340

KATZENBACH & WARREN, 114, 175, 178, 191, 241, 268

KAUFMANN, 32, 110, 145, 151, 201, 238, 242-244, 269

KAY LYN, 71, 196, 279, 301

KELLER, 27, 29-31, 36, 56, 71, 74, 78, 84, 94, 106, 110, 116, 120, 134, 137, 143, 150, 159, 163, 174, 191, 196, 203, 206, 229, 232, 245, 250, 274, 275, 286, 292,

Index

296, 300-302, 305,
311-313, 317, 320
KEMP FURNITURE, 134, 196
KEN MAC, 78
KENMILL, 32, 238
KENNEBUNK WEAVERS, 279
KENNEDY ROCKERS, 148
KENROY, 34, 84, 177, 184, 191
KENT UPHOLSTERY, 84
KENTILE, 28, 313
KESSLER, 27, 56, 78, 84, 94, 116,
157, 163, 203, 206, 235,
266, 268, 279, 310, 314,
318, 320
KETTLER, 27, 29-30, 34, 56, 203,
304
KEVIN CHRISTIAN, 148
KEY CITY, 30, 38, 56, 71, 78, 116,
120, 131, 163, 167, 174,
191, 196, 203, 206, 222,
241, 266, 284, 302, 304,
305, 310, 320
KEYNOTE BY CRAFTWORK, 286
KEYSTONE, 37, 171, 302
KHOURY, 155
KI, 30, 157, 257
KIANI, 37, 314, 325
KICHLER LIGHTING, 177, 184
KIM ORIGINALS, 286
KIMBALL, 25, 26, 31, 33, 37, 38,
71, 78, 84, 94, 106, 114,
116, 120, 134, 161, 167,
175, 188, 196, 200, 203,
206, 214, 218, 229, 235,
241, 247, 250, 253, 259,
266, 270, 274, 275, 279,
286, 300-302, 307, 310,
311, 318, 320, 328, 338
KIMBALL (OFFICE), 94, 94
KIMBALL (PIANOS), 94, 94
KIMBALL 18TH CENTURY, 229
KIMBALL GALLERY, 188, 188
KIMBALL HARMONY WOODS,
279
KIMBALL REPRODUCTIONS,
163
KIMERS FURNITURE, 279
KINCAID, 26-31, 33, 36, 56, 71,
74, 78, 82, 84, 98, 110,
116, 134, 137, 157, 159,
161, 167, 169, 173, 174,
180, 188, 191, 194, 196,
203, 207, 218, 219, 228,
229, 232, 235, 247, 250,
253, 266, 268, 301, 302,
314, 320, 338, 340
KINCAID GALLERY, 82, 82
KINDER HARRIS, 81, 191, 196,
270, 279, 286, 307, 328

KINDRED SINKS, 177, 184
KING CONTRACT, 257
KING HICKORY, 35, 38, 56, 71,
78, 84, 116, 120, 131,
150, 163, 167, 171, 191,
196, 200, 203, 229, 250,
257, 270, 274, 275, 279,
292, 296, 300, 305, 320,
328
KING KOIL, 27, 35, 84, 114, 116,
153, 241
KING MANOR, 78
KING'S CHANDELIER
COMPANY, 219, 335
KINGS ANTIQUE, 279
KINGS CREEK, 56, 78, 84, 279
KINGSDOWN, 27, 57, 71, 78, 84,
93, 96, 98, 101-103, 106,
114, 116, 141, 180, 191,
196, 200, 203, 211, 228,
229, 232, 241, 268, 279,
284, 292, 293, 302, 305,
317, 320
KINGSDOWN BEDDING, 211,
228, 320
KINGSLEY, 37, 38, 57, 114, 116,
143, 171, 191, 203, 207,
279, 314
KINGSLEY-BATES, 84, 114, 116,
143, 171, 191, 279, 314
KINGSTON HULL, 78, 279, 301
KINNEY, 32, 76, 270, 279
KIRK STIEFF, 241
KIRSCH, 39, 75, 106, 129, 130,
166, 178, 201, 207, 245,
252, 254, 295, 315, 324
KITCHLER, 191
KITTINGER, 29, 33, 94, 114, 137,
241, 305, 322
KJ'S FURNITURE OUTLET, 220,
340
KLAUSSNER, 35, 38, 57, 71, 74,
78, 79, 84, 116, 174, 203,
207, 279, 286, 297, 329
KLUDI FAUCETS, 177, 184
KNF, 191, 194, 229
KNIGHT GALLERIES INC, 221,
341
KNOB CREEK, 27, 29, 31, 33, 35,
36, 53, 57, 71, 84, 116,
131, 159, 171, 174, 191,
229, 235, 241, 250, 296,
306-307, 314, 317, 320,
327, 328
KNOLL, 33
KOCH, 26, 29, 35, 36, 84, 137,
159, 163, 177, 184, 200,
203, 235, 247, 253, 270,
279, 300, 304, 313, 328

KOCH & LOWY LAMPS, 159,
191, 207, 250, 270, 279
KOCH METALCRAFT, 200
KOCH ORIGINALS, 26, 29-31, 35,
36, 57, 84, 137, 163, 203,
207, 247, 250, 253, 304
KOFABCO, 287
KOHLER, 149, 177, 184
KRAUS, 28, 213
KRAVET, 32, 39, 71, 78, 137, 145,
146, 151, 157, 159, 191,
210, 238, 250, 254, 268,
270, 279, 296, 299, 309
KREISS, 114, 268
KRISTOLINA, 191
KROEHLER, 38, 74, 191, 228, 230
KROIN FAUCETS, 177, 184
KRUEGER, 257
KRUG, 257
KRUPNICK BROS, 191, 238, 299
KUSCH, 30, 157
KUSHWOOD, 33, 57, 279
KWC DOMO, 149
KWC FAUCETS, 177, 184
KWIK-FILE, 257
L & B, 30, 157, 257
L & S, 78, 84, 200, 211, 241
LA LACQUER WORKS, 84
LA MAISON, 82, 82
LaBARGE, 29-31, 33, 35, 36, 71,
81, 83, 84, 93, 94, 98,
100, 103, 114, 116, 131,
159, 163, 180, 188, 190,
191, 200, 203, 214, 221,
229, 241, 247, 250, 253,
266, 268, 270, 274, 275,
279, 287, 296, 300-302,
305, 314, 318, 320, 322,
327, 328, 331, 338
LaBARGE FACTORY OUTLET,
188, 221, 338
LACASSE, 257
LAFALEGNAMI, 279
LAFONT, 264
LAINE, 30, 34, 37-39, 47, 57, 71,
78, 83, 92, 94, 116, 120,
132, 134, 138, 150, 167,
188, 190, 194, 196, 206,
211, 214, 229, 241, 266,
279, 287, 301, 302, 305,
312, 317, 320, 327, 337
LAKE HICKORY FURNITURE,
222, 335
LAM LEE GROUP, 93
LAMARINA ANTIQUES, 78, 84
LAMBERT, 150, 279
LAMONTAGE, 191, 279
LAMP WAREHOUSE, 34, 342
LANDMARK, 84, 128, 136

LANE, 25, 30-31, 33, 36, 41, 43, 45, 50-51, 55, 59-61, 66, 67, 70, 71, 74, 77, 78, 81-82, 84, 85, 98, 100, 102, 103, 106, 109, 110, 114, 117, 131, 134, 137, 138, 148, 157, 161, 169, 171-175, 180, 188, 189, 191, 194, 199, 200, 202, 203, 205, 214, 222, 224, 228-229, 234-235, 238, 241, 246, 247, 252, 253, 265, 266, 268, 273, 278-279, 284, 286, 287, 292, 293, 296, 297, 299, 304-305, 307, 311-314, 316-318, 325, 331, 338, 340

LANE GALLERY, 188, 224, 338

LANIER, 78

LANSCOT, 32, 201, 238, 242-244, 309

LANSCOT ARLEN, 32, 201, 238, 309

LARGO, 27, 27, 30, 117, 121, 203, 250, 296, 334

LATIMER, 242-244

LAUFEN, 177, 184

LAURA ASHLEY, 32, 57, 76, 178, 252, 258, 259

LAURA LEE DESIGNS, 191

LAUREL LAMPS, 114

LAURIER, 27, 84

LAWINGS FURNITURE, 224, 341

LAWRENCE UNLIMITED, 25, 84, 279

LAZAR, 30, 38, 57, 84, 157, 191, 318

LA-Z-BOY, 5, 1, 35-39, 54, 84, 93, 169, 257, 306, 307, 328

LCN DOOR CLOSERS, 177, 184

LD BRINKMAN, 90

LE CORBUSIER, 145

LEA, 27, 27, 29, 51, 57, 71, 74, 84, 93, 94, 116, 120, 121, 128, 134, 148, 150, 157, 161, 163, 174, 175, 191, 194, 196, 200, 203, 207, 211, 230, 232, 235, 241, 247, 250, 253, 266, 274, 275, 279, 287, 292, 300-302, 305, 307, 310, 311, 314, 320, 328

LEATHER CENTER, 84, 84

LEATHER LINING, 241

LEATHER LOUNGERS, 84

LEATHER SHOP, 225, 268, 292, 338

LEATHER SHOP, THE, 225, 338

LEATHER TECH, 35, 311

LEATHER UNLIMITED, 82, 82

LEATHERCRAFT, 30, 35, 38, 58, 93, 94, 120, 138, 150, 163, 171, 180, 200, 247, 253, 257, 268, 287, 305, 314, 323

LEATHERMAN'S GUILD, 58, 84, 207, 250, 268, 279, 292, 301

LEATHERMARK, 191

LEATHERTREND, 84, 163, 166, 191, 207

LEATHERWORKS, 58, 191, 314

LEBIJOU SINKS, 177, 185

LEDA, 27, 29, 33, 36, 84, 191

LEE INDUSTRIES, 34, 58, 78, 191, 268

LEE JOFA, 114, 191, 238, 241, 268

LEE TABLE PAD, 247, 253

LEE WOODARD, 78

LEE'S CARPET SHOWCASE, 226, 334

LEE/ROWAN, 245

LEEAZANNE, 84, 191, 279

LEEDO, 33, 58, 163, 257, 279, 287, 314

LEES, 28, 28, 58, 90, 169, 213, 226, 261, 314

LEGACY DESIGNS, 279

LEGACY LEATHER, 78, 84

LEGGETT & PLATT, 27, 58, 287

LEGRAND, 191

LEHIGH, 27, 29-31, 33, 36, 78

LEISTERS, 36, 58, 71, 78, 84, 120, 171, 175, 196, 203, 247, 253, 274, 275, 279, 287, 311, 314

LEISTERS OF HANOVER, 230

LEISURE HOUSE, 84, 120

LENNOX, 279

LENOIR HOUSE, 150

LENOX, 58, 58, 166, 191, 224, 274, 275, 287, 304, 314

LEN-DAL CARPETS & RUGS, 28

LEONARD'S OAK WORLD, 78

LEVOLOR, 39, 75, 128, 166, 178, 239, 252, 254, 264, 295, 299, 315, 324

LEXINGTON, 1, 27, 29, 31, 33, 34, 36-39, 71, 72, 78, 81, 84, 92-94, 98, 100, 102, 106-108, 110, 114, 116, 120, 127, 128, 131, 134, 137, 138, 143, 148, 150, 157, 159-161, 163, 167, 169, 174, 175, 180, 188, 191, 196, 200, 203, 207, 211, 214, 222, 226-228, 230, 232, 238, 241, 245, 247, 250, 253, 260, 262, 265, 266, 268, 270, 274, 275, 279, 284, 287, 288, 292, 296, 300-302, 305, 307, 310-312, 314, 317, 318, 320, 322, 327, 328, 330, 331, 338

LEXINGTON GALLERY (BOYLES), 226, 226

LIBERTY, 47, 59, 78, 84, 185, 194, 340

LIBRARY LAMPS, 93, 191

LIEF PETERSON, 84

LIFELINE, 287

LIFESTYLES OF CALIFORNIA, 71, 78, 203, 207

LIGHT & SIGHT, 314

LIGHT SOURCE, 84

LIGHTING, 5, 25, 37, 43, 50, 51, 57, 60, 62, 65-68, 73, 76, 79, 84, 92, 114, 143, 145, 159, 177-178, 184-185, 187, 189, 193, 196, 203, 206, 223, 224, 235, 240, 241, 249, 250, 268, 270, 276, 279-280, 286, 301, 303, 304, 310, 313-314, 335, 340, 342

LIGHTING ENTERPRISES, 191

LIGHTING MATEGRA, 196

LIGHTS UP, 84

LIGNE, 328

LIGO, 74, 78, 84, 169, 247, 253, 279

LIGON IMPORTS, 279

LILLIAN AUGUST, 99, 141, 191, 230, 235, 250, 296

LINA'S INTERIORS, 191

LINCOLN GERARD, 82, 84, 227, 340

LINCOLN GERARD USA INC, 227, 340

LINDEN CLOCKS, 308

LINDY'S FURNITURE COMPANY, 227

LINEAGE, 27, 29, 31, 34-36, 38, 84, 191

LINEAL, 37, 60, 66, 279

LINK, 26, 26, 27, 31, 37, 58, 110, 114, 116, 131, 137, 150, 153, 157, 159, 169, 172, 174, 206, 207, 228-230, 247, 250, 252, 268, 274, 275, 299, 307, 313, 314, 322, 325, 327, 328, 331

LINK TAYLOR, 27, 74, 81, 84, 93, 120, 137, 161, 163, 167, 191, 196, 207, 214, 222,

228, 230, 232, 235, 270, 279, 288, 292, 300, 301, 304, 311, 312, 320
LINRENE, 280
LISTER BY GEEBRO, 280
LITE SOURCE, 34, 84, 257
LITELINE LTD LAMPS, 196
LITTLE BRIDGE LANE, 191
LITTLE MISS LIBERTY, 194
LITTLE ONES, 27
LJ BEST FURNITURE, 228, 342
LLOYD, 36-38, 58, 71, 74, 78, 81, 84, 93, 106, 116, 143, 159, 161, 163, 169, 171, 191, 196, 199, 203, 207, 230, 232, 235, 241, 247, 250, 253, 266, 268, 270, 287, 292, 296, 300, 301, 305, 307, 310, 314, 317, 320, 325, 328
LLOYD FLANDERS, 71, 74, 78, 81, 84, 93, 106, 114, 116, 143, 159, 161, 163, 169, 171, 191, 196, 199, 203, 207, 230, 232, 235, 241, 247, 250, 253, 266, 268, 270, 287, 292, 296, 300, 301, 305, 307, 310, 314, 317, 320, 328
LO BROS, 143
LOCK, 27, 34, 41, 77, 184, 185, 206, 240, 249, 301
LOFTIN-BLACK FURNITURE COMPANY, 229, 342
LOLA LTD, 78
LONG COAST LAMPS, 191
LORRAINE HEADBOARDS, 163
LORTS, 157, 191
LOTFY & SONS, 191
LOTUS ARTS, 92, 191, 280, 314
LOUIS BOWEN, 32, 58, 137, 252
LOUIS DE POORTERE, 191
LOUIS J SOLOMON, 207
LOUNGE SHOP, THE, 230, 336
LOUVERDRAPE, 39, 75, 128, 166, 178, 254, 255, 264, 295, 324
LOWENSTEIN, 30, 157, 207, 257, 268, 304
LT MOSES WILLARD, 84, 191, 222
LUBKE, 196
LUCE LIGHTING, 177, 184
LUCIA DESIGNS, 191
LUI, 280
LUIGI CRYSTAL, 34, 231, 343
LULLABYE, 302
LUMINARIES, 84
LUMINART PICTURES, 280

LUNAR, 191
LUX ART SILKS, 191
LUXURY FABRICS AND INTERIORS, 231, 335
LYNDON, 84, 208
LYNN HANEY, 84
LYNN HOLLYN, 37, 143, 207, 235, 280, 288, 305
LYON SHAW, 29, 58, 71, 74, 78, 81, 84, 93, 114, 116, 120, 137, 143, 161, 163, 169, 171, 191, 199, 203, 207, 230, 235, 247, 250, 253, 266, 270, 274, 275, 280, 287, 300, 301, 320, 328
M & B, 39, 239, 255, 295, 299, 315, 324
M & M NAUTICAL, 161
M&H SEATING, 270
MAC SCULPTURE, 191
MACKIE FURNITURE CO, INC, 232, 336
MACKINTOSH, 145
MACON UMBRELLA, 37, 161, 304
MADDOX, 94, 114, 274, 275
MADE IN THE SHADE, 314
MADISON AVENUE, 32, 191
MADISON FURNITURE, 280
MADISON SQUARE, 58, 71, 72, 78, 84, 93, 94, 101, 106, 107, 114, 116, 120, 131, 137, 150, 159, 163, 171, 191, 203, 207, 214, 230, 235, 241, 247, 250, 253, 266, 268, 274, 275, 280, 284, 287, 300-302, 305, 310, 312, 314, 317, 320, 328, 331
MAENLINE, 32, 146, 238, 299
MAGNOLIA, 242-244, 310
MAGNUSSEN RESIDENTIAL, 163
MAHOGANY HEIRLOOMS, 59, 280
MAHOGANY REPRODUCTIONS, 207
MAIMI METAL, 280
MAIN STREET PENNSYLVANIA HOUSE, 82, 232, 340
MAIR ASTLEY, 28, 213
MAITLAND SMITH, 25, 74, 93, 98, 102, 103, 114, 116, 159, 160, 163, 171, 172, 180, 188, 191, 203, 214, 234, 235, 241, 250, 268, 280, 296, 300, 305, 314, 318, 331, 338, 340

MAITLAND SMITH FACTORY OUTLET, 188, 233, 338
MAITLAND SMITH FURNITURE OUTLET, 233, 340
MAJESTIC MIRRORS, 92
MALABAR GROVE, 172
MALLIN, 59, 207, 280
MALLORY'S FINE FURNITURE, 234, 341
MANCHESTER WOOD, 29, 30, 34, 36-37, 59, 280, 314
MANNINGTON, 213, 226, 314, 319, 321
MANOR HOUSE, 114
MANOR TRADITIONS, 280, 280
MANUEL CANOVAS, 32, 238
MAOR LIGHTING, 191
MAPTIME, 84
MARBLEWORKS, 280
MARBRO LAMPS, 74, 93, 116, 159, 191, 235, 250, 268, 280, 305, 314, 331
MARCELLA, 172
MARGE CARSON, 27, 33, 74, 98, 100, 102, 103, 180, 188, 191, 235, 338
MARGE CARSON GALLERY, 188, 235, 338
MARGLEN, 261
MARIE ALBERT, 84
MARIMEKKO, 32, 59
MARIMONT, 114
MARIO, 32, 71, 78, 81, 93, 166, 200, 207, 287, 312
MARION TRAVIS, 236, 342
MARK SALES CO, INC, 236, 343
MARK THOMAS, 78, 114, 207, 230, 302
MARKEL LIGHTING, 81, 166, 280, 292, 314
MARKET SAMPLE FURNITURE OUTLET, 237, 340
MARLENE'S DECORATOR FABRICS, 237, 342
MARLOW, 35, 71, 78, 94, 163, 191, 196, 203, 222, 230
MARSH CABINETS, 196
MARSHALL JAMES, 280
MART SHIPPING ASSOCIATION, 188
MARTEX, 27, 179
MARTHA ASHER, 134
MARTIN, 29, 34, 84, 201, 238, 259
MARTINSVILLE NOVELTY, 29, 30, 35, 36, 38, 59, 71, 78, 94, 134, 148, 150, 174, 196, 200, 230, 280, 314
MARTY RAE OF LEXINGTON, 238, 343

MARVEL, 163, 257
MARY DALE LAMPS, 134, 196
MARYLAND CLASSICS, 137,
        163, 207, 230, 250, 268,
        280, 287, 300, 305, 310,
        314
MASLAND, 28, 73, 90, 116, 137,
        159, 163, 169, 207, 213,
        241, 250, 261, 268, 305,
        314, 318, 319, 331
MASSON HAMLIN (PIANOS), 94,
        94
MASSOUD, 59, 116, 191
MASTER DESIGN, 29-31, 35, 39,
        59, 78, 84, 120, 128, 196,
        203, 207, 280, 287
MASTER LOCK, 177, 185
MASTERCRAFT, 32, 59, 71, 94,
        101, 116, 159, 191, 238,
        241, 250, 318
MASTERFIELD, 71, 78, 84, 94,
        120, 167, 175, 196, 203,
        280, 292
MASTERLOOMS, 163, 191
MASTERPIECE DESIGN, 78, 84
MASTERPIECE
        REPRODUCTIONS, 78
MATTEO, 191, 261
MAURICE HERBEAU, 177, 184
MAX HOWARD, 84, 191
MAXIM, 35, 177, 185, 191
MAXTON, 25, 84, 191, 287
MAYFAIR, 32, 276
MAYFIELD LEATHER, 239, 338
MAYFLOWER, 32, 146
McENROE, 207, 280, 314
McFARLINS, 191
McGUIRE, 37, 59, 116, 137, 159,
        241, 250, 268, 280
McKAY CUSTOM PRODUCTS,
        78, 81, 150
McKAY TABLE PADS, 74, 93,
        159, 163, 169, 191, 200,
        207, 222, 232, 235, 241,
        250, 268, 274, 275, 287,
        300, 301, 305, 314, 317
McKINLEY LEATHER, 35, 59, 78,
        93, 116, 191, 194, 230,
        280, 287, 305, 312, 323
MDC DIRECT, INC, 239, 334
MEADOWCRAFT, 27, 37, 59, 63,
        71, 78, 84, 93, 114, 163,
        171, 191, 199, 200, 203,
        241, 268, 280, 300-302,
        304, 306, 311, 314, 325
MECKLENBURG FURNITURE,
        240, 335
MEDALLION, 82, 114, 340

MEDALLION FURNITURE, 82,
        241, 340
MELARD, 149
MELINDA TRENT, 84
MENDEL, 78
MER, 191, 270
MERCER, 261, 261
MERRIMAC, 32, 59, 201, 238,
        242-244
MERSMAN, 36, 71, 78, 94, 150,
        167, 196, 207, 274, 275,
        280, 287, 301, 302
METRO MILLS, 146
METROPOLITAN LIGHTING, 191
MEYDA TIFFANY, 34, 191
MIAMI METAL, 59, 81, 318
MICHAEL ARAM, 84
MICHAEL SHOWALTER, 27, 280
MICHAEL THOMAS, 35, 38, 59,
        72, 84, 114, 116, 143,
        159, 171, 191, 207, 214,
        235, 250, 280, 281, 296,
        300-302, 306, 320, 327,
        328
MICHAEL'S, 32, 84, 137, 146
MICHAEL'S TEXTILES, 32, 146
MICHAELIAN & KOHLBERG,
        191
MICHAELS CO, 78, 191, 287, 314
MIDAS FABRIC, 242-243,
        335-336, 341
MIES VAN DER ROHE, 145
MIKASA, 301
MIKHAIL DARAFEEV, 59, 84, 93,
        163, 191, 270, 280, 287,
        328
MILA INTERNATIONAL, 280
MILES, 28, 74, 84, 91, 111, 118,
        157, 171, 213, 214, 313,
        327, 328, 335
MILES TALBOT, 84, 157, 171,
        214, 327, 328
MILL CREEK, 238, 242-244
MILLENDER, 81, 137, 163, 191,
        196, 230, 235, 241, 300,
        301
MILLENIUM, 27, 59, 78, 84, 121,
        191, 207, 215, 280, 287,
        320, 328
MILLER DESK, 33, 59, 84, 94,
        163, 167, 172, 191, 196,
        200, 203, 241, 247, 253,
        257, 270, 280, 301, 317
MILLER IMPORTS, 81, 191
MILLER OFFICE DESKS, 287
MILLER'S - THE WINDOW
        DECOR STORE, 244
MILLIKEN, 32, 73, 191, 280, 314,
        319

MILLS CUSTOM HOUSE
        NUMBERS, 177, 185
MINCEY'S INC, 245, 335
MINI-BLINDS, 95, 255
MINKA, 177, 185, 191
MINOFF LAMPS, 169, 280, 314
MINT HILL LAMPS, 196
MIRAGE, 32, 252, 299
MIRROR CRAFT, 143, 196
MIRROR FAIR, 60, 280
MITCHELL, 32, 299
MOBEL, 71, 74, 78, 84, 121, 150,
        167, 176, 191, 196, 203,
        222, 247, 253, 284, 295,
        302, 314
MOBILIA, 84, 94
MOBY DICK, 287
MODA LIGHTING, 191
MODERN CLASSICS, 84, 145, 157
MODERN UPHOLSTERY CO,
        246, 340
MODULAR CONCEPTS, 196
MODULUS, 301
MODUS, 84
MOEN, 149
MOHAWK, 28, 30, 34, 36, 60, 69,
        78, 84, 90, 163, 191, 203,
        211, 213, 222, 226, 261
MOLLA, 30, 37, 60, 114, 191, 280
MONET, 177, 185
MONITOR, 114
MONROE'S FURNITURE, 246,
        252, 343
MONTAGE, 84, 191, 280, 287
MONTGOMERY, 47, 67, 94, 167,
        171
MONTICELLO, 28, 67, 213, 261
MOON COLLECTION, 84, 157,
        280
MOON/MONTAGE, 287
MOONLIGHT TIFFANY LAMP &
        FIXTURES, 191
MOONLIGHTING, 191
MOOSEHEAD, 27, 31, 33-36, 38,
        60, 71, 78, 84, 93, 106,
        116, 121, 138, 191, 203,
        207, 230, 247, 253, 280,
        292, 302, 314, 317, 320,
        328
MORGAN STEWART, 74, 78, 84,
        121, 188, 191, 203, 230,
        232, 248, 274, 275, 280,
        338
MORGAN STEWART GALLERY,
        188, 248, 338
MORGANTON CHAIR, 74, 84,
        121, 207, 232, 300
MORRIS GREENSPAN, 71, 200,
        207, 274, 275, 302

MOTIF, 32, 137, 155, 207
MOTION ONLY, 34, 114
MOTIONCRAFT, 38, 60, 84, 98,
  100, 103, 114, 116, 159,
  171, 180, 188, 191, 200,
  235, 248, 250, 266, 280,
  287, 296, 314, 318, 328,
  338
MOTIONCRAFT GALLERY, 188,
  248, 338
MOTTAHEDEH, 191, 241, 268,
  280, 331
MP IMPORTS, 191, 280
MR STEAM, 177, 185
MRS H'S HANDLES, 177, 185
MT AIRY, 26, 27, 31, 33, 36, 60,
  71, 74, 78, 79, 84, 93-94,
  106, 116, 121, 131, 138,
  143, 150, 157, 159, 161,
  167, 171, 172, 174, 191,
  196, 200, 203, 207, 230,
  235, 250, 270, 280, 287,
  292, 296, 300-302, 310,
  311, 314, 317, 320, 327,
  331
MUNIZ, 84
MUROBELLO, 191
MURPHY, 27, 78, 134, 148, 174,
  176, 200, 203
MURRAY FEISS, 34, 60, 114, 159,
  177, 185, 196, 200, 207,
  241, 250, 268, 270, 279,
  280, 287, 302, 303
MURROW FURNITURE
  GALLERIES, 249, 342
MY DOG SPOT BEDDING, 84
MY ROOM, 84
MYRTLE DESK, 94, 150, 196, 280
MYSON TOWEL WARMERS,
  177, 185
MYSTIC VALLEY TRADERS, 280
NADEAU, 31, 36, 84, 208
NAFCO, 261, 314, 319
NAGYKERY IMPORTS, 191, 280
NAJARIAN, 27, 84, 230
NAPP DEADY, 287
NAPTIME, 191
NATHAN HALE, 26, 27, 29, 31,
  36, 60, 71, 79, 84, 94,
  106, 121, 131, 138, 167,
  191, 196, 203, 207, 211,
  214, 222, 230, 250, 268,
  280, 287, 292, 295-296,
  300, 314, 317
NATHAN LAGIN LAMPS, 94
NATIONAL ART GALLERY, 188,
  188

NATIONAL BLIND AND
  WALLPAPER
  FACTORY, 251, 335
NATIONAL CAROLINA
  INTERIORS, 246, 252,
  343
NATIONAL CLOCK GALLERY,
  188, 188
NATIONAL DECORATORS, 32,
  254, 334
NATIONAL FURNITURE, 254,
  336
NATIONAL MT AIRY, 26, 27, 31,
  33, 36, 60, 71, 74, 79, 84,
  93, 94, 106, 114, 116,
  121, 131, 138, 143, 150,
  157, 159, 161, 167, 171,
  172, 174, 191, 196, 200,
  203, 207, 230, 235, 250,
  270, 280, 287, 292, 296,
  300-302, 306-307, 310,
  311, 314, 317, 320, 327,
  331
NATURAL DECORATIONS, 191,
  314
NATURAL LIGHT, 60, 81, 84, 157,
  166, 172, 207, 250, 270,
  280, 287, 306, 314
NATUZZI, 35, 74, 84, 92, 163, 191,
  272, 280, 328
NAUTILUS IMPORTS, 200
NDI, 25, 270, 280
NEIDERMEIER, 84
NESSEN, 280
NETTLE CREEK, 114
NETWORK FLOOR COVERING,
  255, 334
NEVERS, 257
NEW CENTURY PICTURE, 287
NEW CREATIONS, 71, 196, 241
NEW ENGLAND BLINDS, 255,
  342
NEW ENGLAND CLOCK, 29, 60,
  79, 84, 200, 258, 308,
  314
NEW ENGLAND UPHOLSTERY,
  146
NEW MARBRO, 331
NEW RIVER ARTISAN, 84, 270,
  280
NEW VISION, 319
NEWPORT BRASS, 177, 185
NEWPORT CABINET, 314
NICHOLAS JAMES, 280
NICHOLS & STONE, 29, 31, 34,
  36, 38, 60, 71, 74, 79, 84,
  106, 107, 110, 114, 116,
  121, 131, 138, 150, 159,
  163, 167, 171, 191, 196,

200, 203, 230, 241, 247,
  250, 253, 266, 268, 280,
  287, 292, 296, 301, 302,
  306-307, 310-312, 314,
  320, 328
NICOLETTI, 84, 85
NJ ROSS, 279
NOBAR FABRICS, 146, 159, 207,
  250
NOBILIS, 273
NOJO, 191
NORA FENTON, 84, 93, 134, 167,
  169, 191, 280, 287, 314,
  328
NORBERT ROESSLER, 191
NORMAN PERRY, 34, 60, 81, 159,
  241, 250, 268, 280, 331
NORMAN ROCKWELL, 235, 270,
  311, 320
NORMAN'S, 32, 106, 114, 146,
  196
NORMAN'S OF SALISBURY, 32,
  106, 114, 146
NORSTAD POTTERY SINKS,
  177, 185
NORTH CAROLINA FURNITURE
  CLEARANCE, 256-256
NORTH HICKORY, 29, 34-35, 38,
  60, 71, 74, 79, 106, 114,
  116, 121, 138, 163, 167,
  196, 200, 207, 230, 268,
  280, 287
NORTH STAR, 79, 196, 207
NORTH STAR GAME TABLES,
  207
NORTHWEST, 7, 8, 23, 28, 213
NORTHWOOD, 32, 39, 71, 79,
  106, 134, 292
NORWELL LIGHTING, 177, 185
NOSTALGIA, 188, 192
NOURY & SONS, 192
NOVA, 32, 83, 95, 190, 257, 279,
  328
NS GUSTIN, 314
NU WOODS, 316
NULCO, 34, 177, 185, 192, 224
NULL INDUSTRIES, 60, 71, 74,
  79, 84, 93, 94, 136, 150,
  163, 167, 174, 192, 196,
  200, 207, 222, 230, 247,
  253, 280, 287, 306, 311,
  312
NUTONE, 149, 177, 185, 192
O & P CHAIR, 287
O'ASIAN, 37, 71, 79, 143, 161,
  196, 230, 241, 301, 306,
  317, 331
OAK CRAFT, 29, 79, 280
OAK HERITAGE, 84

OAKWOOD, 27, 29, 79, 84, 167, 203
OASIS WHIRLPOOLS, 177, 185
OEM IMPORTS, 84, 328
OFFICE IMAGES, 257, 340
OFFICE STAR, 84
OFS, 30, 33, 163, 257
OGGETTI, 33, 192, 280
OHIO TABLE PAD, 85, 203, 266, 292
OIL PAINTINGS, 172
OKLAHOMA CASTING, 166
OKLAHOMA IMPORTING, 270, 280, 287, 304
OLD COUNTRY REPRODUCTIONS, 134, 200
OLD HICKORY, 11, 25, 38, 60, 71, 79, 93, 94, 116, 121, 153, 163, 167, 171, 192, 196, 200, 203, 207, 241, 250, 268, 287, 292, 302, 314, 320
OLD HICKORY TANNERY, 25, 38, 60, 71, 79, 93, 94, 116, 121, 153, 163, 167, 171, 192, 196, 200, 203, 207, 241, 250, 268, 280, 287, 292, 302, 320
OLD SALEM, 58, 67, 235, 292, 311
OLD TOWN CLOCK SHOP, 258, 342
OLD WAVERLY, 207, 235, 250, 280, 287, 314
OLD WORLD WEAVERS, 32, 192
OLDE BRICKYARD COOPER, 287
OLNEY, 71, 140, 343
OLYMPIA LIGHTING, 192, 314
OMNIA, 85, 177, 185
ONDINE, 149
ONE OF A KIND, 85, 192, 205, 328
ORDEREST, 27, 85, 134, 192, 196
ORIENTAL ACCENTS, 81, 166, 192
ORIENTAL LACQUER, 60, 81, 85, 93, 157, 192, 196, 207, 270, 280, 314, 318
ORIENTAL PRODUCTS, 192
ORIENTAL RUGS BY, 131
ORIENTAL WEAVERS, 192, 192, 216
ORIGINALS 22, 157
ORIGO DESIGNS, 192
OSBORNE & LITTLE, 270
OTTO ZENKE, 280
OUTDOOR LIFESTYLE, 192, 257
OW LEE, 37, 60, 117

OXFORD LEATHER, 148
P & J HOME FURNISHINGS AND FABRIC OUTLET, 258
P & P CHAIR, 29, 37, 38, 60, 71, 79, 150, 174, 200, 247, 253, 280, 311, 314
P COLLINS, 32, 192, 238, 242-244, 268, 280
P KAUFMANN, 32, 110, 145, 151, 201, 238, 269
PACE, 280, 280
PACIFIC COAST, 79, 85, 157, 166, 192, 280
PACIFIC RATTAN, 37, 61, 79, 143, 207, 280, 306
PACIFIC WEAVERS, 238
PALAIS ROYAL, 179
PALAZETTI, 280
PALECEK, 25, 61, 172, 200, 230, 241, 270, 280, 287, 301, 314, 328
PALLISER, 27-27, 33-34, 36, 38, 61, 82, 85, 121, 128, 192, 201, 203, 259-260, 280, 323, 340
PALMER HOME COLLECTION, 58, 192, 227, 328
PAMA, 79, 85
PANASONIC, 247, 253
PANDE CAMERON RUGS, 94, 116, 131, 159, 192, 241, 250, 270, 296, 306, 312, 314
PANEL CONCEPTS, 257
PAOLI, 30, 33, 116, 157, 207, 257, 280, 306, 314
PAPER WHITE, 270, 280
PARADIGM, 85
PARADISE MILLS, 135, 135
PARAGON DECORS, 192
PARAGON PICTURES, 85, 121, 134, 166, 172, 196, 280, 287, 301
PARAMOUNT, 85, 134, 260, 340
PARAMOUNT FURNITURE CO INC, 260, 340
PARK AVENUE, 192, 196, 207, 306
PARK IMPORTS, 192
PARK PLACE, 27, 30, 38, 61, 81, 85, 92, 116, 121, 131, 157, 167, 196, 235, 287, 292, 320
PARK PLACE SLEEPERS, 131
PARKER SOUTHERN, 79, 85, 108, 163, 192, 194, 203, 247, 253, 312, 328
PARKER'S CARPET, 261, 334
PARLIAMENT, 85, 280

PASSPORT, 25, 33, 36, 81, 93, 166, 304
PASTEL, 85, 192
PATCRAFT, 213, 261, 319
PAUL BARROW, 32, 145
PAUL DECORATIVE/GREENWICH COLLECTION, 177, 185
PAUL HANSON, 61, 114, 159, 207, 241, 250, 268, 301, 302
PAUL MARSHALL, 134
PAUL ROBERT, 94, 116, 192, 203, 250, 280
PAUL ROBINSON, 85, 280
PAVILLION, 85, 328
PAWLEY'S ISLAND HAMMOCK, 143, 171, 280, 314
PAYNE, 32, 114, 137, 210, 238, 241, 268, 318
PAYNE STREET, 192, 280
PEACHTREE, 32, 145, 146, 242-244, 290, 299, 306, 334
PEACOCK ALLEY, 85, 172, 280
PEARSON, 1, 3, 30-31, 35, 37-39, 61, 71, 79, 82, 85, 93, 94, 106, 114, 116, 120, 131, 138, 143, 150, 157, 160, 162, 163, 188-190, 196, 199, 206, 207, 214, 230, 235, 241, 249, 262, 266, 268, 274, 275, 278, 280, 287, 296, 300-302, 305, 310, 313, 317, 320, 327, 328, 338
PEARSON GALLERY, 188, 262, 338
PEE GEE LAMPS, 196, 200, 207
PEM KAY, 280
PEMBROKE, 79
PENDULES CLOCKS, 192
PENNS CREEK, 85
PENNSBURG WOODCRAFT, 207
PENNSYLVANIA, 14, 26-27, 29, 31, 34, 38-39, 57, 61, 71, 72, 79, 93, 108, 112, 121, 138, 163, 167, 169, 174, 180, 230, 232, 233, 257, 263, 266, 280, 287, 296, 300, 301, 307, 311, 314, 320, 327, 328, 338, 343
PENNSYLVANIA CLASSICS, 27, 31, 61, 71, 72, 79, 85, 92, 93, 110, 114, 116, 121, 138, 163, 167, 192, 203, 207, 230, 241, 257, 266,

Index

270, 280, 287, 300, 311, 320, 327, 328
PENNSYLVANIA HOUSE, 26, 27, 29, 34, 38-39, 57, 61, 85, 92, 108, 112, 114, 116, 169, 180, 192, 203, 207, 232, 233, 241, 263, 270, 296, 301, 307, 314, 338
PENNSYLVANIA HOUSE COLLECTOR'S GALLERY, 262, 340
PENNSYLVANIA HOUSE GALLERY, 188, 263
PENTURA, 85, 192, 328
PEOPLOUNGER, 71, 79, 85, 94, 163, 167, 196, 200, 203, 230, 280, 284, 287
PERFECTION, 79, 94, 196, 306
PERGO, 226
PERIOD BRASS HARDWARE, 177, 185
PERRIN & ROWE, 177, 185
PETER PEPPER, 257
PETERS-REVINGTON, 71, 79, 85, 103, 106, 163, 176, 192, 196, 200, 207, 222, 230, 235, 245, 247, 253, 268, 270, 280, 284, 296, 301, 310, 312, 314, 328
PETITE AMIE CHILDREN'S FURNITURE, 85
PETITES CHOSES, 85
PHASE IV, 287
PHILADELPHIA, 28, 37, 43, 61, 62, 66, 85, 90, 116, 139, 169, 211, 213, 231, 250, 261, 281, 287, 306, 314, 318, 319, 321, 343
PHILADELPHIA CARPET, 37, 116, 169, 213, 250, 287, 306, 314
PHILCO TV/STEREO, 134
PHILIP R, 121
PHILIP WHITNEY, 192
PHILLIP JEFFRIES, 270
PHILLIP REINISCH, 85, 134, 153, 166, 207, 280, 297, 328
PHILLIPS, 32, 38, 61, 85, 192, 263, 328, 340
PHILLIPS FURNITURE, 61, 85, 263, 280, 340
PHOENIX ART, 192, 280, 328
PHOENIX DESIGNS, 257
PHOENIX GALLERIES, 192
PICTURE SOURCE, 85
PIEDMONT DESIGN, 264, 338
PIEFA ART STONE, 192
PIERI, 85, 192
PIERRE DEUX, 238

PIETRARTE, 85, 223
PIETRO CONSTANTIANI, 85
PILGRIM GLASS, 287
PILLIOD FURNITURE, 134
PIMPERNEL, 172
PINDLER & PINDLER, 32, 137, 146, 192, 238, 268, 273
PINE QUARTERS, 85
PINECREST, 114
PINEHURST, 171, 304
PINE-TIQUE, 27, 31, 33-36, 79, 85, 114, 116, 148, 167, 280, 287, 301
PINNACLE, 37, 38, 79, 121, 161, 196, 203, 241, 280, 292, 306
PINTCHIK HOMEWORKS, 264, 342
PIRELLI RUBBER FLOORS, 261
PJ HAMILTON, 130
PLAN HOLD, 257
PLANT, 25, 25, 43, 85
PLANT PLANT, 25, 92, 93, 196, 207, 257, 268, 270, 280, 287, 301, 314, 331
PLANTATION COMFORT, 37, 37, 280
PLANTERS, 49
PLATT, 26-27, 38, 58, 62, 114, 160, 192, 250, 280, 287, 318
PLAZA FURNITURE GALLERY, 265, 336
PLAZA FURNITURE INC, 265, 343
PLEXI-CRAFT QUALITY PRODUCTS CORP, 266, 343
PLYCRAFT, 301
PM MATTRESS, 71
POLOMA PICASSO, 192
POLTROMEC/POLTROARREDO LEATHER, 117
POLYWOOD, 114, 192, 314
POLYWOOD FURNITURE, 114
POMEROY COLLECTION, 192
POMPEII, 62, 85, 102, 103, 116, 192, 235, 270, 280, 328
PORCHER CHINA SINKS & WATERCLOSETS, 177, 185
PORT MERION, 314
PORT ROYAL, 116, 137, 192, 240, 268, 300, 322
PORTER, 28, 28, 32, 213
PORTFOLIO, 238, 242-244
POULIOT, 25, 196, 207, 268, 287, 292, 301, 306, 314
POUNDER DINING, 85

POWELL, 27, 27, 33-36, 62, 85, 163, 192, 204, 280, 314
PRECEDENT, 38, 39, 62, 71, 79, 98, 100, 103, 114, 171, 188, 192, 207, 266, 267, 280, 338
PRECEDENT GALLERY, 188, 267, 338
PREMIER, 10, 29, 35, 77, 96, 116, 131, 179, 189, 240, 242-244, 286, 299, 301
PRESIDENTIAL, 85, 136, 280
PRESTIGE, 207
PRESTIGIOUS, 57, 187
PREVIEW, 38, 62, 74, 116, 157, 163, 197, 204, 207, 280, 318
PRIBA FURNITURE SALES AND INTERIORS, 267, 336
PRICE PFISTER, 149
PRINTER'S ALLEY STORES, 269, 336
PRIVATE LABEL, 62, 85, 152, 315
PRIVILEGE HOUSE, 163, 280
PRO SCAN, 85
PROFILE, 75
PROGRESSIVE, 27, 29, 36, 39, 62, 128
PROVIDENCE RUGS, 207
PULASKI, 25, 27, 30, 31, 36-39, 62-63, 71, 79-81, 85, 93, 94, 106, 121, 128, 134, 138, 143, 150, 157, 160, 161, 163, 167, 169, 174, 176, 189, 192, 197, 200, 204, 207, 211, 214, 215, 222, 230, 232, 234, 235, 238, 241, 245-247, 250, 252, 253, 266, 268, 270, 273, 280, 284, 287, 292, 296, 300-302, 304, 306-307, 310-312, 314, 317, 318, 320, 328
PUZZLE CRAFT, 85
QEW, 247, 253
QUADRILLE, 32, 192
QUAKER, 32, 242-244
QUALITY DINETTE, 134
QUALITY FURNITURE MARKET OF LENOIR, INC, 269, 341
QUALITY HOUSE, 32, 276
QUALITY LAMP, 192
QUEEN, 28, 35, 50, 134, 168, 213, 261, 288, 290, 314, 319, 322, 334
QUEEN ANNE, 35, 288
QUEEN CARPET, 213, 314, 322
QUEEN'S VIEW, 192

QUINTESSA ART, 192
QUINTESSENTIALS-QII, 177, 185
QUOIZEL, 34, 93, 121, 166, 177,
   185, 192, 200, 303
QUORUM, 192
R & M COCO, 299
R&M/COCO, 238
RA SIEGEL, 213
RABY, 85
RAJ, 85, 192
RALEIGH ROAD, 301
RALPH LAUREN, 32, 62, 76, 109,
   238, 252, 258, 259, 299
RALPH LAUREN FABRICS, 192
RALPH LAUREN WALLPAPERS,
   192
RAPIER, 242-244
RATTAN SPECIALTIES, 62, 143
RAVENWOOD, 287
RAYMOND WAITES, 103, 192,
   270
RCA HOME THEATRE, 85
RD STALLION, 28, 213, 261
REDRUM, 32, 146
REFLECTIONS, 79-79, 82, 85,
   163, 177, 184, 188, 190,
   194, 247, 250, 253, 271,
   300, 338, 340
REGAL, 60, 242-244
REGENCY, 32, 71, 79, 85, 148,
   163, 166, 192, 194, 197,
   204, 207, 257, 280, 314
REGENCY FURNITURE, 280
REGENCY HOUSE, 71, 79, 85,
   148, 163, 166, 192, 194,
   197, 204, 207, 257, 314
REGENT, 71
REID LEATHER, 197
REID WATSON PLUMBING, 178,
   185
RELAX-A-CLINER, 38, 148
RELAX-R, 192
RELIABLE BEDDING, 85
RELIABLE MATTRESS, 150
RELIANCE, 62, 62, 166, 172, 192,
   204, 207, 250, 270, 280,
   287
REMARK MFG, 200
REMBRANDT, 34, 62, 85, 166,
   192, 204, 224, 280
REMINGTON, 62, 71, 81, 166,
   197, 200, 204, 207, 224,
   241, 257, 268, 274, 275,
   280, 302, 304, 306, 314
RENOIR, 85
REPLACEMENTS, LTD, 272, 336
REPLOGLE, 197, 200, 301
REPROCRAFTERS, 25, 62, 92,
   121, 192, 280

REPRODUX, 138, 160, 207, 268,
   280, 300
RESOURCE DESIGN, 188, 188
RESTONIC, 27, 35, 71, 106, 128,
   192, 204
REUBENS, 85, 207, 272
REX, 29-31, 38, 71, 79, 85, 93,
   121, 151, 167, 192, 197,
   204, 207, 211, 214, 230,
   247, 250, 253, 266, 270,
   280, 284, 287, 292, 296,
   300-302, 314, 328
RHONEY FURNITURE HOUSE,
   188-188, 273-274
RICHARDSON BROS, 27, 30, 31,
   36, 38, 71, 79, 85, 94,
   106, 121, 131, 138, 163,
   167, 192, 197, 204, 207,
   230, 235, 268, 280, 287,
   296, 301, 310, 314, 328
RICHELIEU, 138
RICHLIGHT LAMP CO, 197
RICHLOOM, 32, 145, 201, 238,
   242-244
RICHMOND, 28, 61, 113, 213,
   261, 269, 343
RIDGEWAY, 25, 29, 63, 71, 79,
   94, 116, 121, 163, 197,
   200, 207, 230, 235, 241,
   258, 270, 280, 287,
   300-302, 306, 308, 320
RIDGEWOOD, 63, 79, 85, 163,
   174, 204, 250, 280, 287,
   306
RIVER OAKS, 79
RIVERSIDE, 27, 29, 45, 63, 71, 79,
   85, 93, 94, 116, 143, 148,
   150, 160, 161, 163, 167,
   169, 174, 176, 180, 192,
   197, 200, 204, 207, 211,
   214, 230, 232, 235, 245,
   247, 250, 253, 270, 274,
   275, 280, 287, 296,
   300-302, 304, 311, 314,
   317, 320, 328
RIVERWALK, 85, 192
RIVIERA, 117
ROBBINS BROS, 211
ROBERO BATH CABINETS, 177,
   185
ROBERT ABBEY LAMPS, 71, 85
ROBERT ALLEN, 32, 63, 72, 114,
   137, 145, 146, 151, 157,
   160, 163, 192, 204, 207,
   210, 235, 238, 250, 254,
   268, 270, 273, 278, 280,
   296, 299, 309, 318
ROBERT BERGELIN, 189, 189
ROBERT GRACE, 85, 192

ROBINSON, 29, 31, 37, 63, 85,
   106, 167, 204, 280, 312
ROBINSON IRON, 280
ROBINSON'S WALLCOVERINGS,
   276, 343
ROCK CITY, 27, 79, 85, 230, 247,
   253, 314
ROCKLAND INDUSTRIES, 32,
   146
ROMLIN LAMPS, 271
ROMWEBER, 27, 34, 36, 63, 114,
   157
RON FISHER, 29, 157, 192, 194
RON HAINER LIGHTING
   DESIGNS, INC, 276, 335
ROOMS TO GROW, 27, 174
ROPPE, 261
ROSALCO, 25, 27, 33, 36, 37, 121,
   197, 204, 280, 287, 306,
   314
ROSE CUMMINGS, 192, 238
ROSE FURNITURE, 8, 277, 340
ROSE JOHNSON, 257
ROSE TRUNKS, 200
ROSECORE CARPETS, 268
ROSENBAUM FINE ARTS, 280
ROSENTHAL NETTER, 207, 274,
   275
ROSS, 27, 78, 166, 167, 197, 200,
   204, 279, 301-303, 305,
   313
ROSSVILLE, 201
ROTHSCHILD, 242-244
ROUGIER, 207
ROUND THE HOUSE
   CASEGOODS, 85
ROWE, 35, 36, 38, 47, 63, 79, 85,
   116, 121, 128, 151, 153,
   177, 185, 189, 192, 194,
   197, 230, 280, 281, 287,
   320, 328, 338
ROWE GALLERY, 189, 281, 338
ROXTON, 85, 287
ROYAL DESIGNS, 192
ROYAL DUTCH CARPETS, 28,
   213
ROYAL HAEGAR LAMPS, 314
ROYAL PATINA, 63, 79, 85, 116,
   171, 192, 280, 287, 328
ROYAL WORCESTER/SPODE,
   314
ROYCE, 63, 280, 287
RR SCHIEBE, 36, 314
RUDD LIGHTING, 257
RUG BARN, 81, 85, 148
RUG HOLD, 192
RUG MARKET, 192
RUG ROOM, THE, 282, 338
RUG STORE, THE, 28, 282, 335

Index

RUPPERSBURG, 287
RUSTIC CRAFTS, 166
RYNONE, 27, 33, 318
S & K PRODUCTS, 287
S & S FABRICS, 32, 146, 299
S & S MILLS, INC, 283, 334
S BENT, 27, 85, 114, 116, 131, 250, 301, 302, 307, 314, 328
S HARRIS, 32, 238
SADEK, 81, 134, 166, 172, 189, 192, 222, 247, 252, 287, 301, 314
SADEK IMPORTS, 81, 134, 166, 172, 287, 314
SAGEFIELD, 163, 192, 270
SALEM, 7, 23, 28, 48, 58, 63, 67, 79, 85, 90, 116, 121, 138, 163, 166, 168, 192, 207, 213, 235, 241, 247, 250, 253, 258, 261, 266, 268, 280, 287, 292, 296, 300, 301, 304, 306, 311, 317, 319, 320, 328, 342
SALEM SQUARE, 63, 79, 85, 116, 121, 138, 163, 166, 192, 207, 241, 247, 250, 253, 266, 268, 280, 287, 296, 300, 301, 304, 306, 317, 320, 328
SALLY STOWE INERIORS, 283, 335
SALOOM, 29, 31, 35, 71, 79, 116, 163, 171, 197, 204, 207, 250, 296
SALTERINI, 36, 37, 63, 85, 114, 153, 304
SALVATORE POLIZZI, 85
SAM MOORE, 29, 29, 30, 38, 63, 79, 85, 93, 121, 157, 163, 189, 192, 204, 207, 230, 235, 247, 250, 253, 266, 268, 280, 284, 287, 296, 304, 307, 314, 318, 328, 339
SAM MOORE GALLERY, 189, 284, 339
SAMAD BROS, 192
SAMARCAND, 192
SAMSONITE, 30, 30, 37, 63, 117, 143, 160, 163, 174, 192, 197, 199, 204, 230, 257, 268, 280, 301, 302
SAMUEL HEATH & SONS, 177, 184
SAMUEL LAWRENCE, 63, 128, 280, 293
SAN DIEGO DESIGNS, 200, 280
SAN MIGUEL TRADING, 280

SANDER, 128
SANDERSON, 32, 192, 238, 280, 299, 309
SANDOWN, 238, 242-244
SANDOWN & BOURNE, 238
SANITAS, 32, 76, 175, 252, 299
SAN-DON, 197
SARATOGA, 85, 192, 272
SARATOGA MARBLE, 85, 272
SARREID, 25, 25, 63, 79, 81, 85, 93, 114, 116, 131, 160, 163, 169, 192, 207, 230, 235, 247, 250, 253, 268, 270, 274, 275, 280, 287, 296, 301, 304, 311, 314, 317, 318, 328, 331
SAUDER, 27, 27, 29, 33, 34, 36, 37, 63, 79
SAXON, 79
SCALAMANDRE, 32, 64, 114, 192, 238, 241, 268, 273, 280, 318
SCHEIBE, 280
SCHLAGE DOOR HARDWARE, 177, 185
SCHNADIG, 31, 36, 38, 56, 64, 79, 84, 85, 153, 163, 197, 204, 207, 280, 287
SCHOLTE TABLE, 192
SCHONBEK, 177, 185, 192, 303
SCHOONBECK, 114, 241, 306
SCHOTT, 39, 114, 160, 163, 241, 250, 300, 301, 311
SCHUMACHER, 32, 64, 71, 79, 114, 137, 146, 160, 178, 192, 193, 204, 207, 210, 230, 238, 241-244, 250, 254, 268, 270, 276, 280, 301, 318
SCHWAB, 257
SCHWARTZ, 71
SCHWEIGER, 34, 36-39, 64, 71, 79, 85, 94, 121, 151, 163, 197, 204, 207, 215, 280, 287, 310
SCULLINI, 81
SEABROOK, 32, 64, 76, 142, 157, 160, 250, 252, 268, 270, 299
SEABROOK WALLCOVERING, 160, 250, 270
SEALY, 27, 35, 71, 79, 98, 114, 121, 128, 131, 151, 157, 161, 167, 176, 180, 197, 200, 207, 209, 214, 241, 245, 247, 250, 253, 268, 280, 287, 292, 302, 317, 320, 328, 331

SEALY BEDDING, 64, 94, 121, 287, 292
SEALY FURNITURE, 85, 192, 314
SEALY FURNITURE OF MARYLAND, 85, 280, 314
SEALY LEATHER, 192
SEALY MATTRESS, 151, 160, 167, 197, 200, 204, 207
SEALY OF CONNECTICUT, 94
SEALY OF MARYLAND, 64, 230, 250
SEASONS OUTDOOR GALLERY, 189, 189
SECOND AVE, 85, 192, 270
SEDGEFIELD, 34, 64, 79, 81, 85, 93, 94, 106, 114, 116, 137, 163, 166, 167, 169, 192, 197, 204, 207, 230, 235, 241, 247, 250, 253, 266, 270, 280, 287, 300, 304, 306, 307, 310, 312, 314, 317, 328
SEDGEFIELD LEATHER, 167
SEDGEWICK RATTAN, 37, 93, 280
SEE IMPORTS, 85, 270, 280
SEIGEL LIGHTING, 303
SELECT MANUFACTURING, 134
SELIG, 64, 79, 94, 116, 197, 207, 230, 241, 302, 317
SEPTEMBER WOODS, 85
SERTA, 27, 35, 64, 71, 79, 85, 93, 121, 131, 134, 138, 157, 160, 161, 163, 167, 174, 192, 197, 200, 204, 207, 211, 221, 230, 241, 247, 250, 253, 266, 268, 270, 274, 275, 280, 287, 292, 296, 300-302, 307, 310-312, 317, 328
SETH THOMAS, 29, 197, 200
SEVEN SEAS OF KEY WEST, 301
SHADOW CATCHER, 85, 287, 328
SHADY LADY, 93, 192
SHAFER SEATING, 197
SHAHEEN, 28, 213
SHALOM BROS, 192
SHARUT, 27, 29, 33-36, 85, 272
SHAW, 28, 29, 37, 58, 61, 69, 71, 74, 78, 81, 84, 90, 93, 94, 106, 114, 116, 120, 137, 143, 150, 159, 161, 163, 169, 171, 191, 196, 199, 200, 203, 207, 213, 226, 230, 235, 241, 247, 250, 253, 261, 266, 268, 270, 274, 275, 280, 287,

300-302, 305, 314, 317, 320, 328, 341
SHAW FURNITURE GALLERIES, 285, 341
SHEFFIELD, 28, 35, 37, 213
SHELBY WILLIAMS, 33, 292, 306
SHELLY'S CUSHIONS, 37, 192, 199, 287, 314
SHELLY'S CUSHIONS & UMBRELLAS, 192, 287
SHENANDOAH, 35, 38, 64, 85, 204, 207, 208
SHEPHERDS DISCOUNT FURNITURE, 288, 335
SHERIDAN, 192, 247, 253
SHERMAG, 27, 33, 38, 49, 85, 106, 192
SHERRILL, 3-3, 31, 35, 36, 39, 50, 62, 64, 93, 94, 114, 116, 160, 172, 189, 192, 193, 197, 204, 207, 234, 235, 240, 247, 250, 253, 266, 268, 271, 278, 286-288, 296, 302, 314, 317, 327, 339
SHERRILL GALLERY, 189, 288, 339
SHERRY KLINE, 85
SHOAL CREEK, 34, 85, 137, 160, 197, 235, 241, 287, 301, 306, 317
SHUFORD, 85, 94, 114, 116, 160, 163, 192, 241, 250, 280, 287, 296, 302, 307, 317, 320, 328
SHUTTER DEPOT, 289, 334
SIBES ACCESSORIES, 177, 185
SIDEX, 29-31, 148
SIDNEY ARTHUR, 85, 163, 194
SIERRA, 85, 130, 274, 275
SIGLA, 280
SIGN OF THE CRAB, 149
SIGNATURE LIGHTING, 81, 222
SIGNATURE RUGS, 192, 280, 287
SILK SURPLUS, 32, 289, 343
SILK TREE FACTORY, 287
SILVER, 30, 36, 37, 64, 135, 163, 207, 217
SILVER QUEEN, THE, 290, 334
SILVER SHOP, 290, 334
SILVESTRI, 197, 200, 280, 314
SIMMONS, 27, 35, 38, 64, 79, 96, 106, 114, 121, 163, 169, 194, 197, 204, 207, 235, 300, 304, 306
SIMPLY SOUTHERN, 71, 79, 167, 172, 204, 222, 235, 250, 314, 320
SINA ORIENTAL RUG, 28, 28

SINGER, 27, 34, 36, 64, 79, 94, 114, 121, 134, 151, 167, 197, 207, 228, 230, 280, 302, 320
SINGER-MANOR HOUSE, 114
SINOUS, 192
SITCOM, 85
SK DINETTES, 320
SK FURNITURE, 29, 31, 200, 207
SK PRODUCTS, 64, 71, 79, 85, 116, 148, 157, 163, 174, 192, 194, 197, 204, 266, 280, 292, 301, 310, 314, 328
SKILLCRAFT, 79, 85, 92, 106, 121, 192, 197, 204, 211, 230, 247, 253, 271, 280, 292, 300, 301, 311, 312, 314
SKYLAND FURNITURE SHOP, 291, 341
SLEEP MASTER, 174
SLEEP SHOP, 292, 292-293
SLEEP WORKS, 27, 38, 85, 192
SLIDE THREE STUDIO, 85
SLIGH, 25, 33, 34, 36, 64, 71, 79, 85, 93, 94, 98, 100, 101, 106, 114, 116, 131, 138, 163, 167, 172, 180, 192, 207, 214, 230, 241, 247, 250, 251, 253, 258, 268, 271, 280, 287, 296, 301, 302, 306, 308, 312, 314, 317, 320, 322, 328
SM HEXTER, 32, 137
SMIDBO ACCESSORIES, 177, 185
SMITH SYSTEMS, 257
SMOKEY MOUNTAIN FURNITURE OUTLET, 293, 341
SNOW CATCHERS, 172
SOBOL HOUSE OF FURNISHINGS, 294, 335
SOFA ART BY G NICOLETTI, 85
SOICHER MARIN, 287, 328
SOIL SHIELD, 191
SOMEREST PICTURES, 85
SOMERSET, 25, 52, 85, 192
SOMMA, 27, 71, 79, 106, 174, 207, 280, 301, 312, 317
SOURCE INTERNATIONAL, 257
SOUTH CONE, 79, 247, 253, 328
SOUTH CORE, 85
SOUTH SEAS, 79, 121, 192, 207, 257, 271, 280, 294, 325, 336

SOUTH SEAS RATTAN, 79, 121, 192, 207, 257, 271, 280, 294, 336
SOUTHAMPTON, 72, 85, 98, 100-102, 114, 116, 138, 172, 192, 235, 241, 250, 268, 280, 287, 296, 307, 314, 317, 328, 331
SOUTHEAST WHOLESALERS, 295, 334
SOUTHERN, 23, 26-27, 29, 33, 36-38, 65, 85, 93, 108, 114, 148, 161, 163, 189, 194, 203, 204, 222, 230, 266, 280, 295, 296, 300, 304, 312, 339
SOUTHERN BRASS BED, 114
SOUTHERN CRAFTSMEN GUILD, 148, 163, 247, 253, 280
SOUTHERN DESIGNS, 189, 189
SOUTHERN FURNITURE, 27, 27, 29, 36, 38, 65, 116, 163, 167, 250, 266, 296, 300, 306, 314, 320
SOUTHERN FURNITURE OF CONOVER, 33, 85, 167, 222, 287, 306
SOUTHERN FURNITURE REPRODUCTIONS, 27, 33, 36, 65, 116, 163, 222, 287, 300, 314
SOUTHERN MANOR, 306
SOUTHERN OF CONOVER, 116, 121, 172, 192, 280
SOUTHERN OFFICE, 33, 161, 304
SOUTHERN REPRODUCTIONS, 93, 235, 328
SOUTHERN TABLE, 71, 280
SOUTHERN TRADITION, 79
SOUTHLAND FURNITURE GALLERIES, 296
SOUTHMARK, 35, 138, 160, 235, 306
SOUTHWEST CO, 280
SOUTHWEST DESIGNS, 280
SOUTHWESTERN IMPORTS, 192
SOUTHWOOD, 25, 26, 31, 33, 35, 36, 38, 65, 71, 72, 79, 85, 94, 98, 100-102, 107, 114, 116, 121, 131, 180, 192, 197, 204, 230, 235, 238, 241, 250, 268, 280, 287, 296, 302, 306-307, 310, 317, 320, 322, 327, 328, 331
SOUTHWOOD REPRODUCTIONS, 71, 72, 79, 94, 121, 192, 235,

241, 268, 280, 302, 322, 327

SOVA & SOVA, 280, 331

SOVEREIGN COLLECTION, 306

SPEAKMAN, 177, 185

SPECTRA GALLERIES, 79

SPECTRUM, 32, 85, 134, 238, 242-244

SPEED QUEEN, 134

SPEER, 72, 74, 81, 114, 116, 160, 172, 192, 222, 235, 250, 280, 287, 292, 300, 304, 318, 331

SPEER COLLECTIBLES, 81, 280, 287, 300, 304

SPEER LAMPS, 74, 116

SPEER LIGHTING, 192, 292

SPINNING WHEEL RUGS, 192, 271

SPIRAL, 85

SPRAGUE & CARLTON, 114, 197

SPRING AIR, 27, 33, 35, 65, 71, 79, 85, 127, 151, 163, 192, 204, 207, 247, 253, 268, 271, 280, 287

SPRING AIR BEDDING, 247, 253, 271

SPRING VALLEY DISCOUNT FURNITURE, 297, 336

SPRING WALL, 121

SPRINGS, 15-16, 62, 134, 331, 332

SPRINGWALL MATTRESS, 85

ST MARTIN'S LANE, 82, 85, 297, 340

ST MARTIN'S LANE LTD, 82, 297, 340

ST THOMAS CHINA, 177, 185

ST THOMAS CREATIONS, 149

ST TIMOTHY, 79, 167, 204, 270, 280, 300, 301

ST TIMOTHY CHAIR, 79, 167, 301

STAINSAFE, 194

STAKMORE, 65, 79, 106, 163, 192, 200, 207, 274, 275, 280, 292, 301, 304, 306, 314

STANDARD OF GARDNER, 114

STANFORD, 38, 65, 85, 160, 171, 192, 235, 280, 300, 307, 314, 327, 328

STANICK, 200

STANLEY, 27, 27, 29-31, 33-34, 36, 37, 39, 63, 65, 79, 82, 85, 92-94, 96, 98, 100, 102, 103, 106-108, 110, 114, 116, 121, 127, 131, 138, 148, 151, 157, 160, 161, 163, 167, 169, 172,

174, 176, 180, 189, 192, 193, 197, 200, 207, 211, 214, 222, 230, 241, 246, 247, 250, 253, 268, 270, 271, 274, 275, 281, 287, 292, 296, 298, 300-302, 304, 306-307, 310-311, 314, 317, 318, 320, 328, 339, 340

STANLEY GALLERY, 82, 189, 216, 298, 339, 340

STAR, 79, 84, 85, 190, 196, 207, 298, 342

STAR CARPET BLIND & WALLCOVERINGS, 298, 342

STARFIRE LIGHTING, 177, 185

STARK CARPETS, 114, 268, 318

STATE OF HICKORY, 71

STATEMENTS, 51, 281

STATESVILLE, 46, 61, 65, 71, 72, 79, 85, 94, 106, 110, 116, 121, 131, 138, 143, 163, 169, 174, 192, 204, 207, 230, 236, 241, 247, 250, 253, 266, 271, 281, 287, 300, 301, 303, 306, 311, 314, 317, 327, 328, 342

STATTON, 26, 26-29, 33, 34, 36, 38, 65, 71, 79, 85, 98, 100, 101, 107, 114, 116, 121, 131, 138, 163, 172, 192, 204, 214, 241, 247, 250, 253, 266, 268, 270, 281, 284, 296, 300, 301, 303, 312, 317, 320, 322, 327, 328

STEAMIST, 177, 185

STEARNS & FOSTER, 27, 71

STEINWORLD, 85

STELLAR CARPET, 28, 213

STERLING, 25, 27, 30-33, 35, 36, 38, 56, 131, 149, 167, 171, 172, 196, 200, 290, 317, 343

STEVE BUSS, 85

STEVENS, 27, 33, 90, 179, 214, 242-244, 261, 299, 300, 335, 341

STEVENS FURNITURE COMPANY, INC, 299, 341

STEVENS OF BOONE, 300, 335

STEWART, 74, 78, 79, 84, 85, 121, 188, 203, 204, 230, 232, 248, 274, 275, 279-281, 307, 338

STICKLEY, 27, 29, 34, 36, 138, 160

STIFFEL, 34, 65, 71, 79, 81, 93, 94, 106, 114, 116, 121, 131, 137, 151, 160, 163, 166, 192, 197, 200, 204, 207, 214, 224, 230, 235, 241, 247, 250, 253, 257, 266, 268, 271, 274, 275, 281, 284, 287, 296, 300, 301, 303, 306, 307, 310, 312, 314, 317, 320, 331

STIFFEL LAMP, 79, 230, 235, 247, 253, 271, 274, 275, 287, 301, 317

STONE ART, 192, 281

STONE COLLECTION, 157, 287

STONE COUNTRY IRONWORKS, 192, 222, 281, 287

STONE INTERNATIONAL, 31, 65, 130, 157

STONE INTL, 85, 160, 163, 207, 281, 287, 306

STONE POINT DECOYS, 301

STONELEIGH, 116, 192, 207, 250

STONEVILLE, 29-31, 71, 79, 85, 134, 163, 169, 176, 204, 228, 274, 275, 281, 287

STONEWASH, 172

STOTTER, 192

STOUT, 29, 30, 32, 34, 38, 146, 207, 238, 242-244, 257, 299

STRAITS, 85

STRATFORD, 38, 65, 71, 79, 151, 161, 163, 197, 204, 207, 230, 281, 303, 314

STRATFORD/STRATOL OUNGER, 163, 204

STRATHROY, 306

STRATOLOUNGER, 35, 37-39, 151, 161, 163, 169, 192, 194, 197, 204, 207, 230, 281, 287, 306

STREETMAN, 71, 79, 151

STROHEIM & ROMANN, 32, 65, 137, 160, 192, 210, 238, 241, 250, 254, 268, 271, 273, 281, 299

STROUPE MIRRORS, 71

STUART, 71, 85, 95, 114, 121, 138, 151, 197, 204, 207, 250, 281, 287, 292, 296, 303, 314, 317

STUBBERON, 331

STUBER STONE, 85

STUCKEY BROTHERS FURNITURE CO, INC, 302, 343

STUDIO, 25, 34, 51, 98, 99, 102, 142, 188, 283, 303, 337, 340
STUDIO OF LIGHTS, 34, 303, 340
STYLE, 1, 1, 3, 30, 31, 45-48, 51, 52, 55, 65, 70, 71, 77, 80, 83, 85, 92, 95, 116, 134, 150, 161-162, 167, 173, 189, 192-194, 196, 204, 206, 229, 240, 251, 261, 268, 271, 274, 275, 278, 281, 286, 291, 301, 303, 305, 313, 314, 335
STYLE CRAFT INTERIORS, 303, 335
STYLE SEATING, 271
STYLE UPHOLSTERY, 65, 71, 85, 167, 192, 194, 274, 275, 281, 314
STYLECRAFT, 34, 38, 65, 79, 85, 128, 166, 204, 207, 261, 287, 297
SUGAR CREEK, 245, 314, 335
SUGAR HILL PINE, 114
SUGATSUNE, 177, 185
SUGGS & HARDIN, 95, 197, 207, 306
SUMMER CLASSICS, 29, 31, 37, 192, 199, 281, 314
SUMTER, 27, 31, 34, 47, 71, 79, 106, 121, 138, 163, 167, 174, 214, 245, 247, 253, 266, 284, 303, 311, 312, 314
SUMTER CABINET, 27, 31, 66, 71, 79, 106, 138, 163, 174, 214, 247, 253, 266, 284, 303, 311, 314
SUN CITY, 85
SUN FLOORING, 28, 214
SUN MILLS, 28, 214
SUNBEAM OUTDOOR, 287
SUNBRELLA, 238
SUNBURST, 85
SUNBURY, 201
SUNNY QUALITY, 85
SUNRISE CARPET, 28, 214
SUNSET LAMPS, 34, 95
SUNWALL, 32, 76, 175
SUNWORTHY, 32, 142, 252, 276, 299
SUPERIOR, 25, 34, 71, 79, 85, 93, 106, 114, 121, 138, 160, 163, 192, 200, 204, 207, 222, 230, 247, 250, 253, 281, 285, 287, 296, 310, 314, 317, 328
SUPREME, 28, 214, 261
SUSTAINABLE LIFESTYLES, 192

SUTTON CARPETS, 168, 214, 319, 322
SUTTON REPRODUCTIONS, 85
SUTTON-COUNCIL FURNITURE COMPANY, 304, 342
SWAIM, 38, 39, 66, 71, 74, 85, 93, 114, 116, 130, 137, 138, 160, 163, 192, 197, 204, 207, 230, 241, 250, 266, 268, 281, 287, 318, 328
SWAN BRASS, 49, 71, 79, 93, 95, 114, 131, 151, 160, 161, 163, 197, 200, 230, 241, 274, 275, 281, 300
SWANSTONE, 149
SYDNEY DAVIS, 299
SYMBOL MATTRESS, 27, 37, 144
SYMPHONY, 95, 299
T & E, 242-244
TAHOE, 247, 253
TAPESTRIES LTD, 81, 161, 192, 271, 281, 287
TARKETT, 213, 214, 226, 261, 314, 319, 322
TAYLOR CLASSICS, 167
TAYLOR KING, 38, 71, 79, 85, 167, 192, 214, 247, 253, 266
TAYLOR WOODCRAFT, 27, 29-31, 36, 38, 66, 71, 79, 93, 95, 106, 116, 138, 160, 204, 207, 230, 235, 250, 271, 281, 287, 296, 301, 310, 314
TAYLORSVILLE, 38, 41, 53, 55, 67, 71, 79, 85, 95, 116, 121, 151, 160, 161, 167, 197, 200, 204, 207, 241, 250, 281, 284, 287, 292, 301, 303
TAYMOR ACCESSORIES, 177, 185
TDU, 85
TECH DESIGN, 85
TECH LIGHTING, 177, 185
TELESCOPE, 29, 37, 66, 71, 79, 81, 93, 114, 117, 161, 163, 169, 171, 174, 192, 197, 199, 200, 232, 281, 287, 306, 314
TELL CITY, 27, 29-31, 34-36, 38, 66, 71, 79, 93, 95, 114, 131, 138, 151, 161, 163, 167, 197, 222, 235, 241, 245, 250, 281, 301, 303, 306, 314, 317
TELLUS, 257
TEMPLE, 71, 114, 138, 151, 163, 167, 174, 192, 197, 207,

241, 247, 250, 253, 274, 275, 281, 287, 292, 296, 301, 303, 311, 317
TEMPLE FURNITURE, 174
TEMPLE STUART, 79, 85, 95, 114, 121, 138, 197, 204, 207, 250, 281, 287, 292, 296, 303, 317
TEMPLE UPHOLSTERY, 71, 95, 151, 163
TERRYCRAFT, 151
TEVIS & DUNLAP, 177, 185
TEXTILLERY, 192
TEXTRA, 192
TFA, 201
THAYER COGGIN, 29, 29-31, 33-36, 38, 39, 66, 74, 79, 81, 85, 93, 95, 114, 116, 151, 160, 163, 192, 197, 200, 204, 230, 250, 268, 271, 274, 275, 278, 281, 287, 300, 306, 317
THC, 177, 185
THE CHAIR CO, 200
THE RUG ROOM, 189
THE WORK STATION, 189
THEODORE & ALEXANDER, 85
TIIEODORE ALEXANDER, 328
THIBAUT, 32, 273
THIEF RIVER LINEN, 192, 271
THOMAS BLAKEMORE, 192
THOMAS HOME FURNISHINGS, 306, 336
THOMAS LIGHTING, 177, 185, 192
THOMAS MOSER, 148
THOMAS OFFICE, 114
THOMASVILLE, 26, 27, 29, 33-36, 38, 47, 48, 50, 52, 65-66, 79, 85, 95-96, 98, 101, 114, 136, 138, 160, 171-172, 180, 188, 189, 197, 199, 207, 214, 228, 229, 235, 250, 268, 281, 287, 307, 314, 327, 328, 339
THOMASVILLE ACCESSORIES, 192
THOMASVILLE CABINET, 26, 197, 207, 235, 287
THOMASVILLE GALLERY, 96, 189, 307, 339
THOMASVILLE LAMP, 281
THONET, 33, 241
THREE COINS, 192, 199, 204
THREE WEAVERS, 287
THROUGH BARN DOOR, 230
THYBONY, 32, 76

Index

TIFFANY, 32, 50, 166, 190-192, 257, 270, 278
TIMBERLAKE, 25, 26, 28, 38, 58, 64, 67, 74, 83, 105, 120, 143, 161, 162, 169, 189, 192, 206, 211, 214, 221, 222, 225, 227, 229, 247, 250, 252, 270, 274, 275, 278, 291, 292, 296, 299, 305, 307, 311, 312, 320
TIMBERLINE, 85
TIMBERWOOD, 85, 328
TIME GALLERY, 29, 308, 336
TIMELESS BEDDING, 85, 121, 169, 192, 197, 222
TIMMERMAN, 85, 148, 163, 167, 192-194, 207, 274, 275, 281
TINSLEY-CLARK, 174
TIOGA MILL OUTLET STORES, INC, 309
TODAY'S HOME UPHOLSTERY, 192
TOEPPERWEINS, 192
TOLTEC, 192
TOM SEELY, 38, 79, 85, 138, 192, 207
TOM THUMB LIGHTING, 192
TOMLIN, 192, 281
TOMLINSON, 29-31, 36, 38, 59, 66, 138, 233, 268, 340
TON JON MIRRORS, 177, 185
TOP BRASS, 34, 166, 192, 287
TOP NOTCH WOODWORK, 148
TOP SERVICE, 309, 343
TOTO, 178, 185
TOU LEMONDE BOCHART, 281
TOUCH OF BRASS, 241
TOUHY, 56, 257
TOWEL WARMERS, 177, 178
TOWER, 28, 214
TOWN SQUARE, 37, 121, 281
TOYO, 134, 166, 197, 274, 275, 287, 301
TRADERS LEAGUE, 200
TRADEWINDS, 37, 66, 71, 79, 200, 241
TRADITION HEIRLOOMS, 287
TRADITION HOUSE, 31, 34, 36, 39, 66, 72, 114, 131, 163, 172, 193, 214, 235, 241, 250, 284, 287, 292, 296, 300, 317, 320
TRADITIONAL HEIRLOOMS, 79, 85, 93, 193, 247, 253, 281, 311, 314
TRADITIONS BY KIMBALL, 163
TRADITIONS FRANCE, 27, 29, 79, 100, 103, 116, 171,

207, 241, 247, 250, 253, 268, 281, 287, 296, 314, 320
TRAFALGAR GARDEN, 200
TRANS PACIFIC, 163
TRANSGLOBE, 193
TRANSPACIFIC, 27, 36, 37, 250, 281
TREES INTERNATIONAL, 304
TREND CLOCKS, 71, 114
TREND HOUSE, 79
TREND WEST, 71, 79
TRENDLINE, 79
TRESSARD, 193
TRI TEX, 242-244
TRIAD BUTCHER BLOCK, 85, 163
TRIAD FURNITURE DISCOUNTERS, 310, 343
TRIARCH INDUSTRIES, 178, 185
TRICA, 85, 271
TRICOMFORT, 193, 199
TRIPLETT'S FURNITURE FASHION, 311, 341
TRIUNE, 257, 281, 287
TRIUNE BUSINESS, 257, 287
TRI-ARC, 193
TRI-LIGHT LIGHTING, 178, 185
TROIS EQLISE, 85
TROPITONE, 37, 66, 71, 79, 81, 85, 93, 95, 114, 116, 131, 144, 157, 160, 161, 163, 167, 171, 193, 197, 199, 200, 204, 207, 211, 241, 247, 250, 253, 268, 271, 274, 275, 281, 287, 292, 296, 300, 301, 303, 304, 307, 310, 314, 317, 320, 328, 331
TROSBY, 114, 116, 193, 250, 258, 268
TROTT FURNITURE CO, 312, 341
TROUTMAN CHAIR, 151, 174, 200, 314
TROUVAILLES, 27, 33, 138, 200, 268
TROY LIGHTING, 34, 193
TRUNKS BY BARBARA, 85
TRYMAR LAMPS, 193
TUBB, 79, 163, 207, 287, 301
TUBB WOODCRAFTERS, 79, 163, 287
TUCKER DESIGNS, 193
TUFENKIAN TIBETAN CARPETS, 281
TUFTEX, 28, 211, 214
TURKART, 85, 287
TURNER, 134

TUSCANA, 193
TWIN RIVER UPHOLSTERY, 134
TWO DAY DESIGNS, 85, 193
TYNDALE, 34, 66, 81, 93, 204, 281, 300, 303, 318
TYPHOON, 37, 71, 79, 197, 258, 271
TYSON FURNITURE COMPANY, INC, 312
ULTIMA, 32, 149
ULTIMATE LAMPS, 85, 281
ULTRUM, 258
UMBRELLA FACTORY, 170
UNICOR, 258
UNION, 26, 26-27, 33-34, 37-39, 66, 80, 95, 114, 197, 204, 241, 281, 301, 311, 316
UNION CITY CHAIR, 30, 31, 38, 204, 281, 311
UNION NATIONAL, 33, 34, 66, 95, 114, 197, 241, 301
UNIQUE, 15, 27, 31, 32, 50, 54, 59, 63, 80, 95, 114, 120, 130, 156, 163, 165, 177, 184, 193, 205, 207, 223, 225, 239, 241, 259, 265, 269, 270, 281, 296
UNIQUE ORIGINALS, 27, 163, 193, 281
UNITED, 8, 45, 85, 175, 193, 252
UNITED DESIGN, 193
UNIVERSAL, 26, 27, 30-31, 34-37, 66, 71, 81, 85, 93, 95, 96, 98, 100, 102, 106, 108, 110, 116, 134, 138, 144, 148, 151, 157, 161, 163, 167, 170, 172, 174, 176, 180, 189, 193, 197, 200, 204, 207, 211, 214, 215, 222, 228, 232, 234, 235, 241, 247, 250, 253, 258, 265, 266, 268, 270, 271, 274, 275, 281, 288, 292, 296, 297, 300-301, 304, 306-307, 310-312, 314, 315, 317, 328, 339
UNIVERSAL GALLERY, 189, 315, 339
UNIVERSAL STATUARY, 287
UPPER DECK, 166
UPS, 13, 39, 45, 128, 164, 165, 169, 216, 223, 237, 238, 242-244, 266, 276, 298, 309, 324
URBAN WOODS, 193
US FURNITURE, 29-31, 38, 39, 47, 85, 197, 204, 230, 247, 253, 281, 287, 310
USA BLIND FACTORY, 315, 343

USA EXPRESS, 32, 316, 342
USA WOODS, 315, 316
UTILITY CRAFT, 316, 340
UTTERMOST, 25, 66, 81, 85, 151, 166, 174, 193, 222, 271, 281, 287
UWHARRIE CHAIR, 67, 79, 85, 121, 163, 207, 230, 281, 311, 314
VAGABOND HOUSE, 79
VALDESE WEAVERS, 201, 238
VALERIE MAKSTELL INTERIORS, 317
VALLI & VALLI HARDWARE, 178, 185
VALRITE LEATHER, 314
VAN LUIT, 32, 175, 178, 193, 252, 268
VAN PATTEN CURIOS, 193
VAN TEAL, 34, 85, 178, 185, 193, 197, 207, 223, 281, 287
VAN TEAL LIGHTING, 178, 185
VANCE, 37, 79, 178, 185, 306
VANCE STAINLESS SINKS, 178, 185
VANGUARD, 25, 27, 34, 67, 71, 79, 85, 92, 93, 95, 96, 106, 116, 121, 137, 138, 160, 163, 166, 168, 170, 189, 197, 200, 235, 241, 247, 250, 253, 266, 268, 271, 274, 275, 296, 300, 301, 303, 310, 317, 318, 320, 322, 327, 328, 339
VANGUARD GALLERY, 189, 318, 339
VARGUS, 207
VAUGHAN, 27, 29-31, 35, 36, 39, 95, 106, 148, 167, 168, 174, 193, 211, 232, 247, 250, 253, 274, 275, 288, 296, 297, 303, 314
VAUGHAN BASSETT, 79, 93, 116, 121, 163, 176, 204, 265, 266, 281, 287, 292
VAXEL LIGHTING, 178, 185
VB WILLIAMS, 27, 134
VELCO, 193, 271
VENEMAN, 37, 85, 171, 193, 247, 253, 281, 287, 307, 314
VENETIAN TRADERS, 193
VENTURE, 30, 36-38, 67, 71, 79, 85, 95, 114, 116, 121, 144, 151, 160, 163, 168, 172, 176, 191, 193, 197, 199, 204, 207, 211, 214, 222, 230, 235, 241, 247, 250, 253, 266, 268, 271, 274, 275, 279, 281, 287,

292, 296, 301, 303, 306-307, 310, 311, 314, 317, 320, 328
VERANDA, 144
VERMONT FURNITURE DESIGNS, 85
VERMONT PRECISION, 27, 29, 67, 85, 207
VERMONT TUBBS, 27, 27, 29, 33, 85, 116, 208, 250
VEROSOL, 75, 178, 254, 264, 295
VERSTEEL, 258
VERTICAL, 136, 178, 254, 255, 326
VICTOR & BISHOP, 261
VICTORIAN CLASSIC, 93, 174, 245, 247, 253, 281, 314
VICTORIUS, 32, 106, 301
VIETRI, 86, 207, 281, 287
VIEWPOINT LEATHER, 67, 86, 204, 327
VILLAGE, 28, 32, 62, 67, 111, 112, 252, 254, 320
VILLAGE CARPET, 28, 319, 341
VILLAGE FURNITURE HOUSE, 112, 319, 341
VILLAGEOUS, 27, 86
VINEYARD, 193
VINTAGE FURNITURE, 314
VIRCO, 30, 157
VIRGINIA GALLERIES, 114, 114, 281
VIRGINIA HOUSE, 27, 29-31, 36, 67, 71, 79, 95, 110, 114, 116, 121, 138, 151, 163, 167, 170, 174, 189, 193, 197, 200, 207, 211, 222, 241, 247, 250, 253, 266, 268, 274, 275, 281, 287, 292, 301, 303, 304, 310, 314, 317, 320, 321, 339
VIRGINIA HOUSE GALLERY, 189, 321, 339
VIRGINIA METALCRAFTERS, 67, 71, 81, 93, 95, 106, 114, 116, 121, 131, 160, 166, 170, 193, 207, 230, 235, 247, 250, 253, 268, 271, 281, 287, 292, 296, 300, 301, 304, 306, 307, 317, 320, 322, 331
VISIONS, 34, 271
VISUAL COMFORT, 281
VITA BATH WHIRLPOOLS, 178, 185
VOGUE, 32, 37, 71, 79, 95, 114, 144, 161, 197, 207, 241, 268, 301, 303, 306, 314

VOGUE RATTAN, 37, 71, 79, 95, 114, 144, 161, 197, 207, 241, 268, 301, 303
VUE LIGHTING, 178, 185
VYMURA, 32, 252
W KING AMBLER, 172, 279, 281
WABON, 301
WALBURG, 207
WALKER, 67, 114, 193, 204, 311
WALKER MARLEN, 67, 193, 204, 311
WALL STREET, 79, 86
WALL TRENDS, 32, 252
WALLBURG, 79
WALLTEX, 32, 178, 252
WAMBOLD, 27, 31, 34-36, 39, 67, 86, 193-194, 204, 281, 301
WAMSUTTA, 35, 52, 53, 179
WARA, 81, 193
WAREHOUSE CARPETS, INC, 321, 334
WARNER, 32, 32, 51, 76, 142, 252, 271
WARREN LLOYD, 114
WATERFORD, 25, 57, 71, 79, 86, 116, 138, 178, 185, 214, 235, 241, 247, 253, 306-307, 314, 317, 320, 328, 331
WATERFORD FURNITURE, 67, 79, 86, 116, 160, 193, 235, 250, 281, 320
WATERLOO, 287
WATSON CHAIR, 281
WATSON OF TAYLORSVILLE, 207
WAVERLY, 32, 67, 72, 100, 110, 114, 137, 145, 146, 151, 160, 163, 178, 189, 201, 204, 210, 231, 235, 238, 241-244, 254, 259, 268, 271, 280-281, 287, 300, 309, 318
WAYBORN, 86
WAYNLINE, 37, 38, 71, 79
WEATHER WICKER, 197
WEATHERCRAFT, 37, 144, 193, 292, 311
WEATHERMASTER, 37, 143, 157, 193, 292, 311
WEAVE, 16, 201, 238
WEAVER WAYSIDE FURNITURE, 322, 343
WEBB, 27, 29-31, 34, 36, 50, 67, 71, 79, 128, 134, 151, 174, 176, 197, 204, 247, 253, 287, 297, 310
WEDGEWOOD, 160, 250, 314

WEDGEWOOD/WATERFORD, 160

WEEKEND RETREAT, 292, 311

WEIMAN, 36, 38, 39, 67, 71, 79, 81, 86, 93, 95, 114, 121, 131, 151, 160, 161, 163, 168, 174, 189, 193, 197, 200, 204, 207, 215, 230, 235, 241, 247, 250, 253, 265, 266, 268, 271, 281, 287, 296, 300, 303, 306, 307, 311, 317, 320, 322, 327, 328, 331, 339

WEIMAN GALLERY, 189, 322, 339

WEINSTOCK, 193

WEISS & BIHELLER, 193

WELLCO, 28, 214, 261

WELLESLEY GUILD, 157, 160, 207, 250, 281, 287

WELLINGTON, 27, 33, 36, 68, 72, 79, 81, 86, 95, 103, 114, 116, 121, 131, 138, 157, 160, 163, 168, 172, 193, 204, 214, 235, 241, 250, 261, 266, 268, 271, 274, 275, 281, 284, 287, 292, 296, 300, 304, 306-307, 310, 314, 320, 322, 328, 331

WELLINGTON HALL, 27, 33, 36, 68, 72, 79, 81, 86, 95, 103, 114, 116, 121, 131, 138, 157, 160, 163, 168, 172, 193, 204, 214, 235, 241, 250, 266, 268, 271, 274, 275, 281, 284, 287, 292, 296, 300, 304, 306-307, 310, 314, 320, 328, 331

WELLINGTON'S COLLECTION, 323

WELLINGTONS FINE LEATHER FURNITURE, 323, 335

WELLS, 71, 79, 95, 323, 334

WELLS INTERIORS INC, 323, 334

WENDY LYNN LAMPS, 86

WESAUNARD, 178, 185

WESCO, 238, 299

WESLEY ALLEN, 27-27, 68, 71, 79, 86, 93, 100, 101, 106, 116, 121, 148, 160, 161, 163, 168, 172, 193, 197, 200, 204, 230, 235, 241, 247, 250, 253, 266, 268, 271, 274, 275, 278, 281, 287, 292, 296, 300, 301, 307, 310-312, 314, 317, 320, 328

WESLEY BOBER, 193

WESLEY HALL, 79, 86, 116, 160, 204, 235, 250, 284, 297, 317, 327, 328

WESTCHESTER LEATHER, 197, 241

WESTERN, 23, 164, 238, 242-244, 309, 313

WESTGATE, 32, 114, 137, 193, 238, 242-244, 250, 254, 268, 271, 281, 299

WESTMOUNT, 142

WESTNOVA, 86

WESTON HALL, 306

WESTWOOD, 34, 71, 93, 197, 200, 204, 230, 301, 303, 314

WHITAKER, 68, 79, 95, 168, 204, 207, 281, 314

WHITE, 16, 26-29, 33, 35, 36, 38, 39, 41, 49, 54, 55, 68, 78, 82, 84, 93, 95, 96, 98, 100, 102, 114, 116, 121, 128, 131, 137, 138, 157, 159, 161, 163, 167, 180, 188, 189, 191, 195-197, 215, 235, 240, 247, 250, 253, 259, 266, 268, 270, 278-281, 286, 296, 299, 303, 305, 306, 310, 313, 317, 318, 320, 327, 328, 337

WHITE OF MEBANE, 68, 95, 281, 306

WHITECRAFT, 27, 33, 37, 68, 110, 114, 144, 163, 193, 194, 200, 207, 235, 241, 281, 303, 306, 310, 325

WHITECREST, 28, 214, 261

WHITEHAUS, 178, 185

WHITEWOOD, 155

WHITNEY RUGS, 271

WHITTAKER & WOODS, 299

WHITTEMORE SHERRILL, 98, 100, 102, 103, 171, 193

WHITTIER, 207

WICKER, 26, 26, 27, 29, 31, 33, 37, 38, 43, 44, 46, 52, 58, 61, 68, 77-78, 93, 105, 116, 148, 153, 172, 173, 187, 197-198, 203, 219, 240, 242, 247, 252, 270, 278, 279, 281, 292-294, 313, 320, 325, 341-342

WICKER GALLERY, THE, 324, 341

WICKER WAREHOUSE INC, 325, 342

WILDERMERE, 189, 189

WILDWOOD, 34, 68, 71, 72, 81, 86, 93, 95, 100, 114, 117, 131, 137, 160, 166, 172, 204, 207, 214, 230, 235, 241, 247, 250, 253, 266, 269, 271, 281, 287, 297, 300, 301, 303, 307, 314, 317, 320, 322, 328, 331

WILKHAHN, 258

WILLIAM ALAN, 38

WILLIAM ALLEN, 68, 71, 79, 86, 115, 137, 138, 151, 197, 200, 207, 250, 269, 281, 287, 297, 303, 304

WILLOW CREEK, 121, 166, 193

WILLSBORO WOOD PRODUCTS, 314

WILSHIRE, 71, 178, 185, 193

WILSHIRE LIGHTING, 178, 185

WILSONART, 281

WILTON, 134, 281

WILTON ARMATALE, 281

WIMBLEDON, 261

WINDEMERE LAMPS, 314

WINDOWARE CATALOG-SMITH & NOBLE, 326

WINDSONG, 281

WINDSOR, 25, 29, 30, 37, 38, 118, 134, 166, 193, 274, 275, 281, 287, 325

WINDSOR OAK COLLECTION, 134

WINDWARD, 118

WINNERS ONLY, 30, 33, 68, 79, 86, 128, 163, 193, 194, 204, 271, 281, 284, 300, 314

WINSOME TRADING, 86

WINSOME WOOD, 222

WINSTON, 7, 23, 37, 58, 68, 71, 79, 81, 86, 93, 106, 115, 117, 121, 138, 144, 161, 163, 170, 171, 174, 193, 197, 199, 200, 204, 207, 230, 235, 241, 247, 250, 253, 258, 266, 269, 271, 281, 287, 297, 300, 301, 303, 306, 307, 314, 317, 328, 331, 342

WISCONSIN, 15, 30, 34, 36, 38, 86, 110, 193, 222, 250, 296, 297, 343

WOLF, 27, 32, 145, 238, 242-244, 309

WOOD & HOGAN, 115, 281

WOOD BLINDS, 254, 255, 315, 326

WOOD CLASSICS, 281

WOOD WORKS, 86

WOOD-ARMFIELD FURNITURE
COMPANY, 327, 340
WOODARD, 30, 30, 36, 37, 68, 78,
81, 86, 93, 95, 115, 117,
144, 157, 160, 163, 171,
193-194, 197, 199, 200,
204, 207, 230, 235, 241,
247, 250, 253, 266, 269,
271, 281, 297, 300, 301,
303, 306, 310, 314, 320,
328, 331
WOODCRAFT, 27, 29, 33, 36, 38,
66, 79, 93, 95, 106, 116,
138, 151, 160, 204, 230,
235, 250, 259, 271, 281,
287, 296, 301, 310, 314,
317
WOODFIELD, 71, 106, 197, 303,
306
WOODLAND, 33, 155
WOODLEE, 71, 79, 95, 241, 269
WOODMARK, 35, 39, 68, 71, 81,
86, 93, 95, 106, 108, 117,
121, 131, 138, 160, 163,
193, 200, 204, 207, 214,
230, 235, 241, 250, 269,
271, 274, 275, 281, 284,
287, 292, 297, 301, 303,

307, 310, 314, 317, 320,
328, 331
WOODSTOCK, 306
WOODWINDS, 316
WOOD-ARMFIELD FURNITURE
CO, 82
WOOD-ARMFIELD FURNITURE
COMPANY, 326, 340
WORK STATION, THE, 328, 339
WORKSPACE, 27, 29, 207
WORLD, 7, 26, 28-29, 31, 32,
36-37, 39, 54, 57-59, 63,
65, 69, 78, 80, 90, 115,
116, 192-193, 204, 207,
214, 224, 227, 231, 261,
281, 291, 303, 322, 329,
341, 343
WORLD GLASS IMPORTS, 193
WORLD OF LEATHER, 329, 341
WORTHINGTON FURNITURE
GALLERY, 330, 339
WRIGHT TABLE, 27, 31, 33, 36,
68, 71, 79, 115, 193, 241,
250, 331
WUNDAWEAVE, 28, 214, 306,
314, 319
XIN YANG, 86
YESTERYEAR, 27, 37, 281, 292

YIELD HOUSE, 27, 30, 34, 38, 68,
86, 320
YORK, 3, 14, 33, 41, 48-52, 60, 62,
64, 67, 76, 86, 109, 133,
142, 179, 210, 223, 252,
254, 264, 266, 276, 289,
299, 309, 336, 343
YORKSHIRE, 35, 68, 79, 86, 121,
144, 168, 193, 200, 202,
207, 230, 250, 269, 281,
306, 310, 328, 343
YOUNG AMERICA, 193
YOUNG'S FURNITURE & RUG
COMPANY, 330, 341
YOUNG-HINKLE, 161, 274, 275,
288, 301
ZAGAROLI, 82, 86, 189, 193,
331-332, 339, 341
ZAGAROLI CLASSICS, 82, 82
ZAKI, 8, 37, 86, 332, 341
ZAKI ORIENTAL RUGS, 8, 332,
341
ZARBIN & ASSOCIATES, 143,
333, 334
ZILO CASEGOODS, 86
ZINISSER, 86
ZIRO DESIGNS, 86

Index

RESOURCES, INC BOOK ORDER FORM

NAME

ADDRESS

CITY- ST   ZIP

Order Information

Quantity		Cost
	THE FINE FURNITURE AND FURISHINGS DISCOUNT SHOPPING GUIDE	$15.95
Book Cost		
Shipping:	($3.00 per book)	
TOTAL		

Payment Method

❑ Check   ❑ Mastercard   ❑ Visa

Card #   EXP:

Signature:

MAIL IN:	**RESOURCES, INC. PO BOX 973 BLOOMFIELD HILLS, MI 48303**
PHONE or FAX:	**800-644-3440**

HOME OFFICE ▶

LEATHER ▶

ACCESSORIES ▶

REPRODUCTIONS ▶

HOLSTERY ▶

LIGHTING ▼ RTA ▼ WALLCOVERING ▼ HARDWARE ▼ ANTIQUES ▼ WINDOWS ▼

RESOURCES, INC BOOK ORDER FORM

NAME

ADDRESS

CITY- ST   ZIP

Order Information

Quantity		Cost
	THE FINE FURNITURE AND FURISHINGS DISCOUNT SHOPPING GUIDE	$15.95
Book Cost		
Shipping:	($3.00 per book)	
TOTAL		

Payment Method

❑ Check   ❑ Mastercard   ❑ Visa

Card #   EXP:

Signature:

MAIL IN:

RESOURCES, INC.
PO BOX 973
BLOOMFIELD HILLS, MI
48303

PHONE or FAX: **800-644-3440**